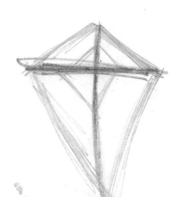

HOLT

GEORGIA

Environmental Science

Karen Arms, Ph.D., J.D.
Savannah, Georgia

HOLT, RINEHART AND WINSTON

A Harcourt Education Company

Orlando • **Austin** • New York • San Diego • London

ABOUT THE AUTHOR

Karen Arms, Ph.D., J.D.

Karen Arms received her Ph.D. in molecular biology from Oxford University and a doctor of law from Cornell University. She was an assistant professor of biology at Cornell University, where she taught introductory biology and courses in science and society. She also taught marine biology at the University of Georgia Marine Biology Station and introductory biology at South College in Savannah, Georgia. In addition to *Holt Environmental Science,* Dr. Arms has written several college-level biology textbooks. Her interest in and concern for the environment led her to form an ecotourism organization that introduces people to the ecosystems of the southeastern coast.

For permission to reprint copyrighted material, grateful acknowledgement is made to the following sources:

Lippincott Williams & Wilkins: Adaptation of "Figure 4: Environmental portion of disease in the major world regions" (retitled "Poor Health by World Region") by Kirk R. Smith from "How Much Global Ill Health Is Attributable to Environmental Factors?" by Kirk R. Smith, Carlos F. Corvalán, and Tord Kjellström from *Epidemiology,* vol. 10, no.5, September 1999, pp. 573–584. Copyright © 1999 by Epidemiology Resources Inc.

Dr. Pim Martens: "Figure 6: Malaria risk by the year 2020" by Pim Martens from *American Scientist November–December 1999* Web site, accessed March 5, 2002, at www.sigmaxi.org/amsci/articles/99articles/Martens.html. Copyright © 1999 by Dr. Pim Martens.

United Nations Population Fund (UNFPA): From "Women and the Environment" from *The State of the World Population 2001,* edited by Alex Marshall. Copyright © 2001 by UNFPA.

ISBN-13: 978-0-03-094762-9
ISBN-10:   0-03-094762-6

3 4 5 6 7 048 09 08

GA2

Georgia

As you read the following pages and work through the unpacking of the Georgia Science Standards, you will discover the big ideas and key concepts that your teacher expects you to learn and understand.

You will see three things:

1 >
what the standard actually says

2 What's it mean?
an explanation to help you understand the big ideas within the standard

3 Review Question
a typical standards Review Question

Georgia

State capitol, Atlanta

Stone Mountain Park

Cloudland Canyon State Park

Characteristics of Science

Habits of Mind

>**SCSh1** Students will evaluate the importance of curiosity, honesty, openness, and skepticism in science.

What's it mean?

Students will know the importance of questioning the world around them, reporting their findings truthfully, keeping an open mind, and thinking critically about scientific ideas. Go to Chapter 2, Tools of Environmental Science, for help.

>**SCSh1.a** Exhibit the above traits in their own scientific activities.

What's it mean?

Do all of the above when learning about science. Go to Chapter 2, Tools of Environmental Science, for help.

Review Question What attribute of a skeptic would contribute to a good scientific mind?
   A. willingness to travel
   B. empathetic nature
   C. desire to conduct experiments
   D. continual questioning of observations

>**SCSh1.b** Recognize that different explanations often can be given for the same evidence.

What's it mean?

Know that different scientists can have different answers to the same question even after looking at the same clues. Go to Chapter 2, Tools of Environmental Science, for help.

Brown thrasher

Cherokee rose

Review Question A newspaper headline says, "Detective Has Theory on How Computers Were Stolen from Warehouse." Which of the following words most accurately reflects the use of the term *theory* in this news paper headline?

A. law
B. fact
C. hypothesis
D. experiment

>**SCSh1.c** Explain that further understanding of scientific problems relies on the design and execution of new experiments which may reinforce or weaken opposing explanations.

What's it mean?

Explain how designing and carrying out new studies helps scientists find the answers to science questions. What we learn from these new studies can help us find new answers that make more sense than older answers. They can also help us find out why old answers are not true. Go to Chapter 2, Tools of Environmental Science, for help.

Review Question A friend notices that ants have started crawling along her kitchen wall. They form a trail on the wall that curves around a dark colored square of paint on the wall. Which of the following is a testable hypothesis that explains the ants' behavior?

A. Dark colors make ants unhappy.
B. All insects prefer light colors over dark colors.
C. Ants avoid walking over dark colored surfaces.
D. The friend's kitchen has ants because it is messy.

Hiking trail

Georgia

Atlanta

>**SCSh2** Students will use standard safety practices for all classroom laboratory and field investigations.

What's it mean?
Students will be careful and safe during science activities in class and on field trips. Go to Safety in the Laboratory for help.

>**SCSh2.a** Follow correct procedures for use of scientific apparatus.

What's it mean?
Follow directions when using laboratory equipment. Go to Chapter 2, Tools of Environmental Science, for help.

Review Question Which of the following is an example of a scientist's physical model?
A. a crash-test dummy for a car company
B. a diagram of the structure of an atom
C. a map of Denver, Colorado
D. a satellite image of South America

>**SCSh2.b** Demonstrate appropriate technique in all laboratory situations.

What's it mean?
Follow directions in all science activities. Go to Chapter 2, Tools of Environmental Science, for help.

Review Question Which of the following readings on a pH meter would indicate that a substance is acidic?
A. 5.0
B. 7.0
C. 9.0
D. none of the above

>**SCSh2.c** Follow correct protocol for identifying and reporting safety problems and violations.

What's it mean?
Follow the teacher's instructions for recognizing when someone is being unsafe and for reporting the unsafe activity or situation. Go to Chapter 2, Tools of Environmental Science, for help.

Review Question Which of the following is not a benefit of incinerating waste?

    A. It reduces the amount of material sent to landfills.

    B. It produces energy in the form of heat.

    C. It can be used to produce electricity.

    D. It neutralizes all of the toxic materials in the waste.

>SCSh3 Students will identify and investigate problems scientifically.

What's it mean?

Students will look at the world and explore it in a scientific way. Go to Chapter 2, Tools of Environmental Science, for help.

>SCSh3.a Suggest reasonable hypotheses for identified problems.

What's it mean?

Make testable, educated guesses to science questions. Go to Chapter 2, Tools of Environmental Science, for help.

Review Question Jane and Jim observed a group of male butterflies by the roadside. As an experiment, they put out different trays full of sand soaked in saltwater and sand soaked in a solution containing nitrogen in an area where butterflies had been seen. Which of the following statements is a testable hypothesis about the experiment?

    A. Male butterflies mate with female butterflies.

    B. Salt is a compound and nitrogen is an element.

    C. Butterflies are never seen in groups except on sandy surfaces.

    D. Butterflies are attracted to salt.

>SCSh3.b Develop procedures for solving scientific problems.

What's it mean?

Design ways to test explanations of science questions. Go to Chapter 2, Tools of Environmental Science, for help.

Review Question A scientist notices that lichen are growing on only one side of all of the rocks in an area. How might the scientist test her idea that the lichen's growth pattern depends on the position of the growing surface?

    A. Observe the rocks for a year and see if the pattern of lichen growth changes during that time.

    B. Collect one of the rocks and place it in a laboratory to observe whether the lichen growth pattern changes.

    C. Place new, lichen-free rocks in the area in different positions and observe whether lichen grow on a particular side of each new rock.

    D. Turn one of the rocks around and observe whether lichen grows on the other side of the rock over a period of a month.

Palm trees, Jekyll Island

>SCSh3.c Collect, organize and record appropriate data.

What's it mean?
Make measurements about the world and write them down. Go to Chapter 2, Tools of Environmental Science, for help.

Review Question The graph below shows the composition (by weight) of municipal solid wastes in the United States. Use this graph to answer the following question.

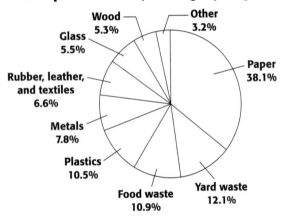

Municipal Solid Waste (Percentage by Weight)

Wood 5.3%
Other 3.2%
Glass 5.5%
Paper 38.1%
Rubber, leather, and textiles 6.6%
Metals 7.8%
Plastics 10.5%
Food waste 10.9%
Yard waste 12.1%

By how much would the amount of municipal waste be reduced if every household in the country composted food and yard wastes?
- A. 12%
- B. 23%
- C. 35%
- D. 41%

>SCSh3.d Graphically compare and analyze data points and/or summary statistics.

What's it mean?
Use graphs and pictures to display and better understand information. Go to Chapter 2, Tools of Environmental Science, for help.

Review Question The bar graph below shows the distribution of lengths in a population of dwarf wedge mussels. Use this graph to answer the following question.

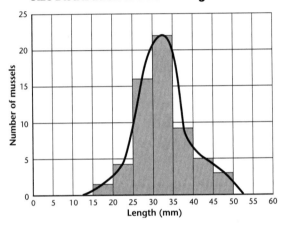

Size Distribution of Dwarf Wedge Mussels

Number of mussels vs *Length (mm)*

What is the most likely size predictable for a mussel randomly drawn from this population?
- A. 15–20 mm
- B. 25–30 mm
- C. 30–35 mm
- D. 40–45 mm

Pink lady slipper

>SCSh3.e Develop reasonable conclusions based on data collected.

What's it mean?

Come up with reasonable explanations for information gathered. Go to Chapter 2, Tools of Environmental Science, for help.

Review Question The graph below shows the population of some reindeer that were introduced to an Alaskan island in 1910. Use the graph to answer the following question.

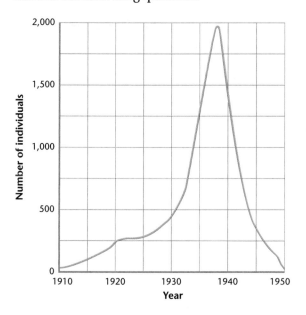

What might have happened in 1937?
A. A major predator species was suddenly killed off.
B. Twice as many births took place than had in 1930.
C. The food resource was probably depleted by 1937.
D. Humans introduced a new source of food for reindeer.

>SCSh3.f Evaluate whether conclusions are reasonable by reviewing the process and checking against other available information.

What's it mean?

Think about whether explanations make sense by looking at the information they came from and checking that they match other information. Go to Chapter 2, Tools of Environmental Science, for help.

Review Question The graph below shows the numbers of various types of species that are officially listed as endangered or threatened in the United States and internationally. Use this graph to answer the following question.

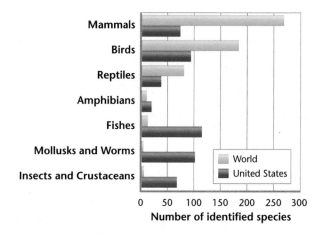

Given this information, which types of species might need further research worldwide?
A. birds and reptiles
B. mammals and birds
C. mammals and fishes
D. insects and crustaceans

Chattahoochee National Forest

>SCSh4 Students use tools and instruments for observing, measuring, and manipulating scientific equipment and materials.

What's it mean?

Students use scientific tools to look at and measure characteristics of various materials. Go to Chapter 2, Tools of Environmental Science, for help.

>SCSh4.a Develop and use systematic procedures for recording and organizing information.

What's it mean?

Design and use careful methods for writing down and organizing data. Go to Chapter 2, Tools of Environmental Science, for help.

Review Question In a research study, a scientist records his observations of half of his subjects with one instrument and the other half with a second, older instrument. How might he be introducing error into his data collection?
- A. Older instruments rarely give accurate measurements.
- B. It takes practice to use newer instruments effectively.
- C. By not introducing a third instrument, he will not be varying his measurements enough.
- D. By using two different instruments, he is introducing differences in data that would not exist with one instrument.

>SCSh4.b Use technology to produce tables and graphs.

What's it mean?

Use drawing tools, graphing calculators, and computers to make tables and graphs for understanding data. Go to Chapter 2, Tools of Environmental Science, for help.

Review Question The graph below shows population projections for the world at different growth rates. Use this graph to answer the following question.

World Population Projections for Different Growth Rates

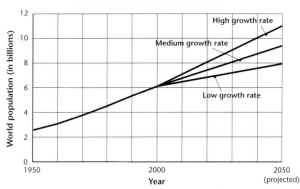

Source: UN Population Division.

What does the chart project as the most likely outcome for the world population?

A. It will be 12 billion in 2050.
B. It will double by the year 2050.
C. It will increase by 25% by the year 2050.
D. It will be between 8 and 11 billion in 2050.

>SCSh4.c Use technology to develop, test, and revise experimental or mathematical models.

What's it mean?

Use scientific tools to come up with scientific explanations, test them, and make them better. Go to Chapter 2, Tools of Environmental Science, for help.

Review Question Scientists are currently unable to make accurate predictions about the rate of global warming because climatic patterns are complex and too many variables must be taken into account to be solved even using today's fastest computers. In the future, how could faster computers influence the predictions of climate change?

A. Faster computers could produce more data.
B. Faster computers could solve more complex equations.
C. Faster computers could reduce the number of variables needed.
D. Faster computers could increase the degree certainty over a prediction.

Answers: SCSh4.a) D, SCSh4.b) D, SCSh4.c) B

Okefenokee Swamp

>SCSh5 Students will demonstrate the computation and estimation skills necessary for analyzing data and developing reasonable scientific explanations.

What's it mean?

Students will show that they know the basic math skills needed to look at data and come up with reasonable scientific explanations for it. Go to Chapter 2, Tools of Environmental Science, for help.

>SCSh5.a Trace the source on any large disparity between estimated and calculated answers to problems.

What's it mean?

Look at methods of measurement and calculation to find the difference between a predicted amount and a calculated amount. Go to Chapter 2, Tools of Environmental Science, for help.

Review Question A scientist finds that a 100 mL sample of seawater has about 4 grams of salt in it. He calculates that a 1L sample of seawater should have ten times that amount, 40 grams of salt. However, he finds that a 1L sample of sea-

water actually has 35 grams of salt. What might explain the difference in the two values?
- A. A larger sample of water can hold more salt than a smaller sample of water.
- B. A 1L sample has more than ten times the amount of water as a 100 mL sample.
- C. It is not possible to compare the amount of salt in two different samples of seawater.
- D. His measurement of the smaller sample was not careful, so his calculation for the larger sample made the error larger.

>SCSh5.b Consider possible effects of measurement errors on calculations.

What's it mean?

Think about the ways that mistakes made during measuring could lead to wrong answers even when the math is correct. Go to Chapter 2, Tools of Environmental Science, for help.

Review Question Which of the following units of measure would be most appropriate for determining the mass of an apple?
- A. gram
- B. kilogram
- C. milligram
- D. centigram

Jekyll Island Historic District

>SCSh5.c Recognize the relationship between accuracy and precision.

What's it mean?

Know the difference between making measurements that are repeatable and making measurements that are close to the actual value. Go to Chapter 2, Tools of Environmental Science, for help.

Review Question A scientist used two methods to find the temperature of a soil sample. Using Method A, she took five measurements that were very different, but they had an average that was close to the expected temperature. Using Method B, she took five measurements that were all very similar, but they were very different from the expected temperature. What can she conclude about the two methods?

   A. Method A is accurate but not precise.
   B. Method B is accurate but not precise.
   C. Both methods are accurate, but only Method A is precise.
   D. Both methods are accurate, but only Method B is precise.

>SCSh5.d Express appropriate numbers of significant figures for calculated data, using scientific notation where appropriate.

What's it mean?

Write answers to the correct number of digits and report very large and very small numbers using powers of ten. Go to Chapter 2, Tools of Environmental Science, for help.

Review Question How many significant digits are in the measurement 0.007 504 kg?

   A. three
   B. four
   C. six
   D. seven

>SCSh5.e Solve scientific problems by substituting quantitative values, using dimensional analysis and/or simple algebraic formulas as appropriate.

What's it mean?

Use mathematical formulas and conversion factors to solve problems. Go to Chapter 2, Tools of Environmental Science, for help.

Review Question The formula for converting Celsius temperatures to Fahrenheit temperatures is given below.

Fahrenheit temperature =
$(1.8 \times$ Celsius temperature$) + 32.0$

What is 33.0 °C expressed in degrees Fahrenheit?

   A. 1.0   C. 64.0
   B. 65.8   D. 91.4

>SCSh6 Students will communicate scientific investigations and information clearly.

What's it mean?

Students will talk about what they observed during laboratory activities. Go to Chapter 2, Tools of Environmental Science, for help.

>SCSh6.a Write clear, coherent laboratory reports related to scientific investigations.

What's it mean?

Write careful reports explaining observations and measurements. Go to Chapter 2, Tools of Environmental Science, for help.

Review Question Why is it important for scientists to write careful reports explaining their observations and measurements?

   A. so that no one can untruthfully claim to have made a discovery first
   B. so that others can repeat their experiments and verify their results
   C. so that the hypotheses can be quickly formulated into theories
   D. so that they can prove that they used a scientific method

>SCSh6.b Write clear, coherent accounts of current scientific issues, including possible alternative interpretations of the data.

What's it mean?

Write clear reports of science topics, such as different ways to explain data. Go to Chapter 2, Tools of Environmental Science, for help.

Review Question How has the construction of irrigation canals and dams enabled the spread of infectious disease?

   A. The construction allows viruses to evolve.

   B. Canals and dams provide sites for waste disposal.

   C. Canals and dams provide increased habitats for vectors.

   D. The construction eliminates the natural predators of pathogens.

>SCSh6.c Use data as evidence to support scientific arguments and claims in written or oral presentations.

What's it mean?

Use information from experiments and research to explain science concepts in written or spoken reports. Go to Chapter 2, Tools of Environmental Science, for help.

Review Question Different scientists classify biomes in different ways. The map below shows one way to classify the biomes in Africa. Use this map to answer the following question.

Biomes of Africa

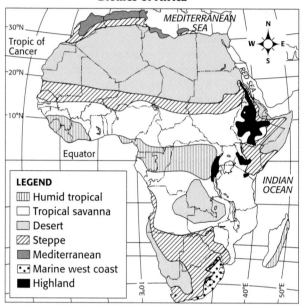

LEGEND
- Humid tropical
- Tropical savanna
- Desert
- Steppe
- Mediterranean
- Marine west coast
- Highland

What can be inferred about the biomes of Africa?

   A. Africa has a large concentration of tropical rain forests.

   B. Africa has a limited number of plant and animal communities.

   C. Africa has all types of plant life because of the many diverse biomes.

   D. Africa has large desert areas that get less than 25.0 cm of precipitation a year.

Georgia fields

>SCSh6.d Participate in group discussions of scientific investigation and current scientific issues.

What's it mean?
Talk about science experiments and science news in groups. Go to Chapter 1, Science and the Environment, for help.

Review Question Which of the following is an effect of the increased burning of fossil fuels on the carbon cycle?
A. More carbonates remain in fossil fuels.
B. More carbon dioxide is absorbed by organisms.
C. More carbon dioxide is absorbed by the atmosphere.
D. More carbohydrates remain buried deep in the ground.

The Nature of Science

>SCSh7 Students analyze how scientific knowledge is developed.

What's it mean?
Students think about how scientists work together to explain the world. Go to Chapter 2, Tools of Environmental Science, for help.

>SCSh7.a The universe is a vast single system in which the basic principles are the same everywhere.

What's it mean?
The basic rules that explain the world work the same way in every part of the universe. Go to Chapter 1, Science and the Environment, for help.

Review Question Though scientists study the world from differing perspectives, what must all scientists take into account?
A. universal laws
B. ecological succession
C. temperature differences
D. the importance of environmental science

>SCSh7.b Universal principles are discovered through observation and experimental verification.

What's it mean?

Scientists discover the basic rules that explain the world by looking carefully at the world and doing experiments. Go to Chapter 2, Tools of Environmental Science, for help.

Review Question In what ways are today's environmental resources like the commons described in the essay "The Tragedy of the Commons"?

 A. The Earth's resources are owned by individuals and can become depleted or polluted.
 B. The Earth's resources are shared by everyone and are being protected from overuse.
 C. The Earth's resources are owned by individuals and are being protected from overuse.
 D. The Earth's resources are shared by everyone and can become depleted or polluted.

>SCSh7.c From time to time, major shifts occur in the scientific view of how the world works. More often, however, the changes that take place in the body of scientific knowledge are small modifications of prior knowledge. Major shifts in scientific views typically occur after the observation of a new phenomenon or an insightful interpretation of existing data by an individual or research group.

What's it mean?

From time to time, there are big changes in the way that scientists think the world works. Usually, only very small changes take place. Big changes in the way that scientists think usually take place after one or more scientists discover something new or find a new way of thinking about an old discovery. Go to Chapter 2, Tools of Environmental Science, for help.

Review Question How did Rachel Carson's book Silent Spring change how people viewed the world?

 A. It prompted new thinking about primate behavior.
 B. It began a renewed public interest in the theory of evolution.
 C. People became aware of the dangers of rapid population growth.
 D. People began to realize that natural resources had to be protected.

Alligator, Okefenokee Swamp

>SCSh7.d Hypotheses often cause scientists to develop new experiments that produce additional data.

What's it mean?
Scientists make educated guesses about how the world works. Then, they design scientific experiments to test these ideas. Go to Chapter 2, Tools of Environmental Science, for help.

Review Question How would a scientist categorize a testable explanation for an observation?
  A. a correlation   C. a hypothesis
  B. an experiment   D. a prediction

>SCSh7.e Testing, revising, and occasionally rejecting new and old theories never ends.

What's it mean?
Scientists are always checking scientific explanations to see if they can be made better or replaced with new ones. Go to Chapter 2, Tools of Environmental Science, for help.

Review Question What attribute of a skeptic contribute to a good scientific mind?
  A. willingness to travel
  B. empathetic nature
  C. desire to conduct experiments
  D. continual questioning of observations

>SCSh8 Students will understand important features of the process of scientific inquiry.

What's it mean?
Students will understand the major steps of the scientific method, the way that scientists work. Go to Chapter 2, Tools of Environmental Science, for help.

>SCSh8.a Scientific investigators control the conditions of their experiments in order to produce valuable data.

What's it mean?
In experiments, scientists make sure to compare measurements with a control group to be certain that they mean something. Go to Chapter 2, Tools of Environmental Science, for help.

Review Question In an experiment, the experimental treatment differs from the control treatment only in the _____ being studied.
  A. experiment
  B. variable
  C. hypothesis
  D. data

Answers: SCSh7.b) D, SCSh7.c) D, SCSh7.d) C, SCSh7.e) D, SCSh8.a) B

George Smith State Park

Georgia

Stone Mountain Park

>**SCSh8.b** Scientific researchers are expected to critically assess the quality of data including possible sources of bias in their investigations' hypotheses, observations, data analyses, and interpretations.

What's it mean?

Scientists should look over their observations, research, and experiments to make sure data are correct even if they don't support the scientists' ideas.. Go to Chapter 2, Tools of Environmental Science, for help.

Review Question If the results of your experiment do not support your hypothesis, you should
- A. publish your results anyway.
- B. consider the results abnormal and continue working.
- C. find a way to rationalize your results.
- D. try another method.

>**SCSh8.c** Scientists use practices such as peer review and publication to reinforce the integrity of scientific activity and reporting.

What's it mean?

Scientists write reports and read each other's reports to be sure that investigations follow scientific methods. Go to Chapter 2, Tools of Environmental Science, for help.

Review Question What happens when an observation is submitted for peer review?
- A. The article is proofread before it is published.
- B. A professor gives a lecture based on a published article.
- C. The results are looked at closely by other scientific experts.
- D. Information on the experimental design is included in published works.

>**SCSh8.d** The merit of a new theory is judged by how well scientific data are explained by the new theory.

What's it mean?

New scientific explanations are considered good if they fit the observations they explain very well. Go to Chapter 2, Tools of Environmental Science, for help.

Review Question How is the merit of a new theory judged?
- A. by how long the new theory has been around
- B. by how many scientists agree with the new theory
- C. by how often the new theory appears in scientific journals
- D. by how well scientific data are explained by the new theory

>SCSh8.e The ultimate goal of science is to develop an understanding of the natural universe which is free of biases.

What's it mean?

The object of science is to come up with a fair and truthful way to explain the world around us. Go to Chapter 2, Tools of Environmental Science, for help.

Review Question Why is it important to use unbiased methods in scientific research?
- A. Unbiased methods are more persuasive to the public.
- B. Unbiased methods produce more data than biased methods.
- C. Unbiased methods are easier to develop than biased methods.
- D. Unbiased methods help scientists to better characterize the natural world.

>SCSh8.f Science disciplines and traditions differ from one another in what is studied, techniques used, and outcomes sought.

What's it mean?

Different braches of science look at different parts of the world, have different ways of studying the world, and look for different answers. Go to Chapter 1, Science and the Environment, for help.

Review Question Which of the following is an important foundation of environmental science?
- A. ecology
- B. economics
- C. meteorology
- D. political science

Content

>SEV1 Students will investigate the flow of energy and cycling of matter within an ecosystem and relate these phenomena to human society.

What's it mean?

In an ecosystem, producers convert solar energy into chemical energy that is then used by the producers themselves and a series of consumers and decomposers. Matter cycles through the ecosystem from producer, through consumers and decomposers, and back to the producers. Similar relationships of resource use exist in human social organization. Go to Chapter 5, How Ecosystems Work, for help.

>SEV1.a Interpret biogeochemical cycles including hydrologic, nitrogen, phosphorus, oxygen, and carbon cycles. Recognize that energy is not recycled in ecosystems.

What's it mean?

Matter is reused in ecosystems through cycles in which water and the elements nitrogen, phosphorus, oxygen, and carbon are used over and over by plants and animals. Sequences of chemical reactions and physical changes in living and in nonliving systems move these substances throughout the ecosystem where they are used by organisms. Energy is not recycled in the ecosystem but instead flows from producers through food webs and food chains. Go to Chapter 5, How Ecosystems Work, for help.

Review Question Which of the following statements about the nitrogen cycle is not true?
- A. Animals get nitrogen by eating plants or other animals.
- B. Plants generate nitrogen in their roots.
- C. Nitrogen moves back and forth between the atmosphere and living things.
- D. Decomposers break down waste to yield ammonia.

>SEV1.b Relate energy changes to food chains, food webs, and to trophic levels in a generalized ecosystem, recognizing that entropy is a primary factor in the loss of usable food energy during movement up the trophic levels.

What's it mean?

In an ecosystem, energy is captured from the sun or, in some cases, heat from the interior of Earth by producers. Energy is transferred to higher levels of the ecosystem as food. At each level, much of the energy is lost as heat to the environment so it is not available to the next level. The amount of food energy available to the top consumers is much less than the amount produced in the ecosystem. Go to Chapter 5, How Ecosystems Work, for help.

Review Question The energy lost between trophic levels
- A. can be captured only by parasitic organisms.
- B. cools the surrounding environment.
- C. is used in the course of normal living.
- D. evaporates in the atmosphere.

>SEV1.c Relate food production and quality of nutrition to population growth and the trophic levels

What's it mean?

One of the factors that limits the population of an organism is the amount of available food. If there is a good supply of nutritional food, the population tends to grow and if food resources are too limited the population falls. The number of species and trophic levels tends to be higher in regions with higher densities of producers. Go to Chapter 8, Understanding Populations, for help.

Review Question What happens to population size between the time it overshoots carrying capacity to when it recovers and stabilizes?

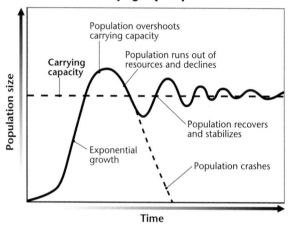

Carrying Capacity

- A. It remains stable.
- B. It declines steadily.
- C. It decreases before it stabilizes.
- D. It continues to increase at a steady rate.

*Fox,
Okefenokee Swamp*

Marta, Atlanta

>SEV1.d Relate the cycling of matter and the flow of energy to the Laws of Conservation of matter and energy. Identify the role and importance of decomposers in the recycling process.

What's it mean?

The Laws of Conservation of matter and energy state that neither matter nor energy is created or destroyed. They are converted to other forms of matter or energy. Decomposers play an important role in the process of converting matter when they break down dead organisms and return nutrient chemicals to the soil, water and atmosphere. Go to Chapter 5, How Ecosystems Work, for help.

Review Question What role do bacteria play during the nitrogen cycle?

- A. Bacteria store nitrogen in wastes.
- B. Bacteria turn nitrogen into phosphates.
- C. Bacteria convert nitrogen into water that can be used by living things.
- D. Bacteria turn nitrogen gas into a form that living things can use.

>SEV1.e Distinguish between abiotic and biotic factors in an ecosystem and describe how matter and energy move between these.

What's it mean?

An ecosystem consists of two parts: biotic factors and abiotic factors. Biotic factors are living things, once-living things, and waste products of living things. Abiotic factors are the non-living part of the environment, such as soil, water, air, and sunlight. Matter and energy can be transferred between biotic and abiotic factors. Go to Chapter 5, How Ecosystems Work, for help.

Review Question Which of the following is an effect of the increased burning of fossil fuels on the carbon cycle?

- A. More carbonates remain in fossil fuels.
- B. More carbon dioxide is absorbed by organisms.
- C. More carbon dioxide is absorbed by the atmosphere.
- D. More carbohydrates remain buried deep in the ground.

Answers: SEV1.b) C, SEV1.c) C, SEV1.d) D, SEV1.e) C

Sapelo Island
lighthouse

>**SEV2** Students will demonstrate an understanding that the Earth is one interconnected system.

What's it mean?

Earth and everything on it are constantly changing. Changes in one part of Earth, for example, the atmosphere, the oceans, or living things, affects other parts. Go to Chapter 3, The Dynamic Earth, for help.

>**SEV2.a** Describe how the abiotic components (water, air, and energy) affect the biosphere.

What's it mean?

The biosphere, all the living things on Earth, is closely related to other parts of the Earth system. Abiotic factors, such as water, air, and the availability of energy, affect the types and number of living things that can live in a particular place. Go to Chapter 4, The Organization of Life, for help.

Review Question How does energy move through most ecosystems on Earth?
   A. from the sun to consumers to producers
   B. from the sun to producers to consumers to decomposers
   C. from the sun to decomposers to producers to consumers
   D. from the sun to consumers to producers back to consumers

>**SEV2.b** Recognize and give examples of the hierarchy of the biological entities of the biosphere (organisms, populations, communities, ecosystems, and biosphere).

What's it mean?

The biosphere consists of all the living things on Earth. Scientists organize the biosphere by levels:

- organism—an individual living thing
- population—a group of organisms of the same species in a geographical area
- community—a group of populations that interact with one another
- ecosystem—a community and its abiotic environment
- biosphere—all the ecosystems on Earth

Go to Chapter 4, The Organization of Life, for help.

Review Question Which of the following pairs of organisms belong to the same population?
A. a dog and a cat
B. a marigold and a geranium
C. a human mother and her child
D. a spider and a cockroach

>SEV2.c Characterize the components that define a Biome.

Abiotic Factors—to include precipitation, temperature and soils.

Biotic Factors—plant and animal adaptations that create success in that biome.

What's it mean?

A biome is a large region with a specific type of climate and certain types of plant and animal communities. The type of plants that grow in a particular region depend on climate conditions and type of soil. The plant and animal life in a biome has adapted to the particular conditions. Go to Chapter 6, Biomes, for help.

Review Question According to the map, which of the following determines the characteristics of a biome?

Biomes of Africa

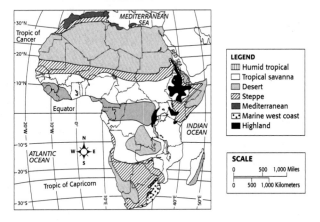

A. geographic borders
B. latitude
C. longitude
D. the Indian Ocean

Answers: SEV2.a) B, SEV2.b) C, SEV2.c) B

Peach tree blossoms

>SEV2.d Characterize the components that define fresh-water and marine systems.

Abiotic Factors—to include light, dissolved oxygen, phosphorus, nitrogen, pH and substrate. Biotic Factors—plant and animal adaptations characteristic to that system.

What's it mean?

Aquatic ecosystems include both freshwater systems, such as rivers and lakes, and saltwater systems, such as oceans and salt marshes. The plants and animals in an aquatic ecosystem have adapted to specific abiotic conditions of the system. Abiotic factors that affect living things in aquatic systems include light, dissolved oxygen, nutrients, acidity, and materials such as rocks and sand. Go to Chapter 7, Aquatic Ecosystems, for help.

Review Question Organisms living in coastal areas must adapt to what changes?

A. water level and degree of salinity
B. water level and amount of sunlight
C. temperature and availability of oxygen
D. temperature and availability of nutrients

>SEV3 Students will describe stability and change in ecosystems.

What's it mean?

Ecosystems change when there is a change in biotic or abiotic factors. A major change, or disturbance, can affect all levels of the ecosystem.

After a disturbance, organisms in an environment follow a pattern of change over time. If no major disturbances occur, eventually, the organisms will grow into a stable community. In a stable ecosystem, there are no major changes until the system is disturbed again. Go to Chapter 5, How Ecosystems Work, for help.

>SEV3.a Describe interconnections between abiotic and biotic factors, including normal cyclic fluctuations and changes associated with climatic change (i.e. ice ages).

What's it mean?

The organisms in an ecosystem depend on abiotic factors to provide such things as water, energy, and shelter. The biotic and abiotic parts of the ecosystem are connected so a change in one affects the other. For example, organisms in an ecosystem will change migration patterns to adapt to changes in climate temperatures. Go to Chapter 5, How Ecosystems Work, for help.

Review Question In which season (in the Northern Hemisphere) does carbon dioxide in the atmosphere decrease as a result of natural processes?

A. fall
B. winter
C. summer
D. spring

Palmyra Plantation at Melon Bluff

Waters Creek

>SEV3.b Explain succession in terms of changes in communities through time to include changes in biomass, diversity, and complexity.

What's it mean?

Ecological succession is a gradual change and replacement of some or all of the species in a community. After a disturbance, an ecosystem undergoes a succession as new plants adapt to conditions and affect the rest of the ecosystem. Each level of an ecological succession includes changes in the number and diversity of living things and how they interact with one another. Go to Chapter 5, How Ecosystems Work, for help.

Review Question Which of the following are most likely to be the pioneer organisms on an area of bare rock?
- A. trees
- B. shrubs
- C. lichens
- D. perennial grasses

>SEV3.c Explain how succession may be altered by traumatic events.

What's it mean?

The succession of populations in an ecosystem can be changed if there is a major change in some factor of the ecosystem. Large scale events such as volcanic eruptions, floods, or fires can disrupt the ecosystem so that the succession of living things changes. Go to Chapter 5, How Ecosystems Work, for help.

Review Question Suppose that a plague eliminates all the primary consumers in an ecosystem. Which of these changes will most likely occur in this ecosystem?
- A. The population of producers will decline rapidly.
- B. The population of secondary consumers will increase.
- C. All organisms in the ecosystem will die out.
- D. Producers will flourish.

>SEV3.d Explain how biotic and abiotic factors influence populations.

What's it mean?

A population, or group of organisms of the same species living in an area, is affected by other factors in the ecosystem. Biotic factors, such as food sources, prey, and competitive populations can allow a population to grow or keep it from growing. Abiotic factors, such as temperature and the availability of water, also determine the number of organisms of a population that can be supported by the ecosystem. Go to Chapter 4, The Organization of Life, for help.

Review Question The graph below shows the change in population of reindeer on an Alaskan Island. Which of the following could not be a factor in the population decrease around 1937?

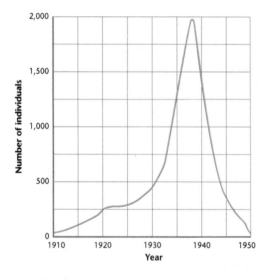

A. Disease decreased the number of predators.
B. Abnormal weather affected food production.
C. The growing population depleted the food supply.
D. A new predator was introduced to the island.

>SEV3.e Describe interactions between individuals (i.e. mutualism, commensalisms, parasitism, predation, and competition).

What's it mean?

Species within an ecosystem can interact in different ways:

- Mutualism is a relationship that benefits both species.
- Commensalism is a relationship that benefits one species but does not help or harm the other species.
- Parasitism occurs when one species lives on another and takes nourishment from it, generally without killing its host.
- Predation occurs when one species feeds on another.
- Competition occurs when different individuals or populations attempt to use the same limited resources.

Go to Chapter 8, Understanding Populations, for help.

Centennial Park, Atlanta

Review Question Which of the interactions listed in the table is harmful to both species?

Interactions Between Two Species

Interaction	Species A	Species B
Competition	Fox	Coyote
Predation	Kit fox	Kangaroo rat
Mutualism	Yucca moth	Yucca
Commensalism	Wren	Cactus

A. commensalism
B. competition
C. mutualism
D. predation

>SEV4 Students will understand and describe availability, allocation and conservation of energy and other resources.

What's it mean?
Earth's resources that are used by humans are limited. Many of them are found only in specific parts of the world. People must make decisions about how resources are to be used, who will use them, and how they can be conserved in order to make best use of the available resources. Go to Unit 5, Mineral and Energy Resources, for help.

>SEV4.a Differentiate between renewable and nonrenewable resources including how different resources are produced, rates of use, renewal rates, and limitations of sources. Distinguish between natural and produced resources.

What's it mean?
Some natural resources are renewable, which means that they are produced from sources that are constantly being formed. Energy produced from the sun, wind, or flowing water is a renewable resource. Nonrenewable resources are materials that are not replaced by nature. These include fossil fuels and uranium for energy production, as well as metals, minerals and other materials mined from Earth. Go to Chapter 17, Nonrenewable Energy, and Chapter 18, Renewable Energy for help.

Review Question Based on the map below, what can be inferred about the use of hydroelectric power in the United States?

Hydroelectric Power

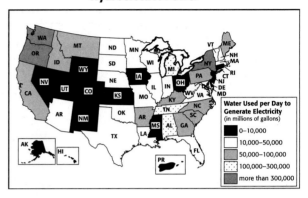

A. There are more dams in Oregon than in Kansas.
B. There is more hydroelectric power used in New Mexico than in Alabama.
C. The upper Midwest uses more water for hydroelectric power than New England.
D. The biggest users of water for hydroelectricity are located along the Mississippi River.

>SEV4.b Describe how technology is increasing the efficiency of utilization and accessibility of resources.

What's it mean?
New technologies have changed how resources are used. As technologies are developed, people are able to reach resources that could not be obtained previously. Other technologies increase the efficiency of existing resources by recycling them or reducing the amount needed for a particular use. Go to Chapter 16, Mining and Mineral Resources, for help.

Review Question Which of the following methods is not a subsurface mining method?
A. quarrying
B. solution mining
C. longwall mining
D. room-and-pillar mining

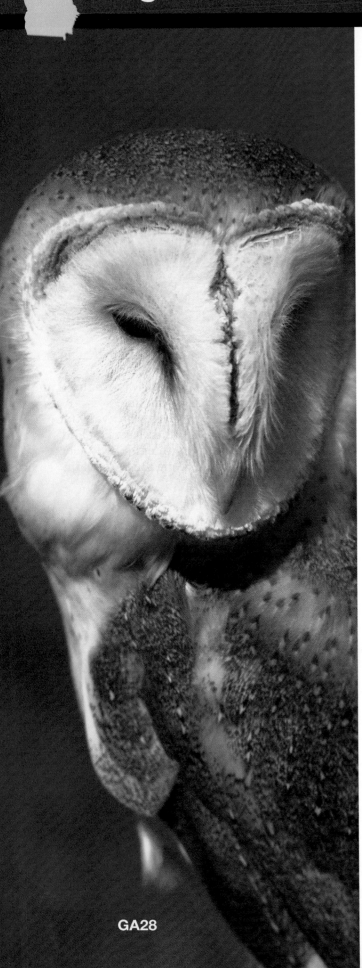

>**SEV4.c** Describe how energy and other resource utilization impact the environment and recognize that individuals as well as larger entities (businesses, governments, etc.) have impact on energy efficiency.

What's it mean?

The production and use of energy and other resources has harmful effect s on the environment and the ecosystems humans need for survival. Because energy use is an important part of our daily lives, individuals can make choices that affect how energy is used. Go to Chapter 21, Economics, Policy, and the Future, for help.

Review Question How can an individual have an effect on global environmental problems?
- A. Buy things that provide only a single use.
- B. Buy paper goods at the local discount store.
- C. Structure daily activities around convenience.
- D. Purchase vegetables that are organically grown.

>**SEV4.d** Describe the relationship of energy consumption and the living standards of societies.

What's it mean?

Energy consumption is related to living standards. Developed nations consume more energy and other resources than less developed nations. Greater levels of production, more travel, and increased consumption all require additional energy. Go to Chapter 17, Nonrenewable Energy, and Chapter 18, Renewable Energy, for help.

Review Question Which of the following statements describes energy consumption trends today?
- A. Developed nations are using less energy per person.
- B. Developing nations are using less energy per person.
- C. Developed nations are using more energy than undeveloped nations.
- D. Developing nations are using more energy than developed nations.

>SEV4.e Describe the commonly used fuels (e.g. fossil fuels, nuclear fuels, etc.) and some alternative fuels (e.g. wind, solar, ethanol, etc.) including the required technology, availability, pollution problems and implementation problems. Recognize the origin of fossil fuels and the problems associated with our dependence on this energy source.

What's it mean?

Fossil fuels provide most energy for human use today. Dependence on fossil fuels has created political and social problems because they are not evenly distributed, and environmental problems such as climate change and acid rain. Because there is a limited supply of fossil fuels, people have developed alternatives, including wind, sun, and ethanol. These fuels also have some limitations, such as the costs of technology development and difficulties in adding them to existing processes. Go to Chapter 17, Nonrenewable Energy, and Chapter 18, Renewable Energy, for help.

Review Question What can be concluded about oil production from the graph?

Past and Predicted Oil Production

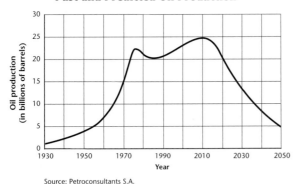

Source: Petroconsultants S.A.

A. Oil production hit its peak in the mid 20th century.
B. Oil production saw a dramatic increase during the 1980s.
C. Oil production continued to increase throughout the 1900s.
D. Oil production more than doubled between 1965 and 1975.

>SEV4.f Describe the need for informed decision making of resource utilization. (i.e. energy and water usage allocation, conservation, food and land, and long-term depletion)

What's it mean?

The survival of individuals and of human societies depends on how limited resources are used. In order to have sustainable use of natural resources, choices have to be made about how energy, water, and other resources will be used, distributed, and conserved. If the best decisions are to be made, people must be informed about choices and consequences. Go to Chapter 21, Economics, Policy, and the Future, for help.

Review Question Which of the following statements about U.S. environmental policy is not true?

A. During most of the 19th century, most Americans were not concerned about environmental consequences.
B. During the 1960s, several individuals had strong effects on public thinking about environmental issues.
C. Before Earth Day 1970, no one in the United States cared about the environment.
D. The Environmental Protection Agency was established at a time of increasing public awareness of environmental problems.

>SEV5 Students will recognize that human beings are part of the global ecosystem and will evaluate the effects of human activities and technology on ecosystems.

What's it mean?

Because humans are part of their ecosystems, changes in the ecosystem affect people and human activities affect the ecosystem.

>SEV5.a Describe factors affecting population growth of all organisms, including humans. Relate these to factors affecting growth rates and carrying capacity of the environment.

What's it mean?

In an ecosystem, the population of species can change. The growth rate of a population is the birth rate minus the death rate. There are a number of things that affect population growth, including the birth rate of the species, the number of predators, and the amount of food and other resources. The carrying capacity of an ecosystem is the maximum population of a species that it can support indefinitely. These principles apply to human populations as well as all other populations. Go to Chapter 8, Understanding Populations, for help.

Review Question If the population size was nearly 2,000 when it overshot carrying capacity, and 1,500 when it was at its lowest amount of decline during its recovery, what is the estimated carrying capacity of the population?

Carrying Capacity

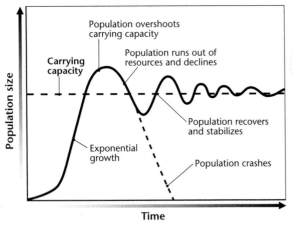

A. 1,600
B. 1,750
C. 1,800
D. 1,950

>SEV5.b Describe the effects of population growth, demographic transitions, cultural differences, emergent diseases, etc. on societal stability.

What's it mean?

The stability of human societies and the interactions among people is affected by the changes in population. The population size in an area and the mix of cultures both affect stability. Some influences on human society include population growth, differences between different cultures, migration, and the spread of diseases. Go to Chapter 9 ,The Human Population, for help.

Review Question A country in the second stage of the demographic transition may have all of the following except
A. increasing agricultural production.
B. improving healthcare and education.
C. decreasing population size.
D. decreasing death rates.

>SEV5.c Explain how human activities affect global and local sustainability.

What's it mean?

Humans affect the ecosystems by activities such as farming, building, and using natural resources. Human activities can increase or decrease sustainability, the ability of the environment to provide the resources that allow the human population to survive. Go to Chapter 14, The Human Population, for help.

Review Question Which of the following is a likely result of deforestation?
A. The amount of carbon dioxide removed from the atmosphere is reduced.
B. Wind blows soil away because the plant cover has been removed.
C. Water runs off the land more rapidly and causes floods.
D. all of the above

>**SEV5.d** Describe the actual and potential effects of habitat destruction, erosion, and depletion of soil fertility associated with human activities.

What's it mean?

Agriculture provides most of the food needed for the human population. For agriculture to continue to sustain the population, good practices are needed. Not using these practices causes the destruction of animal and human habitat, loss of useful soil by erosion, and using up all the nutrients so that soil cannot produce enough crops. Go to Chapter 15, Food and Agriculture, for help.

Review Question Which of the following is an effect of soil erosion?

A. increased crop yields
B. increase in land fertility
C. decrease in desertification
D. decrease in the amount of topsoil

>**SEV5.e** Describe the effects and potential implications of pollution and resource depletion on the environment at the local and global levels (e.g. air and water pollution, solid waste disposal, depletion of the stratospheric ozone, global warming, and land uses).

What's it mean?

The use of resources provides materials needed for human survival but it is also a cause of pollution and damage to the environment. Some of the problems that result from use of energy and other resources include pollution of the atmosphere and water systems, destruction of ozone in the stratosphere, global warming, and changes in land uses. Go to Chapter 13, Atmosphere and Climate Change, for help.

Review Question The development and widespread use of CFCs led to what scientific discovery?

A. CFC molecules are chemically stable.
B. CFC molecules contain chlorine atoms.
C. CFC molecules are destroying the ozone layer.
D. CFC molecules are protecting the ozone layer.

Melon Bluff Nature Center

Answers: SEV5.a) C, SEV5.b) C, SEV5.c) D, SEV5.d) D, SEV5.e) C

>SEV5.f Describe how political, legal, social, and economic decisions may affect global and local ecosystems.

What's it mean?

Local and global ecosystems are affected by human decisions about resource use. Development and removal of resources can cause ecosystems to deteriorate. Decisions to use resources in sustainable ways and to preserve existing resources can prevent deterioration of ecosystems. These decisions can be made by individuals or by societies. Go to Chapter 21, Economics, Policy, and the Future, for help.

Review Question How is the number of national parks related to the size of a country in Central America?

National Parks

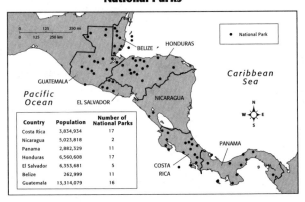

Country	Population	Number of National Parks
Costa Rica	3,834,934	17
Nicaragua	5,023,818	2
Panama	2,882,329	11
Honduras	6,560,608	17
El Salvador	6,353,681	5
Belize	262,999	11
Guatemala	13,314,079	16

A. The bigger countries have more national parks.
B. The smaller countries have more national parks.
C. The countries with the most coastline have more national parks.
D. There is no correlation between a country's size and its national parks.

Answer: SEV5.f) D

Georgia peaches

HOLT

Environmental Science

Karen Arms, Ph.D., J.D.
Savannah, Georgia

HOLT, RINEHART AND WINSTON

A Harcourt Education Company

Orlando • **Austin** • New York • San Diego • London

ABOUT THE AUTHOR

Karen Arms, Ph.D., J.D.

Karen Arms received her Ph.D. in molecular biology from Oxford University and a doctor of law from Cornell University. She was an assistant professor of biology at Cornell University, where she taught introductory biology and courses in science and society. She also taught marine biology at the University of Georgia Marine Biology Station and introductory biology at South College in Savannah, Georgia. In addition to *Holt Environmental Science,* Dr. Arms has written several college-level biology textbooks. Her interest in and concern for the environment led her to form an ecotourism organization that introduces people to the ecosystems of the southeastern coast.

For permission to reprint copyrighted material, grateful acknowledgement is made to the following sources:

Lippincott Williams & Wilkins: Adaptation of "Figure 4: Environmental portion of disease in the major world regions" (retitled "Poor Health by World Region") by Kirk R. Smith from "How Much Global Ill Health Is Attributable to Environmental Factors?" by Kirk R. Smith, Carlos F. Corvalán, and Tord Kjellström from *Epidemiology,* vol. 10, no.5, September 1999, pp. 573–584. Copyright © 1999 by Epidemiology Resources Inc.

Dr. Pim Martens: "Figure 6: Malaria risk by the year 2020" by Pim Martens from *American Scientist November–December 1999* Web site, accessed March 5, 2002, at www.sigmaxi.org/amsci/articles/99articles/Martens.html. Copyright © 1999 by Dr. Pim Martens.

United Nations Population Fund (UNFPA): From "Women and the Environment" from *The State of the World Population 2001,* edited by Alex Marshall. Copyright © 2001 by UNFPA.

ISBN-13: 978-0-03-078136-0
ISBN-10: 0-03-078136-1

6 7 048 09 08

Acknowledgments

CONTRIBUTING WRITERS

Inclusion Specialist

Joan A. Altobelli
Special Education Director
Austin Independent School District
Austin, Texas

John A. Solorio
Multiple Technologies Lab Facilitator
Austin Independent School District
Austin, Texas

Feature Development and Lab Safety Consultants

Michele Benn
Science Teacher
Beaver Falls High School
Beaver Falls, Pennsylvania

Randa Flinn
Science Teacher
Northeast High School
Fort Lauderdale, Florida

Eric Grace, Ph.D.
Science Writer
Victoria, British Columbia, Canada

Natasha Marko
Science Writer
Newmarket, Ontario, Canada

Alyson M. Mike
Science Teacher
East Helena Public Schools
East Helena, Montana

Frank Mustoe, Ph.D.
Science Writer
Barrie, Ontario, Canada

Tammie Niffenegger
Science Chair and Science Teacher
Port Washington High School
Waldo, Wisconsin

Gabriell DeBear Paye
Science and Environmental Technology Lead Teacher
West Roxbury High School
West Roxbury, Massachusetts

Teresa Wilson
Science Writer
Austin, Texas

Teacher Edition Development

Kara R. Dotter
Science Writer
Austin, Texas

Lisa Parks
Science Writer
Seattle, Washington

Meredith Phillips
Science Writer
Brooklyn, New York

Catherine Podeszwa
Science Writer
Duluth, Minnesota

Teresa Wilson
Science Writer
Austin, Texas

ACADEMIC REVIEWERS

Jess F. Adkins, Ph.D.
Assistant Professor of Geochemistry and Global Environment Science
Division of Geological and Planetary Sciences
California Institute of Technology
Pasadena, California

Foster K. Amey, Ph.D.
Associate Professor of Sociology
Department of Sociology and Anthropology
Middle Tennessee State University
Murfreesboro, Tennessee

Mead Allison, Ph.D.
Associate Professor
Department of Geology and Earth Sciences
Tulane University
New Orleans, Louisiana

David M. Armstrong, Ph.D.
Professor
Environmental, Population, and Organismic Biology
University of Colorado
Boulder, Colorado

Paul D. Asimow, Ph.D.
Associate Professor of Geology and Geochemistry
Division of Geological and Planetary Sciences
California Institute of Technology
Pasadena, California

Nolan B. Aughenbaugh, Ph.D.
Professor
Department of Geology and Geological Engineering
University of Mississippi
University, Mississippi

Janice L. Branson
Assistant Professor
School of Agriculture
Tennessee Technological University
Cookeville, Tennessee

Gary Campbell, Ph.D.
Professor of Mineral Economics
School of Business and Economics
Michigan Technological University
Houghton, Michigan

Laura Chenault, D.V.M.
Bulverde, Texas

Marian R. Chertow, Ph.D.
Assistant Professor of Industrial Environmental Management
Yale School of Forestry and Environmental Studies
Yale University
New Haven, Connecticut

Susan L. Cutter, Ph.D.
Carolina Distinguished Professor
Department of Geography
University of South Carolina
Columbia, South Carolina

Susan B. Dickey, R.N., Ph.D.
Associate Professor
Pediatric Nursing
Temple University
Philadelphia, Pennsylvania

Dale Elifrits, Ph.D.
Professor
Department of Physics and Geology
Northern Kentucky University
Highland Heights, Kentucky

Turgay Ertekin, Ph.D.
George E. Trimble Chair in Earth and Mineral Sciences
Professor of Petroleum and Natural Gas Engineering
Department of Energy and Geo-Environmental Engineering
Penn State University
University Park, Pennsylvania

Acknowledgments

Ronald A. Feldman, Ph.D.
Ruth Harris Ottman Centennial Professor for the Advancement of Social Work Education
Director, Center for the Study of Social Work Practice
Columbia University
New York, New York

Linda Gaul, Ph.D.
Epidemiologist
Texas Department of Health
Austin, Texas

Matthew R. Gilligan, Ph.D.
Professor and Program Coordinator, Marine Sciences
Department of Natural Sciences and Mathematics
Savannah State University
Savannah, Georgia

Deborah Jean Gochfeld, Ph.D.
Senior Scientist
National Center for Natural Products Research
University of Mississippi
University, Mississippi

John Goodge, Ph.D.
Associate Professor of Geology
Southern Methodist University
Dallas, Texas

Herbert Grossman, Ph.D.
Associate Professor of Botany and Biology, Retired
Department of Biology
Pennsylvania State University
University Park, Pennsylvania

Mary L. Haasch, Ph.D.
NRC Senior Scientist
U.S. Environmental Protection Agency
Duluth, Minnesota

David Haig, Ph.D.
Associate Professor of Biology
Department of Organismic and Evolutionary Biology
Harvard University
Cambridge, Massachusetts

Vicki Hansen, Ph.D.
Professor of Geological Sciences
Department of Geology
Southern Methodist University
Dallas, Texas

Rosalind Harris, Ph.D.
Professor, Rural Agriculture
Department of Sociology
University of Kentucky
Lexington, Kentucky

Richard Hey, Ph.D.
Professor of Geophysics
School of Ocean and Earth Sciences Technology
University of Hawaii
Honolulu, Hawaii

James C. Hower, Ph.D.
Editor-in-Chief
International Journal of Coal Geology
Senior Scientist
Center for Applied Energy Research
University of Kentucky
Lexington, Kentucky

Steven A. Jennings, Ph.D.
Associate Professor of Geography
Department of Geography and Environmental Studies
University of Colorado
Colorado Springs, Colorado

Elizabeth W. Kleppinger, Ph.D.
Adjunct Professor
Department of Chemistry
Eastern Kentucky University
Richmond, Kentucky

Joel Leventhal, Ph.D.
Emeritus Scientist
U.S. Geological Survey and Diversified Geochemistry
Lakewood, Colorado

Alex Mills, Ph.D.
University of Toronto
Toronto, Ontario, Canada

Joann Mossa, Ph.D.
Associate Professor
Department of Geography
University of Florida
Gainesville, Florida

Gary Mueller, Ph.D.
Associate Professor of Nuclear Engineering
Department of Engineering
University of Missouri
Rolla, Missouri

Barbara Murck, Ph.D.
Director, Environmental Programs
University of Toronto
Mississauga, Ontario, Canada

Emily Niemeyer, Ph.D.
Assistant Professor of Chemistry
Department of Chemistry
Southwestern University
Georgetown, Texas

Bryan Norton, Ph.D.
Professor
School of Public Policy
Georgia Institute of Technology
Atlanta, Georgia

Eva Oberdörster, Ph.D.
Lecturer
Department of Biological Sciences
Southern Methodist University
Dallas, Texas

Hilary Olson, Ph.D.
Research Scientist
Institute of Geophysics
The University of Texas
Austin, Texas

Ken Peace, C.C.E.
Geology Supervisor
Ark Land Company
St. Louis, Missouri

Per F. Peterson, Ph.D.
Professor and Chair
Department of Nuclear Engineering
University of California
Berkeley, California

David Pimentel, Ph.D.
Professor and Agricultural Ecologist
Department of Entomology, Systematics and Ecology
Cornell University
Ithaca, New York

Mary M. Poulton, Ph.D.
Department Head and Associate Professor of Geological Engineering
Department of Mining and Geological Engineering
University of Arizona
Tucson, Arizona

Barron Rector, Ph.D.
Associate Professor and Extension Range Specialist
Texas Agricultural Extension Service
Texas A&M University
College Station, Texas

continued on page 709

CONTENTS IN BRIEF

CONTENTS

INTRODUCTION TO ENVIRONMENTAL SCIENCE   UNIT 1

      EARTH SCIENCE CONNECTION

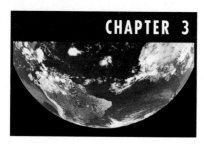
ECOLOGY

UNIT 2

EARTH SCIENCE CONNECTION

MINERAL AND ENERGY RESOURCES

UNIT 5

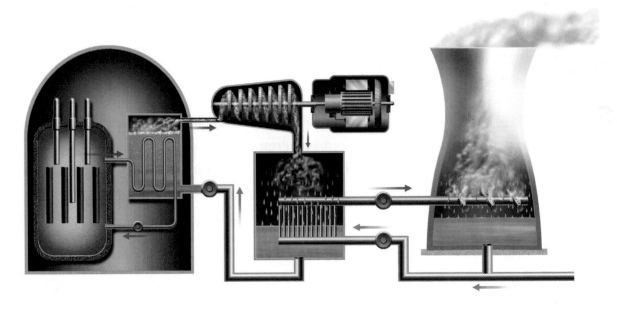

🌐 **EARTH SCIENCE CONNECTION**

OUR HEALTH AND OUR FUTURE

UNIT 6

APPENDIX

Exploration Labs

Skills Practice Labs

Inquiry Labs

QuickLABS

MAPS IN ACTION

FEATURE ARTICLES

Making a Difference

Points of View

Society and the Environment

CASE STUDIES

Safety Symbols

The following safety symbols will appear in this text when you are asked to perform a procedure requiring extra precautions. Once you have familiarized yourself with these safety symbols, turn to pp. 600–603 for safety guidelines to use in all of your laboratory work in environmental science.

 ## EYE PROTECTION

- Wear safety goggles when working around chemicals, acids, bases, flames, or heating devices. Contents under pressure may become projectiles and cause serious injury.
- Never look directly at the sun through any optical device or use direct sunlight to illuminate a microscope.
- Avoid wearing contact lenses in the lab.
- If any substance gets into your eyes, notify your instructor immediately and flush your eyes with running water for at least 15 minutes.

 ## CLOTHING PROTECTION

- Secure loose clothing and remove dangling jewelry. Do not wear open-toed shoes or sandals in the lab.
- Wear an apron or lab coat to protect your clothing when you are working with chemicals.
- If a spill gets on your clothing, rinse it off immediately with water for at least 5 minutes while notifying your instructor.

 ## CAUSTIC SUBSTANCES

- If a chemical gets on your skin, on your clothing, or in your eyes, rinse it immediately and alert your instructor.
- If a chemical is spilled on the floor or lab bench, alert your instructor, but do not clean it up yourself unless your instructor directs you to do so.

 ## CHEMICAL SAFETY

- Always use caution when working with chemicals.
- Always wear appropriate protective equipment. Always wear eye goggles, gloves, and a lab apron or lab coat when you are working with any chemical or chemical solution.
- Never mix chemicals unless your instructor directs you to do so.
- Never taste, touch, or smell chemicals unless your instructor directs you to do so.
- Add an acid or base to water; never add water to an acid or base.
- Never return an unused chemical to its original container.
- Never transfer substances by sucking on a pipet or straw; use a suction bulb.
- Follow instructions for proper disposal.

 ## ANIMAL SAFETY

- Always obtain permission before bringing any animal to school.
- Handle animals carefully and respectfully.
- Wash your hands thoroughly after handling any animal.

 ## PLANT SAFETY

- Wear disposable polyethylene gloves when handling any wild plant.
- Do not eat any part of a plant or plant seed used in the lab.
- Wash hands thoroughly after handling any part of a plant.
- When outdoors, do not pick any wild plants unless your instructor directs you to do so.

 ## ELECTRICAL SAFETY

- Do not place electrical cords in walking areas or let cords hang over a table edge in a way that could cause equipment to fall if the cord is accidentally pulled.

- Do not use equipment that has frayed electrical cords or loose plugs.
- Be sure that equipment is in the "off" position before you plug it in.
- Never use an electrical appliance around water or with wet hands or clothing.
- Be sure to turn off and unplug electrical equipment when you are finished using it.

HEATING SAFETY

- Avoid wearing hair spray or hair gel on lab days.
- Whenever possible, use an electric hot plate instead of an open flame as a heat source.
- When heating materials in a test tube, always angle the test tube away from yourself and others.
- Glass containers used for heating should be made of heat-resistant glass.

SHARP OBJECTS

- Use knives and other sharp instruments with extreme care.
- Never cut objects while holding them in your hands. Place objects on a suitable work surface for cutting.
- Never use a double-edged razor in the lab.

HAND SAFETY

- To avoid burns, wear heat-resistant gloves whenever instructed to do so.
- Always wear protective gloves when working with an open flame, chemicals, solutions, or wild or unknown plants.
- If you do not know whether an object is hot, do not touch it.
- Use tongs when heating test tubes. Never hold a test tube in your hand to heat the test tube.

FIRE SAFETY

- Know the location of laboratory fire extinguishers and fire-safety blankets.
- Know your school's fire-evacuation routes.

GAS SAFETY

- Do not inhale any gas or vapor unless your instructor directs you to do so. Do not breathe pure gases.
- Handle materials prone to emit vapors or gases in a well-ventilated area. This work should be done in an approved chemical fume hood.

GLASSWARE SAFETY

- Check the condition of glassware before and after using it. Inform your teacher of any broken, chipped, or cracked glassware, because it should not be used.
- Do not pick up broken glass with your bare hands. Place broken glass in a specially designated disposal container.

WASTE DISPOSAL

- Clean and decontaminate all work surfaces and personal protective equipment as directed by your instructor.
- Dispose of all broken glass, contaminated sharp objects, and other contaminated materials (biological and chemical) in special containers as directed by your instructor.

HYGIENIC CARE/CLEAN HANDS

- Keep your hands away from your face and mouth.
- Always wash your hands thoroughly when you have finished with an experiment.

To the Student

Like all other sciences, environmental science is a process of satisfying our curiosity about why things are the way they are and about how things happen the way they do. For example, in studying environmental science, you may discover the answers to the following questions.

Q How could the birth of these otters indicate a healthy ecosystem?

Q How could the demise of this seemingly unimportant insect cause severe damage to the rain forest in which it lives?

Q How could the watering of this lawn affect the water quality of a nearby stream?

Q How could a population of iguanas help save a rain forest from destruction?

Q How could recycling an aluminum can help save fossil fuels and reduce both air and water pollution?

Q How could the exhaust from these cars in New York contribute to the decline of salmon in Canada?

Q How could technology used to study weather help us to understand air pollution?

Learning about Environmental Science

You may not have expected to have the questions shown on these pages answered in your study of environmental science. The answers to these questions and many more like them help define this unusual and exciting area of study. In learning about the various aspects of our environment, you will quickly come to understand how interdependent life on Earth is.

In many cases, we know so little about environmental interactions that we can't even begin to predict long-term effects. For example, it took nearly 15 years of study before we understood the relationship between the pesticide DDT and the declining populations of bald eagles. It will take even longer to understand the relationship between pollution and the climate. And what usually happens is that the answer to one question leads to a string of new questions.

Perhaps the most important question to ask at the beginning of this course is: **What do you hope to get out of this environmental science text?**

You may be interested in science and want to know more about the inner workings of our environment. Or you may be interested in learning more about human impact on the environment and what we can do to reduce the negative consequences. You may even want to know more about the environment firsthand so that you can decipher environmental issues for yourself, rather than simply accepting someone else's point of view.

Challenge

Regardless of your reasons for taking this course, my challenge to you is to think for yourself. In reading this textbook, you not only will learn a lot about science, you will learn about the complex issues facing our environment. You will explore different points of view and be exposed to a variety of differing opinions. Don't feel that you have to accept any particular opinion as your own. As your knowledge and skills in environmental science grow, so will your ability to draw your own conclusions.

Karen Arms

How to Use Your Textbook

Your Roadmap for Success with *Holt Environmental Science*

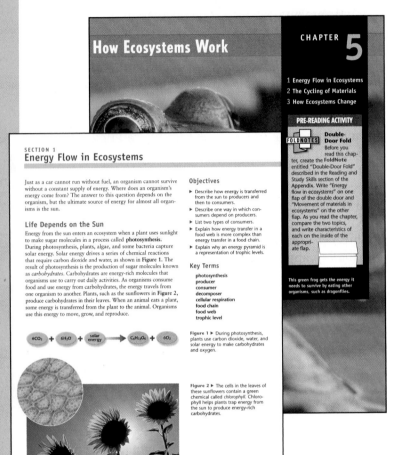

Get Organized

Do the **Pre-Reading Activity** at the beginning of each chapter to create a **FoldNote**, which is a helpful note-taking and study aid. Use the **Graphic Organizer** activity within the chapter to organize the chapter content in a way that you understand.

STUDY TIP Go to the **Reading and Study Skills** section of the Appendix for guidance on making FoldNotes and Graphic Organizers.

Read for Meaning

Read the **Objectives** at the beginning of each section, because they will tell you what you'll need to learn. **Key Terms** are also listed for each section. Each key term is also highlighted in the text. Be sure to answer the **Reading Check** questions and then look in the Appendix to see how you are doing. After reading each chapter, turn to the **Chapter Highlights** page and review the Key Terms and the **Main Ideas,** which are brief summaries of the chapter's key concepts. You may want to do this even before you read the chapter.

STUDY TIP If you don't understand a definition, reread the page on which the term is introduced. The surrounding text should help make the definition easier to understand.

Be Resourceful, Use the Web

Internet Connect boxes in your textbook take you to resources that you can use for science projects, reports, and research papers. Go to **scilinks.org** and type in the SciLinks code to get information on a topic.

Visit go.hrw.com

Find resources and reference materials that go with your textbook at **go.hrw.com.** Enter the keyword HE6 Home to access the home page for your textbook.

Prepare for Tests

Section Reviews and **Chapter Reviews** test your knowledge of the main points of the chapter. Critical Thinking items challenge you to think about the material in different ways and in greater depth. The **Standardized Test Prep** that is located at the end of each chapter helps you sharpen your test-taking abilities.

STUDY TIP Reread the Section Objectives and Chapter Highlights when studying for a test to be sure you know the material.

Use the Appendix

Your **Appendix** contains a variety of resources designed to enhance your learning experience. These resources include **Reading and Study Skills**, a **Math Skills Refresher**, and a **Chemistry Refresher**, which provide helpful study aids. The Appendix also contains features on **Economic Concepts, Environmental Careers**, and **Ecoskills**. In addition, you can find information on **SI Conversions, Mineral Uses**, and a variety of **Maps**.

Figure 10 ▶ Examples of at-risk species and populations in the United States include ❶ the cecropia moth, (declining populations), ❷ the tulip poplar tree (limited distribution), ❸ the crayfish *Cambarus mongalensis* (limited distribution), ❹ the desert pupfish (endangered), and ❺ the northern spotted owl (threatened).

Biodiversity in the United States You may notice that three of the biodiversity hotspots in **Figure 9** are partly within U.S. borders. The United States includes a wide variety of unique ecosystems, including the Florida Everglades, the California coastal region, Hawaii, the Midwestern prairies, and the forests of the Pacific Northwest. The United States holds unusually high numbers of species of freshwater fishes, mussels, snails, and crayfish. Species diversity in the United States is also high among groups of land plants such as pine trees and sunflowers. Some examples of the many species and populations that are at risk of being lost are shown in **Figure 10**.

The California Floristic Province, a biodiversity hotspot, is home to 3,488 native plant species. Of these species, 2,124 are endemic and 565 are threatened or endangered. The threats to this area include the use of land for agriculture and housing, dam construction, overuse of water, destructive recreation, and mining—all stemming from local human population growth.

SECTION 2 Review

1. **Describe** four ways that species are being threatened with extinction globally.

2. **Define** and give examples of *endangered species* and *threatened species*.

3. **List** areas of the Earth that have high levels of biodiversity and many threats to species.

4. **Compare** the amount of biodiversity in the United States to that of the rest of the world.

CRITICAL THINKING

5. **Interpreting Graphics** The biodiversity hot spots shown in Figure 9 share several characteristics besides a great number of species. Look at the map, and name as many shared characteristics as you can.

6. **Expressing Opinions** Which of the various threats to biodiversity do you think will be most difficult to stop? Which are hardest to justify? Write a paragraph to explain your opinion. **WRITING SKILLS**

Section 2 **Biodiversity at Risk** **269**

Visit Holt Online Learning

If your teacher gives you a special password to log onto the **Holt Online Learning** site, you'll find your complete textbook on the Web. In addition, you'll find some great learning tools and practice quizzes. You'll be able to see how well you know the material from your textbook.

SCIENCE

CHAPTER 1
Science and the Environment

CHAPTER 2
Tools of Environmental Science

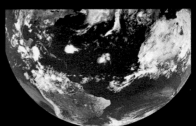

CHAPTER 3
The Dynamic Earth

When they reach adulthood, amphibians, such as these un-hatched salamanders, breathe through their skin, which makes them vulnerable to pollutants in their environment. Scientists closely monitor amphibian species to determine the effects of pollution on the world's ecosystems.

Science and the Environment

1 **Understanding Our Environment**

2 **The Environment and Society**

PRE-READING ACTIVITY

Booklet
Before you read this chapter, create the **FoldNote** entitled "Booklet" described in the Reading and Study Skills section of the Appendix. Label each page of the booklet with a main idea from the chapter. As you read the chapter, write what you learn about each main idea on the appropriate page of the booklet.

More than 2,700 m (9,000 ft) above sea level, a forest ecologist is studying biodiversity in a Costa Rican rain forest. To ascend to the treetops, he shoots an arrow over a branch and hauls himself up with the attached rope.

Understanding Our Environment

SCSh.6.d; SEV.4.a; SEV.5.d; SEV.5.e

When someone mentions the term *environment,* some people think of a beautiful scene, such as a stream flowing through a wilderness area or a rain forest canopy alive with blooming flowers and howling monkeys. You might not think of your backyard or neighborhood as part of the environment. In fact, the environment is everything around us. It includes the natural world as well as things produced by humans. But the environment is also more than what you can see—it is a complex web of relationships that connects us with the world we live in.

What Is Environmental Science?

The students from Keene High School in **Figure 1** are searching the Ashuelot River in New Hampshire for dwarf wedge mussels. The mussels, which were once abundant in the river, are now in danger of disappearing completely—and the students want to know why. To find out more, the students test water samples from different parts of the river and conduct experiments. Could the problem be that sewage is contaminating the water? Or could fertilizer from a nearby lawn be causing algae in the river to grow rapidly and use up the oxygen that the mussels need to survive? Another possible explanation might be that a small dam on the river is disrupting the mussels' reproduction.

The students' efforts have been highly praised and widely recognized. Yet they hope for a more meaningful reward—the preservation of an endangered species. The students' work is just one example of a relatively new field—**environmental science,** the study of the impact of humans on the environment.

Objectives

▶ **Define** *environmental science,* and compare environmental science with ecology.

▶ **List** the five major fields of study that contribute to environmental science.

▶ **Describe** the major environmental effects of hunter-gatherers, the agricultural revolution, and the Industrial Revolution.

▶ **Distinguish** between renewable and nonrenewable resources.

▶ **Classify** environmental problems into three major categories.

Key Terms

environmental science
ecology
agriculture
natural resource
pollution
biodiversity

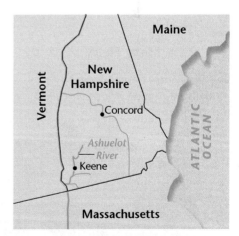

Figure 1 ▶ These students are counting the number of dwarf wedge mussels in part of the Ashuelot River. They hope that the data they collect will help preserve this endangered species.

Connection to History

Rachel Carson Alarmed by the increasing levels of pesticides and other chemicals in the environment, biologist Rachel Carson published *Silent Spring* in 1962. Carson imagined a spring morning that was silent because the birds and frogs were dead after being poisoned by pesticides. Carson's carefully researched book was enthusiastically received by the public and was read by many other scientists, as well as policy makers and politicians. However, many people in the chemical industry saw *Silent Spring* as a threat to their pesticide sales and launched a $250,000 campaign to discredit Carson. Carson's research prevailed, although she died in 1964—unaware that the book she had written was instrumental in the birth of the modern environmental movement.

The Goals of Environmental Science One of the major goals of environmental science is to understand and solve environmental problems. To accomplish this goal, environmental scientists study two main types of interactions between humans and the environment. One area of study focuses on how we use natural resources, such as water and plants. The other area of study focuses on how our actions alter our environment. To study these interactions, environmental scientists must gather and analyze information from many different disciplines.

Many Fields of Study Environmental science is an interdisciplinary science, which means that it involves many fields of study. One important foundation of environmental science is ecology. **Ecology** is the study of how living things interact with each other and with their nonliving environment. For example, an ecologist might study the relationship between bees and the plants that bees pollinate. However, an environmental scientist might investigate how the nesting behavior of bees is influenced by human activities, such as suburban landscaping.

Many other sciences contribute to environmental science. For example, chemistry helps us understand the nature of pollutants. Geology helps us model how pollutants travel underground. Botany and zoology provide information to preserve species. Paleontology, the study of fossils, can help us understand how Earth's climate has changed in the past. Using such information about the past can help us predict how future climate changes could affect life on Earth. **Figure 2** shows a few examples of disciplines that contribute to environmental science.

✓ **Reading Check** How is ecology related to environmental science? (See the Appendix for answers to Reading Checks.)

Figure 2 ▶ Many Fields of Study

▶ This marine biologist (right) is studying a marine mammal called a *manatee*.

▶ This ornithologist (above) is studying the nesting behavior of seabirds called *albatrosses*.

But studying the environment also involves studying human populations, so environmental scientists may use information from the social sciences, which include economics, law, politics, and geography. Social sciences can help us answer questions such as, How do cultural attitudes affect how people use the U.S. national park system? or How does human migration from rural to urban areas affect the local environment? **Table 1** lists some of the major fields of study that contribute to the study of environmental science.

SCI LINKS.
www.scilinks.org
Topic: Careers in Environmental Science
Code: HE80223

Table 1 ▼

Major Fields of Study That Contribute to Environmental Science	
Biology is the study of living organisms.	**Zoology** is the study of animals. **Botany** is the study of plants. **Microbiology** is the study of microorganisms. **Ecology** is the study of how organisms interact with their environment and each other.
Earth science is the study of the Earth's nonliving systems and the planet as a whole.	**Geology** is the study of the Earth's surface, interior processes, and history. **Paleontology** is the study of fossils and ancient life. **Climatology** is the study of the Earth's atmosphere and climate. **Hydrology** is the study of Earth's water resources.
Physics is the study of matter and energy.	**Engineering** is the science by which matter and energy are made useful to humans in structures, machines, and products.
Chemistry is the study of chemicals and their interactions.	**Biochemistry** is the study of the chemistry of living things. **Geochemistry**, a branch of geology, is the study of the chemistry of materials such as rocks, soil, and water.
Social sciences are the study of human populations.	**Geography** is the study of the relationship between human populations and Earth's features. **Anthropology** is the study of the interactions of the biological, cultural, geographical, and historical aspects of humankind. **Sociology** is the study of human population dynamics and statistics.

▶ This geologist is studying a volcano in Hawaii.

▶ This biologist is examining a plant that was grown in a lab from just a few cells.

The Fall of Troy Environmental problems are nothing new. Nearly 3,000 years ago, the Greek poet Homer wrote about the ancient seaport of Troy, which was located beneath a wooded hillside. The Trojans cut down all the trees on the surrounding hills. Without trees to hold the soil in place, rain washed the soil into the harbor. So much silt accumulated in the harbor that large ships could not enter and Troy's economy collapsed. Today, the ruins of Troy are several miles from the sea.

Scientists as Citizens, Citizens as Scientists

Governments, businesses, and cities recognize that studying our environment is vital to maintaining a healthy and productive society. Thus, environmental scientists are often asked to share their research with the world. **Figure 3** shows scientists at a press conference that was held after a meeting on climate change.

Often, the observations of nonscientists are the first step toward addressing an environmental problem. For example, middle-school students first noticed the appearance of deformed frogs in Minnesota lakes. Similarly, the students at Dublin Scioto High School in Ohio, shown in **Figure 3,** study the habitat of endangered box turtles every year. A habitat is a place where an organism usually lives. The students want to find out how the turtles live and what factors affect their nesting and hibernation sites in their habitat. The students track and map the turtles' movements, measure atmospheric conditions, and analyze soil samples. These efforts matter, because the box turtle habitat is threatened. At the end of every year, the students present their findings to city planners, hoping to protect the most sensitive turtle habitats.

Figure 3 ▶ Environmental Science and Public Life Scientists hold a press conference on climate change (above). Students (right) are studying the movements of box turtles.

SECTION 1 Mid-Section Review

1. **Describe** the two main types of interactions that environmental scientists study. Give an example of each.

2. **Describe** the major fields of study that contribute to environmental science.

3. **Explain** why environmental science is an interdisciplinary science.

CRITICAL THINKING

4. **Making Comparisons** What is the difference between environmental science and ecology?

5. **Making Inferences** Read the Ecofact. Propose a solution to prevent the environmental problems of the seaport of Troy described in the Ecofact.
   READING SKILLS

Our Environment Through Time

Wherever humans have hunted, grown food, or settled, they have changed the environment. For example, the land where New York City now stands was once an area where Native Americans hunted game and gathered food, as shown in **Figure 4.** The environmental change that has occurred on Manhattan Island over the last 300 years is immense, yet this period of time is just a "blink" in human history.

Hunter-Gatherers For most of human history, people were *hunter-gatherers,* or people who obtain food by collecting plants and by hunting wild animals or scavenging their remains. Early hunter-gatherer groups were small, and they migrated from place to place as different types of food became available at different times of the year. Even today there are hunter-gatherer societies in the Amazon rain forests of South America and in New Guinea, as shown in **Figure 5.**

Hunter-gatherers affected their environment in many ways. For example, some Native American tribes hunted bison, which live in grasslands. The tribes set fires to burn the prairies and prevent the growth of trees. In this way, the tribes kept the prairies as open grassland where they could hunt bison.

In North America, a combination of rapid climate changes and overhunting by hunter-gatherers may have led to the disappearance of some species of large mammals. These species include giant sloths, giant bison, mastodons, cave bears, and saber-toothed cats. Huge piles of bones have been found in places where hunter-gatherers drove thousands of animals into pits and killed them.

Reading Check Name two ways that hunter-gatherers affected their environment.

Figure 4 ▶ Three hundred years ago, Manhattan was a very different place. This painting shows an area where Native Americans hunted and fished.

Graphic Organizer Comparison Table

Create the **Graphic Organizer** entitled "Comparison Table" described in the Appendix. Label the columns with "Hunter-Gatherers," "The Agricultural Revolution," and "The Industrial Revolution." Label the rows with "Characteristics" and "Effects on the Environment." Then, fill in the table with details about the characteristics and the effects on the environment of each historical period.

Figure 5 ▶ This modern hunter-gatherer group lives in New Guinea, a tropical island off the north coast of Australia.

Figure 6 ▶ This grass, called Eastern gama grass, is thought to be a relative of the modern corn plant. Native Americans may have selectively bred a grass like this to produce corn.

FIELD ACTIVITY

Germinating Corn Many people do not realize how easy it is to grow corn plants from unpopped popcorn kernels. This ancient grass will sprout in a matter of days if it is watered frequently. Place a few popcorn kernels on a wet paper towel, and place the paper towel in a clear plastic cup so that the kernels are visible from the outside. Leave the cup on a windowsill for several days and water it frequently. As your plant grows, see if you can observe any grasslike features. Record your observations in your *EcoLog.*

Figure 7 ▶ For thousands of years humans have burned forests to create fields for agriculture. In this photo, a rain forest in Thailand is being cleared for farming.

The Agricultural Revolution Eventually many hunter-gatherer groups began to collect the seeds of the plants they gathered and to domesticate some of the animals in their environment. **Agriculture** is the practice of growing, breeding, and caring for plants and animals that are used for food, clothing, housing, transportation, and other purposes. The practice of agriculture started in many different parts of the world over 10,000 years ago. This change had such a dramatic impact on human societies and their environment that it is often called the *agricultural revolution.*

The agricultural revolution allowed human populations to grow at an unprecedented rate. An area of land can support up to 500 times as many people by farming as it can by hunting and gathering. As populations grew, they began to concentrate in smaller areas. These changes placed increased pressure on local environments.

The agricultural revolution also changed the food we eat. The plants we grow and eat today are descended from wild plants. During harvest season, farmers collected seeds from plants that exhibited the qualities they desired. The seeds of plants with large kernels or sweet and nutritious flesh were planted and harvested again. Over the course of many generations, the domesticated plants became very different from their wild ancestors. For example, the grass shown in **Figure 6** may be related to the grass that corn was bred from.

As grasslands, forests, and wetlands were replaced with farmland, habitats were destroyed. Slash-and-burn agriculture, shown in **Figure 7**, is one of the earliest ways that land was converted to farmland. Replacing forest with farmland on a large scale can cause soil loss, floods, and water shortages. In addition, much of this converted land was farmed poorly and is no longer fertile. The destruction of farmland had far-reaching environmental effects. For example, the early civilizations of the Tigris-Euphrates River basin collapsed, in part, because the overworked soil became infertile through salt contamination.

Figure 8 ▶ During much of the Industrial Revolution, few limits were placed on the air pollution caused by burning fossil fuels. Locomotives such as these are powered by burning coal.

The Industrial Revolution For almost 10,000 years the tools of human societies were powered mainly by humans or animals. This pattern changed in the middle of the 1700s with the Industrial Revolution, which involved a shift from energy sources such as animal muscle and running water to fossil fuels, such as coal and oil. The increased use of fossil fuels and machines, such as the steam engines shown in **Figure 8**, changed society and greatly increased the efficiency of agriculture, industry, and transportation.

During the Industrial Revolution, the large-scale production of goods in factories became less expensive than the local production of goods. Machinery reduced the amount of land and human labor needed for farming. As fewer people grew their own food, populations in urban areas steadily grew. Fossil fuels and motorized vehicles allowed food and other goods to be transported cheaply across great distances.

Improving Quality of Life The Industrial Revolution introduced many positive changes. Inventions such as the light bulb greatly improved our quality of life. Agricultural productivity increased, and sanitation, nutrition, and medical care vastly improved. Technologies such as the telephone and the portable computer, shown in **Figure 9**, enabled people to work and communicate more easily from any location. Yet with all of these advances, the Industrial Revolution introduced many new environmental problems.

In the 1900s, modern societies began to use artificial substances in place of raw animal and plant products. Plastics and many other artificial materials have made life easier. However, we now understand some of the environmental problems they present. Much of environmental science is concerned with the problems associated with the Industrial Revolution.

Figure 9 ▶ The invention of computers has improved the ways that people work, learn, communicate, and entertain themselves.

✔ **Reading Check** Identify three ways that the Industrial Revolution changed society.

Figure 10 ▶ This photograph was taken in 1968 by the crew of *Apollo 8*. Photographs such as this helped people realize the uniqueness of the planet we share.

Spaceship Earth

Earth has been compared to a ship traveling through space, unable to dispose of waste or take on new supplies as it travels. Earth is essentially a *closed system*—the only thing that enters Earth's atmosphere in large amounts is energy from the sun, and the only thing that leaves in large amounts is heat. A closed system of this sort has potential problems. Some resources are limited, and as the population grows, the resources will be used. In a closed system, there is also the chance that we will produce wastes more quickly than we can dispose of them.

Although the Earth can be thought of as a complete system, environmental problems can occur on different scales: local, regional, or global. For example, your community may be discussing where to build a new landfill, or local property owners may be arguing with environmentalists about the importance of a rare bird or insect. The drinking water in your region may be affected by a polluted river hundreds of miles away. Other environmental problems are global. For example, ozone-depleting chemicals released in Brazil may destroy the ozone layer that everyone on Earth depends on.

CASE STUDY

Lake Washington: An Environmental Success Story

Seattle is located on a narrow strip of land between two large bodies of water. To the west is the Puget Sound, which is part of the Pacific Ocean, and to the east is Lake Washington, which is a deep freshwater lake. During the 1940s and early 1950s, cities on the east side of Lake Washington built 11 sewer systems that emptied into the lake. Unlike raw sewage, this sewage was treated and was not a threat to human health. So, people were surprised by research in 1955 showing that the treated sewage was threatening their lake. Scientists working in Dr. W. T. Edmondson's lab at the University of Washington found a bacterium, *Oscillatoria rubescens,* that had never been seen in the lake before.

Dr. Edmondson knew that in several lakes in Europe, pollution from sewage had been followed by

the appearance of *O. rubescens*. A short time after, the lakes deteriorated severely and became cloudy, smelly, and unable to support fish. The scientists studying Lake Washington realized that they were seeing the beginning of this process.

About this same time, Seattle set up the Metropolitan Problems Advisory Committee, chaired by James Ellis. Dr. Edmondson wrote Ellis a letter that explained what could be expected in the future if action was not taken. The best solution to the problem seemed to be to pump the sewage around the lake and empty it deep into Puget Sound. Although this solution may seem like it would save one body of water by polluting another one, it was actually a good choice. Diluting the sewage in Puget Sound is less of an environmental problem than

allowing it to build up in an enclosed lake.

Cities around the lake had to work together to connect their sewage plants to large lines that would carry the treated sewage to Puget Sound. Because there was no legal way for cities to connect plants

Population Growth: A Local Pressure One reason many environmental problems are so pressing today is that the agricultural revolution and the Industrial Revolution allowed the human population to grow much faster than it had ever grown before. The development of modern medicine and sanitation also helped increase the human population. As shown in **Figure 11**, the human population almost quadrupled during the 20th century. Producing enough food for such a large population has environmental consequences. In the past 50 years, nations have used vast amounts of resources to meet their need for food. Many of the environmental problems that affect us today, such as habitat destruction and pesticide pollution, are the result of feeding the world in the 20th century.

There are many different predictions of population growth for the future. But most scientists think that the human population will almost double in the 21st century before it begins to stabilize. We can expect that the pressure on the environment will continue to increase as the human population and its need for food and resources grows.

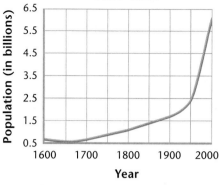

World Population: 1600–2000

Figure 11 ▶ The size of the human population in 2000 was more than 10 times larger than it was just 400 years ago.

▶ Lake Washington is now clean enough for everyone to enjoy.

at the time, Ellis successfully worked for the passage of a bill in the state legislature that set up committees to handle projects of this kind. Newspaper articles and letters to the editor addressed the issue. Public forums and discussion groups were also held.

The first sewage plant was connected in 1963. Today, the lake is clearer than it has been since scientists began their studies of the lake in the 1930s. The story of Lake Washington is an example of how environmental science and public action work together to solve environmental problems. Science was essential to understanding a healthy lake ecosystem, to documenting changes that were beginning to cause problems, and to making predictions about what would happen if changes were made or if nothing was done. Engineers offered practical solutions to the problem of moving the sewage. Legislators and civic leaders addressed the legal problems. Volunteers, local media, and local activists provided public education and pressed to get the problem solved quickly. The clear, blue waters of Lake Washington stand as a monument to citizens' desires to live in a clean, healthy environment and to their ability to work together to make it happen.

CRITICAL THINKING

1. Analyzing Processes Explain how each person and group played a crucial role in the cleanup of Lake Washington.

2. Analyzing Relationships How was the scientists' work similar to the work of the Keene High School students you read about in this section?

QuickLAB

Classifying Resources

Procedure

1. Create a table similar to Table 2.
2. Choose five objects in your classroom, such as a **pencil**, a **notebook**, or a **chair**.
3. Observe your objects closely, and list the resources that comprise them. For example, a pencil is made of wood, graphite, paint, aluminum, rubber, and pumice.
4. Classify the resources you have observed as nonrenewable or renewable.

Analysis

1. What percentage of the resources you observed are renewable? What percentage of the resources are nonrenewable?
2. Hypothesize the origin of three of the resources you observed. If time permits, research the origin of the resources you chose to find out if you were correct.

What Are Our Main Environmental Problems?

You may feel as though the world has an unlimited variety of environmental problems. But we can generally group environmental problems into three categories: resource depletion, pollution, or loss of biodiversity.

Resource Depletion Any natural material that is used by humans is called a **natural resource.** Natural resources can be classified as renewable and nonrenewable as shown in **Table 2.** A *renewable resource* is a resource that can be replaced relatively quickly by natural processes. Fresh water, air, soil, trees, and crops are all resources that can be renewed. Energy from the sun is also a renewable resource. A *nonrenewable resource* is a resource that forms at a much slower rate than the rate that it is consumed. The most common nonrenewable resources are minerals and fossil fuels. Once the supply of a nonrenewable resource is used up, it may take millions of years to replenish it.

Resources are said to be *depleted* when a large fraction of the resource has been used up. **Figure 12** shows a mine where copper, a nonrenewable resource, is removed from the Earth's crust. Some renewable resources can also be depleted. For example, if trees are harvested faster than they can grow naturally in an area, deforestation will result.

Pollution One effect of the Industrial Revolution is that societies began to produce wastes faster than the wastes could be disposed of. These wastes accumulate in the environment and cause pollution. **Pollution** is an undesired change in air, water, or soil that adversely affects the health, survival, or activities of humans or

Table 2 ▼

Renewable and Nonrenewable Resources	
Renewable	**Nonrenewable**
energy from the sun	metals such as iron, aluminum, and copper
water	
wood	nonmetallic materials such as salt, sand, and clay
soil	
air	fossil fuels

Figure 12 ▶ More than 12 million tons of copper have been mined from the Bingham mine in Utah. Once all of the copper that can be profitably extracted is used up, the copper in this mine will be depleted.

other organisms. Human activities produce a great deal of pollution. Air pollution in Mexico City, as shown in **Figure 13**, is dangerously high, mostly because of car exhaust and industrial pollutants.

There are two main types of pollutants. *Biodegradable pollutants* are pollutants that can be broken down by natural processes. They include materials such as human sewage and food wastes. Degradable pollutants are a problem when they accumulate faster than they can be broken down. Pollutants that cannot be broken down by natural processes, such as mercury, lead, and some types of plastic, are called *nondegradable pollutants*. Because nondegradable pollutants do not break down easily, they can build up to dangerous levels in the environment.

Loss of Biodiversity The term **biodiversity** refers to the number and variety of species that live in an area. Earth has been home to hundreds of millions of species. Yet only a fraction of those species are alive today—the others are extinct. Extinction is a natural process, and several large-scale extinctions, or *mass extinctions*, have occurred throughout Earth's history. For example, at the end of the Permian period, 250 million years ago, as much as 95 percent of all species became extinct. So why should we be concerned about the modern extinction of an individual species such as the Tasmanian tiger shown in **Figure 14**?

The organisms that share the world with us can be considered natural resources. We depend on other organisms for food, for the oxygen we breathe, and for many other things. A species that is extinct is gone forever, so a species can be considered a nonrenewable resource. We have only limited information about how modern extinction rates compare with those of other periods in Earth's history. But many scientists think that if current rates of extinction continue, it may cause problems for human populations in the future. Many people also argue that all species have potential economic, ecological, scientific, aesthetic, and recreational value, so it is important to preserve them.

Figure 13 ▶ The problem of air pollution in Mexico City is compounded because the city is located in a valley that traps air pollutants.

Figure 14 ▶ The Tasmanian tiger, native to an island near Australia, was declared extinct in 1986.

SECTION 1 **Review**

1. **Explain** how hunter-gatherers affected the environment in which they lived.

2. **Describe** the major environmental effects of the agricultural revolution and the Industrial Revolution.

3. **Explain** how environmental problems can be local, regional, or global. Give one example of each.

4. **Identify** an example of a biodegradable pollutant.

CRITICAL THINKING

5. **Analyzing Relationships** How did the Industrial Revolution affect human population growth?

6. **Making Inferences** Fossil fuels are said to be nonrenewable resources, yet they are produced by the Earth over millions of years. By what time frame are they considered nonrenewable? Write a paragraph that explains your answer. **WRITING SKILLS**

SECTION 2
The Environment and Society

Objectives

▶ Describe "The Tragedy of the Commons."

▶ Explain the law of supply and demand.

▶ List three differences between developed and developing countries.

▶ Explain what sustainability is, and describe why it is a goal of environmental science.

Key Terms

law of supply and demand
ecological footprint
sustainability

When we think about environmental problems and how to solve them, we have to consider human societies, how they act, and why they do what they do. One way to think about society and the environment is to consider how a society uses common resources. A neighborhood park, for example, is a common resource that people share. On a larger scale, the open ocean is not owned by any nation, yet people from many countries use the ocean for fishing and for transporting goods. How do we decide how to share common resources? In 1968, ecologist Garrett Hardin published an essay titled "The Tragedy of the Commons," which addressed this question.

"The Tragedy of the Commons"

In his essay, Hardin argued that the main difficulty in solving environmental problems is the conflict between the short-term interests of individuals and the long-term welfare of society. To illustrate his point, Hardin used the example of the *commons,* as shown in **Figure 15.** Commons were areas of land that belonged to a whole village. Anyone could graze cows or sheep on the commons. It was in the best short-term interest of an individual to put as many animals as possible on the commons. Individuals thought, If I don't use this resource, someone else will.

However, if too many animals grazed on the commons, the animals destroyed the grass. Then everyone suffered because no one could raise animals on the commons. Commons were eventually replaced by closed fields owned by individuals. Owners were careful not to put too many animals on their land, because overgrazing meant that fewer animals could be raised the next year. The point of Hardin's essay is that someone or some group has to take responsibility for maintaining a resource. If no one takes that responsibility, the resource can be overused and become depleted.

Figure 15 ▶ Hardin observed that when land was held in common (left), individuals tended to graze as many animals as possible. Overgrazing led to the destruction of the land resources. When commons were replaced by enclosed fields owned by individuals (right), people tended to graze only the number of animals that the land could support.

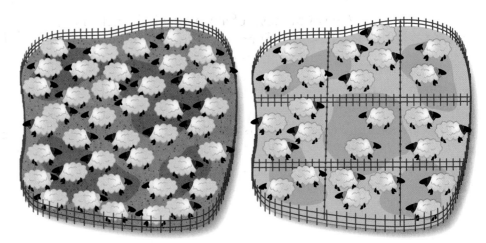

Earth's natural resources are our modern commons. Hardin thought that people would continue to deplete natural resources by acting in their own self-interest to the point of society's collapse. But Hardin did not consider the social nature of humans. Humans live in groups and depend on one another. In societies, we can solve environmental problems by planning, organizing, considering the scientific evidence, and proposing a solution. The solution may override the interests of individuals in the short term, but it improves the environment for everyone in the long term.

Economics and the Environment

In addition to social pressures, economic forces influence how we use resources. Many of the topics you will explore later in this book are affected by economic considerations.

Supply and Demand One basic rule of economics is the **law of supply and demand,** which states that the greater the demand for a limited supply of something, the more that thing is worth. One example of this rule is shown in **Figure 16,** which illustrates the relationship between the production of oil and its price over a period of 20 years. Many environmental solutions have to take the relationship between supply and demand into account. For example, if the supply of oil decreases, we have three choices: pay the higher price, use less oil, or find new sources of energy.

Costs and Benefits The cost of environmental solutions can be high. To determine how much to spend to control air pollution, a community may perform a cost-benefit analysis. A *cost-benefit analysis* balances the cost of the action against the benefits one expects from it. The results of a cost-benefit analysis often depend on who is doing the analysis. To an industry, the cost of pollution control may outweigh the benefits, but to a nearby community, the benefits may be worth the high price. The cost of environmental regulations is often passed on to the consumer or the taxpayer. The consumer then has a choice. He or she can either pay for the more expensive product that meets environmental regulations or seek out a cheaper product that may not have the same environmental safeguards.

Risk Assessment One of the costs of any action is the risk of an undesirable outcome. Cost-benefit analysis involves *risk assessment,* which is one tool that helps us create cost-effective ways to protect our health and the environment. To come up with an effective solution to an environmental problem, the public must perceive the risk accurately. This does not always happen. In one study, people were asked to assess the risk from various technologies. The public generally ranked nuclear power as the riskiest technology on the list, whereas experts ranked it 20th—less risky than riding a bicycle.

✓ Reading Check Use an example to illustrate the law of supply and demand.

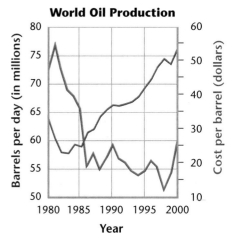

World Oil Production

Source: U.S. Department of Energy.

Figure 16 ▶ Between 1980 and 2000, the production and price of oil changed dramatically. This graph shows how, in general, the price of a barrel of oil increased as the production decreased.

MATHPRACTICE

Market Equilibrium
In economics, the point where supply and demand are in balance is known as *market equilibrium*. In Figure 16, market equilibrium for oil was reached in 1986. What was the cost of a barrel of oil in that year? How many barrels of oil were produced in that year? By how much did the cost of a barrel of oil decline from 1981 to 1986?

Developed and Developing Countries

The decisions and actions of all people in the world affect our environment. But the unequal distribution of wealth and resources around the world influences the environmental problems that a society faces and the choices it can make. The United Nations classifies countries as either developed or developing. *Developed countries* have higher average incomes, slower population growth, diverse industrial economies, and stronger social support systems. They include the United States, Canada, Japan, and the countries of Western Europe. *Developing countries* have lower average incomes, simple and agriculture-based economies, and rapid population growth. Developed and developing countries have different consumption patterns, as shown in **Figure 17**, which affect the environment in different ways.

Population and Consumption

Most environmental problems can be traced back to two root causes. First, the human population in some areas is growing too quickly for the local environment to support it. Second, people are using up, wasting, or polluting many natural resources faster than they can be replaced or cleaned up.

Local Population Pressures When the population in an area grows rapidly, there may not be enough natural resources for everyone in the area to live a healthy, productive life. Often, as people struggle for survival in severely overpopulated regions, forests are stripped bare, topsoil is exhausted, and animals are driven to extinction. Malnutrition, starvation, and disease can be constant threats. Even though there are millions of people starving in developing countries, the human population tends to grow most rapidly in these countries. Food production, education, and job creation cannot keep pace with population growth, so each person gets fewer resources as time goes by. Of the 5.2 billion people in developing countries, fewer than half have access to enough food, safe drinking water, and proper sanitation.

Figure 17 ▶ A food market in Pushkar, India is shown above. The food market shown below is in Goleta, California, in the United States. How do these two food markets show differing consumption trends in India and the U.S.?

Table 3 ▼

	Measurement	U.S.	Japan	Mexico	Indonesia
	Indicators of Development for the United States, Japan, Mexico, and Indonesia				
Health	life expectancy in years	77	81	71.5	68
Population growth	per year	0.8%	0.2%	1.7%	1.8%
Wealth	gross national product per person	$29,240	$32,350	$3,840	$640
Living space	people per square mile	78	829	133	319
Energy use	per person per year (millions of Btu)	351	168	59	18
Pollution	carbon dioxide from fossil fuels per person per year (tons)	20.4	9.3	3.5	2.2
Waste	garbage produced per person per year (kg)	720	400	300	43

Consumption Trends For many people in the wealthier part of the world, life is better than ever before. Many environmental problems are being addressed. In addition, the population has stabilized or is growing slowly. But to support this quality of life, developed countries are using much more of Earth's resources than developing countries are. Developed nations use about 75 percent of the world's resources, even though they make up only about 20 percent of the world's population. This rate of consumption creates more waste and pollution per person than in developing countries, as shown in **Table 3.**

Ecological Footprints One way to express the differences in consumption between nations is as an ecological footprint, as shown in **Figure 18.** An **ecological footprint** shows the productive area of Earth needed to support one person in a particular country. It estimates the land used for crops, grazing, forest products, and housing. It also estimates the ocean area used to harvest seafood and the forest area needed to absorb the air pollution caused by fossil fuels.

Figure 18 ▶ An ecological footprint is a calculation of the amount of land and resources needed to support one person from a particular country. The ecological footprint of a person in a developed country is, on average, four times as large as the footprint of a person in a developing country.

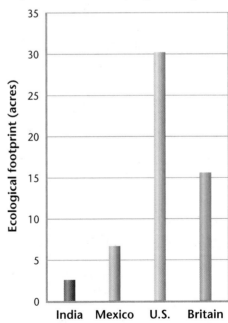

Critical Thinking and the News
Find a news article or watch a news broadcast about a current environmental issue. In your *Ecolog,* write down your initial reaction including your thoughts, feelings, and questions.

Now, look or think again, and answer the following questions:
• Did the report present different sides of the issue? Describe the sides.
• Did the report seem to favor one side over the other? How could you tell?
• Did the report use images, sounds, or words that made you feel a certain way?
• Did the report provide any facts that helped you form an opinion? Try to list the facts.
• Were the sources of the facts provided? Did the sources seem reliable?
• Were the opinions of any expert scientists presented? Who were the scientists?
• Is there any information that was *not* provided that might be important? Give examples.
• When you think about the issue more, does your opinion change?

Figure 19 ▶ Anyone can express an opinion on environmental issues at state and local public hearings.

www.scilinks.org
Topic: Solving
      Environmental
      Problems
Code: HE81424

Environmental Science in Context

As you have learned, environmental problems are complex. Simple solutions are rare, and they sometimes cause more damage than the original problem did. To complicate matters, in recent years, the environment has become a battleground for larger issues that affect human societies. For example, how do you balance the rights of individuals and property owners with the needs of society as a whole? Or, when economic or political refugees emigrate—legally or illegally—what can be done about the devastation they may cause to the local environment? How do human rights relate to the environment?

Critical Thinking and the Environment People on any side of an environmental issue may feel passionately about their cause, and they can distort information and mislead people about the issues. Research done by environmental scientists is often used to make political points or is misrepresented to support controversial viewpoints. In addition to the scientific data, the economic dimensions of an environmental issue can be oversimplified. To further complicate things, the media often sensationalizes environmental issues. So, as you make your own decisions about the environment, it is essential that you use your critical-thinking skills.

Learning to think critically about what you see in newspapers, on TV, and on the Internet will help you make informed decisions. As you explore environmental science further, you should remember a few things. First, be prepared to listen to many viewpoints. People have many different reasons for the opinions they form. Try to understand what those reasons are before reacting to their ideas. If you want your ideas to be heard, it is important that you listen to the opinions of others, as shown in **Figure 19**. Also, identify your own bias. How does it affect the way you interpret the issue?

Second, investigate the source of the information you encounter. Ask yourself if the authors have reason for bias. Also, question the conclusions that are drawn from data. Ask yourself if the data support the claims that are made. Think critically about information posted on the Internet—flashy graphics and persuasive text might be hiding a biased agenda. Finally, gather all the information you can before drawing a conclusion.

A Sustainable World

Despite the differing points of view on the environment, most people support a key goal of environmental science: achieving sustainability. **Sustainability** is the condition in which human needs are met in such a way that a human population can survive indefinitely. A sustainable world is not an unchanging world—technology advances and human civilizations continue to be productive. But at the present time we live in a world that is far from sustainable. The standard of living in developed countries is high because those countries are using resources faster than they can be replaced.

The problems described in this chapter are not insurmountable. Achieving a sustainable world requires everyone's participation. If individual citizens, industries, and governments cooperate, we can move toward sustainability. For example, you read about how Seattle's Lake Washington is cleaner and healthier now than it was 30 years ago. Another example is the bald eagle, which was once on the brink of extinction. Today bald eagles are making a comeback, because of the efforts to preserve their habitat and to reduce pollution from the pesticide DDT.

Nevertheless, our environmental problems are significant and require careful attention and action. The 21st century will be a crucial time in human history. We must find solutions that allow people on all parts of our planet to live in a clean, healthy environment and have the resources they need for a good life.

Reading Check What is a sustainable world?

Figure 20 ▶ These high school students are taking action to improve their environment. They are cleaning up trash that is clogging an urban creek.

Connection to Astronomy

Another Earth? If the environment on Earth changed drastically, would we have anywhere to go? There are no other planets in our solar system with an adequate range of temperatures, a breathable atmosphere, or the resources needed to sustain humans with our present technology. There may be other planets like Earth in the universe, but the closest planets we know of are in other solar systems that are light-years away.

SECTION 2 Review

1. **Describe** three differences between developing and developed nations using the examples in Table 3. Would you classify Mexico as a developing nation? Explain your answer.

2. **Explain** why critical thinking is an important skill in environmental science.

3. **Explain** the law of supply and demand, and give an example of how it relates to the environment.

CRITICAL THINKING

4. **Applying Ideas** The law of supply and demand is a simplification of economic patterns. What other factors might affect the cost of a barrel of oil?

5. **Evaluating Ideas** Write a description of "The Tragedy of the Commons." Do you think that Hardin's essay is an accurate description of the relationship between individuals, society, and the environment? **WRITING SKILLS**

Highlights

1 Understanding Our Environment

Key Terms

environmental science, 5
ecology, 6
agriculture, 10
natural resource, 14
pollution, 14
biodiversity, 15

Main Ideas

▶ Environmental science is an interdisciplinary study of human interactions with the living and nonliving world. One important foundation of environmental science is the science of ecology.

▶ Environmental change has occurred throughout Earth's history.

▶ Hunter-gatherer societies cleared grassland by setting fires and may have contributed to the extinction of some large mammals.

▶ The agricultural revolution caused human population growth, habitat loss, soil erosion, and the domestication of plants and animals.

▶ The Industrial Revolution caused rapid human population growth and the increased use of fossil fuels. Most modern environmental problems began during the Industrial Revolution.

▶ The major environmental problems we face today are resource depletion, pollution, and loss of biodiversity.

2 The Environment and Society

law of supply and demand, 17
ecological footprint, 19
sustainability, 21

▶ "The Tragedy of the Commons" was an influential essay that described the relationship between the short-term interests of the individual and the long-term interests of society.

▶ The law of supply and demand states that when the demand for a product increases while the supply remains fixed, the cost of the product will increase.

▶ Environmental problems in developed countries tend to be related to consumption. In developing nations, the major environmental problems are related to population growth.

▶ Describing how sustainability can be achieved is a primary goal of environmental science.

Using Key Terms

Use each of the following terms in a separate sentence.

1. *agriculture*
2. *natural resource*
3. *pollution*
4. *ecological footprint*
5. *sustainability*

Use the correct key term to complete each of the following sentences.

6. The_____ Revolution was characterized by a shift from human and animal power to fossil fuels.

7. Resources that can theoretically last forever are called _____ resources.

8. _____ is a term that describes the number and variety of species that live in an area.

✔ STUDY TIP

Root Words As you study it may be helpful to learn the meaning of important root words. You can find these roots in most dictionaries. For example, *hydro-* means "water." Once you learn the meaning of this root, you can learn the meanings of words such as *hydrothermal, hydrologist, hydropower,* and *hydrophobic.*

Understanding Key Ideas

9. An important effect that hunter-gatherer societies may have had on the environment was
   a. soil erosion.
   b. extinction.
   c. air pollution.
   d. All of the above

10. An important effect of the agricultural revolution was
    a. soil erosion.
    b. habitat destruction.
    c. plant and animal domestication.
    d. All of the above

11. Which of the following does *not* describe an effect of the Industrial Revolution?
    a. Fossil fuels became important energy sources.
    b. The amount of land and labor needed to produce food increased.
    c. Artificial substances replaced some animal and plant products.
    d. Machines replaced human muscle and animal power.

12. Pollutants that are not broken down by natural processes are
    a. nonrenewable.
    b. nondegradable.
    c. biodegradable.
    d. Both (a) and (c)

13. All of the following are renewable resources *except*
    a. energy from the sun.
    b. minerals.
    c. crops.
    d. fresh water.

14. In his essay, "The Tragedy of the Commons," one factor that Garrett Hardin failed to consider was
    a. the destruction of natural resources.
    b. human self-interest.
    c. the social nature of humans.
    d. None of the above

15. The term used to describe the productive area of Earth needed to support the lifestyle of one person in a particular country is called
    a. supply and demand.
    b. the ecological footprint.
    c. the consumption crisis.
    d. sustainability.

Short Answer

16. Give an example of how environmental science might involve geology and chemistry.

17. Can biodegradable pollutants cause environmental problems? Explain your answer.

18. In what ways are today's environmental resources like the commons described in the essay "The Tragedy of the Commons"?

19. How could environmental concerns conflict with your desire to improve your standard of living?

20. If you were evaluating the claims made on a Web site that discusses environmental issues what types of information would you look for?

21. Can species be considered natural resources? Explain your answer.

Interpreting Graphics

The graphs below show the difference in energy consumption and population size in developed and developing countries. Use the graphs to answer questions 22–24.

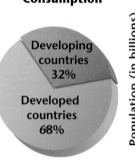

Commercial Energy Consumption

Developing countries 32%

Developed countries 68%

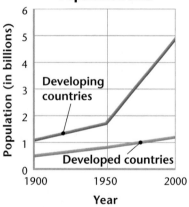

Population Size

22. Describe the differences in the energy consumption and population growth of developed and developing countries.

23. Do you think that the percentage of commercial energy consumed by developing countries will increase or decrease? Explain your answer.

24. Why is information on energy consumption represented in a pie graph, while population size is shown in a line graph?

Concept Mapping

25. Use the following terms to create a concept map: *geology, biology, ecology, environmental science, chemistry, geography,* and *social sciences.*

Critical Thinking

26. **Analyzing Ideas** Are humans part of the environment? Explain your answer.

27. **Drawing Conclusions** Why do you think that fossil fuels were not widely used until the Industrial Revolution? Write a paragraph that describes your thoughts. **WRITING SKILLS**

28. **Evaluating Assumptions** Once the sun exhausts its fuel and burns itself out, it cannot be replaced. So why is the sun considered a renewable resource?

29. **Evaluating Assumptions** Read the description of the Industrial Revolution. Were all the effects of the Industrial Revolution negative? Explain your answer. **READING SKILLS**

Cross-Disciplinary Connection

30. **Demographics** Obtain the 1985 and 2000 census reports for your town or city. Look for changes in demographic characteristics, such as population size, income, and age. Make a bar graph that compares some of the characteristics you chose. How does your city or town compare with national trends? What might be some of the environmental implications of these trends?

Portfolio Project

31. **Make a Diagram** Many resources can be traced to energy from the sun. For example, plants living in swamps millions of years ago used energy from the sun to grow. Over time, some of these plants became coal deposits. When we burn coal today, we are using energy that radiated from the sun millions of years ago. Choose a resource, and create a diagram that traces the resource back to energy from the sun.

MATH SKILLS

Use the table below to answer questions 32–34.

	U.S.	Japan	Indonesia
People per square mile	78	829	319
Garbage produced per person per year	720 kg	400 kg	43 kg

32. **Analyzing Data** Make a bar graph that compares the garbage produced per person per year in each country.

33. **Making Calculations** Calculate how much garbage is produced each year per square mile of each country listed in the table.

34. **Evaluating Data** Use the information in the table to evaluate the validity of the following statement: In countries where population density is high, more garbage is produced per person.

WRITING SKILLS

35. **Communicating Main Ideas** Briefly describe the relationship between humans and the environment through history.

36. **Writing Persuasively** Write a persuasive essay explaining the importance of science in a debate about an environmental issue.

37. **Outlining Topics** Write a one-page outline that describes population and consumption in the developing and developed world.

READING SKILLS

Read the passage below, and then answer the questions that follow.

Think about what you did this morning. From the moment you got up, you were making decisions and acting in ways that affect the environment. The clothes you are wearing, for example, might be made of cotton. Several years ago the fibers of cotton in your shirt might have sprouted as seedlings in Egypt or Arizona. The cotton seedlings were probably irrigated with water diverted from a nearby river or lake. Chemicals such as pesticides, herbicides, and fertilizers helped the seedlings grow into plants. Furthermore, the metals in the machines that harvested the cotton were mined from the Earth's crust. In addition, the vehicles that brought the shirt to the store where you bought it were powered by fossil fuels. Fossil fuels came from the bodies of tiny organisms that lived millions of years ago. All of these connections can make environmental science a complex and interesting field.

1. According to the passage, which of the following conclusions is true?
   a. Decisions we make in everyday life do not affect our environment.
   b. Cotton comes from minerals in the Earth's crust.
   c. Many different things in the environment are connected and interrelated.
   d. There is no connection between a cotton shirt and the resources needed to grow a field of cotton.

2. Which of the following statements best describes the meaning of the term *irrigation*?
   a. Irrigation is a connection between living things in the environment.
   b. Irrigation is the artificial process by which water is supplied to plants.
   c. Irrigation is the process of diverting water from a stream or lake.
   d. Irrigation is the process by which cotton seedlings grow into plants.

Understanding Concepts

Directions (1–4): For *each* question, write on a separate sheet of paper the letter of the correct answer.

1 How do scientists characterize a nonrenewable resource?
 A. a resource that is used by humans
 B. a resource that cannot be replaced
 C. a resource that can be replaced relatively quickly
 D. a resource that takes more time to replace than to deplete

2 Which of the following is an important foundation of environmental science?
 F. ecology
 G. economics
 H. meteorology
 I. political science

3 Which of the following phrases describes the term biodiversity?
 A. species that have become extinct
 B. the animals that live in an area
 C. species that look different from one another
 D. the number and variety of species that live in an area

4 Energy from the sun, water, air, wood, and soil are all examples of what kind of energy?
 F. ecological energy
 G. organic energy
 H. renewable energy
 I. solar energy

Directions (5–6): For *each* question, write a short response.

5 Pollution is created when societies produce wastes faster than they can be disposed of. Identify the two main types of pollutants.

6 Economic forces influence the use of natural resources. One rule of economics is the law of supply and demand. Analyze how economic forces affect the usage of nonrenewable resources.

Reading Skills

Directions (7–9): Read the passage below. Then answer the questions.

Early hunter-gatherer groups began to collect the seeds of the plants they gathered and to domesticate animals in their environment. This practice of agriculture started in many parts of the world more than 10,000 years ago, and had such a dramatic impact on human societies and their environment that it is often called the agricultural revolution. An area of land could now support up to 500 times as many people by farming than it could by hunting and gathering. As populations grew, they began to concentrate in smaller areas.

As grasslands, forests, and wetlands were replaced with farmland, habitat was destroyed. In addition, much of the converted land was farmed poorly and became infertile. The destruction of farmland had far-reaching environmental effects.

7 The practice of gathering seeds and domesticating some animals led to
 A. a reduction in the kinds of food people ate
 B. the extension of the prairies as open grassland
 C. the disappearance of some species of large mammals
 D. a growth in population at an unprecedented rate

8 In what ways did the agricultural revolution increase pressure on local environments?

9 What happened to human populations as they became larger?
 F. They began to concentrate in smaller areas.
 G. They remained dispersed.
 H. They became hunter-gatherers.
 I. Most became extinct.

Interpreting Graphics

Directions (10–13): For *each* question below, record the correct answer on a separate sheet of paper.

10 Population growth can result in what ethical environmental problem, addressed by ecologist Garrett Hardin in "The Tragedy of the Commons"?
   A. the conflict between water resources and industrial growth
   B. the conflict between forest resources and the lumber companies
   C. the conflict between political interests and international energy use
   D. the conflict between individual interests and the welfare of society

The line graph below shows the world population between the years 1600 and 2000. Use this graph to answer questions 11 and 12.

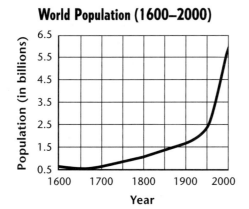

World Population (1600–2000)

11 What was the total population increase between the years 1600 and 1900?
   F. 0.6 billion
   G. 0.9 billion
   H. 1.0 billion
   I. 1.5 billion

12 If the rate of growth from 1900–1950 had been the same as the rate of growth from 1950–2000, what would the world population have been at the end of the century?
   A. more than 7 billion
   B. more than 10 billion
   C. more than 15 billion
   D. more than 20 billion

13 Which of the following characterizes the environmental consequences of the current population trend?
   F. More people mean more housing construction.
   G. The need for food and resources is growing rapidly.
   H. The standard of living has risen around the world.
   I. There is no connection between population growth and environment.

Test TIP

When reading a graph that shows a change in some variable over time, keep in mind that the steepness and direction of a curve indicate the relative rate of change at a given point in time.

Exploration Lab: FIELD ACTIVITY

Objectives

▶ **Survey** an area of land and determine the land's physical features and the types of organisms that live there.

▶ **USING SCIENTIFIC METHODS** **Identify** possible relationships between the organisms that live in the area of land you surveyed.

Materials

hand lens
markers or felt-tip pens of
  several different colors
notebook
pen or pencil
poster board
stakes, (4)
string, about 50 m
tape measure or metric ruler

optional materials: field guides to
  insects or plants

▶ **Marking a Site** Use stakes and string to mark a site that you will observe in detail.

What's in an Ecosystem?

How well do you know the environment around your home or school? You may walk through it every day without noticing most of the living things it contains or thinking about how they survive. Ecologists, on the other hand, observe organisms and seek to understand how they interact. In this lab, you will play the role of an ecologist by closely observing part of your environment.

Procedure

1. Use a tape measure or meter stick to measure a 10 m × 10 m site to study. Place one stake at each corner of the site. Loop the string around each stake, and run the string from one stake to the next to form boundaries for the site.

2. Survey the site, and then prepare a site map of the physical features of the area on the poster board. For example, show the location of streams, sidewalks, trails, or large rocks, and indicate the direction of any noticeable slope.

3. Create a set of symbols to represent the organisms at your site. For example, you might use green triangles to represent trees, blue circles to represent insects, or brown squares to represent animal burrows or nests. At the bottom or side of the poster board, make a key for your symbols.

4. Draw your symbols on the map to show the location and relative abundance of each type of organism. If there is not enough space on your map to indicate the specific kinds of plants and animals you observed, record them in your notebook.

5. In your notebook, record any observations of organisms in their environment. For example, note insects feeding on plants or seeking shelter under rocks. Also describe the physical characteristics of your study area. Consider the following characteristics:

   a. **Sunlight Exposure** How much of the area is exposed to sunlight?
   b. **Soil** Is the soil mostly sand, silt, clay, or organic matter?
   c. **Rain** When was the last rain recorded for this area? How much rain was received?
   d. **Maintenance** Is the area maintained? If so, interview the person who maintains it and find out how often the site is watered, fertilized, treated with pesticides, and mowed.
   e. **Water Drainage** Is the area well drained, or does it have pools of water?
   f. **Vegetation Cover** How much of the soil is covered with vegetation? How much of the soil is exposed?

6. After completing these observations, identify a 2 m × 2 m area that you would like to study in more detail. Stake out this area, and wrap the string around the stakes.

7. Use your hand lens to inspect the area. Be careful not to disturb the soil or the organisms. Then record the types of insects and plants you see.

8. Collect a small sample of soil, and observe it with your hand lens. Record a description of the soil and the organisms that live in it.

Analysis

1. **Organizing Data** Return to the classroom, and display your site map. Use your site map, your classmates' site maps, and your notes to answer the following questions. Write your answers in your notebook.

2. **Analyzing Data** Write one paragraph that describes the 10 m × 10 m site you studied.

3. **Analyzing Data** Describe the 2 m × 2 m site you studied. Is this site characteristic of the larger site?

Conclusions

4. **Interpreting Conclusions** What are the differences between the areas that your classmates studied? Do different plants and animals live in different areas?

5. **Making Predictions** As the seasons change, the types of organisms that live in the area you studied may also change. Predict how your area might change in a different season or if a fire or flood occurred. If possible, return to the site at different times throughout the year and record your observations.

▶ **Site Maps** Your site map should be as detailed as possible, and it should include a legend.

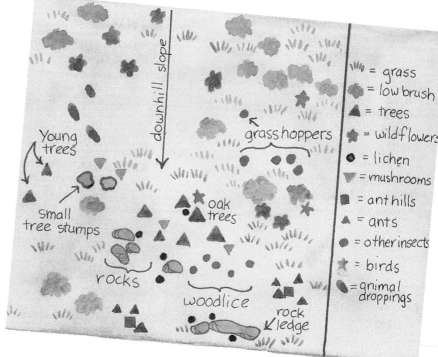

Extension

1. **Asking Questions** Based on what you have learned, think of a question that explores how the components of the area you observed interact with each other. For example, you might want to consider the influence of humans on the site; study a particular predator/prey relationship; or explore the effects of physical features, such as water or sunlight, on the growth or behavior of organisms. Write a description of how you would investigate this topic. **WRITING SKILLS**

CHICKEN OF THE TREES

In the stillness of predawn, the air warms over the Carara Biological Preserve in Costa Rica. Several thousand eggs in sun-heated incubators just below the surface of the Earth stir in response. Within these eggs are tiny iguanas—lizards that will eventually emerge, grow to a length of 1.5 m to 2.0 m (5 ft to 6.5 ft), and weigh up to 6 kg (13 lb).

What's going on here? Well, these giant lizards are being raised so that they can be released into the rain forest. It's part of a project led by German-born scientist Dr. Dagmar Werner. Her goal is to help restore an iguana population that has been severely reduced in the past several decades.

The lizard has suffered from the effects of hunting, pollution, and habitat destruction by people who clear the rain forest for farming. Prime iguana habitat is at the edge of the forest—where a combination of open areas, scrub, and trees occur. Historically, these areas are the type of habitat that humans most often destroy when converting forestland to farmland. People cut down the forest at its edges—which just happens to be prime habitat for iguanas and other plants and animals.

Back at the Iguana Ranch

Dr. Werner's "iguana ranch" preserve has artificial nests where females can lay their eggs in a predator-free environment. After they hatch, the young lizards are placed in a temperature- and humidity-controlled incubator and given a special diet. As a result, the iguanas grow faster and stronger and are better protected from predators than their noncaptive counterparts.

In the first five years of her project, more than 80,000 iguanas were released into the wild. Ordinarily, less than 2 percent of all iguanas survive to adulthood in the wild, but Dr. Werner's iguanas have a 77 percent survival rate. Dr. Werner knows this because after she releases the iguanas into the rain forest, the lizards are tracked and monitored to determine whether they have successfully adapted to life in the wild.

Passing It On

Since the 1980s, Dr. Werner has improved the iguanas' chances of survival by breeding them and releasing thousands of young iguanas into the wild. But Dr. Werner soon realized that this effort was not enough, so she began training other people to do the same.

Because she knew there was no time to lose, Dr. Werner took an immediate and drastic approach to solving the problem. She combined her captive-breeding program at the preserve with an education program that shows farmers that there is more than one way to make a profit from the rain forest. Instead

▶ These are iguanas at the Carara Biological Preserve in Costa Rica.

▶ Dr. Werner and an associate discuss how the iguana can be farmed.

of raising cattle (and cutting down rain forest to do so), she encourages local farmers to raise iguanas, which can be released into the wild or sold for food. Known as the "chicken of the trees," this lizard has been a favored source of meat among native rain-forest inhabitants for thousands of years.

Not only do farmers profit from the sale of iguana meat, they also produce iguana leather and other handicrafts from the lizard.

Fundación Pro Iguana Verde

With Dr. Werner's methods, farmers can release many iguanas into the wild and earn a good living. But convincing farmers to use her methods hasn't been easy. According to Dr. Werner, "Many locals have never thought of wild animals as creatures that must be protected in order to survive. That's why so many go extinct." To get her message across, Dr. Werner has established the Fundación Pro Iguana Verde (the Green Iguana Foundation). This organization sponsors festivals and education seminars in local communities. These activities promote the traditional appeal of the iguana, increase civic pride in the animal, and heighten awareness about the iguana's economic importance.

By demonstrating that the needs of all concerned parties can be met when attempting to save an endangered species, Dr. Werner has revolutionized the concepts of species preservation and economic development. This hard-working scientist has hit upon a solution that may encourage farmers throughout Central America to "have their lizards and eat them too."

▶ Dr. Werner has established an innovative way to raise the number of iguanas living in the wild.

What Do You Think?

How does Dr. Werner's project protect iguanas and help local farmers too? Why do you think that she trains farmers to raise and value iguanas—what could her larger goal be? Can you think of a similar project that would be suitable for your area?

Tools of Environmental Science

1 Scientific Methods
2 Statistics and Models
3 Making Informed Decisions

PRE-READING ACTIVITY

FOLDNOTES

Key-Term Fold

Before you read this chapter, create the **FoldNote** entitled "Key-Term Fold" described in the Reading and Study Skills section of the Appendix. Write a key term from the chapter on each tab of the key-term fold. Under each tab, write the definition of the key term.

This photograph shows a researcher filming a Weddell seal in Antarctica. Although scientists often use sophisticated tools in their work, their most important tools are those they carry with them—their senses and their habits of mind.

Scientific Methods

SCSh.1.a; SCSh.1.b; SCSh.1.c; SCSh.2.b;
SCSh.3.c; SCSh.3.e; SCSh.6.a; SCSh.6.d;
SCSh.7.b; SCSh.7.e; SCSh.8.a; SCSh.8.b;
SCSh.8.c; SCSh.8.d; SCSh.8.e

The word *science* comes from the Latin verb *scire,* meaning "to know." Indeed, science is full of amazing facts and ideas about how nature works. But science is not just something you know; it is also something you do. This chapter explores how science is done and examines the tools scientists use.

The Experimental Method

You have probably heard the phrase, "Today scientists discovered..." How do scientists make these discoveries? Scientists make most of their discoveries using the *experimental method.* This method consists of a series of steps that scientists worldwide use to identify and answer questions. The first step is observing.

Observing Science usually begins with observation. Someone notices, or observes, something and begins to ask questions. An **observation** is a piece of information we gather using our senses— our sight, hearing, smell, and touch. To extend their senses, scientists often use tools such as rulers, microscopes, and even satellites. For example, a ruler provides our eyes with a standard way to compare the lengths of different objects. The scientists in **Figure 1** are observing the tail length of a tranquilized wolf with the help of a tape measure. Observations can take many forms, including descriptions, drawings, photographs, and measurements.

Students at Keene High School in New Hampshire have observed that dwarf wedge mussels are disappearing from the Ashuelot River, which is located near their school. The students have also observed that the river is polluted. These observations prompted the students to take the next step in the experimental method—forming hypotheses.

Objectives

▶ List and describe the steps of the experimental method.

▶ Describe why a good hypothesis is not simply a guess.

▶ Describe the two essential parts of a good experiment.

▶ Describe how scientists study subjects in which experiments are not possible.

▶ Explain the importance of curiosity and imagination in science.

Key Terms

observation
hypothesis
prediction
experiment
variable
experimental group
control group
data
correlation

Figure 1 ▶ These scientists are measuring the tail of a tranquilized wolf. What questions could these observations help the scientists answer?

QuickLAB

Hypothesizing and Predicting

Procedure

1. Place a **baking tray** on a table, and place a **thin book** under one end of the tray.

2. Place **potting soil, sand,** and **schoolyard dirt** in three piles at the high end of the baking tray.

3. Use a **toothpick** to poke several holes in a **paper cup.**

4. Write down a hypothesis to explain why soil gets washed away when it rains.

5. Based on your hypothesis, predict which of the three soils will wash away most easily.

6. Pour **water** into the cup, and slowly sprinkle water on the piles.

Analysis

1. What happened to the different soils?

2. Revise your hypothesis, if necessary, based on your experiment.

Figure 2 ▶ The diagram below shows the trends observed by the students at Keene High School. Site 1 is upstream. Site 3 is downstream.

Hypothesizing and Predicting Observations give us answers to questions, but observations almost always lead to more questions. To answer a specific question, a scientist may form a hypothesis. A **hypothesis** (hie PAHTH uh sis) is a testable idea or explanation that leads to a scientific investigation. A hypothesis is more than a guess. A good hypothesis follows from what you already know and can be tested.

The Keene High School students observed two trends: that the number of dwarf wedge mussels on the Ashuelot River is declining over time and that the number of dwarf wedge mussels decreases at sites downstream from the first study site. These trends are illustrated in **Figure 2.** Students tested the water in three places and found that the farther downstream they went, the more phosphate the water had. Phosphates are chemicals in many fertilizers.

Armed with their observations, the students might make the following hypothesis: *phosphate fertilizer from a lawn is washing into the river and killing dwarf wedge mussels.* To test their hypothesis, the students make a **prediction,** a logical statement about what will happen if the hypothesis is correct. The students might make the following prediction: *mussels will die when exposed to high levels of phosphate in their water.*

It is important that the students' hypothesis—high levels of phosphate are killing the mussels—can be disproved. If students successfully raised mussels in water that has high phosphate levels, their hypothesis would be incorrect. Every time a hypothesis is disproved, the number of possible explanations for an observation is reduced. By eliminating possible explanations a scientist can zero in on the best explanation with more confidence.

✓ **Reading Check** What is the difference between a hypothesis and a prediction? (See the Appendix for answers to Reading Checks.)

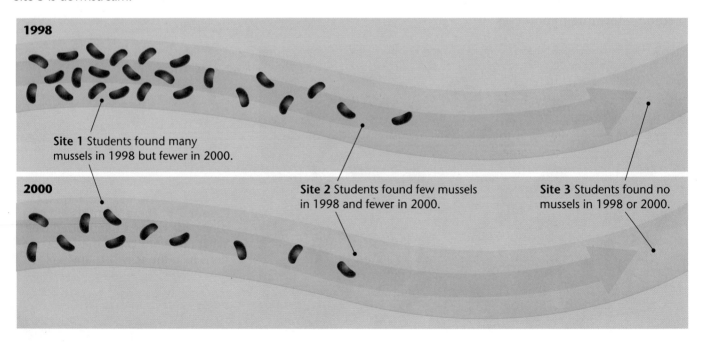

1998

Site 1 Students found many mussels in 1998 but fewer in 2000.

2000

Site 2 Students found few mussels in 1998 and fewer in 2000.

Site 3 Students found no mussels in 1998 or 2000.

Experimenting The questions that arise from observations often cannot be answered by making more observations. In this situation scientists usually perform one or more experiments. An **experiment** is a procedure designed to test a hypothesis under controlled conditions.

Experiments should be designed to pinpoint cause-and-effect relationships. For this reason, good experiments have two essential characteristics: a single variable is tested, and a control is used. The **variable** (VER ee uh buhl) is the factor of interest, which, in our example, would be the level of phosphate in the water. To test for one variable, scientists usually study two groups or situations at a time. The variable being studied is the only difference between the groups. The group that receives the experimental treatment is called the **experimental group.** In our example, the experimental group would be those mussels that receive phosphate in their water. The group that does not receive the experimental treatment is called the **control group.** In our example, the control group would be those mussels that do not have phosphate added to their water. If the mussels in the control group thrive while most of those in the experimental group die, the experiment's results support the hypothesis that phosphates from fertilizer are killing the mussels.

The Experimental Method In Action at Keene High School

▶ **Keene High School** students are conducting an experiment to study the effect of phosphate levels on the growth rates of freshwater mussels.

Keene High School students collected mussels (nonendangered relatives of the dwarf wedge mussel) and placed equal numbers of them in two aquariums. They ensured that the conditions in the aquariums were identical—same water temperature, food, hours of light, and so on. The students added a measured amount of phosphate to the aquarium of the experimental group. They added nothing to the aquarium of the control group.

A key to the success of an experiment is changing only one variable and having a control group. What would happen if the aquarium in which most of the mussels died had phosphate in the water and was also warmer? The students would not know if the phosphate or the higher temperature killed the mussels.

Another key to experimenting in science is *replication*, or recreating the experimental conditions to make sure the results are consistent. In this case, using six aquariums—three control and three experimental—

would help ensure that the results are not simply due to chance.

CRITICAL THINKING

1. Applying Ideas Why did the students ensure that the conditions in both aquariums were identical?

2. Evaluating Hypothesis How would you change the hypothesis if mussels died in both aquariums?

Figure 3 ► This scientist is analyzing his data with the help of a computer.

Table 1 ▼

Pollutant Concentrations (mg/L)		
Site	Nitrates	Phosphates
1	0.3	0.02
2	0.3	0.06
3	0.1	0.07

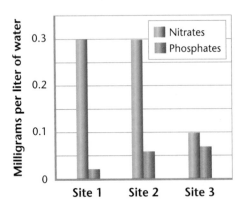

Figure 4 ► This graph and the table above it compare the concentrations of phosphates and nitrates in the Ashuelot River in 2000. Site 1 is upstream of Sites 2 and 3.

Organizing and Analyzing Data Keeping careful and accurate records is extremely important in science. A scientist cannot rely on experimental results that are based on sloppy observations or incomplete records. The information that a scientist gathers during an experiment, which is often in numeric form, is called **data.**

Organizing data into tables and graphic illustrations helps scientists analyze the data and explain the data clearly to others. The scientist in **Figure 3** is analyzing data on pesticides in food. Graphs are often used by scientists to display relationships or trends in the data. Graphs are especially useful for illustrating conclusions drawn from an experiment.

One common type of graph is called a *bar graph*. Bar graphs are useful for comparing the data for several things in one graph. **Figure 4** shows the data in **Table 1** in the form of a bar graph. Look at the data for Site 3 in the bar graph. The data show that the concentration of phosphates is higher at Site 3 than at Sites 1 and 2, and the concentration of nitrates is lower than at Sites 1 and 2.

Drawing Conclusions Scientists determine the results of their experiment by analyzing their data and comparing the outcome of their experiment with their prediction. Ideally, this comparison provides scientists with an obvious conclusion. But often the conclusion is not obvious. For example, in the mussel experiment, what if three mussels died in the control tank and five died in the experimental tank? The students could not be certain that phosphate is killing the mussels. Scientists often use mathematical tools to help them determine whether such differences are meaningful or are just a coincidence. Scientists also repeat their experiments.

Repeating Experiments Although the results from a single experiment may seem conclusive, scientists look for a large amount of supporting evidence before they accept a hypothesis. The more often an experiment can be repeated with the same results, in different places and by different people, the more sure scientists become about the reliability of their conclusions.

Communicating Results Scientists publish their results to share what they have learned with other scientists. When scientists think their results are important, they usually publish their findings as a scientific article. A scientific article includes the question the scientist explored, reasons why the question is important, background information, a precise description of how the work was done, the data that were collected, and the scientist's interpretation of the data.

The Correlation Method

Whenever possible, scientists study questions by using experiments. But many questions cannot be studied experimentally. The question "What was Earth's climate like 60 million years ago?" cannot be studied by performing an experiment because the scientists are 60 million years too late. "Does smoking cause lung cancer in humans?" cannot be studied experimentally because doing experiments that might injure people would be unethical.

When using experiments to answer questions is impossible or unethical, scientists test predictions by examining **correlations,** or associations between two or more events. For example, scientists know that the relative width of a ring on a tree trunk is a good indicator of the amount of rainfall the tree received in a given year. Trees produce wide rings in rainy years and narrow rings in dry years. Scientists have used this knowledge to investigate why the first European settlers at Roanake Island, Virginia (often called the Lost Colony) disappeared and why most of the first settlers at Jamestown, Virginia, died. As shown in **Figure 5,** the rings of older trees on the Virginia coast indicate that the Lost Colony and the Jamestown Colony were founded during two of the worst droughts the coast had experienced in centuries. The scientists concluded that the settlers may have starved because the famine made it hard to grow food.

Although correlation studies are useful, correlations do not necessarily prove cause-and-effect relationships between two variables. For example, the correlation between increasing phosphate levels and a declining mussel population on the Ashuelot River does not prove that phosphates harm mussels. Scientists become more sure about their conclusions if they find the same correlation in different places and as they eliminate other possible explanations.

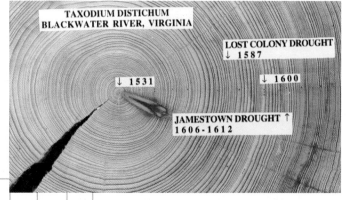

Figure 5 ▶ This cross section of a baldcypress from southeastern Virginia (above) shows a record of rainfall beginning in 1531. The graph translates the relative tree ring width into what is called a *drought index,* which allowed scientists to compare rainfall between different years.

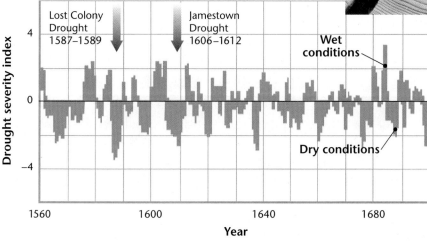

Source: *Science.*

Discovering Penicillin Alexander Fleming discovered penicillin by accident. Someone left a window open near his dishes of bacteria, and the dishes were infected with spores of fungi. Instead of throwing the dishes away, Fleming looked at them closely and saw that the bacteria had died on the side of a dish where a colony of green *Penicillium* mold had started to grow. If he had not been a careful observer, penicillin might not have been discovered. You may find *Penicillium* yourself on moldy bread.

Scientific Habits of Mind

Scientists actually approach questions in many different ways. But good scientists tend to share several key habits of mind, or ways of approaching and thinking about things.

Curiosity Good scientists are endlessly curious. Jane Goodall, pictured in **Figure 6,** is an inspiring example. She studied a chimpanzee troop in Africa for years. She observed the troop so closely that she came to know the personality and behavior of each member of the troop and greatly contributed to our knowledge of that species.

The Habit of Skepticism Good scientists also tend to be skeptical, which means that they don't believe everything they are told. For example, 19th century doctors were taught that men and women breathe differently—men use the diaphragm (the sheet of muscle below the rib cage) to expand their chest, whereas women raise their ribs near the top of their chest. Finally, a female doctor found that women seemed to breathe differently because their clothes were so tight that their ribs could not move far enough to pull air into their lungs.

Openness to New Ideas As the example above shows, skepticism can go hand in hand with being open to new ideas. Good scientists keep an open mind about how the world works.

Figure 6 ▶ Jane Goodall is famous for her close observations of chimpanzees—observations fueled in part by her endless curiosity.

Intellectual Honesty A scientist may be certain that a hypothesis is correct before it has been fully tested. But when an experiment is repeated, the results may differ from those obtained the first time. A good scientist will consider the possibility that the new results may be accurate, even if this means that the hypothesis might be wrong.

Imagination and Creativity
Good scientists are not only open to new ideas but able to conceive of new ideas themselves. The ability to see patterns where others do not, or to imagine things that others cannot, allows a good scientist to expand the boundaries of what we know.

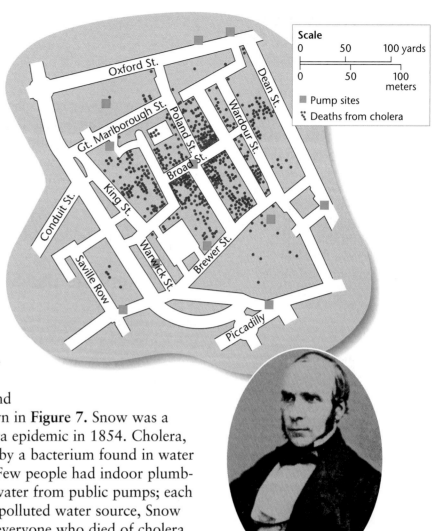

An example of an imaginative and creative scientist is John Snow, shown in **Figure 7**. Snow was a physician in London during a cholera epidemic in 1854. Cholera, a potentially fatal disease, is caused by a bacterium found in water that is polluted with human waste. Few people had indoor plumbing in 1854. Most people got their water from public pumps; each pump had its own well. To find the polluted water source, Snow made a map showing the homes of everyone who died of cholera. The map also showed the public water pumps. In this example of a correlation study, he found that more deaths occurred around a pump in Broad Street than around other pumps in the area. London authorities ended the cholera epidemic by shutting off the Broad Street pump. Using observation, imagination, and creativity, Snow solved an environmental problem and saved lives.

Figure 7 ▶ John Snow (bottom) created his famous spot map (top), which enabled him to see a pattern that no one had noticed before.

✔ **Reading Check** How did drawing a map of London help John Snow solve the cholera problem in 1854?

SECTION 1 Review

1. **Describe** the steps of the experimental method.

2. **Name** three scientific habits of mind and explain their importance.

3. **Explain** why a hypothesis is not just a guess.

4. **Explain** how scientists try to answer questions that cannot be tested with experiments.

CRITICAL THINKING

5. **Analyzing Methods** Read the description of experiments. Describe the two essential parts of a good experiment, and explain their importance.
   READING SKILLS

6. **Analyzing Relationships** How can a scientist be both skeptical and open to new ideas at the same time? Write a one-page story that describes such a situation. **WRITING SKILLS**

Statistics and Models

Objectives

▶ Explain how scientists use statistics.

▶ Explain why the size of a statistical sample is important.

▶ Describe three types of models commonly used by scientists.

▶ Explain the relationship between probability and risk.

▶ Explain the importance of conceptual and mathematical models.

Key Terms

statistics
mean
distribution
probability
sample
risk
model
conceptual model
mathematical model

Environmental science provides a lot of data that need to be organized and interpreted before they are useful. **Statistics** is the collection and classification of data that are in the form of numbers. People commonly use the term statistics to describe numbers, such as the batting record of a baseball player. Sportswriters also use the methods of statistics to translate a player's batting record over many games into a batting average, which allows people to easily compare the batting records of different players.

How Scientists Use Statistics

Scientists are also interested in comparing things, but scientists use statistics for a wide range of purposes. Scientists rely on and use statistics to summarize, characterize, analyze, and compare data. Statistics is actually a branch of mathematics that provides scientists with important tools for analyzing and understanding their data.

Consider the experiment in which students studied mussels to see if the mussels were harmed by fertilizer in their water. Students collected data on mussel length and phosphate levels during this experiment. Some mussels in the control group grew more than some mussels in the experimental group, yet some grew less. How could the students turn this data into meaningful numbers?

Statistics Works with Populations Scientists use statistics to describe statistical populations. A *statistical population* is a group of similar things that a scientist is interested in learning about. For example, the dwarf wedge mussels shown in **Figure 8** are part of the population of all dwarf wedge mussels on the Ashuelot River.

Figure 8 ▶ Students found these dwarf wedge mussel shells in a muskrat den. These mussels are part of the statistical population of all dwarf wedge mussels on the Ashuelot River.

What Is the Average? Although statistical populations are composed of similar individuals, these individuals often have different characteristics. For example, in the population of students in your classroom, each student has a different height, weight, and so on.

The Keene High School students measured the lengths of dwarf wedge mussels in a population, as shown in **Figure 8**. They added the lengths of the mussels and then divided by the number of mussels. This gave the average length of the mussels, which in statistical terms is called the mean. The **mean** is the number obtained by adding the data for a characteristic and dividing this sum by the number of individuals. The mean provides a single measure for a given characteristic of a population. Scientists can compare different populations by comparing their means. The mean length of the mussels in **Figure 9** is about 30 mm.

The Distribution The bar graph in **Figure 9** shows the lengths of dwarf wedge mussels in a population. The pattern that the bars create when viewed as a whole is called the *distribution*. A **distribution** is the relative arrangement of the members of a statistical population. In **Figure 9**, the lengths of the individuals are arranged between 15 and 50 mm.

The overall shape of the bars, which rise to form a hump in the middle of the graph, is also part of the distribution. The line connecting the tops of the bars in **Figure 9** forms the shape of a bell. The graphs of many characteristics of populations, such as the heights of people, form bell-shaped curves. A bell-shaped curve indicates a *normal distribution*. In a normal distribution, the data are grouped symmetrically around the mean.

Reading Check How was the mean length of the dwarf wedge mussel population calculated?

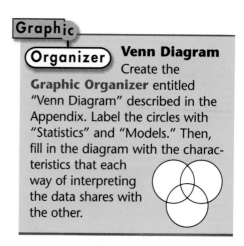

Graphic Organizer **Venn Diagram** Create the **Graphic Organizer** entitled "Venn Diagram" described in the Appendix. Label the circles with "Statistics" and "Models." Then, fill in the diagram with the characteristics that each way of interpreting the data shares with the other.

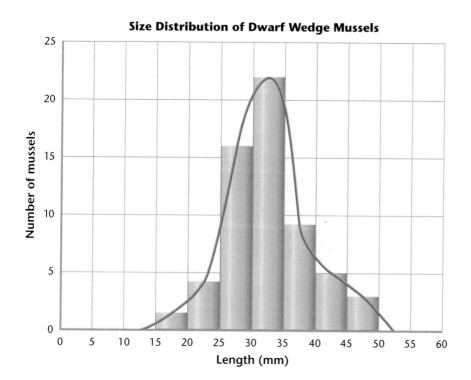

Size Distribution of Dwarf Wedge Mussels

Length (mm) — horizontal axis
Number of mussels — vertical axis

Figure 9 ▶ This bar graph shows the distribution of lengths in a population of dwarf wedge mussels. For example, the second bar from the left indicates that the population studied contained four mussels between 20 and 25 mm long.

What Is the Probability? The chance that something will happen is called **probability**. For example, if you toss a penny, what is the probability that it will come up heads? Most people would say "half and half," and they would be right. The chance of a tossed penny coming up heads is ½, which can also be expressed as 0.5 or 50%. In fact, probability is usually expressed as a number between 0 and 1 and written as a decimal rather than as a fraction. Suppose the penny comes up heads 7 out of 10 times. Does this result prove that the probability of a penny coming up heads is 0.7? No, it does not. So what is the problem?

The problem is that the *sample size*—the number of objects or events sampled—is too small to yield an accurate result. In statistics, a **sample** is a group of individuals or events selected to represent the population. If you toss a penny 10 times, your sample size is 10. If you continue tossing 1,000 times, you are almost certain to get about 50% heads and 50% tails. In this example, the sample is the number of coin tosses you make, while the population is the total number of coin tosses possible. Scientists try to make sure that the samples they take are large enough to give an accurate estimate for the whole population.

Statistics in Everyday Life

You have probably heard, "There is a 50 percent chance of rain today." **Figure 10** shows an example of a natural event that we often associate with probability—a thunderstorm. You encounter statistics often and use them more than you may think. People are constantly trying to determine the chance of something happening. A guess or gut instinct is probably just an unconscious sense of probability.

Understanding the News The news contains statistics every day, even if they are not obvious. For example, a reporter may say, "A study shows that forest fires increased air pollution in the city last year." We could ask many statistical questions about this news item. We might first ask what the average amount of air pollution in the city is. We could gather data on air pollution levels over the past 20 years and graph them. Then we could calculate the mean, and ask ourselves how different last year's data are from the average. We might graph the data and look at the distribution. Do this year's pollution levels seem unusually high compared to levels in other years? Recognizing and paying attention to statistics will make you a better consumer of information, including information about the environment.

Figure 10 ▶ Most people are familiar with statistics regarding the weather, such as the chance, or probability, of a thunderstorm.

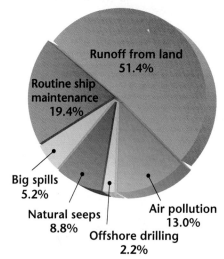

Figure 11 ▶ The graph below shows the sources of oil that pollute the ocean. The photo at left shows an oil spill off the coast of Galveston, Texas. Big oil spills are a relatively minor source of oil pollution.

Runoff from land 51.4%
Routine ship maintenance 19.4%
Big spills 5.2%
Natural seeps 8.8%
Offshore drilling 2.2%
Air pollution 13.0%

Thinking About Risk In scientific terms, **risk** is the probability of an unwanted outcome. For example, if you have a 1 in 4 chance of failing a class, the risk of failing is ¼, or 0.25. **Figure 11** shows a well-publicized environmental problem—oil spills. But as you can see in the pie graph, the risk of pollution from large oil spills is much smaller than the risk of oil pollution from everyday sources.

The most important risk we consider is the risk of death. Most people overestimate the risk of dying from sensational causes, such as terrorism, and underestimate the risk from common causes, such as smoking. Likewise, most citizens overestimate the risk of sensational environmental problems and underestimate the risk of ordinary ones, as shown in **Table 2.**

Table 2 ▼

Perceptions of Risk by Experts and Ordinary Citizens		
	High risk	**Low risk**
Experts	ozone depletion; global climate change	oil spills; radioactive materials; water pollution
Citizens	ozone depletion; radioactive waste; oil spills	global climate change; water pollution

Source: U.S. Environmental Protection Agency.

Figure 12 ▶ This plastic model of a DNA molecule is an example of a physical model.

Models

You are probably already familiar with models. Museums have models of ships, dinosaurs, and atoms. Architects build models of buildings. Even crash-test dummies are models. **Models** are representations of objects or systems. Although people usually think of models as things they can touch, scientists use several different types of models to help them learn about our environment.

Physical Models All of the models mentioned above are physical models. *Physical models* are three-dimensional models you can touch. Their most important feature is that they closely resemble the object or system they represent, although they may be larger or smaller.

One of the most famous physical models was used to discover the structure of DNA. The two scientists who built the structural model of DNA knew information about the size, shape, and bonding qualities of the subunits of DNA. With this knowledge, the scientists created model pieces that resembled the subunits and the bonds between them. These pieces helped them figure out the possible structures of DNA. Discovering the structure of DNA furthered other research that helped scientists understand how DNA replicates in a living cell. **Figure 12** shows a modern model of a DNA molecule. The most useful models teach scientists something new and help to further other discoveries.

Graphical Models Maps and charts are the most common examples of *graphical models*. Showing someone a road map is easier than telling him or her how to get somewhere. An example of a graphical model is the map of the Denver, Colorado, area in **Figure 13**. Scientists use graphical models to show things such as the positions of the stars, the amount of forest cover in a given area, and the depth of water in a river or along a coast.

Geofact

Fossil-Fuel Deposits Fossil fuels, such as coal and oil, are often buried deep underground in particular rock formations. We find fossil fuels by drilling for rocks that indicate the presence of fossil fuels and then we make models of where the coal or oil is likely to be found.

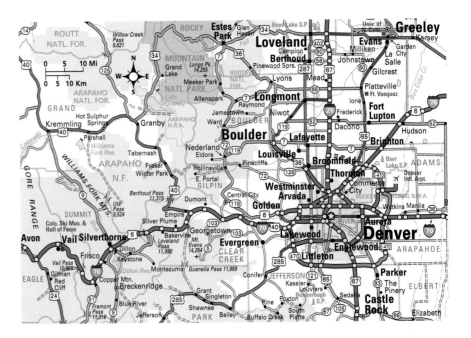

Figure 13 ▶ This map of the Denver, Colorado, area is an example of a graphical model.

Conceptual Models A **conceptual model** is a verbal or graphical explanation of how a system works or is organized. A flow-chart diagram is an example of a type of conceptual model. A flow-chart uses boxes linked by arrows to illustrate what a system contains and how those contents are organized.

Consider this example. Suppose that a scientist wants to know how mercury, a poisonous metal, moves through the environment to reach people after the mercury is released from burning coal. The scientist would use an understanding of mercury in the environment to build a conceptual model, as shown in **Figure 14.** Scientists often create such diagrams to help them understand how a system works—what components the system contains, how they are arranged, and how they affect one another.

Conceptual models are not always diagrams. They can also be verbal descriptions or even drawings of how something works or is put together. For example, the model of an atom as a large ball circled by smaller balls is a conceptual model of the structure of an atom. As this example shows, an actual model can be more than one type. An atomic model made of plastic balls is both a conceptual model and a physical model.

Reading Check How does building a conceptual model help scientists in their work?

FIELD ACTIVITY

Conceptual Model Accompany your class outdoors. Observe your surroundings, and write down observations about what you see. In your *Ecolog*, draw a conceptual model of something you observe. Your model should represent a system with components that interact, such as a small community of organisms.

SCLINKS.
www.scilinks.org
Topic: Using Models
Code: HE81588

Conceptual Model of Mercury Contamination

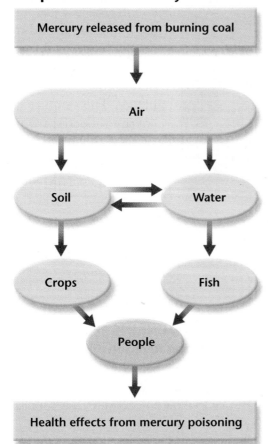

Figure 14 ▶ This conceptual model shows how mercury released from burning coal could end up reaching people, where it could cause poisoning.

Mathematical Models A **mathematical model** is one or more equations that represents the way a system or process works. You can represent many common situations using math models.

For example, suppose that the grapes in a fruit basket at home are getting moldy. You notice that every day the mold covers two more grapes. Here is a mathematical model for the number of moldy grapes on Tuesday:

$$M_{Tue} = M_{Mon} + 2, \text{ where } M = \text{number of moldy grapes}$$

Mathematical models are especially useful in cases with many variables, such as the many things that affect the weather.

Because mathematical models use numbers and equations, people may think the models are always right. But weather models, for example, sometimes predict rain on dry days. In fact, people are the ones who interpret data and write the equations.

If the data or the equations are wrong, the model will not be realistic and so will provide incorrect information. Like all models, mathematical models are only as good as the data that went into building them.

People may think of mathematical models as being confined to blackboards and paper, but scientists can use the models to create amazing, useful images. Look at the image of the San Francisco Bay Area in **Figure 15.** This is a "false color" digital satellite image. The satellite measures energy reflected from the Earth's surface. Scientists use mathematical models to relate the amount of energy reflected from objects to the objects' physical condition.

Figure 15 ▶ This is a satellite image of the San Francisco Bay Area. Scientists use mathematical models to understand the terrain from the way objects on the surface reflect light. In this image, healthy vegetation is red.

SECTION 2 **Review**

1. **Explain** why sample size is important in determining probability.

2. **Explain** what "the mean number of weeds in three plots of land" means.

3. **Describe** three types of models used by scientists.

CRITICAL THINKING

4. **Analyzing Relationships** Explain the relationship between probability and risk.

5. **Applying Ideas** Write a paragraph that uses examples to show how scientists use statistics. **WRITING SKILLS**

6. **Evaluating Ideas** Why are conceptual and mathematical models especially powerful?

SECTION 3
Making Informed Decisions

Scientific research is an essential first step to solve environmental problems. However, many other factors must also be considered. How will the proposed solution affect people's lives? How much will it cost? Is the solution ethical? Questions like these require an examination of **values,** which are principles or standards we consider important. What values should influence decisions that affect the environment? **Table 3** lists some values that often affect environmental decisions. You might think of others as well.

An Environmental Decision-Making Model

Forming an opinion about an environmental issue is often difficult and may seem overwhelming. It helps to have a systematic way of analyzing the issues and deciding what is important. One way to guide yourself through this process is to use a decision-making model. A **decision-making model** is a conceptual model that provides a systematic process for making decisions.

Figure 16 shows one possible decision-making model. The first step of the model is to gather information. In addition to watching news reports and reading about environmental issues, you should listen to well-informed people on all sides of an issue. Then consider which values apply to the issue. Explore the consequences of each option. Finally, evaluate all of the information to make a decision.

✔ **Reading Check** Why is a decision-making model helpful for making environmental decisions?

Table 3 ▼

Values That Affect Environmental Decision Making	
Value	**Definition**
Aesthetic	what is beautiful or pleasing
Economic	the gain or loss of money or jobs
Environmental	the protection of natural resources
Educational	the accumulation and sharing of knowledge
Ethical/moral	what is right or wrong
Health	the maintenance of human health
Recreational	human leisure activities
Scientific	understanding of the natural world
Social/cultural	the maintenance of human communities and their values and traditions

Objectives

▶ Describe three values that people consider when making decisions about the environment.

▶ Describe the four steps in a simple environmental decision-making model.

▶ Compare the short-term and long-term consequences of two decisions regarding a hypothetical environmental issue.

Key Terms

value
decision-making model

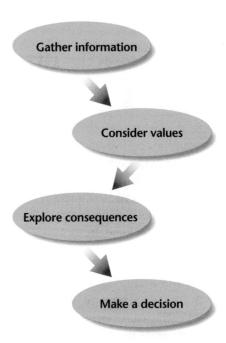

Figure 16 ▶ The diagram above shows a simple decision-making model.

A Hypothetical Situation

Consider the following hypothetical example. In the town of Pleasanton, in Valley County, biologists from the local college have been studying the golden-cheeked warbler, shown in **Figure 17**. The warblers have already disappeared from most areas around the state, and the warbler population is declining in Valley County. The biologists warn county officials that if the officials do not take action, the state fish and wildlife service may list the bird as an endangered species.

Pleasanton is growing rapidly, and much of the new development is occurring outside the city limits. This development is destroying warbler habitat. Valley County already has strict environmental controls on building, but these controls do not prevent the clearing of land.

Several groups join together to propose that the county buy several hundred acres of land where the birds are known to

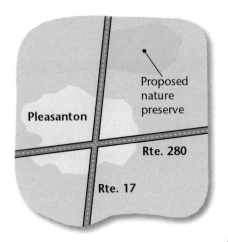

Figure 17 ▶ The map (above) shows the proposed nature preserve, which would be home to warblers like the one pictured (right).

Saving the Everglades: Making Informed Decisions

The Florida Everglades is an enormous, shallow freshwater marsh. The water in the Everglades slowly flows from Lake Okeechobee to Florida Bay. Much of the marsh is filled with sawgrass, mangroves, and other water-loving plants. It is also home to wildlife, from 40 species of fish to panthers, alligators, and wading birds such as herons and roseate spoonbills.

In the 1880s, marshlands were considered wastelands. Developers began to drain the Everglades. They replaced marsh with houses and sugarcane fields. Between 1940 and 1971, the Army Corps of Engineers built dikes, canals, and pumping stations that drained even more water. The Corps also straightened the Kissimmee River, which runs into Lake Okeechobee.

Scientists have shown that what remains of the Everglades is dying. Its islands and mangrove swamps are vanishing, its water is polluted with fertilizer from farms, and its wading-bird colonies are much smaller than before. These effects have economic consequences. Because much of the Everglades' water has been diverted from Florida Bay into the Atlantic Ocean, the towns of southeast Florida are running out of fresh water and much of the marine life in Florida Bay has died.

In the 1990s, a commission reported that the destruction of the Everglades had jeopardized the state's tourism industry, farming, and the economic future of south Florida. The solution was obvious—undo the water diversion dikes and dams and restore water to the Everglades.

▶ The roseate spoonbill is a colorful resident of the Everglades.

breed and save that land as a nature preserve. The groups also propose limiting development on land surrounding the preserve. The group obtains enough signatures on a petition to put the issue to a vote, and the public begins to discuss the proposal.

Some people who own property within the proposed preserve oppose the plan. These property owners have an economic interest in this discussion. They believe that they will lose money if they are forced to sell their land to the county instead of developing it.

Other landowners support the plan. They fear that without the preserve the warbler may be placed on the state's endangered species list. If the bird is listed as endangered, the state will impose a plan to protect the bird that will require even stricter limits on land development. People who have land near the proposed preserve think their land will become more valuable. Many residents of Pleasanton look forward to hiking and camping in the proposed preserve. Other residents do not like the idea of more government regulations on how private property can be used.

The Everglades There are 112 threatened or endangered plant and animal species in the Florida Everglades, according to the U.S. Fish & Wildlife Service.

SC*L*INKS.

www.scilinks.org
Topic: Environmental Decision Making
Code: HE80525

▶ **The Everglades** can be thought of as a shallow, slow-moving river that empties into Florida Bay.

In 2000, the $7.8 billion Everglades Restoration Plan was signed into law. The plan was put together by groups that had been fighting over the Everglades for decades: environmentalists, politicians, farmers, tourism advocates, and developers. Over the course of 5 years, members from the groups met and crafted a plan. At first people were afraid to break up into committees for fear that other people would make deals behind their backs. The director instituted social gatherings, and the members got to know and trust each other.

In the end, no one was completely satisfied, but all agreed that they would be better off with the plan than without it. Already Florida has restored 7 miles of the Kissimmee River to its original path. Native plants are absorbing some of the pollution that has killed an estimated $200 million worth of fish and wildfowl. The Everglades Restoration Plan is not perfect, but the process of creating and approving it shows how science and thoughtful negotiation can help solve complex environmental problems.

CRITICAL THINKING

1. Analyzing Processes Explain why it was so difficult for people to agree on how to restore the Everglades.

2. Analyzing Relationships If your county decided to build a landfill, do you think the decision-making process would resemble the Everglades example?

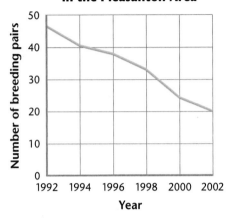

Warbler Population in the Pleasanton Area

Number of breeding pairs — Year: 1992, 1994, 1996, 1998, 2000, 2002

Figure 18 ▶ The population of golden-cheeked warblers in the Pleasanton area has declined in recent years.

How to Use the Decision-Making Model

The hypothetical situation in Pleasanton can be used to illustrate how to use the decision-making model. Michael Price is a voter in Valley County who will vote on whether the county should create a nature preserve to protect the golden-cheeked warbler. The steps Michael took to make his decision about the proposal are outlined below.

Gather Information Michael studied the warbler issue thoroughly by watching local news reports, reading the newspaper, learning more about golden-cheeked warblers from various Web sites, and attending forums where the issues were discussed. An example of scientific information that Michael considered includes the graph of warbler population decline in **Figure 18**. Several of the arguments on both sides made sense to him.

Consider Values Michael made a table similar to **Table 4** to clarify his thoughts. The values listed are environmental, economic, and recreational. Someone else might have thought other values were more important to consider.

Table 4 ▼

Should Valley County Set Aside a Nature Preserve?			
	Environmental	**Economic**	**Recreational**
Positive short-term consequences	Habitat destruction in the nature preserve area is slowed or stopped.	Landowners whose property was bought by the county receive a payment for their land. Property outside the preserve area can be developed with fewer restrictions.	Parts of the preserve are made available immediately for hiking and picnicking.
Negative short-term consequences	Environmental controls are made less strict in parts of the county outside the preserve area.	Property owners inside the preserve area do not make as much money as if they had developed their land. Taxpayers must pay higher taxes to buy preserve land.	Michael could not think of any negative short-term consequences.
Positive long-term consequences	The population of warblers increases, and the bird does not become endangered. Other species of organisms are also protected. An entire habitat is preserved.	Property near the preserve increases in value because it is near a natural area. Businesses move to Valley County because of its beauty and recreational opportunities, which results in job growth. The warbler is not listed as endangered, which avoids stricter controls on land use.	Large areas of the preserve are available for hiking and picnicking. Landowners near the preserve may develop campgrounds with bike trails, swimming, and fishing available on land adjacent to the preserve.
Negative long-term consequences	Other habitat outside the preserve may be damaged by overdevelopment.	Taxpayers must continue to pay for maintaining the preserve. Taxpayers lose the tax revenue that this land would have provided if it was developed.	State officials might restrict some recreational activities on private land within the preserve.

Explore Consequences Michael decided that in the short term the positive and negative consequences listed in his table were almost equally balanced. He saw that some people would suffer financially from the plan, but others would benefit. Taxpayers would have to pay for the preserve, but all the residents would have access to land that was previously off-limits because it was privately owned. Some parts of the county would have more protection from development, and some would have less.

The long-term consequences of the plan helped Michael make his decision. He realized that environmental values were an important factor. The idea of a bird becoming extinct distressed him. Also, protecting warbler habitat now would cost less than doing it later under a state-imposed plan.

Michael considered that there were long-term benefits to add to the analysis as well. He had read that property values were rising more rapidly in counties with land for recreation. He found that people would pay more to live in counties that have open spaces. Michael had found that Valley County had very little preserved land. He thought that creating the preserve would bring the county long-term economic benefits. He also highly valued the aesthetic and recreational benefits a preserve would offer, such as the walking trail in **Figure 19.**

Make A Decision Michael chose to vote for the nature preserve. Other people who looked at the same table of pros and cons might have voted differently. If you lived in Valley County, how would you have voted?

As you learn about issues affecting the environment, both in this course and in the future, use this decision-making model as a starting point to making your decisions. Make sure to consider your values, weigh pros and cons, and keep in mind both the short-term and long-term consequences of your decision.

Reading Check How did considering long-term consequences help Michael make a decision about creating a nature preserve in Valley County?

Figure 19 ▶ Land set aside for a nature preserve can benefit people as well as wildlife.

SECTION 3 **Review**

1. **Explain** the importance of each of the four steps in a simple decision-making model.

2. **List** and define three possible values to consider when making environmental decisions.

3. **Describe** in a short paragraph examples of two situations in which environmental values come into conflict with other values. **WRITING SKILLS**

CRITICAL THINKING

4. **Making Decisions** Pick one of the situations you described in question 3. Make a decision-making table that shows the positive and negative consequences of either of two possible decisions.

5. **Analyzing Ideas** Suggest how to make the decision-making model presented here more powerful.

Highlights

1 Scientific Methods

Key Terms

observation, 33
hypothesis, 34
prediction, 34
experiment, 35
variable, 35
experimental
  group, 35
control group, 35
data, 36
correlation, 37

Main Ideas

▶ Science is a process by which we learn about the world around us. Science progresses mainly by the experimental method.

▶ The experimental method involves making observations, forming a hypothesis, performing an experiment, interpreting data, and communicating results.

▶ In cases in which experiments are impossible, scientists look for correlations between different phenomena.

▶ Good scientists are curious, creative, honest, skeptical, and open to new ideas.

2 Statistics and Models

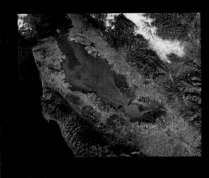

statistics, 40
mean, 41
distribution, 41
probability, 42
sample, 42
risk, 43
model, 44
conceptual model, 45
mathematical
  model, 46

▶ Scientists use statistics to classify, organize, and interpret data.

▶ Measures such as means and probabilities are used to describe populations and events.

▶ Statistics provides a powerful tool for evaluating information about the environment.

▶ Scientists use models, including conceptual and mathematical models, to understand the systems they study.

3 Making Informed Decisions

value, 47
decision-making
  model, 47

▶ Making environmental decisions involves gathering information, considering values, and exploring consequences.

▶ Decisions about the environment should be made thoughtfully. Using a decision-making model will provide you with a systematic process for making knowledgeable decisions.

▶ Making a table that lists positive and negative short-term and long-term consequences will help you recognize and weigh your values about an environmental decision.

Using Key Terms

Use each of the following terms in a separate sentence.

1. *experiment*
2. *correlation*
3. *model*
4. *distribution*
5. *values*

For each pair of terms, explain how the meanings of the terms differ.

6. *hypothesis* and *prediction*
7. *risk* and *probability*
8. *distribution* and *population*
9. *sample* and *population*

✔ **STUDY TIP**

Imagining Examples To understand how key terms apply to actual examples, work with a partner and take turns describing an environmental problem and explaining how the key terms relate to the problem.

Understanding Key Ideas

10. Scientists form _____ hypotheses to answer questions.
    a. accurate
    b. short
    c. mathematical
    d. testable

11. Risk is the _____ of a negative outcome.
    a. sample
    b. statistic
    c. probability
    d. event

12. If the results of your experiment do not support your hypothesis, you should
    a. publish your results anyway.
    b. consider the results abnormal and continue working.
    c. find a way to rationalize your results.
    d. try another method.

13. In a population, characteristics such as size will often be clustered around the
    a. sample.
    b. mean.
    c. distribution.
    d. collection.

14. Models used by scientists include
    a. conceptual models.
    b. variable models.
    c. physical models.
    d. Both (a) and (c)

15. Reading scientific reports is an example of
    a. assessing risk.
    b. considering values.
    c. gathering information.
    d. exploring consequences.

16. A conceptual model represents a way of thinking about
    a. relationships.
    b. variables.
    c. data.
    d. positions.

17. In an experiment, the experimental treatment differs from the control treatment only in the _____ being studied.
    a. experiment
    b. variable
    c. hypothesis
    d. data

18. To fully understand a complex environmental issue, you may need to consider
    a. economics.
    b. values.
    c. scientific information.
    d. All of the above

19. Scientists _____ experiments to make sure the results are meaningful.
    a. perform
    b. repeat
    c. conclude
    d. communicate

Short Answer

20. Explain the statement, "A good scientist is one who asks the right questions."

21. Explain the role of a control group in a scientific experiment.

22. How are statistics helpful for evaluating information about the environment?

23. Explain why environmental scientists use mathematical models.

24. How does making a table help you evaluate the values and concerns you have when making a decision?

Interpreting Graphics

The graph below shows the change in size of a shoreline alligator population over time. Use the graph to answer questions 25–27.

25. What happened to the density of alligators between 1986 and 1988?

26. What happened to the trend in the alligator concentration between 1994 and 1998?

27. How many times greater was the alligator population in 1986 than it was in 2000?

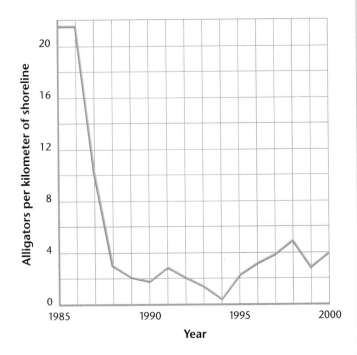

Concept Mapping

28. Use the following terms to create a concept map: *control group, experiment, experimental group, prediction, data, observations, conclusions,* and *hypothesis.*

Critical Thinking

29. Drawing Conclusions What does a scientist mean by the statement, "There is an 80 percent probability that a tornado will hit this area within the next 10 years"?

30. Making Inferences How does a map of Denver allow you to navigate around the city?

31. Evaluating Assumptions Are complicated models always more accurate? Write a paragraph that uses examples to explain your answer. **WRITING SKILLS**

32. Interpreting Statistics Explain what the following statement proves: "We sampled pet owners and found that three out of five surveyed own dogs and two out of five surveyed own cats."

Cross-Disciplinary Connection

33. Language Arts The word *serendipity,* which means "luck in finding something accidentally," came from a Persian fairy tale called *The Three Princes of Serendip.* In the story, each of the princes discovers something by accident. Research and write a short report on a serendipitous discovery about the environment. **WRITING SKILLS**

Portfolio Project

34. Make a Poster Choose an environmental issue in your area. You can choose a real-life problem that you have heard about on the news, such as improving the sewage system or building a new landfill, or you can choose a project that you think should be considered. Research the issue at your school or local library. Prepare a poster listing the groups of people likely to be involved in the decision and the factors that may be taken into consideration, including economic, social, and environmental factors.

MATH SKILLS

This table shows the results of an experiment that tested the hypothesis that butterflies are attracted to some substances but not to others. Twenty-four trays containing four substances were placed in random order on a sandbank to see if butterflies landed on the trays. The number of butterflies that landed on each type of tray and stayed for more than 5 min during a 2 h period was recorded in the table. Use the data in the table below to answer questions 35–36.

Butterfly Feeding Preferences				
	Sugar solution	Nitrogen solution	Water	Salt solution
Number of butterflies attracted	5	87	7	403

35. **Evaluating Data** Do the results in the table show that butterflies are attracted to salt solution but not any other substance? Why or why not? What other data would you like to see to help you evaluate the results of this experiment?

36. **Analyzing Data** Are there any controls shown in this table?

WRITING SKILLS

37. **Communicating Main Ideas** How is the experimental method an important scientific tool?

38. **Writing Persuasively** Write a letter to the editor of your local paper outlining your opinion on a local environmental issue.

READING SKILLS

Read the passage below, and then answer the questions that follow.

Jane and Jim observed a group of male butterflies by the roadside. Jane said that this behavior was called puddling and that the butterflies were counting each other to see if there was room to set up a territory in the area. Jim said he did not think butterflies could count each other and suggested the butterflies were feeding on nitrogen in the sand. Jane agreed that the butterflies appeared to be feeding, but she said that they may not be feeding on nitrogen, because female butterflies need more nitrogen than males.

Jim and Jane decided to perform some experiments on the butterflies. They put out trays full of sand in an area where butterflies had been seen. Two trays contained only sand. Two contained sand and water, two contained sand and a salt solution, and two contained sand and a solution containing nitrogen. Butterflies came to all the trays, but they stayed for more than 1 min only at the trays that contained the salt solution.

1. Which of the following statements is a testable hypothesis about the experiment?
   a. Male butterflies mate with female butterflies.
   b. Salt is a compound and nitrogen is an element.
   c. Butterflies are never seen in groups except on sandy surfaces.
   d. Butterflies are attracted to salt.

2. Which of the following conclusions is supported by the observations Jane and Jim made?
   a. Male butterflies can count each other.
   b. The butterflies were probably feeding on nitrogen in the sand.
   c. The butterflies were probably feeding on salts in the sand.
   d. Female butterflies need less nitrogen than male butterflies.

Standardized Test Prep

Understanding Concepts

Directions (1–4): For *each* question, write on a separate sheet of paper the letter of the correct answer.

1 How would a scientist categorize a testable explanation for an observation?
 A. a correlation
 B. an experiment
 C. a hypothesis
 D. a prediction

2 What happens when an observation is submitted for peer review?
 F. The article is proofread before it is published.
 G. A professor gives a lecture based on a published article.
 H. The results are looked at closely by other scientific experts.
 I. Information on the experimental design is included in published works.

3 Which of the following is an example of a scientist's physical model?
 A. a crash-test dummy for a car company
 B. a diagram of the structure of an atom
 C. a map of Denver, Colorado
 D. a satellite image of South America

4 What attribute of a skeptic would contribute to a good scientific mind?
 F. willingness to travel
 G. empathetic nature
 H. desire to conduct experiments
 I. continual questioning of observations

Directions (5–6): For *each* question, write a short response.

5 A penny is tossed and comes up heads 7 out of 10 times. Is the probability that it will be heads on the next toss 70%? Why or why not?

6 A mean is the number obtained by adding up the data for a given characteristic of a statistical population, and dividing the sum by the total number of individuals in the given population. Why do scientists calculate the mean of a statistical population?

Reading Skills

Directions (7–9): Read the passage below. Then answer the questions.

We use statistics everyday. Weather experts report the forecast in terms of probabilities, such as "There is a 50 percent chance of rain today." People are constantly guessing the possibility that something will or will not happen. A guess is one of the ways we express probability.

In scientific terms, risk is the probability of an unwanted outcome. Most people overestimate the risk of dying from sensational causes, such as terrorism, and underestimate the risk from common causes such as smoking. Likewise, most citizens overestimate the risk of sensational environmental problems such as oil spills, and underestimate the risk of ordinary ones, like ozone depletion. However, when decisions must be made on proposals affecting the environment, it is important that all the benefits and risks of the possible action are calculated.

7 Assess which of the following experts would perceive as having the **highest** risk.
 A. the threat of global climate change
 B. the radioactivity from the waste of a nuclear power plant
 C. the possibility of a tidal wave reaching a highly populated land mass
 D. the danger of widespread water pollution

8 How would a scientist define the term risk?
 F. the likelihood of something good
 G. a chance event
 H. the probability of an unwanted outcome
 I. a benefit that is overestimated

9 How could a decision-making model be helpful for estimating the benefits and risks of a proposal?
 A. It would eliminate uncertainty.
 B. It would create a digital image.
 C. It would predict the outcome of the decision.
 D. It would allow consideration of all the variables.

Interpreting Graphics

Directions (10–13): For *each* question below, record the correct answer on a separate sheet of paper.

The bar graph below shows the distribution of lengths in a population of dwarf wedge mussels. Use this graph to answer questions 10 through 13.

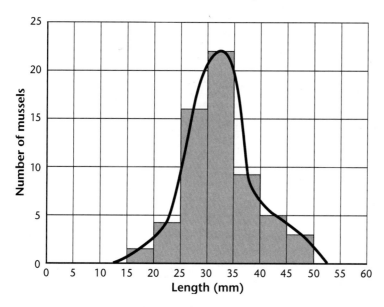

Size Distribution of Dwarf Wedge Mussels

10 What type of distribution does this bell-shaped curve depict?
  F. asymmetric
  G. correlative
  H. normal
  I. random

11 How many mussels are less than 25 mm in length?
  A. 6
  B. 9
  C. 12
  D. 15

12 Determine the total size of this statistical population of dwarf wedge mussels.
  F. 60
  G. 70
  H. 80
  I. 90

13 What is the **most** likely size predictable for a mussel randomly drawn from this population?
  A. 15–20 mm
  B. 25–30 mm
  C. 30–35 mm
  D. 40–45 mm

Test TIP

Probability is the chance of an outcome occurring. The highest probability occurs in the group with the largest number of individuals.

Skills Practice Lab: OBSERVATION

Objectives

▶ **USING SCIENTIFIC METHODS** **Formulate** a hypothesis about the relationship between temperature and fermentation by yeast.

▶ **USING SCIENTIFIC METHODS** **Test** your hypothesis.

▶ **Analyze** your data.

▶ **Explain** whether your data support or refute your hypothesis.

Materials

beakers, 100 mL (3)
beakers, 400 mL (3)
clock
delivery tubes, rubber or plastic (3)
graph paper
ice cubes
solution of yeast, corn syrup, and water
stoppers, no. 2, one-hole (3)
test tubes, 20 mm × 200 mm (3)
thermometer

▶ **Step 3** Carbon dioxide bubbles will be released from the delivery tube.

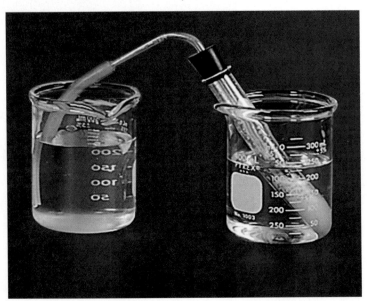

Scientific Investigations

A scientist considers all the factors that might be responsible for what he or she observes. Factors that can vary and that can be measured are called *variables*. The variable that you experimentally manipulate is the *independent variable*. The variable that you think will respond to this manipulation is the *dependent variable*.

You can practice the scientific method as it relates to everyday observations, such as the observation that bread dough rises when it is baked. According to a bread recipe, you dissolve a package of yeast in warm water and add flour, corn syrup, salt, and oil. Yeast is a microorganism that plays an important role in making bread. Yeast obtains energy by converting sugar to alcohol and carbon dioxide gas in a process called *fermentation*. The carbon dioxide forms bubbles, which make the bread dough rise. But what role, if any, does temperature play in this process? In this investigation, you will work as part of a team to try to answer these questions. Together, you will form a hypothesis and conduct an experiment that tests your hypothesis.

Procedure

1. Restate the question relating temperature to fermentation in yeast as a hypothesis.

2. Set up three test tubes containing yeast, water, and corn syrup stoppered with a gas-delivery tube. Label the test tubes "A", "B", and "C". Place each test tube in a water bath of different temperature. Place tube A in a water bath cooled by a few ice cubes, place tube B in room-temperature water, and place tube C in a warm water bath.

3. Allow the apparatus to sit for 5 min. Then place the open end of the delivery tube under water and begin to collect data on gas production. For the next 10 min, count the number of gas bubbles released from each tube, and record your data in the table on the next page.

4. Prepare a graph of data by placing time on the *x*-axis and the total number of gas bubbles released on the *y*-axis. Plot three curves on the same graph, and label each with the temperature you recorded for each test tube. Compare your graph with that of three other teams before handing in your report.

Carbon Dioxide Bubbles Released by Yeast										
Time (min)	1	2	3	4	5	6	7	8	9	10
Tube A:_____										
Tube B:_____										
Tube C:_____										

DO NOT WRITE IN THIS BOOK

Analysis

1. **Classifying Data** Which set of conditions is most similar to the conditions for the bread dough in the recipe? Why were two other conditions used in this experiment?

2. **Classifying Data** What was the independent variable in this experiment? Explain your answer.

3. **Classifying Data** What was the dependent variable in this experiment? Explain your answer.

Conclusions

4. **Drawing Conclusions** Write a conclusion for this experiment. Describe how the independent and dependent variables are related. Tell how the data supports your conclusion.

5. **Evaluating Results** What does temperature have to do with making bread dough rise?

6. **Evaluating Methods** Why did you compare your results with those of other teams before writing your conclusions?

7. **Applying Conclusions** Science is not just something you know but also something you do. Explain this statement in light of what you have learned in this investigation.

Extension

1. **Designing Experiments** Formulate a new hypothesis about the effect of different types of sugar on carbon dioxide production by yeast. Test your new hypothesis under controlled conditions. Did your results support your hypothesis? Research the types of sugar you used, and write a short explanation for your findings.

▶ **Recording Data** Count the number of bubbles produced under each experimental condition and record the data in a table.

A TOPOGRAPHIC MAP OF KEENE, NEW HAMPSHIRE

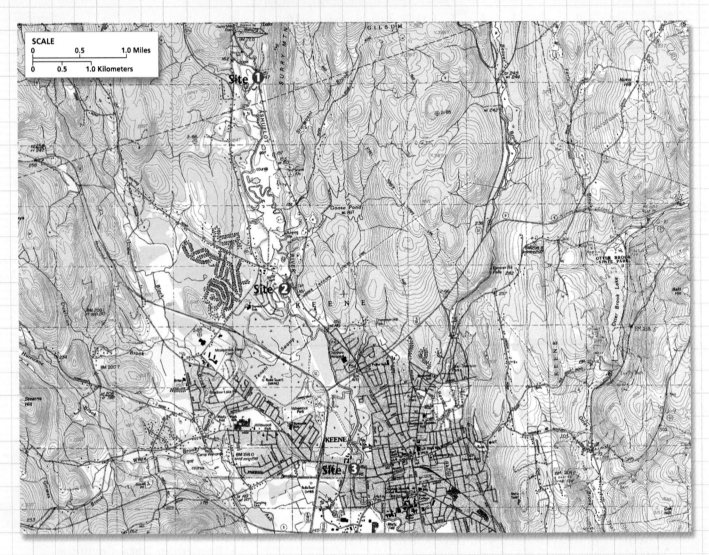

MAP SKILLS

Topographic maps use contour lines to indicate areas that share a common elevation. Where the lines are close together, the terrain is steep. Where the lines are far apart, the landscape is flat. In this map, the Ashuelot River flows downhill from Site 1 to Site 3. Use the map to answer the questions below.

1. **Using a Key** Use the scale at the top of the map to calculate the distance between Sites 1 and 2 and between Sites 2 and 3.

2. **Understanding Topography** Are the hills to the east and west of the town of Keene more likely to

drain into the river around Site 3 or Site 2? Explain your answer.

3. **Identifying Trends** Which site is more likely to be polluted? Explain your answer.

4. **Analyzing Data** Trace the sections of the Ashuelot River between each site to determine the length of stream between each site.

5. **Interpreting Landforms** A flood plain is an area that is periodically flooded when a river overflows its banks. Interpret the contour lines to locate the flood plain of the Ashuelot River.

BATS AND BRIDGES

A large colony of Mexican free-tailed bats lives under the Congress Avenue Bridge in Austin, Texas. These bats eat millions of insects a night, so they are welcome neighbors. Communities around the country and around the world have learned of the bats and have asked Austin for help in building bat-friendly bridges. But all that the people of Austin knew was that the bats appeared after the Congress Avenue Bridge was rebuilt in the 1980s. What attracted the bats? The people of Austin had to do a little research.

A Crevice Will Do

In the wild, bats spend the day sleeping in groups in caves or in crevices under the flaking bark of old trees. They come back to the same place every day to roost. Deep crevices in tree bark are rare now that many of our old forests have been cut down, and many bats are in danger of extinction.

In the 1990s, the Texas Department of Transportation and Bat Conservation International, a non-profit organization located in Austin, set out to discover what made a bridge attractive to bats. They collected data on 600 bridges, including some that had bat colonies and some that did not. They answered the following questions: Where was the bridge located? What was it made of? How was it constructed? Was it over water or land? What was the temperature under the bridge? How was the land around the bridge used?

Some Bridges are Better

Statistical analysis of the data revealed a number of differences between bridges occupied by bats and bridges unoccupied by bats. Which differences were important to the bats and which were not? The researchers returned to the Congress Avenue Bridge in Austin to find out. Crevices under the bridge appeared to be crucial, and the crevices had to be the right size. Free-tailed bats appeared to prefer crevices 1 to 3 cm wide and about 30 cm deep in hidden corners of the bridge, and they preferred bridges made of concrete, not steel.

The scientists looked again at their data on bridges. They discovered that 62 percent of bridges in central and southern Texas that had appropriate crevices were occupied by bats. Now, the Texas Department of Transportation is adding bat houses to existing bridges that do not have crevices. These houses are known as Texas Bat-Abodes, and they can make any bridge bat friendly.

Bat Conservation International is collecting data on bats and bridges everywhere. Different bat species may have different preferences. A Texas Bat-Abode might not attract bats to a bridge in Minnesota or Maine. If we can figure out what features attract bats to bridges, we can incorporate these features into new bridges and make more bridges into bat-friendly abodes.

▶ **Mexican free-tailed bats** leave their roost under the Congress Avenue Bridge in Austin, Texas, to hunt for insects.

What Do You Think?

Many bridges in the United States could provide roosting places for bats. Do you think communities should try to establish colonies of bats under local bridges? How should communities make this decision, and what information would they need to make it wisely?

The Dynamic Earth

1 The Geosphere

2 The Atmosphere

3 The Hydrosphere and Biosphere

PRE-READING ACTIVITY

FOLDNOTES

Pyramid Before you read this chapter, create the FoldNote entitled "Pyramid" described in the Reading and Study Skills section of the Appendix. Label the sides of the pyramid with "Geosphere," "Atmosphere," "Hydrosphere," and "Biosphere." As you read the chapter, write information you learn about each category under the appropriate flap.

Landmasses are moving slowly across our planet's surface. The atmosphere is a swirling mix of gases and vapor. Our planet, which may appear placid from space, is always changing.

The Geosphere

SCSh.7.a; SEV.1.a; SEV.1.e

EARTH SCIENCE **CONNECTION**

Molten rock from Earth's interior flows over the surface of the planet, and violent eruptions blow the tops off volcanoes. Hurricanes batter beaches and change coastlines. Earthquakes shake the ground and topple buildings and freeway overpasses. None of this activity is caused by people. Instead, it is the result of the dynamic state of planet Earth. What are the conditions that allow us to survive on a constantly changing planet?

The Earth as a System

The Earth consists of rock, air, water, and living things that all interact with each other. Scientists divide this system into four parts. As shown in **Figure 1,** the four parts are the geosphere (rock), the atmosphere (air), the hydrosphere (water), and the biosphere (living things).

The solid part of the Earth that consists of all rock, as well as the soils and loose rocks on Earth's surface, makes up the **geosphere.** Most of the geosphere is located in Earth's interior. At the equator, the average distance through the center of the Earth to the other side is 12,756 km. The atmosphere is the mixture of gases that makes up the air we breathe. Nearly all of these gases are found in the first 30 km above the Earth's surface. The hydrosphere makes up all of the water on or near the Earth's surface. Much of this water is in the oceans. Water is also found in the atmosphere, on land, and in the soil. The biosphere is made up of parts of the geosphere, the atmosphere, and the hydrosphere. The biosphere is the part of the Earth where life exists. It is a thin layer at Earth's surface that extends from about 9 km above the Earth's surface down to the bottom of the ocean.

Objectives

▶ Describe the composition and structure of the Earth.

▶ Describe the Earth's tectonic plates.

▶ Explain the main cause of earthquakes and their effects.

▶ Identify the relationship between volcanic eruptions and climate change.

▶ Describe how wind and water alter the Earth's surface.

Key Terms

geosphere
crust
mantle
core
lithosphere
asthenosphere
tectonic plate
erosion

Figure 1 ▶ The Earth is an integrated system that consists of the geosphere, the atmosphere, the hydrosphere, and the biosphere (inset).

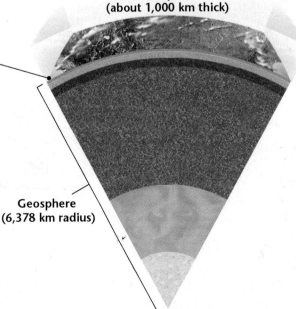

Atmosphere
(about 1,000 km thick)

Geosphere
(6,378 km radius)

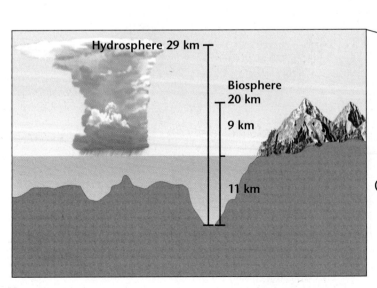

Hydrosphere 29 km

Biosphere
20 km

9 km

11 km

Discovering Earth's Interior

Studying the Earth beneath our feet is not easy. The deepest well that has been drilled into Earth's interior is only about 12 km deep. An alternative method must be used to study the interior of the Earth. Scientists can use *seismic waves* to learn about Earth's interior. Seismic waves are the waves that travel through Earth's interior during an earthquake. If you have ever tapped a melon to see if it is ripe, you know that the state of the melon's interior affects the sound you detect. Similarly, a seismic wave is altered by the nature of the material through which it travels. As shown in **Figure 2,** seismologists measure changes in the speed and direction of seismic waves that penetrate the interior of the planet. By doing this, seismologists have learned that the Earth is made up of different layers and have inferred what substances make up each layer.

The Composition of the Earth Scientists divide Earth into three layers—the crust, the mantle, and the core—based on their composition. These layers are composed of progressively denser materials toward the center of the Earth. Figure 3 shows a cross section of the Earth. Earth's thin outer layer, the **crust,** is composed almost entirely of light elements. The crust makes up less than 1 percent of the Earth's mass. The crust is the Earth's thinnest layer. It is 5 km to 8 km thick beneath the oceans and is 20 km to 70 km thick beneath the continents. The **mantle,** which is the

Figure 2 ▶ Seismologists have measured changes in the speed and direction of seismic waves that travel through Earth's interior. Through this process, they have learned that the Earth is made up of different layers.

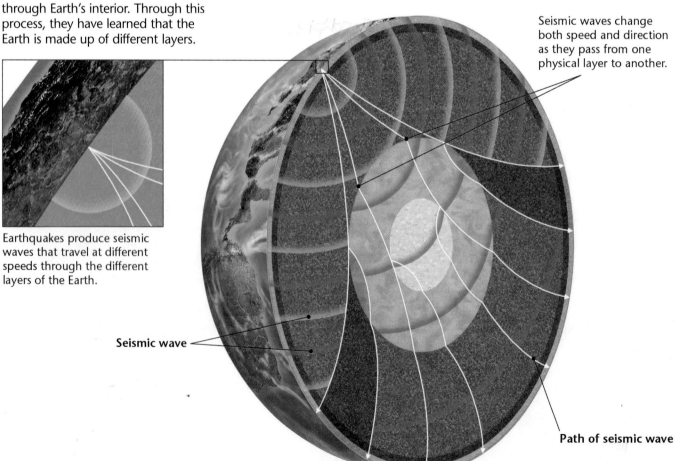

Earthquakes produce seismic waves that travel at different speeds through the different layers of the Earth.

Seismic waves change both speed and direction as they pass from one physical layer to another.

Seismic wave

Path of seismic wave

layer beneath the crust, makes up 64 percent of the mass of the Earth. The mantle is approximately 2,900 km thick and is made of rocks of medium density. Earth's innermost layer is the **core.** The core is composed of the densest elements. It has a radius of approximately 3,400 km.

The Structure of the Earth If we consider the physical properties of each layer, instead of their chemistry, the Earth can be divided into five layers. Earth's outer layer is the **lithosphere.** It is a cool, rigid layer, 15 km to 300 km thick, that includes the crust and uppermost part of the mantle. It is divided into huge pieces called *tectonic plates.* The **asthenosphere** is the layer beneath the lithosphere. The asthenosphere is a plastic, solid layer of the mantle made of rock that flows very slowly and allows tectonic plates to move on top of it. Beneath the asthenosphere is the mesosphere, the lower part of the mantle.

The Earth's outer core is a dense liquid layer. At the center of the Earth is the dense, solid inner core, which is made up mostly of the metals iron and nickel. The temperature of the inner core is estimated to be between 4,000°C to 5,000°C. It is solid because it is under enormous pressure. Earth's outer and inner core together make up about one-third of Earth's mass.

✓ **Reading Check** Which of Earth's physical layers is liquid? (See the Appendix for answers to Reading Checks.)

Figure 3 ▶ Earth's Layers Scientists divide the Earth into different layers based on composition and physical properties.

Compositional Layers

Crust 5–70 km thick; the solid, brittle, outermost layer of the Earth; continental crust is thick and made of lightweight materials, whereas oceanic crust is thin and made of denser materials

Mantle 2,900 km thick; the layer of the Earth between the crust and the core; made of dense, iron-rich minerals

Core 3,428 km radius; a sphere of hot, dense nickel and iron at the center of the Earth

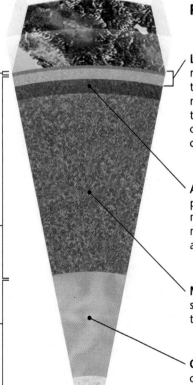

Physical Layers

Lithosphere 15–300 km thick; the cool, rigid, outermost layer of the Earth; consists of the crust and the rigid, uppermost part of the mantle; divided into huge pieces called tectonic plates, which move around on top of the asthenosphere and can have both continental and oceanic crust

Asthenosphere 250 km thick; the solid, plastic layer of the mantle between the mesosphere and the lithosphere; made of mantle rock that flows very slowly, which allows tectonic plates to move on top of it

Mesosphere 2,550 km thick; the "middle sphere"; the lower layer of the mantle between the asthenosphere and the outer core

Outer Core 2,200 km thick; the outer shell of Earth's core; made of liquid nickel and iron

Inner Core 1,228 km radius; a sphere of solid nickel and iron at the center of the Earth

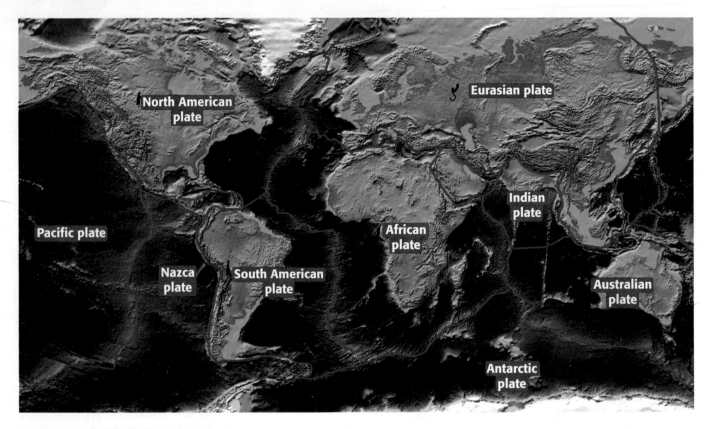

Figure 4 ▶ Earth's lithosphere is divided into pieces called *tectonic plates*. The tectonic plates are moving in different directions and at different speeds.

Plate Tectonics

You learned that the lithosphere—the rigid, outermost layer of the Earth—is divided into pieces called **tectonic plates.** These plates glide across the underlying asthenosphere in much the same way as a chunk of ice drifts across a pond. The continents are located on tectonic plates and move around with them. The major tectonic plates include the Pacific, North American, South American, African, Eurasian, and Antarctic plates. **Figure 4** illustrates the major tectonic plates and their direction of motion.

Plate Boundaries Much of the geologic activity at the surface of the Earth takes place at the boundaries between tectonic plates. Plates may move away from one another, collide with one another, or slip past one another. Enormous forces are generated at tectonic plate boundaries, where the crust is pulled apart, is squeezed together, or is constantly slipping. The forces produced at the boundaries of tectonic plates can cause mountains to form, earthquakes to shake the crust, and volcanoes to erupt.

Plate Tectonics and Mountain Building When tectonic plates collide, slip by one another, or pull apart, enormous forces cause rock to break and buckle. Where plates collide, the crust becomes thicker, is pushed up, and eventually forms a mountain range. As shown in **Figure 5,** the Himalaya Mountains in south-central Asia began to form when the Eurasian tectonic plate and the Indian tectonic plate began to push into each other about 50 million years ago.

Earthquakes

A *fault* is a break in the Earth's crust along which blocks of the crust slide relative to one another. When rocks that are under stress suddenly break along a fault, a series of ground vibrations is set off. These vibrations of the Earth's crust caused by slippage along a fault are known as *earthquakes*. Earthquakes are occurring all of the time, but many are so small that we cannot feel them. Other earthquakes are enormous movements of the Earth's crust that cause widespread damage.

The Richter scale is used by scientists to quantify the amount of energy released by an earthquake. The measure of the energy released by an earthquake is called *magnitude*. The smallest magnitude that can be felt is approximately 2.0, and the largest magnitude that has ever been recorded is 9.5. Each increase of magnitude by one whole number indicates the release of 31.7 times more energy than the whole number below it. For example, an earthquake of magnitude 6.0 releases 31.7 times the energy of an earthquake of magnitude 5.0. Earthquakes that cause widespread damage have magnitudes of 7.0 and greater.

Figure 5 ▶ The Himalaya Mountains are still growing today because the tectonic plate containing Asia and the tectonic plate containing India continue to collide.

Where Do Earthquakes Occur? Areas of the world where earthquakes occur are shown on the map in **Figure 6.** As you can see from the map, the majority of earthquakes take place at or near tectonic plate boundaries. Over the past 15 million to 20 million years, large numbers of earthquakes have occurred along the San Andreas fault, which runs almost the entire length of California. The San Andreas fault is the line where parts of the North American plate and the Pacific plate are slipping past one another.

Reading Check What is meant by the magnitude of an earthquake?

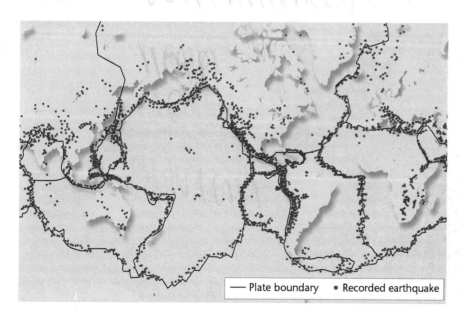

Plate boundary • Recorded earthquake

Figure 6 ▶ The largest and most active earthquake zones lie along tectonic plate boundaries.

Can Animals Predict Earthquakes? Can animals that live close to the site of an earthquake detect changes in their physical environment prior to an earthquake? Documentation of unusual animal behavior prior to earthquakes can be found as far back as 1784. Examples of this odd behavior include zoo animals refusing to enter shelters at night, snakes and small mammals abandoning their burrows, and wild birds leaving their usual habitats. These behaviors reportedly happened within a few days, hours, or minutes of earthquakes.

Earthquake Hazard Despite much study, scientists cannot predict when earthquakes will take place. However, information about where they are most likely to occur can help people prepare for them. An area's earthquake-hazard level is determined by past and present seismic activity. The Maps in Action activity located at the end of this chapter shows earthquake-hazard levels for the contiguous United States.

Earthquakes are not restricted to high-risk areas. In 1886, an earthquake shook Charleston, South Carolina, which is considered to be in a medium-risk area. Because the soil beneath the city is sandy, this earthquake caused extensive damage. During shaking from a strong earthquake, sand acts like a liquid and causes buildings to sink. In areas that are prone to earthquakes, it is worth the extra investment to build bridges and buildings that are at least partially earthquake resistant. Earthquake-resistant buildings are slightly flexible so that they can sway with the ground motion.

Volcanoes

A *volcano* is a mountain built from magma—melted rock—that rises from the Earth's interior to its surface. Volcanoes are often located near tectonic plate boundaries where plates are either colliding or separating from one another. Volcanoes may occur on land or under the sea, where they may eventually break the ocean surface as islands. As **Figure 7** shows, the majority of the world's active volcanoes on land are located along tectonic plate boundaries that surround the Pacific Ocean.

Figure 7 ▶ The Ring of Fire
Tectonic plate boundaries are places where volcanoes usually form. The Ring of Fire contains nearly 75 percent of the world's active volcanoes that are on land. A large number of people live on or near the Ring of Fire.

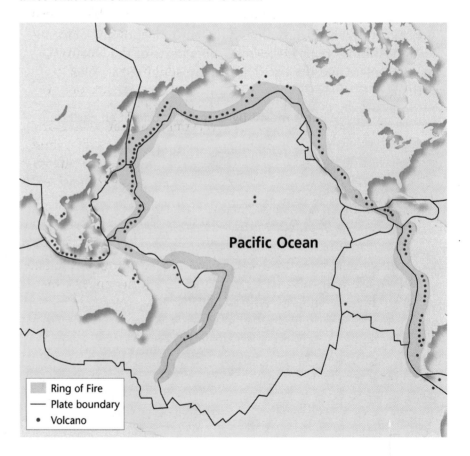

Pacific Ocean

Ring of Fire
— Plate boundary
• Volcano

Local Effects of Volcanic Eruptions A volcano erupts when the pressure of the magma inside becomes so great that it blows open the solid surface of the volcano. Some volcanoes have magma flowing out of them all the time, so the pressure never builds up and they never erupt. Volcanic eruptions can be devastating to local economies and can cause great human loss. Clouds of hot ash, dust, and gases can flow down the slope of a volcano at speeds of up to 200 km/h and sear everything in their path. During an eruption, volcanic ash can mix with water and produce a mudflow. In addition, ash that falls to the ground can cause buildings to collapse under its weight, bury crops, and damage the engines of vehicles. Volcanic ash may also cause breathing difficulties.

Global Effects of Volcanic Eruptions Major volcanic eruptions, such as the eruption of Mount St. Helens shown in **Figure 8**, can change Earth's climate for several years. In large eruptions, clouds of volcanic ash and sulfur-rich gases may reach the upper atmosphere. As the ash and gases spread across the planet, they can reduce the amount of sunlight that reaches the Earth's surface. This reduction in sunlight can cause a drop in the average global surface temperature. In the 1991 eruption of Mount Pinatubo in the Philippines, the amount of sunlight that reached the Earth's surface was estimated to have decreased by 2 to 4 percent. As a result, the average global temperature dropped by several tenths of a degree Celsius over a period of several years.

Figure 8 ▶ On May 18, 1980, Mount St. Helens in Washington State erupted. Sixty-three people lost their lives, and 400 km² of forest were destroyed in an eruption that blew away the top 410 m of the volcano.

Graphic Organizer Comparison Table

Create the **Graphic Organizer** entitled "Comparison Table" described in the Appendix. Label the columns with "Local Effects" and "Global Effects." Label the rows with "Volcanic Eruptions" and "Earthquakes." Then, fill in the table with details about the characteristics and the effects of each type of natural disaster.

Erosion

Forces at the boundaries of tectonic plates bring rock to the surface of the Earth. At the Earth's surface, rocks are altered by other forces. The Earth's surface is continually battered by wind and scoured by running water, which moves rocks around and changes their appearance. The removal and transport of surface material is called **erosion**. Erosion wears down rocks and makes them smoother as time passes. The older a mountain range is, the longer the forces of erosion have acted on it. This information helped geologists learn that the round-topped Appalachian Mountains in the eastern United States are older than the jagged Rocky Mountains in the west.

Water Erosion Erosion by both rivers and oceans can produce dramatic changes on Earth's surface. Waves from ocean storms can erode coastlines to give rise to a variety of spectacular landforms. Over time, rivers can carve deep gorges into the landscape, as shown in **Figure 9.**

Wind Erosion Like moving water, wind can also change the landscape of our planet. In places where plants grow, their roots hold soil in place. But in places where there are few plants, wind can blow soil away very quickly. Beaches and deserts, which have loose, sandy soil, are examples of places where few plants grow. Soft rocks, such as sandstone, erode more easily than hard rocks, such as granite, do. In parts of the world, spectacular rock formations are sometimes seen where pinnacles of hard rock stand alone because the softer rock around them has been eroded by wind and/or water.

Figure 9 ▶ Over long periods of time, erosion can produce spectacular landforms on Earth's surface.

SECTION 1 Review

1. **Name** and describe the physical and compositional layers into which scientists divide the Earth.

2. **Explain** the main cause of earthquakes and their effects.

3. **Describe** the effects that a large-scale volcanic eruption can have on the global climate.

4. **Describe** how wind and water alter the Earth's surface.

CRITICAL THINKING

5. **Analyzing Processes** How might the surface of the Earth be different if it were not divided into tectonic plates?

6. **Compare and Contrast** Read about the effects of erosion on mountains on this page. From what you have read, describe the physical features you would associate with a young mountain range and an old mountain range. READING SKILLS

SECTION 2
The Atmosphere

Objectives

▶ Describe the composition of the Earth's atmosphere.

▶ Describe the layers of the Earth's atmosphere.

▶ Explain three mechanisms of heat transfer in Earth's atmosphere.

▶ Explain the greenhouse effect.

Key Terms

atmosphere
troposphere
stratosphere
ozone
radiation
conduction
convection
greenhouse effect

Earth is surrounded by a mixture of gases known as the **atmosphere.** Nitrogen, oxygen, carbon dioxide, and other gases are all parts of this mixture. Earth's atmosphere changes constantly as these gases are added and removed. For example, animals remove oxygen from the atmosphere when they breathe in and add carbon dioxide when they breathe out. Plants take in carbon dioxide and add oxygen to the atmosphere when they produce food. Gases can be added to and removed from the atmosphere in ways other than through living organisms. A volcanic eruption adds gases. A vehicle both adds and removes gases.

The atmosphere also insulates Earth's surface. This insulation slows the rate at which the Earth's surface loses heat. The atmosphere keeps Earth at temperatures at which living things can survive.

Composition of the Atmosphere

Figure 10 shows the percentages of gases that make up Earth's atmosphere. Nitrogen makes up 78 percent of the Earth's atmosphere. It enters the atmosphere when volcanoes erupt and when dead plants and animals decay. Oxygen, the second most abundant gas in Earth's atmosphere, is primarily produced by plants. Other gases, including argon, carbon dioxide, methane, and water vapor, make up the rest of the atmosphere.

In addition to gases, the atmosphere contains many types of tiny, solid particles, or atmospheric dust. Atmospheric dust is mainly soil but includes salt, ash from fires, volcanic ash, particulate matter from combustion, skin, hair, bits of clothing, pollen, bacteria and viruses, and tiny, liquid droplets called *aerosols.*

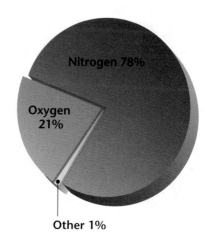

Figure 10 ▶ Nitrogen and oxygen make up 99 percent of the composition of the atmosphere.

Figure 11 ▶ This sunrise scene that was taken from space captures the tropopause, the transitional zone that separates the troposphere (yellow layer) from the stratosphere (white layer). The tropopause is the illuminated brown layer.

Section 2   **The Atmosphere**   **71**

Air Pressure Earth's atmosphere is pulled toward Earth's surface by gravity. As a result of the pull of gravity, the atmosphere is denser near Earth's surface. Almost the entire mass of Earth's atmospheric gases is located within 30 km of our planet's surface. Fewer gas molecules are found at altitudes above 30 km; less pressure at these altitudes pushes downward on atmospheric gases. The air also becomes less dense as elevation increases, so breathing at higher elevations is more difficult.

Layers of the Atmosphere

The atmosphere is divided into four layers based on temperature changes that occur at different distances above the Earth's surface. **Figure 12** shows the four layers of Earth's atmosphere.

The Troposphere The atmospheric layer nearest Earth's surface is the troposphere. The **troposphere** extends to about 18 km above Earth's surface. Almost all of the weather occurs in this layer, as shown in **Figure 13**. The troposphere is Earth's densest atmospheric layer. Temperature decreases as altitude increases in the troposphere.

The Mesosphere In geology, the term *mesosphere,* which means "middle sphere," refers to the 2,550 km thick physical layer of the Earth that lies below the asthenosphere. The mesosphere is also the name of the atmospheric layer that extends from 50 to 80 km above Earth's surface.

Figure 12 ▶ The layers of the atmosphere differ in temperature and pressure. The red line indicates temperature, and the green line indicates pressure in pascals.

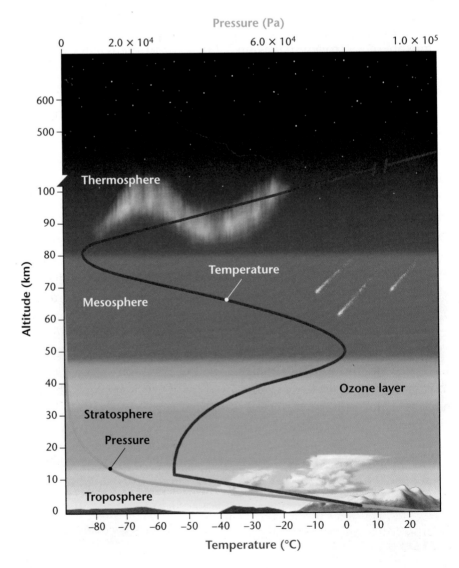

The Stratosphere Above the troposphere is the stratosphere. The **stratosphere** extends from about 18 km to an altitude of about 50 km. Temperatures rise as altitude increases in the stratosphere. This happens because ozone in the stratosphere absorbs the sun's ultraviolet (UV) energy and warms the air. **Ozone,** O_3, is a molecule made up of three oxygen atoms. Almost all the ozone in the atmosphere is concentrated in the ozone layer in the stratosphere. Ozone reduces the amount of UV radiation that reaches Earth. UV radiation can harm humans and other organisms.

The Mesosphere The layer above the stratosphere is the *mesosphere*. This layer extends to an altitude of about 80 km. The mesosphere is the coldest layer of the atmosphere, and its temperatures have been measured as low as –93°C.

The Thermosphere The atmospheric layer farthest from Earth's surface is the *thermosphere*. In the thermosphere, nitrogen and oxygen absorb solar radiation, which results in temperatures above 2,000°C. Despite these high temperatures, the thermosphere would not feel hot to us. Air particles that strike one another transfer heat. The air in the thermosphere is so thin that air particles rarely collide, so little heat is transferred.

Nitrogen and oxygen atoms in the lower region of the thermosphere (about 80 km to 550 km above Earth's surface) absorb harmful solar radiation, such as X rays and gamma rays. This absorption causes atoms to become electrically charged. Electrically charged atoms are called *ions*. The lower thermosphere is called the *ionosphere*. Sometimes ions radiate energy as light. This light often glows in spectacular colors in the night skies near the Earth's North and South Poles, as shown in **Figure 14.**

✓ **Reading Check** How does ozone in the stratosphere affect life on the Earth's surface?

Figure 13 ▶ Scientists on board a research plane from the National Oceanic and Atmospheric Administration (NOAA) are making measurements of temperature, humidity, barometric pressure, and wind speed as they fly over the eye of a hurricane.

Figure 14 ▶ The *aurora borealis,* or Northern Lights, can be seen in the skies around Earth's North Pole.

QuickLAB

The Heat Is On!

Procedure

1. Fill two **250 mL beakers** with **water**. Use a **thermometer** to record the initial temperature of the water in both beakers. The temperature of the water should be the same for both beakers.

2. Wrap one beaker with **white paper**, and wrap one with **black paper**. Secure the paper with a piece of **tape**.

3. Place a **150 W floodlight** 50 cm away from the beakers, and turn the light on.

4. Record the temperature of the water in both beakers at 1 min, 5 min, and 10 min.

Analysis

1. By what mechanism is energy being transferred to the beakers? Explain your answer.

Energy in the Atmosphere

As shown in **Figure 15,** energy from the sun is transferred in Earth's atmosphere by three mechanisms: radiation, convection, and conduction. **Radiation** is the transfer of energy across space and in the atmosphere. When you stand before a fire or a bed of coals, the heat you feel has reached you by radiation. **Conduction** is the flow of heat from a warmer object to a colder object when the objects are placed in direct physical contact. **Convection** is the transfer of heat by air currents. Hot air rises and cold air sinks. Thus, if you hold your hand above a hot iron, you will feel the heat because a current of hot air rises up to your hand.

Heating of the Atmosphere Solar energy reaches the Earth as electromagnetic radiation, which includes visible light, infrared radiation, and ultraviolet light. Our planet only receives about two-billionths of this energy. But this seemingly small amount of radiation contains a tremendous amount of energy. As shown in **Figure 15,** about half of the solar energy that enters the atmosphere passes through and reaches Earth's surface. The rest is absorbed or reflected in the atmosphere by clouds, gases, and dust, or it is reflected by the Earth's surface. On a sunny day, rocks may become too hot to touch. If the Earth's surface continually absorbed energy, it would get hotter and hotter.

Figure 15 ▶ Thermal Radiation
Three important mechanisms responsible for transferring heat in the atmosphere are ❶ radiation, ❷ conduction, and ❸ convection.

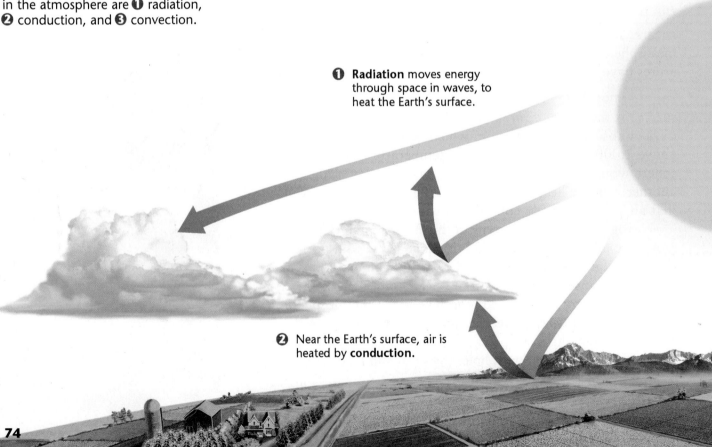

❶ **Radiation** moves energy through space in waves, to heat the Earth's surface.

❷ Near the Earth's surface, air is heated by **conduction.**

This does not happen, because the oceans and the land radiate the energy they have absorbed back into the atmosphere.

You may have noticed that dark-colored objects become much hotter in the sun than light-colored objects. Dark-colored objects absorb more solar radiation than light-colored objects, so dark-colored objects have more energy to release as heat. This is one reason the temperature in cities is higher than the temperature in the surrounding countryside.

The Movement of Energy in the Atmosphere Air that is constantly moving upward, downward, or sideways causes Earth's weather. In the troposphere, currents of less dense air, warmed by the Earth's surface, rise into the atmosphere and currents of denser cold air sink toward the ground. As a current of air rises into the atmosphere, it begins to cool. Eventually, the air current becomes more dense than the air around it and sinks instead of continuing to rise. So, the air current moves back toward Earth's surface until it is heated by the Earth and becomes less dense. Then, the air current begins to rise again. The continual process of warm air rising and cool air sinking moves air in a circular motion, called a *convection current*. A convection current is shown in **Figure 15**.

✔ **Reading Check** Why does cool air sink and warm air rise in the atmosphere?

Ecofact

Lost Weekend Have you ever complained about how it always seems to rain on the weekends? If you live on the East Coast, you might actually have a point. Researchers recently found that the mid-Atlantic states have a 30 to 40 percent greater chance of rain on the weekends. Why? Researchers suggest that the automobile exhaust that accumulates in the atmosphere over the course of the work week has actually caused weather patterns in this area to shift. By Friday, the exhaust levels are high enough to trigger rain over the weekend, which cleanses the atmosphere for another week.

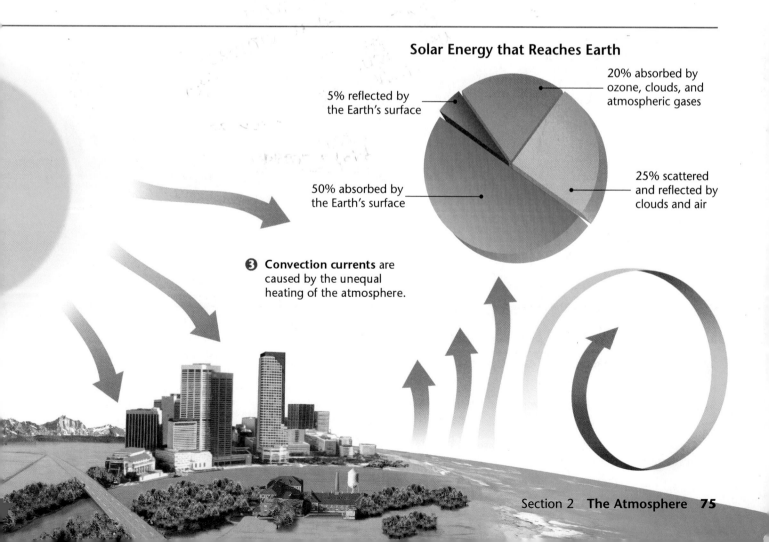

Solar Energy that Reaches Earth

5% reflected by the Earth's surface

20% absorbed by ozone, clouds, and atmospheric gases

50% absorbed by the Earth's surface

25% scattered and reflected by clouds and air

❸ **Convection currents** are caused by the unequal heating of the atmosphere.

FIELD ACTIVITY

Exploring the Greenhouse Effect Some of your classmates and teachers probably drive to school. Given what you know about the reflection and absorption of heat, go to the parking lot on a sunny day and hypothesize which cars will have the hottest interiors. Base your hypothesis on such variables as the color of car interiors and whether the windows are tinted or untinted. Record your observations in your *Ecolog*.

Figure 16 ▶ The gases in the atmosphere act like a layer of glass. Both glass and the gases in the atmosphere allow solar energy to pass through. But glass and some of the gases in the atmosphere absorb heat and stop the heat from escaping into space.

The Greenhouse Effect

The gases in Earth's atmosphere act like the glass in the car shown in **Figure 16.** Sunlight that penetrates Earth's atmosphere heats the surface of the Earth. The Earth's surface radiates heat back to the atmosphere, where some of the heat escapes into space. The remainder of the heat is absorbed by greenhouse gases, which warms the air. Heat is then radiated back toward the surface of the Earth. This process, in which gases trap heat near the Earth, is known as the **greenhouse effect.** Without the greenhouse effect, the Earth would be too cold for life to exist.

The gases in our atmosphere that trap and radiate heat are called *greenhouse gases*. None of the greenhouse gases have a high concentration in Earth's atmosphere. The most abundant greenhouse gases are water vapor, carbon dioxide, methane, and nitrous oxide. The quantities of carbon dioxide and methane in the atmosphere vary considerably as a result of natural and industrial processes, and the amount of water varies because of natural processes.

❶ Sunlight passes through the glass into the car.

❷ The interior absorbs radiant energy, changing it into heat.

❸ The glass in the car stops most of the heat from escaping, increasing the temperature inside the car.

SECTION 2 **Review**

1. **Describe** the composition of Earth's atmosphere.

2. **Describe** a characteristic of each layer of the atmosphere.

3. **Explain** the three mechanisms of heat transfer in Earth's atmosphere.

4. **Describe** the role of greenhouse gases in Earth's atmosphere.

CRITICAL THINKING

5. **Analyzing Processes** Read about the density of Earth's atmosphere under the heading "Air Pressure." Write a paragraph that explains why Earth's atmosphere becomes less dense with increasing altitude above Earth. **WRITING SKILLS**

6. **Analyzing Processes** How does human activity change some greenhouse-gas levels?

The Hydrosphere and Biosphere

 SCSh.7.a; SCSh.9.c; SEV.1.d; SEV.2.b

 EARTH SCIENCE **CONNECTION**

Life on Earth is restricted to a very narrow layer around the Earth's surface. In this layer, called the *biosphere*, everything that organisms need to survive can be found. One of the requirements of living things is liquid water.

The Hydrosphere and Water Cycle

The hydrosphere includes all of the water on or near the Earth's surface. The hydrosphere includes water in the oceans, lakes, rivers, wetlands, polar icecaps, soil, rock layers beneath Earth's surface, and clouds.

The continuous movement of water into the air, onto land, and then back to water sources is known as the **water cycle,** which is shown in **Figure 17. Evaporation** is the process by which liquid water is heated by the sun and then rises into the atmosphere as water vapor. Water continually evaporates from Earth's oceans, lakes, streams, and soil, but the majority of the water evaporates from the oceans. In the process of **condensation,** water vapor forms water droplets on dust particles. These water droplets form clouds, in which the droplets collide, stick together, and create larger, heavier droplets. These larger droplets fall from clouds as rain in a process called **precipitation.** Precipitation may also take the form of snow, sleet, or hail.

Objectives

▶ Name the three major processes in the water cycle.

▶ Describe the properties of ocean water.

▶ Describe the two types of ocean currents.

▶ Explain how the ocean regulates Earth's temperature.

▶ Discuss the factors that confine life to the biosphere.

▶ Explain the difference between open and closed systems.

Key Terms

water cycle
evaporation
condensation
precipitation
salinity
fresh water
biosphere

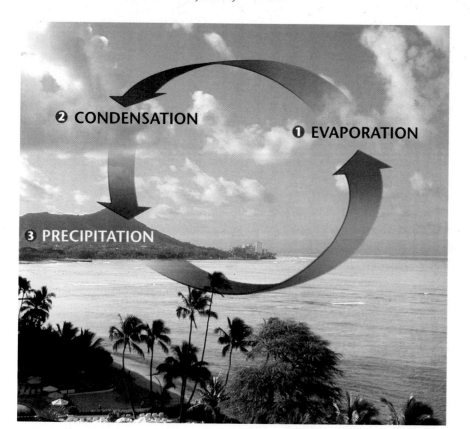

❷ CONDENSATION

❶ EVAPORATION

❸ PRECIPITATION

Figure 17 ▶ The major processes of the water cycle include ❶ evaporation, ❷ condensation, and ❸ precipitation.

Submarine Volcanoes Geologists estimate that approximately 80 percent of the volcanic activity on Earth takes place on the ocean floor. Most of this activity occurs as magma slowly flows onto the ocean floor where tectonic plates pull away from each other. But enormous undersea volcanoes are also common. Off the coast of Hawaii, a submarine volcano called the *Loihi Seamount* rises 5,185 m from the ocean floor. Loihi is just 915 m below the ocean's surface, and in several thousand years, this volcano may become the next Hawaiian Island.

Earth's Oceans

We talk about the Atlantic Ocean, the Pacific Ocean, the Arctic Ocean, and the Indian Ocean. However, if you look at **Figure 18**, you see that these oceans are all joined. This single, large, interconnected body of water is called the *world ocean*. Its waters cover a little over 70 percent of the Earth's surface. As we will see, the world ocean plays many important roles in regulating our planet's environment.

The largest ocean on Earth is the Pacific Ocean. It covers a surface area of approximately 165,640,000 km² and has an average depth of 4,280 m. The deepest point on the ocean floor is in the Pacific Ocean. This point is called the Challenger Deep and is located east of the Philippine Islands at the bottom of the Mariana Trench. The Challenger Deep is 11,033 m below sea level, which is deeper than Mount Everest is tall. Oceanographers often divide the Pacific Ocean into the North Pacific and South Pacific based on the direction of surface current flow in each half of the Pacific Ocean. Surface currents in the Pacific move in a clockwise direction north

CASE STUDY

Hydrothermal Vents

The light from your tiny research submarine illuminates the desert-like barrenness of the deep-ocean floor. Suddenly, the light catches something totally unexpected—an underwater oasis teeming with sea creatures that no human has laid eyes on before. At the center of this community is a tall chimney-like structure from which a column of black water is rising.

This scene is much like the one that John Corliss and John Edmond witnessed when they discovered the first deep-sea hydrothermal vents and the odd community of creatures that inhabit them. Corliss's and Edmond's discovery was made during a dive in the submarine *Alvin* in early 1977. The dive site was in the eastern Pacific Ocean near the Galápagos Islands. Since the original

dive, many more hydrothermal vents have been located on the ocean bottom.

Hydrothermal vents are openings in the ocean floor where super-hot, mineral-rich waters stream into the ocean. Hydrothermal vents form where tectonic plates are separating and where deep fractures are opening in the Earth's crust. Water seeps down into some of these fractures to a depth where it is heated by molten rock and enriched with minerals. The water returns to the ocean floor through other fractures and then pours into the ocean. Water often streams through structures called *chimneys*. Chimneys form when the minerals in the vent water—mostly iron and sulfur—precipitate as the

▶ Superheated, mineral-rich water streams through a chimney at a hydrothermal vent on the floor of the Pacific Ocean.

water cools from above 100°C to less than 50°C. The tallest chimney reported to date is 49 m. Vent

of the equator, whereas surface currents flow in a counterclockwise direction south of the equator.

The second largest ocean on Earth is the Atlantic Ocean. It covers a surface area of 81,630,000 km², which is about half the area of the Pacific Ocean. Like the Pacific Ocean, the Atlantic Ocean can be divided into a north half and a south half based on the directions of surface current flow north and south of the equator.

The Indian Ocean covers a surface area of 73,420,000 km² and is the third-largest ocean on Earth. It has an average depth of 3,890 m.

The smallest ocean is the Arctic Ocean, which covers 14,350,000 km². The Arctic Ocean is unique because much of its surface is covered by floating ice. This ice, which is called *pack ice*, forms when either waves or wind drive together frozen seawater, known as sea ice, into a large mass.

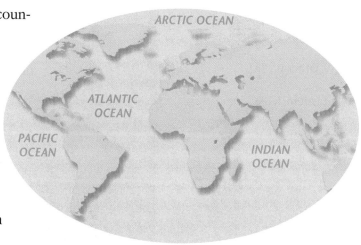

Figure 18 ▶ The Pacific, Atlantic, Indian, and Arctic Oceans are interconnected into a single body of water, the world ocean, which covers 70 percent of Earth's surface.

▶ Over 300 species of organisms have been found in hydrothermal vent communities, including species of tube worms that may grow to a length of 3 m.

water can reach temperatures as high as 400°C.

The pressure at the ocean bottom is tremendous. No sunlight penetrates these depths, and hydrothermal vents spew minerals into their surroundings. Still, at least 300 species of organisms—all new to scientists—live near hydrothermal vents. These organisms include tube worms, giant clams, mussels, shrimp, crabs, sea anemones, and octopuses.

How is life at hydrothermal vents possible? Bacteria that live

EARTH SCIENCE CONNECTION

in vent communities can use hydrogen sulfide escaping from the vents as an energy source. Some animals that live in vent communities consume these bacteria to obtain their energy. Other animals have bacteria living inside their bodies that supply them with energy.

CRITICAL THINKING

1. Applying Processes Some scientists have suggested that life may have originated in or near hydrothermal vents because vent organisms are able to obtain their energy from chemicals in the absence of sunlight. Does this suggestion seem realistic?

2. Making Predictions How might the creatures that live in hydrothermal vent communities be of benefit to humankind in the future?

Ocean Water The difference between ocean water and fresh water is that ocean water contains more salts. These salts have dissolved out of rocks on land and have been carried down rivers into the ocean over millions of years. Underwater volcanic eruptions also add salts to the ocean.

Most of the salt in the ocean is sodium chloride, which is made up of the elements sodium and chlorine. **Figure 19** shows the concentration of these and other elements in ocean water. The **salinity** of ocean water is the concentration of all the dissolved salts it contains. The average salinity of ocean water is 3.5 percent by weight. The salinity of ocean water is lower in places that get a lot of rain or in places where fresh water flows into the sea. Salinity is higher where water evaporates rapidly and leaves the salts behind.

Other 0.7%
Potassium 1.1%
Calcium 1.2%
Sulfur 3.7%
Magnesium 7.7%
Chlorine 55.0%
Sodium 30.6%

Figure 19 ▶ This pie graph shows the percentages by weight of dissolved solids found in ocean water. Sodium and chlorine, the two elements that form salt, are the most important dissolved solids in ocean water.

Temperature Zones **Figure 20** shows the temperature zones of the ocean. The surface of the ocean is warmed by the sun. In contrast, the depths of the ocean, where sunlight never reaches, have temperatures only slightly above freezing. Surface waters are stirred up by waves and currents, so the warm surface zone may be as much as 350 m deep. Below the surface zone is the thermocline, which is a layer about 300 to 700 m deep where the temperature falls rapidly with depth. If you have ever gone swimming in a deep lake in the summer, you have probably encountered a shallow thermocline. The boundary between the warm and cold water is the thermocline.

Figure 20 ▶ Water in the ocean can be divided into three zones based on temperature.

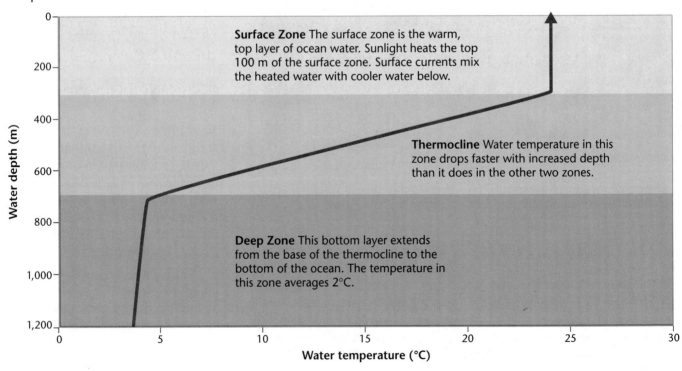

Surface Zone The surface zone is the warm, top layer of ocean water. Sunlight heats the top 100 m of the surface zone. Surface currents mix the heated water with cooler water below.

Thermocline Water temperature in this zone drops faster with increased depth than it does in the other two zones.

Deep Zone This bottom layer extends from the base of the thermocline to the bottom of the ocean. The temperature in this zone averages 2°C.

A Global Temperature Regulator One of the most important functions of the world ocean is to absorb and store energy from sunlight. This capacity of the ocean to absorb and store energy from sunlight regulates temperatures in Earth's atmosphere.

The world ocean absorbs over half the solar radiation that reaches the planet's surface. The ocean both absorbs and releases heat more slowly than land does. As a consequence, the temperature of the atmosphere changes much more slowly than it would if there were no ocean on Earth. If the ocean did not regulate atmospheric and surface temperatures, the temperature would be too extreme for life on Earth to exist.

Local temperatures in different areas of the planet are also regulated by the world ocean. Currents that circulate warm water cause the land areas they flow past to have a more moderate climate. For example, the British Isles are warmed by the Gulf Stream, which moves warm waters from lower latitudes toward higher latitudes, as shown in **Figure 21.**

✓ **Reading Check** How does the absorption and release of heat by the ocean differ from the absorption and release of heat by land?

MATHPRACTICE

The Influence of the Gulf Stream The temperature of the British Isles is moderated by the Gulf Stream. Plymouth, England, and Winnipeg, Canada, are located at approximately 50° north latitude. Plymouth, which is located in the southwest of England near the Atlantic Ocean, has average low temperatures of 4°C in December, 3°C in January, and 3°C in February. Winnipeg, which is located in the interior of North America, has average low temperatures of –18°C in December, –23°C in January, and –20°C in February. What is the difference in average low temperatures in degrees Celsius between Plymouth and Winnipeg?

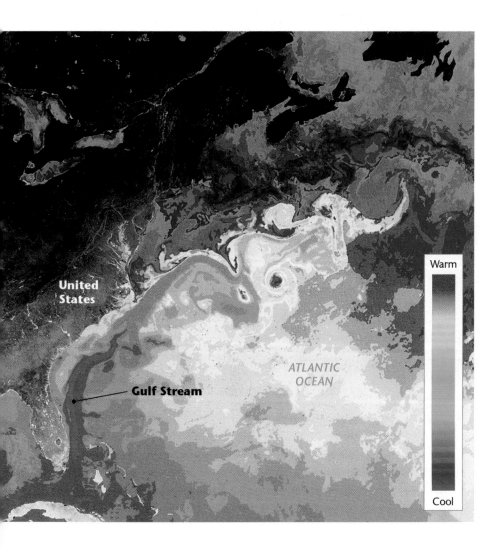

United States

Gulf Stream

ATLANTIC OCEAN

Warm

Cool

Figure 21 ▶ In this infrared satellite image, the Gulf Stream is moving warm water (shown in red, orange, and yellow) from lower latitudes into higher latitudes. The British Isles are warmed by the waters of the Gulf Stream.

Ocean Currents Streamlike movements of water that occur at or near the surface of the ocean are called surface currents. Surface currents are wind driven and result from global wind patterns. **Figure 22** shows the major surface currents of the world ocean. Surface currents may be warm-water currents or cold-water currents. Currents of warm water and currents of cold water do not readily mix with one another. Therefore, a warm-water current like the Gulf Stream can flow for hundreds of kilometers through cold water without mixing and losing its heat.

Surface currents can influence the climates of land areas they flow past. As we have seen, the Gulf Stream moderates the climate in the British Isles. The Scilly Isles in England are as far north as Newfoundland in northeast Canada. However, palm trees grow on the Scilly Isles, where it never freezes, whereas Newfoundland has long winters of frost and snow.

Deep currents are streamlike movements of water that flow very slowly along the ocean floor. Deep currents form when the cold, dense water from the poles sinks below warmer, less dense ocean water and flows toward the equator. The densest and coldest ocean water is located off the coast of Antarctica. This cold water sinks to the bottom of the ocean and flows very slowly northward to produce a deep current called the Antarctic Bottom Water. The Antarctic Bottom Water creeps along the ocean floor for thousands of kilometers and reaches a northernmost point of approximately 40° north latitude. It takes several hundred years for water in this deep current to make this trip northward.

Figure 22 ▶ The oceans' surface currents circulate in different directions in each hemisphere.

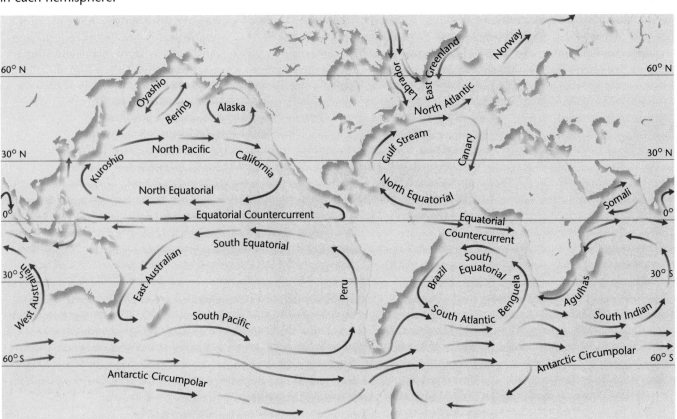

Fresh Water

Most of the water on Earth is salt water in the ocean. A little more than 3 percent of all the water on Earth is **fresh water.** Most of the fresh water is locked up in icecaps and glaciers that are so large they are hard to imagine. For instance, the ice sheet that covers Antarctica is as large as the United States and is up to 3 km thick. The rest of Earth's fresh water is found in lakes, rivers, wetlands, the soil, rock layers below the surface, and in the atmosphere.

River Systems A river system is a network of streams that drains an area of land. A river system contains all of the land drained by a river, including the main river and all its tributaries. As shown in **Figure 23,** *tributaries* are smaller streams or rivers that flow into larger ones. Some river systems are enormous. For example, most of the precipitation that falls between the Rocky Mountains in the west and the Appalachian Mountains in the east eventually drains into the Mississippi River. The Mississippi River system covers about 40 percent of the contiguous United States.

Groundwater

Rain and melting snow sink into the ground and run off the land. Some of this water ends up in streams and rivers, but most of it trickles down through the ground and collects as *groundwater.* Groundwater fulfills the human need for fresh drinking water and supplies water for many agricultural and industrial uses. But groundwater accounts for less than 1 percent of all the water on Earth.

Aquifers A rock layer that stores and allows the flow of groundwater is called an *aquifer.* The surface of the land where water enters an aquifer is called a *recharge zone.* **Figure 24** shows the location of aquifers in the contiguous United States.

Figure 23 ▶ This photo shows a network of tributaries flowing into a river in the wetlands of southern Louisiana.

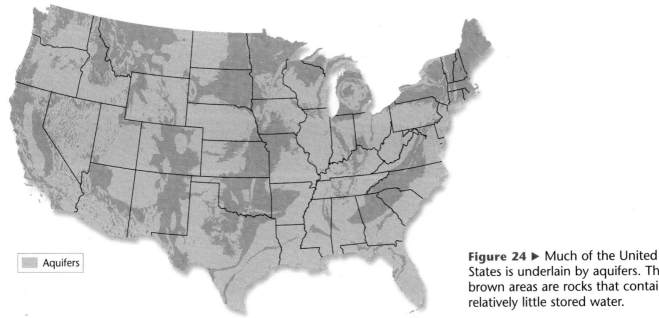

Aquifers

Figure 24 ▶ Much of the United States is underlain by aquifers. The brown areas are rocks that contain relatively little stored water.

The Biosphere

If the Earth were an apple, the biosphere would be its skin. This comparison illustrates how small the layer of the Earth that can support life is in relation to the size of the planet. The **biosphere** is the narrow layer around Earth's surface in which life can exist. The biosphere is made up of the uppermost part of the geosphere, most of the hydrosphere, and the lower part of the atmosphere. The biosphere extends about 12 km into the ocean and about 9 km into the atmosphere.

Life exists on Earth because of several important factors. Most life requires liquid water, moderate temperatures, and a source of energy. The materials that organisms require must continually be cycled. Gravity allows a planet to maintain an atmosphere and to cycle materials. Suitable combinations of the things that organisms need to survive are found only in the biosphere.

The biosphere is located near Earth's surface because most of the sunlight is available near the surface. Plants on land and in the ocean are shown in **Figure 25**. Plants need sunlight to produce their food, and almost every other organism gets its food from plants and algae. Most of the algae float at the surface of the ocean. These tiny, free-floating, marine algae are known as phytoplankton. Except for bacteria that live at hydrothermal vents, most of the organisms that live deep in the ocean feed on dead plants and animals that drift down from the surface.

Reading Check What makes life possible in the biosphere?

Figure 25 ▶ This illustration of the biosphere shows the concentration of plant life on land and in the ocean. The colors represent different concentrations of plant life in different regions.

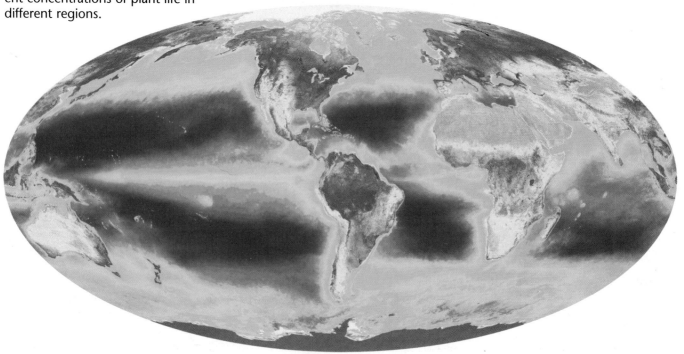

Ocean chlorophyll concentration

Low   High

Amount of land vegetation

Low   High

Energy Flow in the Biosphere

When an organism in the biosphere dies, its body is broken down and the matter in its body becomes available to other organisms. This matter is continually recycled. Energy, however, must be supplied constantly. The Eden Project, shown in **Figure 26**, is a closed system that models this flow of matter and energy.

In a *closed system*, energy enters and leaves the system, but matter does not. The Earth is a closed system because the only thing that enters in significant amounts is energy from the sun, and the only thing that leaves in significant amounts is heat. Energy from the sun is used by plants in the biosphere to make their food. When an animal eats a plant, the energy stored in the plant is transferred to the animal. The animal, in turn, may be eaten by another animal. At each stage in the food chain, some of the energy is lost to the environment as heat, which is eventually lost into space.

In an *open system*, both matter and energy are exchanged between a system and the surrounding environment. The Earth was once an open system. Matter was added to the early Earth as it was hit by comets and meteorites. Now, however, little matter reaches the Earth this way.

Figure 26 ▶ The Eden Project is an attempt to model the biosphere. In this project, plants from all over the world live in a closed system. The Eden Project is housed within a series of domes that were constructed in an old clay pit in England.

SECTION 3 Review

1. **Name** and describe each of the three major processes in the water cycle.

2. **Describe** the properties of ocean water.

3. **Describe** the two types of ocean currents.

4. **Name** two factors that confine living things to the biosphere.

CRITICAL THINKING

5. **Analyzing Processes** Read about the ocean's role in regulating temperature under the heading "A Global Temperature Regulator." How might Earth's climate change if the land area on Earth were greater than the area of the world ocean? **READING SKILLS**

6. **Analyzing Relationships** Why is the human body considered an open system?

1 The Geosphere

Key Terms

geosphere, 63
crust, 64
mantle, 65
core, 65
lithosphere, 65
asthenosphere, 65
tectonic plate, 66
erosion, 70

Main Ideas

▶ The solid part of the Earth that consists of all rock, and the soils and sediments on Earth's surface, is the geosphere.

▶ Earth's interior is divided into layers based on composition and structure.

▶ Earth's surface is broken into pieces called *tectonic plates*, which collide, separate, or slip past one another.

▶ Earthquakes, volcanic eruptions, and mountain building are all events that occur at the boundaries of tectonic plates.

▶ Earth's surface features are continually altered by the action of water and wind.

2 The Atmosphere

Key Terms

atmosphere, 71
troposphere, 72
stratosphere, 73
ozone, 73
radiation, 74
conduction, 74
convection, 74
greenhouse effect, 76

Main Ideas

▶ The mixture of gases that surrounds the Earth is called the *atmosphere*.

▶ The atmosphere is composed almost entirely of nitrogen and oxygen.

▶ Earth's atmosphere is divided into four layers based on changes in temperature that take place at different altitudes.

▶ Heat is transferred in the atmosphere by radiation, conduction, and convection.

▶ Some of the gases in Earth's atmosphere slow the escape of heat from Earth's surface in what is known as the greenhouse effect.

3 The Hydrosphere and Biosphere

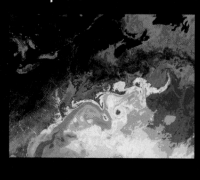

Key Terms

water cycle, 77
evaporation, 77
condensation, 77
precipitation, 77
salinity, 80
fresh water, 83
biosphere, 84

Main Ideas

▶ The hydrosphere includes all of the water at or near Earth's surface.

▶ Water in the ocean can be divided into three zones—the surface zone, the thermocline, and the deep zone—based on temperature.

▶ The ocean absorbs and stores energy from sunlight, regulating temperatures in the atmosphere.

▶ Surface currents in the ocean affect the climate of the land they flow near.

▶ The biosphere is the narrow layer at the surface of the Earth where life can exist.

▶ Earth is a closed system because energy enters and leaves Earth, but matter does not.

Using Key Terms

Use each of the following terms in a separate sentence.

1. *tectonic plate*
2. *erosion*
3. *radiation*
4. *ozone*
5. *salinity*

For each pair of terms, explain how the meanings of the terms differ.

6. *lithosphere* and *asthenosphere*
7. *conduction* and *convection*
8. *crust* and *mantle*
9. *evaporation* and *condensation*

STUDY TIP

The Importance of Nouns Most multiple-choice questions center around the definitions of nouns. When you study, pay attention to the definitions of nouns that appear to be important in the text. These nouns will often be boldfaced key terms or italicized secondary terms.

Understanding Key Ideas

10. The thin layer at Earth's surface where life exists is called the
    a. geosphere.
    b. atmosphere.
    c. hydrosphere.
    d. biosphere.

11. The thin layer of the Earth upon which tectonic plates move around is called the
    a. mantle.
    b. asthenosphere.
    c. lithosphere.
    d. outer core.

12. Seventy-eight percent of Earth's atmosphere is made up of
    a. oxygen.
    b. hydrogen.
    c. nitrogen.
    d. carbon dioxide.

13. The ozone layer is located in the
    a. stratosphere.
    b. mesosphere.
    c. thermosphere.
    d. troposphere.

14. Convection is defined as the
    a. transfer of energy across space.
    b. direct transfer of energy.
    c. trapping of heat near the Earth by gases.
    d. transfer of heat by currents.

15. Which of the following gases is *not* a greenhouse gas?
    a. water vapor
    b. nitrogen
    c. methane
    d. carbon dioxide

16. Liquid water turns into gaseous water vapor in a process called
    a. precipitation.
    b. convection.
    c. evaporation.
    d. condensation.

17. Currents at the surface of the ocean are moved mostly by
    a. heat.
    b. wind.
    c. salinity.
    d. the mixing of warm and cold water.

18. Which of the following statements about the biosphere is *not* true?
    a. The biosphere is a system closed to matter.
    b. Energy enters the biosphere in the form of sunlight.
    c. Nutrients in the biosphere must be continuously recycled.
    d. Matter is constantly added to the biosphere.

Short Answer

19. How do seismic waves give scientists information about Earth's interior?

20. Explain the effect of gravity on Earth's atmosphere.

21. Explain how convection currents transport heat in the atmosphere.

22. Why does land that is near the ocean change temperature less rapidly than land that is located farther inland?

23. Why is life on Earth confined to such a narrow layer near the Earth's surface?

Interpreting Graphics

The map below shows the different amounts of chlorophyll in the ocean. Chlorophyll is the pigment that makes plants and algae green. Chlorophyll identifies the presence of marine algae. The red and orange colors on the map show the highest amounts of chlorophyll, the blue and purple colors on the map show the smallest amounts of chlorophyll. Use the map to answer questions 24–25.

24. Is there a greater concentration of marine algae at location A or at location B?

25. What conclusion can you reach about conditions in the parts of the ocean where marine algae may prefer to live?

Chlorophyll Content

High   Low

Concept Mapping

26. Use the following terms to create a concept map: *geosphere, crust, mantle, core, lithosphere, asthenosphere,* and *tectonic plate.*

Critical Thinking

27. **Making Predictions** The eruption of Mount Pinatubo in 1991 reduced global temperature by several tenths of a Celsius degree for several years. Write a paragraph predicting what might happen to Earth's climate if several large-scale eruptions took place at the same time? **WRITING SKILLS**

28. **Analyzing Processes** Read about the heating of Earth's surface and the absorption of incoming solar radiation under the heading "Heating of the Atmosphere." How might the Earth be different if the Earth's surface absorbed greater or lesser percentages of radiation? **READING SKILLS**

29. **Analyzing Processes** Surface currents are deflected by continental landmasses. How might the pattern of Earth's surface currents change if the Earth had no landmasses? Where on the world ocean might the majority of warm surface currents be located? Where would the cold surface currents be located?

Cross-Disciplinary Connection

30. **History** Scientists believe that some human migration between distant landmasses may have taken place on rafts powered only by the wind and ocean currents. Look at Figure 22, which shows the Earth's surface currents. Hypothesize potential migratory routes these early seafarers may have followed.

Portfolio Project

31. **Plotting Seismic Activity** Most earthquakes take place near tectonic plate boundaries. Using the encyclopedia, the Internet, or another source, find at least 20 locations where major earthquakes took place during the 20th century. Plot these locations on a map of the world that shows Earth's tectonic plates. Did the majority of earthquakes occur at or near tectonic plate boundaries?

MATH SKILLS

Use the graph below to answer questions 32–33.

32. Analyzing Data Rearrange the oceans in order of highest depth-to-area ratio to lowest depth-to-area ratio.

33. Making Calculations On the graph, you are given the average depths of the four oceans. From these data, calculate the average depth of the world ocean.

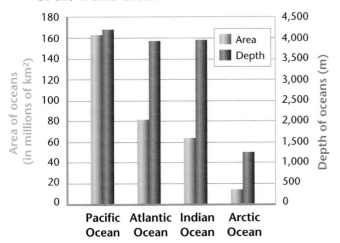

WRITING SKILLS

34. Communicating Main Ideas Describe the three important ways in which the movement of energy takes place in Earth's atmosphere.

35. Writing Persuasively Write a persuasive essay that explains why the Earth today should be regarded as a closed system for matter rather than an open system.

36. Outlining Topics Write a one-page outline that describes some of the important inter-actions that take place in the Earth system.

READING SKILLS

Read the passage below, and then answer the questions that follow.

Researchers at Ohio State University have developed a video camera that photographs the foamy bubbles left when a wave breaks on a beach. Software analyzes images from the camera and uses the movement of the foam to calculate the speed and direction of currents along the shore. How do we know that the software produces an accurate picture of the currents? To test the software, researchers set up a video camera on the beach at Duck, North Carolina, where dozens of underwater sensors already measure currents directly. A comparison of the currents detected by the video camera and by the sensors showed a close match. The Ohio State University researchers believe data from the video camera would be even more accurate if the camera were directly above the breaking waves. The researchers' next step will be to mount the camera on a blimp suspended over a beach in Monterey, California.

1. According to the passage, which of the following conclusions is true?
   a. The video camera uses wave speed to calculate the direction and speed of currents.
   b. Underwater sensors are less accurate at measuring currents than video cameras.
   c. Video cameras do not measure currents directly.
   d. Underwater sensors detect the movement of foam.

2. What is the importance of foam in measuring currents?
   a. Foam can be measured directly by both video cameras and underwater sensors.
   b. The movement of foam can be used to calculate the direction and speed of a current.
   c. Foam from breaking waves can be detected by placing a video camera at any point on a beach.
   d. both (b) and (c)

Understanding Concepts

Directions (1–4): For *each* question, write on a separate sheet of paper the letter of the correct answer.

1 What is the cool, rigid, outermost layer of the Earth?
A. the asthenosphere
B. the geosphere
C. the lithosphere
D. the mesosphere

2 The collision of tectonic plates creates what geologic feature?
F. mesosphere
G. inner core
H. mountains
I. hydrothermal vents

3 What determines the weather we experience on Earth?
A. movement of water over land masses
B. gases trapping heat near Earth's surface
C. absorption of radiation by the thermosphere
D. air constantly moving through Earth's atmosphere

4 What is the difference between evaporation and condensation?
F. Evaporation is the first stage of the water cycle; condensation is the last stage.
G. Evaporation is the change from water to vapor; condensation is the change from vapor to water.
H. Evaporation is the process where water is heated by the sea; condensation is the process where water droplets fall from clouds.
I. Evaporation is the process where water vapor forms droplets; condensation is the process where water vapor forms clouds.

Directions (5–6): For *each* question, write a short response.

5 Differentiate between the three compositional layers of Earth.

6 What is the purpose of the Richter scale?

Reading Skills

Directions (7–9): **Read the passage below. Then answer the questions.**

A volcano is a mountain built from melted rock that rises from the Earth's interior to its surface. Volcanoes may occur on land or under the sea, where they eventually break the ocean surface as islands. They are often located near tectonic plate boundaries.

Volcanic eruptions can be devastating to local economies, cause great human loss, and affect global climate for several years. In large eruptions, clouds of volcanic ash and sulfur-rich gases may reach the upper atmosphere. In addition, ash that falls to the ground can cause buildings to collapse under its weight, bury crops, and damage the engines of vehicles.

Major volcanic eruptions, such as the eruption of Mount St. Helens, can change Earth's climate for several years.

7 Where are most of the Earth's volcanoes located?
A. within tropical rain forests
B. near Mount St. Helens
C. near the Antarctic
D. near tectonic plate boundaries

8 What happens during a large volcanic eruption?
F. The ash causes islands to form.
G. The ash rises from the Earth's interior.
H. The ash and sulfur-rich gases may reach the upper atmosphere.
I. The ash falls to the ground and produces dust storms.

9 Volcanic eruptions can have a global effect on the Earth by
A. changing the Earth's climate for several years
B. changing tectonic plates
C. changing local economies
D. causing buildings to collapse

Interpreting Graphics

Directions (10–12): For *each* question below, record the correct answer on a separate sheet of paper.

10 Which of the following statements is true?
  F. The world ocean covers 70% of Earth's surface.
  G. The world ocean is the body of water south of Africa.
  H. The world ocean has little effect on Earth's environment.
  I. The world ocean consists of the Atlantic and Pacific Oceans.

The illustration below shows elements in the ocean's water. Use it to answer question 11.

Elements in Ocean Water

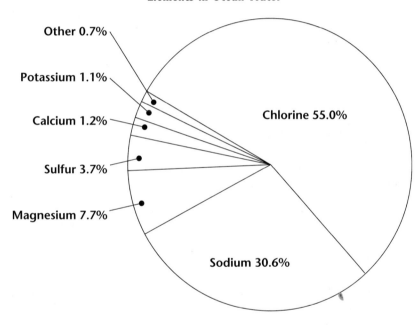

11 What fraction of ocean salinity is not sodium and chlorine?
  A. 12.1%
  B. 14.6%
  C. 12.4%
  D. 14.4%

12 The Atlantic Ocean covers 81,630,000 km² of Earth's surface area and the Pacific Ocean covers 165,640,000 km². How much more surface area is covered by the Pacific Ocean than the Atlantic Ocean, in millions of km²?
  F. 72
  G. 84
  H. 96
  I. 108

Test TIP

If you come upon a word you do not know, try to identify its prefix, suffix, or root. Sometimes knowing even one part of the word will help you answer the question.

CHAPTER 2

Exploration Lab: MODELING

Objectives

▶ **Examine** models that show how the forces generated by wave action build, shape, and erode beaches.

▶ **USING SCIENTIFIC METHODS**
Hypothesize ways in which beaches can be preserved from the erosive forces of wave activity.

Materials

metric ruler
milk cartons, empty, small (2)
pebbles
plaster of Paris
plastic container (large) or long wooden box lined with plastic
rocks, small
sand, 5 to 10 lb
wooden block, large

▶ **Step 2** Use a wooden block to generate waves at the end of the container opposite the beach.

Beaches

Almost one-fourth of all of the structures that have been built within 150 m of the U.S. coastline, including the Great Lakes, will be lost to beach erosion over the next 60 years, according to a June 2000 report released by the Federal Emergency Management Agency (FEMA). The supply of sand for most beaches has been cut off by dams built on rivers and streams that would otherwise carry sand to the sea. Waves generated by storms also erode beaches. Longshore currents, which are generated by waves that break at an angle to a shoreline, transport sediment continuously and change the shape of a shoreline.

You will now observe a series of models. These models will help you understand how beaches can be both washed away and protected from the effects of waves and longshore currents.

Procedure

1. One day before you begin the investigation, make two plaster blocks. Mix a small amount of water with plaster of Paris until the mixture is smooth. Add five or six small rocks to the mixture for added weight. Pour the plaster mixture into the milk cartons. Let the plaster harden overnight. Carefully peel the milk cartons away from the plaster.

2. Prepare a wooden box lined with plastic or other similar large, shallow container. Make a beach by placing a mixture of sand and small pebbles at one end of the container. The beach should occupy about one-fourth the length of the container. See step 2. In the area in front of the sand, add water to a depth of 2 to 3 cm. Use the large wooden block to generate several waves by moving the block up and down in the water at the end of the container opposite the beach. Continue this wave action until about half the beach has moved. Record your observations.

3. Remove the water, and rebuild the beach. In some places, breakwaters have been built offshore in an attempt to protect beaches from washing away. Build a breakwater by placing two plaster blocks across the middle of the container. Using the metric ruler, leave a 4 cm space between the blocks. See step 3. Use a wooden block to generate waves. Describe the results.

4. Drain the water, and make a new beach along one side of the container for about half its length. See step 4. Using the wooden block, generate a series of waves from the same end of the container as the end of the beach. Record your observations.

5. Rebuild the beach along the same side of the container. A jetty or dike can be built out into the ocean to intercept and break up a longshore current. Make a jetty by placing one of the small plaster blocks in the sand. See step 5. As you did in the previous steps, use the wooden block to generate waves. Describe the results.

6. Remove the wet sand, and put it in a container. Dispose of the water. (Note: Follow your teacher's instructions for disposal of the sand and water. Never pour water containing sand into a sink.)

Analysis

1. **Describing Events** In step 2 of the procedure, what happened to the beach when water was first poured into the container? What happened to the particles of fine sand? Predict what would happen to the beach if it had no source of additional sand.

2. **Analyzing Results** In step 3 of the procedure, did the breakwater help protect the beach from washing away?

3. **Describing Events** What happened to the beach that you made in step 4 of the procedure? What happened to the shape of the waves along the beach?

4. **Analyzing Results** What effect did the jetty have on the beach that you made in step 5 of the procedure?

Conclusions

5. **Drawing Conclusions** What can be done to preserve a beach area from being washed away as a result of wave action and longshore currents?

6. **Drawing Conclusions** What can be done to preserve a beach area that has been changed as a result of excessive use by people?

Extension

1. **Building Models** Make a beach that would be in danger of being washed away by a longshore current. Based on what you have learned, build a model in which the beach would be preserved by a breakwater or jetties. Explain how your model illustrates ways in which longshore currents can be intercepted and broken up.

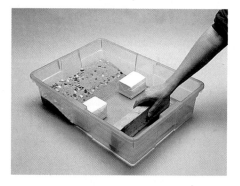

▶ **Step 3** Build a breakwater by placing two plastic blocks across the middle of the container.

▶ **Step 4** Make a beach lengthwise along one side of the container. The length of the beach should equal one-half the length of the container.

▶ **Step 5** Place one of the small plaster blocks in the sand to make a jetty.

EARTHQUAKE HAZARD MAP OF THE CONTIGUOUS UNITED STATES

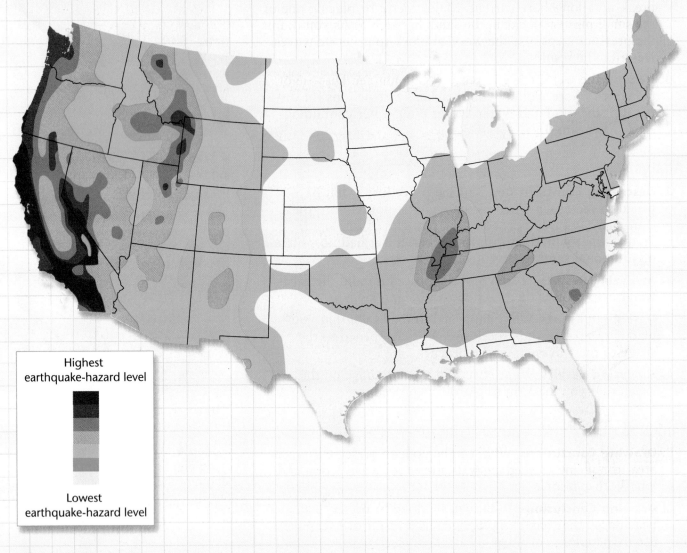

Highest earthquake-hazard level

Lowest earthquake-hazard level

MAP SKILLS

Use the earthquake-hazard map of the contiguous United States to answer the questions below.

1. **Using a Key** Which area of the contiguous United States has a very high earthquake-hazard level?

2. **Using a Key** Determine which areas of the contiguous United States have very low earthquake-hazard levels.

3. **Analyzing Relationships** In which areas of the contiguous United States would scientists most likely set up earthquake-sensing devices?

4. **Inferring Relationships** Most earthquakes take place near tectonic plate boundaries. Based on the hazard levels, where do you think a boundary between two tectonic plates is located in the United States?

5. **Forming a Hypothesis** The New Madrid earthquake zone passes through southeastern Missouri and western Tennessee and has experienced some of the most widely felt earthquakes in U.S. history. Yet this earthquake zone lies far from any tectonic plate boundary. Propose a hypothesis that would explain these earthquakes.

SOCIETY & the Environment

TRACKING OCEAN CURRENTS WITH TOY DUCKS

Scientists usually study ocean currents by releasing labeled drift bottles from various points and recording where they are found. However, only about 2 percent of drift bottles are recovered, so this type of research takes a long time. A large toy spill is helping scientists track surface currents in the Pacific Ocean.

Toys Ahoy!

In 1993, thousands of bathtub toys were found on Alaskan beaches. When oceanographers heard about this, they placed advertisements in newspapers up and down the Alaskan coast asking people who found the toys to call them. They discovered that in 1992 a container ship that was traveling northwest of Hawaii ran into a storm. Several containers were washed overboard and burst open. One of these held 29,000 plastic toys. Ten months later, the toys—blue turtles, yellow ducks, red beavers, and green frogs—began washing up near Sitka, Alaska. In the following years, toys began to be found farther north, in the Bering Sea. The map below shows where the containers went overboard and where the toys were found.

The Data in the Deep Blue Sea

Obviously, the toys had traveled east from where they were spilled. But what did this reveal about the currents in the North Pacific? The answer is not as obvious as it might seem. First, floating objects are moved by wind as well as by currents. The floating toys stuck up about 4 cm above the water, which may have caused them to be moved by the wind as well as by currents. The toys started out in cardboard and plastic packages. Did the packages make them sink when they were first released? To find the answer, scientists obtained some of the packaged toys from the manufacturer in China and dropped them in buckets of sea water. The glue in the packaging dissolved within a day and released the toys. So it was obvious that the toys had floated most of the way to where they were found.

Experiments showed how fast the toys moved under the influence of wind without any current. The toys had floated past a weather station where many drift bottles had been released and also past the place where 61,000 shoes had fallen off a ship in 1990. About two percent of the shoes were recovered in Alaska. Comparing data from the toys and the shoes with other data from as far back as 1946, the researchers concluded that the current across the northeast Pacific Ocean changes little from year to year. But the data showed that in 1990 and 1992 the current was unusually far north.

Data that help us understand ocean currents and many other natural processes come not just from scientific experiments. Data sometimes come from the most unusual sources.

▶ This map is a computer simulation that shows the possible trajectory of the toys and their estimated locations on certain dates as they floated across the Pacific Ocean from the point of the spill to recovery points in Alaska.

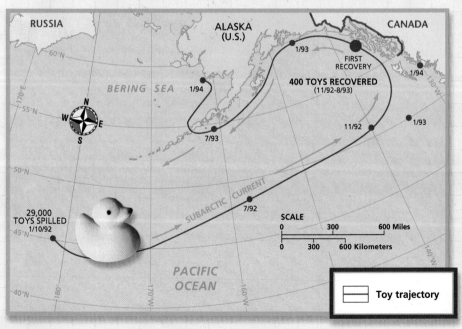

What Do You Think?

Take a look at Figure 22. If the toys continue to be carried by surface currents, where might they be found in the future? How might the height of the toys above the water's surface have influenced the speed at which they traveled?

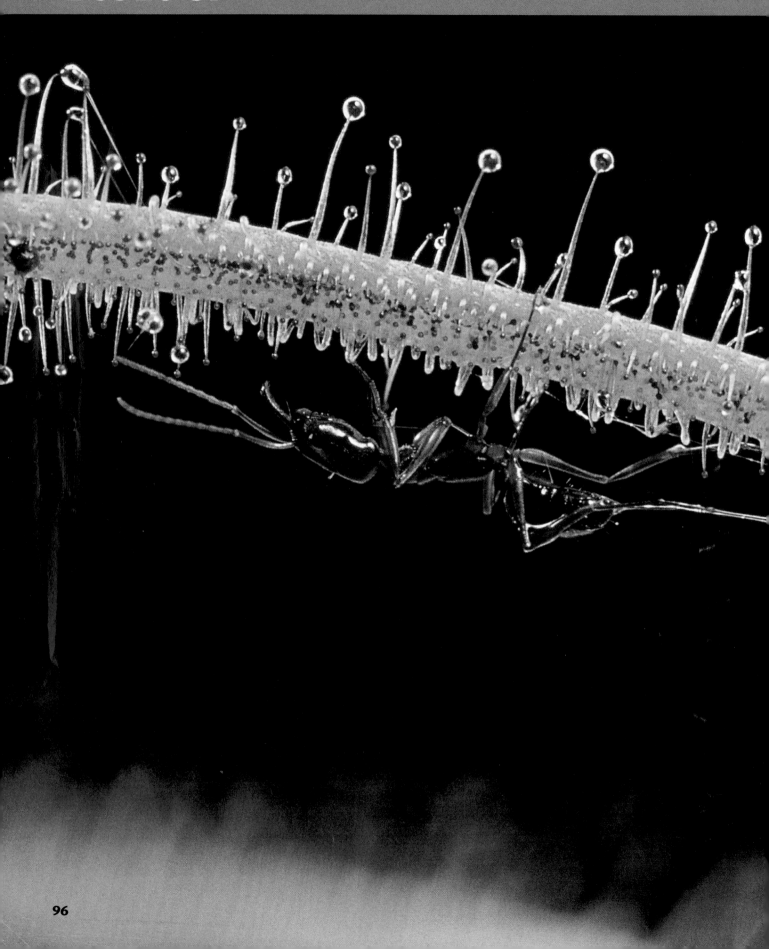

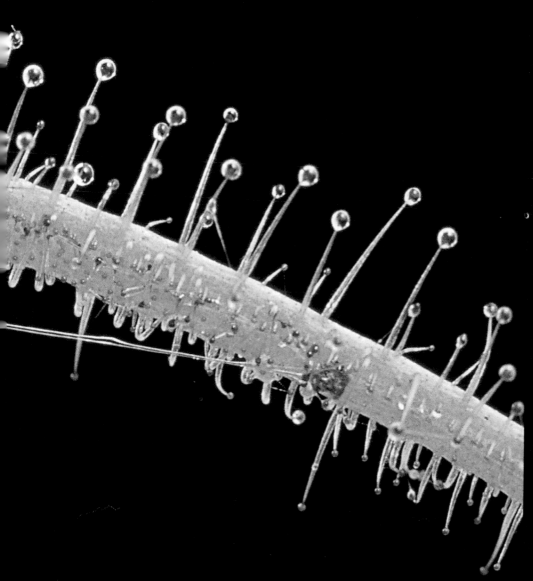

CHAPTER 4

The Organization
of Life

CHAPTER 5

How Ecosystems Work

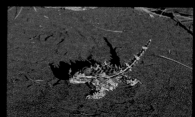

CHAPTER 6

Biomes

CHAPTER 7

Aquatic Ecosystems

This Australian plant called the
fork-leafed sundew gets the nutrients that it needs to survive by
dissolving insects that get stuck
on its sticky tips.

The Organization of Life

PRE-READING ACTIVITY

FOLDNOTES

Layered Book
Before you read this chapter, create the **FoldNote** entitled "Layered Book" described in the Reading and Study Skills section of the Appendix. Label the tabs of the layered book with "Ecosystem," "Population," "Community," and "Habitat." As you read the chapter, write information you learn about each category under the appropriate flap.

A coral reef is an ecosystem that contains a wide variety of species. How many different species can you find in this photograph?

Ecosystems: Everything Is Connected

SCSh.7.c

You may have heard the concept that in nature everything is connected. What does this mean? Consider the following example. In 1995, scientists interested in controlling gypsy moths, which kill oak trees, performed an experiment. The scientists removed most mice, which eat young gypsy moths, from selected plots of oak forest. The number of gypsy moth eggs and young increased dramatically. The scientists then added acorns to the plots. Mice eat acorns. The number of mice soon increased, and the number of gypsy moths declined as the mice ate them as well.

This result showed that large acorn crops can suppress gypsy moth outbreaks. Interestingly, the acorns also attracted deer, which carry parasitic insects called ticks. Young ticks soon infested the mice. Wild mice carry the organism that causes Lyme disease. Ticks can pick up the organism when they bite mice. Then the ticks can bite and infect humans. This example shows that in nature, things that we would never think are connected— mice, acorns, ticks, and a human disease—can be linked to each other in a complex web.

Defining an Ecosystem

The mice, moths, oak trees, deer, and ticks in the previous example are all part of the same ecosystem. An **ecosystem** (EE koh SIS tuhm) is all of the organisms living in an area together with their physical environment. An oak forest is an ecosystem. The coral reef on the opposite page is an ecosystem. Even a vacant lot, as shown in **Figure 1,** is an ecosystem.

Objectives

▶ **Distinguish** between the biotic and abiotic factors in an ecosystem.

▶ **Describe** how a population differs from a species.

▶ **Explain** how habitats are important for organisms.

Key Terms

ecosystem
biotic factor
abiotic factor
organism
species
population
community
habitat

www.scilinks.org
Topic: Ecosystems
Code: HE80466

Figure 1 ▶ This vacant lot is actually a small ecosystem. It includes various organisms, including plants and insects, as well as soil, air, and sunlight.

Figure 2 ▶ Like all ecosystems, this coastal region in France contains certain basic components. What components can you identify?

Geofact

The Living Soil Soil, which is part of nearly all ecosystems on land, is formed in part by living organisms, which break down dead leaves and organisms. Small, plantlike organisms even help break down rocks!

Figure 3 ▶ This caribou is a biotic factor in a cold, northern ecosystem in Denali National Park, Alaska.

Ecosystems Are Connected People often think of ecosystems as isolated from each other, but ecosystems do not have clear boundaries. Things move from one ecosystem into another. Soil washes from a mountain into a lake, birds migrate from Michigan to Mexico, and pollen blows from a forest into a field.

The Components of an Ecosystem

In order to survive, ecosystems need certain basic components. These are energy, mineral nutrients, carbon dioxide, water, oxygen, and living organisms. As shown in **Figure 2**, plants and soil are two of the most obvious components of most land ecosystems. The energy in most ecosystems comes from the sun.

To appreciate how all of the things in an ecosystem are connected, think about how a car works. The engine alone is made up of hundreds of parts that all work together. If even one part breaks, the car might not run. Likewise, if one part of an ecosystem is destroyed or changes, the entire system may be affected.

Biotic and Abiotic Factors An ecosystem is made up of both living and nonliving things. **Biotic factors** are the living and once living parts of an ecosystem, including all of the plants and animals. Biotic factors include dead organisms, dead parts of organisms, such as leaves, and the organisms' waste products. **Abiotic** (ay bie AHT ik) **factors** are the nonliving parts of the ecosystem. Abiotic factors include air, water, rocks, sand, light, and temperature. **Figure 3** shows several biotic and abiotic factors in an Alaskan ecosystem.

Scientists organize living things into levels. **Figure 4** shows how an ecosystem fits into the organization of living things.

✔ **Reading Check** What is the difference between a biotic factor and an abiotic factor? (See the Appendix for answers to Reading Checks.)

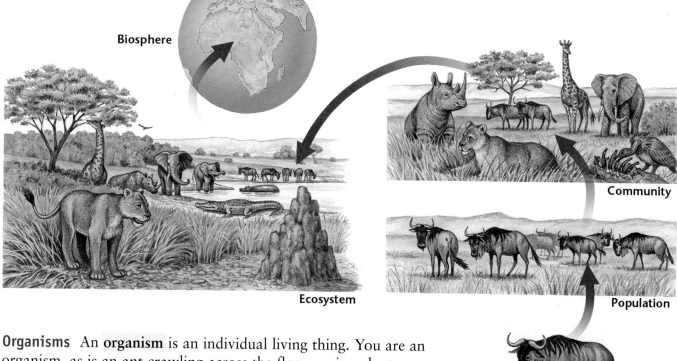

Biosphere

Ecosystem

Community

Population

Organism

Figure 4 ▶ An individual organism is part of a population, a community, an ecosystem, and the biosphere.

Organisms An **organism** is an individual living thing. You are an organism, as is an ant crawling across the floor, an ivy plant on the windowsill, and a bacterium in your intestines.

A **species** is a group of organisms that can mate to produce fertile offspring. All humans, for example, are members of the species *Homo sapiens*, while all black widow spiders are members of the species *Latrodectus mactans*. Every organism is a member of a species.

Populations Members of a species may not all live in the same place. Field mice in Maine and field mice in Florida will never interact even though they are members of the same species. An organism lives as part of a population. A **population** is all the members of the same species that live in the same place at the same time. For example, all the field mice in a corn field make up one population of field mice.

An important characteristic of a population is that its members usually breed with one another rather than with members of other populations. The bison in **Figure 5** (right) will usually mate with another member of the same herd, just as the wildflowers (left) will usually be pollinated by other flowers in the same field.

Figure 5 ▶ Two of the populations shown here are a population of purple-flowered musk thistle (left) and a herd of bison (right).

Communities Every population is part of a **community,** a group of various species that live in the same place and interact with each other. A community is different from an ecosystem because a community is made up only of biotic components. A pond community, for example, includes all of the populations of plants, fish, and insects that live in and around the pond. All of the living things in an ecosystem belong to one or more communities.

Communities differ in the types and numbers of species they have. A land community is often characterized by the types of plants that are dominant. These plants determine the other organisms that can live in this community. For example, the dominant plant in a Colorado forest might be its ponderosa pine trees. This pine community will have animals, such as squirrels, that live in and feed on these trees.

Figure 6 ▶ Salamanders, such as this red-backed salamander, live in habitats that are moist and shaded.

Habitat

The squirrels mentioned above live in a pine forest. All organisms live in particular places. The place an organism lives is called its **habitat.** A howler monkey's habitat is the rain forest and a cactus's habitat is a desert. The salamander shown in **Figure 6** is in its natural habitat, the damp forest floor.

Every habitat has specific biotic and abiotic factors that the organisms living there need to survive. A coral reef contains sea water, coral, sunlight, and a wide variety of other organisms. If any of these factors change, then the habitat changes.

Organisms tend to be very well suited to their natural habitats. Indeed, animals and plants cannot usually survive for long periods of time away from their natural habitats. For example, a fish that lives in the crevices of a coral reef will die if the coral reef is destroyed.

✓ **Reading Check** Why is an organism's habitat important for that organism? (See the Appendix for answers to Reading Checks.)

SECTION 1 Review

1. **List** the abiotic and biotic factors you see in the northern ecosystem in Figure 3.

2. **Describe** a population not mentioned in this section.

3. **Describe** which factors of an ecosystem are not part of a community.

4. **Explain** the difference between a population and a species.

CRITICAL THINKING

5. **Analyzing Relationships** Write your own definition of the term *community,* using the terms *biotic factors* and *abiotic factors.* **WRITING SKILLS**

6. **Understanding Concepts** Why might a scientist say that an animal is becoming rare because of habitat destruction?

Evolution

SEV 2 a; SEV3a; SEV3b; SEV3d

Organisms tend to be well suited to where they live and what they do. **Figure 7** shows a chameleon (kuh MEEL ee uhn) capturing an insect. Insects are not easy to catch, so how does the chameleon do it? Chameleons can change the color and pattern of their skin, and then blend into their backgrounds. Their eyes are raised on little, mobile turrets that enable the lizards to look around without moving. An insect is unlikely to notice such an animal sitting motionless on a branch. When the insect moves within range, the chameleon shoots out an amazingly long tongue to grab the insect.

Evolution by Natural Selection

In 1859, English naturalist Charles Darwin observed that organisms in a population differ slightly from each other in form, function, and behavior. Some of these differences are *hereditary* (huh RED i TER ee)—that is, passed from parent to offspring. Darwin proposed that the environment exerts a strong influence over which individuals survive to produce offspring. Some individuals, because of certain traits, are more likely to survive and reproduce than other individuals. Darwin used the term **natural selection** to describe the survival and reproduction of organisms with particular traits.

Darwin proposed that over many generations natural selection causes the characteristics of populations to change. A change in the genetic characteristics of a population from one generation to the next is known as **evolution**.

✓ Reading Check **How is natural selection related to the process of evolution?**

Objectives

▶ Explain the process of evolution by natural selection.

▶ Explain the concept of adaptation.

▶ Describe the steps by which a population of insects becomes resistant to a pesticide.

Key Terms

natural selection
evolution
adaptation
artificial selection
resistance

Connection to **Geology**

Darwin and Fossils In the 1800s, fossil hunting was a popular hobby. The many fossils that people found started arguments about where fossils come from. Darwin's theory of evolution proposed that fossils are the remains of extinct species from which modern species evolved. When his book on the theory of evolution was first published in 1859, it became an immediate bestseller.

SCILINKS.
www.scilinks.org
Topic: Evolution
Code: HE80546

Figure 7 ▶ A chameleon catches an unsuspecting insect that has strayed within range of the lizard's long, fast-moving tongue.

Nature Selects Darwin thought that nature selects for certain traits, such as sharper claws or lighter feathers, because organisms with these traits are more likely to survive and reproduce. For example, lions that have the trait of sharper claws can kill their prey more easily than lions with duller claws. Thus, lions with sharper claws are more likely to survive and reproduce. Over time, the lion population includes a greater and greater proportion of lions with sharper claws. As the populations of a given species change, so does the species. **Table 1** summarizes the premises of Darwin's theory of evolution by natural selection. Darwin proposed his theory after drawing a conclusion based on these premises.

Table 1 ▼

Evolution by Natural Selection	
Premises	**Conclusion**
1. Individuals in a population vary in each generation.	Based on these four premises, individuals with genetic traits that make them more likely to grow up and reproduce in the existing environment will become more common in the population from one generation to the next.
2. Some of these variations are genetic, or inherited.	
3. More individuals are produced than live to grow up and reproduce.	
4. Individuals with some genes are more likely to survive and reproduce than individuals with other genes.	

Darwin's Finches

Before Charles Darwin formulated his theory of evolution, he sailed around the coast of South America. The plants and animals he saw had a great effect on his thinking about how modern organisms had originated. He was surprised by the organisms he saw on islands because they were often unusual species found nowhere else.

He was particularly impressed by the organisms in the Galápagos Islands, an isolated group of volcanic islands in the Pacific Ocean west of Ecuador. The islands contain 13 unique species of birds, which have become known as Darwin's finches. All the species look generally similar,

but different species have differently specialized bills adapted to eating different types of food. Some species have large, parrotlike bills adapted to cracking big seeds, some species have slim bills that are used to sip nectar from flowers, and some species have even become insect eaters. Darwin speculated that all the Galápagos finches had evolved from a single species of seed-eating finch that found its way to the islands from the South American mainland. Populations of the finches became established on the various islands, and the finches that survived were those able to eat what they found on their island.

▶ Notice the beaks in the two species of Darwin's finches. What do you think these finches eat?

Princeton University biologists Peter and Rosemary Grant have spent 25 years studying Darwin's finches on Daphne Major, one of the Galápagos Islands. Here, one

Figure 8 shows an example of evolution in which a population of deer become isolated in a cold area. Many die, but some have genes for thicker, warmer fur. These deer are more likely to survive, and their young with thick fur are also more likely to survive to reproduce. The deer's thick fur is an **adaptation,** an inherited trait that increases an organism's chance of survival and reproduction in a certain environment.

Figure 8 ▶ These steps show the evolution of thicker fur in a population of deer.

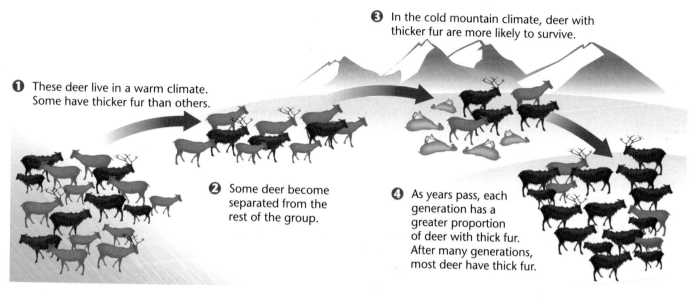

❸ In the cold mountain climate, deer with thicker fur are more likely to survive.

❶ These deer live in a warm climate. Some have thicker fur than others.

❷ Some deer become separated from the rest of the group.

❹ As years pass, each generation has a greater proportion of deer with thick fur. After many generations, most deer have thick fur.

species, the medium ground finch, has a short, stubby beak and eats seeds as well as a few insects. The ground finches have few predators. The Grants found that the main factor that determined whether a finch lived or died was how much food was available. During a long drought in 1977, many plants died and the small seeds that the finches

eat became scarce. Only finches that had large beaks survived. Large beaks allowed them to eat larger seeds from the larger plants that had survived the drought.

The finches that survived the drought passed their genes for large beaks to their offspring. Two years later, the Grants found that the beaks of medium ground finches on Daphne Major were nearly 4 percent larger, on average, than they had been before the drought. The Grants had observed evolution occurring in birds over a short period of time, something that had seldom been seen before.

Two factors make the Galápagos Islands well suited for researching evolution. First, there are few plant species in the community, so the finches have little choice in their

food source. Second, shifts in rainfall determine which plants live and die, further limiting the finches' food sources.

The islands are strongly influenced by El Niño and La Niña weather patterns. These weather patterns produce alternating periods of very wet and very dry weather in a relatively short time. The plants vary, depending on the weather pattern, exerting different selective pressures on the animals that depend on the plants for food.

CRITICAL THINKING

1. Analyzing Relationships Could the finches that evolved bigger beaks in this study evolve smaller beaks some day?

Figure 9 ▶ This Hawaiian honey-creeper is using its curved beak to sip nectar from a lobelia flower.

Coevolution Organisms evolve adaptations to other organisms and to their physical environment. The process of two species evolving in response to long-term interactions with each other is called *coevolution* (koh EV uh LOO shuhn). One possible example is shown in **Figure 9.** The honeycreeper's beak is long and curved, which lets it reach the nectar at the base of the long, curved flower. The flower has evolved structures that cause the bird to get pollen on its head as it sips the nectar. When the bird moves to another flower, some of the pollen rubs off. In this way, the bird helps lobelia plants reproduce. The honeycreeper's adaptation for obtaining more nectar is a long, curved beak. The plant has two adaptations for greater pollination. One is sweet nectar, which attracts the birds. The other is a flower structure that forces pollen onto a bird's head when the bird sips the nectar.

Evolution by Artificial Selection

Many populations of plants and animals do not live in the wild but are cared for by humans. People control how these organisms reproduce and therefore how they evolve. The two species in **Figure 10** are closely related. Over thousands of years, humans bred the ancestors of today's wolves to produce the variety of dog breeds. The selective breeding of organisms by humans for specific characteristics is called **artificial selection.**

The fruits, grains, and vegetables we eat were also produced by artificial selection. By selecting for traits such as size and sweetness, farmers directed the evolution of crop plants. As a result, crops produce fruits, grains, and roots that are larger, sweeter, and easier to harvest than their wild relatives. Native Americans cultivated the ancestor of today's corn from a grasslike plant in the mountains of Mexico. Modern corn is very different from the wild plant that was its ancestor.

✓ Reading Check How is artificial selection different from natural selection?

MATHPRACTICE

Plumper Pumpkins
Each year a farmer saves and plants only the seeds from his largest pumpkins. Suppose that he starts with pumpkins that average 5 kg and each year grows pumpkins that are 3 percent more massive, on average, than those he grew the year before. What will be the average mass of his pumpkins after 10 years?

Figure 10 ▶ As a result of artificial selection, the Chihuahua on the right looks very different from its wolf ancestor on the left.

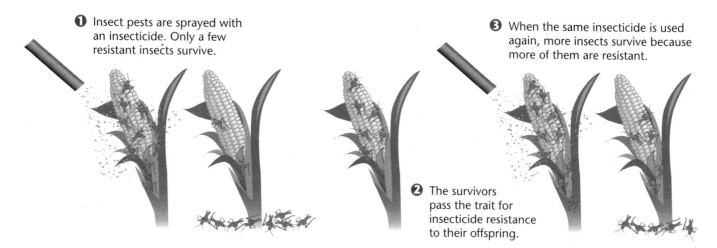

❶ Insect pests are sprayed with an insecticide. Only a few resistant insects survive.

❸ When the same insecticide is used again, more insects survive because more of them are resistant.

❷ The survivors pass the trait for insecticide resistance to their offspring.

Evolution of Resistance

Sometimes humans cause populations of organisms to evolve unwanted adaptations. You may have heard about insect pests that are resistant to pesticides and about bacteria that are resistant to antibiotics. What is resistance, and what does it have to do with evolution?

Resistance is the ability of one or more organisms to tolerate a particular chemical designed to kill it. An organism may be resistant to a chemical when it contains a gene that allows it to break the chemical down into harmless substances. By trying to control pests and bacteria with chemicals, humans promote the evolution of resistant populations.

Pesticide Resistance Consider the evolution of pesticide resistance among corn pests, as shown in **Figure 11**. A pesticide is sprayed on corn to kill grasshoppers. Most of the grasshoppers die, but a few survive. The survivors happen to have a version of a gene that protects them from the pesticide. The surviving insects pass on the gene to their offspring. Each time the corn is sprayed, insects that are resistant to the pesticide will have a greater chance of survival and reproduction. As a result, the insect population will evolve to include more and more resistant members.

Figure 11 ▶ The evolution of resistance to a pesticide starts when the pesticide is sprayed on the corn. Most of the insects are killed, but a few resistant ones survive. After each spraying, the insect population contains a larger proportion of resistant organisms.

FIELD ACTIVITY

Artificial Selection Look around your school grounds and the area around your home for possible examples of artificial selection. Observe and report on any examples you can find.

Dogs are one example of artificial selection mentioned in this chapter, but you will probably find many more plant examples. Record your observations in your *EcoLog*.

SECTION 2 **Review**

1. **Explain** what an adaptation is, and provide three examples.

2. **Explain** the process of evolution by natural selection.

3. **Describe** one way in which artificial selection can benefit humans.

4. **Explain** how a population of insects could become resistant to a pesticide.

CRITICAL THINKING

5. **Understanding Concepts** Read the description of evolution by natural selection in this section and describe the role that the environment plays in the theory. **READING SKILLS**

6. **Identifying Relationships** A population of rabbits evolves thicker fur in response to a colder climate. Is this an example of coevolution? Explain your answer.

SCSh.2.a; SCSh.2.b; SCSh.3.a; SCSh.3.c; SCSh.3.d; SCSh.3.e; SCSh.4.a; SCSh.6.a; SCSh.6.b; SCSh.6.c; SCSh.9.c; SEV.2.a; SEV.2.b

SECTION 3
The Diversity of Living Things

Objectives

▶ Name the six kingdoms of organisms and identify two characteristics of each.

▶ Explain the importance of bacteria and fungi in the environment.

▶ Describe the importance of protists in the ocean environment.

▶ Describe how angiosperms and animals depend on each other.

▶ Explain why insects are such successful animals.

Key Terms

Archaebacteria
Eubacteria
fungus
protist
gymnosperm
angiosperm
invertebrate
vertebrate

Life on Earth is incredibly diverse. Take a walk in a park, and you will see trees, birds, insects, and maybe fish in a stream. All of these organisms are living, but they are all very different from one another.

Most scientists classify organisms into six *kingdoms*, as described in **Table 2,** based on different characteristics. Members of the six kingdoms get their food in different ways and are made up of different types of *cells*, the smallest unit of biological organization. The cells of animals, plants, fungi, and protists contain a *nucleus* (NOO klee uhs), which consists of a membrane that surrounds a cell's genetic material. Bacteria, fungi, and plants all have *cell walls*, structures that surround their cells and provide them with support.

Archaebacteria and Eubacteria

Organisms in the kingdoms Archaebacteria and Eubacteria share a lot of features, even though they are not closely related. They are microscopic, single-celled organisms that usually have cell walls and reproduce by dividing in half. Unlike all other organisms, members of Archaebacteria and Eubacteria lack nuclei. **Archaebacteria** are often found in extreme places, such as hot springs. **Eubacteria** are very common and can be found in soil and animal bodies. Many types of eubacteria are commonly referred to as bacteria.

Table 2 ▼

The Kingdoms of Life		
Kingdom	**Characteristics**	**Examples**
Archaebacteria	single celled; lack cell nuclei; reproduce by dividing in half; often found in harsh environments	methanogens (live in swamps and produce methane gas) and extreme thermophiles (live in hot springs)
Eubacteria	single celled; lack cell nuclei; reproduce by dividing in half; incredibly common	proteobacteria (common in soils and in animal intestines) and cyanobacteria (also called *blue-green algae*)
Fungi	absorb their food through their body surface; have cell walls; most live on land	yeasts, mushrooms, molds, mildews, and rusts
Protists	most single celled but some have many cells; most live in water	diatoms, dinoflagellates (red tide), amoebas, trypanosomes, paramecia, and *Euglena*
Plants	many cells; make their own food by photosynthesis; have cell walls	ferns, mosses, trees, herbs, and grasses
Animals	many cells; no cell walls; ingest their food; live on land and in water	corals, sponges, worms, insects, fish, reptiles, birds, and mammals

Bacteria and the Environment Bacteria play many important roles in the environment. Some kinds of bacteria break down the remains and wastes of other organisms and return nutrients to the soil. Others recycle mineral nutrients, such as nitrogen and phosphorous. For example, certain kinds of bacteria play a very important role by converting nitrogen in the air into a form that plants can use. Nitrogen is important because it is a main component of proteins and genetic material.

Bacteria also allow many organisms, including humans, to extract certain nutrients from their food. The bacteria in **Figure 12** are *Escherichia coli,* or *E. coli,* a bacterium found in the intestines of humans and other animals. Here, *E. coli* helps digest food and release vitamins that humans need. A different form of *E. coli* can cause severe food poisoning.

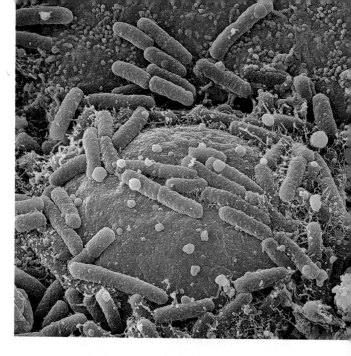

Figure 12 ▶ The long, orange objects in the image above are *E. coli* bacteria as they appear under a microscope.

Fungi

A **fungus** (plural, *fungi*) is an organism whose cells have nuclei and cell walls. A mushroom is the reproductive structure of a fungus. The rest of the fungus is an underground network of fibers. These fibers absorb food from decaying organisms in the soil.

Fungi get their food by releasing chemicals that help break down organic matter, and then absorbing the nutrients. The bodies of most fungi are a huge network of threads that grow through the soil, dead wood, or other material on which the fungi are feeding. Like bacteria, fungi play an important role in the environment by breaking down the bodies and body parts of dead organisms.

Like bacteria, some fungi cause diseases, such as athlete's foot. Other fungi add flavor to food. The fungus in blue cheese, shown in **Figure 13**, gives the cheese its strong flavor. And fungi called *yeasts* produce the gas that makes bread rise.

> **Reading Check** Name one way that bacteria and fungi are similar and one way that they are different.

Graphic Organizer **Spider Map** Create the **Graphic Organizer** entitled "Spider Map" described in the Appendix. Label the circle "Kingdoms." Create a leg for each kingdom. Then, fill in the map with details about the organisms in each kingdom.

Figure 13 ▶ A mushroom (left) is the reproductive structure of a fungus that lives in the soil. The cheese (above) gets its taste and its blue color from a fungus.

Protists

Most people have some idea what bacteria and fungi are, but few could define a protist. **Protists** are a diverse group of one-celled organisms and their many-celled relatives. Some, such as amoebas, are animallike. Others, such as the kelp in **Figure 14**, are plantlike. Still others are more like fungi. Most protists are one-celled microscopic organisms. This group includes amoebas and *diatoms* (DIE uh TAHMS). Diatoms, shown in **Figure 14**, float on the ocean surface. The most infamous protist is *Plasmodium*, the one-celled organism that causes the disease malaria. From an environmental standpoint, the most important protists are probably algae. Algae are plantlike protists that can make their own food using the sun's energy. Green pond "scum" and seaweed are examples of algae. Algae range in size from the giant kelp to the one-celled *phytoplankton*, which are the initial source of food in most ocean and freshwater ecosystems.

Plants

Plants are many-celled organisms that have cell walls and that make their own food using the sun's energy. Most plants live on land, where the resources a plant needs are separated between the air and the soil. Sunlight, oxygen, and carbon dioxide are in the air, and minerals and water are in the soil. Plants have roots that access water and nutrients in the soil and leaves that collect light and gases in the air. Leaves and roots are connected by *vascular tissue,* a system of tubes that carries water and food. Vascular tissue has thick cell walls, so a wheat plant or a tree is like a building supported by its plumbing.

Lower Plants The first land plants had no vascular tissue, and they also had swimming sperm. As a result, these early plants could not grow very large and had to live in damp places. Their descendants alive today are small plants such as mosses. Ferns and club mosses were the first vascular plants. Some of the first ferns were as large as small trees. Tree ferns still live in the tropics and in New Zealand today. Some examples of lower plants are shown in **Figure 15**.

Figure 15 ▶ Lower plants, such as these mosses and ferns, live in damp places because they need water to reproduce.

Gymnosperms Pine trees and other evergreens with needle-like leaves are gymnosperms (JIM noh SPUHRMZ). **Gymnosperms** are woody plants that produce seeds, but their seeds are not enclosed in fruits. Gymnosperms such as pine trees are also called *conifers* because their seeds are inside cones, as shown in **Figure 16.**

Gymnosperms have several adaptations that allow them to live in drier conditions than lower plants can. Gymnosperms produce *pollen,* which protects and moves sperm between plants. These plants also produce *seeds,* which protect developing plants from drying out. And a conifer's needle-like leaves lose little water. Much of our lumber and paper comes from gymnosperms.

Angiosperms Most land plants today are **angiosperms** (AN jee oh SPUHRMZ), flowering plants that produce seeds in fruit. All of the plants in **Figure 17** are angiosperms. The flower is the reproductive structure of the plant. Some angiosperms, such as grasses, have small flowers that produce pollen that is carried by the wind. Other angiosperms have large flowers that attract insects or birds to carry their pollen to other plants. Many flowering plants depend on animals to disperse their seeds and carry their pollen. For example, a bird that eats a fruit will drop the seeds elsewhere, where they may grow into new plants.

Most land animals could not survive without flowering plants. Most of the food we eat, such as wheat, rice, beans, oranges, and lettuce, comes from flowering plants. Building materials and fibers, such as oak and cotton, also come from flowering plants.

✓ Reading Check How do angiosperms depend on animals, and how do animals depend on angiosperms?

Figure 16 ▶ This gymnosperm has male and female reproductive structures called *cones.*

QuickLAB

Pollen and Flower Diversity

Procedure

1. Use a **cotton swab** to collect pollen from a common **flowering plant.**
2. Tap the cotton swab on a **microscope slide** and cover the slide with a **cover slip.**
3. Examine the slide under a **microscope,** and draw the pollen grains in your *EcoLog.*
4. Repeat this exercise with a **grass plant in bloom.**

Analysis

1. Based on the structure of the flower and the pollen grains, explain which plant is pollinated by insects and which is pollinated by wind.

Figure 17 ▶ This meadow contains a wide array of angiosperms, including grasses, trees, and wildflowers.

Animals

Animals cannot make their own food like plants can. They have to take in food from their environment. In addition, animal cells have no cell walls, so animals' bodies are soft and flexible. Some animals have evolved hard skeletons against which their muscles can pull to move their bodies. As a result, animals are much more mobile than plants and all animals move around in their environments during at least one stage in their lives.

Invertebrates Animals that lack backbones are **invertebrates** (in VUHR tuh brits). Many invertebrates live attached to hard surfaces in the ocean and filter their food out of the water. These organisms move around only when they are larvae (juveniles). At this early stage of life, they are part of the ocean's floating plankton. Filter feeders include corals, various worms, and mollusks such as clams and oysters. **Figure 18** shows a variety of invertebrates. Other invertebrates, including squid in the ocean and insects on land, move around actively in search of food.

More insects exist on Earth than any other type of animal. Insects have a waterproof external skeleton that keeps them from losing water in dry environments. Insects move quickly and they reproduce quickly. Also, most insects can fly. Their small size allows them to live on little food and to hide from enemies in small spaces, such as a seed or in the hair of a mammal.

Many insects and plants have evolved together and depend on each other to survive. Insects carry pollen from male parts of flowers to female parts of flowers to fertilize a plant's egg, which develops into a fruit. Without insect pollinators, we would not have tomatoes, cucumbers, apples, and many other crops. Insects also eat other insects that we consider to be pests. But, humans and insects are often enemies. Bloodsucking insects transmit human diseases, such as malaria, sleeping sickness, and West Nile virus. Insects probably do more damage indirectly, however, by eating our crops.

Figure 18 ▶ Examples of invertebrates include the banana slug (left), the leaf-footed bug (middle), and the cuttlefish (right).

Figure 19 ▶ Examples of vertebrates include the toco toucan (left), the blue-spotted stingray (middle), and the snow leopard (right).

Vertebrates Animals that have backbones are called **vertebrates.** Members of three vertebrate groups are shown in **Figure 19.** The first vertebrates were fish, but today most vertebrates live on land. Amphibians, which include toads, frogs, and salamanders, are partially aquatic. Nearly all amphibians must return to water to lay their eggs.

The first vertebrates to complete their entire life cycle on land were the reptiles, which today include turtles, lizards, snakes, and crocodiles. These animals have an almost waterproof egg, which allows the egg to hatch on land, away from predators in the water.

Birds are warm-blooded vertebrates with feathers. Bird eggs have hard shells. Adult birds keep their eggs and young warm until they develop insulating layers of fat and feathers. *Mammals* are warm-blooded vertebrates that have fur and feed their young milk. The ability to maintain a high body temperature allows birds and mammals to live in cold areas, where other animals cannot survive.

Eco fact

Conserving Water Arthropods and vertebrates are the only two groups of animals that have adaptations that prevent dehydration so effectively that some of them can move about freely on land on a dry, sunny day.

SECTION 3 **Review**

1. **Describe** how animals and angiosperms depend on each other. Write a short paragraph to explain your answer. **WRITING SKILLS**

2. **Describe** the importance of protists in the ocean.

3. **Name** the six kingdoms of life, and give two characteristics of each.

4. **Explain** the importance of bacteria and fungi in the environment.

CRITICAL THINKING

5. **Analyzing Relationships** Explain how the large number and wide distribution of angiosperm species is related to the success of insects.

6. **Understanding Concepts** Write a short paragraph that compares the reproductive structures of gymnosperms and angiosperms. **WRITING SKILLS**

CHAPTER 4

Highlights

1 Ecosystems: Everything Is Connected

Key Terms

Main Ideas

▶ Ecosystems are composed of many interconnected parts that often interact in complex ways.

▶ An ecosystem is all the different organisms living in an area as well as the physical environment.

▶ Organisms live as populations of one species in communities with other species. Each species has its own habitat, or type of place that it lives.

2 Evolution

Key Terms

Main Ideas

▶ The naturalist Charles Darwin used the term natural selection to describe the survival and reproduction of organisms with particular traits.

▶ Darwin proposed that natural selection is responsible for evolution—a change in the genetic characteristics of a population from one generation to the next.

▶ By selecting which domesticated animals and plants breed, humans cause evolution by artificial selection.

▶ We have unintentionally selected for pests that are resistant to pesticides and for bacteria that are resistant to antibiotics.

3 The Diversity of Living Things

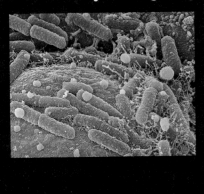

Key Terms

Main Ideas

▶ Organisms can be divided into six kingdoms, which are distinguished by the types of cells they possess and how they obtain their food.

▶ Bacteria and fungi play the important environmental roles of breaking down dead organisms and recycling nutrients.

▶ Gymnosperms, which include the conifers, are the earliest plants with seeds. Angiosperms are flowering plants.

▶ Insects, invertebrates that are the most successful animals on Earth, affect humans in both positive and negative ways.

▶ Vertebrates, or animals with backbones, include fish, amphibians, reptiles, birds, and mammals.

Using Key Terms

Use each of the following terms in a separate sentence.

1. *adaptation*
2. *invertebrate*
3. *abiotic factor*
4. *habitat*
5. *species*

For each pair of terms, explain how the meanings of the terms differ.

6. *community* and *population*
7. *evolution* and *natural selection*
8. *gymnosperm* and *angiosperm*
9. *bacteria* and *protists*

✔ **STUDY TIP**

Make an Outline After reading each section, summarize the main ideas into a short outline, leaving space between each entry. Then write the key terms under the subsection in which they are introduced, followed by a short definition for each.

Understanding Key Ideas

10. Which of the following pairs of organisms belong to the same population?
    a. a dog and a cat
    b. a marigold and a geranium
    c. a human mother and her child
    d. a spider and a cockroach

11. Which of these phrases does *not* describe part of the process of evolution by natural selection?
    a. the environment contains limited resources
    b. organisms produce more offspring than will survive to reproduce
    c. communities include populations of several species
    d. organisms in a population differ in their traits

12. Which of the following components of an ecosystem are *not* abiotic factors?
    a. wind
    b. small rocks
    c. sunlight
    d. tree branches

13. Some snakes produce a powerful poison that paralyzes their prey. This poison is an example of
    a. resistance.
    b. an adaptation.
    c. a reptile.
    d. an abiotic factor.

14. Angiosperms called roses come in a variety of shapes and colors as a result of
    a. natural selection.
    b. coevolution.
    c. different ecosystems.
    d. artificial selection.

15. Single-celled organisms that live in swamps and produce methane gas are
    a. protists.
    b. archaebacteria.
    c. fungi.
    d. eubacteria.

16. Which of the following statements about protists is *not* true?
    a. Most of them live in water.
    b. Some of them cause diseases in humans.
    c. They contain genetic material.
    d. Their cells have no nucleus.

17. Which of the following statements about plants is *not* true?
    a. They make their food from oxygen and water through photosynthesis.
    b. Land plants have cell walls that help hold their stems upright.
    c. They have adaptations that help prevent water loss.
    d. Plants absorb nutrients through their roots.

Short Answer

18. List the five components that an ecosystem must contain to survive indefinitely.

19. What is the difference between biotic and abiotic factors in an ecosystem?

20. What is the difference between adaptation and evolution?

21. Describe the three steps by which a population of insects becomes resistant to a pesticide.

22. List the six kingdoms of organisms and the characteristics of each kingdom.

Interpreting Graphics

Below is a graph that shows the number of aphids on a rose bush during one summer. The roses were sprayed with a pesticide three times, as shown. Use the graph to answer questions 23 and 24.

23. What evidence is there that the pesticide killed aphids?

24. Aphids have a generation time of about 10 days. Is there any evidence that the aphids evolved resistance to the pesticide during the summer? Explain your answer.

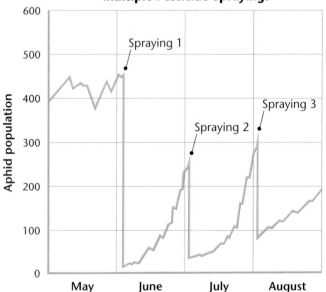

Aphid Population Changes Over Multiple Pesticide Sprayings

Concept Mapping

25. Use the following terms to create a concept map: *ecosystem, abiotic factor, biotic factor, population, species, community,* and *habitat.*

Critical Thinking

26. Analyzing Ideas Can a person evolve? Read the description of evolution in this chapter and explain why or why not. `READING SKILLS`

27. Making Inferences A scientist applies a strong fungicide, a chemical that kills fungi, to an area of forest soil every week during October and November. How might this area look different from the surrounding ground at the end of the experiment?

28. Drawing Conclusions In what building in your community do you think bacteria are evolving resistance to antibiotics most rapidly? Explain your answer.

29. Evaluating Assumptions Many people assume that the human population is no longer evolving. Do you think these people are right? Explain your answer.

Cross-Disciplinary Connection

30. Geography Find out how the isolation of populations on islands has affected their evolution. Research a well-known example, such as the animals and plants of Madagascar, the Galápagos Islands, or the Hawaiian Islands. Write a short report on your findings. `WRITING SKILLS`

Portfolio Project

31. Study an Ecosystem Observe an ecosystem near you, such as a pond or a field. Identify biotic and abiotic factors and as many populations of organisms as you can. Do not try to identify the organisms precisely. Just list them, for example, as spiders, ants, grass, not as a specific type. Make a poster showing the different populations. Put the organisms into columns to show which of the kingdoms they belong to.

MATH SKILLS

Use the graph below to answer questions 32–33.

32. **Analyzing Data** The graph below shows the mass of different types of organisms found in a meadow. How much greater is the mass of the plants than that of the animals?

33. **Analyzing Data** What is the ratio of the mass of the bacteria to the mass of the fungi?

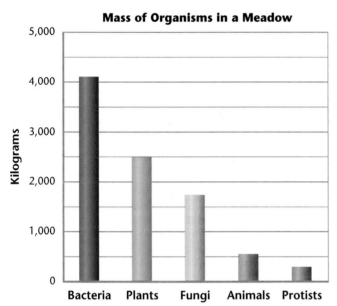

Mass of Organisms in a Meadow

READING SKILLS

Read the passage below, and then answer the questions that follow.

Some Central American acacia trees, called *ant acacias,* have a mutually beneficial relationship with ants that live on them. The trees have several structures that benefit the ants. The trees have hollow thorns in which the ants live, glands that produce sugary nectar, and swollen leaf tips, which the ants remove and feed to their larvae.

The ants reduce the damage that other organisms do to the tree. They remove dust, fungus spores, and spider webs. They destroy seedlings of other plants that sprout under the tree, so that the tree can obtain water and nutrients without competition from other plants. The ants sting animals that try to eat the tree.

Proof that the ants are valuable to the acacia tree comes from studies in which the ants are removed. Fungi invade the tree, it is eaten by herbivores, and it grows more slowly. When ants are removed from the tree, it usually dies in a few months.

1. According to the passage, which of the following statements is not true?
   a. Ants and ant acacias have evolved a relationship beneficial to both of them.
   b. The ants prevent fungi from growing on the acacia.
   c. The tree would benefit from not having ants.
   d. The ants benefit from living on the tree.

2. What is the advantage to an acacia of not having other plants grow nearby?
   a. Ants cannot crawl onto the acacia from the other plants.
   b. The acacia keeps more ants for itself.
   c. This reduces competition for water and nutrients.
   d. This reduces competition for fungi.

WRITING SKILLS

34. **Communicating Main Ideas** Why is evolution considered to be such an important idea in biology?

35. **Outlining Topics** Outline the essential steps in the evolution of pesticide resistance in insects.

Understanding Concepts

Directions (1–4): For *each* question, write on a separate sheet of paper the letter of the correct answer.

1 What is the term for the area where organisms live together with their physical environment?
A. biome
B. biosphere
C. ecosystem
D. population

2 Which of the following describes the theory of natural selection?
F. Organisms with desired traits are selected for reproduction.
G. Heredity determines which organisms will survive in their environment.
H. Traits are developed in organisms in response to interaction with other organisms.
I. Organisms with strong survival traits are more likely to pass on the traits in reproduction.

3 What inherited trait increases an organism's chance of survival and reproduction in a certain environment?
A. adaptation
B. characteristic
C. evolution
D. natural selection

4 What are the six kingdoms of life?
F. Archaebacteria, Eubacteria, Fungi, Protists, Plants, Animals
G. Eubacteria, Fungi, Protists, Plants, Land Animals, Marine Animals
H. Archaebacteria, Fungi, Plantlike Protists, Animal-like Protists, Plants, Animals
I. Bacteria, Fungi, Protists, Flowering Plants, Non-flowering Plants, Animals

Directions (5–6): For *each* question, write a short response.

5 Everything in nature is connected. Use the concept of interdependence to analyze how an ecosystem works.

6 Describe one of the important roles of bacteria.

Reading Skills

Directions (7–9): Read the passage below. Then answer the questions.

Ecosystems are composed of many interconnected parts that often interact in complex ways. People often think of ecosystems as isolated from each other, but ecosystems do not have clear boundaries. Things move from one ecosystem into another.

Ecosystems are made up of both living and nonliving things. Biotic factors are the living and once-living parts of an ecosystem, including all the plants and animals. Biotic factors include dead organisms, dead parts of organisms, such as leaves, and the organisms' waste products. The biotic parts of an ecosystem interact with the abiotic factors, the nonliving parts of the ecosystem. There are different levels in the ecological organization, from the individual organism to the biosphere.

7 What is one example of an abiotic factor?
A. armadillo
B. carnation
C. robin
D. rock

8 Why would it be incorrect to describe ecosystems as being isolated from each other?
F. All ecosystems have different species.
G. Things can move from one ecosystem into another because ecosystems do not have clear boundaries.
H. Ecosystems have biotic and abiotic factors.
I. Both ecosystems and communities have biotic and abiotic factors.

9 State the kinds of biotic factors that would be found in an ocean ecosystem.

Interpreting Graphics

Directions (10–12): For *each* question below, record the correct answer on a separate sheet of paper.

The map below shows changes in forest cover in Costa Rica over 40 years. Use this map to answer questions 10 through 12.

Forest Cover in Costa Rica

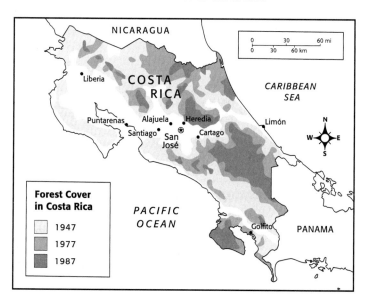

10 Approximately what percentage of Costa Rica was covered by forest in 1947?
   A. 25%
   B. 33%
   C. 50%
   D. 75%

11 What conclusion can be drawn about the forest cover of Costa Rica?
   F. Most of the remaining forests are near cities.
   G. The remaining forests are concentrated along the western coast.
   H. Costa Rica lost more than half of its forest cover in less than 50 years.
   I. Deforestation has accounted for little change in Costa Rica's environment.

12 What can be inferred about organisms adapted to living in trees in Costa Rica?
   A. Organisms that are adapted for living in trees will continue to thrive across the country.
   B. Organisms that are adapted for living in trees will be eliminated from the country's environment.
   C. Organisms that are adapted for living in trees will continue to thrive in areas that used to have forest.
   D. Organisms that are adapted for living in trees will thrive in forested areas but struggle in areas that no longer have trees.

Test *TIP*

Allow a few minutes at the end of the test-taking period to check for mistakes made in marking answers.

Inquiry Lab: DESIGN YOUR OWN

Objectives

▶ **USING SCIENTIFIC METHODS** **Observe** the behavior of brine shrimp.

▶ **USING SCIENTIFIC METHODS** **Identify** a variable, and design an experiment to test the effect of the variable on habitat selection by brine shrimp.

Materials

- aluminum foil
- brine shrimp culture
- corks sized to fit tubing
- Detain™ or methyl cellulose
- fluorescent lamp or grow light
- funnel
- graduated cylinder or beaker
- hot-water bag
- ice bag
- metric ruler
- Petri dish
- pipet
- plastic tubing, 40cm × 1cm, clear, flexible
- screen, pieces
- screw clamps
- tape
- test-tube rack
- test tubes with stoppers

How Do Brine Shrimp Select a Habitat?

Different organisms are adapted for life in different habitats. For example, brine shrimp are small crustaceans that live in saltwater lakes. Organisms select habitats that provide the conditions, such as a specific temperature range and amount of light, to which they are best adapted. In this investigation, you will explore habitat selection by brine shrimp and determine which environmental conditions they prefer.

Procedure

Establish a Control Group

1. To make a test chamber and to establish a control group, divide a piece of plastic tubing into four sections by making a mark at 10 cm, 20 cm, and 30 cm from one end. Label the sections "1", "2", "3", and "4".

2. Place a cork in one end of the tubing. Then transfer 50 mL of brine shrimp culture to the tubing. Place a cork in the other end of the tubing. Set the tube aside, and let the brine shrimp move about the tube for 30 min.

3. After 30 min, divide the tubing into four sections by placing a screw clamp at each mark on the tubing. While someone in your group holds the corks firmly in place, tighten the middle clamp at 20 cm and then tighten the other two clamps.

4. Remove the cork from the end of section 1 and pour the contents of section 1 into a test tube labeled "1." Repeat this step for the other sections by loosening the screw clamps and pouring the contents of each section into their corresponding test tubes.

5. To get an accurate count for the number of brine shrimp in each test tube, place a stopper on test tube 1, and invert the tube gently to distribute the shrimp. Use a pipet to transfer a 1 mL sample of the culture to a Petri dish. Add a few drops of Detain™ to the sample so that the brine shrimp move slower. Count and record the number of brine shrimp in the Petri dish.

▶ **Making a Test Chamber** Use a screw clamp to divide one section of tubing from another.

6. Empty the Petri dish, and take two more 1 mL samples of brine shrimp from test tube 1. Calculate the average of the three samples recorded for test tube 1.

7. Repeat steps 5 and 6 for each of the remaining test tubes to count the number of brine shrimp in each section of tubing.

▶ **Brine Shrimp** These crustaceans have specific habitat preferences.

Ask a Question

8. Write a question you would like to explore about brine shrimp habitat selection. For example, you can explore how temperature or light affects brine shrimp. To explore the question, design an experiment that uses the materials listed for this lab.

9. Write a procedure and a list of safety precautions for your group's experiment. Have your teacher approve your procedure and precautions before you begin the experiment.

10. Set up and conduct your group's experiment.

Analysis

1. **Constructing Graphs** Make a bar graph of your data. Plot the environmental variable on the x-axis and the number of brine shrimp on the y-axis.

2. **Evaluating Results** How did the brine shrimp react to changes in the environment?

3. **Evaluating Methods** Why did you have to have a control in your experiment?

4. **Evaluating Methods** Why did you record the average of three samples to count the number of brine shrimp in each test tube in steps 6 and 7?

Conclusions

5. **Drawing Conclusions** What can you conclude from your results about the types of habitat that brine shrimp prefer?

Extension

1. **Formulating Hypotheses** Now that you have observed brine shrimp, write a hypothesis about how brine shrimp select a habitat that could be explored with another experiment, other than the one you performed in this lab. Formulate a prediction based on your hypothesis.

2. **Evaluating Hypotheses** Conduct an experiment to test your prediction. Write a short explanation of your results. Did your results support your prediction? Explain your answer.

Making a difference

BUTTERFLY ECOLOGIST

Imagine millions of butterflies swirling through the air like autumn leaves, clinging in tightly packed masses to tree trunks and branches, and covering low-lying forest vegetation like a luxurious, moving carpet. According to Alfonso Alonso-Mejía, this is quite a sight to see.

Every winter Alfonso climbs up to the few remote sites in central Mexico where about 150 million monarch butterflies spend the winter. He is researching the monarchs because he wants to help preserve their habitat and the butterflies themselves. His work helped him earn a Ph.D. in ecology from the University of Florida.

Monarchs are famous for their long-distance migration. The butterflies that eventually find their way to Mexico come from as far away as the northeastern United States and southern Canada. Some of them travel an amazing 3,200 km before reaching central Mexico.

Wintering Habitat at Risk

Unfortunately, the habitat that the monarchs travel long distances to reach is increasingly threatened by illegal logging and other human activities. Logging reduced the size of the wintering region by approximately 90 percent over a 30-year period, from about 1970 to 2000. Mexico has set aside five of the known butterfly sites as sanctuaries, but even these are endangered by people who cut down fir trees for fuel or money.

Alfonso's work is helping Mexican conservationists better understand and protect monarch butterflies. Especially important is Alfonso's discovery that the monarchs depend on bushlike vegetation, called *understory vegetation,* that grows beneath the fir trees.

Keeping Warm

Alfonso's research showed that when the temperature falls below freezing, as it often does in the mountains where the monarchs winter, understory vegetation can mean the difference between life and death for some monarchs. These conditions are life threatening to the monarchs because low temperatures (–1°C to 4°C, or 30°F to 40°F) limit their movement. In fact, the butterflies are not even able to fly at such low temperatures. They can only crawl. At even colder temperatures (–7°C to –1°C, or 20°F to 30°F), monarchs resting on the forest floor may freeze to death. But if the forest has understory vegetation, the monarchs can slowly climb the vegetation until they are at least 10 cm above the ground, where it is warmer. This tiny difference in elevation can provide a microclimate that is warm enough to ensure the monarchs' survival.

▶ **Butterfly Man** Alfonso examines a monarch as part of his efforts to understand its ecology.

▶ Monarch Sanctuaries Monarch butterflies spend the winter at forested sites just above Mexico City.

The importance of understory vegetation was not known before Alfonso did his research. Now, thanks to Alfonso's work, Mexican conservationists will better protect the understory vegetation. And the Mexican government has passed a new decree that protects monarchs in areas the butterflies are known to use.

The Need for Conservation

Although the monarchs continue to enjoy the forests where they overwinter, those forests are still threatened. There is little forest left in this area, and the need for wood increases each year. Alfonso hopes his efforts will help protect the monarch both now and in the future.

Now that he has completed his Ph.D., Alfonso is devoting himself to preserving monarchs and other organisms. He works as director for conservation and development for the Smithsonian Institutions

▶ A Sea of Orange At their overwintering sites in Mexico, millions of monarchs cover trees and bushes in a fluttering carpet of orange and black.

Monitoring and Assessment of Biodiversity (MAB) program.

Information...

If you are interested in learning more about monarchs, including their spectacular migration, visit the Website for Monarch Watch. Monarch Watch is an organization based at the University of Kansas that is dedicated to educating people about the monarch and promoting its conservation.

What Do You Think?

As a migrating species, monarchs spend part of their lives in the United States and part in Mexico. Should the U.S. and Mexico cooperate in their efforts to understand and manage the monarch? Should nations set up panels to manage other migrating species, such as many songbirds?

How Ecosystems Work

1 Energy Flow in Ecosystems
2 The Cycling of Materials
3 How Ecosystems Change

PRE-READING ACTIVITY

Double-Door Fold

Before you read this chapter, create the **FoldNote** entitled "Double-Door Fold" described in the Reading and Study Skills section of the Appendix. Write "Energy flow in ecosystems" on one flap of the double door and "Movement of materials in ecosystems" on the other flap. As you read the chapter, compare the two topics, and write characteristics of each on the inside of the appropriate flap.

This green frog gets the energy it needs to survive by eating other organisms, such as dragonflies.

SECTION 1
Energy Flow in Ecosystems

Just as a car cannot run without fuel, an organism cannot survive without a constant supply of energy. Where does an organism's energy come from? The answer to this question depends on the organism, but the ultimate source of energy for almost all organisms is the sun.

Life Depends on the Sun

Energy from the sun enters an ecosystem when a plant uses sunlight to make sugar molecules in a process called **photosynthesis.** During photosynthesis, plants, algae, and some bacteria capture solar energy. Solar energy drives a series of chemical reactions that require carbon dioxide and water, as shown in **Figure 1.** The result of photosynthesis is the production of sugar molecules known as *carbohydrates.* Carbohydrates are energy-rich molecules that organisms use to carry out daily activities. As organisms consume food and use energy from carbohydrates, the energy travels from one organism to another. Plants, such as the sunflowers in **Figure 2,** produce carbohydrates in their leaves. When an animal eats a plant, some energy is transferred from the plant to the animal. Organisms use this energy to move, grow, and reproduce.

Objectives

▶ Describe how energy is transferred from the sun to producers and then to consumers.

▶ Describe one way in which consumers depend on producers.

▶ List two types of consumers.

▶ Explain how energy transfer in a food web is more complex than energy transfer in a food chain.

▶ Explain why an energy pyramid is a representation of trophic levels.

Key Terms

photosynthesis
producer
consumer
decomposer
cellular respiration
food chain
food web
trophic level

$$6CO_2 \; + \; 6H_2O \; + \; \text{solar energy} \; \longrightarrow \; C_6H_{12}O_6 \; + \; 6O_2$$

Figure 1 ▶ During photosynthesis, plants use carbon dioxide, water, and solar energy to make carbohydrates and oxygen.

Figure 2 ▶ The cells in the leaves of these sunflowers contain a green chemical called *chlorophyll.* Chlorophyll helps plants trap energy from the sun to produce energy-rich carbohydrates.

Figure 3 ▶ Transfer of Energy
Almost all organisms depend on the sun for energy. Plants like the clover shown above get energy from the sun. Animals like the rabbit and coyote get their energy by eating other organisms.

From Producers to Consumers When a rabbit eats a clover plant, the rabbit gets energy from the carbohydrates the clover plant made through photosynthesis. If a coyote eats the rabbit, some of the energy is transferred from the rabbit to the coyote. In **Figure 3,** the clover is the producer. A **producer** is an organism that makes its own food. Producers are also called *autotrophs,* or self-feeders. The rabbit and the coyote are **consumers,** organisms that get their energy by eating other organisms. Consumers are also called *heterotrophs,* or other-feeders. In **Figure 3,** the clover, rabbit, and coyote get their energy from the sun. Some producers get energy directly from the sun by absorbing it through their leaves. Consumers get energy indirectly from the sun by eating producers or other consumers.

An Exception to the Rule: Deep-Ocean Ecosystems The bottom of the ocean off the coast of Ecuador is teeming with life. Scientists found large communities of worms, clams, crabs, mussels, and barnacles living near thermal vents in the ocean floor.
These deep-ocean communities exist in total darkness, where photosynthesis cannot occur. So where do these organisms get their energy? Bacteria, such as those pictured in **Figure 4,** live in some of these organisms and use hydrogen sulfide to make their own food. Hydrogen sulfide is present in the hot water that escapes from the cracks in the ocean floor. Therefore, the bacteria are producers. The bacteria are eaten by the other underwater organisms and thus support a thriving ecosystem.

Figure 4 ▶ The tube worms (above) depend on bacteria that live inside them to survive. The bacteria (right) use energy from hydrogen sulfide to make their own food.

✔ **Reading Check** How do producers and consumers get energy from the sun? (See the Appendix for answers to Reading Checks.)

What Eats What

Table 1 below classifies organisms by the source of their energy. Consumers that eat only producers are called *herbivores*, or plant eaters. Rabbits are herbivores and so are cows, sheep, deer, grasshoppers, and many other animals. Consumers, such as lions and hawks, that eat only other consumers are called *carnivores*, or flesh eaters. You already know that humans are consumers, but what kind of consumers are we? Because most humans eat both plants and animals, we are called *omnivores*, or eaters of all. Bears, pigs, and cockroaches are other examples of omnivores. Some consumers get their food by breaking down dead organisms and are called **decomposers.** Bacteria and fungi are examples of decomposers. The decomposers allow the nutrients in the rotting material to return to the soil, water, and air.

MATHPRACTICE

A Meal Fit for a Grizzly Bear Grizzly bears are omnivores that can eat up to 15 percent of their body weight per day when eating salmon and up to 33 percent of their body weight when eating fruits and other vegetation. How many pounds of salmon can a 200 lb grizzly bear eat in one day? How many pounds of fruits and other vegetation can the same bear eat in one day?

Table 1 ▼

What Eats What in an Ecosystem		
	Energy source	**Examples**
Producer	makes its own food through photosynthesis or chemical sources	grasses, ferns, cactuses, flowering plants, trees, algae, and some bacteria
Consumer	gets energy by eating producers or other consumers	mice, starfish, elephants, turtles, humans, and ants
Types of Consumers in an Ecosystem		
	Energy source	**Examples**
Herbivore	producers	cows, sheep, deer, and grasshoppers
Carnivore	other consumers	lions, hawks, snakes, spiders, sharks, alligators, and whales
Omnivore	both producers and consumers	bears, pigs, gorillas, rats, raccoons, cockroaches, some insects, and humans
Decomposer	breaks down dead organisms in an ecosystem and returns nutrients to the soil, water, and air	fungi and bacteria

Figure 5 ▶ Bears, such as the grizzly bear below, are omnivores. Grizzly bears eat other consumers, such as salmon, but they also eat various plants.

Chemical Equations Chemical reactions are represented by chemical equations. A chemical equation is a shorthand description of a chemical reaction using chemical formulas and symbols. The starting materials in a reaction are called *reactants*, and the substances formed from a reaction are called *products*. The number of atoms of each element in the reactants equals the number of atoms of those elements in the products to make a balanced equation.

Cellular Respiration: Burning the Fuel

So far, you have learned how organisms get energy. But how do they use the energy they get? To understand the process, use yourself as an example. Suppose you have just eaten a large meal. The food you ate contains a lot of energy. Your body gets the energy out of the food by using the oxygen you breathe to break down the food. By breaking down the food, your body obtains the energy stored in the food.

The process of breaking down food to yield energy is called **cellular respiration,** which occurs inside the cells of most organisms. This process is different from *respiration,* which is another name for breathing. During cellular respiration, cells absorb oxygen and use it to release energy from food. As you can see in **Figure 6,** the chemical equation for cellular respiration is essentially the reverse of the equation for photosynthesis. During cellular respiration, sugar and oxygen combine to yield carbon dioxide, water, and, most importantly, energy.

Figure 6 ▶ Through cellular respiration, cells use glucose and oxygen to produce carbon dioxide, water, and energy.

$$C_6H_{12}O_6 + 6O_2 \longrightarrow 6CO_2 + 6H_2O + energy$$

CASE STUDY

DDT in an Aquatic Food Chain

In the 1950s and 1960s, something strange was happening in the estuaries near Long Island Sound, near New York and Connecticut. Birds of prey, such as ospreys and eagles, that fed on fish in the estuaries had high concentrations of the pesticide DDT in their bodies. But when the water in the estuaries was tested, it had low concentrations of DDT.

What accounted for the high levels of DDT in the birds? Poisons that dissolve in fat, such as DDT, can become more concentrated as they move up a food chain in a process called *biological magnification.* When the pesticide enters the water, algae and bacteria take in the poison. When fish eat the algae and bacteria, the poison dissolves into the fat of the fish rather than diffusing back into the water. Each time a bird feeds

on a fish, the bird accumulates more DDT in its fatty tissues. In some estuaries on Long Island Sound, DDT

concentrations in fatty tissues of organisms were magnified almost 10 million times from the bottom to the

▶ A high concentration of DDT decreases the thickness and the strength of eggshells of many birds of prey.

You use a part of the energy you obtain through cellular respiration to carry out your daily activities. Every time you walk, breathe, read a book, think, or play a sport, you use energy. The energy you obtain is also used to make more body tissues and to fight diseases so that you grow and stay healthy. Excess energy you obtain is stored as fat or sugar. All living things use cellular respiration to get the energy they need from food molecules. Even organisms that make their own food through photosynthesis use cellular respiration to obtain energy from the carbohydrates they produce.

Energy Transfer

Each time one organism eats another organism, a transfer of energy occurs. We can trace the transfer of energy as it travels through an ecosystem by studying food chains, food webs, and trophic levels. Food chains, food webs, and trophic levels can tell us how energy is transferred, as well as how *much* energy is transferred, between organisms in an ecosystem. Studying the paths of energy between organisms can also tell us which organisms in an ecosystem depend on other organisms to survive.

Connection to Biology

Calories from Food The substances your body needs to survive and grow come from food. Carbohydrates, proteins, and fats are major sources of energy for the body. The energy content of food can be found by burning a dry food sample in a special calorimeter. Both carbohydrates and proteins provide 4 Calories (Cal) of energy per gram, while fats provide 9 Cal of energy per gram.

▶ Poisons such as DDT have the greatest affect on organisms at the top of food chains. For example, the osprey shown here would have a greater concentration of DDT in its body than the perch it's about to eat.

top of the food chain. Large concentrations of DDT may kill an organism, weaken its immune system, cause deformities, or impair its ability to reproduce. DDT can also weaken the shells of bird eggs. When eggs break too soon, bird embryos die. Therefore, the effects of these chemicals cause a tremendous drop in the population of carnivorous bird species.

The U.S. government recognized DDT as an environmental contaminant and in 1972 banned its sale except in emergencies. The aquatic food chains immediately started to recover, and the populations of ospreys and eagles started to grow.

Food chains are still not free of DDT. DDT is still legal in some countries, where it is used in large quantities to eliminate mosquitoes that carry the disease malaria. As a result, migratory birds may be exposed to DDT while wintering in locations outside the United States.

CRITICAL THINKING

1. Analyzing Processes DDT does not dissolve readily in water. If it did, how would the accumulation of the pesticide in organisms be affected?

2. Evaluating Information Even though DDT is harmful to the environment, why is it still used in some countries?

Figure 7 ▶ Energy is transferred from one organism to another in a food chain, such as the one shown below. Algae are the producers in this ocean food chain.

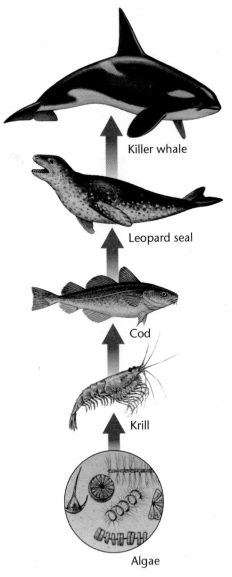

Killer whale

Leopard seal

Cod

Krill

Algae

Food Chains and Food Webs A **food chain** is a sequence in which energy is transferred from one organism to the next as each organism eats another organism. **Figure 7** shows a typical food chain in an ocean ecosystem. Algae are eaten by krill, which are eaten by cod. The cod are eaten by leopard seals, which are eaten by killer whales.

Energy flow in an ecosystem is more complex than energy flow in a simple food chain. Ecosystems almost always contain many more species than a single food chain shows. In addition, most organisms, including humans, eat more than one kind of food. So a food web, such as the one shown in **Figure 8**, includes more organisms and multiple food chains linked together. A **food web** shows many feeding relationships that are possible in an ecosystem.

Trophic Levels Each step through which energy is transferred in a food chain is known as a **trophic level**. In **Figure 8**, the algae are in the bottom trophic level, the krill are in the next level, and so on. Each time energy is transferred from one organism to another, some of the energy is lost as heat and less energy is available to organisms at the next trophic level. Some of the energy is lost during cellular respiration. Organisms use much of the remaining energy to carry out the functions of living, such as producing new cells, regulating body temperature, and moving.

Reading Check What is the difference between a food web and a food chain?

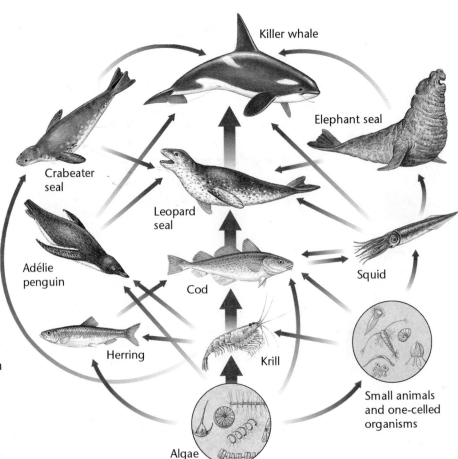

Killer whale

Crabeater seal

Adélie penguin

Leopard seal

Elephant seal

Cod

Squid

Herring

Krill

Small animals and one-celled organisms

Algae

Figure 8 ▶ This food web shows how the largest organisms, such as a killer whale, depend on the smallest organisms, such as algae, in an ocean ecosystem.

About 90 percent of the energy at each trophic level is used in these ways. The remaining 10 percent of the energy becomes part of the organism's body and is stored in its molecules. This 10 percent that is stored is all that is available to the next trophic level when one organism consumes another organism.

Energy Pyramids One way to visualize the loss of energy from one trophic level to the next trophic level is to draw an energy pyramid like the one shown in **Figure 9**. Each layer in the energy pyramid represents one trophic level. Producers form the base of the pyramid, the lowest trophic level, which contains the most energy. Herbivores contain less energy and make up the second level. Carnivores that feed on herbivores form the next level, and carnivores that feed on other carnivores make up the top level. Organisms in the upper trophic levels store less energy than herbivores and producers. A pyramid is a good way to illustrate trophic levels because the pyramid becomes smaller toward the top, where less energy is available.

How Energy Loss Affects an Ecosystem The decreased amount of energy at each trophic level affects the organization of an ecosystem. First, because so much energy is lost at each level, there are fewer organisms at the higher trophic levels. For example, zebras and other herbivores outnumber lions on the African savanna by about 1,000 to 1. In this example, there simply are not enough herbivores to support more carnivores.

Second, the loss of energy from trophic level to trophic level limits the number of trophic levels in an ecosystem. Ecosystems rarely have more than four or five trophic levels because the ecosystem does not have enough energy left to support higher levels. For example, a lion typically needs up to 250 km² of land to hunt for food. Therefore, an animal that feeds on lions would have to expend a lot of energy to harvest the small amount of energy available at the top trophic level. The organisms that do feed on organisms at the top trophic level are usually small, such as parasitic worms and fleas that require a very small amount of energy.

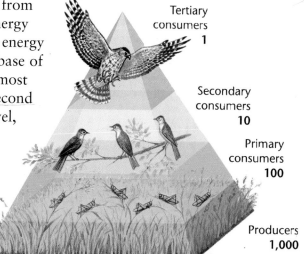

Figure 9 ▶ This energy pyramid shows how energy is lost from one trophic level to the next. The grass at the bottom level stores 1,000 times more energy than the hawk at the top level.

Tertiary consumers
1

Secondary consumers
10

Primary consumers
100

Producers
1,000

*SCi*LINKS.
www.scilinks.org
Topic: Foods Chains, Food Webs, and Trophic Levels
Code: HE80595

SECTION 1 **Review**

1. **Describe** how energy is transferred from one organism to another.

2. **Describe** the role that producers play in an ecosystem.

3. **Explain** the difference between an herbivore and an omnivore.

4. **Compare** energy transfer in a food chain to energy transfer in a food web.

CRITICAL THINKING

5. **Interpreting Graphics** Look at Figure 8. What feeding relationships does the crabeater seal have?

6. **Inferring Relationships** Read the paragraph under the heading "Trophic Levels" in this section. Could more people be supported by 20 acres of land if they ate only plants instead of both plants and animals? Explain your answer. **READING SKILLS**

The Cycling of Materials

Objectives

▶ Describe the short-term and long-term process of the carbon cycle.

▶ Identify one way that humans are affecting the carbon cycle.

▶ List the three stages of the nitrogen cycle.

▶ Describe the role that nitrogen-fixing bacteria play in the nitrogen cycle.

▶ Explain how the excess use of fertilizer can affect the nitrogen and phosphorus cycles.

Key Terms

carbon cycle
nitrogen-fixing bacteria
nitrogen cycle
phosphorus cycle

What will happen to the next ballpoint pen you buy? You will probably use it until its ink supply runs out and then throw it away. The plastic and steel the pen is made of will probably never be reused. By contrast, materials in ecosystems are constantly reused. In this section, you will read about three cycles by which materials are reused—the carbon cycle, the nitrogen cycle, and the phosphorus cycle.

The Carbon Cycle

Carbon is an essential component of proteins, fats, and carbohydrates, which make up all organisms. The **carbon cycle** is a process by which carbon is cycled between the atmosphere, land, water, and organisms. As shown in **Figure 10**, carbon enters a short-term cycle in an ecosystem when producers, such as plants, convert carbon dioxide in the atmosphere into carbohydrates during photosynthesis. When consumers eat producers, the consumers obtain carbon from the carbohydrates. As the consumers break down the food during cellular respiration, some of the carbon is released back into the atmosphere as carbon dioxide. Organisms that make their own food through photosynthesis also release carbon dioxide during cellular respiration.

Some carbon enters a long-term cycle. For example, carbon may be converted into *carbonates,* which make up the hard parts of bones and shells. Bones and shells do not break down easily.

Figure 10 ▶ The Carbon Cycle
Carbon moves between air, water, soil, and organisms. What role do plants play in the carbon cycle?

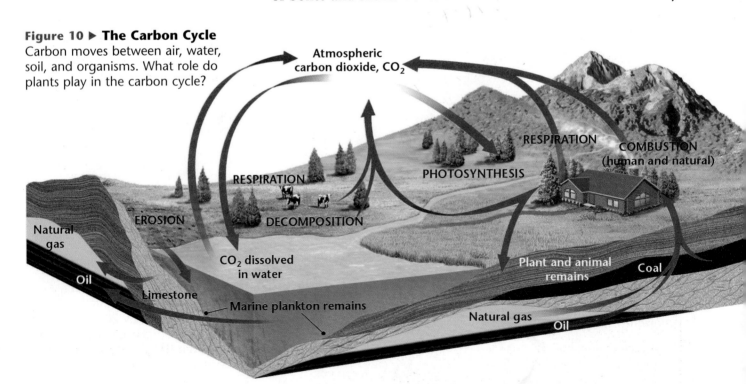

Over millions of years, carbonate deposits have produced huge formations of limestone rocks. Limestone is one of the largest *carbon sinks,* or carbon reservoirs, on Earth.

Some carbohydrates in organisms are converted into fats, oils, and other molecules that store energy. The carbon in carbohydrates and these other molecules may be released into the soil or air after an organism dies. These molecules can form deposits of coal, oil, and natural gas underground. The deposits are known as *fossil fuels.* Fossil fuels are made up of carbon compounds from the bodies of organisms that died millions of years ago.

How Humans Affect the Carbon Cycle When we burn fossil fuels, we release carbon into the atmosphere as carbon dioxide. Cars, factories, and power plants rely on these fossil fuels to operate. In the year 2000, vehicles, such as the truck in **Figure 11,** were the source of one-third of all carbon dioxide emitted in the United States. Each year, about 6 billion metric tons of carbon are released into the atmosphere as carbon dioxide by the burning of fossil fuels and the natural burning of wood in forest fires. About half of this carbon dioxide remains in the atmosphere. As a result, the amount of carbon dioxide in the atmosphere has steadily increased.

Increased levels of carbon dioxide may contribute to global warming, which is an overall increase in the temperature of the Earth. What happens to the carbon dioxide that does not remain in the atmosphere? Scientists estimate that, each year, over a billion metric tons of carbon dioxide dissolves into the ocean, which is a carbon sink. Plants probably absorb the remaining carbon dioxide.

Reading Check How can driving a car affect the carbon cycle?

Figure 11 ▶ This truck releases carbon into the atmosphere when it burns fuel to operate.

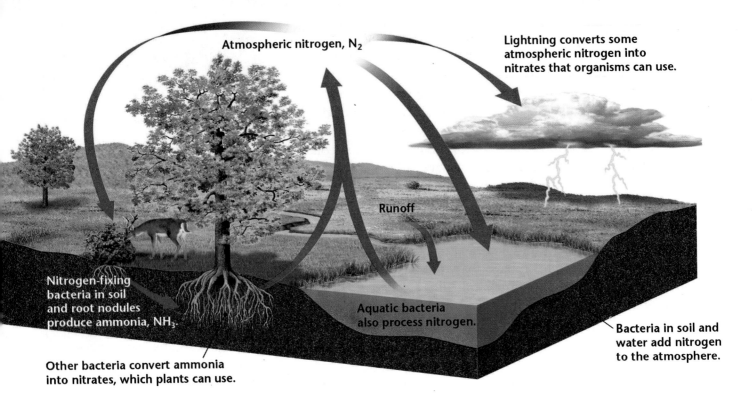

Atmospheric nitrogen, N₂

Lightning converts some atmospheric nitrogen into nitrates that organisms can use.

Runoff

Nitrogen-fixing bacteria in soil and root nodules produce ammonia, NH₃.

Aquatic bacteria also process nitrogen.

Bacteria in soil and water add nitrogen to the atmosphere.

Other bacteria convert ammonia into nitrates, which plants can use.

Figure 12 ▶ The Nitrogen Cycle
Nitrogen could not be cycled in the atmosphere without nitrogen-fixing bacteria. What role do animals play in the nitrogen cycle?

Figure 13 ▶ The swellings on the roots of this soybean plant are called *nodules*. Nitrogen-fixing bacteria, shown magnified at the top right, live inside the nodules of some plants.

The Nitrogen Cycle

All organisms need nitrogen to build *proteins,* which are used to build new cells. Nitrogen makes up 78 percent of the gases in the atmosphere. However, most organisms cannot use atmospheric nitrogen. It must be altered, or fixed, before organisms can use it. The only organisms that can fix atmospheric nitrogen into chemical compounds are a few species of bacteria known as **nitrogen-fixing bacteria.** All other organisms depend upon these bacteria to supply nitrogen. Nitrogen-fixing bacteria are a crucial part of the **nitrogen cycle,** a process in which nitrogen is cycled between the atmosphere, bacteria, and other organisms. As shown in **Figure 12,** bacteria take nitrogen gas from the air and transform it into molecules that living things can use.

Nitrogen-fixing bacteria, shown in **Figure 13,** live in nodules on the roots of plants called *legumes.* Legumes include beans, peas, and clover. The bacteria use sugars provided by the legumes to produce nitrogen-containing compounds such as nitrates. The excess nitrogen fixed by the bacteria is released into the soil. In addition, some nitrogen-fixing bacteria live in the soil rather than inside the roots of legumes. Plants that do not have nitrogen-fixing bacteria in their roots get nitrogen from the soil. Animals get nitrogen by eating plants or other animals, both of which are sources of usable nitrogen.

Decomposers and the Nitrogen Cycle In the nitrogen cycle, nitrogen moves between the atmosphere and living things. Some of the nitrogen that cycles from the atmosphere to living things is released to the soil with the help of bacteria. These decomposers are essential to the nitrogen cycle because they break down wastes, such as urine, dung, leaves, and other decaying plants and animals and return the nitrogen that these wastes contain to the soil. If decomposers did not exist, much of the nitrogen in ecosystems would be stored forever in wastes, corpses, and other parts of organisms. After decomposers return the nitrogen to the soil, bacteria transform a small amount of the nitrogen into nitrogen gas, which then returns to the atmosphere. So, most of the nitrogen that enters an ecosystem stays within the ecosystem. It cycles between organisms and the soil, and is constantly reused.

The Phosphorus Cycle

The element phosphorus is part of many molecules that make up the cells of living organisms. For example, phosphorus is needed to form bones and teeth in animals. Plants get the phosphorus they need from soil and water, while animals get their phosphorus by eating plants or other animals that have eaten plants. The **phosphorus cycle** is the movement of phosphorus from the environment to organisms and then back to the environment. This cycle is slow and does not normally include the atmosphere because phosphorus rarely occurs as a gas.

As shown in **Figure 14,** phosphorus may enter soil and water in a few ways. When rocks erode, small amounts of phosphorus dissolve as phosphate in soil and water. Plants absorb phosphates in the soil through their roots. In addition, phosphorus is added to soil and water when excess phosphorus is excreted in waste from organisms and when organisms die and decompose. Some phosphorus also washes off the land and eventually ends up in the ocean. Many phosphate salts are not soluble in water, so they sink to the bottom of the ocean and accumulate as sediment.

SCILINKS.
www.scilinks.org
Topic: Nitrogen Cycle
Code: HE81036

Geofact

Minerals in Your Mouth
Phosphorus is the 11th most abundant element in the Earth's crust and occurs naturally as phosphate in the mineral apatite. Apatite can exist in igneous, metamorphic, and sedimentary rocks as well as in your teeth and bones.

Figure 14 ▶ The Phosphorus Cycle Phosphorus moves from phosphate deposits in rock to the land, then to living organisms, and finally to the ocean.

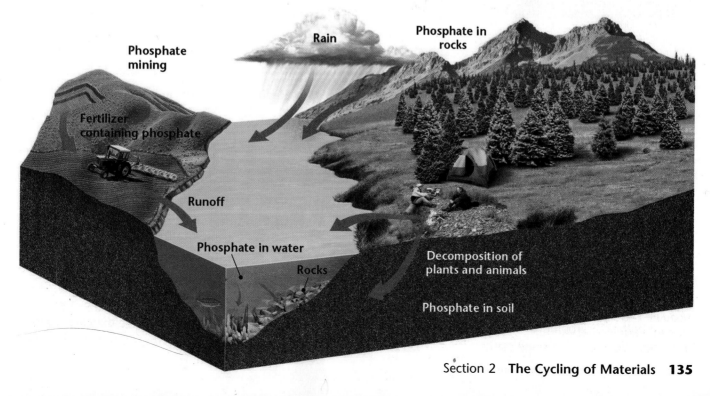

Figure 15 ▶ More than 30 percent of fertilizer may flow with runoff from farmland into nearby waterways. Large amounts of fertilizer in water can cause an excessive growth of algae (below).

Fertilizers and the Nitrogen and Phosphorus Cycles People often apply fertilizers to stimulate and maximize plant growth. Fertilizers contain both nitrogen and phosphorus. If excessive amounts of fertilizer are used, the fertilizer can enter terrestrial and aquatic ecosystems through runoff. Excess nitrogen and phosphorus in an aquatic ecosystem or nearby waterway can cause rapid and overabundant growth of algae, which results in an *algal bloom*. An algal bloom, as shown in **Figure 15,** is a dense, visible patch of algae that occurs near the surface of water. Algal blooms, along with other plants and the bacteria that break down dead algae, can deplete an aquatic ecosystem of important nutrients such as oxygen. Fish and other aquatic organisms need oxygen to survive.

Acid Precipitation We affect the nitrogen cycle when we burn fuel, because nitric oxide is released into the atmosphere. Nitric oxide can combine with oxygen and water vapor in the atmosphere to form nitric acid. Nitric acid can dissolve in rain and snow, which contributes to acid precipitation.

✓ **Reading Check** How do algal blooms harm aquatic ecosystems?

SECTION 2 **Review**

1. **Describe** the two processes of the carbon cycle.

2. **Describe** how the burning of fossil fuels affects the carbon cycle.

3. **Explain** how the excessive use of fertilizer affects the nitrogen cycle and the phosphorus cycle.

4. **Explain** why the phosphorus cycle occurs more slowly than both the carbon cycle and the nitrogen cycle.

CRITICAL THINKING

5. **Making Comparisons** Write a short paragraph that describes the importance of bacteria in the carbon, nitrogen, and phosphorus cycles. What role do bacteria play in each cycle? **WRITING SKILLS**

6. **Applying Ideas** What is one way that a person can help to reduce the level of carbon dioxide in the atmosphere? Can you think of more than one way?

SECTION 3

SCSh.2.a; SCSh.2.b; SCSh.3.c; SCSh.3.e;
SCSh.6.a; SCSh.6.b; SCSh.6.c; SEV.1.a;
SEV.1.b; SEV.1.d; SEV.1.e; SEV.5.c

How Ecosystems Change

Ecosystems are constantly changing. A forest hundreds of years old may have been a shallow lake a thousand years ago. A dead tree falls and lets sunlight reach the forest floor. The sunlight causes some seeds to germinate, and soon wildflowers and shrubs cover the forest floor. Mosses, shrubs, and small trees cover the concrete of a demolished city building. These are all examples of an environmental change called ecological succession.

Ecological Succession

Ecological succession is a gradual process of change and replacement of some or all of the species in a community. Ecological succession may take hundreds or thousands of years. Each new community that arises makes it harder for the previous community to survive. For example, the younger beech trees in **Figure 16** will have a hard time competing with older beech trees for sunlight. However, if a shade-loving species of tree began to grow in the forest, the new species might replace the smaller beech trees.

Primary succession is the type of succession that occurs on a surface where no ecosystem existed before, such as on rocks or sand dunes. **Secondary succession,** the more common type of succession, occurs on a surface where an ecosystem has previously existed. Secondary succession occurs in ecosystems that have been disturbed or disrupted by humans or animals, or by natural processes such as storms, floods, earthquakes, and volcanoes.

✓ **Reading Check** How is secondary succession different from primary succession?

Objectives

▶ List two types of ecological succession.

▶ Explain how a pioneer species contributes to ecological succession.

▶ Explain what happens during old-field succession.

▶ Describe how lichens contribute to primary succession.

Key Terms

ecological succession
primary succession
secondary succession
pioneer species
climax community

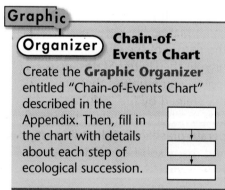

Graphic Organizer

Chain-of-Events Chart
Create the **Graphic Organizer** entitled "Chain-of-Events Chart" described in the Appendix. Then, fill in the chart with details about each step of ecological succession.

Figure 16 ▶ Taller beech trees compete with shorter, young beech trees for sun and make it hard for the younger trees to survive.

Section 3   **137**

Figure 17 ▶ When Mount St. Helens erupted in 1980, much of the forest around the volcano was destroyed.

Secondary Succession In 1980, the volcano Mount St. Helens erupted in Washington State. The eruption at Mount St. Helens has been described as one of the worst volcanic disasters because more than 44,460 acres of forest were burned and flattened by the force of hot ash and other volcanic debris, as shown in **Figure 17**. After the eruption, plants began to colonize the volcanic debris. Such plants are called **pioneer species**—the first organisms to colonize any newly available area and begin the process of ecological succession. Over time, pioneer species will make the new area habitable for other species. If you visited Mount St. Helens today, you would find secondary succession. **Figure 18** shows how after 12 years, plants and flowers had covered most of the lava and new trees and shrubs had started to grow. If these organisms at Mount St. Helens continue to grow, over time they will eventually form a climax community. A **climax community** is a final and stable

Communities Maintained by Fire

Fires set by lightning or human activities occasionally sweep through large areas. Burned areas undergo secondary succession. In the forests of the Rocky Mountains, for example, burned areas are rapidly colonized by fireweed, which clothes the slopes with purple flowers. In some places, fire determines the nature of the climax community. In the United States, ecological communities that are maintained by fire include the chaparral of California, the temperate grassland of the Midwest, and many southern and western pine forests.

Plants native to these communities are adapted to living with fire. A wildfire that is not unusually hot may not harm fire-adapted pine trees, but it can kill deciduous trees—those trees that lose their leaves in winter. Seeds of

▶ Fireweed is one type of plant that colonizes land after the land has been burned by fire.

some species will not germinate until exposed to temperatures of several hundred degrees. When a fire sweeps through a forest, the fire kills plants on the ground and stimulates the seeds to germinate.

Longleaf pines have a strange growth pattern. When they are young, they have long needles that reach down to the ground. The trees remain only about a half of a meter high for many years, while they store nutrients. If a fire occurs, it sweeps through the tops of the tall trees that survived the last fire. The young longleaf pines near the ground may escape the fire. Then, the young pines use their stored food to grow very rapidly. A young pine can grow as much as 2 m each year. Soon the young pines are tall enough so that a fire near the ground would not harm them.

If regular fires are prevented in a fire-adapted community, deciduous trees may invade the area. These trees form a thick barrier near the ground. In addition, their dead leaves and branches pile up on the ground

community. Even though a climax community continues to change in small ways, this type of community may remain the same through time if it is not disturbed.

Fire and Secondary Succession Natural fires caused by lightning are a natural cause of secondary succession in some communities, as discussed in the Case Study below. Some species of trees, such as the Jack pine, can release their seeds only after they have been exposed to the intense heat of a fire. Minor forest fires remove accumulations of brush and deadwood that would otherwise contribute to major fires that burn out of control. Some animal species also depend on occasional fires because they feed on the vegetation that sprouts after a fire has cleared the land. Therefore, foresters sometimes allow natural fires to burn unless the fires are a threat to human life or property.

Figure 18 ▶ The photo above was taken 12 years after the eruption of Mount St. Helens and shows secondary succession.

▶ These young lodgepole pine trees have started growing after a devastating forest fire.

▶ This firefighter is helping to maintain a controlled fire in South Dakota.

and form extra fuel for fires. When a fire does occur, it is hotter and more severe than usual. The fire destroys not only the deciduous trees but also the pines. It may end up as a devastating wildfire.

Although it may seem odd, frequent burning is essential to preserve many plant communities and the animals that depend on them. This is the reason the U.S. National Park Service adopted the policy of letting fires in national parks burn if

they do not endanger human life or property.

This policy caused a public outcry when fires burned Yellowstone National Park in 1988, because people did not understand the ecology of fire-adapted communities. The fires later became an opportunity for visitors to learn about the changes in an ecosystem after a fire.

CRITICAL THINKING

1. Understanding Processes
Explain how a longleaf pine tree might be more likely to survive a forest fire than a deciduous tree, such as a maple or oak tree.

2. Understanding Concepts
Why must controlled fires be set in some ecosystems? What are the advantages? What are the disadvantages?

| Year 1: annual plants | Year 2: perennial plants and grasses | Year 3–10: shrubs | About year 20: young pine forest | After about 150 years: mature oak forest |

Figure 19 ▶ The illustration above shows what an abandoned farm area might look like during old-field succession. Why do you think young oak trees begin to appear around year 20?

FIELD ACTIVITY

Investigating Succession
Explore two or three blocks in your neighborhood, and find evidence of succession. Make notes in your *EcoLog* about the location and the evidence of succession that you observe. Pay attention to sidewalks, curbs, streets, vacant lots, and buildings, as well as parks, gardens, fields, and other open areas. Create a map from your data that identifies where succession is taking place in your neighborhood.

Old-field Succession Another example of secondary succession is *old-field succession*, which occurs when farmland is abandoned. When a farmer stops cultivating a field, grasses and weeds quickly grow and cover the abandoned land. The pioneer grasses and weeds grow rapidly and produce many seeds to cover large areas.

Over time, taller plants, such as grasses, grow in the area. These plants shade the ground, keeping light from the shorter plants. The long roots of the taller plants also absorb most of the water in the soil. The pioneer plants soon die from lack of sunlight and water. As succession continues, the taller plants are deprived of light and water by growing trees. Finally, slower-growing trees, such as oaks, hickories, beeches, and maples, take over the area and block sunlight to the smaller trees. As shown in **Figure 19,** the area can eventually establish a climax community dominated by a mature oak forest.

Primary Succession On new islands created by volcanic eruptions, in areas exposed when a glacier retreats, or on any other surface that has not previously supported life, primary succession can occur. Primary succession is much slower than secondary succession because primary succession begins where there is no soil. It can take several hundred to several thousand years to produce fertile soil naturally. Imagine that a glacier melts and exposes an area of bare rock. The first pioneer species to colonize the bare rock will probably be bacteria and lichens, which can live without soil. Lichens, as shown in **Figure 20,** are important early pioneers in primary succession. They are the colorful, flaky patches that you see on trees and rocks. A lichen is a producer that is actually composed of two different species, a fungus and an alga. The alga photosynthesizes, while the fungus absorbs nutrients from rocks and holds water. Together, they begin to break down the rock.

As the growth of the lichen breaks down the rock, water may freeze and thaw in cracks, which further breaks up the rock. Soil slowly accumulates as dust particles in the air are trapped in cracks in the rock. Dead remains of lichens and bacteria add to the soil in the cracks. Mosses may increase in number and break up the rock even more. When the mosses die, they decay and add nutrients to the growing pile of soil. Thus, fertile soil forms from the broken rock, decayed organisms, water, and air. Primary succession can also be seen in any city street, as shown in **Figure 20**. Mosses, lichens, and weeds can establish themselves in cracks in a sidewalk or building. As well, fungi and mosses can invade a roof that needs repair. Even New York City would eventually turn into a cement-filled woodland if it were not constantly maintained.

Reading Check What is an example of primary succession in a city?

SCⁱ**LINKS**
www.scilinks.org
Topic: Ecological
        Succession
Code: HE80461

Figure 20 ▶ Lichens (left) are colonizing a boulder in Wyoming. Over a long period of time, lichens can break down rock into soil. Plants that grow through cracks in city sidewalks (below) can also be described as pioneers of primary succession.

SECTION 3 **Review**

1. **Compare** primary and secondary succession.

2. **Describe** what role a pioneer species plays during the process of ecological succession.

3. **Explain** why putting out forest fires may be damaging in the long run.

4. **Describe** the role lichens play in primary succession. Write a short paragraph to explain your answer. **WRITING SKILLS**

CRITICAL THINKING

5. **Analyzing Processes** Over a period of 1,000 years, a lake becomes a maple forest. Is this process primary or secondary succession? Explain your answer.

6. **Analyzing Relationships** How are lichens similar to the pioneer species that colonize abandoned farm areas? How are they different?

CHAPTER 5 Highlights

1 Energy Flow in Ecosystems

Key Terms

photosynthesis, 125
producer, 126
consumer, 126
decomposer, 127
cellular respiration, 128
food chain, 130
food web, 130
trophic level, 130

Main Ideas

▶ The majority of the Earth's organisms depend on the sun for energy. Producers harness the sun's energy directly through photosynthesis, while consumers use the sun's energy indirectly by eating producers or other consumers.

▶ The paths of energy transfer can be followed through food chains, food webs, and trophic levels.

▶ Only about 10 percent of the energy that an organism consumes is transferred to the next trophic level when the organism is eaten.

2 The Cycling of Materials

Key Terms

carbon cycle, 132
nitrogen-fixing bacteria, 134
nitrogen cycle, 134
phosphorus cycle, 135

Main Ideas

▶ Materials in ecosystems are recycled and reused by natural processes.

▶ Carbon, nitrogen, and phosphorus are essential for life. Each of these elements follows a recognizable cycle.

▶ Humans can affect the cycling of materials in an ecosystem through activities such as burning fossil fuels and applying fertilizer to soil.

3 How Ecosystems Change

Key Terms

ecological succession, 137
primary succession, 137
secondary succession, 137
pioneer species, 138
climax community, 138

Main Ideas

▶ After a disturbance, organisms in an environment follow a pattern of change over time, known as ecological succession.

▶ Primary succession occurs on a surface where no ecosystem existed before. Secondary succession occurs on a surface where an ecosystem existed before.

▶ Climax communities are made up of organisms that take over an ecosystem and remain until the ecosystem is disturbed again.

Using Key Terms

Use each of the following terms in a separate sentence.

1. *photosynthesis*
2. *trophic level*
3. *carbon cycle*
4. *nitrogen-fixing bacteria*
5. *decomposers*

For each pair of terms, explain how the meanings of the terms differ.

6. *producer* and *consumer*
7. *primary succession* and *secondary succession*
8. *nitrogen cycle* and *phosphorus cycle*
9. *food chain* and *food web*

✔ **STUDY TIP**

Taking Multiple-Choice Tests When you take multiple-choice tests, be sure to read all of the choices before you pick the correct answer. Be patient, and eliminate choices that are obviously incorrect.

Understanding Key Ideas

10. Which of the following statements is *not* true of consumers?
    a. They get energy indirectly from the sun.
    b. They are also called *heterotrophs*.
    c. They make their own food.
    d. They sometimes eat other consumers.

11. Which of the following is correctly arranged from the lowest trophic level to the highest trophic level?
    a. bacteria, frog, eagle, raccoon
    b. algae, deer, wolf, hawk
    c. grass, mouse, snake, eagle
    d. grass, bass, minnow, snake

12. Communities of bacteria have been found living thousands of feet underwater. Which of the following statements is a proper conclusion to draw about these bacteria?
    a. Somehow they are conducting photosynthesis.
    b. They are living on borrowed time.

c. They were somehow introduced by human activities.
d. They use an energy source other than sunlight.

13. Which of the following pairs of organisms probably belong to the same trophic level?
    a. humans and bears
    b. bears and deer
    c. humans and cows
    d. both (a) and (c)

14. The energy lost between trophic levels
    a. can be captured only by parasitic organisms.
    b. cools the surrounding environment.
    c. is used in the course of normal living.
    d. evaporates in the atmosphere.

15. From producer to secondary consumer, about what percentage of energy is lost?
    a. 10 percent
    b. 90 percent
    c. 99 percent
    d. 100 percent

16. Which of the following statements about the nitrogen cycle is *not* true?
    a. Animals get nitrogen by eating plants or other animals.
    b. Plants generate nitrogen in their roots.
    c. Nitrogen moves back and forth between the atmosphere and living things.
    d. Decomposers break down waste to yield ammonia.

17. Which of the following are most likely to be the pioneer organisms on an area of bare rock?
    a. trees
    b. shrubs
    c. lichens
    d. perennial grasses

18. Excessive use of fertilizer that contains nitrogen and phosphorus
    a. affects the carbon cycle.
    b. may cause algal blooms in waterways.
    c. causes soil erosion.
    d. contributes to primary succession.

Short Answer

19. Explain the relationship between cellular respiration and photosynthesis.

20. Why is the number of trophic levels that can exist limited?

21. Why are decomposers an essential part of an ecosystem?

22. Write a short paragraph that explains why the phosphorus cycle occurs slower than the carbon and nitrogen cycles. **WRITING SKILLS**

23. Describe what happens to carbon dioxide in the carbon cycle.

Interpreting Graphics

Use the diagram to answer questions 24–26.

24. How many organisms depend on the squid as a source of food?

25. If the population of Adélie penguins decreased drastically, what effect would this have on elephant seals?

26. What role do algae play in this food web?

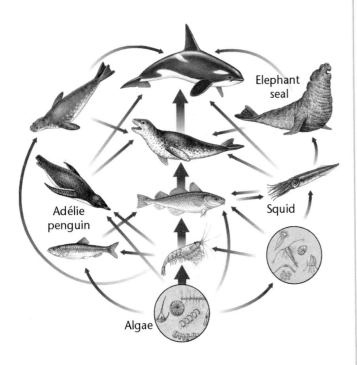

Elephant seal

Adélie penguin

Squid

Algae

Concept Mapping

27. Use the following terms to create a concept map: *algae, humans, solar energy, carnivores, consumers, producers, directly, herbivores, indirectly,* and *omnivores.*

Critical Thinking

28. Comparing Processes How are producers and decomposers opposites of each other?

29. Inferring Relationships Abandoned fields in the southwestern part of the United States are often taken over by mesquite trees, which can grow in nutrient-poor soil. If the land is later cleared of mesquite, the soil is often found to be enriched with nitrogen and is more suitable for crops. What might be the reason for this phenomenon?

30. Understanding Concepts Read the description under the head "What Eats What" in this chapter, and explain why decomposers are considered to be consumers. **READING SKILLS**

31. Drawing Conclusions Suppose that a plague eliminates all the primary consumers in an ecosystem. What will most likely happen to organisms in other trophic levels in this ecosystem?

Cross-Disciplinary Connection

32. Mathematics If a lake contains 600,000 kg of plankton and the top consumers are a population of 40 pike, which each weigh an average of 15 kg, how many trophic levels does the lake contain? Make a graph or pyramid that illustrates the trophic levels.

Portfolio Project

33. Researching Local Succession Do a special project on succession. Find areas in your community that have been cleared of vegetation and left unattended at different times in the past. Ideally, you should find several areas that were cleared at different times, including recently and decades ago. Photograph each area, and arrange the pictures to show how succession takes place in your geographic region.

Use the data in the table below to answer questions 34–35.

Percentage of Fertilizer Use per Year	
Region of the World	Percentage
North America	17
Asia	52
Africa	3
Europe	18
Latin America and the Caribbean	8
Oceania	2

34. Making Calculations If 137.25 million metric tons of fertilizer is used worldwide per year, how many million metric tons does Asia use?

35. Graphing Data Make a bar graph that compares the percentage of fertilizer use in different regions worldwide per year.

36. Communicating Main Ideas Describe the importance of the carbon, nitrogen, and phosphorus cycles to humans.

37. Writing from Research Research information on how countries regulate carbon dioxide emissions. Write an essay that describes the laws regulating carbon dioxide emissions and the solutions some countries have devised to decrease the amount of carbon dioxide emitted.

Read the passage below, and then answer the questions that follow.

The Peruvian economy and many sea birds depend on normal atmospheric conditions. But sometimes, usually in December, the normal east-to-west winds do not form over the Pacific Ocean. Instead, winds push warm water eastward toward the coast of South America. The warm surface water cuts off the upwelling of nutrients. This event is called El Niño, which means "the child," because it happens near Christmas.

Because all convection cells are linked in the atmosphere, the effects of El Niño extend beyond Peru. Under a strong El Niño, northeastern Australia can suffer summer drought, which leads to reduced grain production. The southeastern United States gets higher rainfall in El Niño years, which boosts agriculture and decreases forest fires.

1. According to the passage, a possible cause of reduced grain production in Australia is
   a. a rate of convection that is higher than the average rate.
   b. an amount of rainfall that is higher than the average amount.
   c. a reduced fish population.
   d. a summer drought.

2. According to the passage, which of the following statements is true?
   a. The effects of El Niño do not extend beyond Peru.
   b. During El Niño years, the U.S. agricultural industry suffers.
   c. El Niño is caused by winds that push warm water eastward toward South America.
   d. Australia's agricultural industry benefits the most from strong winds during El Niño.

Understanding Concepts

Directions (1–4): For *each* question, write on a separate sheet of paper the letter of the correct answer.

1 How does energy move through most ecosystems on Earth?
   A. from the sun to consumers to producers
   B. from the sun to producers to consumers to decomposers
   C. from the sun to decomposers to producers to consumers
   D. from the sun to consumers to producers back to consumers

2 Which of the following statements indicates an understanding of the importance of energy to life on Earth?
   F. Many organisms on Earth require energy for their life processes.
   G. All organisms on Earth require energy for their life processes.
   H. Energy is required for the most important life processes on Earth.
   I. The most important organisms on Earth require energy for their life purposes.

3 What role do bacteria play during the nitrogen cycle?
   A. Bacteria store nitrogen in wastes.
   B. Bacteria turn nitrogen into phosphates.
   C. Bacteria convert nitrogen into water.
   D. Bacteria turn nitrogen gas into a form that living things can use.

4 What is the process that breaks down food to yield energy called?
   F. cellular digestion
   G. cellular respiration
   H. decomposition
   I. photosynthesis

Directions (5): Write a short response for the question.

5 Ecological succession is the gradual process of changes in a community. Describe the succession process that occurs when farmland is abandoned.

Reading Skills

Directions (6–8): Read the passage below. Then answer the questions.

Carbon is an essential component of proteins, fats, and carbohydrates, which make up all organisms. The carbon cycle is one of the processes by which materials are reused in an ecosystem. This process cycles carbon between the atmosphere, land, water, and organisms. Carbon enters a short-term cycle in an ecosystem when producers convert carbon dioxide into carbohydrates during photosynthesis. When consumers eat producers, the consumers obtain carbon from the carbohydrates. As the consumers break down the food during cellular respiration, some of the carbon is released back into the atmosphere.

Some carbon enters a long-term cycle. Carbon may be converted into carbonates, which make up the hard parts of bones and shells. Over millions of years, carbonate deposits produce huge formations of limestone rock. Limestone is one of the largest carbon reservoirs on Earth.

6 During what process do producers convert carbon dioxide into carbohydrates?
   A. Carbon dioxide is converted into carbohydrates during the carbon cycle.
   B. Carbon dioxide is converted into carbohydrates during cellular respiration.
   C. Carbon dioxide is converted into carbohydrates during the eating process.
   D. Carbon dioxide is converted into carbohydrates during photosynthesis.

7 Which of the following groups are producers?
   F. animals
   G. decomposers
   H. herbivores
   I. plants

8 How is carbon converted into limestone rock?

Interpreting Graphics

Directions (9–11): For *each* question below, record the correct answer on a separate sheet of paper.

The map below shows carbon dioxide output from the burning of fossil fuels in different regions of the world. Use this map to answer questions 9 and 10.

Carbon Dioxide Output From Fossil Fuels

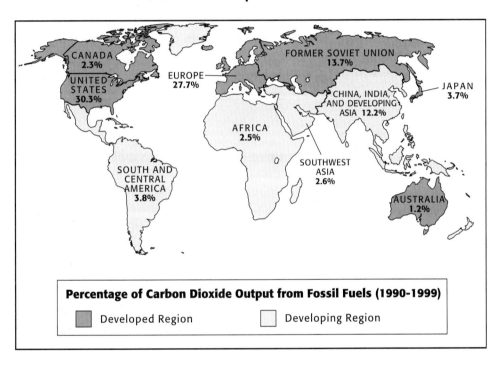

CANADA
2.3%

UNITED
STATES
30.3%

EUROPE
27.7%

FORMER SOVIET UNION
13.7%

JAPAN
3.7%

CHINA, INDIA,
AND DEVELOPING
ASIA 12.2%

AFRICA
2.5%

SOUTHWEST
ASIA
2.6%

SOUTH AND
CENTRAL
AMERICA
3.8%

AUSTRALIA
1.2%

Percentage of Carbon Dioxide Output from Fossil Fuels (1990-1999)

☐ Developed Region   ☐ Developing Region

9 Which continent has the lowest percentage of carbon dioxide output?
A. Asia
B. Australia
C. Europe
D. North America

10 What regions are responsible for the highest percentage of carbon dioxide output?
F. developed regions in the western hemisphere
G. developed regions in the eastern hemisphere
H. developing regions in the western hemisphere
I. developing regions in the eastern hemisphere

11 Which of the following is an effect of the increased burning of fossil fuels on the carbon cycle?
A. More carbonates remain in fossil fuels.
B. More carbon dioxide is absorbed by organisms.
C. More carbon dioxide is absorbed by the atmosphere.
D. More carbohydrates remain buried deep in the ground.

Test TIP

The key helps you interpret the map and get information about the different types of regions.

Exploration Lab: OBSERVATION

Objectives

▶ **Examine** the remains of an owl's diet.

▶ **USING SCIENTIFIC METHODS** **Construct** a food chain based on your observations.

Materials

disposable gloves
dissecting needle
dissecting pan
egg cartons
forceps
owl pellet(s)
piece of white paper
small animal identification
    field guide that includes skull
    illustrations

Dissecting Owl Pellets

Owls are not known as finicky eaters. They prey on almost any animal that they can swallow whole. Like many other birds, owls have an interesting adaptation—a special structure called a gizzard. The gizzard acts as a filter and prevents the indigestible parts of their prey, such as fur, feathers, and bones, from passing into their intestines. These indigestible parts are passed to a storage pouch, where they accumulate. A few hours after consuming a meal, the owl coughs up the accumulated indigestible material, which has been compressed into a pellet. By examining such a pellet, you can tell what the owl ate. In addition, by examining the remains of the owl's prey found in the pellet, you can get a good idea of what the prey ate. Using this information, you can construct a food chain of the owl and its prey.

Procedure

1. Work in groups of three or four. Place an owl pellet in the dissecting pan, and remove it from its aluminum-foil casing.

2. Examine the owl pellet. Using the dissecting needle and forceps, carefully break apart the owl pellet. Separate the fur or feathers from the bones. Be careful not to damage the small bones. Place the bones onto a piece of white paper.

3. Identify the major components of the pellet.

4. If the pellet contains remains from more than one organism, determine as best as you can how many different animals and species are present.

5. Attempt to group the remains by type of organism. Count the number of skulls to find out how many prey were in the pellet. Decide which bones belong with which skulls. Then try to assemble complete skeletons. Sample skeletal diagrams are shown below.

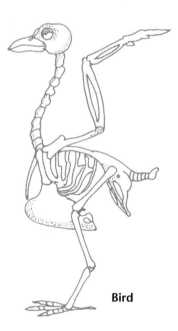

Bird

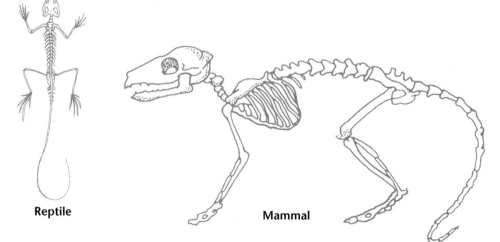

Reptile

Mammal

▶ **Types of Organisms** Use these drawings to help you determine if the organism you put together is a bird, mammal, or reptile.

6. Closely examine the skulls of each prey. Compare the skulls to the diagrams of skulls on this page. What purpose do the teeth or bills seem to have—tearing flesh, chewing plant parts, or grinding seeds? If you are able to identify the prey, find out their typical food sources.

7. On a separate piece of paper, construct a simple food chain based on your findings.

8. Compare your findings with those of other groups of students.

Analysis

1. **Examining Data** How many skeletons were you able to make from your pellet? What kinds of animals did you identify in the owl pellet?

2. **Organizing Data** Compare your findings with those of your classmates by using the following questions:

   a. What animals were represented most often in the pellets?

   b. What common traits do these animals have?

   c. How many animals found in the pellets were herbivores? How many were carnivores?

Conclusions

3. **Interpreting Information** What biological relationships were you able to determine from your examination of the owl pellet?

4. **Evaluating Data** How many different trophic levels are represented by the animals you found in the pellet?

5. **Drawing Conclusions** Most owls hunt at night and sleep during the day. From that information, what can you infer about their prey?

Extension

1. **Research and Communications** Research information on an owl species and the types of organisms found in its habitat. Make a poster of a food web, including the owl species. Be sure to include producers, consumers, and decomposers.

▶ **Identify the Prey** Use these drawings to identify the owl's prey.

Shrew

Vole

Mouse

Mole

Frog

Snake

Rat

Rabbit

DOPPLER RADAR TRACKING OF BATS AND INSECTS IN CENTRAL TEXAS

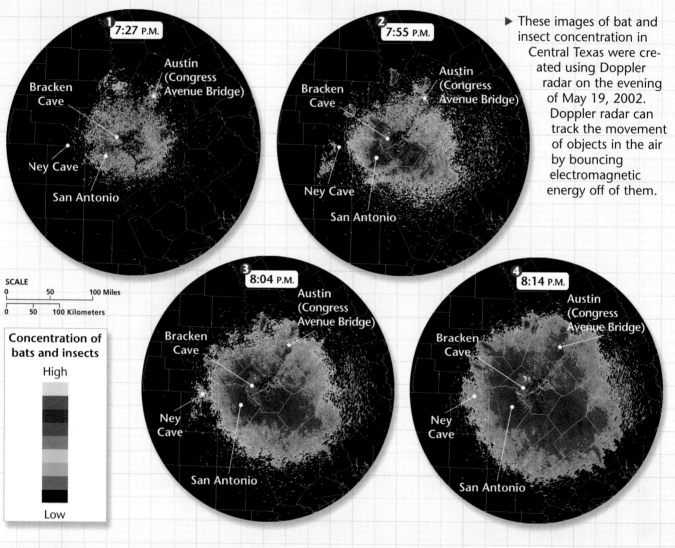

▶ These images of bat and insect concentration in Central Texas were created using Doppler radar on the evening of May 19, 2002. Doppler radar can track the movement of objects in the air by bouncing electromagnetic energy off of them.

SCALE

Concentration of bats and insects

High

Low

MAP SKILLS

Use the Doppler radar images of bats and insects in Central Texas to answer the questions below.

1. **Analyzing Data** At what time was the bat and insect concentration the lowest? At what time was the bat and insect concentration the highest?

2. **Using a Key** Use the concentration key to determine which area of Central Texas has the highest concentration of bats and insects at 8:14 P.M.

3. **Analyzing Data** Approximately how many kilometers wide is the concentration of bats and insects at 7:27 P.M.? at 8:14 P.M.?

4. **Inferring Relationships** Bracken Cave is home to 20 million bats that eat millions of pounds of insects nightly. Approximately how far is Bracken Cave from the city of San Antonio? If the bat population in the cave drastically decreased, what effect would this decrease have on the people living in San Antonio and Central Texas?

5. **Identifying Trends** These Doppler radar images of bats and insects were taken in the beginning of the summer season. How might these four images look in the month of December?

EATING THE BAIT

Most of the food we eat comes from agriculture and farming, but we also rely heavily on the fishing industry to provide us with fresh fish. Because of a high demand for fish, however, many fish species have been overharvested. Many organisms depend on these *fisheries*, places where fish are caught, to survive. The swordfish and cod fisheries of the North Atlantic and the salmon fishery off the northwestern coast of the United States are examples of fisheries that have become depleted. These fisheries now contain so few fish that harvesting the fish is not economical.

▶ **Overfishing** of organisms from higher trophic levels has forced the commercial fishing industry to harvest organisms in lower trophic levels in order to fulfill the demand for fresh fish.

Fishing Down the Food Chain

Fish such as cod, tuna, and snapper are top carnivores in ocean food chains and food webs. As these fish have disappeared, species from lower trophic levels have begun to appear in fish markets. Fish that were once swept back into the sea when they were caught in nets by accident are now being kept and sold. Organisms from lower trophic levels such as mullet, squid, mackerel, and herring, which were typically used as bait to catch larger fish, now appear on restaurant menus.

According to data from the United Nations on worldwide fish harvests, the overall trophic level at which most fish are caught has declined since the 1950s. Overfishing of organisms in lower trophic levels disrupts food chains and food webs. If the food webs of ocean ecosystems collapse, the commercial fishing industry will also collapse. For example, in the North Atlantic cod fisheries, the cod began to disappear, so the fishers concentrated on the cods' prey, which is shrimp. Cod are higher trophic level organisms, while shrimp are in the lower trophic levels and feed on algae and detritus. If the shrimp become overfished, the cod and other organisms that depend on both the shrimp and cod to survive are affected.

Creating Sustainable Fisheries

One aim of environmental science is to determine how fisheries can be managed so that they are sustainable or capable of supplying the same number of fish to be harvested each year. However, few, if any, countries manage their

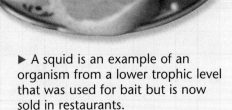

▶ A squid is an example of an organism from a lower trophic level that was used for bait but is now sold in restaurants.

fisheries in this way. Almost all countries permit unsustainable, large harvests. One solution to overfishing is to establish "no-take" zones. These are areas of the sea where no fishing is permitted. Studies have shown that fish populations grow rapidly in "no-take" zones. When a population grows in a "no-take zone," the higher trophic level organisms leave the zone and become available to fishers. "No-take" zones help populations recover and allow food chains and food webs to remain intact.

What Do You Think?

The next time you go to a fish market or seafood restaurant, take note of the different types of species for sale. Write down the names of the species, and try to assign each species to a trophic level. How many of the species for sale belong to lower trophic levels? How many belong to higher trophic levels? How do prices differ between the species for sale?

Biomes

1 What Is a Biome?

2 Forest Biomes

3 Grassland, Desert, and Tundra Biomes

PRE-READING ACTIVITY

FOLDNOTES

Four-Corner Fold

Before you read this chapter, create the **FoldNote** entitled "Four-Corner Fold" described in the Reading and Study Skills section of the Appendix. Label each flap of the four-corner fold with "Forest Biomes," "Grassland Biomes," "Desert Biomes," and "Tundra Biomes." As you read the chapter, define each biome, and write characteristics of each biome on the appropriate fold.

This thorny devil lives in the desert of Australia. The grooves in its rough skin help it collect water to drink. Water from rain or condensation lands on its back and runs along the tiny grooves to its mouth.

What Is a Biome?

 SEV.2.c

Earth is covered by many types of ecosystems. Ecologists group these ecosystems into larger areas known as biomes. A **biome** is a large region characterized by a specific type of climate and certain types of plants and animal communities. The map in **Figure 1** shows the locations of the world's major land, or terrestrial, biomes. In this chapter, you will take a tour through these terrestrial biomes—from lush rain forests to scorching deserts and the frozen tundra. When you read about each biome, notice the adaptations of the organisms to their very different environments.

Biomes and Vegetation

Biomes are described by their vegetation because the plants that grow in a certain region are the most noticeable characteristics of that region. The plants, in turn, determine the other organisms that can live there. For example, mahogany trees grow in tropical rain forests because they cannot survive cold, dry weather. Organisms that depend on mahogany trees live where trees grow.

Plants in a particular biome have these adaptations that enable them to survive there. These adaptations include size, shape, and color. For example, plants that grow in the tundra tend to be short because they cannot obtain enough water to grow larger. They also have a short summer growing season. Desert plants, such as cactuses, do not have leaves. Instead, cactuses have specialized structures to conserve and retain water.

✔ **Reading Check** How are ecosystems related to biomes? (See the Appendix for answers to Reading Checks.)

Objectives

▶ **Describe** why vegetation is used to name a biome.

▶ **Explain** how temperature and precipitation determine which plants grow in an area.

▶ **Explain** how latitude and altitude affect which plants grow in an area.

Key Terms

biome
climate
latitude
altitude

Figure 1 ▶ The ecosystems of the world can be grouped into regions called *biomes*. These biomes, shown below, are named for the vegetation that grows there.

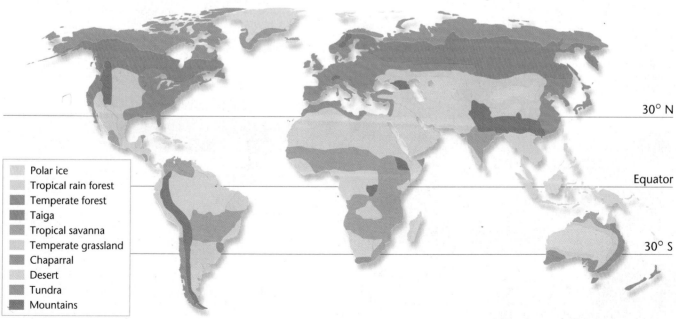

Polar ice
Tropical rain forest
Temperate forest
Taiga
Tropical savanna
Temperate grassland
Chaparral
Desert
Tundra
Mountains

30° N

Equator

30° S

Figure 2 ▶ The soil of the tundra biome is frozen most of the year. Plants such as these have about two months in summer to grow and reproduce before temperatures become too cold again.

Figure 3 ▶ Temperature and precipitation help determine the type of vegetation in an ecosystem. As temperature and precipitation decrease, the climate of an area becomes drier and vegetation becomes sparser.

Biomes and Climate

Biomes are defined by their plant life, but what factors determine which plants can grow in a certain area? The main factor is climate. **Climate** refers to the weather conditions, such as temperature, precipitation, humidity, and winds, in an area over a long period of time. Temperature and precipitation are the two most important factors that determine a region's climate.

Temperature and Precipitation Most organisms are adapted to live within a certain range of temperatures and will not survive at temperatures too far outside of their range. Plants are also affected by the length of the growing season, as shown in **Figure 2**.

Precipitation also limits the organisms that are found in a biome. All organisms need water. The larger an organism is, the more water it needs. For example, biomes that do not receive enough rainfall to support large trees support communities dominated by small trees, shrubs, and grasses. In biomes where rainfall is not frequent, the vegetation is mostly made up of cactuses and desert shrubs. In extreme cases, lack of rainfall results in no plants, no matter what the temperature is. As shown in **Figure 3**, the higher the temperature and precipitation are, the taller and denser the vegetation is. Notice how much more vegetation exists in a hot, wet tropical rain forest than in a dry desert.

✓ **Reading Check** Why does temperature limit which plants can grow in a certain biome?

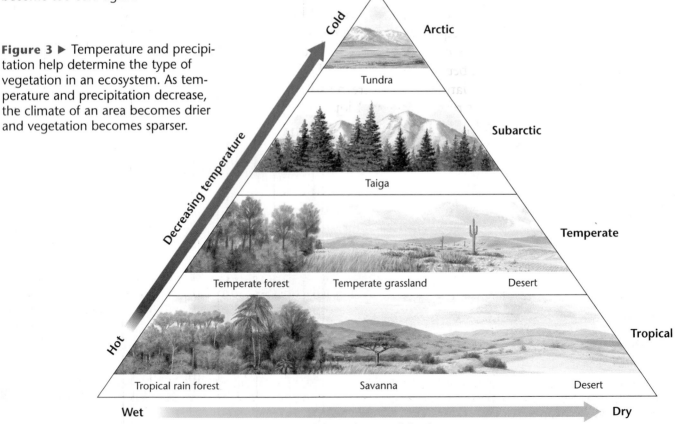

Mountains (ice and snow)

Tundra (herbs, lichens, and mosses)

Taiga (coniferous forests)

Temperate deciduous forests

Tropical rain forests

Altitude

Tropical rain forests

Temperate deciduous forests

Taiga

Tundra

Polar ice

Latitude

Figure 4 ▶ Latitude and altitude affect climate and vegetation in similar ways.

Latitude and Altitude Biomes and vegetation vary with latitude and altitude. **Latitude** is the distance north or south of the equator and is measured in degrees. **Altitude** is the height of an object above sea level. Climate varies with latitude and altitude. For example, climate gets colder as latitude and altitude increase. So, climate also gets colder as you move farther up a mountain.

Figure 4 shows that as latitude and altitude increase, biomes and vegetation change. For example, the trees of tropical rain forests usually grow closer to the equator, while the mosses and lichens of the tundra usually grow closer to the poles. The land located in the temperate region, between about 30° and 60° north latitudes and 30° and 60° south latitudes, is where most of the food in the world is grown. This region includes biomes such as temperate forests and grasslands, which usually have the moderate temperatures and fertile soil that are ideal for agriculture.

SC*LINKS*®
www.scilinks.org
Topic: Biomes
Code: HE80158

SECTION 1 **Review**

1. **Describe** how plants determine the name of a biome.

2. **Explain** how temperature affects which plants grow in an area.

3. **Explain** how precipitation affects which plants grow in an area.

4. **Define** *latitude* and *altitude.* How is latitude different from altitude? How do these factors affect the organisms that live in a biome?

CRITICAL THINKING

5. **Making Inferences** The equator passes through the country of Ecuador. But the climate in Ecuador can range from hot and humid to cool and dry. Write a short paragraph that explains what might cause this range in climate. **WRITING SKILLS**

6. **Analyzing Relationships** Look at Figure 1, and locate the equator and 30° north latitude. Which biomes are located between these two lines?

Forest Biomes

Objectives

▶ List three characteristics of tropical rain forests.

▶ Name and describe the main layers of a tropical rain forest.

▶ Describe one plant in a temperate deciduous forest and an adaptation that helps the plant survive.

▶ Describe one adaptation that may help an animal survive in the taiga.

▶ Name two threats to the world's forest biomes.

Key Terms

tropical rain forest
emergent layer
canopy
epiphyte
understory
temperate rain forest
temperate deciduous forest
taiga

The air is hot and heavy with humidity. You walk through the shade of the tropical rain forest, step carefully over tangles of roots and vines, and brush past enormous leaves. Life is all around you, but you see little vegetation on the forest floor. Birds call, and monkeys chatter from above.

Tropical Rain Forests

Of all the biomes in the world, forest biomes are the most widespread and are home to the greatest diversity of plants, animals, and other organisms. Trees need a lot of water, so forests exist where precipitation is plentiful. Tropical forests, temperate forests, and taiga are the main forest biomes.

Tropical rain forests are located in a belt around the Earth near the equator, as shown in **Figure 5**. They help regulate world climate and play vital roles in the nitrogen, oxygen, and carbon cycles. Tropical rain forests are always humid and warm and get about 200 to 450 cm of rain a year. Because they are near the equator, tropical rain forests get strong sunlight year-round and maintain a relatively constant temperature year-round. This climate is ideal for a wide variety of plants and animals, as shown in **Figure 6**. The warm, wet conditions also nourish more species of plants than any other biome does. While one hectare (10,000 m^2) of temperate forest usually contains a few species of trees, the same area of tropical rain forest may contain more than 100 species.

▶ Glasswing butterflies live in the rain forests of Costa Rica.

▶ The *Rafflessia keithii* flower grows in the rain forests of Borneo.

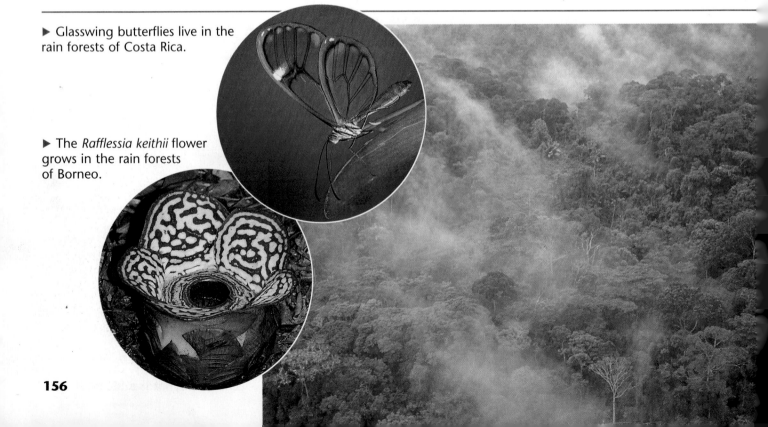

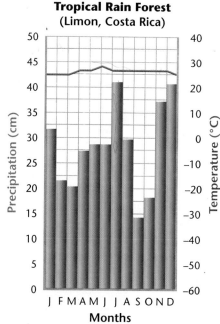

Tropical Rain Forest
(Limon, Costa Rica)

Nutrients in Tropical Rain Forests You might think that the diverse plant life grows on rich soil, but it does not. Most nutrients are within plants, not within soil. Organic matter decays quickly in hot, wet conditions. Decomposers on the rain-forest floor break down organic matter and return the nutrients to the soil, but plants quickly absorb the nutrients. Some trees in a tropical rain forest support fungi that feed on dead organic matter on the rain-forest floor. In this relationship, the fungi transfer the nutrients from the dead organic matter directly to the tree.

The nutrients are removed so efficiently from the soil in a tropical rain forest that water running out of the soil may be as clear as distilled water. Most tropical soils that are cleared of plants for agriculture lack nutrients and cannot support crops for more than a few years. Many of the trees form above-ground roots, called buttresses or braces, that grow sideways from the trees and provide the trees with extra support in the thin soil.

Figure 5 ▶ The world's tropical rain forests have heavy rainfall during much of the year and fairly constant, high temperatures.

Figure 6 ▶ Species of Tropical Rain Forests

▶ These mountain gorillas live in the rain forests of Rwanda.

▶ The tropical rain forests in the Andes mountains in Ecuador are among the wettest places on Earth.

▶ Scarlet macaws live in the trees of rain forests of Peru.

Emergent layer

Upper canopy

Lower canopy

Understory

Bright light

Filtered light

Dense shade

Figure 7 ▶ The plants in tropical rain forests form distinct layers. The plants in each layer are adapted to a particular level of light. The taller trees absorb the most light, while the plants near the forest floor are adapted to growing in the shade.

Layers of the Rain Forest In tropical rain forests, different types of plants grow in different layers, as shown in **Figure 7.** The four main layers above the forest floor are the emergent layer, the upper canopy, the lower canopy, and the understory. The top layer is called the **emergent layer.** This layer consists of the tallest trees, which reach heights of 60 to 70 m. Trees in the emergent layer grow and emerge into direct sunlight.

The next layer, considered the primary layer of the rain forest, is called the **canopy.** Trees in the canopy can grow more than 30 m tall. The tall trees form a dense layer that absorbs up to 95 percent of the sunlight. The canopy can be split into an upper canopy and a lower canopy. The lower canopy receives less light than the upper canopy does. Plants called **epiphytes,** such as the orchid in **Figure 8,** use the entire surface of a tree as a place to live. Epiphytes grow on tall trees for support. Some grow high in the canopy, where their leaves can reach the sunlight needed for photosynthesis. Growing on tall trees also allows them to absorb the water and nutrients that run down the tree after it rains. Most animals that live in the rain forest live in the canopy because they depend on the abundant flowers and fruits that grow there.

Below the canopy, very little light reaches the next layer, called the **understory.** Trees and shrubs that are adapted to shade grow here. Most plants in the understory do not grow more than 3.5 m tall. Herbs with large, flat leaves grow on the forest floor. These plants capture the small amount of sunlight that penetrates the understory. Most of our house plants are native to tropical rain-forest floors. Because they are adapted to low levels of light, they are able to grow indoors.

Reading Check In which layer of the rain forest is most of the animal life found?

Species Diversity in Rain Forests

The tropical rain forest is the biome with the greatest amount of species diversity. The diversity of rain-forest vegetation has led to the evolution of a diverse community of animals. Most rain-forest animals are specialists that use specific resources in particular ways. Some rain-forest animals have amazing adaptations for capturing prey, and other animals have adaptations that they use to escape predators. For example, the collared anteater in **Figure 8** uses its long tongue to reach insects in small cracks and holes where other animals cannot reach. The wreathed hornbill (shown below) uses its strong, curved beak to crack open nutshells. Insects, such as the Costa Rican mantis in **Figure 8,** use camouflage to avoid predators. These insects may be shaped like leaves or twigs.

Ecofact

A Little Land, A Lot of Species

Tropical rain forests cover less than 7 percent of Earth's land surface but contain at least 50 percent of all the plant and animal species in the world.

Figure 8 ▶ Examples of plant and animal adaptations in the tropical rain forest include ❶ the long tongue of a collared anteater, ❷ the strong, curved beak of a wreathed hornbill, ❸ the shape of a Costa Rican mantis, and ❹ an orchid attached to a tall tree.

Threats to Rain Forests Tropical rain forests once covered about 20 percent of Earth's surface. Today, they cover only about 7 percent. Every minute of every day, 100 acres of tropical rain forest are cleared for logging operations, agriculture, or oil exploration. *Habitat destruction* occurs when land inhabited by an organism is destroyed or altered. Habitat destruction is the usual reason for a species becoming extinct.

An estimated 50 million people live in tropical rain forests. These people are also threatened by habitat destruction. Their food, building materials, culture, and traditions come from and are uniquely connected to the rain forest. The loss of this habitat destroys their way of life.

Plants and animals that live in rain forests are also threatened by trading. Many plant species found only in tropical rain forests are valuable and marketable to industries. Animals are threatened by exotic-pet trading. Some exotic-pet traders illegally trap animals, such as parrots, and sell them in pet stores at high prices.

✓ **Reading Check** What are two main threats to the organisms that live in tropical rain forests?

SCiLINKS.
www.scilinks.org
Topic: Threats to
Rain Forests
Code: HE81521

CASE STUDY

Deforestation, Climate, and Floods

A plant absorbs water from the soil through its roots and transports the water to its stems and leaves. Water then evaporates from pores in plant leaves into the atmosphere through a process called *transpiration*. A large tree may transpire as much as 5 tons of water on a hot day. Water absorbs heat when it evaporates. Therefore, the temperature is much cooler under a tree on a hot day than under a wood or brick shelter. Trees that provide shade around homes keep homes much cooler in the summer.

When rain falls on a forest, much of the rain is absorbed by plant roots and transpired into the air as water vapor. Water vapor forms rain clouds. Much of this water will fall as rain somewhere downwind from the forest. Because of the role trees play in

transpiration, *deforestation,* the clearing of trees, can change the climate. If a forest is cut down or replaced by smaller plants, much of the rainfall is not absorbed by plants. Instead, the rain runs off the soil and causes flooding as well as soil erosion. The climate downwind from the forest becomes drier.

Deforestation led to the disastrous flooding of the Yangtze River in China in 1998. More than 2,000 people died in the floods, and at least 13 million people had to leave their homes. When the Yangtze River flooded, the water poured into a flood plain where over 400 million people lived. It is estimated that 85 percent of the forest in the Yangtze River basin has been cut down. The millions of tons of water that these trees once absorbed now

▶ A man makes his way past flooded buildings in his street on a makeshift raft after the Yangtze River flooded in July 1998. Water of the Yangtze River reached record-high levels.

flow freely down the river and spread across fields and into towns during the seasonal monsoon rains.

Deforestation has also caused terrible floods in places such as Bangladesh. The Ganges River starts high in the Himalaya Mountains and flows through Bangladesh. Deforestation of the Himalaya

Temperate Forests

Temperate rain forest occurs in North America, Australia, and New Zealand. Temperate rain forests have large amounts of precipitation, high humidity, and moderate temperatures. The Pacific Northwest shown, in **Figure 9,** houses North America's only temperate rain forest, where tree branches are draped with mosses and tree trunks are covered in lichens. The forest floor is blanketed with lush ferns. Evergreen trees that are 90 m tall, such as the Sitka spruce and the Douglas fir, dominate the forest. Other large trees, such as western hemlock, Pacific silver fir, and redwood, can also be found in temperate rain forests.

Even though the temperate rain forest of the Pacific Northwest is located north of most other rain forests, it still maintains a moderate temperature year-round. The temperate rain forest also rarely freezes because the nearby Pacific Ocean waters keep temperatures mild by blowing cool ocean wind over the forest. As this ocean wind meets the coastal mountains, a large amount of rainfall is produced. The rainfall keeps the temperate rain forest cool and moist.

Figure 9 ▶ The only temperate rain forest in North America is located in the Pacific Northwest, as shown above in Olympic National Park in Washington State.

▶ Deforestation reduces the amount of water that is absorbed by plants after it rains. The more trees that are cleared from a forest, the more likely a flood will occur in that area.

Mountains left few trees to stop the water flowing down the mountain. So, most of the water flows into the river when it rains. Heavy rains have eroded and carried away so much soil from the slopes of the mountains that the soil has formed a new island in the Bay of Bengal, which is off the coast of Bangladesh.

People are beginning to understand the connection between deforestation and floods. People held protests in northern Italy in 2000 after floods covered a town that had

never been flooded before. The townspeople claimed that authorities had permitted developers to cover the hills with homes. These developers cut down most of the trees and covered much of the land with asphalt. After heavy rains, the water was no longer absorbed by trees and soil, so the water flowed down the hills and flooded the town.

CRITICAL THINKING

1. Identifying Relationships
How might deforestation in China and other countries affect the overall climate of the Earth?

2. Analyzing a Viewpoint
Imagine that you are a city council member and must vote on whether to clear a forest so that a mall can be built. List the pros and cons of each viewpoint. After reviewing your list, how would you vote? Explain your answer.

Temperate Deciduous Forest
(Stuttgart, Germany)

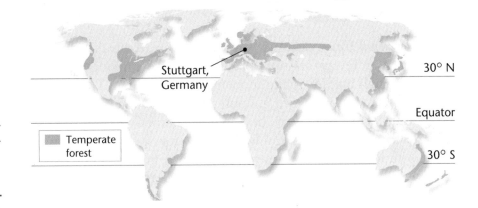
Stuttgart,
Germany

Temperate
forest

30° N

Equator

30° S

Figure 10 ▶ The difference between summer and winter temperatures in temperate deciduous forests is extreme.

Figure 11 ▶ The change of seasons in a temperate deciduous forest in Michigan is shown below.

Temperate Deciduous Forests

If you walk through a North American deciduous forest in the fall, you will immerse yourself in color. Leaves in every shade of orange, red, and yellow crackle beneath your feet. Most birds have flown south. The forest is quieter than it was in the summer. You see mostly chipmunks and squirrels gathering and storing the food they will need during the long, cold winter.

In **temperate deciduous forests,** trees drop their broad, flat leaves each fall. These forests once dominated vast regions of the Earth, including parts of North America, Europe, and Asia. Today, temperate deciduous forests are generally located between 30° and 50° north latitudes, as shown in **Figure 10.** The range of temperatures in a temperate deciduous forest can be extreme, and the growing season lasts for only four to six months. Summer temperatures can soar to 35°C. Winter temperatures often fall below freezing, so little water is available for plants. Just as temperatures change with the seasons, so does the vegetation, as shown in **Figure 11.** Although there is enough moisture for decomposition, temperatures are low during the winter. As a result, organic matter decomposes fairly slowly. This means that the soil contains more organic matter and nutrients than the soil in a tropical rain forest.

Plants of Temperate Deciduous Forests Like the plants of tropical rain forests, the plants in deciduous forests grow in layers. Tall trees, such as maple, oak, and birch, dominate the forest canopy. Small trees and shrubs cover the understory. Because the floor of a deciduous forest gets more light than the floor of a rain forest does, more plants such as ferns, herbs, and mosses grow in a deciduous forest.

Temperate-forest plants are adapted to survive seasonal changes. In the fall, most deciduous trees begin to shed their leaves. In the winter, moisture in the soil changes to ice, which causes the remaining leaves to fall to the ground. Herb seeds, bulbs, and rhizomes (underground stems) become dormant in the ground and are insulated by the soil, leaf litter, and snow. In the spring, when the sunlight increases and the temperature rises, trees grow new leaves, seeds germinate, and rhizomes and roots grow new shoots and stems.

Animals of Temperate Deciduous Forests The animals of temperate deciduous forests are adapted to use the forest plants for food and shelter. Squirrels eat the nuts, seeds, and fruits in the treetops. Bears feast on the leaves and berries of the forest plants. Grasshoppers, such as the one shown in **Figure 12**, eat almost all types of vegetation found throughout the forest. Deer and other herbivores nibble leaves from trees and shrubs.

Many birds nest in the relative safety of the canopy. Most of these birds are migratory. Because many birds cannot survive harsh winters, each fall they fly south for warmer weather and more available food. Each spring, they return north to nest and feed. Animals that do not migrate use various strategies for surviving the winter. For example, some mammals reduce their activity so that they do not need as much food for energy.

Figure 12 ▶ Grasshoppers, woodpeckers, and deer are among the many animals that live in the temperate deciduous forest.

Taiga

The **taiga** is the northern coniferous forest that stretches in a broad band across the Northern Hemisphere just below the Arctic Circle. As shown in **Figure 13,** winters are long (6 to 10 months) and have average temperatures that are below freezing and often fall to –20°C. Many trees seem like straight, dead shafts of bark and wood—until you look up and see their green tops. Plant growth is most abundant during the summer months because of nearly constant daylight and larger amounts of precipitation.

Figure 13 ▶ The taiga has long, cold winters and small amounts of precipitation, as shown in the climatogram below.

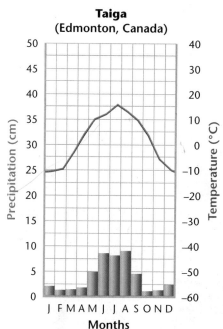

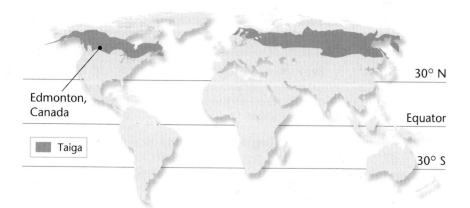

Plants of the Taiga A conifer is a tree with needle-like leaves and seeds that develop in cones. The shape of the leaves and their waxy coating prevent the tree from losing too much water. This is especially important when the ground is frozen and the roots cannot replace lost water by absorbing more from the soil. As **Figure 14** shows, many conifers are shaped like a large cone. The cone-like shape helps to prevent snow from building up on the branches and causing the branches to break under the weight.

Conifer needles contain substances that make the soil acidic when the needles fall to the ground. Most plants cannot grow in acidic soil, which is one reason the forest floor of the taiga has few plants. In addition, soil forms slowly in the taiga because the climate and acidity of the fallen leaves slow decomposition.

Animals of the Taiga The taiga has many lakes and swamps that in summer attract birds that feed on aquatic organisms. Many birds migrate south to avoid winter in the taiga. Because food is scarce during the winter, some year-round residents, such as jumping mice, burrow underground to hibernate. As shown in **Figure 15**, some animals, such as snowshoe hares, have adapted to avoid predation by lynxes, wolves, and foxes by shedding their brown summer fur and growing white fur that camouflages them in the winter snow.

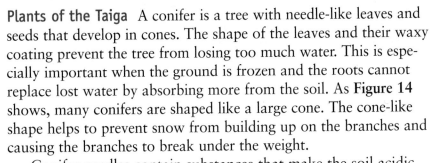

Figure 14 ▶ The taiga has cold winter temperatures, a small amount of annual precipitation, and coniferous trees. The seeds of conifers are protected inside tough cones like the one above. Also, the narrow shape and waxy coating of conifer needles help the tree retain water.

Figure 15 ▶ In the taiga, a snowshoe hare's fur changes color according to the seasons to help camouflage the animal from predators.

SECTION 2 **Review**

1. **List** three characteristics of tropical rain forests.

2. **Name** the main layers of a tropical rain forest. What kinds of plants grow in each layer?

3. **Describe** two ways in which tropical rain forests of the world are being threatened.

4. **Describe** how a plant survives the change of seasons in a temperate deciduous forest. Write a short paragraph to explain your answer. **WRITING SKILLS**

CRITICAL THINKING

5. **Evaluating Information** Which would be better suited for agricultural development: the soil of a tropical rain forest or the soil of a temperate deciduous forest? Explain your answer.

6. **Identifying Relationships** How does a snowshoe hare avoid predation by other animals during the winter in a taiga biome? How might this affect the animal that depends on the snowshoe hare for food?

Grassland, Desert, and Tundra Biomes

SCSh.2.b; SCSh.3.c; SCSh.3.d; SCSh.3.e;
SCSh.6.a; SCSh.6.b; SCSh.6.c; SCSh.6.d;
SCSh.9.c; SEV.2.c; SEV.2.d

EARTH SCIENCE **CONNECTION**

In areas with too little precipitation for large trees to survive, the biomes are dominated by smaller plants. Where there is almost no rainfall at all, few plants can grow and we find desert. Thus, warm areas with little precipitation are characterized by savanna and desert biomes. Temperate areas have grassland, chaparral, and desert biomes, and cold areas have tundra and desert biomes.

Savannas

Parts of Africa, western India, northern Australia, and some parts of South America are covered by grassland called *savanna*. A **savanna** is a tropical biome dominated by grasses, shrubs, and small trees. As **Figure 16** shows, rain falls mainly during the wet season, which lasts for only a few months of the year. This is the only time that plants can grow. The plants support an amazing variety of herbivores, such as antelopes, giraffes, and elephants, as well as the predators that hunt them—cheetahs, lions, and hyenas, for example.

Plants of the Savanna Because most of the rain falls during the wet season, plants must be able to survive prolonged periods of time without water. During the dry season, plants lose their leaves or die down to the ground. When the rain returns, they start to grow again. Many plants have large, horizontal root systems so they can draw water from as large an area as possible. The coarse savanna grasses have vertical leaves that expose less of their surface area to the hot sun to further help the grasses conserve water. Some trees of the savanna also lose their leaves during the dry season to conserve water. Trees and shrubs often have thorns or sharp leaves that keep hungry herbivores away.

✔ **Reading Check** Name two herbivores and two predators that savanna plants support.

Objectives

▶ Describe the difference between tropical and temperate grasslands.

▶ Describe the climate in a chaparral biome.

▶ Describe two desert animals and the adaptations that help them survive.

▶ Describe one threat to the tundra biome.

Key Terms

savanna
temperate grassland
chaparral
desert
tundra
permafrost

Figure 16 ▶ Savannas have periods of heavy rainfall followed by periods of drought.

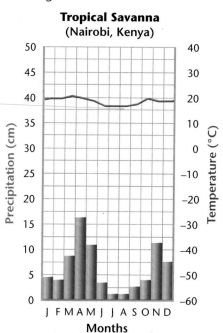

Tropical Savanna
(Nairobi, Kenya)

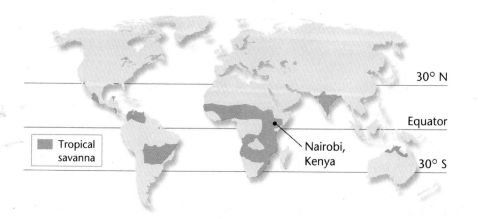

Figure 17 ▶ Herbivores of the savanna, such as the elephants shown here, range widely in search of food.

Geofact

Deep Soil Gravel or sand becomes fertile soil when decomposers slowly break down organic matter such as dead leaves. Decomposers work most effectively in hot, wet weather. As a result, the world's deepest soil is in grasslands. In temperate grassland biomes, winters are cold and summers are dry, which causes leaves to break down slowly. So, organic matter builds up over time. Some North American prairies had more than 2 m of topsoil when the first farmers arrived.

Animals of the Savanna Grazing herbivores, such as the elephants shown in **Figure 17,** have adopted a migratory way of life. They follow the rains to areas of newly sprouted grass and watering holes. Some predators follow and stalk migratory animals for food. Many savanna animals give birth only during the rainy season, when food is most abundant and the young are more likely to survive. Also, some species of herbivores eat vegetation at different heights than other species do. For example, small gazelles graze on grasses, black rhinos browse on shrubs, and giraffes feed on tree leaves.

Temperate Grasslands

Temperate grassland covers large areas of the interior of continents, where there is moderate rainfall, but still too little for trees to grow. The prairies in North America, the steppes in Asia, the veldt in South Africa, and the pampas in South America are temperate grasslands. Their locations are shown in **Figure 18.** Two examples of temperate grasslands are shown in **Figure 19.**

Mountains often play a crucial role in maintaining grasslands. For example, in North America, rain clouds moving from the west release most of their moisture as they pass over the Rocky Mountains. As a result, the shortgrass prairie just east of the Rockies receives so little rain that it looks almost like a desert.

Figure 18 ▶ Temperate grasslands are characterized by small amounts of rainfall, periodic droughts, and high temperatures in the summer.

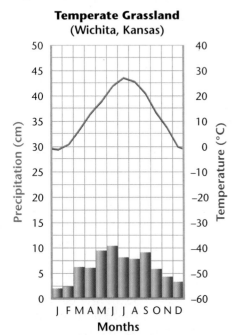

Temperate Grassland
(Wichita, Kansas)

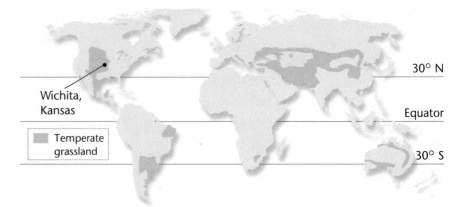

The amount of rain increases as you move east, which permits the growth of taller grasses and some shrubs. Grassland plants dry out in the summer, so lightning strikes often start fires.

Plants of Temperate Grasslands Temperate grassland vegetation consists of grasses and wildflowers. Although there is only a single layer of vegetation, many species may be present. Shrubs and trees grow only where the soil contains extra water, usually on the banks of streams.

The root systems of grassland plants form dense layers that survive drought and fire. **Figure 20** shows how the heights of grasses and the depths of their roots vary.

Grasslands are highly productive because of their fertile soil. The summer is hot and the winter is cold, so the plants die back to their roots in the winter. Low temperatures in the winter slow decomposition. As a result, the rate at which dead plants decay is slower than the rate at which new vegetation is added each year. Over time, organic matter accumulates in the soil. This means that grasslands have the most fertile soil in the world. Most grasslands have been converted to farmland for growing crops such as wheat and corn.

Shortgrass prairie (about 25 cm rain per year)	Mixed or middlegrass prairie (about 50 cm rain per year)	Tallgrass prairie (up to 88 cm rain per year)

Connection to **History**

The State of Bison More than 60 million bison once roamed the temperate grasslands of North America. But these large grass-eating mammals were almost brought to extinction by the late 1800s because of hunting by western settlers. By 1889, fewer than 1,100 bison remained in North America! The first bill to save the bison was introduced by Congress in 1874. In 1903, President Theodore Roosevelt started the National Wildlife Refuge System to provide protected areas for bison and other animals. Today, North America has more than 200,000 bison.

Figure 20 ▶ The height of grassland plants and the depth of their roots depend on the amount of rainfall that the grasslands receive.

Figure 21 ▶ Prairie dogs, such as those shown here, live in temperate grasslands. Prairie dogs live in colonies and burrow in the ground to build mounds, holes, and tunnels.

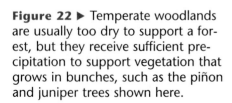
Animals of Temperate Grasslands Grazing animals, such as pronghorn antelope and bison, have large, flat back teeth for chewing the coarse prairie grasses. Other grassland animals, such as badgers, prairie dogs, and burrowing owls, live protected in underground burrows as shown in **Figure 21.** The burrows shield the animals from fire and weather and protect them from predators on the open grasslands.

Threats to Temperate Grasslands Farming and overgrazing have changed the grasslands. Grain crops cannot hold the soil in place as well as native grasses can because the roots of crops are shallow and the soil is ploughed regularly, so soil erosion eventually occurs. Erosion is also caused by overgrazing. When grasses are constantly eaten and trampled, the grasses cannot regenerate or hold the soil. This constant use can change fruitful grasslands into less productive, desertlike biomes.

Chaparral

Temperate woodland biomes have fairly dry climates but receive enough rainfall to support more plants than a desert does. One type of temperate woodlands consists of scattered tree communities made up of coniferous trees such as piñon pines and junipers, as shown in **Figure 22.**

The chaparral is a temperate shrubland biome that is found in all fives parts of the world with a Mediterranean climate. These areas have moderately dry, coastal climates, with little or

Figure 22 ▶ Temperate woodlands are usually too dry to support a forest, but they receive sufficient precipitation to support vegetation that grows in bunches, such as the piñon and juniper trees shown here.

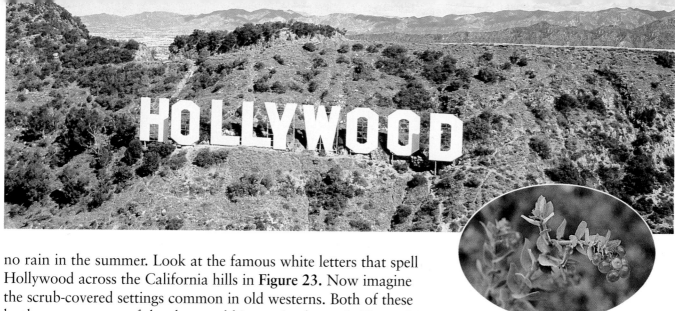

no rain in the summer. Look at the famous white letters that spell Hollywood across the California hills in **Figure 23**. Now imagine the scrub-covered settings common in old westerns. Both of these landscapes are part of the chaparral biome. As shown in **Figure 24**, chaparral is located in the middle latitudes, about 30° north and south of the equator.

Figure 23 ▶ The chaparral biome in the Hollywood hills is home to plants such as the manzanita, which is shown above.

Plants of the Chaparral Most chaparral plants are low-lying, evergreen shrubs and small trees that tend to grow in dense patches. Common chaparral plants include chamise, manzanita, scrub oak, olive trees, and herbs, such as sage and bay. These plants have small, leathery leaves that retain water. The leaves also contain oils that promote burning, which is an advantage because natural fires destroy trees that might compete with chaparral plants for light and space. Chaparral plants are so well adapted to fire that they can resprout from small bits of surviving plant tissue.

Animals of the Chaparral A common adaptation of chaparral animals is camouflage, which is shape or coloring that allows an animal to blend into its environment. Animals such as quail, lizards, chipmunks, and mule deer have a brownish-gray coloring that lets them move through the brush without being noticed.

Figure 24 ▶ Chaparral biomes are located in areas that have Mediterranean climates.

Threats to the Chaparral Worldwide, the greatest threat to chaparral is human development. Because chaparral biomes get a lot of sun, are near the oceans, and have a mild climate year-round, humans tend to develop the land for commercial and residential use.

✓ **Reading Check** How does camouflage help chaparral animals?

Santa Barbara, California

Chaparral

30° N

Equator

30° S

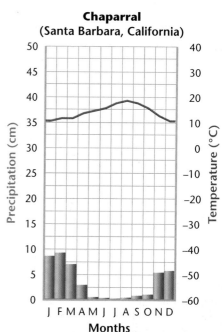

Chaparral
(Santa Barbara, California)

Precipitation (cm)

Temperature (°C)

J F M A M J J A S O N D

Months

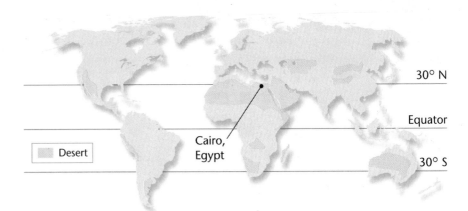

Desert
(Cairo, Egypt)

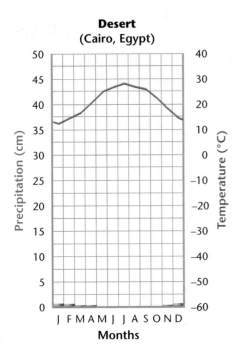

30° N

Equator

30° S

Cairo, Egypt

Desert

Figure 25 ▶ Deserts are the driest places on Earth. They typically receive less than 25 cm of precipitation a year.

Deserts

When some people think of a desert, they think of the hot sand that surrounds the Egyptian pyramids. Other people picture the Sonoran Desert and its mighty saguaro cactuses, or the magnificent rock formations of Monument Valley in Arizona and Utah. Many kinds of deserts are located throughout the world, but one characteristic that they share is that they are the driest places on Earth.

Deserts are areas that have widely scattered vegetation and receive very little rain. In extreme cases, it never rains and there is no vegetation. The distribution of Earth's deserts is shown in **Figure 25.** Even in hot deserts near the equator, there is so little insulating moisture in the air that the temperature changes rapidly during a 24-hour period. The temperature may go from 40°C (104°F) during the day to near-freezing at night. Deserts are often located near mountain ranges, which block the passage of rain clouds.

▶ The flapnecked chameleon lives in the deserts of Botswana.

▶ The Sonoran Desert in Arizona appears lush with plant life just after the winter rains.

Plants of the Desert All desert plants have adaptations for obtaining and conserving water, which allow the plants to live in dry, desert conditions. Plants called *succulents,* such as cactuses, have thick, fleshy stems and leaves that store water. Their leaves also have a waxy coating that prevents water loss. Sharp spines on cactuses keep thirsty animals from devouring the plant's juicy flesh. Rainfall rarely penetrates deeply into the soil, so many plants' roots spread out just under the surface of the soil to absorb as much rain as possible.

Many desert shrubs drop their leaves during dry periods and grow new leaves when it rains again. When conditions are too dry, some plants die and drop seeds that stay dormant in the soil until the next rainfall. Then, new plants quickly germinate, grow, and bloom before the soil becomes dry again. Some desert plants have adapted so that they can survive even if their water content drops to as low as 30 percent of their mass. Water levels below 50 to 75 percent are fatal for most plants.

Animals of the Desert Reptiles, such as Gila monsters and rattlesnakes, have thick, scaly skin that prevents water loss. Amphibians, such as the spadefoot toad, survive scorching desert summers by *estivating*—burying themselves in the ground and sleeping through the dry season. Some animals, such as the elf owl shown in **Figure 26,** nest in cactuses to avoid predators. Desert insects and spiders are covered with body armor that helps them retain water. In addition, most desert animals are nocturnal, which means they are active mainly at night or at dusk, when the air is cooler.

Figure 26 ▶ Desert plants survive harsh conditions by growing deep roots to reach groundwater and by having specialized structures that limit the loss of water. Desert animals bury themselves underground or burrow in cactuses to avoid extreme temperatures and predators.

▶ Elf owls burrow in cactuses to avoid hot temperatures during the day.

▶ This sidewinder has a unique way of moving so that only small portions of its body are in contact with the hot sands at any one time.

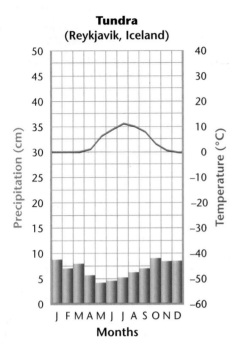

Tundra
(Reykjavik, Iceland)

Figure 27 ▶ The precipitation that the tundra biome receives remains frozen much of the year.

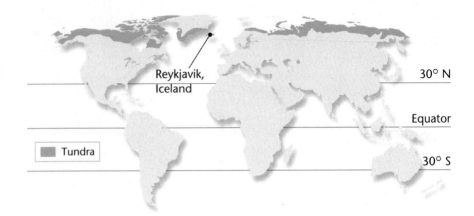

Reykjavik, Iceland

30° N

Equator

30° S

☐ Tundra

Graphic
Organizer **Venn Diagram**
Create the **Graphic Organizer** entitled "Venn Diagram" described in the Appendix. Label the circles with "Tundra" and "Desert." Then, fill in the diagram with characteristics that each biome shares with the other.

Tundra

The **tundra** biome is located in northern arctic regions, as shown in **Figure 27**. The winter is too cold and dry to permit the growth of trees in this biome. In many areas of the tundra, the deeper layers of soil, called **permafrost,** are permanently frozen throughout the year. As a result, the topsoil is very thin. In the summer, when the thin topsoil layer thaws, the tundra landscape becomes quite moist and spongy and is dotted with bogs. These wet areas are ideal breeding grounds for enormous numbers of swarming insects, such as mosquitoes and black flies, and for the many birds that feed on the insects.

Vegetation of the Tundra **Figure 28** shows the Alaskan tundra in the summer. Mosses and lichens, which can grow without soil, cover vast areas of rocks in the tundra. The soil is thin, so plants have wide, shallow roots to help anchor them against the icy winds. Most flowering plants of the tundra, such as campion and gentian, are short. Growing close to the ground keeps the plants out of the wind and helps them absorb heat from the sunlit soil during the brief summer. Woody plants and perennials such as willow and birch have evolved dwarf forms and grow flat or grow along the ground.

Figure 28 ▶ During its brief summer, the Alaskan tundra is covered by flowering plants and lichens.

Figure 29 ▶ Many migratory animals, such as geese (left) and caribou (below), return to the tundra each year to breed.

Animals of the Tundra Millions of migratory birds fly to the tundra to breed in the summer. Food is abundant in the form of plants, mollusks, worms, and especially insects. Caribou, shown in **Figure 29,** migrate throughout the tundra in search of food and water. Wolves roam the tundra and prey on caribou, moose, and smaller animals, such as lemmings, mice, and hares. These animals burrow underground during the winter but they are still active. Many animals that live in the tundra year-round, such as arctic foxes, lose their brown fur and grow white fur that camouflages them with the winter snow. These animals are also extremely well insulated.

Threats to the Tundra The tundra is one of the most fragile biomes on the planet. Its food chains are relatively simple, so they are easily disrupted. Because conditions are so extreme, the land is easily damaged and slow to recover. Until recently, the tundra was undisturbed by humans. But oil has been located in some tundra regions, such as in northern Alaska. Oil exploration, extraction, and transport has disrupted the habitats of the plants and animals in many parts of the tundra. Pollution caused by spills or leaks of oil and other toxic materials may also poison the food and water sources of the organisms that live in the tundra. 🌐

MATHPRACTICE

U.S. Oil Production On average, the United States produces an estimated 8.1 million barrels of oil per day. How many millions of barrels of oil does the United States produce in 1 year? If all of the oil-producing countries of the world produce an estimated 74.13 million barrels of oil per day, what percentage of worldwide oil does the United States produce?

SECTION 3 Review

1. **Describe** two desert animals and the adaptations that help them survive.

2. **Describe** how tropical grasslands differ from temperate grasslands.

3. **Compare** the plants that live in deserts with the plants that live in the tundra biome.

4. **Describe** one threat to the tundra biome.

CRITICAL THINKING

5. **Making Inferences** Former grasslands are among the most productive farming regions. Read the description of temperate grasslands in this section and explain why this statement is true. **READING SKILLS**

6. **Analyzing Relationships** Explain why elephants and caribou, which live in very different biomes, both migrate.

Section 3 **Grassland, Desert, and Tundra Biomes** **173**

1 What Is a Biome?

Key Terms

biome, 153
climate, 154
latitude, 155
altitude, 155

Main Ideas

▶ Scientists classify the ecosystems of the world into large areas called *biomes*.

▶ Biomes are described by their plant life because specific climate conditions support the growth of specific types of vegetation.

▶ Climate determines which plants can grow in an area. Latitude and altitude affect climate in similar ways.

2 Forest Biomes

Key Terms

tropical rain forest, 156
emergent layer, 158
canopy, 158
epiphyte, 158
understory, 158
temperate rain forest, 161
temperate deciduous forest, 162
taiga, 163

Main Ideas

▶ Major forest biomes include tropical rain forest, temperate rain forest, temperate deciduous forest, temperate evergreen forest, and taiga.

▶ Tropical rain forests have high rainfall and high temperatures throughout the year. They are the most diverse of all biomes.

▶ Temperate forests experience seasonal variations in precipitation and temperature. Their vegetation is adapted to surviving these changes.

▶ Forest biomes are threatened by deforestation through logging, ranching, and farming.

3 Grassland, Desert, and Tundra Biomes

Key Terms

savanna, 165
temperate grassland, 166
chaparral, 168
desert, 170
tundra, 172
permafrost, 172

Main Ideas

▶ Savannas are located north and south of tropical rain forests and have distinct wet seasons.

▶ Temperate grasslands get too little rainfall to support trees. Grasslands are dominated mostly by different types of grasses and flowering plants.

▶ Deserts are the driest biomes on Earth.

▶ Plants and animals found in each biome adapt to the environment in which they live.

Using Key Terms

Use each of the following terms in a separate sentence.

1. *biome*
2. *climate*
3. *epiphyte*
4. *tundra*
5. *permafrost*

For each pair of terms, explain how the meanings of the terms differ.

6. *understory* and *canopy*
7. *latitude* and *altitude*
8. *chaparral* and *desert*
9. *tropical rain forest* and *temperate deciduous forest*

✔ **STUDY TIP**

Concept Maps Remembering words and understanding concepts are easier when information is organized in a way that you recognize. For example, you can use key terms and key concepts to create a concept map that links them together in a pattern you will understand and remember.

Understanding Key Ideas

10. Approximately what percentage of the Earth's species do tropical rain forests contain?
    a. 7 percent
    b. 20 percent
    c. 40 percent
    d. 50 percent

11. Animal species of the tropical rain forest
    a. compete more for available resources than species native to other biomes do.
    b. have adaptations that minimize competition.
    c. have adaptations to cope with extreme variations in climate.
    d. are never camouflaged.

12. Migration of animals in the savanna is mostly a response to
    a. predation.
    b. altitude.
    c. rainfall.
    d. temperature.

13. Spadefoot toads survive the dry conditions of the desert by
    a. migrating to seasonal watering holes.
    b. finding underground springs.
    c. burying themselves in the ground.
    d. drinking cactus juice.

14. The tundra is most suitable to a vertebrate that
    a. requires nesting sites in tall trees.
    b. is coldblooded.
    c. has a green outer skin for camouflage.
    d. can migrate hundreds of kilometers each summer.

15. A biome that has a large amount of rainfall, high temperatures, and poor soil is a
    a. temperate woodland.
    b. temperate rain forest.
    c. tropical rain forest.
    d. savanna.

16. The two main factors that determine where organisms live are
    a. soil type and precipitation.
    b. temperature and precipitation.
    c. altitude and precipitation.
    d. temperature and latitude.

17. Which of the following biomes contains large trees?
    a. savanna
    b. temperate rain forest
    c. chaparral
    d. desert

18. The most common types of plants in the taiga biome are
    a. deciduous trees.
    b. short shrubs.
    c. coniferous trees.
    d. grasses.

Short Answer

19. Unlike the jungles you see in movies, the floor of an undisturbed tropical rain forest usually has little vegetation. Explain why it lacks vegetation.

20. What is the relationship between root systems and erosion in a grassland ecosystem?

21. How might a mountain affect where particular types of biomes are located?

22. Well-preserved mammoths have been found buried in the tundra. Explain why the tundra preserves animal remains well.

23. How does deforestation contribute to a change in climate and increase the chance of floods in a biome?

Interpreting Graphics

Use the diagram below to answer questions 24–26.

24. Why are tall trees found in the taiga but not in the tundra?

25. As moisture decreases, what happens to the amount of vegetation in an area?

26. What does the diagram tell you about the temperature of and precipitation in temperate grasslands?

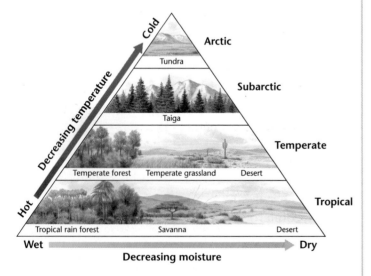

Concept Mapping

27. Use the following terms to create a concept map: *threats to an ecosystem, erosion, overgrazing, logging, grasslands, rain forests, tundra, deserts, oil extraction,* and *irrigation.*

Critical Thinking

28. **Comparing Processes** American prairies and Asian steppes contain different plant species but are dominated by grasses. Write a short paragraph that explains why the two grasslands contain different species but the same types of plants. **WRITING SKILLS**

29. **Classifying Information** Read the description of tropical rain forests in this chapter, and list two factors that are responsible for the biodiversity of this biome. Describe two reasons for the decline of tropical rain forests. **READING SKILLS**

30. **Analyzing Relationships** If you took a population of squirrels from the southeastern United States and introduced them into a Central American rain forest, they would probably not survive. Why do you think the squirrels would not survive even though they are naturally adapted to life in a forest?

31. **Making Inferences** How might prairie fires set from natural and human causes have affected the evolution of fire resistance in prairie grasses?

Cross-Disciplinary Connection

32. **Geography** Use a world map to find locations of the various biomes. Then, make a poster that contains photos or illustrations of plants and animals native to each biome.

Portfolio Project

33. **Food Webs in Your Biome** Do a special project on the ecosystems in your biome. Use field guides to find out what plants and animals live in your biome. Then, draw a food web that shows how organisms in each ecosystem could be related.

MATH SKILLS

Use the table below to answer quesions 34–35.

Amount of Tropical Rainforest		
Country	Amount of tropical rain forest (km²)	Amount of annual deforestation (km²/y)
A	1,800,000	50,000
B	55,000	3,300
C	22,000	6,000
D	530,000	12,000
E	80,000	700

34. **Making Calculations** What percentage of tropical rain forest is being destroyed each year in country A? in country D?

35. **Interpreting Statistics** According to the table, which country's tropical rain forest will be completely destroyed first? Which country's rain forest will be completely destroyed last?

WRITING SKILLS

36. **Communicating Main Ideas** Describe the importance of conserving the biomes of the world. What can you do to help conserve the world's biomes?

37. **Writing From Research** Choose one biome and research the threats that exist against it. Write a short essay that describes the threats and any actions that are being taken to help save the biome.

READING SKILLS

Read the passage below, and then answer the questions that follow.

The Tropics and other regions of high biodiversity include some of the economically poorest countries on Earth. These countries are trying to use their natural resources to build their economies and to raise the standard of living for their citizens. Several conservation strategies offer ways for developing countries to benefit economically from preserving their biodiversity.

For example, in a *debt-for-nature swap*, richer countries or private conservation organizations pay some of the debts of a developing country. In exchange, the developing country agrees to take steps to protect its biodiversity, such as setting up a preserve or launching an education program for its citizens. Another idea to help local people make money from intact ecosystems is to set up a national park to attract tourists. People who want to see the ecosystem and its unique organisms will pay money for nature guides, food, and lodging. This idea is called *ecotourism*.

1. The main objective of both a *debt-for-nature swap* and *ecotourism* is
   a. economic gain.
   b. education of citizens.
   c. preservation of biodiversity.
   d. Both (a) and (c)

2. According to the passage, which of the following statements is true?
   a. Regions of high biodiversity are not worth saving.
   b. Intact ecosystems are ecosystems that are most developed.
   c. A debt-for-nature swap is an example of international compromise.
   d. Launching education programs for citizens does not help protect ecosystems.

Understanding Concepts

Directions (1–4): For *each* question, write on a separate sheet of paper the letter of the correct answer.

1 Which of the following describes a biome?
 A. all the areas on Earth that are life-supporting
 B. weather conditions in an area for a specific time period
 C. a region characterized by specific climate and organism communities
 D. an area where the animal population interacts with its abiotic environment

2 What type of forest has the greatest biodiversity?
 F. taiga forest
 G. temperate deciduous forest
 H. temperate rain forest
 I. tropical rain forest

3 What is the diversity of the species in an area dependent on?
 A. plant life
 B. rainfall
 C. sunlight
 D. temperature

4 What are the main factors that determine weather?
 F. altitude, latitude, precipitation, temperature
 G. altitude, latitude, precipitation, vegetation
 H. air currents, altitude, temperature, vegetation
 I. air currents, precipitation, temperature, vegetation

Directions (5–6): For *each* question, write a short response.

5 A temperate grassland is a biome that is dominated by grasses and that has very few trees. How are temperate grasslands threatened by overgrazing?

6 Compare and contrast the tundra and desert biomes.

Reading Skills

Directions (7–8): Read the passage below. Then answer the questions.

When rain falls on a forest, much of the rain is absorbed by plant roots and transpired into the air as water vapor. The water vapor forms rain clouds. Much of the water in the clouds will fall as rain somewhere downwind from the forest. Clearing the trees results in deforestation, which can change the climate.

Deforestation led to the disastrous flooding of the Yangtze River in China in 1998. More than 2,000 people died in the floods, and at least 13 million people had to leave their homes. It is estimated that 85 percent of the forest in the Yangtze River basin has been cut down. So the millions of tons of water these trees once absorbed now flows freely down the river and spreads across the fields into towns during the seasonal monsoon rains.

7 How could future flooding on the Yangtze River be avoided?
 A. replanting crops
 B. rebuilding homes
 C. replanting trees
 D. rebuilding walls

8 Examine the climate change produced by deforestation.

Directions (9): Read the passage below. Then answer the question.

Tropical rain forests are located in a belt around the Earth near the equator. The climate is ideal for a wide variety of plants and animals. In tropical rain forests, different types of plants grow in different layers. The main layers above the forest floor are, in order from top to bottom, the emergent layer, the canopy, and the understory.

9 Which layer of a tropical rain forest receives the least sunlight, and why?

Interpreting Graphics

Directions (10–13): For *each* question below, record the correct answer on a separate sheet of paper.

Different scientists classify biomes in different ways. The map below shows one way to classify the biomes in Africa. Use this map to answer questions 10 through 13.

Biomes of Africa

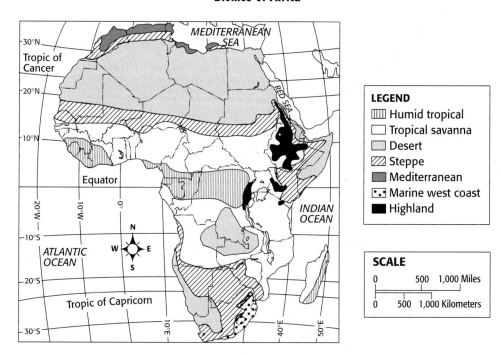

10 What can be inferred about the biomes of Africa?
  F. Africa has a large concentration of tropical rain forests.
  G. Africa has a limited number of plant and animal communities.
  H. Africa has all types of plant life because of the many diverse biomes.
  I. Africa has large desert areas that get less than 25.0 cm of precipitation a year.

11 Which biome covers the most surface area in Africa?
  A. desert   **C.** Mediterranean
  B. highland   **D.** steppe

12 According to the map, which of the following determines the characteristics of a biome?
  F. geographic borders   **H.** longitude
  G. latitude   **I.** the Indian ocean

13 What geographic features are near 10°N, 40°E?
  A. mountains   **C.** rivers
  B. plains   **D.** volcanoes

Test TIP

When several questions refer to the same graph, table or map, answer the questions you are most sure of first.

Exploration Lab: FIELD ACTIVITY

Objectives

▶ **Collect** information from international, national, and local resources about the biome in which you live.

▶ **USING SCIENTIFIC METHODS** **Perform** field observations to identify the name of the biome in which you live.

Materials

binoculars (optional)
field guide to local flora and
  fauna
globe or atlas
graph paper (optional)
notebook
pencil or pen
ruler

▶ **Climatograms** The temperature and precipitation for Austin, Texas is shown in this climatogram.

Identify Your Local Biome

In what biome do you live? Do you live in a temperate deciduous forest, a desert, or a temperate grassland, such as a prairie or savanna? In this lab, you will explore certain characteristics of the biome in which you live. With the information you gather, you will be able to identify which biome it is.

Procedure

1. Use a globe or atlas to determine the latitude at which you live. Record this information.

2. Consider the topography of the place where you live. Study the contour lines on a map or surface variations on a globe. What clues do you find that might help identify your biome? For example, is your area located near a mountain or an ocean? Record your findings.

3. Prepare a climatogram of your area. A climatogram is a graph that shows average monthly values for two factors: temperature and precipitation. Temperature is expressed in degrees Celsius and is plotted as a smooth curve. Precipitation values are given in centimeters and are plotted as a histogram.

   To make a climatogram of your area, obtain monthly averages of precipitation and temperature for one year from your local TV or radio weather station. Make a data table, and record these values. Next, draw the vertical and horizontal axes of your climatogram in your notebook or on graph paper. Then, show the temperature scale along the vertical axis on the right side of the graph and the precipitation scale along the vertical axis on the left side of the graph. Show months of the year along the horizontal axis. Finally, plot your data.

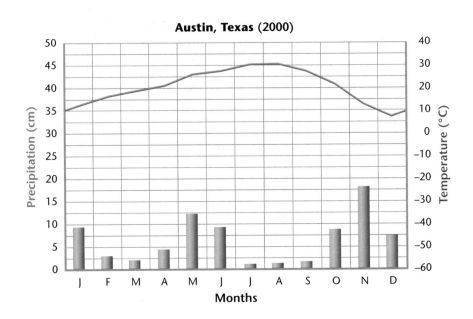

4. Go outside to observe the plants growing in your area. Bring a field guide, and respond to the following items in your notebook.

   a. Sketch or describe as many plants that are common in your area as you can. Use your field guide to identify each of these species.

   b. Describe three or more adaptations of each plant to the local climate.

   c. Which of the plants that you observed are native to your area? Which have been introduced by humans? Which of the introduced plants can survive on their own in local conditions? Which of the introduced plants require extensive human care to remain alive?

   d. Look for evidence that animals have left behind—footprints, nests, dens or burrows, hair or feathers, scratches, or urine markings. Sketch or describe as many different animal species as possible. Identify each species by using your field guide.

   e. Describe three or more adaptations that each animal has developed in order to survive in local climatic conditions.

Analysis

1. **Analyzing Data** Compare your local climatogram to the biome climatograms shown in this chapter. Which biome has a climatogram most similar to your climatogram?

2. **Analyzing Results** Consider your latitude, topographical findings, and observations of local plants and animals. Combine this information with your climatogram, and determine which biome best matches the area in which you live.

Conclusions

3. **Evaluating Results** Does your climatogram match any of the seven major terrestrial climatograms shown in the chapter? Explain how any differences between your biome and the biome in the chapter that your biome most clearly matches might influence the adaptations of local animals and plants.

4. **Applying Conclusions** Organisms create features of the biome in which they live. What features of your biome are created by the organisms that live there?

▶ **Biomes** These two cities are located in two different biomes. Stamford, Vermont (top) is located in a temperate deciduous forest, and Tucson, Arizona (bottom) is located in a desert.

Extension

1. **Classifying Information** Name the three plant adaptations and the three animal adaptations that you observed. Explain in detail how each of these adaptations meets the conditions of your biome.

Making a difference

A LITTLE PIECE OF CAJUN PRAIRIE

Cajun prairie is a distinct grassland, named for the settlers who lived there. It once covered more than 2.5 million acres of southwest Louisiana. Today, only about 100 acres of Cajun prairie remain. If the work of two biologists and many volunteers pays off, however, a little piece of Cajun prairie will always exist in Louisiana.

"I think that saving Cajun prairie is important because once it is gone, you cannot bring it back," says Charles Allen, a retired professor from the University of Louisiana and the botanist for Louisiana's Fort Polk. "There are plants and animals there that have never been tested for uses by humans. We could be losing a plant that would cure cancer, or provide food or fiber," he says.

Allen and biologist Malcolm Vidrine, a professor of biology at Louisiana State University in Eunice, have been working for almost two decades to restore Cajun prairie.

Although Cajun prairie and the tallgrass prairies of the Midwest both belong to the temperate grassland biome, Cajun prairie soil has unique characteristics. It is made of tight, heavy clays that formed as a result of coastal flooding and rains. This soil, combined with frequent lightning fires, makes it difficult for trees to grow but easy for prairie plants to flourish.

Settling on the Prairie

In the mid-1700s, many French Acadians, also known as Cajuns, arrived in Louisiana from Nova Scotia, Canada. They sustained themselves for over 100 years by fishing, hunting, and some farming. They also sustained their environment because their lifestyle caused little damage to the prairie.

The establishment of the railroad in the late 1800s brought new settlers to farm the rich land. These settlers brought with them new, more intensive agricultural practices and established herds of cattle that overgrazed the vegetation. By the early 20th century, most of the Cajun prairie had disappeared.

▶ Charles Allen is shown here collecting seeds from a compass plant at a Cajun prairie remnant. The leaves of the compass plant face east to catch the sun.

Today, the Cajun prairie ecosystem is labelled as "imperiled globally" by the Nature Conservancy, an organization dedicated to preserving natural communities. There are now fewer than 100 acres of Cajun prairie left in Louisiana. The railroad led to the near disappearance of the prairie, but it has also played an important role

▶ Cajun prairie, preserved on this 10-acre site, once covered nearly 10 percent of Louisiana.

▶ Volunteers such as these students used seeds and sod gathered from remnants to create a new Cajun prairie habitat in Eunice, Louisiana.

▶ To maintain the habitat, volunteers remove nonnative vegetation such as this vasey grass.

in saving the last remaining pieces of prairie. The remaining prairie is mostly in remnants of small, narrow strips along railroad right-of-ways. Because the railroad owned these pieces of land, they were never farmed.

The Eunice Cajun Prairie Restoration Project

In the late 1980s, Allen and Vidrine located as many remnant strips as they could. They chose 10 of the strips and studied them carefully. They found almost 500 species of plants in the 10 strips.

The Eunice Cajun Prairie Restoration Project began in the summer of 1988. Its goal was to restore and preserve a small Cajun prairie in the city of Eunice, Louisiana.

A 10-acre site in Eunice was mowed, and herbicide was used to destroy the nonnative vegetation. Volunteers from local elementary and high schools collected bags of seeds from Cajun prairie plants

growing in the remnant strips. That winter, controlled burns were used to prepare the site. On a designated planting day, the students spread the seeds they had collected. The site was then lightly tilled. Sod was removed from the remnant strips and replanted at the Eunice site during the next three seasons.

Restoration is an ongoing effort. Yearly controlled burns maintain the habitat. The fires destroy shrubs and trees, but do not kill most of the prairie plants. Spot herbicides are used on the more pervasive nonnative species, such as the Chinese tallow tree, the most threatening nonnative species for the prairie. The seeds of this tree are easily spread when birds eat the seeds and deposit them in droppings.

Today, nearly 300 native Cajun prairie species, including little bluestem, Eastern gama grass, blazing stars, and hairy sunflower, have been reestablished at the site. As well, the rare wild coco orchid

(Eulophia ecrista) has been found at the site. This is a very positive sign because few of these orchids have been found in the remnant strips or in Louisiana. Much of the Eunice site is now almost completely Cajun prairie.

What Do You Think?

Are there threatened habitats in your area? What factors do you think led to the loss of these habitats? Is it possible for people to settle in a habitat without having a negative impact? How were the Cajuns able to sustain themselves on the prairie without destroying the habitat?

Aquatic Ecosystems

1 Freshwater Ecosystems
2 Marine Ecosystems

PRE-READING ACTIVITY

Two-Panel Flip Chart
Before you read this chapter, create the **FoldNote** entitled "Two-Panel Flip Chart" described in the Reading and Study Skills section of the Appendix. Label the flaps of the two-panel flip chart with "Freshwater Ecosystems" and "Marine Ecosystems." As you read the chapter, write information you learn about each category under the appropriate flap.

Manatees live in both freshwater and saltwater ecosystems. Manatees are herbivores and will eat at least 27 kg (60 lb) of aquatic plants per day.

Freshwater Ecosystems

SCSh.2.a; SCSh.2.b; SCSh.3.a; SCSh.3.c; SCSh.6.b; SCSh.6.c; SEV.2.d

The types of organisms in an aquatic ecosystem are mainly determined by the water's *salinity*—the amount of dissolved salts the water contains. As a result, aquatic ecosystems are divided into freshwater ecosystems and marine ecosystems.

Freshwater ecosystems include the sluggish waters of lakes and ponds, such as the lake shown in **Figure 1,** and the moving waters of rivers and streams. They also include areas where land, known as a **wetland,** is periodically underwater. Marine ecosystems include the diverse coastal areas of marshes, swamps, and coral reefs as well as the deep, vast oceans.

Characteristics of Aquatic Ecosystems

Factors such as temperature, sunlight, oxygen, and nutrients determine which organisms live in which areas of the water. For instance, sunlight reaches only a certain distance below the surface of the water, so most photosynthetic organisms live on or near the surface.

Organisms that live in aquatic ecosystems are grouped by their location and by their adaptations. Three groups of aquatic organisms include plankton, nekton, and benthos. **Plankton** are organisms that cannot swim against currents, so they are drifters. Drifting plants, called *phytoplankton*, are the food base for most aquatic ecosystems. The majority of phytoplankton are microscopic. Drifting animals, which may be microscopic or as large as a jellyfish, are called *zooplankton*. **Nekton** are free-swimming organisms, such as fish, turtles, and whales. **Benthos** are bottom-dwelling organisms, such as mussels, worms, and barnacles. Many benthic organisms live attached to hard surfaces. Organisms called decomposers, which break down dead organisms, are also present in aquatic ecosystems.

Objectives

▶ Describe the factors that determine where an organism lives in an aquatic ecosystem.

▶ Describe the littoral zone and the benthic zone that make up a lake or pond.

▶ Describe two environmental functions of wetlands.

▶ Describe one threat against river ecosystems.

Key Terms

wetland
plankton
nekton
benthos
littoral zone
benthic zone
eutrophication

Figure 1 ▶ Lake Louise in Alberta, Canada, is an example of a freshwater ecosystem.

Figure 2 ▶ Amphibians, such as this bullfrog, live in or near lakes and ponds.

SCI**LINKS**®
www.scilinks.org
Topic: Lakes and Ponds
Code: HE80846

Figure 3 ▶ In a pond or lake ecosystem, the most diverse and abundant life occurs near the shore, where sunlight and nutrients are plentiful. In the open water, sunlight at and near the surface supports drifting phytoplankton.

Lakes and Ponds

Lakes, ponds, wetlands, rivers, and streams make up the various types of freshwater ecosystems. Lakes, ponds, and wetlands can form naturally where groundwater reaches the Earth's surface. As well, beavers can create ponds by damming up streams. Humans intentionally create artificial lakes by damming flowing rivers and streams to use them for power, irrigation, water storage, and recreation.

Life in a Lake Lakes and ponds can be structured into horizontal and vertical zones. In the nutrient-rich **littoral zone** near the shore, aquatic life is diverse and abundant. Plants, such as cattails and reeds, are rooted in the mud underwater, and their upper leaves and stems emerge above the water. Plants that have floating leaves, such as pond lilies, are rooted here also. Farther from the shore, in the open water, there are no rooted plants. Here, phytoplankton make their own food by *photosynthesis*. As shown in **Figure 3**, nutrients and sunlight influence the location and types of organisms in a pond or lake ecosystem.

Some bodies of fresh water have areas so deep that there is too little light for photosynthesis. In these deep areas, bacteria and other decomposers live on dead plants and animals that drift down from above. Fish adapted to cooler water also live there. Eventually, dead and decaying organisms reach the **benthic zone,** the bottom of a pond or lake, which is inhabited by decomposers, insect larvae, and clams.

Some animals that live in lakes and ponds have interesting adaptations that help them obtain what they need to survive. Water beetles use the hairs under their bodies to trap surface air so that they can breathe during their dives for food. Whiskers help catfish sense food as they swim over dark lake bottoms. In regions where lakes partially freeze in winter, amphibians burrow into the littoral mud to avoid freezing temperatures.

Sunlight

LITTORAL ZONE

BENTHIC ZONE

Decomposers

Phytoplankton and zooplankton

How Nutrients Affect Lakes **Eutrophication** is an increase in the amount of nutrients in an aquatic ecosystem. A lake that has a large amount of algae and plant growth due to nutrients, as shown in **Figure 4,** is known as a *eutrophic lake.* As the amount of plants and algae grows, the number of bacteria feeding on the decaying organisms also grows. These bacteria use the oxygen dissolved in the lake water. Eventually, the reduced amount of oxygen kills oxygen-loving organisms. Lakes naturally become eutrophic over a long period of time. However, eutrophication can be accelerated by runoff. Runoff is precipitation, such as rain, that can carry sewage, fertilizers, or animal wastes from land into bodies of water.

Freshwater Wetlands

Freshwater wetlands are areas of land that are covered with fresh water for at least part of the year. The two main types of freshwater wetlands are marshes and swamps. *Marshes* contain nonwoody plants, such as cattails, while *swamps* are dominated by woody plants, such as trees and shrubs.

Wetlands perform several important environmental functions, as shown in **Table 1.** Wetlands act as filters or sponges because they absorb and remove pollutants from the water that flows through them. Therefore, wetlands improve the water quality of lakes, rivers, and reservoirs downstream. Wetlands also control flooding by absorbing extra water when rivers overflow, which protects farms and urban and residential areas from damage. Many of the freshwater game fish caught in the United States each year use the wetlands for feeding and spawning. In addition, these areas provide a home for native and migratory wildlife, including the blue herons shown in **Figure 5.** Wetland vegetation also traps carbon that would otherwise be released as carbon dioxide, which may be linked to rising atmospheric temperatures.

✔ **Reading Check** How can wetlands reduce damage that is caused by flooding? (See the Appendix for answers to Reading Checks.)

Figure 4 ▶ A eutrophic lake, like the one above, contains large amounts of plants as a result of high levels of nutrients.

Figure 5 ▶ Wetlands provide habitat for many plants and animals, including the great blue herons shown below.

Table 1 ▼

Environmental Functions of Wetlands

- trapping and filtering sediments, nutrients, and pollutants, which keep these materials from entering lakes, reservoirs, and oceans

- reducing the likelihood of a flood, protecting agriculture, roads, buildings, and human health and safety

- buffering shorelines against erosion

- providing spawning grounds and habitat for commercially important fish and shellfish

- providing habitat for rare, threatened, and endangered species

- providing recreational areas for activities such as fishing, bird-watching, hiking, canoeing, photography, and painting

Figure 6 ▶ This map shows the locations of large freshwater wetlands in the United States.

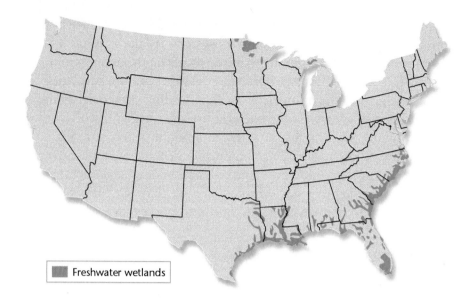

Freshwater wetlands

Marshes As shown in **Figure 6**, most freshwater wetlands in the United States are located in the Southeast. The Florida Everglades is the largest freshwater wetland in the United States. Freshwater marshes tend to occur on low, flat lands and have little water movement. In shallow waters, plants such as reeds, rushes, and cattails root themselves in the rich bottom sediments. As shown in **Figure 7**, the leaves of these and other plants stick out above the surface of the water year-round.

The benthic zones of marshes are nutrient rich and contain plants, numerous types of decomposers, and scavengers. Waterfowl, such as grebes and ducks, have flat beaks adapted for sifting through the water for fish and insects. Water birds, such as herons, have spearlike beaks that they use to grasp small fish and to probe for frogs buried in the mud. Marshes also attract many migratory birds from temperate and tropical habitats.

The salinity of marshes varies. Some marshes have slightly salty (brackish) water, while other marshes have water that is as salty as ocean water. The organisms that live in and around a marsh are generally adapted to the specific range of salinities of its water.

Figure 7 ▶ A marsh is a type of wetland that contains nonwoody plants.

Swamps Swamps occur on flat, poorly drained land, often near streams. The species of trees and shrubs in a swamp depend on the salinity of the water and the climate of the area. For example, mangroves are trees that grow in saltwater swamps in tropical climates. Freshwater swamps are the ideal habitat for many amphibians, such as frogs and salamanders, because of the continuously moist environment. Swamps also attract birds, such as wood ducks, that nest in hollow trees near or over the water. Reptiles, such as the American alligator in **Figure 8,** are the predators of swamps and will eat almost any organism that crosses their path.

Human Impact on Wetlands Wetlands were previously considered to be wastelands that provide breeding grounds for disease-carrying insects. Therefore, many have been drained, filled, and cleared for farms or residential and commercial development, as shown in **Figure 9.** For example, the Florida Everglades once covered 8 million acres of south Florida, but now covers less than 2 million acres. The important role of wetlands as purifiers of wastewater and in flood prevention is now recognized. Wetlands are vital habitats for wildlife. Law and the federal government protect many wetlands, and most states now prohibit the destruction of certain wetlands.

MATHPRACTICE

Wetland Conversion
From 1982 to 1992, approximately 1.6 million acres of wetlands on nonfederal lands in the United States were converted for other uses. Fifty-seven percent of the wetlands were converted into land for development. Twenty percent of the wetlands were converted into land for agriculture. How many acres of land were converted into land for development? How many acres of land were converted into land for agriculture?

Figure 9 ▶ The wetland above has been drained for agricultural purposes. Wetlands such as the one above typically serve as breeding areas for ducks. The oil rig on the left is located in a marsh along the coast of Louisiana.

Rivers

Many rivers originate from snow melt in mountains. At its headwaters, a river is usually cold and full of oxygen and runs swiftly through a shallow riverbed. As a river flows down a mountain, it becomes warmer, wider, and slower, containing more vegetation and less oxygen. **Figure 10** compares the water flow of two sections of two different rivers. A river changes with the land and the climate through which it flows. Runoff, for example, may wash nutrients and sediment from the surrounding land into a river. These materials affect the growth and health of the organisms in the river.

Life in a River Near the churning headwaters, mosses anchor themselves to rocks by using rootlike structures called *rhizoids*. Trout and minnows are adapted to the cold, oxygen-rich headwaters. Trout are powerful swimmers and have streamlined bodies that present little resistance to the strong current. Downstream, plants such as the crowfoot set roots in the river's rich sediment. The leaves of some plants, such as the arrowhead, vary in shape according to the strength of the river's current. Fish such as catfish and carp also live in the calmer waters.

Rivers in Danger Communities and industries affect the health of rivers. People draw water from rivers to use in homes and manufacturing. People may also use rivers to dispose of their sewage and garbage. These practices have polluted rivers with toxins. The toxins have killed river organisms and made river fish unsuitable for eating. Today, runoff from the land puts pesticides and other poisons into rivers and coats riverbeds with toxic sediments. As well, dams alter the ecosystems in and around a river.

Figure 10 ▶ A river changes dramatically as it flows from a mountaintop to flat land.

✓ **Reading Check** What effect can runoff have on the health of organisms that live in and around a river?

SECTION 1 Review

1. **List** two factors that determine where an organism lives in an aquatic ecosystem.

2. **Compare** the littoral zone of a lake with the benthic zone of a lake.

3. **List** two environmental functions that wetlands provide. How do these functions affect you?

4. **Describe** one threat against river ecosystems.

CRITICAL THINKING

5. **Identifying Relationships** A piece of garbage that is thrown into a stream may end up in a river or an ocean. What effects might one piece of garbage have on an aquatic ecosystem? What effects might 100 pieces of garbage have on an aquatic ecosystem?

6. **Analyzing Processes** Write a short paragraph that explains how fertilizing your yard and applying pesticides can affect the health of a river ecosystem.
   WRITING SKILLS

Marine Ecosystems

SCSh.2.a; SCSh.2.b; SCSh.3.b; SCSh.3.c;
SCSh.3.e; SCSh.4.a; SCSh.5.a; SCSh.6.a;
SCSh.6.d; SEV.2.d; SEV.5.a

Marine ecosystems are ecosystems that contain salt water. Such ecosystems are found in and around the world's oceans. In the open water, the amount of sunlight and available nutrients vary from one part of an ocean to another. In coastal areas, the water level and salinity usually change during the day.

Coastal Wetlands

Coastal land areas that are covered by salt water for all or part of the time are known as *coastal wetlands*. Coastal wetlands provide habitat and nesting areas for many fish and wildlife. Coastal wetlands also absorb excess rain, which protects areas from flooding, they filter out pollutants and sediments, and they provide recreational areas for boating, fishing, and hunting.

Estuaries Many coastal wetlands form in estuaries. An **estuary** is an area in which fresh water from a river mixes with salt water from the ocean. As the two bodies of water meet, currents form and cause mineral-rich mud and dissolved nutrients to fall to the bottom. **Figure 11** illustrates how the waters mix in such a way that the estuary becomes a nutrient trap. These nutrients then become available to producers, and in some shallow areas, marsh grass will grow in the mud. Estuaries are very productive ecosystems because they constantly receive fresh nutrients from the river. The surrounding land, such as the mainland or a peninsula, protects estuaries from the harsh force of ocean waves.

Objectives

▶ Explain why an estuary is a very productive ecosystem.

▶ Compare salt marshes and mangrove swamps.

▶ Describe two threats to coral reefs.

▶ Describe two threats to ocean organisms.

Key Terms

estuary
salt marsh
mangrove swamp
barrier island
coral reef

SC*LINKS*.

www.scilinks.org
Topic: Estuaries
Code: HE80536

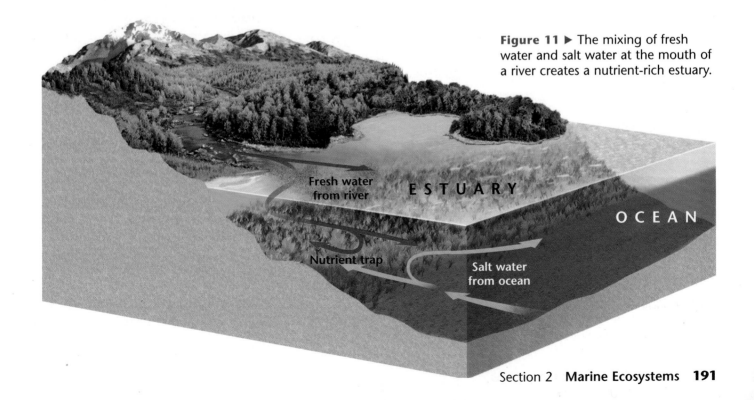

Figure 11 ▶ The mixing of fresh water and salt water at the mouth of a river creates a nutrient-rich estuary.

Fresh water from river

ESTUARY

OCEAN

Nutrient trap

Salt water from ocean

QuickLAB

Estuaries

Procedure

1. Place a few drops of **red food coloring** in a **test tube** filled with **water.**

2. In a separate **test tube**, add **salt water** and a few drops of **yellow food coloring.**

3. Gently place some of the fresh water solution on top of the salt water solution.

Analysis

1. How do fresh water and salt water interact in an estuary?

Plants and Animals of Estuaries For a week each spring, horseshoe crabs, shown in **Figure 12,** crawl out of the ocean and onto the beaches of Delaware Bay. In the shallow areas along the shore, the crabs mate and lay billions of eggs. Many migrating shorebirds depend on these eggs for food.

Estuaries support many marine organisms because estuaries receive plenty of light for photosynthesis and plenty of nutrients for plants and animals. Rivers supply nutrients that have been washed from the land, and because the water is shallow, sunlight can reach all the way to the bottom of the estuary. The light and nutrients support large populations of rooted plants as well as plankton. The plankton in turn provide food for larger animals, such as fish. Dolphins, manatees, otters, and other mammals often feed on fish and plants in estuaries. Oysters, barnacles, and clams live anchored to marsh grass or rocks and feed by filtering plankton out of the water. Organisms that live in estuaries are able to tolerate variations in salinity because the salt content of the water varies as fresh water and salt water mix when tides go in and out.

CASE STUDY

Restoration of the Chesapeake Bay

The Chesapeake Bay is the largest estuary in the United States. The bay produces large amounts of seafood each year, supports many species of wildlife, and provides recreation for millions of people.

However, the ecosystems of the bay are threatened by several environmental problems. For example, pollution builds up because the small tide flushes pollutants out of the bay very slowly. Pollution builds up because only a very narrow opening joins the bay and the ocean. By 1980, the Chesapeake Bay was severely polluted with toxic industrial chemicals. Pesticides as well as excess nutrients ran into the bay from housing developments, farms, and wastewater (including sewage). Marsh grasses and plankton were dying, and fish, oysters, and crabs were disappearing. Birds of prey, such as bald eagles, had

almost vanished. Therefore, fishers, environmentalists, and residents became alarmed and launched campaigns to save the bay.

Restoring Chesapeake Bay habitats and water quality is not easy. Maryland and Virginia, the main bordering states of the bay, have different environmental laws. Also, the bay's watershed covers parts of four other states. Interested groups would have to work together if they were to restore the bay. The Chesapeake Bay Program was set up as a partnership between the Environmental Protection Agency, the District of Columbia, Maryland, Pennsylvania, Virginia, and citizen advisory groups. Goals included reducing chemical pollution, removing dams that prevented fish from migrating, and reforesting river banks to reduce soil erosion.

Chesapeake Bay Watershed

▶ The Chesapeake Bay forms where the Potomac, Rappahannock, and other rivers meet the Atlantic Ocean.

Remarkable progress has been made in the last 20 years. About half of the wastewater flowing into

Estuaries provide protected harbors, access to the ocean, and connection to a river. As a result, many of the world's major ports are built on estuaries. Of the 10 largest urban areas in the world, 6 were built on estuaries. These 6 cities are Tokyo, New York, Shanghai, Buenos Aires, Rio de Janeiro, and Bombay.

Threats to Estuaries Estuaries in populated areas were often used as solid waste landfills. The landfills were then developed and used as building sites. This practice occurred widely in California, which now has plans to restore some of its estuary wetlands. The pollutants that damage estuaries are the same pollutants that damage other aquatic ecosystems: sewage, industrial waste, and agricultural runoff. Most of these pollutants eventually break down over time, but estuaries cannot cope with the excessive amounts produced by dense human populations.

Figure 12 ▶ Horseshoe crabs go to the Delaware Bay, an estuary between New Jersey and Delaware, to lay their eggs.

▶ This great egret lives in one of the estuaries that borders the Chesapeake Bay.

the bay is now biologically treated to remove pollutants and excess nutrients. Bald eagles are back, and industry has reduced the chemical pollutants released into the bay by nearly 70 percent. Planting trees has restored forested buffers to about 60 percent of the river banks, and populations of fish, such as striped bass, are increasing.

However, the number of people in the bay area is increasing and the number of miles these people drive

each year has increased even faster. In the last 30 years, miles traveled by vehicles increased four times as fast as the population. This has led to runoff from streets and lawns and pollution from vehicle exhaust, all of which harm the bay. The oyster harvest has decreased and the forested part of the bay's watershed is still decreasing.

You can help save your local watershed in the following ways: by reducing the number of miles you

drive, trying to conserve electricity and water, planting native vegetation, using only a small amount of fertilizer or water on your lawn or garden, and properly disposing of hazardous wastes such as motor oil, antifreeze, and cleaning fluids. You can help by picking up trash that others leave behind. You can also join a citizens group to help preserve estuaries.

CRITICAL THINKING

1. Predicting Consequences If the Chesapeake Bay Program had never been founded, what might have happened to the Chesapeake Bay? Explain how one organism may have been affected.

2. Identifying Relationships How may the use of less fertilizer on plants and lawns help the Chesapeake Bay and other estuaries?

Figure 13 ▶ Mangrove swamps are found along warm, tropical coasts and are dominated by salt-tolerant mangrove trees.

Ecofact

Mangrove Swamps Mangroves cover 180 billion square meters of tropical coastlines around the world. The largest single mangrove swamp is 5.7 billion square meters, located in the Sundarbans of Bangladesh. This single mangrove swamp provides habitat for the Bengal tiger and helps supply approximately 300,000 people with food, fuel, building materials, and medicines.

Figure 14 ▶ This barrier island is located off the coast of Long Island, New York. Barrier islands are separated from the mainland and help protect the shore of the mainland from erosion.

Salt Marshes In estuaries, where rivers deposit their load of mineral-rich mud, **salt marshes** form. Here, thousands of acres of salt marsh support a community of clams, fish, and aquatic birds. The marsh also acts as a nursery in which many species of shrimps, crabs, and fishes find protection when they are small. As they grow to maturity and migrate to the sea, they are eaten by larger fish or caught by commercial fisheries. Salt marshes, like other wetlands, absorb pollutants and protect inland areas.

Mangrove Swamps Mangroves, such as those shown in **Figure 13**, are several species of small trees adapted for growing in shallow salt water. Most mangroves have wide, above-ground root systems for support. Dense growths of mangrove trees in swampy areas called **mangrove swamps** are found in tropical and subtropical zones. Mangrove swamps help to protect the coastline from erosion and reduce the damage from storms. They provide habitat for about 2,000 animal species. Like salt marshes, mangrove swamps have been filled with waste or used for development projects in many parts of the world.

Rocky and Sandy Shores Rocky shores have many more plant and animal species than sandy shores do. The rocks anchor seaweed and the many animals that live on it, such as sea anemones, mussels, and sponges. Life on sandy shores, although less diverse, is abundant in the water and in the sand and sediments. In the water and on land, animals are adapted to the effects of drying and exposure at low tide. At low tide, birds poke and prod about for animals that have not attached themselves firmly enough or buried themselves deeply enough to escape the tidal pull.
Barrier islands, such as the one in **Figure 14**, often run parallel to sandy shores. These islands help to protect the mainland and the coastal wetlands from storms and ocean waves.

✔ **Reading Check** Name two things that a salt marsh has in common with a mangrove swamp.

Figure 15 ▶ Coral reefs are found in warm, shallow waters, where there is enough light for photosynthesis. Coral reefs support a great diversity of species.

Graphic Organizer — Cause-and-Effect Map

Create the **Graphic Organizer** entitled "Cause-and-Effect Map" described in the Appendix. Label the effect with "Disappearing Coral Reefs." Then, fill in the map with causes of disappearing coral reefs and details about the causes and effects.

Coral Reefs

Coral reefs are limestone ridges built by tiny coral animals called *coral polyps* and the algae that live inside them. Coral polyps secrete skeletons of limestone (calcium carbonate), which slowly accumulate and form coral reefs. Thousands of species of plants and animals live in the cracks of coral reefs, which makes coral reefs among the most diverse ecosystems on Earth.

Because reef-building corals live only in warm salt water where there is enough light for photosynthesis, coral reefs are found in shallow, clear tropical seas. **Figure 15** shows the locations of coral reefs. Only the outer layer of a reef contains living corals, which build their rock homes with the help of the photosynthetic algae that live within them. Corals, such as those shown in **Figure 16,** are predators that never chase their prey. Their stinging polyps capture small animals that float or swim close to the reef. Because of their convoluted shape, coral reefs provide a habitat for a magnificent variety of fish, snails, clams, sponges and many other types of organisms.

Coral Reefs in Danger Coral reefs are fragile ecosystems. If the surrounding water is too hot or cold for too long, or if it is too muddy, polluted, or high in nutrients, the algae that live in the corals will leave or die. As a result, the corals turn white, a condition called *coral bleaching*. If coral bleaching occurs often or long enough, coral animals and the reefs they build will die.

Since the twentieth century, bleaching events have been occurring more frequently, mainly due to human activities. About 50 percent of the world's coral reefs are now in danger of destruction. In addition, global warming, oil spills, and polluting runoff have been linked to the destruction of coral reefs. As well, overfishing upsets the balance of a reef ecosystem by devastating fish populations. Because coral reefs grow slowly, a reef may not be able to repair itself when parts of it are stressed or destroyed.

Figure 16 ▶ Coral reefs (bottom) are built by tiny coral animals called coral polyps. The stinging polyps of fire coral (top) capture animals by poisoning them.

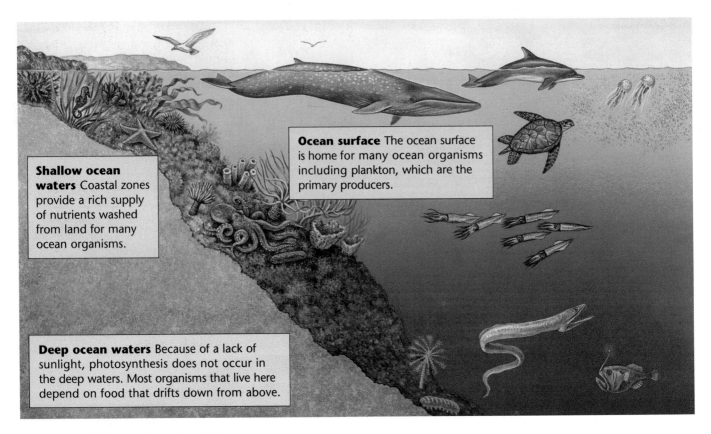

Shallow ocean waters Coastal zones provide a rich supply of nutrients washed from land for many ocean organisms.

Ocean surface The ocean surface is home for many ocean organisms including plankton, which are the primary producers.

Deep ocean waters Because of a lack of sunlight, photosynthesis does not occur in the deep waters. Most organisms that live here depend on food that drifts down from above.

Figure 17 ▶ The amount of sunlight available determines which organisms can live in each layer of the ocean.

FIELD ACTIVITY

Make a Miniature Aquatic Ecosystem Make your own aquarium by collecting organisms from an aquatic ecosystem near your home or school. Be sure to collect some water from the aquatic ecosystem. Bring your collection back to school and set up an aquarium. If necessary, research the Internet to find out the special care that your ecosystem may require. Examine a few drops of your collected water under the microscope. Be sure to look for algae or other forms of life. Record and draw your observations in your *EcoLog.* Observe and record the changes you see in your aquarium over the next 3 weeks. What conditions are needed to keep your miniature ecosystem healthy?

Oceans

Because water absorbs light, sunlight that plants can use for photosynthesis penetrates only about 100 m (330 ft) into the ocean. As a result, much of the ocean's life is concentrated in the shallow, coastal waters. Here, sunlight penetrates to the bottom and rivers wash nutrients from the land. Seaweed and algae grow anchored to rocks, and phytoplankton drift on the surface. Invertebrates and fish that feed on these plants are also concentrated near the shore.

Plants and Animals of Oceans In the open ocean, phytoplankton grow only in areas where there is enough light and nutrients. As a result, the open ocean is one of the least productive of all ecosystems. Phytoplankton have buoyancy devices, such as oil bubbles, that prevent them from sinking into deep water, which is too dark for photosynthesis. The sea's smallest herbivores are the zooplankton, which live near the surface with the phytoplankton they eat. The zooplankton include jellyfish, tiny shrimp, and the larvae of fish and bottom-dwelling animals, such as oysters and lobsters. Fish feed on the plankton as do marine mammals such as whales.

The depths of the ocean are perpetually dark, so most food at the ocean floor consists of dead organisms that fall from the surface. Decomposers, filter feeders, and the organisms that eat them live in the deep areas of the ocean. **Figure 17** illustrates the types of organisms that may be found in the layers of the ocean at various depths, depending on available sunlight.

Threats to the Oceans Although oceans are huge, they are steadily becoming more polluted. Most ocean pollution arises from activities on land. For example, runoff from fertilized fields may cause algal blooms, some of which are poisonous. Waste from cities and industries, fertilizers, and sewage running off the land are the main sources of coastal pollution in the United States.

Overfishing and certain fishing methods are also destroying some fish populations. Immense trawl nets can entangle organisms that are larger than the holes in the nets. Marine mammals such as dolphins, which must breathe air, can drown in the nets. Some ships illegally discard fishing lines into the ocean, where they can strangle and kill animals such as the sea lion in **Figure 18.**

Figure 18 ▶ This sea lion was strangled by a fishing net off the coast of California.

Arctic and Antarctic Ecosystems The arctic ecosystems at the North and South Poles are marine ecosystems because nearly all the food comes from the ocean and seas.

The Arctic Ocean is rich in nutrients from the surrounding land masses. It supports large populations of plankton, which feed a rich diversity of fish in the open water and under the ice. The fish are food for ocean birds, whales, and seals. Beluga whales, shown in **Figure 19,** feed on nearly 100 different arctic organisms. Fish and seals also provide food for polar bears and people on land.

The Antarctic is the only continent never colonized by humans. Even during the summer, only a few plants grow at the rocky edges of the continent. As in the Arctic, plankton form the basis of the Antarctic food web. They nourish large numbers of fish, whales, and birds such as penguins, which cannot fly because their wings have evolved for swimming.

✔ **Reading Check** What are two threats to organisms that live in the ocean?

Figure 19 ▶ Beluga whales inhabit the Arctic Ocean.

SECTION 2 **Review**

1. **Explain** why estuaries are very productive ecosystems. Why are estuaries vulnerable to the effects of pollution?

2. **Compare** salt marshes with mangrove swamps.

3. **Describe** two factors that can damage coral reefs.

4. **List** two ways in which animals of the oceans are threatened.

CRITICAL THINKING

5. **Predicting Consequences** Suppose that the sea level suddenly rose by 100 m. What would happen to the world's coral reefs? Explain.

6. **Analyzing Processes** Read the description of estuaries in this section, and explain why cities are often built on estuaries. How would building a city on an estuary affect the plants and animals living in the estuary? **READING SKILLS**

1 Freshwater Ecosystems

Key Terms

wetland, 185
plankton, 185
nekton, 185
benthos, 185
littoral zone, 186
benthic zone, 186
eutrophication, 187

Main Ideas

▶ Aquatic ecosystems can be classified as freshwater ecosystems or marine ecosystems. The plants and animals in aquatic ecosystems are adapted to specific environmental conditions.

▶ Freshwater ecosystems include lakes, ponds, freshwater wetlands, rivers, and streams. The types of freshwater ecosystems are classified by the depth of the water, the speed of the water flow, and the availability of minerals, sunlight, and oxygen.

▶ Freshwater wetlands serve many functions within ecosystems. They trap and filter sediments and pollutants; reduce the likelihood of a flood; and buffer shorelines against erosion.

2 Marine Ecosystems

estuary, 191
salt marsh, 194
mangrove swamp, 194
barrier island, 194
coral reef, 195

▶ Marine ecosystems are identified by the presence of salt water and include coastal wetlands, coral reefs, oceans, and polar ecosystems.

▶ Estuaries are among the most productive of ecosystems because they constantly receive fresh nutrients from a river and from an ocean. Estuaries provide habitat for a multitude of plants and animals.

▶ Coral reefs are susceptible to destruction because they must remain at tropical temperatures and they must receive a large amount of sunlight. Coral reefs provide habitat for approximately one-fourth of all marine species.

▶ Almost every person has an impact on aquatic ecosystems. Through understanding how we affect aquatic ecosystems, we can reduce the negative effects we have on them.

Using Key Terms

Use each of the following terms in a separate sentence.

1. *wetland*
2. *mangrove swamp*
3. *estuary*
4. *eutrophication*
5. *benthos*

For each pair of terms, explain how the meanings of the terms differ.

6. *littoral zone* and *benthic zone*
7. *plankton* and *nekton*
8. *salt marsh* and *barrier island*
9. *wetland* and *coral reef*

✔ **STUDY TIP**

Graph Skills Taking the following steps when reading a graph will help you correctly interpret the information. Be sure to read the title so that you understand what the graph represents. If the graph has axes, read the titles of both the *x*- and the *y*-axis. Examine the range of values on both the *x*- and the *y*-axis. Finally, examine the data on the graph, reading them from left to right, and put into words what you think the graph represents.

Understanding Key Ideas

10. Wetlands are important to fisheries in the United States because
    a. wetlands are the easiest place to catch fish.
    b. wetlands are the breeding grounds for insects that are eaten by fish.
    c. wetlands provide the most desirable species of fish.
    d. many of the fish caught each year use wetlands for feeding and spawning.

11. Animals that live in estuaries
    a. tend to produce few offspring.
    b. are usually found in unpolluted environments.
    c. must be adapted to varying levels of salinity.
    d. are adapted to cold-water conditions.

12. Bacteria can kill organisms in eutrophic lakes by
    a. feeding on decaying plants and animals.
    b. reducing oxygen dissolved in the water.
    c. Both (a) and (b)
    d. Neither (a) nor (b)

13. Arctic ecosystems are considered marine ecosystems because
    a. arctic ecosystems contain an enormous amount of frozen sea water.
    b. arctic ecosystems are inhabited by few organisms.
    c. sunlight is limited.
    d. phytoplankton form the basis of arctic food webs.

14. Which of the following statements does *not* describe a function of wetlands?
    a. Wetlands buffer shorelines against erosion.
    b. Wetlands provide spawning grounds for commercially important fish and shellfish.
    c. Wetlands filter pollutants.
    d. Wetlands make good hazardous waste dumpsites.

15. Tiny animals, called *coral polyps*, that secrete limestone create
    a. barrier islands.
    b. coral reefs.
    c. swamps.
    d. salt marshes.

16. Mangrove trees grow
    a. along riverbanks.
    b. in freshwater wetlands.
    c. in tropical areas and in subtropical areas.
    d. in the benthic zones of lakes.

17. The Florida Everglades
    a. is the largest freshwater marsh in the United States.
    b. protects threatened and endangered wildlife.
    c. provides habitat for migratory birds.
    d. All of the above

18. Which of the following actions is an example of how humans affect wetlands?
    a. draining a wetland to create farmland
    b. clearing a wetland to build a housing development
    c. using a wetland as a landfill
    d. all of the above

Short Answer

19. How does the phrase "the best of both worlds" relate to an estuary?

20. Explain the difference between the types of organisms that make up these classes: plankton, nekton, and benthos.

21. List three functions of wetlands.

22. Describe what happens when a lake is considered to be eutrophic.

23. What type of vegetation dominates mangrove swamps?

Interpreting Graphics

The pie graph below shows the percentage of coral reefs at risk in the world. Use the pie graph to answer questions 24–26.

24. What percentage of coral reefs are still living?

25. If there is a total of 255,300 km² of coral reefs in the world, how many square kilometers of coral reefs are at a high risk of being destroyed?

26. How many square kilometers of coral reefs are at a medium risk of being destroyed? Assume there is a total of 255,300 km² coral reefs in the world.

Status of the World's Coral Reefs

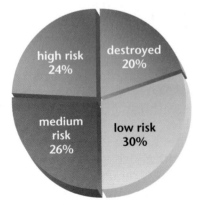

Source: Global Coral Reef Monitoring Network

Concept Mapping

27. Use the following terms to create a concept map: *lakes, estuaries, aquatic ecosystems, coral reefs, freshwater wetlands, freshwater ecosystems, rivers, oceans, marshes, marine ecosystems, swamps, coastal ecosystems,* and *mangrove swamps.*

Critical Thinking

28. Analyzing Relationships Write a short paragraph that explains the relationship between the speed of a river and the oxygen content of a river. **WRITING SKILLS**

29. Determining Cause and Effect Explain what may happen if the use of fertilizer on farms and lawns around an estuary is not controlled.

30. Making Comparisons Read the paragraph under the heading "Threats to Estuaries" in this chapter. How do these threats compare with those described under the heading "Threats to the Oceans"? **READING SKILLS**

31. Analyzing Relationships Explain why planting trees along a riverbank might benefit a river ecosystem.

Cross-Disciplinary Connection

32. Demography Six out of 10 of the largest urban areas were built on estuaries. Three of these cities are Tokyo, New York, and Rio de Janeiro. Research the population of each of these cities, and predict what may happen if population numbers continue to increase.

Portfolio Project

33. Research a Local Aquatic Ecosystem Observe an aquatic ecosystem near your school or home. This ecosystem can be as simple as a pond or stream or as complex as a lake or estuary. Observe the color of the water and the types of plants and animals. Record any interactions among the organisms that you observe. When you have recorded all of your data and observations, write a one-page report on the aquatic ecosystem.

Use the graph below to answer questions 34–35.

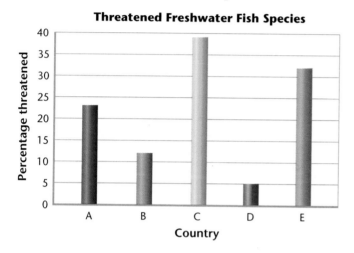

Threatened Freshwater Fish Species

Percentage threatened (y-axis: 0 to 40)
Country (x-axis: A, B, C, D, E)

34. **Analyzing Data** The graph below illustrates the percentage of freshwater fish species that are threatened in specific countries. What percentage of freshwater fish species are threatened in country B? in country D?

35. **Evaluating Data** If the number of freshwater fish species in country C totals 599 different species, how many of these species are threatened?

 WRITING SKILLS

36. **Communicating Main Ideas** What effect does overfishing have on estuaries? What effect does overfishing have on oceans?

37. **Writing from Research** Research endangered marine mammals of ocean and polar ecosystems. Write a one-page report on the factors that have caused these mammals to become endangered.

 READING SKILLS

Read the passage below, and then answer the questions that follow.

In the United States during the last 200 years, over 99 percent of native prairies have been replaced with farmland or urban development and most of the old-growth forests have been cut. Loss of so many of these habitats has resulted in losses of biodiversity.

A new discipline, called *conservation biology,* seeks to identify and maintain natural areas. In areas where human influence is greater, such as agricultural areas, former strip mines, and drained wetlands, biologists may have to reverse major changes and replace missing ecosystem components. For example, returning a strip-mined area to grassland may require contouring the land surface, introducing bacteria to the soil, planting grass and shrub seedlings, and even using periodic fires to manage the growth of vegetation. Restoring an area to its natural state is called *restoration ecology.*

1. Which of the following phrases describes a likely task of a restoration ecologist?
   a. raising funds needed to create a national park
   b. returning missing ecosystem components to a drained wetland
   c. educating citizens about the need to protect a local habitat
   d. both (a) and (b)

2. Based on the passage, which of the following statements is true?
   a. Former strip mines tend to have a high level of biodiversity.
   b. A conservation biologist would most likely oppose the development of areas around the Grand Canyon.
   c. Periodic fires in some ecosystems do not help manage excess growth of vegetation.
   d. Most prairie ecosystems located in the United States have been preserved.

Understanding Concepts

Directions (1–5): For *each* question, write on a separate sheet of paper the letter of the correct answer.

1 Organisms living in coastal areas must adapt to what changes?
   A. water level and degree of salinity
   B. water level and amount of sunlight
   C. temperature and availability of oxygen
   D. temperature and availability of nutrients

2 Bleaching events lead to the destruction of what kind of marine ecosystem?
   F. coastal wetlands
   G. coral reefs
   H. mangrove swamps
   I. salt marshes

3 Which of the following correctly lists types of organisms in aquatic ecosystems from shallowest to deepest?
   A. plankton, nekton, benthos
   B. plankton, benthos, nekton
   C. benthos, plankton, nekton
   D. benthos, nekton, plankton

4 What is the difference between swamps and marshes?
   F. Marshes attract birds, swamps attract amphibians.
   G. Marshes are freshwater, swamps are saltwater.
   H. Marshes contain non-woody plants, swamps contain woody plants.
   I. Marshes are mostly in the southeast U.S., swamps in the northeast U.S.

5 Which of the following would be considered among the most productive ecosystems?
   A. barrier island
   B. estuary
   C. river
   D. salt marsh

Directions (6–7): For *each* question, write a short response.

6 Most ocean pollution arises from activity on land. How does land pollution end up in the oceans?

7 Aquatic ecosystems are divided into two types—marine and freshwater. Compare and contrast marine and freshwater ecosystems.

Reading Skills

Directions (8–10): Read the passage below. Then answer the questions.

Wetlands perform several important environmental functions. Some wetlands are used to produce commercially important products, such as cranberries. But wetlands were once considered to be wastelands that provide breeding grounds for insects. Therefore, many have been drained, filled, and cleared for farms or residential and commercial development. For example, the Florida Everglades once covered 8 million acres of south Florida, but now it covers less than 2 million acres. From 1982 to 1992 alone, 57 percent of wetlands were converted into land for development. Wetlands are vitally important as habitats for wildlife, and their important role in the environment is now recognized.

8 Which of the following is **not** an environmental function of wetlands?
   F. Wetlands are important as habitats for wildlife.
   G. Wetlands may be converted into land for development.
   H. Wetlands may be used to grow commercial products, such as cranberries.
   I. Wetlands trap and filter sediments and pollutants.

9 By approximately how much has the area of the Florida Everglades in south Florida decreased?
   A. 40 percent
   B. 75 percent
   C. 5 percent
   D. 60 percent

10 What could be inferred as the cause of scientific awareness of the importance of wetlands?

Interpreting Graphics

Directions (11–13): For *each* question below, record the correct answer on a separate sheet of paper.

The table below shows organisms whose presence or absence can be indicators of water quality. Use this table to answer questions 11 through 13.

Living Water Quality Indicators

Most sensitive species Caddisfly larvae, hellgrammites, stonefly larvae, mayfly nymphs, gilled snails, and water penny larvae	mayfly nymph caddisfly larvae
Moderately sensitive species Clams, cranefly larvae, crayfish, damselfly nymphs, dragonfly nymphs, scuds, predacious diving beetle larvae, sowbugs, fishfly larvae, and alderfly larvae	dragonfly nymph predacious diving beetle larva
Tolerant species Aquatic worms, blackfly larvae, leeches, midge larvae, and pouch snails	midge larva leeches

11 If a water sample contains mayfly nymphs, what can you conclude about the water quality of the area where the sample was taken?
  F. The area has generally poor water quality.
  G. The area has generally good water quality.
  H. The water quality cannot be determined from such a sample.
  I. The water in the area has been chemically treated for pollutants.

12 What group of organisms could be seen **only** in a sample taken from unpolluted water?
  A. leeches and caddisfly larvae
  B. leeches and dragonfly nymphs
  C. leeches and midge larvae
  D. leeches and predacious diving beetle larvae

13 Water sample A contains only leeches. Water sample B contains leeches and predacious diving beetle larvae. What comparison can be made between samples A and B?
  F. Both samples A and B have the same water quality.
  G. Both samples came from the same water source.
  H. Sample A has relatively poorer water quality than sample B.
  I. Sample B has relatively poorer water quality than sample A.

Test TIP

Imagine the increasing levels of pollution that would affect water quality and cause particular species to disappear.

Skills Practice Lab: OBSERVATION

Objectives

▶ **USING SCIENTIFIC METHODS** **Observe** the effects of nitrates and phosphates on an aquatic ecosystem.

▶ **Compare** the growth of organisms in different levels of nutrients.

▶ **Predict** possible effects nitrates and phosphates would have on an aquatic ecosystem in your area.

Materials

distilled water
eyedropper
fertilizer, household use
fluorescent lamp
graduated cylinder
guide to pond life identification
jars, 1 qt (3)
microscope
microscope slides with coverslips
plastic wrap
pond water that contains viable
  organisms
stirring rod
wax pencil

▶ **Step 5** Observe a drop of pond water under the microscope.

Eutrophication: Too Much of a Good Thing?

Plants depend on nutrients such as phosphates and nitrates to survive. However, when people release large amounts of these nutrients into rivers and lakes, *artificial eutrophication* can occur. In artificial eutrophication, nutrients cause algae and plant life to grow rapidly and then die off and decay. When microorganisms decompose the algae and plant matter, they use up oxygen in the water, which causes the death of fish and other animals that depend on oxygen for survival. Eutrophication is commonly caused by phosphates, which are often found in detergents, and by nitrates, which are found in animal wastes and fertilizers. In this lab, you will observe artificial eutrophication in an aquatic ecosystem.

Procedure

1. Working with your team, use a wax pencil to label one jar "Control," a second jar "Fertilizer," and a third jar "Excess fertilizer."

2. Put 750 mL of distilled water in each of the three jars. Read the label on the fertilizer container to determine the recommended dilution of fertilizer for watering plants. To the "Fertilizer" jar, add the amount of fertilizer recommended for a quart of water. To the "Excess fertilizer" jar, add 10 times this amount of fertilizer. Stir the contents of each jar thoroughly to dissolve the fertilizer.

3. Obtain a sample of pond water. Stir it gently but thoroughly to ensure that the organisms in it are evenly distributed. Measure 100 mL of pond water into each of the three jars.

4. Cover each jar loosely with plastic wrap. Place all three jars about 20 cm from a fluorescent lamp. (Do not place the jars in direct sunlight, as this may cause them to heat up too much.)

5. Observe a drop of pond water from your sample, under the microscope. On a sheet of paper, draw at least four different organisms that you see. Determine whether the organisms are algae (usually green) or consumers (usually able to move). Describe the total number and type of organisms that you see.

6. Based on what you have learned about eutrophication, make a prediction about how the pond organisms will grow in each of the three jars.

7. Observe the jars when you first set them up and at least once every three days for the next 3 weeks. Make a data table to record the date, color, odor, and any other observations you make for each jar.

8. When life-forms begin to be visible in the jars (probably after a week), use an eyedropper to remove a sample of organisms from each jar and observe the sample under the microscope. Record your observations.

9. At the end of your 3-week observation period, again remove a sample from each jar and observe it under the microscope. Draw at least four of the most abundant organisms that you see, and describe how the number and type of organisms have changed.

▶ **Step 7** Record your observations of the jars every 3 days for 3 weeks.

Analysis

1. **Describing Events** After three weeks, which jar shows the most abundant growth of algae? What may have caused this growth?

2. **Analyzing Data** Did you observe any effects on organisms other than algae in the jar that had the most abundant algae growth? Explain.

Conclusions

3. **Applying Conclusions** Did your observations match your predictions? Explain.

4. **Drawing Conclusions** How can artificial eutrophication be prevented in natural water bodies?

Extension

1. **Designing Experiments** Modify the experiment by using household dishwashing detergent instead of household fertilizer. Are the results different?

2. **Research and Communications** Research the watersheds that are located close to your area. How might activities such as farming and building affect watersheds?

MAPS in action

WETLANDS IN THE UNITED STATES, 1780s Vs. 1980s

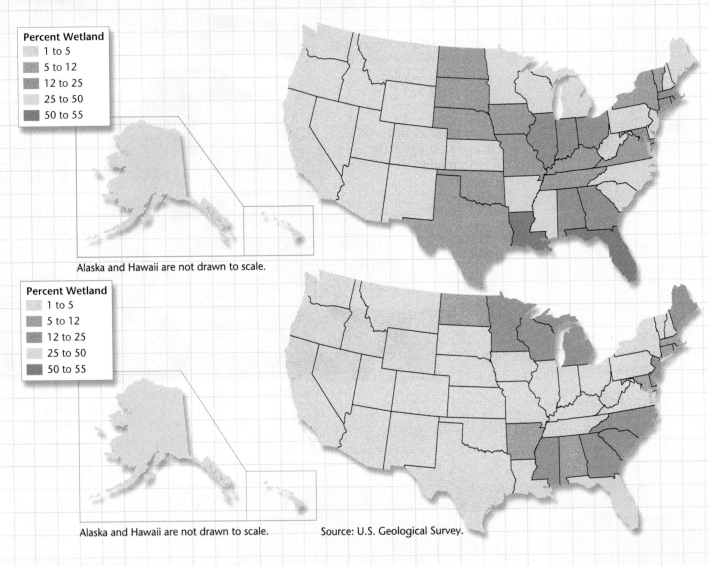

Percent Wetland
- 1 to 5
- 5 to 12
- 12 to 25
- 25 to 50
- 50 to 55

Alaska and Hawaii are not drawn to scale.

Percent Wetland
- 1 to 5
- 5 to 12
- 12 to 25
- 25 to 50
- 50 to 55

Alaska and Hawaii are not drawn to scale.   Source: U.S. Geological Survey.

MAP SKILLS

Use the maps of wetland loss in the United States to answer the questions below.

1. **Using a Key** Use the key to determine how many states had a decrease in wetland distribution from 5 to 12 percent to 1 to 5 percent.

2. **Analyzing Data** Is there any state on the map of wetland distribution in the 1980s that has the same percentage of wetland distribution as it did in the 1780s? If so, how many?

3. **Analyzing Data** Which states have had the greatest decrease in wetland distribution since the 1780s?

4. **Making Inferences** What might have caused Florida's and Louisiana's wetlands to decrease in distribution?

5. **Using a Key** Use the key to determine how many states had a decrease in wetland distribution from 25 to 50 percent to 12 to 25 percent.

6. **Identifying Trends** If these trends of wetland loss continue, what might a map of wetland distribution of the United States look like circa 2040?

HURRICANE KATRINA AND NEW ORLEANS

The city of New Orleans was built in the Mississippi River Delta, about 100 miles upriver from the Gulf of Mexico. This city is vulnerable to flooding from the Mississipppi River, Lake Pontchartrain to the north, and heavy rainfall from tropical storms. In addition, hurricanes that pass over the coast can create storm surges, waves up to 30 feet high.

To help protect New Orleans from flooding, engineers and city planners built levees and flood walls along the river banks and lakeshore. They constructed pumps to move floodwater from lower-lying areas through canals into Lake Pontchartrain. Despite these measures, Hurricane Katrina overwhelmed the city in late August, 2005. Hundreds of people were killed, and hundreds of thousands were left homeless. Analyses of the catastrophe concluded that human-made changes in the natural environment were partly responsible for the damage.

Protection from the Sea

The low-lying land of the Mississippi River Delta is a transitional area between the land and the ocean. It consists of saltwater and freshwater marshes, mud flats, and creeks, collectively known as coastal wetlands. Winds and currents move loose sediment to build up barrier islands. These islands shelter the coastal wetlands and mainland from the ocean. Plants growing in the wetlands trap sediment and help to stabilize the land. The Louisiana coast has about 40 percent of all the coastal marshes in the continental United States. These coastal wetlands are an important habitat for crustaceans, mollusks, fish, and birds. As well, they filter out pollutants from the river, absorb floodwater, and help to supply fresh water to aquifers.

Eroding the Barrier Islands

As levees confined the flow of the Mississippi River, sediment carried by the river was flushed farther out into the Gulf of Mexico. The sediment was no longer deposited to build up more land.

Canals that were built through the barrier islands to handle river traffic increased the erosion of the coastal wetlands. Soil dug from the canals was piled on the banks, smothering vegetation that had helped to hold the banks in place. The increased speed and volume of the water in the canals washed away more soil from the barrier islands. As the barrier islands eroded, the marshes and land behind them were left exposed and were washed away.

The Impact of Katrina

Most of the damage from Hurricane Katrina was caused by rising water that overflowed or broke through the levees.

A wide shipping canal funneled a storm surge from the ocean into the city. The storm surge broke through the banks of the canal. Other canals, built to drain water into Lake Pontchartrain, had their flow reversed as the water level in the lake rose. Eventually, the city's drainage system failed when most of the pumping stations were submerged.

▶ Over 80 percent of New Orleans was submerged by floodwater when Hurricane Katrina struck in August, 2005.

What Do You Think?

Many engineers and environmental scientists had predicted that the risk of flooding in New Orleans had been increased by poorly designed levees and canals, and by massive erosion. Should a large city have been built in such an unstable environment?

This school of young striped cat-fish near the coast of Australia gathers into a huge, writhing ball to defend against predators. Forming a ball makes the fish look like one large organism, and the fish's stripes may make it hard for a predator to see individual fish.

Understanding Populations

PRE-READING ACTIVITY

FOLDNOTES

Three-Panel Flip Chart
Before you read this chapter, create the **FoldNote** entitled "Three-Panel Flip Chart" described in the Reading and Study Skills section of the Appendix. Label the flaps of the chart with "Population," "Niche," and "Species Interaction." As you read the chapter, write information you learn about each category under the appropriate panel.

Orcas (also called killer whales) hunt sea lions. The interaction between these groups affects the number of individuals and the behavior of individuals in each group.

How Populations Change in Size

SCSh.2.a; SCSh.2.b; SCSh.3.a; SCSh.3.b;
SCSh.3.c; SCSh.3.d; SCSh.4.a; SCSh.4.b;
SCSh.4.c; SCSh.5.a; SCSh.5.b; SCSh.6.a;
SCSh.6.b; SCSh.6.c; SEV.3.e

Biologist Charles Darwin once calculated that a single pair of elephants could theoretically produce 19 million descendants within 750 years. Darwin made the point that the actual number of elephants is limited by their environment.

One way to study the relationship of elephants with their environment is at the level of populations. Such a study would include tracking the number of elephants in an area and observing the animals' interactions with their environment.

What Is a Population?

A **population** is all the members of a species living in the same place at the same time. The bass in an Iowa lake make up one population. **Figure 1** shows other examples of populations. A population is a reproductive group because organisms usually breed with members of their own population. For example, daisies in an Ohio field will breed with each other and not with daisies in a Maryland population. The word *population* refers to the group in general and also to the size of the population—the number of individuals it contains.

Objectives

▶ Describe the three main properties of a population.

▶ Describe exponential population growth.

▶ Describe how the reproductive behavior of individuals can affect the growth rate of their population.

▶ Explain how population sizes in nature are regulated.

Key Terms

population
density
dispersion
growth rate
reproductive potential
exponential growth
carrying capacity

Figure 1 ▶ The palm trees on an island (left) and a school of fish (below) are examples of populations.

Figure 2 ▶ Populations may have very different sizes, densities, and dispersions. Flamingos (right) are usually found in huge, dense flocks, while most snakes (above) are solitary and dispersed randomly.

QuickLAB

Population Growth

Procedure

1. Model the change in size of a population by applying the equation at right.

2. Start with **100 g (3.5 oz) of dry beans.** Count out five beans to represent the starting population of a species.

3. Assume that each year 20 percent of the beans each have two offspring. Also assume that 20 percent of the beans die each year.

4. Calculate the number of beans to add or subtract for 1 y. Round your calculations to whole numbers. Add to or remove beans from your population as appropriate.

5. Continue modeling your population changes over the course of 10 y. Record each change.

Analysis

1. Make a graph of your data. Describe the changes in your population.

Properties of Populations

Populations may be described in terms of size, density, or dispersion, as shown in **Figure 2.** A population's **density** is the number of individuals per unit area or volume, such as the number of bass per cubic meter of water in a lake. A population's **dispersion** is the relative distribution or arrangement of its individuals within a given amount of space. A population's dispersion may be *even, clumped,* or *random.* Size, density, dispersion, and other properties can be used to describe populations and to predict changes within them.

How Does a Population Grow?

A population gains individuals with each new offspring or birth and loses them with each death. The resulting population change over time can be represented by the equation below. A change in the size of a population over a given period of time is that population's **growth rate.** The growth rate is the *birth rate* minus the *death rate.*

Over time, the growth rates of populations change because birth rates and death rates increase or decrease. Growth rates can be positive, negative, or zero. For a population's growth rate to be zero, the average number of births must equal the average number of deaths. A population would remain the same size if each pair of adults produced exactly two offspring, and each of those offspring survived to reproduce. If the adults in a population are not replaced by new births, the growth rate will be negative and the population will shrink.

How Fast Can a Population Grow?

A female sea turtle may lay 2,000 eggs in her lifetime. **Figure 3** shows newly hatched sea turtles leaving their nests for the ocean. If all of them survived, the turtle population would grow rapidly. But they do not all survive. Populations usually stay about the same size from year to year because various factors kill many individuals before they can reproduce. These factors control the sizes of populations.

Reproductive Potential A species' *biotic potential* is the fastest rate at which its populations can grow. This rate is limited by the maximum number of offspring that each member of the population can produce, which is called its **reproductive potential.** Some species have much higher reproductive potentials than others. Darwin calculated that it could take 750 years for a pair of elephants to produce 19 million descendants. In contrast, a bacterium can produce 19 million descendants in a few days or weeks.

Reproductive potential increases when individuals produce more offspring at a time, reproduce more often, and reproduce earlier in life. Reproducing earlier in life has the greatest effect on reproductive potential. Reproducing early shortens the *generation time,* the average time it takes a member of the population to reach the age when it reproduces.

Small organisms, such as bacteria, have short generation times. These organisms can reproduce when they are only a few hours or a few days old. As a result, their populations can grow quickly. In contrast, large organisms, such as elephants and humans, become sexually mature after a number of years. The human generation time is about 20 years, so humans have a much lower reproductive potential than insects.

Exponential Growth Populations sometimes undergo **exponential growth,** which means they grow faster and faster. For example, if a pair of dogs gives birth to 6 puppies, there will be 6 dogs in one generation. If each pair in that generation has 6 puppies, there will be 18 dogs in the next generation. The following generation will contain 54 dogs, and so on. If the number of dogs is plotted versus time on a graph, it will have the shape shown in **Figure 4.**

Exponential growth occurs in nature only when populations have plenty of food and space, and have little or no competition or predators. For example, populations of European dandelions and starlings imported into the United States initially underwent exponential growth. Similar population explosions occur when bacteria or molds grow on a new source of food.

Reading Check Under what conditions does exponential population growth take place? (See the Appendix for answers to Reading Checks.)

Figure 3 ▶ Most organisms have a reproductive potential that far exceeds the number of their offspring that will survive. Very few of these baby sea turtles will survive long enough to breed.

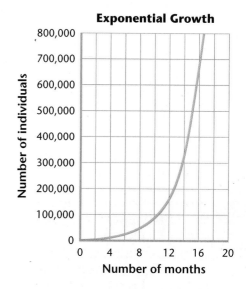

Figure 4 ▶ Population growth is graphed by plotting population size over a period of time. Exponential population growth will look like the curve shown here.

What Limits Population Growth?

Because natural conditions are neither ideal nor constant, populations cannot grow forever and rarely grow at their reproductive potential. Eventually, resources are used up or the environment changes, and deaths increase or births decrease. Under the forces of natural selection in a given environment, only some members of any population will survive and reproduce. Thus, the properties of a population may change over time.

Carrying Capacity The blue line in **Figure 5** represents a population that seems to be limited to a particular size. This theoretical limit, shown by the dashed yellow line, is called *carrying capacity*. The **carrying capacity** of an ecosystem for a particular species is the maximum population that the ecosystem can support indefinitely. A population may increase beyond this number, but it cannot stay at this increased size. Because ecosystems change, carrying capacity is difficult to predict or calculate exactly. However, carrying capacity may be estimated by looking at average population sizes or by observing a population crash after a certain size has been exceeded.

The history of rabbits in Australia demonstrates both exponential growth and carrying capacity. Originally, there were no rabbits in the native ecosystems of Australia. When rabbits were introduced there in 1859, their numbers increased rapidly because they had plenty of vegetation to eat, no competition, and no predators. But eventually, disease and starvation caused the rabbit population to crash. Over time, the vegetation recovered, and the rabbit population increased again. The population continues to increase and decrease, but less dramatically.

Ecofact

Carrying Capacity of Islands
Islands are good places to study carrying capacity because islands have clear boundaries. The Pribilof Islands off the coast of Alaska were the site of a well-studied population explosion and crash. In 1911, 25 reindeer were introduced on one of the islands. By 1938, the herd had grown to 2,000 animals. The reindeer ate mostly lichens, which grow back very slowly. By 1950, there were only 8 reindeer alive on the island.

Figure 5 ▶ An example of carrying capacity is shown by the dashed yellow line in the graph (right). When rabbits were introduced into Australia (below), their population quickly exceeded the carrying capacity of the area. Rabbits have eaten all the vegetation around this water hole.

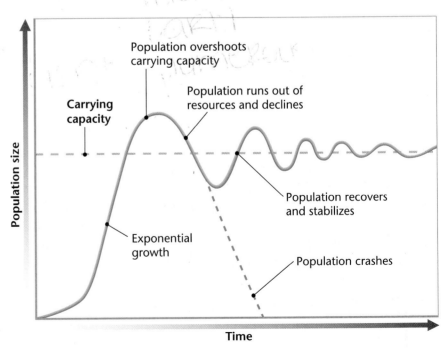

Resource Limits A species reaches its carrying capacity when it consumes a particular natural resource at the same rate at which the ecosystem produces the resource. That natural resource is then called a *limiting resource* for the species in that area. For example, plant growth is limited by supplies of water, sunlight, and mineral nutrients. The supply of the most severely limited resources determines the carrying capacity of an environment for a particular species at a particular time.

Competition Within a Population The members of a population use the same resources in the same ways, so they will eventually compete with one another as the population approaches its carrying capacity. An example is mealworm larvae in a sack of flour. Adults of this beetle will find a sack of flour, lay their eggs in the sack, and leave. Most of the first larvae to hatch will have plenty of flour to eat and will grow to adulthood. However, the sack has a limited amount of food, and mealworms from eggs that were laid later may not have enough food to survive to adulthood.

Instead of competing directly for a limiting resource, members of a species may compete indirectly for social dominance or for a territory. A *territory* is an area defended by one or more individuals against other individuals. The territory is of value not only for the space but also for the shelter, food, or breeding sites it contains. Competition within a population is part of the pressure of natural selection. Many organisms expend a large amount of time and energy competing with members of the same species. Some examples of competition within species are shown in **Figure 6**.

Reading Check Describe one example of competition among members of a population.

Figure 6 ▶ Members of a population often compete with each other. These plants (above) are growing over each other as they compete for light. These wolves (left) are competing for food and for social dominance.

MATHPRACTICE

Growth Rate A growth rate is a change in a population's size over a specific period of time.

$$\text{growth rate} = \frac{\text{change in population}}{\text{time}}$$

Imagine a starting population of 100 individuals. If there were 10 births and 5 deaths in a given year, what was the population's growth rate for the year? In the next year, if there were 20 births and 10 deaths, what would the new growth rate be? If births increased by 10 and deaths increased by 5 for each of the next 5 years, how would you describe the growth of this population?

Figure 7 ▶ The way a disease spreads through a population is affected by the population's density. These pine trees have been infected by a disease carried by the southern pine beetle. This disease has spread rapidly through U.S. timber forests.

Connection to History

Density and Disease The black plague of 14th-century Europe was spread in a density-dependent pattern. About one-third of Europe's population died from the highly contagious disease. Most of the deaths occurred in the crowded towns of the time, and fewer deaths occurred in the countryside.

Figure 8 ▶ Weather events usually affect every individual in a similar way, so such events are considered density-independent regulation.

Two Types of Population Regulation

Population size can be limited in ways that may or may not depend on the density of the population. Causes of death in a population may be *density dependent* or *density independent*.

When a cause of death in a population is *density dependent*, deaths occur more quickly in a crowded population than in a sparse population. This type of regulation happens when individuals of a population are densely packed together, such as when a population is growing rapidly. Limited resources, predation, and disease often result in higher rates of death in dense populations than in sparse populations. The pine trees in **Figure 7** are infected with a disease that is spreading in a density-dependent pattern. Many of the same kind of pine tree are growing close to each other, so a disease-carrying beetle easily spreads the disease from one tree to another.

When a cause of death is *density independent*, a certain proportion of a population dies regardless of the population's density. This type of regulation affects all members of a population in a general or uniform way. Severe weather and natural disasters are often density-independent causes of death. The winter storm shown in **Figure 8** froze crops and fruiting trees regardless of the density of plants in the area.

SECTION 1 Review

1. **Compare** two populations in terms of size, density, and dispersion. Choose any populations you know of.

2. **Describe** exponential population growth.

3. **Describe** three methods by which the reproductive behavior of individuals can affect the growth rate of a population.

4. **Explain** how population sizes in nature are regulated.

CRITICAL THINKING

5. **Making Predictions** How accurately do you think the future size of a population can be predicted? What information might be needed to make a prediction?

6. **Compare and Contrast** Read the description of the populations of rabbits in Australia and reindeer in the Pribilof Islands. List the similarities and differences between these two histories. **READING SKILLS**

How Species Interact with Each Other

SCSh.6.d; SEV.3.e; SEV.5.a; SEV.5.b

What's the difference between lions in a zoo and lions in the wild? In the wild, lions are part of a community and a food web. In the African savanna, lions hunt zebras, fight with hyenas, and are fed upon by fleas and ticks. Interactions like these were part of the evolution of the lions that you see in zoos. Any species is best understood by looking at all of the relationships the species has within its native communities.

An Organism's Niche

The unique role of a species within an ecosystem is its **niche** (NICH). A niche includes the species' physical home, the environmental factors necessary for the species' survival, and all of the species' interactions with other organisms. A niche is different from a habitat. An organism's *habitat* is a location. However, a niche is an organism's pattern of use of its habitat.

A niche can also be thought of as the functional role, or job, of a particular species in an ecosystem. For example, American bison occupied the niche of large grazing herbivores on American grasslands. Kangaroos occupy a similar niche on Australian grasslands. Herbivores often interact with carnivores, such as lions, if they both exist in the same habitat. Some parts of a lion's niche are shown in **Figure 9.**

Objectives

▶ Explain the difference between niche and habitat.

▶ Give examples of parts of a niche.

▶ Describe the five major types of interactions between species.

▶ Explain the difference between parasitism and predation.

▶ Explain how symbiotic relationships may evolve.

Key Terms

niche
competition
predation
parasitism
mutualism
commensalism
symbiosis

Figure 9 ▶ Parts of a lion's niche are shown here. Can you think of other parts?

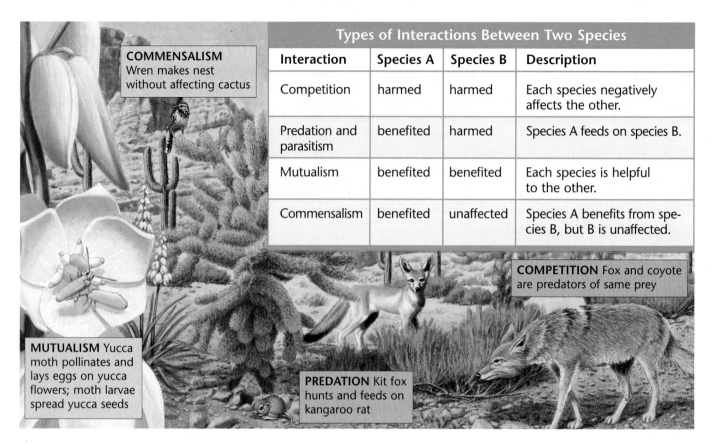

COMMENSALISM
Wren makes nest without affecting cactus

Types of Interactions Between Two Species			
Interaction	Species A	Species B	Description
Competition	harmed	harmed	Each species negatively affects the other.
Predation and parasitism	benefited	harmed	Species A feeds on species B.
Mutualism	benefited	benefited	Each species is helpful to the other.
Commensalism	benefited	unaffected	Species A benefits from species B, but B is unaffected.

COMPETITION Fox and coyote are predators of same prey

MUTUALISM Yucca moth pollinates and lays eggs on yucca flowers; moth larvae spread yucca seeds

PREDATION Kit fox hunts and feeds on kangaroo rat

Figure 10 ▶ There are five major types of species interactions.

FIELD ACTIVITY

Observing Competition You can study competition between bird species at home or at school. Build a bird feeder using a plastic milk jug, a metal pie pan, or some other inexpensive material. Fill the feeder with unsalted bread crumbs, sunflower seeds, or commercial birdseed.

Observe the birds that visit the feeder. Sit quietly in the same spot, and make observations at the same time each day for several days in a row.

In your *EcoLog,* keep a record that includes data about the kinds of birds that use the feeder, the kinds of seeds that the birds prefer, the factors that affect how much the birds eat, and the kinds of birds that are better competitors for the birdseed.

Ways in Which Species Interact

The five major types of species interactions, summarized in **Figure 10,** are competition, predation, parasitism, mutualism, and commensalism. These categories are based on whether each species causes benefit or harm to the other species in a given relationship. Keep in mind that the benefit or harm is in terms of total effects over time. Also note that other types of interaction are possible. Many interactions between species are indirect, and some interactions do not fit a category clearly.

Competition

For most organisms, competition is part of daily life. Seed-eating birds compete with each other for seed at a bird feeder, and weeds compete for space in a sidewalk crack. **Competition** is a relationship in which different individuals or populations attempt to use the same limited resource. Each individual has less access to the resource and so is harmed by the competition.

Competition can occur both within and between species. We have learned that members of the same species must compete with each other because they require the same resources—they occupy the same niche. When members of different species compete, we say that their niches *overlap,* which means that both species use some of the same resources in a habitat.

✓ Reading Check What determines how a species interaction is categorized?

Indirect Competition Species can compete even if they never come into direct contact with each other. Suppose that one insect species feeds on a certain plant during the day and that another species feeds on the same plant during the night. Because they use the same food source, the two species are indirect competitors. Similarly, two plant species that flower at the same time may compete for the same pollinators even if the plants do not compete in any other way. Humans rarely interact with the insects that eat our food crops, but those insects are still competing with us for food.

Adaptations to Competition When two species with similar niches are placed together in the same ecosystem, we might expect one species to be more successful than the other species. The better-adapted species would be able to use more of the resources. But in the course of evolution, adaptations that decrease competition will also be advantageous for species whose niches overlap.

One way competition can be reduced between species is by dividing up the niche in time or space. *Niche restriction* occurs when each species uses less of the niche than it is capable of using. Niche restriction is observed in closely related species that use the same limited resources within a habitat. For example, two similar barnacle species compete for space in the intertidal zone of rocky shorelines. One of the species, *Chthamalus stellatus,* is found only in the upper level of the zone when the other species is present. But when the other species is removed from the area, *C. stellatus* is found at deeper levels, as shown in **Figure 11.** In the presence of competition, the actual niche used by a species may be smaller than the potential niche. Ecologists have observed various other ways of dividing up a niche among groups of similar species.

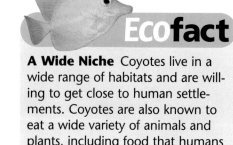

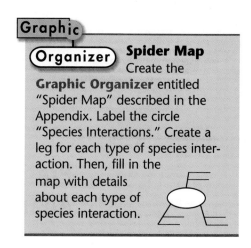

Graphic Organizer **Spider Map**
Create the **Graphic Organizer** entitled "Spider Map" described in the Appendix. Label the circle "Species Interactions." Create a leg for each type of species interaction. Then, fill in the map with details about each type of species interaction.

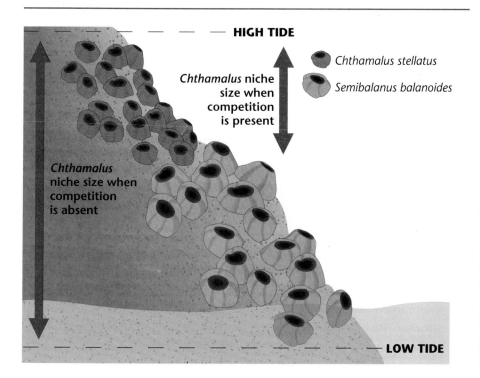

HIGH TIDE

Chthamalus niche size when competition is present

○ *Chthamalus stellatus*
○ *Semibalanus balanoides*

Chthamalus niche size when competition is absent

LOW TIDE

Figure 11 ▶ The barnacle species *Chthamalus stellatus* uses less of its potential niche when competing for space with a similar barnacle species, *Semibalanus balanoides.*

Predation

An organism that feeds on another organism is called a *predator*, and the organism that is fed upon is the *prey*. This kind of interaction is called **predation.** Examples of predation include snakes eating mice, bats eating insects, or whales consuming krill. **Figure 12** shows a predatory bird with its captured prey.

Predation is not as simple to understand as it seems. We may think of predators as meat-eating animals, but there can be less obvious kinds of predators. In complex food webs, a predator may also be the prey of another species. Most organisms have evolved some mechanisms to avoid or defend against predators.

Some predators eat only specific types of prey. For example, the Canadian lynx feeds mostly on snowshoe hares during the winter. In this kind of

CASE STUDY

Predator-Prey Adaptations

Most organisms are vulnerable to predation, so there is strong selective pressure for adaptations that serve as defenses against predators.

Many animals are *camouflaged*— disguised so that they are hard to see even when they are in view. Visual camouflage is very obvious to us, because vision is the dominant sense in humans. Many predators also have keen vision. An animal's camouflage usually disguises its recognizable features. The eyes are the most recognizable part of the animal, and hundreds of species have black stripes across their eyes for disguise. Dark bands of color, such as those on many snakes, may also break up the apparent bulk of the animal's body.

Some predators do not chase their prey but wait for the prey to come near enough to be caught. Praying mantises and frogs are examples of these types of predators. Such predators are usually camouflaged so that the prey does not notice them waiting to attack.

Animals, and more often plants, may contain toxic chemicals that harm or deter predators. Many animals that have chemical defenses have a striking coloration. This *warning coloration* alerts potential predators to stay away and protects the prey species from damage. Patterns with black stripes and red, orange, or yellow are common in many species of bees, wasps, skunks, snakes, and poisonous frogs.

Warning coloration works well against predators that can learn and that have good vision.

▶ Patterns of black and red, orange, or yellow are common warning signs.

During the course of evolution, members of several well-protected species have come to resemble each other. For example, both bees and wasps often have black and yellow stripes. This is an example of *mimicry* of one species by another. The advantage of mimicry is that the more individual organisms that have the same pattern, the less chance any one individual has of being killed. Also, predators learn to avoid all animals that have similar warning patterns.

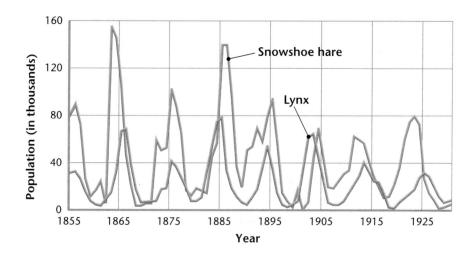

Figure 13 ▶ Populations of predators depend on populations of prey, so changes in one of these populations may be linked to changes in the other. This graph shows population estimates over time for Canadian lynx and their favorite food, snowshoe hares.

close relationship, the sizes of each population tend to increase and decrease in linked patterns, as shown in **Figure 13**. However, many predators will feed on whichever type of prey is easiest to capture.

▶ Both predators and prey may exhibit adaptations such as camouflage or mimicry. The spider that looks like an ant (left) is a predator of insects. The protective quills of this porcupine (right) are a simple but effective way to repel predators.

Occasionally, a harmless species is a mimic of a species that has chemical protection. You have probably tried to get away from insects that you thought were wasps or bees. In fact, some of them were probably flies. Several species of harmless insects have evolved to mimic wasps and bees. On the other hand, sometimes a predator may look like another, less threatening species. Some species of spiders may be mistaken for ants or other types of insects.

A simple defense against predation is some type of *protective covering*. The quills of a porcupine, the spines of a cactus, and the shell of a turtle are all examples of protective covering.

CRITICAL THINKING

1. Making Comparisons For each of these types of adaptations, give an additional example that you have seen or heard of.

2. Determining Cause and Effect Write a paragraph to explain how one of these adaptations might have evolved. **WRITING SKILLS**

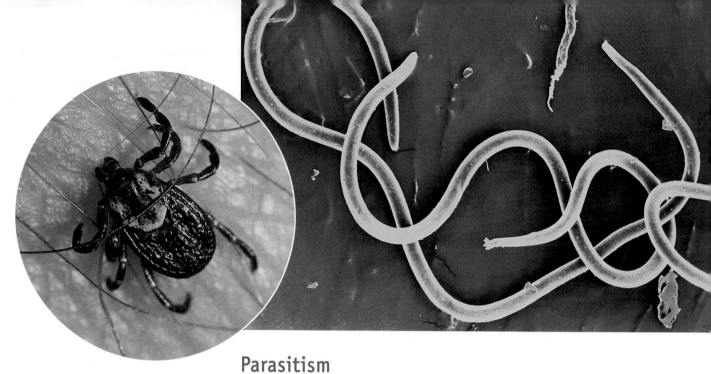

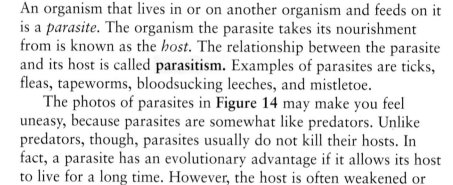

Figure 14 ▶ Parasites such as ticks (left) and intestinal worms (right) could be harmful to you. You probably try to avoid these parasites, almost as if they were predators. In what ways are parasites like predators?

Parasitism

An organism that lives in or on another organism and feeds on it is a *parasite*. The organism the parasite takes its nourishment from is known as the *host*. The relationship between the parasite and its host is called **parasitism.** Examples of parasites are ticks, fleas, tapeworms, bloodsucking leeches, and mistletoe.

The photos of parasites in **Figure 14** may make you feel uneasy, because parasites are somewhat like predators. Unlike predators, though, parasites usually do not kill their hosts. In fact, a parasite has an evolutionary advantage if it allows its host to live for a long time. However, the host is often weakened or exposed to disease by the parasite.

Mutualism

Many species depend on another species for survival. In some cases, neither organism can survive alone. A close relationship between two species in which each species provides a benefit to the other is called **mutualism.** Certain species of bacteria in your intestines form a mutualistic relationship with you. These bacteria help break down food that you could not otherwise digest or produce vitamins that your body cannot make. In return, you give the bacteria a warm, food-rich habitat.

Another case of mutualism happens in the ant acacia trees of Central America, shown in **Figure 15.** Most acacia trees have spines that protect them against plant-eating animals, but the ant acacias have an additional protection—an ant species that lives only on these trees. The trees provide these ants shelter within hollow thorns as well as sugary nectar glands and nutrient-rich leaf tips. In turn, the ants defend the tree against herbivores.

Figure 15 ▶ These acacia trees in Central America have a mutualistic relationship with these ants. The trees provide food and shelter to the ants, and the ants defend the tree.

✔ **Reading Check** Why is the relationship between ants and ant acacia trees categorized as mutualistic?

Figure 16 ▶ Some orchids have a commensal relationship with certain species of trees. The orchid benefits from growing on the tree, because the orchid is exposed to more rain and sunlight than if it grew on the ground. The tree is not harmed or helped by the orchid.

Commensalism

A relationship in which one species benefits and the other species is neither harmed nor helped is called **commensalism.** An example is the relationship between certain orchids and trees, shown in **Figure 16.** The orchid grows around the tree's branches without harming the tree. The height exposes the orchid to rain and sunlight. Another example of commensalism is when birds nest in trees, but only if the birds do not harm the tree. Even a seemingly harmless activity might affect another species.

Symbiosis and Coevolution

A relationship in which two species live in close association is called **symbiosis.** Many types of species interactions are considered symbiotic in some cases. Symbiosis is most often used to describe a relationship in which at least one species benefits.

Over time, species in close relationships may *coevolve.* These species may evolve adaptations that reduce the harm or improve the benefit of the relationship. Recall that harm and benefit are measured in total effects over time. For example, coevolution can be seen in the relationships of flowering plants and their pollinators. Many types of flowers seem to match the feeding habits of certain species of insects or other animals that spread pollen.

Connection to Biology

An Ecosystem in Your Body
Our health is affected by our relationships with microorganisms in our digestive system, skin, and other parts of our body. For example, live-culture yogurt is considered a healthy food because the kinds of bacteria it contains are beneficial to us. The bacteria assist our digestion of dairy products and also compete with other microorganisms, such as yeast, that might cause infections.

SCLINKS.
www.scilinks.org
Topic: Coevolution
Code: HE80309

SECTION 2 Review

1. **List** as many parts as you can of the niche of an organism of your choice.

2. **Give examples** of species that have the same habitat but not the same niche that a lion has.

3. **Describe** the five types of species interactions.

CRITICAL THINKING

4. **Making Comparisons** Read the definition of parasites and predators, and then explain how parasites differ from predators. **READING SKILLS**

5. **Analyzing Relationships** Choose an example of mutualism, and then describe the long process by which the relationship could have evolved.

1 How Populations Change in Size

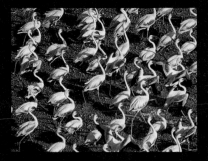

Key Terms

population, 211
density, 212
dispersion, 212
growth rate, 212
reproductive potential, 213
exponential growth, 213
carrying capacity, 214

Main Ideas

▶ Each population has specific properties, including size, density, and pattern of dispersion.

▶ When a population has few limits on its growth, it may undergo exponential growth. This is the fastest possible growth rate of the population.

▶ When a population has few limits to its growth, it may have an exponential growth rate. Usually, population growth is limited by factors such as disease and competition.

▶ Carrying capacity is the maximum population a habitat can support over a long period of time.

▶ A population that grows rapidly may be subject to density-dependent regulation.

2 How Species Interact with Each Other

niche, 217
competition, 218
predation, 220
parasitism, 222
mutualism, 222
commensalism, 223
symbiosis, 223

▶ The niche of an organism is its pattern of use of its habitat and its interactions with other organisms.

▶ Interactions between species are categorized based on the relative benefit or harm that one species causes the other. The categories are competition, predation, parasitism, mutualism, and commensalism.

▶ Competition between species occurs when their niches overlap. The competition may be direct or indirect.

▶ Pairs of species that have close relationships often evolve adaptations that either increase the benefit of or reduce the harm from the relationship.

Using Key Terms

Use each of the following terms in a separate sentence.

1. *reproductive potential*
2. *carrying capacity*
3. *competition*
4. *symbiosis*

For each pair of terms, explain how the meanings of the terms differ.

5. *niche* and *habitat*
6. *predator* and *prey*
7. *predation* and *parasitism*
8. *mutualism* and *commensalism*

✔ **STUDY TIP**

Review with a Partner To review the main ideas of the text, try summarizing with a partner. Take turns reading a passage, and then try to summarize aloud what you have read. Try not to look back at the text. Then, discuss and review the text with your partner to check your understanding.

Understanding Key Ideas

9. In which of the following pairs do both organisms belong to the same population?
   a. a rose and a carnation
   b. a zebra and a horse
   c. two residents of New York City
   d. two similar species of monkeys

10. A population of some species is most likely to grow exponentially
    a. if the species is already very common in the area.
    b. when the species moves into a new area of suitable habitat.
    c. when it uses the same habitat as a similar species.
    d. if the population size is already large.

11. A population will most likely deplete the resources of its environment if the population
    a. grows beyond carrying capacity.
    b. must share resources with many other species.
    c. moves frequently from one habitat to another.
    d. has a low reproductive potential.

12. The growth rate of a population of geese will probably increase within a year if
    a. more birds die than are hatched.
    b. several females begin laying eggs at younger ages than their mothers did.
    c. most females lay two eggs instead of three during a nesting season.
    d. some birds get lost during migration.

13. Which of the following is an example of competition between species?
    a. two species of insects feeding on the same rare plant
    b. a bobcat hunting a mouse
    c. a lichen, which is an alga and a fungus living as a single organism
    d. a tick living on a dog

14. Which of the following statements about parasitism is true?
    a. The presence of a parasite does not affect the host.
    b. Parasitism is a cooperative relationship between two species.
    c. Parasites always kill their hosts.
    d. Parasitism is similar to predation.

15. Ants and acacia trees have a mutualistic relationship because
    a. they are both adapted to a humid climate.
    b. they are part of the same ecosystem.
    c. they benefit each other.
    d. the ants eat parts of the acacia tree.

16. Which of the following is an example of coevolution?
    a. flowers that can be pollinated by only one species of insect
    b. rabbits that invade a new habitat
    c. wolves that compete with each other for territory
    d. bacteria that suddenly mutate in a lab

Short Answer

17. A tapeworm lives in the intestines of a cow and feeds by absorbing food that the cow is digesting. What kind of relationship is this? Explain your answer.

18. Explain how two species can compete for the same resource even if they never come in contact with each other.

19. Snail kites are predatory birds that feed only on snails. The kites use their hooked, needle-like beaks to pull snails from their shells. Explain how these specialized beaks might have evolved in these birds.

20. What would happen to the population of snail kites mentioned in question 19 if the snails' habitat was destroyed? Explain your answer.

Interpreting Graphics

The graph below shows the population of some reindeer that were introduced to an Alaskan island in 1910. Use the graph to answer questions 21–23.

21. Describe this population's changes over time.

22. What might have happened in 1937?

23. Is it possible to estimate the island's carrying capacity for reindeer? Explain your answer.

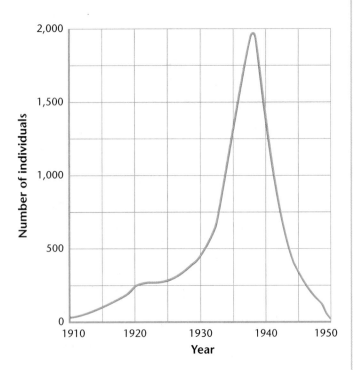

Concept Mapping

24. Use the following terms to create a concept map: *symbiosis, predation, predator, prey, parasitism, parasite, host, mutualism,* and *commensalism.*

Critical Thinking

25. Analyzing Relationships Read the explanations of competition and predation. If one species becomes extinct, and then soon after, another species becomes extinct, was their relationship most likely competition or predation? Explain your answer. **READING SKILLS**

26. Evaluating Hypotheses Scientists do not all agree on the specific carrying capacity of Earth for humans. Why might this carrying capacity be difficult to determine?

27. Evaluating Conclusions A scientist finds no evidence that any of the species in a particular community are competing and concludes that competition never played a role in the development of this community. Could this conclusion be valid? Write a paragraph to explain your answer. **WRITING SKILLS**

Cross-Disciplinary Connection

28. Health Viruses are the cause of many infectious diseases, such as common colds, flu, and chickenpox. Viruses can be passed from one person to another in many different ways. Under what conditions do you think viral diseases will spread most rapidly between humans? What can be done to slow the spread of these viruses?

Portfolio Project

29. Create a Niche Map Create a visual representation of the niche of an organism of your choice. Research the organism's habitat, behaviors, and interactions with other species. If possible, observe the organism (without disturbing it) for a day or more. Create a piece of art to show all of the interactions that this organism has with its environment.

MATH SKILLS

Use the equation below to answer questions 30–31.

Change in population size = Births − Deaths

30. **Extending an Equation** The equation gives the change in a population over a given amount of time (for example, an increase of 100 individuals in one year). Use the two parts on the right side of the equation to write an inequality that would be true if the population were increasing. Rewrite the inequality for a decreasing population.

31. **Analyzing an Equation** Suppose you are studying the small town of Hill City, which had a population of 100 people in the first year of your study. One year later, 10 people have died, and only 9 mothers have given birth. Yet the population has increased to 101. How could this increase happen?

WRITING SKILLS

32. **Communicating Main Ideas** Why do population sizes not grow indefinitely?

33. **Creative Writing** Write a science fiction story about life without competition.

34. **Writing from Research** Find information in encyclopedias or natural history references about different kinds of mutualism. Summarize the similarities and differences between the various relationships. Focus on the ways in which each species benefits from the other species.

READING SKILLS

Read the passage below, and then answer the questions that follow.

Excerpt from Charles Darwin, On the Origin of Species, *1859.*

I should premise that I use the term struggle for existence in a large and metaphorical sense, including dependence of one being on another, and including (which is more important) not only the life of the individual, but success in leaving progeny. Two canine animals in a time of dearth, may truly be said to struggle with each other which shall get food and live. But a plant on the edge of the desert is said to struggle for life against the drought, though more properly it should be said to be dependent on the moisture. A plant which annually produces a thousand seeds, of which on average only one comes to maturity, may more truly be said to struggle with the plants of the same and other kinds which already clothe the ground . . . In these several senses, which pass into each other, I use for convenience sake the general term of struggle for existence.

1. Which of the following statements best describes the author's main purpose in this passage?
   a. to describe the process of reproduction
   b. to persuade the reader that all animals struggle for existence
   c. to explain the meaning of the author's use of the phrase *struggle for existence*
   d. to argue that life in the desert depends on moisture

2. Which of the following statements most closely matches what the author means by the phrase *struggle for existence*?
   a. whenever plants or animals interact in nature
   b. whenever plants or animals compete to survive and to produce offspring
   c. when plants produce many more seeds than are likely to grow
   d. when animals compete for food during difficult times

Understanding Concepts

Directions (1–4): For *each* question, write on a separate sheet of paper the letter of the correct answer.

1 What determines the carrying capacity of an environment?
A. growth rates
B. limiting resources
C. natural selection
D. territorial size

2 Which of the following statements can be made about competition between organisms in a particular ecosystem?
F. Organisms rarely compete with members of their own species.
G. Organisms compete directly when they require the same resources.
H. Organisms only compete when supplies of a resource are unlimited.
I. Organisms only compete for resources when their populations are small.

3 Which of the following describes a species' niche?
A. the unique role the species plays in an ecosystem
B. the physical location where the species can be found on Earth
C. the adaptation of a species population to its physical environment
D. the maximum number of offspring all members of that species can produce

4 Which of the following expressions is used to calculate the change in population size?
F. births plus deaths
G. births plus deaths plus population
H. births minus deaths
I. births minus deaths plus population

Directions (5–6): For *each* question, write a short response.

5 Explain the difference between density dependent and density independent deaths in a population.

6 What are two ways a species can reduce competition when organisms in the same niche use very similar resources?

Reading Skills

Directions (7–9): Read the passage below. Then answer the questions.

A population is all the members of a species living in the same place at the same time. A population is a reproductive group because organisms usually breed with members of their own population. The maximum number of offspring that each member of a population can produce determines the population's reproductive potential. Reproductive potential increases when individuals produce more offspring at a time, reproduce more often, or reproduce earlier in life. Reproducing earlier in life has the greatest effect on reproductive potential. Reproducing early reduces the generation time, the average amount of time it takes a member of a population to reach the age when it reproduces.

Populations sometimes undergo exponential growth, which means they grow faster and faster. In exponential growth, a larger number of individuals is added to the population in each succeeding time period.

7 Which of the following has the highest reproductive potential?
A. bacteria
B. cattle
C. elephants
D. humans

8 What would reduce a population's reproductive potential?
F. increase the number of survivors
G. decrease the number of predators
H. increase the number of descendants
I. decrease the number of offspring

9 When can exponential growth occur in a population?
A. when the brood size of the population increases
B. when the generation time of a population is shortened
C. when the population has plenty of food and little or no competition
D. when the dispersion of the population becomes random

Interpreting Graphics

Directions (10–12): For *each* question below, record the correct answer on a separate sheet of paper.

Use the table below to answer question 10.

Interactions Between Two Species

Interaction	Species A	Species B
Competition	Fox	Coyote
Predation	Kit fox	Kangaroo rat
Mutualism	Yucca moth	Yucca
Commensalism	Wren	Cactus

10 Which of the interactions listed in the table is harmful to both species?

F. commensalism   **H.** mutualism

G. competition   **I.** predation

Use the illustration below to answer questions 11 and 12.

Carrying Capacity

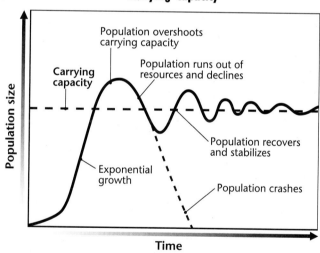

11 What happens to population size between the time it overshoots carrying capacity to when it recovers and stabilizes?

A. It remains stable.   **C.** It decreases before it stabilizes.

B. It declines steadily.   **D.** It continues to increase at a steady rate.

12 If the population size was nearly 2,000 when it overshot carrying capacity, and 1,500 when it was at its lowest amount of decline during its recovery, what is the estimated carrying capacity of the population?

F. 1,600   **H.** 1,800

G. 1,750   **I.** 1,950

Test TIP

Test questions may not be arranged in order of increasing difficulty. If you are unable to answer a question, mark it and move on to another question.

Objectives

▶ **USING SCIENTIFIC METHODS** **Observe, record, and graph** the growth and decline of a population of yeast cells in an experimental environment.

▶ **USING SCIENTIFIC METHODS** **Predict** the carrying capacity of an environment for a population.

▶ **Infer** the limiting resource of an environment.

Materials

compound microscope
methylene blue solution, 1%
micrometer, stage type or
  eyepiece disc for microscope
microscope slide, with coverslip
  (5)
pipet, 1 mL (5)
test tube (5)
yeast culture, in an Erlenmeyer
  flask (5)

▶ **Budding Yeast** This live, budding yeast cell is magnified 3,025 times by a scanning electron microscope.

Studying Population Growth

You have learned that a population will keep growing until limiting factors slow or stop this growth. How do you know when a population has reached its carrying capacity? In this lab, you will observe the changes in a population of yeast cells. The cells will grow in a container and have limited food over several days.

Procedure

1. Your teacher will prepare several cultures of household baker's yeast (fungi of the genus *Saccharomyces*) in flasks. Each yeast culture will have grown for a different period of time in the same type of environment. Each flask will have been prepared with 500 mL lukewarm water, 1 g of active dry yeast, and 20 g of sugar. The sugar is the only food source for the yeast.

2. Make two data tables like the one shown below. One table will contain your observations of living yeast cells, and the other table will be for observations of dead yeast cells.

Cell Counts						
Time (h)	1	2	3	4	Average	Class Average
0						
12						
24						
36						
48						

DO NOT WRITE IN THIS BOOK

3. Take a sample of yeast culture from the first flask (Time 0). Swirl the flask gently to mix the yeast cells evenly, and then immediately use the pipet to transfer 1 mL of yeast culture to a test tube. Add two drops of methylene blue solution to the test tube. The methylene blue will stain the dead yeast cells a deep blue but will not stain the living cells.

4. Make a wet mount by placing a small drop of your mixture of yeast and methylene blue on a microscope slide. Cover the slide with a coverslip.

5. Observe the mounted slide under the low power of a compound microscope. (Note: Adjust the light so that you can clearly see both stained and unstained cells.) After focusing, switch the microscope to high power (400× or 1,000×).

6. Count the live (unstained) yeast cells and the dead (stained) cells that you see through the microscope. Use the micrometer ruler, or ask your teacher for the best counting method. Record the numbers of live cells and dead cells in your data tables.

7. Move the microscope slide slightly, and then make another count of the number of living and dead cells that you can see. Repeat this step until you have made four counts of the cells on the slide.

8. Calculate and record the average number of live cells per observation. Record this number in your data table. Do the same calculation for the dead cells.

9. Predict how many live and dead cells you expect to count in the samples from the other flasks. Record your prediction.

10. Repeat steps 3–8 for each of the flasks to obtain data that represents the growth of a population over a 48-hour period.

11. Clean up your work area, and store all lab equipment appropriately. Ask your teacher how to dispose of the yeast samples and any extra or spilled chemicals.

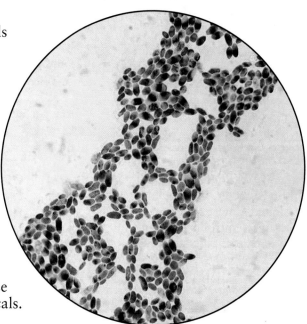

▶ **Stained Yeast Cells** These yeast cells have been stained with methylene blue and magnified 1,000 times with a microscope. Methylene blue gives a deep blue color to dead yeast cells but not to live yeast cells.

Analysis

1. **Analyzing Data** Share your data with the rest of the class. Calculate and record the class averages for each set of observations.

2. **Constructing Graphs** Graph the changes in the average numbers of live yeast cells and dead yeast cells over time. Plot the average number of cells per observation on the *y*-axis and the time (in hours from start of culture) on the *x*-axis.

3. **Describing Events** Describe the general population changes you observed in the yeast cultures over time.

Conclusions

4. **Evaluating Methods** Why were several counts taken and then averaged for each time period?

5. **Evaluating Results** Were your predictions of the yeast cell counts close to the actual average counts? How close were your predictions relative to the variation among all the samples?

6. **Applying Conclusions** Did the yeast cell populations appear to reach a certain carrying capacity? What was the limiting resource in the experimental environment of the flasks?

Extension

1. **Designing Experiments** Form a hypothesis about another factor that might limit the yeast's population growth, and explain how you would test this hypothesis.

POINTS of view

WHERE SHOULD THE WOLVES ROAM?

The gray wolf was exterminated from much of the northwestern United States by the 1920s. Ranchers and federal agents killed the animal to protect livestock. The Rocky Mountain gray wolf was listed as an endangered species in 1973. Then in the 1980s, the U.S. Fish and Wildlife Service began a plan to restore wolf populations in the United States. The agency decided to reintroduce wolves into certain areas. Biologists looked for areas where wolves could have large habitats and enough food. Three areas were chosen, as shown in the figure below.

Between 1995 and 1996, 64 wolves were released in Yellowstone National Park and 34 wolves were released in central Idaho. The original goal was to have breeding populations of at least 100 wolves in each location by 2002. This goal has now become reality.

The wolf reintroduction efforts remain controversial. Some people would prefer that the wolves become extinct. On the other side, some people think that

the government has not done enough to protect wolf populations. Read the following points of view, and then analyze the issue for yourself.

Wolves Should Not Be Reintroduced

Some opponents of the reintroduction plan argue that wolves are not truly endangered. Biologists estimate that hundreds of wolves live in Minnesota, and thousands live in Alaska and Canada. Because there are large numbers of wolves in the wild, some people feel that wolves should not receive special treatment as endangered species.

Many hunters also oppose the plan to reintroduce wolves. Both hunters and wolves hunt for large game animals such as deer, elk, or moose. Hunters believe the wolves might create too much competition for the game animals. Some studies suggest that populations of game animals will decrease if hunted by both humans and wolves.

▶ **A wild wolf** is a now rare sight in most of the United States. Efforts to reintroduce and protect wolf populations are controversial.

Hunters point out that hunting is an important part of the economies of the western states. Also, licensed hunting has become part of the way large parks and wildlife preserves are managed. Hunting is sometimes allowed by park and game managers to control wildlife populations. Hunting fees also help fund wildlife management efforts, such as habitat improvement and biological studies.

Ranchers are among the people who most strongly oppose wolf reintroduction. Ranchers worry that wolves will kill their livestock. Ranchers argue that they cannot afford to lose their livestock. Even though there is a program to pay ranchers for lost livestock, the program will last

▶ **The breeding range of the gray wolf** (far left) has been lost in most of the United States. The U.S. government has reintroduced wolves into parts of Montana, Wyoming, and Idaho (left).

Map (far left)
- Current range
- Historic range (includes the current range)

Map (right)
- Glacier National Park
- MONTANA
- Yellowstone National Park
- IDAHO
- WYOMING
- --- Park boundary
- Wolf reintroduction zones

only as long as wolves are classified as an endangered species. When there are many wolves again in the target areas, the wolf will no longer have endangered status. Ranchers point out that the payment program will disappear when it would be needed most.

Other groups that oppose wolf reintroduction include groups that use public lands for activities such as logging or mining. These groups worry that protection for the wolves may lead to the prevention of other uses of land in the target areas.

Wolves Should Be Reintroduced

A basic argument in favor of wolf reintroduction is that the federal government must uphold the law by trying to restore wolf populations in the United States. But supporters of wild wolves give other reasons too.

Many environmentalists and scientists believe that the reintroduction plan could restore a balance to the Yellowstone ecosystem. Predation by wolves would keep the herds of elk, moose, and deer from growing too dense and overgrazing the land.

The argument that wolves help control wild herds is like the argument in favor of hunting. Some wolf supporters even say that licensed hunting of wolves should be allowed. In this way, hunters might support the reintroduction plans, and populations of both wolves and game animals could be managed.

In response to ranchers' concerns that wolves will attack their livestock, biologists say that this is not likely to be a problem. There

▶ **The International Wolf Center in Minnesota** tries to educate the public about wolves. The center's "Wolves and Humans" exhibit is shown here.

is evidence that most wolves prefer to hunt wild animals rather than domestic animals. Wolves rarely attack livestock when large herds of wild game are nearby. In fact, from 1995 to 1997, fewer than five wolf attacks on livestock were reported in the United States.

Still, some supporters of reintroduction have tried to address the concerns of ranchers. One group raised money to pay ranchers for livestock killed by wolves. Other groups conduct studies and educational programs or talk with local landowners. Most wolf supporters are trying to create reintroduction plans that will work for both humans and wolves.

In response to fears that the wolves pose a danger to humans, supporters say this is also unlikely. There have been no verified attacks on humans by healthy wolves in North America. Wolf experts insist that wolves are shy

animals that prefer to stay away from people.

Most wolf supporters admit that there are only a few places where wolves may live without causing problems. Supporters of the plan believe that the target areas are places where wolves can carry out a natural role without causing problems for humans.

What Do You Think?

Like many plans to protect endangered species, the plan to reintroduce wolves causes some people to weigh their own interests against the needs of a single species. Do you feel that the decision is a simple one? Can you think of other ways to look at this issue? Explain your answers.

The Human Population

CHAPTER 9

1 Studying Human Populations

2 Changing Population Trends

PRE-READING ACTIVITY

Table Fold
Before you read this chapter, create the **FoldNote** entitled "Table Fold" described in the Reading and Study Skills section of the Appendix. Label the columns of the table fold with "Changes in Human Population," and "Effects of Population Change." Label the rows with "Before 1700," "From 1700 to 2000," and "From 2000 to 2050 and Beyond." As you read the chapter, write examples of each topic under the appropriate column.

China has one of the largest populations in the world, with more than 1 billion people. However, China's population is projected to stop growing by the year 2050, mostly because Chinese families are having fewer children.

SECTION 1
Studying Human Populations

SCSh.2.b; SCSh.3.c; SCSh.3.d; SCSh.4.a;
SCSh.5.a; SCSh.6.a; SCSh.6.b; SCSh.6.c;
SEV.5.a; SEV.5.b

The human population of Earth grew faster in the 20th century than it ever has before. This rapid growth has led to environmental problems around the globe. We therefore must try to understand and predict changes in human populations.

Demography is the study of populations, but most often refers to the study of human populations. Demographers study the historical size and makeup of the populations of countries in order to make comparisons and predictions. Demographers also study properties that affect population growth, such as economics and social structure. Countries are often grouped by demographers into two general categories. *Developed countries* have higher average incomes, slower population growth, and diverse industrial economies. *Developing countries* have lower average incomes, simple and agriculture-based economies, and rapid population growth.

The Human Population Over Time

After growing slowly for thousands of years, the human population grew rapidly in the 1800s, as shown in **Figure 1.** The human population underwent *exponential growth*, meaning that population growth rates increased during each decade. These increases were mostly due to increases in food production and improvements in hygiene that came with the industrial and scientific revolutions. However, it is unlikely that the Earth can sustain this growth for much longer.

Objectives

▶ Describe how the size and growth rate of the human population has changed in the last 200 years.

▶ Define four properties that scientists use to predict population sizes.

▶ Make predictions about population trends based on age structure.

▶ Describe the four stages of the demographic transition.

▶ Explain why different countries may be at different stages of the demographic transition.

Key Terms

demography
age structure
survivorship
fertility rate
migration
life expectancy
demographic transition

Figure 1 ▶ After growing slowly for thousands of years, the human population grew rapidly in the 1800s. What caused this change?

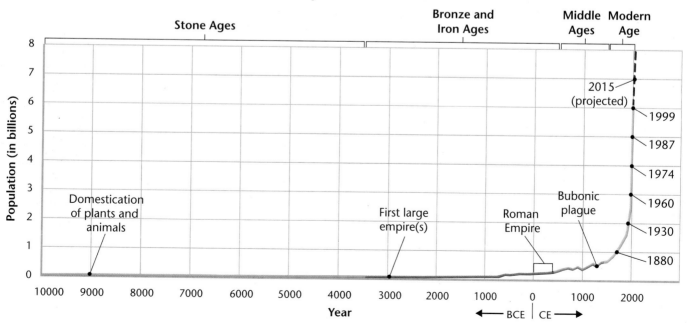

World Population Over Time

Section 1   **Studying Human Populations**   **235**

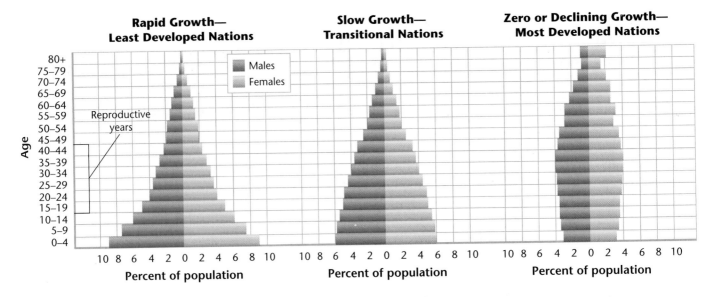

Rapid Growth—Least Developed Nations

Slow Growth—Transitional Nations

Zero or Declining Growth—Most Developed Nations

Males
Females

Reproductive years

Age
80+
75–79
70–74
65–69
60–64
55–59
50–54
45–49
40–44
35–39
30–34
25–29
20–24
15–19
10–14
5–9
0–4

10 8 6 4 2 0 2 4 6 8 10
Percent of population

10 8 6 4 2 0 2 4 6 8 10
Percent of population

10 8 6 4 2 0 2 4 6 8 10
Percent of population

Figure 2 ▶ Age-Structure Diagrams These graphs allow demographers to compare the distribution of ages and sexes in a population. Each graph shows a typical shape for a population with a particular rate of growth. Note that people between 15 and 44 years of age are most likely to produce children.

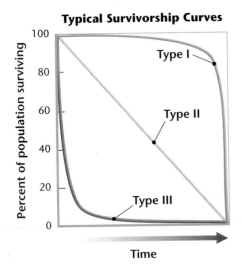

Typical Survivorship Curves

Percent of population surviving
100
80
60
40
20
0

Type I
Type II
Type III

Time

Figure 3 ▶ Survivorship curves show how much of the population survives to a given age. Both Type I and Type III survivorship may result in populations that remain the same size or grow slowly.

Forecasting Population Size

Will your community need more schools in the next 20 years, or will it need more retirement communities? Will people move in and create demand for more roads and utility services? Demographers look at many properties of populations to predict such changes. Population predictions are often inaccurate, however, because human behavior can change suddenly.

Age Structure Demographers can make many predictions based on **age structure**—the distribution of ages in a specific population at a certain time. For example, if a population has more young people than older people, the population size will likely increase as the young people grow up and have children. Age structure can be graphed in a *population pyramid*, a type of double-sided bar graph like those shown in **Figure 2**. The figure shows typical age structures for countries that have different rates of growth. Countries that have high rates of growth usually have more young people than older people. Countries that have slow growth or no growth usually have an even distribution of ages.

Survivorship Another way to predict population trends is to study survivorship. **Survivorship** is the percentage of members of a group that are likely to survive to any given age. To predict survivorship, a demographer studies a group of people born at the same time and notes when each person dies. The results plotted on a graph might look like one of the types of *survivorship curves* in **Figure 3**. Wealthy developed countries such as Japan and Germany currently have a Type I survivorship curve because most people live to be very old. Type II populations have a similar death rate at all ages. Type III survivorship is the pattern in very poor human populations in which many children die.

✓ **Reading Check** How can a population pyramid help demographers predict changes in a population over time? (See the Appendix for answers to Reading Checks.)

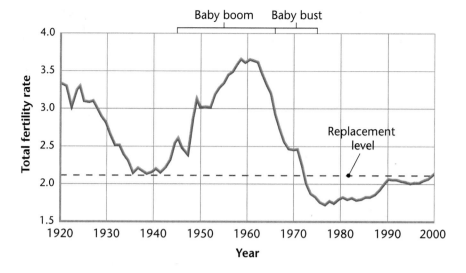

Baby boom Baby bust

Figure 4 ▶ The total fertility rate in the United States went through many changes from 1900 to 2000. The *baby boom* was a period of high fertility rates, and the *baby bust* was a period of decreasing fertility.

Fertility Rates The number of babies born each year per 1,000 women in a population is called the **fertility rate.** Demographers also calculate the *total fertility rate,* or the average number of children a woman gives birth to in her lifetime.

A graph of historical total fertility rates for the United States is shown in **Figure 4.** In 1972, the total fertility rate dropped below replacement level for the first time in U.S. history. *Replacement level* is the average number of children each parent must have in order to "replace" themselves in the population. This number is about 2.1, or slightly more than 2, because not all children born will survive and reproduce.

Total fertility rates in the United States remained below replacement level for most of the 1990s. However, the population continued to grow, as shown in **Figure 5.** One reason for this growth was that the children of the baby boom grew up and had children.

Migration Another reason the population continued to grow was that immigration increased. The movement of individuals between areas is called **migration.** Movement into an area is *immigration* and movement out of an area is *emigration.* Migration between and within countries is a significant part of population change. The populations of many developed countries might be decreasing if not for immigration.

MATHPRACTICE

Extending the Equation for Population Change
The following equation is a simple way to calculate the change in a population over a period of time:

$$\text{change in population} = (births - deaths)$$

However, this equation does not account for changes due to migration. Rewrite the equation to include *immigration* and *emigration.*

Next, create an example word problem that would require the use of this new equation. Trade problems with a classmate, and try to solve the classmate's new word problem.

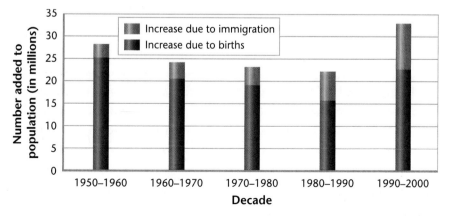

Source: U.S. Census Bureau.

Figure 5 ▶ The population of the United States has continued to grow in the last century because of births as well as immigration.

Figure 6 ▶ Preventive medicine, sanitation, and better nutrition have increased life expectancy in many parts of the world.

Figure 7 ▶ Since 1900, average life expectancy has increased worldwide (red line), although it remains lower in less developed countries (blue and purple lines).

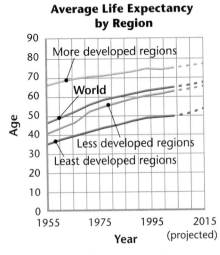

Average Life Expectancy by Region

More developed regions
World
Less developed regions
Least developed regions

Age

1955   1975   1995   2015 (projected)
Year

Source: UN Population Division.

Declining Death Rates

The dramatic increase in Earth's human population in the last 200 years has happened because death rates have declined more rapidly than birth rates. Death rates have declined mainly because more people now have access to adequate food, clean water, and safe sewage disposal. The discovery of vaccines in the 20th century also contributed to declining death rates, especially among infants and children. These factors are shown in **Figure 6.**

Life Expectancy The average number of years members of a population are likely to live is their **life expectancy.** Life expectancy is most affected by *infant mortality,* the death rate of infants less than a year old. In 1900, worldwide life expectancy was about 40 years and the infant mortality rate was very high. By 2000, the rate of infant mortality was less than one-third of the rate in 1900. The graph in **Figure 7** shows that average life expectancy has increased to more than 67 years worldwide. For people in many developed countries, life expectancy is 80 years or more.

Expensive medical care is not needed to prevent infant deaths. The infant mortality rate differs greatly among countries that have the same average income. Instead, infant health is more affected by the parents' access to education, food, fuel, and clean water. Babies need to be fed well and kept clean and warm. If these basic needs are met, most children will have a good chance of surviving.

Meanwhile, new threats to life expectancy arise as populations become denser. Contagious diseases such as AIDS and tuberculosis are a growing concern in a world where such diseases can spread quickly. Life expectancy in many Southern African countries has been reduced in recent decades due to the AIDS epidemic.

The Demographic Transition

In most developed countries, populations have stopped growing. How can populations quadruple in one century, then stop growing or shrink in the next century? The **demographic transition** is a model that describes how economic and social changes affect population growth rates. The model is based on observations of the histories of many developed countries. The graph in **Figure 8** compares trends in birth rates, death rates, and population sizes during the four stages of the transition.

Stages of the Transition In the first stage of the demographic transition, a society is in a preindustrial condition. The birth rate and the death rate are both at high levels and the population size is stable. Most of the world was in this condition until about 1700, when the scientific and industrial revolutions began.

In the second stage, a population explosion occurs. Death rates decline as hygiene, nutrition, and education improve. But birth rates remain high, so the population grows very fast. During this stage, the population can double in less than 30 years.

In the third stage of the demographic transition, population growth slows because the birth rate decreases. As the birth rate becomes close to the death rate, the population size stabilizes. However, the population is much larger than before the demographic transition. In most countries that have passed through the transition, the population quadrupled during the 20th century.

In the fourth stage, the birth rate drops below replacement level, so the size of the population begins to decrease. It has taken from one to three generations for the demographic transition to occur in most developed countries.

Reading Check Which stage of the demographic transition is characterized by a high birth rate and a declining death rate?

www.scilinks.org
Topic: Demographic Transition
Code: HE80386

The Population Clock The Earth's human population is increasing by 2.4 people each second, which accounts for births and deaths. This means Earth gains over 200,000 people per day, or over 75 million per year.

Figure 8 ▶ The four stages of the demographic transition are shown here from left to right. Note the changes in population size with changing birth and death rates. Do you think that all countries will fit this pattern?

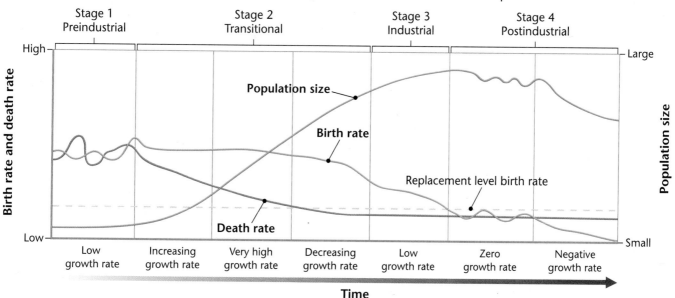

Women and Fertility The factors most clearly related to a decline in birth rates are increasing education and economic independence for women. In the demographic transition model, the lower death rate of the second stage is usually the result of increased levels of education. Educated women find that they do not need to bear as many children to ensure that some will survive. Also, the women may learn family planning techniques. They are able to contribute to their family's increasing prosperity by working, while spending less energy bearing and caring for children. Some countries that want to reduce birth rates have placed a priority on the education of females, as shown in **Figure 9.**

Large families are valuable in communities in which children work or take care of older family members. But as countries modernize, parents are more likely to work away from home. If parents must pay for child care, children may become a financial burden rather than an asset. The elderly will not need the support of their children if pensions are available. All of these reasons contribute to lower birth rates. Today, the total fertility rate in developed countries is about 1.6 children per woman, while in developing countries, the rate is about 3.1 children per woman.

SCI**LINKS**.

www.scilinks.org
Topic: Human
Demographics
Code: HE80767

Figure 9 ▶ These women in Bolivia are learning to read. Many countries include the education of women in development efforts.

SECTION 1 Review

1. **Describe** how the size and growth rate of the human population has changed in the last 200 years.

2. **Define** four properties that scientists use to predict population sizes.

3. **Explain** what we can predict about a population's likely growth rates based on its current age structure.

4. **Describe** the four stages of the demographic transition.

CRITICAL THINKING

5. **Analyzing Relationships** Read the description of life expectancy in this section. Explain why the oldest people in a population may be much older than the average life expectancy. **READING SKILLS**

6. **Evaluating Theories** Do you think that all countries will follow the pattern of the demographic transition? Explain your answer.

Changing Population Trends

Some countries have followed the model of the demographic transition—they have reached large and stable population sizes and have increased life expectancies. But throughout history, and currently in many parts of the world, populations that have high rates of growth create environmental problems. A rapidly growing population uses resources at an increased rate and can overwhelm the infrastructure of a community. **Infrastructure** is the basic facilities and services that support a community, such as public water supplies, sewer lines, power plants, roads, subways, schools, and hospitals. The symptoms of overwhelming population growth include suburban sprawl, overcrowded schools, polluted rivers, barren land, and inadequate housing, as shown in **Figure 10.** You may have seen some of these problems in your community.

Problems of Rapid Growth

People cannot live without sources of clean water, fuel, and land that can be farmed to produce food. A rapidly growing population can use resources faster than the environment can renew them, unless resources come from elsewhere. Standards of living decline when wood is removed from local forests faster than it can grow back, or when wastes overwhelm local water sources. Vegetation, water, and land are the resources most critically affected by rapid growth.

Objectives

▶ Describe three problems caused by rapid human population growth.

▶ Compare population growth problems in more-developed countries and less developed countries.

▶ Analyze strategies countries may use to reduce their population growth.

▶ Describe worldwide population projections into the next century.

Key Terms

infrastructure
arable land
urbanization
least developed countries

Land Area per Person If each person alive on Earth in the year 2000 was given an equal portion of existing surface land, each person would get about 7.3 acres (0.025 km², or about four football fields). In the year 2050, each person might get 4.8 acres of land (0.016 km², or about two and a half football fields).

Figure 10 ▶ Rapid population growth can put pressure on water sources, land, and materials used for fuel or shelter. The makeshift housing shown here is one consequence of unmanaged growth.

Figure 11 ▶ Gathering fuel is part of daily survival in many developing countries. If there is not enough wood to use for fuel, people may have to burn crop residue. This can lead to soil erosion and lower agricultural productivity.

Graphic Organizer **Spider Map** Create the **Graphic Organizer** entitled "Spider Map" described in the Appendix. Label the circle "Problems of Rapid Population Growth." Create a leg for each problem of rapid population growth. Then, fill in the map with details about each problem of rapid population growth.

Figure 12 ▶ This woman is washing clothes in the Rio Grande on the U.S.-Mexico border. In areas that have no sewage or water treatment systems, people may use the same water supply for drinking, bathing, washing, and sewage disposal.

A Shortage of Fuelwood Women in Myanmar gathering firewood are shown in **Figure 11.** In many of the poorest countries, wood is the main fuel source. When populations are stable, people use fallen tree limbs for fuel, which does not harm the trees. When populations grow rapidly, deadwood does not accumulate fast enough to provide enough fuel. People begin to cut down living trees. Parts of Africa, Asia, and India have been cleared of vegetation by people collecting fuelwood.

A supply of fuel ensures that a person can boil water and cook food. In many parts of the world, water taken directly from wells or public supplies is not safe to drink because it contains waterborne parasites or other diseases. The water can be sterilized by boiling it, but fuel is needed to do so. Also, food is often unsafe or harder to digest unless it is cooked. Without enough fuelwood, many people suffer from disease and malnutrition.

Unsafe Water In places that lack infrastructure, the local water supply may be used not only for drinking and washing but also for sewage disposal. As a result, the water supply becomes a breeding ground for organisms that cause diseases such as dysentery, typhoid, and cholera.

Many cities have populations that are doubling every 15 years, and water systems cannot be expanded fast enough to keep up with this growth. In 2001, over 1 billion people worldwide lacked safe drinking water and more than 3 million died of diseases that were spread through water. The Rio Grande, shown in **Figure 12,** is one example of an unsafe water source used by many people.

Lima, Peru, is another example of an area with unsafe water. More than half of the population of Lima is housed in shanty-towns that have no plumbing. The bacteria that cause cholera thrived in Lima's unmanaged water sources in 1991. In that year, Lima's population suffered the first epidemic of cholera that had occurred in the Western Hemisphere in 75 years.

Impacts on Land People prefer to live where they have easy access to resources. Growing populations may have a shortage of **arable land,** which is land that can be used to grow crops. Growing populations also make trade-offs between competing uses for land such as agriculture, housing, or natural habitats.

For example, Egypt's population of 73 million is growing at 2 percent per year. For food and exportable products, Egypt depends on farming within the Nile River valley, shown in **Figure 13.** Most of the country is desert, and less than 4 percent of Egypt's land is arable. However, the Nile River valley is also where most Egyptians live. Egyptians continue to build housing on what was once farmland, which reduces Egypt's available arable land.

Much of the world's population is undergoing **urbanization,** the movement of people from rural areas to cities. In the United States, people often find work in the cities but move into suburban areas around the cities. This *suburban sprawl* leads to traffic jams, inadequate infrastructure, and the reduction of land for farms and wildlife habitat. Meanwhile, housing within cities becomes more costly, more dense, and in shorter supply.

✔ Reading Check How has rapid population growth affected arable land in Egypt?

FIELD ACTIVITY

Does Your Local Area Have Population Pressures? Take an informal survey of your community's population trends. Gather information by taking a walk, reading the local newspaper, or by contacting your local government or chamber of commerce offices.

Try to answer the following questions:

- Is your local population growing or shrinking? How much change is due to migration?

- What growth-related problems are citizens and government planners aware of?

- What solutions are being proposed or debated?

Record your results in your *EcoLog.*

Figure 13 ▶ Egypt's population is mostly crowded into the narrow Nile River valley. The United States has more arable land, but suburban sprawl (left) creates many problems.

Nile River valley

International Development
The United Nations (UN) has an important role in understanding and assisting the development of nations. The UN holds conferences, publishes research, creates treaties, manages international programs, and dispenses funds.

The UN also creates formal designations, such as *least developed countries*. Demographers, foreign aid programs, and international treaties may use these designations.

A Demographically Diverse World

As you have seen, demographers may categorize countries as either developed or developing. However, demographers may prefer the terms *more developed* and *less developed* to describe countries or regions, because the reality of development is complex and politically sensitive.

Not every country in the world is progressing through each stage of the demographic transition according to the model. Some countries now have modern industries, but incomes remain low. A few countries have achieved stable and educated populations with little industrialization. Some countries seem to remain in the second stage of the model. These countries have rapid population growth, but are unable to make enough educational and economic gains to reduce the birth rate and move into the third stage.

In recent years, the international community has begun to focus on the **least developed countries.** These countries show few signs of development and in some cases have increasing death rates, while birth rates remain high. Least developed countries are officially identified by the United Nations. These countries may be given priority for foreign aid and development programs to address their population and environmental problems.

CASE STUDY

Thailand's Population Challenges

Population growth is a major concern for many developing countries. But the options are limited for a country that has a poor economy and growing demands for limited resources. Thailand is one country that has effectively and purposefully slowed its population growth.

Around 1970, Thailand's population was growing at a rate of more than 3 percent per year, and the average Thai family had 6.4 children. The country had increasing environmental problems, such as air pollution in major cities and unsafe water supplies. Thailand's emissions of carbon dioxide from burning fossil fuels almost doubled between 1990 and 1997. In Thailand's capital, Bangkok, one-ninth of residents

▶ **Bangkok, Thailand** is one of the most crowded and polluted cities in the world. However, population growth is slowing in Thailand, and some environmental problems are starting to be solved.

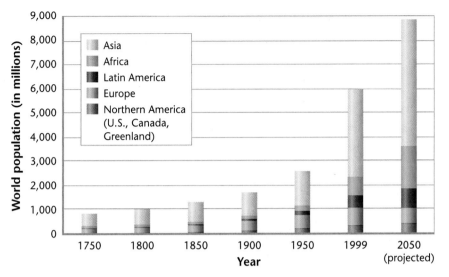

Source: UN Population Division.

Figure 14 ▶ Growth rates vary in different parts of the world. Which regions will contribute the most growth?

Growth rates for different parts of the world are shown in **Figure 14.** Populations are relatively stable in Europe, the United States, Canada, Russia, South Korea, Thailand, China, Japan, Australia, and New Zealand. In contrast, populations are still growing rapidly in less developed regions. Most of the world's population is now within Asia.

SC*i*LINKS.
www.scilinks.org
Topic: Developed and Developing Countries
Code: HE80397

Thailand's Population Strategies

- improved healthcare for mothers and children

- openness of the people, government, and community leaders to changing social traditions

- cooperation of private and nonprofit organizations with the government

- increases in women's rights and ability to earn income

- economic incentives such as building loans for families who participated in family planning programs

- creative family-planning programs promoted by popular government leaders

- high literacy rates of women (80 percent in 1980 and 94 percent in 2000)

How did Thailand make such major changes with limited resources? Demographers believe the changes are due to the combination of strategies shown in the table at left.

CRITICAL THINKING

1. Applying Ideas For what reasons could Thailand be described as a developing country in the 1970s? In what ways was it able to change?

2. Expressing Viewpoints Do you approve of all of the strategies that the government of Thailand employed in order to reduce their population growth? Do the goals justify the strategies they used? Write a persuasive paragraph to defend your opinion. **WRITING SKILLS**

have respiratory problems, and many people die of waterborne diseases each year.

In 1971, Thailand's government adopted a policy to reduce Thailand's population growth. The policy included increased education for women, greater access to healthcare and contraceptives, and economic incentives

to parents who have fewer children. Fifteen years later, the country's population growth rate had been cut to about 1.6 percent. By 2000, the growth rate had fallen to 1.1 percent and the age structure was more evenly distributed. These changes also reflected a decline in the infant mortality rate.

Figure 15 ▶ China has implemented a long campaign to reduce birth rates. Strategies have included economic rewards for single-child families, and advertising such as the billboard shown here.

Table 1 ▼

ICPD Goals for 2015
• Provide universal access to a full range of safe and reliable family-planning methods and related reproductive health services.
• Reduce infant mortality rates to below 35 infant deaths per 1,000 live births and mortality rates of children under five years old to below 45 deaths per 1,000 live births.
• Close the gap in maternal mortality between developing and developed countries. Achieve a maternal mortality rate below 60 deaths per 100,000 live births.
• Increase life expectancy at birth to more than 75 years. In countries with the highest mortality, increase life expectancy at birth to more than 70 years.
• Achieve universal access to and completion of primary education. Ensure the widest and earliest possible access by girls and women to secondary and higher levels of education.

Source: UN Population Fund.

Managing Development and Population Growth

Humans throughout history have witnessed the negative effects of population growth. Today, less developed countries know that continued population growth can limit their economic development. The governments of some countries, such as China, Thailand, and India, have tried to reduce birth rates using public advertising, as shown in **Figure 15**, family planning programs, economic incentives, or legal punishments.

In 1994, the United Nations held the International Conference on Population and Development (ICPD). This conference involved debates about the relationships between population, development, and environment. **Table 1** shows the main goals that resulted from the conference. Many countries favor stabilizing population growth through investments in development, especially through improvements in women's status. In fact, worldwide fertility rates are dropping, as shown in **Figure 16**.

✓ **Reading Check** What are two examples of strategies that a government might use to try to limit population growth?

Figure 16 ▶ Worldwide Trends in Fertility Most countries' fertility rates are dropping toward replacement level.

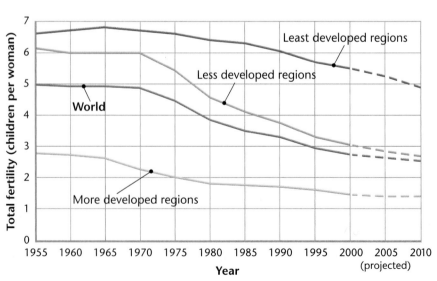

Source: UN Population Division.

Growth Is Slowing

The human population of the world is now more than 6 billion and is still increasing. The worldwide population growth rate peaked at about 87 million people per year between 1985 and 1990. In contrast, the population grew by only 81 million people per year from 1990 to 1995.

Fertility rates have declined since about 1970 in both more-developed and less developed regions. However, rates are still much higher in less developed regions. Demographers predict that this trend will continue and that worldwide population growth will be slower in this century than in the last century. If current trends continue, most countries will have replacement level fertility rates by 2050. If so, world population growth would eventually stop.

Projections to 2050 United Nations projections of world population growth to 2050 are shown in **Figure 17**. The medium-growth line assumes that worldwide fertility rates will decline to replacement level by 2050. The high- and low-growth lines would result from higher or lower fertility rates. Most demographers predict the medium growth rate and a world population of 9 billion in 2050.

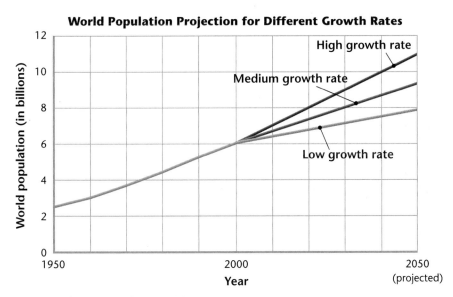

World Population Projection for Different Growth Rates

High growth rate
Medium growth rate
Low growth rate

Source: UN Population Division.

QuickLAB

Estimating Fertility Rates

Procedure

1. Your goal is to estimate the average fertility rate of the mothers of students in your school. Design and conduct a quick survey of other students in the school.

2. Create one or two survey questions that will collect the needed information. Be sure that the questions are sensitive to personal differences and are not judgmental.

3. Devise a method to make the survey anonymous. You might simply pass out a questionnaire to another class.

4. Get your teacher's approval for your survey questions and method, and then conduct your survey.

Analysis

1. Analyze your results, and prepare a short summary of your findings.

Figure 17 ▶ Current fertility trends will result in a world population of about 9 billion in 2050 (middle line). Economic or political changes could lead to higher or lower numbers.

SECTION 2 Review

1. **Describe** three problems caused by rapid human population growth.

2. **Compare** population growth in more-developed countries to population growth in less developed countries.

3. **Describe** worldwide population projections for the next 50 years.

CRITICAL THINKING

4. **Analyzing a Viewpoint** Write a comparison of the pros and cons of the strategies nations have used to reduce population growth. **WRITING SKILLS**

5. **Analyzing Relationships** Do you think that simply changing birth rates will cause a nation to undergo further development?

1 Studying Human Populations

Key Terms

demography, 235
age structure, 236
survivorship, 236
fertility rate, 237
migration, 237
life expectancy, 238
demographic
  transition, 239

Main Ideas

▶ Human population growth has accelerated in the last few centuries. The main reasons for this growth were improvements in hygiene and increases in food production, which accompanied the industrial and scientific revolutions.

▶ Demographers try to predict population trends using data such as age structure, survivorship, fertility rates, migration, and life expectancy.

▶ In the demographic transition model, countries progress through four stages of change in birth rates, death rates, and population size.

2 Changing Population Trends

infrastructure, 241
arable land, 243
urbanization, 243
least developed
  countries, 244

▶ When a growing population uses resources faster than they can be renewed, the resources most critically affected are fuelwood, water, and arable land.

▶ In this century, countries may be labeled more developed or less developed. Not all countries are going through the demographic transition in the same way that the more-developed countries did.

▶ Some countries attempt to reduce birth rates directly through public advertising, family planning programs, economic incentives, or legal punishments for their citizens.

Using Key Terms

Use each of the following terms in a separate sentence.

1. *demography*
2. *demographic transition*
3. *infrastructure*
4. *least developed countries*

For each pair of terms, explain how the meanings of the terms differ.

5. *age structure* and *survivorship*
6. *infant mortality* and *life expectancy*
7. *death rate* and *fertility rate*
8. *urbanization* and *migration*

✔ STUDY TIP

Quantitative Terms Look for key terms in the graphs in this chapter. In your *EcoLog,* copy the graphs and write brief descriptions of how key terms may relate to the graphs and to other key terms. For example, copy Figure 3, and write "High infant mortality results in low life expectancy and Type III survivorship."

Understanding Key Ideas

9. Age structure data include all of the following *except*
   a. the number of members of a population who are between 5 and 11 years old.
   b. the ratio of males to females in a population.
   c. the amount of population change due to immigration or emigration.
   d. the ratio of older people to younger people in a population.

10. Human population growth accelerated in recent centuries mostly because of
    a. the bubonic plague.
    b. better hygiene and food.
    c. the discovery of electricity.
    d. improved efficiency of fuel use.

11. Which countries have Type I survivorship?
    a. the most developed countries
    b. the least developed countries
    c. countries in the second stage of the demographic transition
    d. countries in the first stage of the demographic transition

12. The demographic transition is a(n)
    a. untested hypothesis.
    b. natural law.
    c. model based on observed patterns.
    d. international law.

13. A country in the second stage of the demographic transition may have all of the following *except*
    a. increasing agricultural production.
    b. improving healthcare and education.
    c. decreasing population size.
    d. decreasing death rates.

14. Which of the following resources is likely to be impacted the most by a rapidly growing population?
    a. clothing
    b. food
    c. housing
    d. water

15. Which of the following diseases is often spread through unsafe public water sources?
    a. dysentery
    b. flu
    c. chickenpox
    d. AIDS

16. Which of the following uses of wood is the most important for basic human needs?
    a. heating the home
    b. boiling water
    c. making tools
    d. building shelter

17. In this century, the world population is likely to
    a. remain the same.
    b. continue to grow exponentially.
    c. decline rapidly because fertility rates are already below replacement level.
    d. stabilize after fertility rates fall below replacement level.

Short Answer

18. What are the main reasons that life expectancy has increased worldwide?

19. How does the age structure of a population help predict future population growth?

20. What is the relationship between education and fertility rates in a human population?

21. Which properties of a population change during the demographic transition?

22. Which key resources are impacted the most by rapidly growing populations?

23. Which regions of the world are generally more developed? less developed?

Interpreting Graphics

The graph below shows each region's contribution to world population growth. Use the graph to answer questions 24–26.

24. Which region(s) are projected to increase in population size?

25. Which region(s) are projected to decline in population size?

26. Can you assume that all the countries within each region have the same growth patterns? Explain your answer.

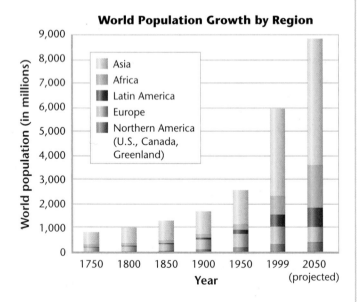

World Population Growth by Region

Legend:
- Asia
- Africa
- Latin America
- Europe
- Northern America (U.S., Canada, Greenland)

World population (in millions) vs. Year (1750, 1800, 1850, 1900, 1950, 1999, 2050 (projected))

Concept Mapping

27. Use the following terms to create a concept map: *rapid human population growth, demographic transition, survivorship, fertility rate, fuelwood, water,* and *land.*

Critical Thinking

28. Analyzing Predictions Why are human population trends difficult to predict? Describe an example of an event that would change most demographic predictions.

29. Analyzing Methods In what ways does the study of human populations differ from the study of wildlife ecology?

30. Identifying Relationships What other factors, besides those already mentioned, might have an effect on fertility rates in a given population?

31. Evaluating Theories Write an evaluation of the demographic transition as a theory of how populations will develop. How useful is the demographic transition model in predicting the future? What assumptions are made by the theory? What criticisms could be made of the theory? **WRITING SKILLS**

Cross-Disciplinary Connection

32. Careers Demographers are employed by many kinds of organizations including governments, health organizations, and insurance companies. How can their skills be useful to each of these organizations?

33. Social Studies Find out the demographic history, for the last 100 years, of a developing country of your choice. Explain how closely this country's pattern of development follows the demographic transition model.

Portfolio Project

34. Research Demographic Trends Look up population statistics for your local city, county, or state. Read and take notes about recent demographic trends and predictions for the next few decades. Make a summary of your findings. **READING SKILLS**

MATH SKILLS

Use the graph below to answer questions 35–37.

35. **Analyzing Data** At which times did the fertility rate change most drastically in the United States?

36. **Graphing Data** Sketch a copy of the graph below. Smooth the bumps to give an idea of general trends.

37. **Drawing Conclusions** On your new graph, draw a second line to show the changes in population size that you would predict to result from the given fertility rates over time.

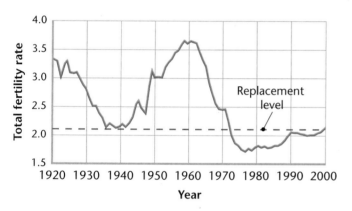

WRITING SKILLS

38. **Writing Persuasively** Write an opinion article for a newspaper or magazine. Argue either for or against a policy related to immigration or family planning.

39. **Writing Using Research** Look up recent census data from your city, county, or state. Write a paragraph that describes the major demographic trends of the last few years.

READING SKILLS

Read the passage below, and then answer the questions that follow.

Excerpt from UN Population Fund, The State of World Population 2001, *2001.*

Worldwide, women have primary responsibility for rearing children and ensuring sufficient resources to meet their needs. In the rural areas of developing countries, women are also the main managers of essential household resources like clean water, fuel for cooking and heating, and fodder for domestic animals.

Women make up more than half of the world's agricultural workforce. They grow crops for the home and market and often produce most staple crops. In the world's poorest countries, women head almost a quarter of rural households.

However, although women have the primary responsibility for managing resources, they usually do not have control. National law or local customs often deny women the right to secure title or inherit land, which means they have no collateral to raise credit and improve their conditions.

Women often lack rights in other aspects of their lives, reinforcing gender inequalities. High fertility and large families are still a feature of rural life, though the rationale has long since passed. In part, this reflects women's lack of choice in the matter.

1. Which of the following are *not* cited in the passage as major responsibilities of women?
   a. management of household resources
   b. agricultural work
   c. government leadership
   d. rearing children

2. The passage implies that improving women's rights would lead to
   a. the ability of women to earn more money.
   b. increased availability of fuel.
   c. poorer rural households.
   d. larger families.

Understanding Concepts

Directions (1–4): **For *each* question, write on a separate sheet of paper the letter of the correct answer.**

1 How did the human population change in the last 200 years?
  A. increased at a decelerated rate
  B. increased at an accelerated rate
  C. decreased at a decelerated rate
  D. decreased at an accelerated rate

2 Which of the following has the **most** effect on the infant mortality rate?
  F. Parents have a college education.
  G. Parents live in a quiet suburban area.
  H. Parents are in the higher income brackets.
  I. Parents keep a baby fed, clean and warm.

3 Why have populations in most developed countries stopped growing?
  A. In most developed countries, immigration has decreased and emigration increased.
  B. In most developed countries, contagious diseases have reduced life expectancies.
  C. In most developed countries, birth rates have decreased to a level close to the death rate.
  D. In most developed countries, industrial development that created progress has moved to less developed countries.

4 What is the term for the average number of years people in a population are likely to live?
  F. age structure
  G. demographic transition
  H. life expectancy
  I. migration pattern

Directions (5–6): **For *each* question, write a short response.**

5 During a period of population growth, the resources most critically affected are fuelwood, water, and arable land. Explain how the supply of fuelwood is affected by human population growth.

6 Describe two of the factors used to predict human population size.

Reading Skills

Directions (7–8): **Read the passage below. Then answer the questions.**

  Growing populations often make trade-offs between competing uses for land such as agriculture, housing, or natural habitats. Much of the world's population is undergoing urbanization, the movement of people from rural areas to cities. In the United States, many cities are becoming large metropolitan areas. People often work in the cities but live in nearby suburbs. This leads to suburban sprawl, traffic jams, inadequate infrastructure, and the reduction of land for farms, ranches, and wildlife habitat.

7 How does urbanization affect agriculture?
  A. It reduces land available for crops.
  B. It reduces land available for housing.
  C. It reduces the safety of the water supply.
  D. It reduces the variety of foodstuffs.

8 Give an example of a situation where a population must decide how to use limited land resources, and the foreseeable effect of that decision.

Directions (9): **Read the passage below. Then answer the question.**

  The demographic transition model describes how population changes can occur. The model is based on observations of the history of many developed countries. The theory behind the model is that industrial development causes economic and social progress that then affects population growth rates.

9 What is the basis for the demographic transition model?
  F. the industrial development of developed countries
  G. economic and social progress in developing countries
  H. observations of the history of all countries
  I. observations of the history of many developed countries

Interpreting Graphics

Directions (10–12): For *each* question below, record the correct answer on a separate sheet of paper.

The graph below shows population projections for the world at different growth rates. Use this graph to answer questions 10 through 12.

World Population Projection For Different Growth Rates

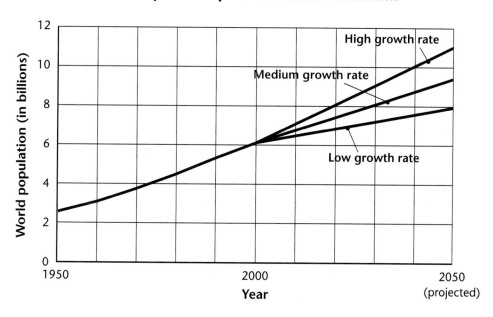

10 Which of the following can be inferred from the medium growth rate predicted?
  A. Migration will no longer add to the overall population growth.
  B. Life expectancy will decrease more rapidly in less-developed countries.
  C. Most countries will have reached replacement level fertility rates by 2050.
  D. More-developed countries will have greater growth than less-developed countries.

11 What does the chart project as the most likely outcome for the world population?
  F. It will be 12 billion in 2050.
  G. It will double by the year 2050.
  H. It will increase by 25% by the year 2050.
  I. It will be between 8 and 11 billion in 2050.

12 By how many billions of people did the population increase between 1950 and 2005?
  A. 2   **C.** 4
  B. 3   **D.** 5

Test *TIP*

When solving a math problem, be sure to examine the units involved closely.

Objectives

▶ **USING SCIENTIFIC METHODS** **Predict** which variable has a greater effect on population growth rates.

▶ **Calculate** changes for a given population over a 50-year period.

▶ **Graph** the resulting population's age structure by creating a population pyramid.

▶ **Compare** the effects of fertility variables on population growth rates.

Materials

calculator or computer
colored pencils or markers
graph paper
notebook
pen or pencil
ruler

▶ **Age Structure** You will make an age-structure diagram, such as this graph of the U.S. population in 2000.

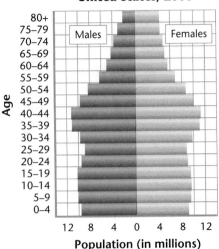

United States, 2000

How Will Our Population Grow?

If you were a demographer, you might be asked to determine how a population is likely to change in the future. You have learned that the rate of population growth is affected by both the number of children per family and the age at which people have children. But which factor has a greater effect? To explore this question, you will use age-structure diagrams—also called population pyramids—such as the one shown below.

Procedure

1. In this lab you will calculate future population trends for an imaginary city. To compare how fertility variables may affect population growth, each group of students will test the effects of different assumptions. Assume the following about the population of this city:

Assumptions About the Population
• Half the population is male and half is female.
• Every woman will have all of her children during a given five-year period of her life.
• Everyone who is born will live to the age of 85 and then die.
• No one will move into or out of the city.

2. Your teacher will divide the class into four groups. Each group will project population growth using the following assumptions:

	Assumptions About the Women in the Population	
Group	**Each woman gives birth to**	**While in the age range of**
A	5 children	15–19
B	5 children	25–29
C	2 children	15–19
D	2 children	25–29

3. Predict which of the four groups will have the greatest population growth in 50 years. Write down the order you would predict for the relative size of the groups from largest population to smallest population.

4. The table at right shows the population of our imaginary city for the year 2000. Use the data in the table to make an age-structure diagram (population pyramid) for the city. Use the example diagram at left to help you.

5. Make a table similar to the one shown at right. Add columns for the years 2005, 2010, and for every fifth year until the year 2050.

6. Calculate the number of 0- to 4-year-olds in the year 2005. To do this, first determine how many women will have children between 2000 and 2005. Remember that half of the population in each age group is female, and that members of the population will reproduce at specific ages. Multiply the number of child-bearing women by the number of children that each woman will have. For example, Group A will have 12,500 new births by 2005.

7. Fill in the entire column for the year 2005. Determine the number of people in each age group by "shifting" each group from 2000. For example, the number of 5- to 9-year-olds in 2005 will equal the number of 0- to 4-year-olds in 2000.

8. Calculate the total population for each five-year period.

9. Repeat the process described in steps 3–8 for each column, to complete the table through the year 2050.

Analysis

1. **Constructing Graphs** Plot the growth of the population on a line graph. You may want to use a computer to graph the results.

2. **Constructing Graphs** Make a population pyramid for the population in 2050.

Conclusions

3. **Evaluating Data** Compare your graphs with the graphs of the other three groups. Were your predictions correct?

4. **Drawing Conclusions** Which variable had a greater effect on population growth—the number of children each woman had or the age at which each woman had children?

5. **Interpreting Information** Did any of the groups show no growth in the population? Explain these results.

Extension

1. From the age-structure diagram on the previous page, what would you predict to happen to the U.S. population in the next 20 years? in the next 50 years? What parts of the age structure are most important to these predictions?

Population in Each Age Group, 2000–2050			
Age	2000	2005	2010
80+	100		
75–79	500		
70–74	600		
65–69	700		
60–64	800		
55–59	900		
50–54	1,000		
45–49	1,250		
40–44	1,500		
35–39	2,000		
30–34	2,500		
25–29	3,000		
20–24	4,000		
15–19	5,000		
10–14	6,500		
5–9	8,000	10,000	
0–4	10,000	12,500	
Total	48,350		
Females that give birth	2,500		
New births	12,500		

▶ **Sample Population Data** Use this table as an example to calculate the age structure for each generation of your imaginary population. Add columns for five-year periods up to 2050. Examples of some of Group A's results are shown in red.

EARTH SCIENCE CONNECTION

FERTILITY RATES AND FEMALE LITERACY IN AFRICA

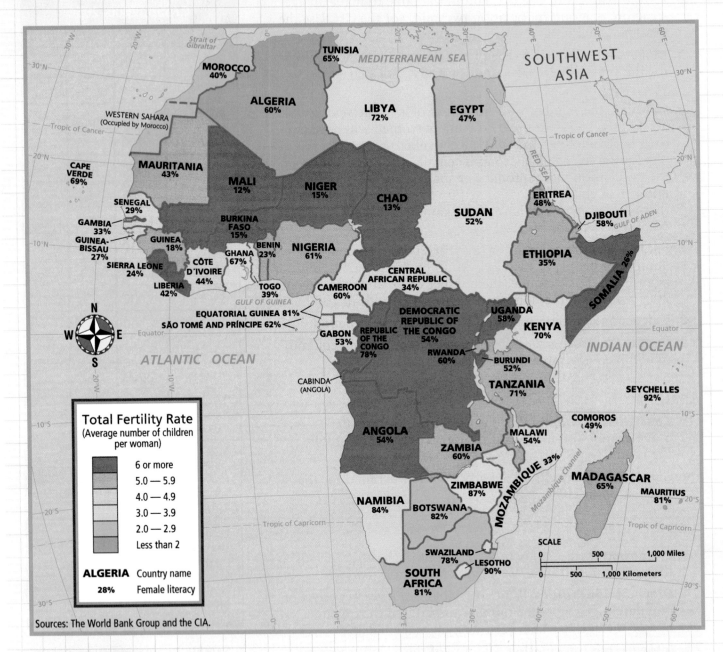

Sources: The World Bank Group and the CIA.

MAP SKILLS

Use the map of Africa to answer the questions below.

1. **Describing Locations** Which regions of Africa have the highest female literacy (percentage of females who can read and write)? the lowest female literacy? Which regions have the highest fertility rates? the lowest fertility rates?

2. **Analyzing Data** Choose 20 countries and make a graph comparing the total fertility rates and female literacy of each country.

3. **Comparing Data** Worldwide, the average total fertility rate is about 2.8 children per woman, and the average female literacy is 74 percent. How does Africa compare with the rest of the world in both aspects?

SOCIETY & the Environment

LOST POPULATIONS: WHAT HAPPENED?

At various points in human history, entire populations have disappeared and left mysterious remains such as the Egyptian pyramids and the Anasazi pueblos in the southwestern United States. Why did these people and their civilizations disappear? Archeologists sometimes find evidence that environmental destruction was one of the reasons the populations disappeared.

Easter Island

On Easter Island in the Pacific Ocean, the first European visitors were amazed to find huge stone heads that were miles from the quarries where the heads had been made. It seemed impossible that the islanders could have moved the heads. There were no horses, oxen, or carts on the island and there were also no trees, which could have been used as rollers to move the heads. The islanders were using grass and reeds to make fires because the island was barren grassland. The island had no tree or shrub that was more than 3 m tall.

A Changed Environment

Researchers have now shown that Easter Island was very different when it was first colonized by Polynesians around 400 CE. In the oldest garbage heaps on the island, archaeologists have found that one-third of the bones came from dolphins. To hunt dolphins, the islanders must have had strong canoes made of wood from tall trees. Pollen grains, which are used to identify plants, show that the island was once covered by a forest that contained many species found nowhere else in the world.

But by 1600 CE, trees were rare and the Easter Island palm tree was extinct. The palm seeds were probably eaten by rats that the Polynesians had brought to the island. With the destruction of the forest, every species of native land

▶ These large stone figures found on Easter Island were made by a civilization that has disappeared.

bird also became extinct, and the human population crashed.

The people of Easter Island destroyed their environment by overusing its natural resources and introducing new species such as chickens and rats. The people were reduced from a complex civilization to a primitive lifestyle. Easter Island is a small-scale example of what ecologists worry could happen to Earth's entire human population.

▶ These ruins in New Mexico were built by the Chaco Anasazi civilization around 900 CE. Environmental changes are thought to have affected this population.

What Do You Think?

Industrialized countries have started to invest in environmental improvements, such as replanting forests that have been destroyed and protecting endangered species. Do you think this makes these countries safe from the kind of environmental disasters that destroyed the Easter Island civilization?

Biodiversity

1 What Is Biodiversity?

2 Biodiversity at Risk

3 The Future of Biodiversity

PRE-READING ACTIVITY

FOLDNOTES

Tri-Fold
Before you read this chapter, create the **FoldNote** entitled "Tri-Fold" described in the Reading and Study Skills section of the Appendix. Write what you know about biodiversity in the column labeled "Know." Then, write what you want to know in the column labeled "Want." As you read the chapter, write what you learn about biodiversity in the column labeled "Learn."

How many species are in this photo? Scientists know that this region of Central Texas is home to an unusual number of unique species. However, many more species remain unknown to science, both in faraway jungles and in our own backyards.

What Is Biodiversity?

SCSh.2.b; SCSh.3.c; SCSh.4.a; SCSh.9.c

Every day, somewhere on Earth, several unique species of organisms become *extinct* as the last members of the species die—often because of human actions. Scientists are not sure how many species are becoming extinct or even how many species there are on Earth. How much extinction is natural? Can we—or should we—prevent extinctions? The study of biodiversity helps us think about these questions, but does not give us all the answers.

A World Rich in Biodiversity

The term **biodiversity,** short for "biological diversity," usually refers to the number of different species in a given area. Certain areas of the planet, such as tropical rain forests, contain an extraordinary variety of species. The complex relationships between so many species are hard to study, but humans may need to understand and preserve biodiversity for our own survival.

Unknown Diversity The study of biodiversity starts with the unfinished task of cataloging all the species that exist on Earth. As shown in **Figure 1,** the number of species known to science is about 1.7 million, most of which are insects. However, the actual number of species on Earth is unknown. Most scientists agree that we have not studied Earth's species adequately, but they accept an estimate of greater than 10 million for the total number of species. New species are considered *known* when they are collected and described scientifically. Unknown species exist in remote wildernesses, deep in the oceans, and even in cities.

✔ Reading Check What determines whether a species is known or unknown? (See the Appendix for answers to Reading Checks.)

Objectives

▶ Describe the diversity of species types on Earth, relating the difference between known numbers and estimated numbers.

▶ List and describe three levels of biodiversity.

▶ Explain four ways in which biodiversity is important to ecosystems and humans.

▶ Analyze the potential value of a single species.

Key Terms

biodiversity
gene
keystone species
ecotourism

Figure 1 ▶ Number of Species on Earth About 1.7 million species on Earth are known to science. Many more species are *estimated* to exist, especially species of smaller organisms. Scientists continue to revise these estimates.

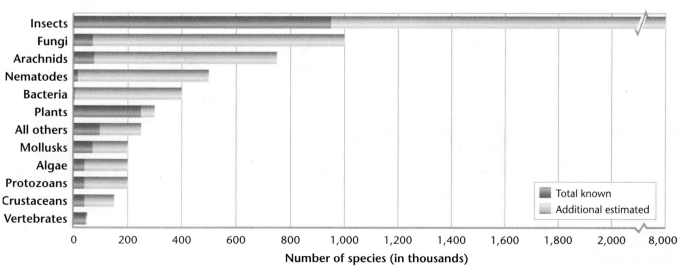

Source: World Conservation Monitoring Center.

Figure 2 ▶ Scientists continue to find and describe new species. Specimens may be stored in collections such as this one of tropical birds, with tags that say where and when they were found.

Figure 3 ▶ The sea otters of North America are an example of a keystone species, upon which a whole ecosystem depends.

Levels of Diversity Biodiversity can be studied and described at three levels. *Species diversity* refers to the number of different species in an area. This kind of diversity has received the most attention and is most often what is meant by *biodiversity*. *Ecosystem diversity* refers to the variety of habitats, communities, and ecological processes within and between ecosystems. *Genetic diversity* refers to all the different *genes* contained within all members of a population. A **gene** is a piece of DNA that codes for a specific trait that can be inherited by an organism's offspring.

Benefits of Biodiversity

Biodiversity can affect the stability of ecosystems and the sustainability of populations. In addition, there are many ways that humans clearly use and benefit from the variety of life-forms on Earth. Biodiversity may be more important than we realize.

Species Are Connected to Ecosystems We depend on healthy ecosystems to ensure a healthy biosphere that has balanced cycles of energy and nutrients. Species are part of these cycles. When scientists study any species closely, they find that it plays an important role in an ecosystem. Every species is probably either dependent on or depended upon by at least one other species in ways that are not always obvious. When one species disappears from an ecosystem, a strand in a food web is removed. How many threads can be pulled from the web before it collapses? We often do not know the answer until it is too late.

Some species are so clearly critical to the functioning of an ecosystem that they are called **keystone species.** One example of a keystone species is the sea otter. **Figure 3** shows how the loss of sea otter populations led to the loss of the kelp beds along the U.S. Pacific coast and how the recovery of otter populations led to the recovery of the kelp populations.

❶ In the 1800s, sea otters were hunted for their fur. They disappeared from the Pacific coast of the U.S.

❷ Sea urchins, with no more predators, multiplied and ate all of the kelp. The kelp beds began to disappear from the area.

❸ In 1937, a small group of surviving otters was discovered. With protection and scientific efforts, the otter populations grew.

❹ The otters once again preyed on the sea urchins. The kelp beds regenerated.

Species and Population Survival Genetic diversity within populations is critical to species survival. Genetic diversity increases the chance that some members of a population will survive environmental changes. Small and isolated populations are less likely to survive such changes. When a population shrinks, its genetic diversity decreases as though it is passing through a bottleneck, represented in **Figure 4.** Even if the population can increase again, its genetic diversity will be reduced. Then, members of the population may become more likely to inherit genetic diseases.

Medical, Industrial, and Agricultural Uses People throughout history have used the variety of organisms on Earth for food, clothing, shelter, and medicine. About one quarter of the drugs prescribed in the United States are derived from plants. Almost all antibiotics are derived from chemicals found in fungi. **Table 1** lists some plants from which medicines are derived.

For some industries, undiscovered and poorly studied species represent a source of potential products. New chemicals and industrial materials may be developed from chemicals discovered in all kinds of species. The scientific community continues to find new uses for biological material and genetic diversity.

✔ **Reading Check** Why is genetic diversity important for the survival of a species?

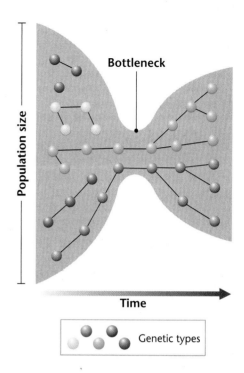

Figure 4 ▶ When a population is reduced to a few members, this creates a *bottleneck* of reduced genetic diversity. The genetic diversity of the population is greater before the bottleneck than after it.

Table 1 ▼

Common Medicines Derived from Plants		
Medicine	**Origin**	**Use**
Neostigmine	calabar bean (Africa)	treatment of glaucoma and basis for synthetic insecticides
Turbocurarine	curare vine (South America)	surgical muscle relaxant; treatment of muscle disorders; and poison for arrow tips
Vincristine, vinblastine	rosy periwinkle (Madagascar)	treatment of pediatric leukemia and Hodgkin's disease
Bromelain	pineapple (South America)	treatment to control tissue inflammation
Taxol	Pacific yew (North America)	anticancer agent
Novacaine, cocaine	coca plant (South America)	local anesthetic and basis for many other anesthetics
Cortisone	wild yam (Central America)	hormone used in many drugs
L-dopa (levodopa)	velvet bean (tropical Asia)	treatment of Parkinson's disease
Reserpine	Indian snakeroot (Malaysia)	treatment to reduce high blood pressure

www.scilinks.org
Topic: Biodiversity
Code: HE80151
Topic: Medicines from Plants
Code: HE80934

Figure 5 ▶ A produce market in Bolivia shows a diversity of native foods. Food crops that originated in the American tropics include corn, tomatoes, squash, and many types of beans and peppers.

Table 2 ▼

Origins of Some Foods
North America, Central America, and South America
• corn (maize), tomato, bean (pinto, green, and lima), peanut, potato, sweet potato, avocado, pumpkin, pineapple, cocoa, vanilla, and pepper (green, red, and chile)
Northeastern Africa, Central Asia, and Near East
• wheat (several types), sesame, chickpea, fig, lentil, carrot, pea, okra, date, walnut, coffee, cow, goat, pig, and sheep
India, East Asia, and Pacific Islands
• soybean, rice, banana, coconut, lemon, lime, orange, cucumber, eggplant, turnip, tea, black pepper, and chicken

Humans benefit from biodiversity every time they eat. Most of the crops produced around the world originated from a few areas of high biodiversity. Some examples of crop origins are shown in **Figure 5** and **Table 2**. Most new crop varieties are *hybrids*, crops developed by combining genetic material from more than one population. Depending on too few plant varieties for food is risky. For example, famines have resulted when an important crop was wiped out by disease. But some crops have been saved from diseases by being crossbred with wild plant relatives. In the future, new crop varieties may come from species not yet discovered.

Ethics, Aesthetics, and Recreation Some people believe that we should preserve biodiversity for ethical reasons. They believe that species and ecosystems have a right to exist whether or not they have any other value. To people of some cultures and religions, each organism on Earth is a gift with a higher purpose.

People also value biodiversity for aesthetic or personal enjoyment—keeping pets, camping, picking wildflowers, or watching wildlife. Some regions earn the majority of their income from **ecotourism,** a form of tourism that supports the conservation and sustainable development of ecologically unique areas.

SECTION 1 **Review**

1. **Describe** the general diversity of species on Earth in terms of relative numbers and types of organisms. Compare known numbers to estimates.

2. **Describe** three levels of biodiversity. Which level is most commonly meant by *biodiversity?*

3. **Explain** how biodiversity is important to ecosystems, and give examples of how it is important to humans.

CRITICAL THINKING

4. **Analyzing a Viewpoint** Is it possible to put a price on a single species? Explain your answer.

5. **Predicting Consequences** What is your favorite type of organism? If this organism were to go extinct, how would you feel? What would you be willing to do to try to save it from extinction? Write a short essay describing your reaction. **WRITING SKILLS**

Biodiversity at Risk

SCSh.2.b; SCSh.3.c; SCSh.3.d; SCSh.3.e;
SCSh.3.f; SCSh.6.a; SCSh.6.d; SEV.1.a;
SEV.1.d; SEV.1.e

About 65 million years ago, a series of changes in the Earth's climate and ecosystems caused the extinction of about half the species on Earth. The extinction of many species in a relatively short period of time is called a *mass extinction*. Earth has experienced several mass extinctions, as shown in **Figure 6**. It takes millions of years for biodiversity to rebound after a mass extinction.

Current Extinctions

Scientists are warning that we are in the midst of another mass extinction. The rate of extinction is estimated to have increased by a multiple of 50 since 1800. Between 1800 and 2100, up to 25 percent of all species on Earth may have become extinct. The current mass extinction is different from those of the past because humans are the primary cause of the extinctions.

Species Prone to Extinction Cockroaches and rats are not likely to become extinct because they have large populations that adapt easily to many habitats. But species with small populations in limited areas can easily become extinct. Species that are especially at risk of extinction include those that migrate, those that need large or special habitats, and those that are exploited by humans.

An **endangered species** is a species that is likely to become extinct if protective measures are not taken immediately. A **threatened species** is a species that has a declining population and that is likely to become endangered if it is not protected. Additional categories of risk exist for certain legal and biological purposes.

✓ Reading Check Why do scientists warn that a mass extinction is occurring now?

Objectives

▶ Define and give examples of *endangered* and *threatened species.*

▶ Describe several ways that species are being threatened with extinction globally.

▶ Explain which types of threats are having the largest impact on biodiversity.

▶ List areas of the world that have high levels of biodiversity and many threats to species.

▶ Compare the amount of biodiversity in the United States to that of the rest of the world.

Key Terms

endangered species
threatened species
exotic species
poaching
endemic species

Figure 6 ▶ Biodiversity has generally increased over time, as indicated here by the numbers of marine families. The past five mass extinctions were probably caused by global climate changes.

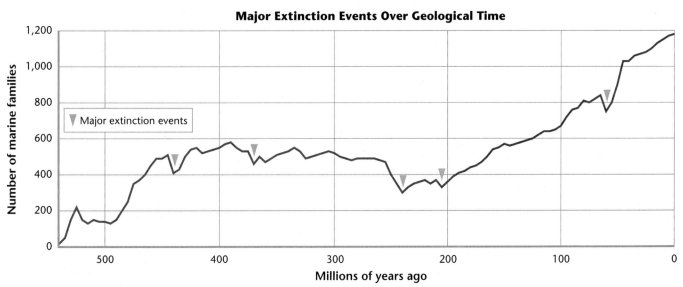

Major Extinction Events Over Geological Time

Number of marine families vs. Millions of years ago

▼ Major extinction events

Table 3 ▼

Species Known to Be Threatened or Extinct Worldwide			
Type of species	Number threatened (all categories of risk)	Number extinct (since ~1800)	Percent of species that may be threatened
Mammals	1,130	87	26
Birds	1,183	131	12
Reptiles	296	22	3.3
Amphibians	146	5	3.1
Fishes	751	92	3.7
Insects	555	73	0.054
Other crustaceans	555	73	1.03
Mollusks and worms	944	303	1.3
Plants	30,827	400	0.054

Source: UN Environment Programme.

Figure 7 ▶ The purple area on the map below shows the range of the Florida panther when settlers first arrived in the southeastern United States. Fewer than 100 of this cougar subspecies (right) remain in the wild.

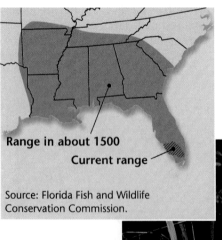

Range in about 1500

Current range

Source: Florida Fish and Wildlife Conservation Commission.

How Do Humans Cause Extinctions?

In the past 2 centuries, human population growth has accelerated and so has the rate of extinctions. The numbers of worldwide species known to be threatened, endangered, or recently extinct are listed in **Table 3**. The major human causes of extinction today are the destruction of habitats, the introduction of nonnative species, pollution, and the overharvesting of species.

Habitat Destruction and Fragmentation As human populations grow, we use more land to build homes and harvest resources. In the process, we destroy and fragment the habitats of other species. It is estimated that habitat loss causes almost 75 percent of the extinctions now occurring.

Due to habitat loss, the Florida panther is one of the most endangered animals in North America. The panther and its historical range are shown in **Figure 7**. Two hundred years ago, cougars—

a species that includes panthers and mountain lions—ranged from Alaska to South America. Cougars require expansive ranges of forest habitat and large amounts of prey. Today, much of the cougars' habitat has been destroyed or broken up by roads, canals, and fences. In 2003, fewer than 100 Florida panthers made up the only remaining wild cougar population east of the Mississippi River.

Invasive Exotic Species

An **exotic species** is a species that is not native to a particular region. Even such familiar organisms as cats and rats are considered to be exotic species when they are brought to regions where they never lived before. Exotic species can threaten native species that have no natural defenses against them. The invasive fire ants in **Figure 8** threaten livestock, people, and native species throughout the southeastern United States.

Harvesting, Hunting, and Poaching

Excessive hunting and harvesting of species can also lead to extinction. In the United States in the 1800s and 1900s, 2 billion passenger pigeons were hunted to extinction and the bison was hunted nearly to extinction. Thousands of rare species worldwide are harvested and sold for use as pets, houseplants, wood, food, or herbal medicine.

Many countries now have laws to regulate hunting, fishing, harvesting, and trade of wildlife. However, these activities continue illegally, a crime known as **poaching.** In poor countries especially, local species are an obvious source of food, medicine, or income. Moreover, not all threatened species are legally protected.

Pollution

Pesticides, cleaning agents, drugs, and other chemicals used by humans are making their way into food webs around the globe. The long-term effects of chemicals may not be clear until after many years of use. The bald eagle is a well-known example of a species that was endangered because of a pesticide known as DDT. Although DDT is now illegal to use in the United States, it is still manufactured here and used around the world.

Connection to Ecology

Extinction and Global Change
Scientists have worried for some time that environmental pollutants might cause drastic changes in our atmosphere and biosphere. However, it is difficult to draw a direct link from global changes to specific extinctions.

In recent decades, scientists have observed a worldwide decline in amphibian species. Unlike most cases of habitat loss or overhunting, there are no clear causes for these extinctions. But there is growing evidence to indicate two probable causes: the pollution of water sources with hormone-like chemicals and increased UV radiation exposure due to the thinning of the Earth's ozone layer.

Figure 8 ▶ Mounds made by imported fire ants cover many fields in the southeastern United States. As with many invasive exotic species, these ants had no natural predators and little competition from native species when they were first brought into the country by accident.

Areas of Critical Biodiversity

Some parts of the world contain a greater diversity of species than others. An important feature of such areas is that they have a large portion of **endemic species,** meaning species that are native to and found only within a limited area. Ecologists often use the numbers of endemic species of plants as an indicator of overall biodiversity, because plants form the basis of ecosystems on land. Ecologists increasingly point out the importance of biodiversity in oceans, though marine ecosystems are also complex and poorly understood.

Tropical Rain Forests The remaining tropical rain forests cover less than 7 percent of the Earth's land surface. Yet biologists estimate that over half of the world's species live in these forests. Most of these species have never been described. Unknown numbers of species are disappearing as tropical forests are cleared for farming or cattle grazing. Meanwhile, tropical forests are among the few places where some native people maintain traditional lifestyles and an intimate knowledge of their forest homes. The case study below explains the increasing value of such knowledge in the global marketplace.

CASE STUDY

A Genetic Gold Rush in the Rain Forests

How much is a species worth? To some people, there is money to be made in centers of biodiversity such as rain forests. Thus, the Amazon rain forest in South America is witnessing an increase in visitors—not just tourists, but scientists seeking genes, glory, or enlightenment into the mysteries of these quickly disappearing treasures.

To biologists, the prospect of discovering new species may be a chance at fame. The first scientist to collect and describe a species often gets to choose a name for that species. For other scientists, researching the unknown inner workings of the rain forests is an adventure similar to the adventures of explorers charting new lands.

But like the quests of early European explorers of the Americas, some reasons to venture into the wilderness may be economic. The *biotechnology* industry is based on the application of biological science to create new products such as drugs. This industry depends on Earth's variety of organisms—especially their genetic material—for research and development.

In fact, the Brazilian government has taken notice of the increased international interest in the Amazon's amazing biological assets. The government has claimed the right to tax or patent any genetic material harvested from within its borders.

Other researchers are more interested in another special feature of the Amazon—native peoples. Some Amazonian natives, such as the Yanomamö, are still living a lifestyle of intimate connection to their forest

▶ This botanist is researching the uses of rain-forest plants and other species with the help of local people.

Coral Reefs and Coastal Ecosystems Coral reefs occupy a small fraction of the marine environment yet contain the majority of the biodiversity there. Reefs provide millions of people with food and tourism revenue. They protect coasts from waves and are sources of new chemicals. But reefs are poorly studied and are not well protected by laws. Nearly 60 percent of Earth's coral reefs are threatened by human activities, such as overfishing and pollution. Similar threats affect coastal ecosystems, such as swamps, marshes, shores, and kelp beds. Coastal areas are travel routes for many migrating species as well as links to ecosystems on land.

Islands When an island rises from the sea, it is colonized by a limited number of species from the mainland. These colonizing species may then evolve into several new species. Thus, islands often hold a very distinct but limited set of species. For example, the Hawaiian Islands have 28 species of an endemic family of birds called *honeycreepers*. Honeycreepers and many other island species are endangered by competition from exotic species.

Reading Check Why is the biodiversity of coral reefs and coastal ecosystems threatened?

Geofact

The World's Largest Reef The Great Barrier Reef of Australia is the largest and probably the oldest reef system in the world. It stretches for 2,000 km (1,250 mi) and consists of 3,400 individual reefs.

▶ The Yanomamö are among the few native peoples of the tropical rain forests who still live traditional lifestyles and use their knowledge of the forests to meet all of their needs.

for their use of the skin excretions of poison dart frogs for hunting.

Often, researchers originally learned of a useful species from a local shaman, or healer. Biochemistry researchers have been amazed by the complex combinations of new chemicals they have discovered in many rain-forest species. Some of these chemicals are already being used in research and medicine.

CRITICAL THINKING

1. Expressing Viewpoints To whom do you think the genetic material of the rain forests should belong? What are some ways this benefit of biodiversity might be shared with the whole world?

home, in much the same way as they have for thousands of years.

An important value of such native peoples is their vast knowledge of the variety of species in the ecosystems where they live. Their knowledge includes more than just being able to recognize or name species. For example, the Yanomamö make use of thousands of plants, fungi, and animals for food, drugs, weapons, and art. Amazonian natives such as the Yanomamö are probably best known

Biodiversity Hotspots The most threatened areas of high species diversity on Earth have been labeled *biodiversity hotspots.* Twenty-five of these areas, shown in **Figure 9**, have been identified by international conservationists. The hotspot label was developed by ecologists in the late 1980s to identify areas that have high numbers of endemic species but that are also threatened by human activities. Most of these hotspots have lost at least 70 percent of their original natural vegetation. The hotspots include mostly tropical rainforests, coastal areas, and islands. In Madagascar, for example, only 18 percent of the original forests remain. More than 80 percent of Madagascar's 10,000 flowering plant species are endemic, as are 91 percent of its 300 reptile species. All 33 species of lemur, which make up a tenth of the world's primate species, are found only in Madagascar.

Figure 9 ▶ Conservationists have identified these 25 *biodiversity hotspots* (green). Examples of endangered species from some areas are shown.

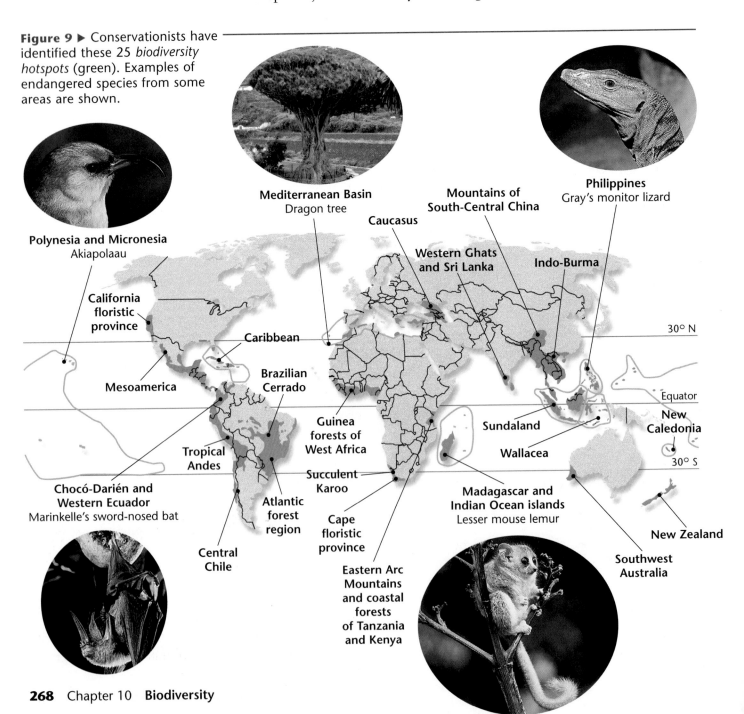

Mediterranean Basin
Dragon tree

Mountains of
South-Central China

Caucasus

Western Ghats
and Sri Lanka

Indo-Burma

Philippines
Gray's monitor lizard

Polynesia and Micronesia
Akiapolaau

California
floristic
province

Caribbean

30° N

Mesoamerica

Brazilian
Cerrado

Equator

Sundaland

New
Caledonia

Tropical
Andes

Guinea
forests of
West Africa

Wallacea

30° S

Chocó-Darién and
Western Ecuador
Marinkelle's sword-nosed bat

Atlantic
forest
region

Succulent
Karoo

Madagascar and
Indian Ocean islands
Lesser mouse lemur

New Zealand

Central
Chile

Cape
floristic
province

Southwest
Australia

Eastern Arc
Mountains
and coastal
forests
of Tanzania
and Kenya

Figure 10 ▶ Examples of at-risk species and populations in the United States include ❶ the cecropia moth, (declining populations), ❷ the tulip poplar tree (limited distribution), ❸ the crayfish *Cambarus mongalensis* (limited distribution), ❹ the desert pupfish (endangered), and ❺ the northern spotted owl (threatened).

Biodiversity in the United States You may notice that three of the biodiversity hotspots in **Figure 9** are partly within U.S. borders. The United States includes a wide variety of unique ecosystems, including the Florida Everglades, the California coastal region, Hawaii, the Midwestern prairies, and the forests of the Pacific Northwest. The United States holds unusually high numbers of species of freshwater fishes, mussels, snails, and crayfish. Species diversity in the United States is also high among groups of land plants such as pine trees and sunflowers. Some examples of the many species and populations that are at risk of being lost are shown in **Figure 10**.

The California Floristic Province, a biodiversity hotspot, is home to 3,488 native plant species. Of these species, 2,124 are endemic and 565 are threatened or endangered. The threats to this area include the use of land for agriculture and housing, dam construction, overuse of water, destructive recreation, and mining—all stemming from local human population growth.

SECTION 2 **Review**

1. **Describe** four ways that species are being threatened with extinction globally.

2. **Define** and give examples of *endangered species* and *threatened species.*

3. **List** areas of the Earth that have high levels of biodiversity and many threats to species.

4. **Compare** the amount of biodiversity in the United States to that of the rest of the world.

CRITICAL THINKING

5. **Interpreting Graphics** The biodiversity hot spots shown in Figure 9 share several characteristics besides a great number of species. Look at the map, and name as many shared characteristics as you can.

6. **Expressing Opinions** Which of the various threats to biodiversity do you think will be most difficult to stop? Which are hardest to justify? Write a paragraph to explain your opinion. **WRITING SKILLS**

The Future of Biodiversity

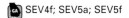

SEV4f; SEV5a; SEV5f

Objectives

▶ List and describe four types of efforts to save individual species.

▶ Explain the advantages of protecting entire ecosystems rather than individual species.

▶ Describe the main provisions of the Endangered Species Act.

▶ Discuss ways in which efforts to protect endangered species can lead to controversy.

▶ Describe three examples of worldwide cooperative efforts to prevent extinctions.

Key Terms

germ plasm
Endangered Species Act
habitat conservation plan
Biodiversity Treaty

Slowing the loss of species is possible, but to do so we must develop new approaches to conservation and sensitivity to human needs around the globe. In this section, you will read about efforts to save individual species and to protect entire ecosystems.

Saving Species One at a Time

When a species is clearly on the verge of extinction, concerned people sometimes make extraordinary efforts to save the last few individuals. These people hope that a stable population may be restored someday.

Captive-Breeding Programs Sometimes, wildlife experts may attempt to restore the population of a species through *captive-breeding* programs. These programs involve breeding species in captivity, with the hope of reintroducing populations to their natural habitats. One example of a captive-breeding program involves the California condor, shown in **Figure 11.**

Condors are scavengers. They typically soar over vast areas in search of dead animals to eat. Habitat loss, poaching, and lead poisoning brought the species near extinction. In 1986, the nine remaining wild California condors were captured by wildlife experts to protect the birds and to begin a breeding program. Birds bred in captivity were released into the wild in the hope that they would breed there. By 2005, there were 121 condors in the wild, a few of them juveniles that had hatched from eggs laid in the wild. The survival of this species remains doubtful.

Preserving Genetic Material One way to save the essence of a species is by preserving its genetic material. **Germ plasm** is any form of genetic material, such as that contained within the reproductive, or germ, cells

Figure 11 ▶ The California condor (above) nearly became extinct in the 1980s. A captive-breeding program (right) is returning some condors to the wild.

of plants and animals. Germ-plasm banks store germ plasm for future use in research or species-recovery efforts. Material may be stored as seeds, sperm, eggs, or pure DNA. Germ plasm is usually stored in special controlled environments, such as that shown in **Figure 12,** to keep the genetic material intact for many years. Farmers and gardeners also preserve germ plasm when they save and share seeds.

Zoos, Aquariums, Parks, and Gardens The original idea of zoos was to put exotic animals on display. However, in some cases, zoos now house the few remaining members of a species and are perhaps the species' last hope for survival. Zoos, wildlife parks, aquariums, and botanical gardens are living museums of the world's biodiversity. Botanical gardens, such as the one shown in **Figure 13,** house about 90,000 species of plants worldwide. Even so, these kinds of facilities rarely have enough resources or knowledge to preserve more than a fraction of the world's rare and threatened species.

More Study Needed Ultimately, saving a few individuals does little to preserve a species. Captive species may not reproduce or survive again in the wild. Also, small populations are vulnerable to infectious diseases and genetic disorders caused by inbreeding. Conservationists hope that these strategies are a last resort to save species.

Figure 12 ▶ This scientist is handling samples of genetic material that are preserved in controlled conditions. The samples may be able to reproduce organisms many years from now.

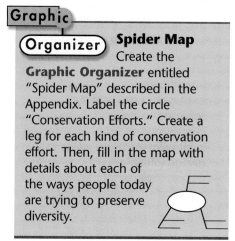

Graphic Organizer **Spider Map** Create the **Graphic Organizer** entitled "Spider Map" described in the Appendix. Label the circle "Conservation Efforts." Create a leg for each kind of conservation effort. Then, fill in the map with details about each of the ways people today are trying to preserve diversity.

Figure 13 ▶ This botanical garden is contained within a clear dome in Queen Elizabeth Park in Vancouver, Canada. The dome houses over 500 species of plants from all over the world as well as over 100 species of tropical birds.

Figure 14 ▶ Another conservation strategy is to promote more creative and sustainable land uses. This coffee crop is grown in the shade of native tropical trees instead of on cleared land. This practice is restoring habitat for many migrating songbirds.

SCI LINKS.
www.scilinks.org
Topic: Preserving
Ecosystems
Code: HE81214

QuickLAB

Design a Wildlife Preserve

Procedure

1. Imagine you have enough money and political support to set aside some land in your community to be habitat for local wildlife. Your goal is to decide which areas to preserve.

2. Find out which species in your area would need this protection the most, where they currently exist, and what their habitat needs are.

3. Use a **colored pencil** to draw some proposed preserve areas on a copy of a **local map.**

Analysis

1. Explain why you chose the areas you did. Can you connect or improve any existing areas of habitat? How could you reduce various threats to the species?

Preserving Habitats and Ecosystems

The most effective way to save species is to protect their habitats. But a species confined to a small area could be wiped out by a single natural disaster. Some species require a large range to find adequate food, find a suitable mate, and rear their young. Therefore, protecting the habitats of endangered and threatened species often means preserving or managing large areas.

Conservation Strategies Most conservationists now give priority to protecting entire ecosystems rather than individual species. By protecting entire ecosystems, we may be able to save most of the species in an ecosystem instead of only the ones that have been identified as endangered. The public has begun to understand that Earth's biosphere depends on all its connected ecosystems.

To protect biodiversity worldwide, conservationists focus on the hotspots described in the previous section. However, they also support additional strategies. One strategy is to identify areas of native habitat that can be preserved, restored, and linked into large networks. Another promising strategy is to promote products that have been harvested with sustainable practices, such as the shade-grown coffee shown in **Figure 14.**

More Study Needed Conservationists emphasize the need for more serious study of ecosystems. Only in recent decades has there been research into such basic questions as, How large does a protected preserve have to be to maintain a certain number of species? How much fragmentation can a particular ecosystem tolerate? The answers may be years or decades away, but decisions affecting biodiversity continue to be made based on available information.

✔ **Reading Check** Why does protecting the habitat of threatened and endangered species involve large areas?

Legal Protections for Species

Many nations have laws and regulations designed to prevent the extinction of species, and those in the United States are among the strongest. Even so, there is controversy about how to enforce such laws and about how effective they are.

U.S. Laws In 1973, the U.S. Congress passed the **Endangered Species Act** and has amended it several times since. This law, summarized in **Table 4,** is designed to protect plant and animal species in danger of extinction. Under the first provision, the U.S. Fish and Wildlife Service (USFWS) must compile a list of all endangered and threatened species in the United States. As of 2005, 1,272 species of plants and animals were listed as endangered or threatened. Dozens more are considered for the list each year. The second main provision of the act protects listed species from human harm. Anyone who harms, buys, or sells any part of these species is subject to a fine. The third provision prevents the federal government from carrying out any project that jeopardizes a listed species.

Recovery and Habitat Conservation Plans Under the fourth main provision of the Endangered Species Act, the USFWS must prepare a *species recovery plan* for each listed species. These plans often propose to protect or restore habitat for each species. However, attempts to restrict human uses of land can be controversial. Real-estate developers may be prohibited from building on their own land because it contains critical habitat for a species. People may lose income when land uses are restricted and may object when their interests are placed below those of another species.

Although battles between developers and environmentalists are widely publicized, in most cases compromises are eventually worked out. One form of compromise is a **habitat conservation plan**—a plan that attempts to protect one or more species across large areas of land through trade-offs or cooperative agreements. The region of California shown in **Figure 15** is part of a habitat conservation plan.

Table 4 ▼

Major Provisions of the Endangered Species Act
• The U.S. Fish and Wildlife Service (USFWS) must compile a list of all endangered and threatened species.
• Endangered and threatened animal species may not be caught or killed. Endangered and threatened plants on federal land may not be uprooted. No part of an endangered and threatened species may be sold or traded.
• The federal government may not carry out any project that jeopardizes endangered species.
• The U.S. Fish and Wildlife Service must prepare a species recovery plan for each endangered and threatened species.

Figure 15 ▶ This region of San Diego, California, is home to several endangered species. A habitat conservation plan attempts to protect these species by managing a large group of lands in the area.

Figure 16 ▶ Scenes like this one of elephant tusk poaching were common before the worldwide ban on the sale of ivory as part of CITES.

MATHPRACTICE

Measuring Risk There are many ways to categorize a species' degree of risk of extinction. The IUCN and the Nature Conservancy have multiple ranks for species of concern, ranging from "presumed extinct" to "secure." According to one study of 20,500 species in the United States, 1,400 of those species were at some risk. Calculate this number of species at risk as a percentage. Use this percentage to estimate how many species may be at risk around the world.

International Cooperation

At the global level, the International Union for the Conservation of Nature and Natural Resources (IUCN) facilitates efforts to protect species and habitats. This organization is a collaboration of almost 200 government agencies and over 700 private conservation organizations. The IUCN publishes *Red Lists* of species in danger of extinction around the world. The IUCN also advises governments on ways to manage their natural resources, and works with groups like the World Wildlife Fund to sponsor conservation projects.

International Trade and Poaching One product of the IUCN has been an international treaty called *CITES* (the Convention on International Trade in Endangered Species). The CITES treaty was the first effective effort to stop the slaughter of African elephants. Elephants were being killed by poachers who would sell the ivory tusks. Efforts during the 1970s and 1980s to limit the sale of ivory did little to stop the poaching. Then in 1989, the members of CITES proposed a worldwide ban on all trade in ivory, hoping to prevent scenes like those in **Figure 16**.

Some people worried that making ivory illegal might increase the rate of poaching instead of decrease it. They argued that illegal ivory, like illegal drugs, might sell for a higher price. But after the ban was enacted, the price of ivory dropped, and elephant poaching declined dramatically.

The Biodiversity Treaty One of the most ambitious efforts to tackle environmental issues on a worldwide scale was the United Nations Conference on Environment and Development, also known as the first *Earth Summit*. More than 100 world leaders and 30,000 other participants met in 1992 in Rio de Janeiro, Brazil.

✔ **Reading Check** Describe one way in which the IUCN helps to protect species and habitats.

An important result of the Earth Summit was an international agreement called the **Biodiversity Treaty.** The treaty's goal is to preserve biodiversity and ensure the sustainable and fair use of genetic resources in all countries. However, the treaty took many years to be adopted into law by the U.S. government. Some political groups objected to the Treaty, especially to the suggestion that economic and trade agreements should take into account any impacts on biodiversity that might result from the agreements. The international community will thus continue to have debates like those that have surrounded the Endangered Species Act in the United States.

Figure 17 ▶ These Greenpeace activists are blocking the path of a Japanese whaling ship. Do you think this is an effective way to protect species?

Private Conservation Efforts

Many private organizations work to protect species worldwide, often more effectively than government agencies. The World Wildlife Fund encourages the sustainable use of resources and supports wildlife protection. The Nature Conservancy has helped purchase millions of hectares of habitat preserves in 29 countries. Conservation International helps identify biodiversity hotspots and develop ecosystem conservation projects in partnership with other organizations and local people. Greenpeace International organizes direct and sometimes confrontational actions, such as the one shown in **Figure 17,** to counter environmental threats.

Balancing Human Needs

Attempts to protect species often come into conflict with the interests of the world's human inhabitants. Sometimes, an endangered species represents a source of food or income. In other cases, a given species may not seem valuable to those who do not understand the species' role in an ecosystem. Many conservationists feel that an important part of protecting species is making the value of biodiversity understood by more people.

FIELD ACTIVITY

Simple Biodiversity Assessment Discover the diversity of weeds and other plants in a small area. Yards, gardens, and vacant lots are good places to conduct such a study. Mark off a 0.5 m² section. Use a field guide to identify every plant species that you can. At least identify how many different kinds of plants there are. You may want to sketch or photograph some of the plants. Then count the number of each kind of plant you identified. Record your results in your *EcoLog*.

SECTION 3 Review

1. **Describe** four types of efforts to save individual species.

2. **Explain** the advantages of protecting entire ecosystems rather than individual species.

3. **Describe** the main provisions of the Endangered Species Act.

4. **Give** examples of worldwide cooperative efforts to prevent extinctions.

CRITICAL THINKING

5. **Analyzing Methods** Read the headings in this section. Which type of effort to preserve species do you think is most worthwhile? **READING SKILLS**

6. **Comparing Viewpoints** Discuss ways in which efforts to protect species can lead to controversy.

7. **Inferring Relationships** Why was a complete ban of ivory sales more effective than a limited ban?

1 What Is Biodiversity?

Key Terms

biodiversity, 259
gene, 260
keystone species, 260
ecotourism, 262

Main Ideas

▶ Biodiversity usually refers to the number of different species in a given area.

▶ The study of biodiversity starts with the unfinished task of identifying and cataloging all species on Earth. Although scientists disagree about the probable number of species on Earth, they do agree that we need to study biodiversity more thoroughly.

▶ Humanity benefits from biodiversity in several ways and perhaps in some unknown ways.

2 Biodiversity at Risk

endangered species, 263
threatened species, 263
exotic species, 265
poaching, 265
endemic species, 266

▶ Many scientists are now concerned that loss of biodiversity is the most challenging environmental issue we face.

▶ The most common cause of extinction today is the destruction of habitats by humans. Unregulated hunting and the introduction of nonnative species also contribute to extinctions.

▶ Certain areas of the world contain a greater diversity of species than other areas. An important feature of such areas is that they have a large portion of endemic species.

▶ The United States has a very important role in preserving biodiversity.

3 The Future of Biodiversity

germ plasm, 270
Endangered Species Act, 273
habitat conservation plan, 273
Biodiversity Treaty, 275

▶ Most major conservation efforts now concentrate on protecting entire ecosystems rather than individual species.

▶ The Endangered Species Act establishes protections for endangered and threatened species in the United States. The act has generated some controversy and has been amended several times.

▶ International cooperation has led to increased recognition and protection of biodiversity worldwide.

▶ The desire to protect biodiversity often conflicts with other human interests.

Using Key Terms

Use each of the following terms in a separate sentence.

1. *keystone species*
2. *ecotourism*

For each pair of terms, explain how the meanings of the terms differ.

3. *hunting* and *poaching*
4. *endemic species* and *exotic species*
5. *endangered species* and *threatened species*
6. *gene* and *germ plasm*
7. *CITES* and *Biodiversity Treaty*

✔ **STUDY TIP**

Use a Map As you review the chapter, refer to an atlas, to the maps in the Appendix, or to previous chapters about biomes to compare information. Draw your own map or make a list of the locations of some of the interesting species and ecosystems that you learn about.

Understanding Key Ideas

8. The term *biodiversity* refers to
   a. the variety of species on Earth.
   b. the extinction of the dinosaurs.
   c. habitat destruction, invasive exotic species, and poaching.
   d. the fact that 40 percent of prescription drugs come from living things.

9. Most of the living species known to science
   a. are large mammals.
   b. live in deserts.
   c. live in the richer countries of the world.
   d. are insects.

10. Some species are so important to the functioning of an ecosystem that they are called
    a. threatened species.
    b. keystone species.
    c. endangered species.
    d. extinct species.

11. A mass extinction is
    a. a rapid increase in biodiversity.
    b. the introduction of exotic species.
    c. the extinction of many species in a short period of time.
    d. a benefit to the environment.

12. When sea otters disappeared from the Pacific coast of North America,
    a. the area became overrun with kelp.
    b. the number of fish in the kelp beds increased.
    c. the number of sea urchins in the kelp beds increased.
    d. the area became overrun with brown seaweed.

13. Which of the following statements about the Endangered Species Act is *not* true?
    a. Parts of an endangered animal, such as feathers or fur, may be traded or sold but only if the animal is not killed.
    b. A species is considered endangered if it is expected to become extinct in the near future.
    c. The federal government cannot carry out a project that may jeopardize an endangered plant.
    d. A recovery plan is prepared for all animals that are listed as endangered.

14. Because of efforts by the Convention on International Trade in Endangered Species (CITES),
    a. the poaching of elephants increased.
    b. the cost of ivory worldwide increased.
    c. the international trade of ivory was banned worldwide.
    d. a captive-breeding program for elephants was established.

15. Emphasizing the preservation of entire ecosystems will
    a. cause the economic needs of farmers to suffer in order to save a single species.
    b. decrease biodiversity, especially in tropical rain forests, coral reefs, and islands.
    c. throw the food webs of many ecosystems out of balance.
    d. save many unknown species from extinction.

Short Answer

16. When was hunting a major cause of extinctions in the United States?

17. What are exotic species, and how do they endanger other species?

18. Why do biologists favor using an ecosystem approach to preserve biodiversity?

19. Describe three ways that preserving biodiversity can come into conflict with human interests.

Interpreting Graphics

The graph below shows the numbers of various types of species that are officially listed as endangered or threatened in the United States and internationally. Use the graph to answer questions 20–23.

20. Do these numbers necessarily reflect *all* species that may be in danger? Explain your answer.

21. Which types of species might be underrepresented here?

22. Compare the United States and world listings. What trends do you see in the types of species listed?

23. Given this information, which types of species might need further research worldwide?

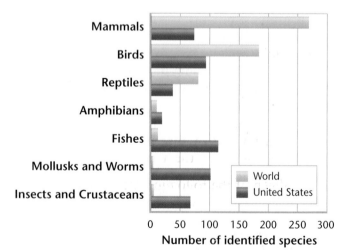

Concept Mapping

24. Use the following terms to create a concept map: *biodiversity, species, gene, ecosystem, habitat loss, poaching, exotic species, germ plasm, captive breeding programs,* and *habitat preservation.*

Critical Thinking

25. **Comparing Processes** Read the passage in this chapter that describes current extinctions. How are the extinctions that are occurring currently different from most extinctions in the past? **READING SKILLS**

26. **Analyzing Methods** With unlimited funding, could zoos and captive-breeding programs restore most endangered animal populations? Explain your answers.

27. **Determining Cause and Effect** How might the loss of huge tracts of tropical rain forests have an effect on other parts of the world?

Cross-Disciplinary Connection

28. **Literature** Try to remember or find some children's stories that include wild animals that are currently endangered, threatened, or extinct. Write a description of how these animals are portrayed in the stories. Also compare the animals in the stories to what you know about the real animals. **WRITING SKILLS**

29. **Geography** Obtain a list of the plants and animals that are endangered in your state. Find out where these species live, and mark the locations on a map of your state. Research the effects of habitat loss on species in your county or in surrounding areas.

Portfolio Project

30. **Endangered Species Outreach** Create a special project about one endangered species of your choice. Consider using a poster, an oral presentation, or a video to inform your classmates about your chosen species or to persuade them of the importance of saving the species.

MATH SKILLS

Use the table below to answer questions 31–32.

31. **Analyzing Data** Which of the types of species in the table below are most accurately described? What do the numbers indicate about how well various species are studied?

32. **Applying Quantities** Which of the types of species may represent the greatest unknown loss of biodiversity? Which type of species is probably least important for further research into biodiversity?

Estimates of Knowledge of Earth's Species

Type of species	Number of species described	Described species as % of total	Number threatened or extinct	Accuracy of estimates
Bacteria	4,000	0.40	(unknown)	very poor
Vertebrates	52,000	94.55	3,843	good
Crustaceans	40,000	26.67	628	moderate
Plants	270,000	84.38	31,277	good

WRITING SKILLS

33. **Writing Persuasively** Write a letter to the editor of a publication or to an elected representative in which you express your opinion regarding protections of endangered species that might affect your local area.

34. **Outlining Topics** Outline the major strategies for protecting biodiversity that have been described in this chapter. List pros and cons of each strategy.

READING SKILLS

Read the passage below, and then answer the questions that follow.

Excerpt from M. Reaka-Kudla, D. Wilson, and E. Wilson, eds., Biodiversity II, *1996.*

Aside from the academic tradition of biodiversity, another powerful influence, related to biodiversity, brought our culture to its current level of technological development: the exploration of the New World. From the thirteenth to the nineteenth centuries, technological developments in navigation allowed European voyagers to embark on an unprecedented exploration of the globe. These expeditions revolutionized knowledge of the geography, human culture, and biology of the world at the time. This ultimately led to a reevaluation of human society's place in the world and an understanding of the evolution of all living things. But the exploration also allowed the acquisition of untold wealth in living and non-living natural resources, which was brought back from the New World and invested in the culture of western Europe.

1. What do the authors probably mean by the term *influence?*
   a. a force of cultural change
   b. a new type of scientific discovery
   c. a source of geographic information
   d. a form of navigation

2. Which of the following are not mentioned by the authors as factors in our current level of technological development?
   a. geographical information
   b. knowledge of a variety of species
   c. new forms of government
   d. evolutionary theory

3. Which of the following did the authors most likely discuss in the paragraph just *before* this passage?
   a. natural resources of the New World
   b. religious beliefs of native peoples
   c. academic tradition of European biology
   d. history of European expeditions

Understanding Concepts

Directions (1–4): For *each* question, write on a separate sheet of paper the letter of the correct answer.

1 Which of the following phrases describes the term genetic biodiversity?
A. the variety of habitats found in an ecosystem
B. the variety of species present in an ecosystem
C. the differences between populations of species
D. the different genes contained within members of a population

2 What species are critical to the survival of an ecosystem?
F. bottleneck species   H. exotic species
G. endemic species   I. keystone species

3 Which of the following describes a species that is likely to become endangered?
A. insects that have to adapt to an urban environment
B. small mammals that live in urban ecosystems
C. birds that can only survive in rural ecosystems
D. mammals that need an undeveloped habitat to breed successfully

4 Why is international cooperation crucial to securing future biodiversity?
F. Wildlife protection laws vary from country to country.
G. Poaching is the most important reason for a species population decline.
H. Habitat destruction and other causes of extinction cross international borders.
I. Protecting species sometimes conflicts with the interests of human populations.

Directions (5–6): For *each* question, write a short response.

5 Why could private or non-governmental agencies be more effective in protecting species than government agencies?

6 Compare endangered species with threatened species.

Reading Skills

Directions (7–10): Read the passage below. Then answer the questions.

Scientists are developing new methods of conservation in an attempt to preserve species on the verge of extinction. Captive-breeding programs try to restore the population of a species. Another approach is to preserve germ plasm. Germ plasm is any form of genetic material, such as that contained within the reproductive, or germ, cells of plants or animals. Germ-plasm banks store seeds, sperm, eggs, or pure DNA in special controlled environments. Farmers and gardeners also preserve germ plasm when they save and share seeds.

7 One way that scientists are trying to preserve species on the verge of extinction is by
A. logging tropical rain forests
B. developing new methods of conservation
C. removing species from the endangered list
D. abandoning new methods of conservation

8 What is the aim of captive-breeding programs?
F. to increase the population size of a species to double its former size
G. to restore the animal kingdom
H. to restore germ plasm
I. to restore the population of a species

9 What is stored at germ-plasm banks?
A. seeds, sperm, eggs, or pure DNA
B. seeds that are not used by farmers and gardeners
C. animals from captive-breeding programs that were not able to survive in the wild
D. instructions about how to restore a species when it becomes extinct

10 Compare the genetic material in germ-plasm banks wih the seeds saved and shared by farmers and gardeners.

Interpreting Graphics

Directions (11–14): For *each* question below, record the correct answer on a separate sheet of paper.

The graph below shows the number of families of marine organisms that existed millions of years ago. Use this graph to answer questions 11 and 12.

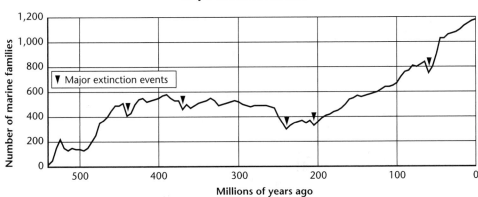

Major Extinction Events

11 How has the biodiversity of marine families changed over the last 500 million years?
F. It has increased.
G. It has decreased slightly.
H. It has remained the same.
I. It has decreased significantly.

12 What is the average number of families of marine organisms lost in a major extinction event?
A. 25   **C.** 100
B. 75   **D.** 150

13 If 90 families were lost in an extinction event that lasted 10 million years, and each family contained 200 species, how many species were lost every 100,000 years during that period?
F. 90   **H.** 200
G. 180   **I.** 360

14 What do we know about the number of individual species currently living on Earth?
A. There are no new species being found.
B. All the species that exist on Earth have been cataloged.
C. About 1.7 million species are known to exist.
D. There are more trees and mammals than there are insects.

Test TIP

Converting the largest numbers to scientific notation may help you simplify your calculations.

CHAPTER 10

Exploration Lab: FIELD ACTIVITY

Objectives

▶ **USING SCIENTIFIC METHODS** **Observe and measure** differences in species diversity between two locations.

▶ **USING SCIENTIFIC METHODS** **Graph and analyze** data collected to reflect differences in species diversity.

▶ **Evaluate** the possible reasons for observed differences in biodiversity.

▶ **USING SCIENTIFIC METHODS** **Infer** other human activities that may influence local biodiversity.

Materials

graph paper
hand lens
meterstick or tape measure
pen or pencil
string or chalk line

optional materials: local-area field guides for plants, animals, and soil organisms; shovel or trowel

▶ **Step 2** Measure and mark off sample areas for your observation and counts of species diversity.

Differences In Diversity

Biodiversity is most obvious and dramatic in tropical rain forests and coral reefs, but you do not have to travel that far to observe differences in species diversity or to see the effects that humans can have on biodiversity.

Recall that biodiversity is most often defined as the number of different species that are present in a given area. This measure can be estimated by making a sample count of species within a representative area. It is often easiest and most effective to collect or observe small organisms, such as insects and soil dwellers, or stationary organisms, such as plants and trees. In this activity, you will investigate the differences in species diversity in two areas that are close to each other, but that are affected differently by humans. You may work in teams or groups.

Procedure

1. Choose two sites for your analysis. Site 1 should be an area that has been greatly affected by humans, such as your school building and the surrounding sidewalks, parking area, or groomed lawns. Site 2 should be an area within view of site 1 but that is less affected by humans, such as a wooded area or a vacant lot overgrown with weeds. If directed by your teacher, you may choose more than two sites. Also ask your teacher about your sample square size.

2. At each site, measure a 5 m × 5 m square area using the meterstick or tape measure. You might use the edge of a building as a side of your square, or you might use trees as the corners. Mark the measurement of the area with string or a chalk line, as shown in the photograph.

3. Observe each site carefully, and record a detailed description of each site. Include as many features as possible, such as location, soil condition, ways the area is used, amount of sun or rain exposure, and other factors that might affect the organisms that exist there.

4. For each site, create a table like the table below.

Species Counts Per Site		
Species type	**Site number ___**	**Site number ___**
Animals		
Plants		
Fungi and other soil organisms		

5. Using your hand lens, find as many different species as possible within the site. Record each new species by placing a slash or tick mark in the column for each different species identified in each general category. You do not need to identify every organism by scientific name, but using field guides may help you have an idea of what you are finding. You may also make more specific categories (such as birds, insects, grasses, and trees) if you are able. Be careful not to disturb the area unnecessarily.

6. Repeat steps 2–5 for each site. If directed by your teacher, compare your data with those of other groups.

7. After you have made and recorded all of your observations, put away your materials and restore anything you disturbed at the sites.

Analysis

1. **Constructing Graphs** Create a bar graph of the number of species counted at each site. As directed by your teacher, you may combine all species counts into one total per site or graph each category of organisms separately.

2. **Analyzing Results** Based on your observations of the organisms found at the sites, which area reflected a higher level of biodiversity?

3. **Interpreting Results** What factors may have contributed to the differences in biodiversity at the sites?

Conclusions

4. **Drawing Conclusions** What can you conclude about the effect of human activities on biodiversity?

5. **Applying Conclusions** What other human activities, besides those you observed directly, could have affected the biodiversity present at your sites?

6. **Evaluating Methods** Do you feel that the method used in this lab was an effective way to identify biodiversity in an area? Why or why not? How could it have been improved?

Extension

1. **Research and Communications** If you were able to use local field guides, what can you generalize about the organisms that you were able to identify? Pay attention to aspects such as how easily recognized each organism is, how common it is in your local area, where it is found outside of your area, or what other unique facts are known about the biology or habitat needs of the organism.

▶ **Step 5** Observe and record how many different types of organisms you find within each sample area.

DR. E. O. WILSON: CHAMPION OF BIODIVERSITY

Dr. Edward Osborne Wilson deserves some of the credit for the fact that this book includes a chapter called "Biodiversity." A few decades ago, the word *biodiversity* was used by few scientists and was found in few dictionaries. Dr. Wilson has helped make the concept and value of biodiversity widely recognized, through his extensive research, publishing, organizing, and social advocacy.

Since his early career as a pioneer in the fields of entomology and sociobiology, Dr. Wilson has gained recognition for many additional accomplishments. He has written two Pulitzer Prize-winning nonfiction books, and has received the National Medal of Science and dozens of other scientific awards and honors. Wilson is widely recognized as one of the most influential scientists and citizens of our time.

It All Started with Bugs

Even before his scientific career, Wilson developed a fascination with insects and the natural world. He always had high expectations of himself but made the best of circumstances. Although his parents were divorced and his father's government career required frequent moves, Wilson found companionship in the woods of the southern United States or the museums of Washington, D.C. After injuries damaged his vision and hearing, Wilson focused his scientific skills on the smaller forms of life.

By the time he earned his master's degree at the University of Alabama at the age of 20, Wilson was well known as a promising *entomologist*—an expert on the insect world. His specialty is the study of ants and their complex social behaviors. So it makes sense that Wilson next went to study at Harvard University, home to the world's largest ant collection. While at Harvard, he earned his Ph.D., conducted field research around the world, collected more than 100 previously undescribed species, and wrote several books on insect physiology and social organization. He eventually became curator of the Museum of Entomology at Harvard.

Clearly, Wilson has a passion for insects. "There is a very special pleasure in looking in a microscope and saying I am the first person to see a species that may be millions of years old," he says. Some of Wilson's research has focused on the social behavior of ants. Among other important scientific findings, Wilson was the first to demonstrate that ant behavior and communication is based mostly on chemical signals.

From Insects to Humans

In 1971, Wilson published *The Insect Societies,* which surveyed the evolution of social organization among wasps, ants, bees, and termites. Wilson began to extend his attempts to understand the relationship of biology and social behavior to other animals, including humans. In 1975, Wilson published a controversial book exploring these new ideas, called *Sociobiology.* Now an accepted branch of science, sociobiology is the study of the biological basis of social behavior in animals, including humans.

During Wilson's studies of the behavior of ants and other social insects, he became interested in the

▶ Dr. Wilson with one of his favorite subjects—ants.

insects' role in the ecosystems where he studied them. Some of his research involved camping for months at a time in a remote wilderness such as the Amazon basin, carefully studying the activities of certain species. His writings include amazing tales of watching huge colonies of "driver" ants swarm out over an area, capturing and killing a great many other species in their path.

If you have ever played the popular computer game *SimAnt*™, Dr. Wilson again deserves credit for providing the inspiration. In 1990, Wilson received his second Pulitzer Prize for co-authoring *The Ants,* an enormous encyclopedia of the ant world. In addition to describing 8,800 known species of ants, the book details the great variations among ant species in terms of anatomy, biochemistry, complex social behaviors, and especially their critical role in many ecosystems. Wilson reminds us that ants "are some of the most abundant and diverse of the Earth's 1.4 million species. They're among the little creatures that run the earth. If ants and other small animals were to disappear, the Earth would rot. Fish, reptiles, birds—and humans—would crash to extinction."

Onward to Biodiversity

As with many great scientists, each thing Dr. Wilson studies leads him to new questions and new ideas. During his research in remote lands, Wilson spent time reflecting and writing on the nature of ecosystems, the importance of biodiversity, and the role of humans in relation to these. In 1992, he put many of these ideas into another popular book called *The Diversity of Life*. This book combined Wilson's engaging writing style and personal expertise with the latest ecological research.

▶ Dr. Wilson (center) speaks to politicians and the public about the need to conserve our planet's biodiversity.

The book showed both how such incredible biodiversity has evolved on the Earth and how this asset is being lost because of current human activities. The book clearly explained for the general public many of the problems and potential solutions regarding biodiversity that we have studied in this chapter.

Urgent Work

Despite his fame, Wilson is a soft-spoken fellow who would prefer to live a quiet life with his research and with his family in their home in the woods of Massachusetts. But the urgent problem of species loss makes Wilson willing to face the public. "Humanity is entering a bottleneck of overpopulation and environmental degradation unique in history. We need to carry every species through the bottleneck . . . Along with culture itself, they will be the most precious gift we can give future generations."

In 1986, Wilson served as one of the leaders of the first National Forum on Biodiversity, and then as editor of *Biodiversity,* the resulting collection of reports. Wilson continues to engage in public and private meetings with scientists and policy makers around the globe, urging them to support conservation efforts based on sound science.

Dr. Wilson recently began promoting the need for a global biodiversity survey. This project would involve an international scientific effort on par with the Human Genome Project. Wilson states that "to describe and classify all of the species of the world deserves to be one of the great scientific goals of the new century."

What Do You Think?

Do you find insects interesting? Could you imagine yourself as an entomologist? Do you think that Dr. Wilson made a goal early in his life to be an internationally famous conservationist? What has led him to take on this role?

4

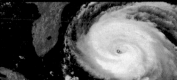

For thousands of years, humans
have altered the environment to
grow food. These rice paddies in
China are built to trap water from
the monsoon rains.

Water

CHAPTER 11

1 Water Resources
2 Water Use and Management
3 Water Pollution

PRE-READING ACTIVITY

Layered Book

Before you read this chapter, create the **FoldNote** entitled "Layered Book" described in the Reading and Study Skills section of the Appendix. Label the tabs of the layered book with "Water Resources," "Water Use," "Water Management," and "Water Pollution." As you read the chapter, write information you learn about each category under the appropriate flap.

This composite photograph shows what an iceberg might look like if you could see the entire iceberg.

SECTION 1
Water Resources

SCSh.9.d; SEV.5.e

EARTH SCIENCE CONNECTION

The next time you drink a glass of water, think about where the water came from. Did you know that some of the water in your glass may have been part of a rainstorm that pounded the Earth long before life existed? Or that water may have been part of a dinosaur that lived millions of years ago. Some of the water we drink today has been around since water formed on Earth billions of years ago. Water is essential to life on Earth. Humans can survive for more than a month without food, but we can live for only a few days without water.

Two kinds of water are found on Earth. Fresh water—the water that people can drink—contains little salt. Salt water—the water in oceans—contains a higher concentration of dissolved salts. Most human uses for water, such as drinking and agriculture, require fresh water.

The Water Cycle

The Earth is often called "the Water Planet" because it has an abundance of water in all forms: solid, liquid, and gas. Water is a renewable resource because it is circulated in the water cycle, as shown in **Figure 1.** In the water cycle, water molecules travel between the Earth's surface and the atmosphere. Water evaporates at the Earth's surface and leaves behind salts and other impurities. Water vapor, which is a gas, rises into the air. As water vapor rises through the atmosphere, the gas cools and condenses into drops of liquid water that form clouds. Eventually the water in clouds falls back to Earth and replenishes the Earth's fresh water. The oceans are an important part of the water cycle because almost all of Earth's water is in the oceans.

Objectives

▶ Describe the distribution of Earth's water resources.

▶ Explain why fresh water is one of Earth's limited resources.

▶ Describe the distribution of Earth's surface water.

▶ Describe the relationship between groundwater and surface water in a watershed.

Key Terms

surface water
river system
watershed
groundwater
aquifer
porosity
permeability
recharge zone

Figure 1 ▶ The water cycle is the continuous movement of water between Earth and its atmosphere.

CONDENSATION

PRECIPITATION

EVAPORATION

Global Water Distribution

To understand why fresh water is such a limited resource, you have to understand how little fresh water is found on Earth. Although 71 percent of the Earth's surface is covered with water, nearly 97 percent of Earth's water is salt water in oceans and seas. **Figure 2** illustrates this relationship. Of the fresh water on Earth, about 77 percent is frozen in glaciers and polar icecaps. Only a small percentage of the water on Earth is liquid fresh water that humans can use. The fresh water we use comes mainly from lakes and rivers and from a relatively narrow zone beneath the Earth's surface.

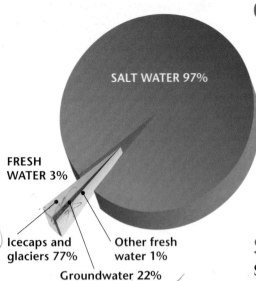

SALT WATER 97%

FRESH WATER 3%

Icecaps and glaciers 77%

Other fresh water 1%

Groundwater 22%

Figure 2 ▶ This pie graph shows the distribution of water on Earth. What percentage of the Earth's fresh water is in a form that humans can use?

Surface Water

Surface water is fresh water on Earth's land surface. Surface water is found in lakes, rivers, streams, and wetlands. Throughout history, people have built cities, towns, and farms near reliable sources of surface water. Some of the oldest cities in the world were built near rivers. Today, most large cities depend on surface water for their water supplies. Rivers, lakes, and streams provide drinking water, water to grow crops, food such as fish and shellfish, power for industry, and a means of transportation by boat.

✔ **Reading Check** Why do most large cities depend on surface water? (See the Appendix for answers to Reading Checks.)

Figure 3 ▶ **Watersheds of the World** This map shows the Earth's major watersheds. The highlighted area of the satellite image below shows that the Mississippi River watershed covers almost half of the United States.

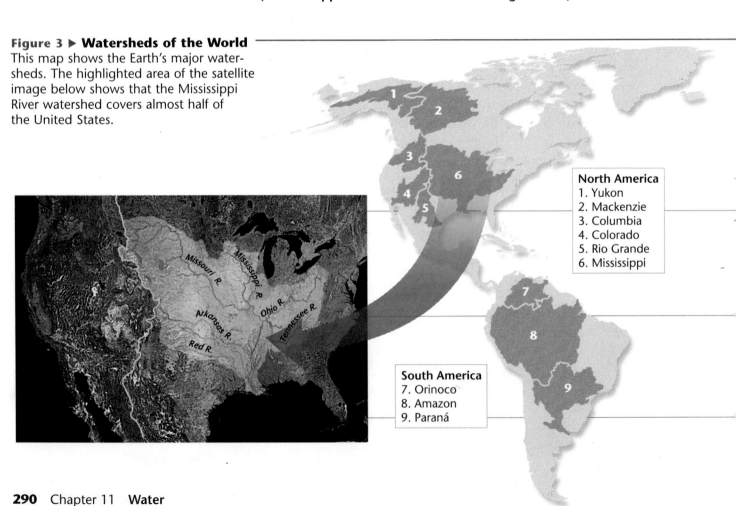

Missouri R.

Mississippi R.

Ohio R.

Arkansas R.

Tennessee R.

Red R.

North America
1. Yukon
2. Mackenzie
3. Columbia
4. Colorado
5. Rio Grande
6. Mississippi

South America
7. Orinoco
8. Amazon
9. Paraná

River Systems Have you ever wondered where all the water in a river comes from? Streams form as water from falling rain and melting snow drains from mountains, hills, plateaus, and plains. As streams flow downhill, they combine with other streams and form rivers. The more streams that run into a river, the larger the river becomes. As streams and rivers move across the land, they form a flowing network of water called a **river system.** If a river system is viewed from above, it can look like the roots of a tree that are feeding into a trunk. The Mississippi, the Amazon, and the Nile are enormous river systems because they collect the water that flows from vast areas of land. The Amazon River system is the largest river system in the world—it drains an area of land that is nearly the size of Europe.

Watersheds The area of land that is drained by a river is known as a **watershed.** The watershed of the Mississippi River is shown in the satellite image in **Figure 3.** Pollution anywhere in a watershed may end up polluting a river. The amount of water that enters a watershed varies throughout the year. Rapidly melting snow as well as spring and summer rains can dramatically increase the amount of water in a watershed. Other times of the year, the river system that drains a watershed may be reduced to a trickle. Communities that depend on rivers for water can be severely affected by these changes to the river system.

Connection to Biology

Ganges River Dolphins The Ganges River dolphin is one of the world's few freshwater dolphin species. This dolphin is almost completely blind, but it can easily navigate through silty river water by using sonar.

SCI**LINKS**
www.scilinks.org
Topic: Watersheds
Code: HE81636

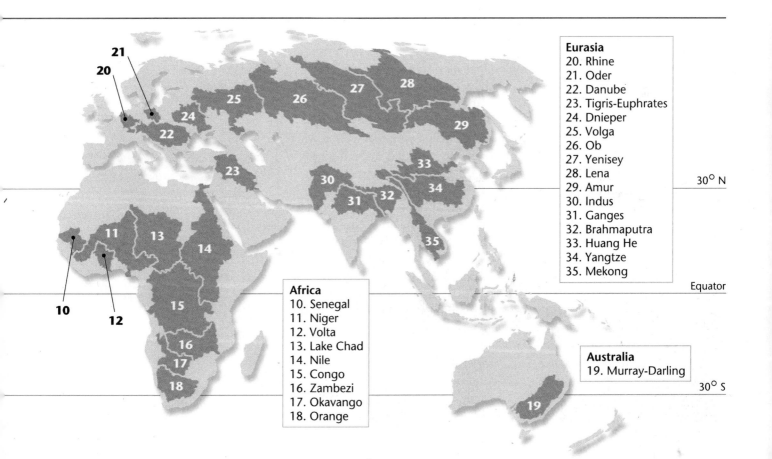

Eurasia
20. Rhine
21. Oder
22. Danube
23. Tigris-Euphrates
24. Dnieper
25. Volga
26. Ob
27. Yenisey
28. Lena
29. Amur
30. Indus
31. Ganges
32. Brahmaputra
33. Huang He
34. Yangtze
35. Mekong

30° N

Equator

Africa
10. Senegal
11. Niger
12. Volta
13. Lake Chad
14. Nile
15. Congo
16. Zambezi
17. Okavango
18. Orange

Australia
19. Murray-Darling

30° S

Groundwater

Most of the fresh water that is available for human use cannot be seen—it exists underground. When it rains, some of the water that falls onto the land flows into lakes and streams. But much of the water percolates through the soil and down into the rocks beneath. Water beneath the Earth's surface in sediment and rock formations is called **groundwater.**

As water travels beneath the Earth's surface, it eventually reaches a level where the rocks and soil are saturated with water. This level is known as the *water table*. In wet regions, the water table may be at the Earth's surface and a spring of fresh water may flow out onto the ground. But in deserts, the water table may be hundreds of meters beneath the Earth's surface. The water table is actually not as level as its name implies. The water table has peaks and valleys that match the shape of the land above it. Just as surface water flows downhill, groundwater tends to flow slowly from the peaks of the water table to the valleys.

Reading Check How can the location of the water table in wet regions be different from its location in deserts?

The Ogallala Aquifer: An Underground Treasure

Anyone who has eaten food produced in the United States has probably enjoyed the benefits of the Ogallala Aquifer, one of the largest known aquifers in the world. This enormous underground water system formed from glaciers that melted at the end of the last Ice Age, 12,000 years ago. Today, the Ogallala Aquifer supplies about one-third of all the groundwater used in the United States.

People began to use the Ogallala Aquifer extensively for irrigation in the 1940s. With help from this ancient water source, farmers turned the Great Plains into one of the most productive farming regions in the world. For many years, farmers seemed to enjoy a limitless supply of fresh water. But in recent years, the Ogallala Aquifer has started to show its limits. Water is being withdrawn from the aquifer 10 to 40 times faster than it is being replaced. In some places, the water table has dropped more than 30 m (100 ft) since pumping began.

Humans are not the only living things that depend on the Ogallala Aquifer. In some areas, the aquifer flows onto the surface and creates wetlands, which are a vital habitat for many organisms, especially birds. These wetlands are often the first habitats to disappear when the water table falls.

Many people are working together to try to conserve the Ogallala Aquifer. For example, some farmers have begun to limit irrigation during bird migrations in order to allow surface-water levels

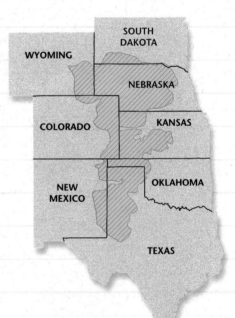

► **The Ogallala Aquifer** holds about 4 quadrillion liters of water—enough to cover the United States to a depth of 0.5 m (1.5 ft).

Aquifers An underground formation that contains groundwater is called an **aquifer.** The water table forms the upper boundary of an aquifer. Most aquifers consist of materials such as rock, sand, and gravel that have a lot of spaces where water can accumulate. As well, groundwater can dissolve rock formations, such as those made of limestone, and fill vast caves with water, which creates underground lakes. Aquifers are an important water source for many cities and for agriculture.

Porosity and Permeability Although most rocks appear solid, many kinds of rocks contain small holes, or pore spaces. **Porosity** is the percentage of the total volume of a rock that has spaces (pores). Water in an aquifer is stored in the pore spaces and flows from one pore space to another. The more porous a rock is, the more water it can hold. The ability of rock or soil to allow water to flow through it is called **permeability.** Materials such as gravel that allow the flow of water are *permeable*. Materials such as clay or granite that do not allow the flow of water are *impermeable*. The most productive aquifers usually form in permeable materials, such as sandstone, limestone, or layers of sand and gravel.

SCi
LINKS.
www.scilinks.org
Topic: Groundwater
Code: HE80699
Topic: Aquifers
Code: HE80089

EARTH SCIENCE  **CONNECTION**

▶ **Sandhill cranes** are among the many kinds of birds that rely on water from the Ogallala Aquifer.

CRITICAL THINKING

1. Applying Ideas Most of the water in the Ogallala Aquifer came from glaciers that melted thousands of years ago. What is the aquifer's primary water source today?

2. Expressing Viewpoints Do you think residents of the Great Plains are the only people who have an interest in conserving the Ogallala Aquifer? Write an editorial that expresses your viewpoint.
WRITING SKILLS

to rise. Other farmers have adopted water-saving irrigation systems and are planting crops such as wheat or grain sorghum, which require less water than corn or cotton.

Many farmers and other residents of the Great Plains recognize the value of the Ogallala Aquifer and are fighting to preserve it. They are pressuring politicians to replace policies that encourage wasting water with policies that promote water conservation. These efforts may help save this underground treasure.

Figure 4 ▶ Groundwater and the Water Table
Aquifers are underground formations that hold water. Impermeable rock can be porous or nonporous, but only permeable rock allows water to pass through it.

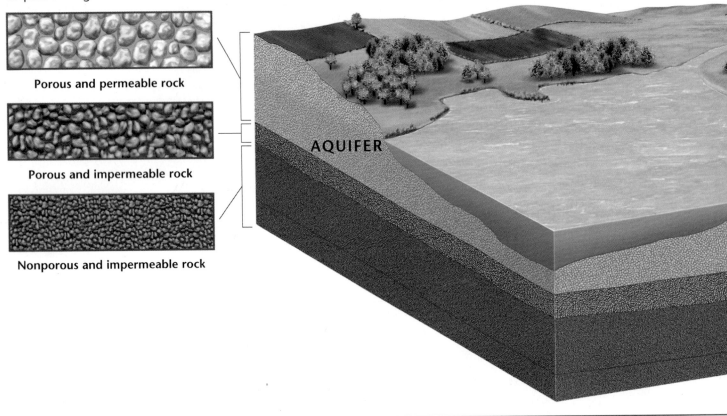

Porous and permeable rock

Porous and impermeable rock

Nonporous and impermeable rock

AQUIFER

The Recharge Zone To reach an aquifer, surface water must travel down through permeable layers of soil and rock. Notice the permeable layers above the aquifer in **Figure 4.** An area of the Earth's surface from which water percolates down into an aquifer is called a **recharge zone.** Recharge zones are environmentally sensitive areas because any pollution in a recharge zone can also enter the aquifer.

The size of an aquifer's recharge zone is affected by the permeability of the surface above the aquifer. Structures such as buildings and parking lots can act as impermeable layers to reduce the amount of water entering an aquifer. Communities should carefully manage recharge zones, because surface water can take a very long time to refill an aquifer. In fact, aquifers can take tens of thousands of years to recharge.

Wells If you go nearly anywhere on Earth and dig a hole deep enough, you will eventually find water. A hole that is dug or drilled to reach groundwater is called a well. For thousands of years, humans have dug wells to reach groundwater. We dig wells because groundwater may be a more reliable source of water than surface water in some areas and because water is filtered

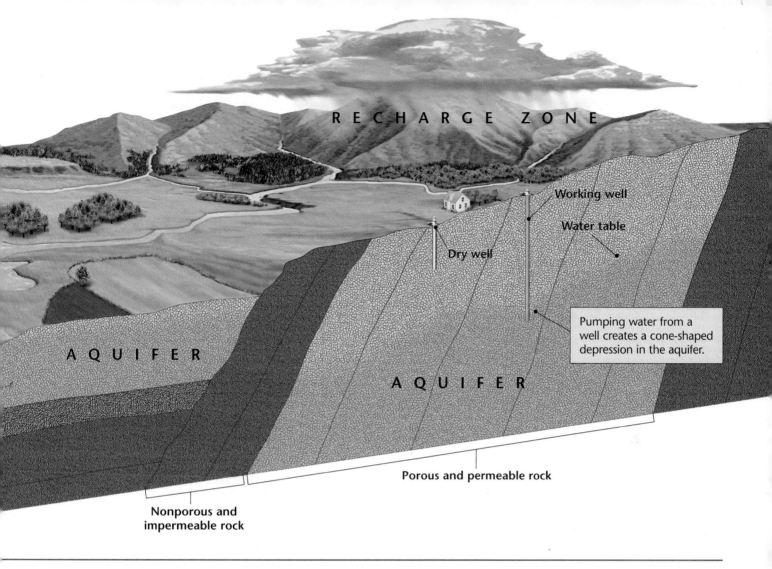

RECHARGE ZONE

Working well

Dry well

Water table

Pumping water from a well creates a cone-shaped depression in the aquifer.

AQUIFER

AQUIFER

Porous and permeable rock

Nonporous and impermeable rock

and purified as it travels underground. The height of the water table changes seasonally, so wells are drilled to extend below the water table. However, if the water table falls below the bottom of the well during a drought, the well will dry up. In addition, if groundwater is removed faster than it is recharged, the water table may fall below the bottom of a well. To continue supplying water, the well must be drilled deeper.

SECTION 1 **Review**

1. **Describe** the distribution of water on Earth. Where is most of the fresh water located?

2. **Explain** why fresh water is considered a limited resource.

3. **Explain** why pollution in a watershed poses a potential threat to the river system that flows through it.

4. **Describe** how water travels through rock.

CRITICAL THINKING

5. **Making Comparisons** Read the description of aquifers. Why is an underground lake an aquifer?
   READING SKILLS

6. **Analyzing Relationships** Describe the relationship between groundwater and surface water in a watershed. What human activities in a recharge zone can affect the groundwater?

SECTION 2
Water Use and Management

EARTH SCIENCE · CONNECTION

Objectives

▶ Identify patterns of global water use.

▶ Explain how water is treated so that it can be used for drinking.

▶ Identify how water is used in homes, in industry, and in agriculture.

▶ Describe how dams and water diversion projects are used to manage freshwater resources.

▶ Identify five ways that water can be conserved.

Key Terms

potable
pathogen
dam
reservoir
desalination

You may have heard the expression "We all live downstream." When a water supply is polluted or overused, everyone living downstream can be affected. The number of people who rely on the Earth's limited freshwater reserves is increasing every day. In fact, a shortage of clean, fresh water is one of the world's most pressing environmental problems. According to the World Health Organization, more than 1 billion people lack access to a clean, reliable source of fresh water.

Global Water Use

To understand the factors that affect the world's supply of fresh water, we must first explore how people use water. **Figure 5** shows the three major uses for water—residential use, agricultural use, and industrial use.

Most of the fresh water used worldwide is used to irrigate crops. Patterns of water use are not the same everywhere, however. The availability of fresh water, population sizes, and economic conditions affect how people use water. In Asia, agriculture accounts for more than 80 percent of water use, whereas it accounts for only 38 percent of water use in Europe. Industry accounts for about 19 percent of the water used in the world. The highest percentage of industrial water use occurs in Europe and North America. Globally, about 8 percent of water is used by households for activities such as drinking and washing.

Residential Water Use

There are striking differences in residential water use throughout the world. For example, the average person in the United States uses about 300 L (80 gal) of water every day. But in India, the

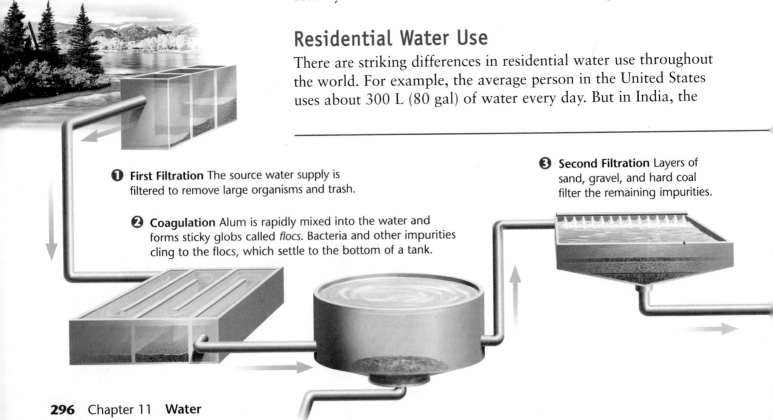

❶ **First Filtration** The source water supply is filtered to remove large organisms and trash.

❷ **Coagulation** Alum is rapidly mixed into the water and forms sticky globs called *flocs*. Bacteria and other impurities cling to the flocs, which settle to the bottom of a tank.

❸ **Second Filtration** Layers of sand, gravel, and hard coal filter the remaining impurities.

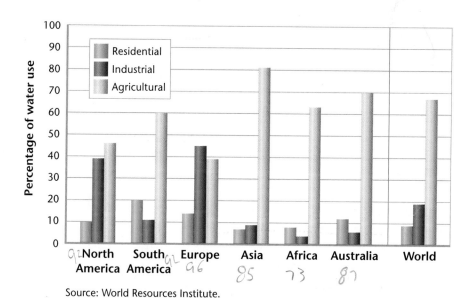

Source: World Resources Institute.

Figure 5 ▶ Europe is the only continent that uses more water for industry than for agriculture.

average person uses only 41 L of water every day. In the United States, only about half of residential water use is for activities inside the home, such as drinking, cooking, washing, and toilet flushing. The remainder of the water used residentially is used outside the home for activities such as watering lawns and washing cars. **Table 1** shows how the average person in the United States uses water.

Water Treatment Most water must be treated to make it **potable,** or safe to drink. Water treatment removes elements such as mercury, arsenic, and lead, which are poisonous to humans even in low concentrations. These elements are found in polluted water, but they can also occur naturally in groundwater. Water treatment also removes **pathogens,** which are organisms that cause illness or disease. Bacteria, viruses, protozoa, and parasitic worms are common pathogens. Pathogens are found in water contaminated by sewage or animal feces. There are several methods of treating water to make it potable. **Figure 6** shows a common drinking water treatment method that includes both physical and chemical treatment.

Table 1 ▼

Daily Water Use in the United States (per Person)	
Use	Water (L)
Lawn watering and pools	95
Toilet flushing	90
Bathing	70
Brushing teeth*	10
Cleaning (inside and outside)	20
Cooking and drinking	10
Other	5

*with water running
Source: U.S. Environmental Protection Agency.

Figure 6 ▶ **Drinking-Water Treatment**

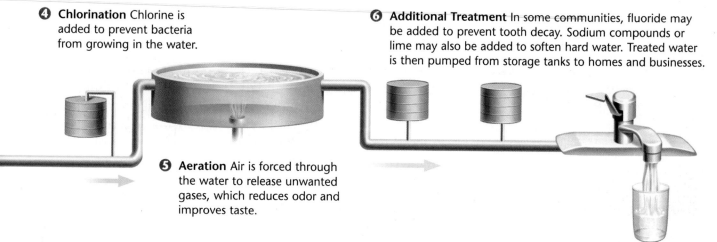

❹ **Chlorination** Chlorine is added to prevent bacteria from growing in the water.

❻ **Additional Treatment** In some communities, fluoride may be added to prevent tooth decay. Sodium compounds or lime may also be added to soften hard water. Treated water is then pumped from storage tanks to homes and businesses.

❺ **Aeration** Air is forced through the water to release unwanted gases, which reduces odor and improves taste.

Industrial water use (world) 19%

Other water use (world) 81%

Figure 7 ▶ Water is a very important industrial resource. These nuclear power plant cooling towers release the steam produced from water used to cool a nuclear reactor.

Industrial Water Use

Industry accounts for 19 percent of water used in the world. Water is used to manufacture goods, to dispose of waste, and to generate power. The amount of water needed to manufacture everyday items can be astounding. For instance, nearly 1,000 L of water are needed to produce 1 kg of aluminum, and almost 500,000 L of water are needed to manufacture a car.

Most of the water that is used in industry is used to cool power plants, as shown in **Figure 7**. Power-plant cooling systems usually pump water from a surface water source such as a river or lake, carry the water through pipes in a cooling tower, and then pump the water back into the source. The returned water is usually warmer than the source, but it is generally clean and can be reused.

Agricultural Water Use

Did you know that it can take nearly 300 L (80 gal) of water to produce one ear of corn? That's as much water as an average person in the United States uses in a day! Agriculture accounts for 67 percent of the water used in the world. Plants require a lot of water to grow, and as much as 80 percent of the water used in agriculture evaporates and never reaches plant roots.

Irrigation Fertile soil is sometimes found in areas of the world that do not have abundant rainfall. In regions where rainfall is inadequate, extra water can be supplied by irrigation. *Irrigation* is a method of providing plants with water from sources other than direct precipitation. The earliest form of irrigation probably involved flooding fields with water from a nearby river.

✓ **Reading Check** How does the amount of water used for industry compare with the amount of water used for agriculture?

Many different irrigation techniques are used today. For example, some crops, such as cotton, are irrigated by shallow, water-filled ditches, as shown in **Figure 8.** In the United States, high-pressure overhead sprinklers are the most common form of irrigation. This method of irrigation is inefficient because nearly half the water evaporates and never reaches the plant roots. Irrigation systems that use water more efficiently are becoming more common.

Figure 8 ▶ High-pressure overhead sprinklers (left) are inefficient because a lot of water is lost to evaporation. Water-filled ditches (above) irrigate cotton seedlings.

Water Management Projects

For thousands of years, humans have altered streams and rivers to make them more useful. Nearly two thousand years ago, the Romans built aqueducts, huge canals that brought water from the mountains to the dry areas of France and Spain. One such aqueduct is shown in **Figure 9.** Some of these aqueducts are still used today. Engineering skills have improved since the time of the Romans, and water projects have become more complex.

People often live in areas where the natural distribution of surface water is inadequate. Water management projects, such as dams and water diversion canals, are designed to meet their needs. Water management projects can have various goals, such as bringing in water to make a dry area habitable, creating a reservoir for recreation or drinking water, or generating electric power. Water management projects have changed the American Southwest and have proved that if water can be piped in, people can live and grow crops in desert areas.

Figure 9 ▶ This aqueduct in Spain was built almost two thousand years ago by the Romans.

Water Diversion Projects To supply dry regions with water, all or part of a river can be diverted into canals that carry water across great distances. **Figure 10** shows a canal that diverts the Owens River in California to provide drinking water for Los Angeles. Another river, the Colorado River, is diverted to provide water for several states. The Colorado River begins as a glacial stream in the Rocky Mountains and quickly grows larger as other streams feed into it. As the river flows south, however, it is divided to meet the needs of seven western states. So much of the Colorado River's water is diverted for irrigation and drinking water in states such as Arizona, Utah, and California that the river often runs dry before it reaches Mexico and flows into the Gulf of California. In fact, the Colorado River reaches the Gulf only in the wettest years.

Dams and Reservoirs A **dam** is a structure built across a river to control the river's flow. When a river is dammed, an artificial lake, or **reservoir,** is formed behind the dam. Water from a reservoir can be used for flood control, drinking water, irrigation, recreation, and industry. Dams are also built to generate electrical energy. Hydroelectric dams use the power of flowing water to turn a turbine that generates electrical energy. About 20 percent of the world's electrical energy is generated by hydroelectric dams, such as the one shown in **Figure 11.**

Although dams provide many benefits, interrupting a river's flow can also have far-reaching consequences. When the land behind a dam is flooded, people are often displaced and entire ecosystems can be destroyed. It is estimated that 50 million people around the world have been displaced by dam projects. Dams also affect

Figure 10 ▶ This canal carries water more than 300 km across mountains and deserts to supply drinking water to Los Angeles, California.

Figure 11 ▶ Dams, such as this one in Zimbabwe, are built to manage freshwater resources.

the land below them. As a river enters a reservoir, it slows down and deposits some of the sediment it carries. This fertile sediment builds up behind a dam instead of enriching the land farther down the river. As a result, the farmland below a dam may become less productive. Dam failure can be another problem—if a dam bursts, people living along the river below the dam can be killed. In the United States, the era of large dam construction is probably over. But in developing countries, such as Brazil, India, and China, the construction of large dams continues.

Water Conservation

As water sources become depleted, water becomes more expensive. This is because wells must be dug deeper, water must be piped greater distances, and polluted water must be cleaned up before it can be used. Water conservation is one way that we can help ensure that everyone will have enough water at a reasonable price.

Water Conservation in Agriculture Most of the water loss in agriculture comes from evaporation, seepage, and runoff, so technologies that reduce these problems help to conserve water. *Drip irrigation systems* offer a promising step toward conservation. Shown in **Figure 12**, drip irrigation systems deliver small amounts of water directly to plant roots by using perforated tubing. Water is released to plants as needed and at a controlled rate. These systems are sometimes managed by computer programs that coordinate watering times by using satellite data. A well-designed drip irrigation system loses very little water.

Water Conservation in Industry As water resources have become more expensive, many industries have developed water conservation plans. The most widely used water conservation plans involve the recycling of cooling water and wastewater. Instead of discharging used water into a nearby river, businesses often recycle water. Thus, the production of 1 kg of paper now uses less than 30 percent of the water it required 50 years ago. Small businesses are also helping conserve water. Denver, Colorado, was one of the first cities to realize the value of conserving water in business. The city pays small businesses to conserve water. This saves money for the city and businesses, and also makes more water available for other uses.

✓ Reading Check What are two ways in which water is conserved in industry?

Figure 12 ▶ Drip irrigation systems use perforated tubing to deliver water directly to plant roots.

Figure 13 ▶ This xeriscaped yard in Arizona features plants that are native to the state. What kinds of plants are native to your region?

Table 2 ▼

What You Can Do to Conserve Water
• Take shorter showers, and avoid taking baths unless you keep the water level low.
• Install a low-flow shower head in your shower.
• Install inexpensive, low-flow aerators in your water faucets at home.
• Purchase a modern, low-flow toilet, install a water-saving device in your toilet, or simply place a water-filled bottle inside your toilet tank to reduce the water used for each flush.
• Do not let the water run while you are brushing your teeth.
• Fill up the sink basin rather than letting the water run when you are shaving, washing your hands or face, or washing dishes.
• Wash only full loads in your dishwasher and washing machine.
• Water your lawn sparingly.

Water Conservation at Home Although households use much less water than agriculture or industry, a few changes to residential water use will make a significant contribution to water conservation. People can conserve water by changing a few everyday habits and by using only the water that they need. Some of these conservation methods are shown in **Table 2.**

Water-saving technology, such as low-flow toilets and shower heads, can also help reduce household water use. These devices are required in some new buildings. As well, many cities pay residents to install water-saving equipment in older buildings.

About one-third of the water used by the average household in the United States is used for landscaping. To conserve water, many people water their lawns at night to reduce the amount of water lost to evaporation. Another way people save water used outside their home is a technique called *xeriscaping* (ZIR i SKAY ping). Xeriscaping involves designing a landscape that requires minimal water use. **Figure 13** shows one example of xeriscaping in Arizona.

Can one person make a difference? When you multiply one by the millions of people who are trying to conserve water—in industry, on farms, and at home—you can make a big difference.

Solutions for the Future

In some places, conservation alone is not enough to prevent water shortages. As populations grow, other sources of fresh water need to be developed. Two possible solutions are desalination and transporting fresh water.

Desalination Some coastal communities rely on the oceans to provide fresh water. **Desalination** (DEE SAL uh NAY shuhn) is the process of removing salt from salt water. Some countries in drier parts of the world, such as the Middle East, have built desalination plants to provide fresh water. Most desalination plants heat salt water and collect the fresh water that evaporates. **Figure 14** shows one such plant in Kuwait. Because desalination consumes a lot of energy, the process is too expensive for many nations to consider.

Transporting Water In some areas of the world where freshwater resources are not adequate, water can be transported from other regions. For example, the increasing number of tourists visiting some Greek islands in the Mediterranean Sea have taxed the islands' freshwater supply. As a result, ships travel regularly from the mainland towing enormous plastic bags full of fresh water. The ships anchor in port, and fresh water is then pumped onto the islands. This solution is also being considered in the United States, where almost half of the available fresh water is in Alaska. Scientists are exploring the possibility of filling huge bags with water from Alaskan rivers and then towing the bags down the coast to California, where fresh water is often in short supply.

Because 77 percent of the Earth's fresh water is frozen in icecaps, icebergs are another potential freshwater source. For years, people have considered towing icebergs to communities that lack fresh water. But an efficient way to tow icebergs is yet to be discovered.

SC*L*INKS.
www.scilinks.org
Topic: Water
Conservation
Code: HE81625

Figure 14 ▶ Most desalination plants, such as this one in Kuwait, use evaporation to separate salt from ocean water.

SECTION 2 **Review**

1. **Describe** the patterns of global water use for each continent shown in the bar graph in Figure 5.

2. **Describe** the drinking water treatment process in your own words.

3. **Describe** the benefits and costs of dams and water diversion projects.

4. **List** at least three things you can do to help conserve the world's water supply.

CRITICAL THINKING

5. **Making Comparisons** Write a description of the evaporative method of desalination using terms from the water cycle. **WRITING SKILLS**

6. **Identifying Alternatives** Describe three ways that communities can increase their freshwater resources.

SECTION 3
Water Pollution

Objectives

▶ Compare point-source pollution and nonpoint-source pollution.

▶ Classify water pollutants by five types.

▶ Explain why groundwater pollution is difficult to clean up.

▶ Describe the major sources of ocean pollution, and explain the effects of pollution on ecosystems.

▶ Describe six major laws designed to improve water quality in the United States.

Key Terms

water pollution
point-source pollution
nonpoint-source pollution
wastewater
artificial eutrophication
thermal pollution
biomagnification

You might think that you can tell if a body of water is polluted by the way that the water looks or smells, but sometimes you can't. There are many different forms of water pollution. **Water pollution** is the introduction of chemical, physical, or biological agents into water that degrade water quality and adversely affect the organisms that depend on the water. Almost all of the ways that we use water contribute to water pollution. However, the two underlying causes of water pollution are industrialization and rapid human population growth.

In the last 30 years, developed countries have made great strides in cleaning up many polluted water supplies. Despite this progress, some water is still dangerously polluted in the United States and in other countries. In developing parts of the world, water pollution is a big problem. Industry is usually not the major cause of water pollution in developing countries. Often, the only water available for drinking in these countries is polluted with sewage and agricultural runoff, which can spread waterborne diseases. To prevent water pollution, people must understand where pollutants come from. As you will learn, water pollution comes from two types of sources: point and nonpoint sources.

Figure 15 ▶ Point-source pollution comes from a single, easily identifiable source. In this photo, the waste from an iron mine is being stored in a pond.

Table 3 ▼

Sources of Point Pollution

- leaking septic-tank systems
- leaking storage lagoons for polluted waste
- unlined landfills
- leaking underground storage tanks that contain chemicals or fuels such as gasoline
- polluted water from abandoned and active mines
- water discharged by industries
- public and industrial waste-water treatment plants

Point-Source Pollution

When you think of water pollution, you probably think of a single source, such as a factory, a wastewater treatment plant, or a leaking oil tanker. These are all examples of **point-source pollution,** which is pollution discharged from a single source. **Table 3** lists some additional examples of point-source pollution. Point-source pollution can often be identified and traced to a source. But even when the source of the pollution is known, enforcing cleanup may be difficult.

Nonpoint-Source Pollution

Nonpoint-source pollution comes from many different sources that are often difficult to identify. For example, a river can be polluted by runoff from any of the land in its watershed. If a farm, a road, or any other land surface in a watershed is polluted, runoff from a rainstorm can carry the pollution into a nearby river, stream, or lake. **Figure 16** shows common sources of nonpoint pollutants. **Table 4** lists some additional causes of nonpoint pollution.

Because nonpoint pollutants can enter bodies of water in many different ways, they are extremely difficult to regulate and control. The accumulation of small amounts of water pollution from many sources is a major pollution problem—96 percent of the polluted bodies of water in the United States were contaminated by nonpoint sources. Controlling nonpoint-source pollution depends to a great extent on public awareness of the effects of activities such as spraying lawn chemicals and using storm drains to dispose of used motor oil.

FIELD ACTIVITY

Identifying Sources of Pollution Walk around your neighborhood, and record potential sources of nonpoint pollution. See Table 4 for examples. Count the number of potential sources of nonpoint pollution, and suggest ways to reduce each source of pollution in your *EcoLog*.

Table 4 ▼

Nonpoint Sources of Pollution
• chemicals added to road surfaces (salt and other de-icing agents)
• water runoff from city and suburban streets that may contain oil, gasoline, animal feces, and litter
• pesticides, herbicides, and fertilizer from residential lawns, golf courses, and farmland
• feces and agricultural chemicals from livestock feedlots
• precipitation containing air pollutants
• soil runoff from farms and construction sites
• oil and gasoline from personal watercraft

Figure 16 ▶ Sources of Nonpoint Pollution Examples of nonpoint-source pollution include ❶ livestock polluting water holes that can flow into streams and reservoirs, ❷ oil on a street, which can wash into storm sewers and then drain into waterways, and ❸ thousands of watercraft, which can leak gasoline and oil.

Table 5 ▼

Pollutant Types and Sources		
Type of pollutant	Agent	Major sources
Pathogens	disease-causing organisms, such as bacteria, viruses, protozoa, and parasitic worms	mostly nonpoint sources: sewage or animal feces, livestock feedlots, and poultry farms; sewage from overburdened wastewater treatment plants
Organic matter	animal and plant matter remains, feces, food waste, and debris from food-processing plants	mostly nonpoint sources
Organic chemicals	pesticides, fertilizers, plastics, detergents, gasoline and oil, and other materials made from petroleum	mostly nonpoint sources: farms, lawns, golf courses, roads, wastewater, unlined landfills, and leaking underground storage tanks
Inorganic chemicals	acids, bases, salts, and industrial chemicals	point sources and nonpoint sources: industrial waste, road surfaces, wastewater, and polluted precipitation
Heavy metals	lead, mercury, cadmium, and arsenic	point sources and nonpoint sources: industrial discharge, unlined landfills, some household chemicals, and mining processes; heavy metals also occur naturally in some groundwater
Physical agents	heat and suspended solids	point sources and nonpoint sources: heat from industrial processes and suspended solids from soil erosion

Principal Water Pollutants

There are many different kinds of water pollutants. **Table 5** lists some common types of pollutants and some of the possible sources of each pollutant.

Wastewater

Do you know where water goes after it flows down the drain in a sink? The water usually flows through a series of sewage pipes that carry it—and all the other wastewater in your community— to a wastewater treatment plant. **Wastewater** is water that contains waste from homes or industry. At a wastewater treatment plant, water is filtered and treated to make the water clean enough to return to a river or lake.

Treating Wastewater A typical residential wastewater treatment process is illustrated in **Figure 17.** Most of the wastewater from homes contains biodegradable material that can be broken down by living organisms. For example, wastewater from toilets and kitchen sinks contains animal and plant wastes, paper, and soap, all of which are biodegradable. But wastewater treatment plants may not remove all of the harmful substances in water. Some household and industrial wastewater and some storm-water runoff contains toxic substances that cannot be removed by the standard treatment.

Sewage Sludge One of the products of wastewater treatment is *sewage sludge*, the solid material that remains after treatment. When sludge contains dangerous concentrations of toxic chemicals, it must be disposed of as hazardous waste. The sludge is often incinerated, and then the ash is buried in a secure landfill. Sludge can be an expensive burden to towns and cities because the volume of sludge that has to be disposed of every year is enormous.

The problem of sludge disposal has led many communities to look for new uses for this waste. If the toxicity of sludge can be reduced to safe levels, sludge can be used as a fertilizer. Sludge can also be combined with clay to make bricks for buildings.

Reading Check Why is it so expensive to dispose of sewage sludge?

Connection to History

***Cryptosporidium* Outbreak** In 1993, a pathogen called *Cryptosporidium parvum* contaminated the municipal water supply of Milwaukee, Wisconsin. The waterborne parasite caused more than 100 deaths, and 400,000 people experienced a flulike illness. *Cryptosporidium* is found in animal feces, but the parasite usually occurs in low levels in water supplies. The outbreak in Milwaukee was probably caused by an unusual combination of heavy rainfall and agricultural runoff that overburdened the city's water treatment plants.

Figure 17 ▶ **Wastewater Treatment Process**

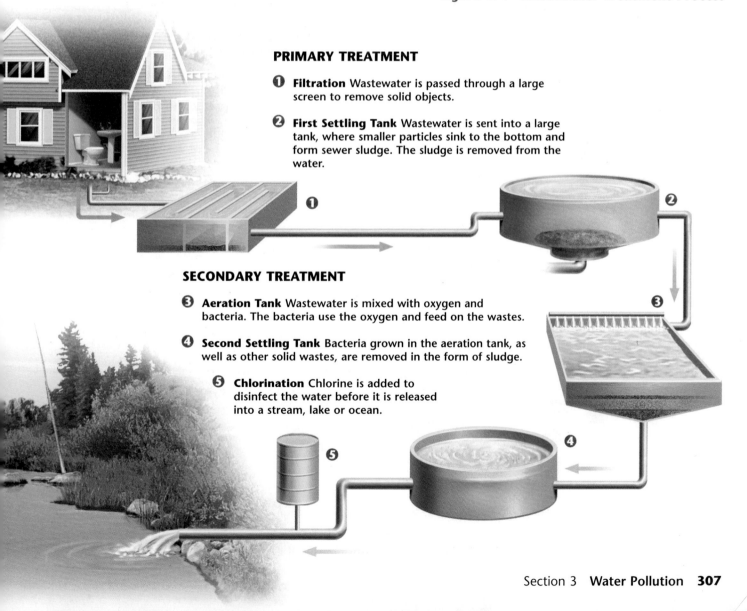

PRIMARY TREATMENT

❶ **Filtration** Wastewater is passed through a large screen to remove solid objects.

❷ **First Settling Tank** Wastewater is sent into a large tank, where smaller particles sink to the bottom and form sewer sludge. The sludge is removed from the water.

SECONDARY TREATMENT

❸ **Aeration Tank** Wastewater is mixed with oxygen and bacteria. The bacteria use the oxygen and feed on the wastes.

❹ **Second Settling Tank** Bacteria grown in the aeration tank, as well as other solid wastes, are removed in the form of sludge.

❺ **Chlorination** Chlorine is added to disinfect the water before it is released into a stream, lake or ocean.

Artificial Eutrophication

Most nutrients in water come from organic matter, such as leaves and animal waste, that is broken down into mineral nutrients by decomposers such as bacteria and fungi. Nutrients are an essential part of any aquatic ecosystem, but an overabundance of nutrients can disrupt an ecosystem. When lakes and slow-moving streams contain an abundance of nutrients, they are eutrophic (yoo TROH fik).

Eutrophication is a natural process. When organic matter builds up in a body of water, it will begin to decay and decompose. The process of decomposition uses up oxygen. As oxygen levels decrease, the types of organisms that live in the water change over time. For example, as a body of water becomes eutrophic, plants take root in the nutrient-rich sediment at the bottom. As more plants grow, the shallow waters begin to fill in. Eventually, the body of water becomes a swamp or marsh.

The natural process of eutrophication is accelerated when inorganic plant nutrients, such as phosphorus and nitrogen, enter the water from sewage and fertilizer runoff. Eutrophication caused by humans is called **artificial eutrophication.** Fertilizer from farms, lawns, and gardens is the largest source of nutrients that cause artificial eutrophication. Phosphates in some laundry and dishwashing detergents are another major cause of eutrophication. Phosphorus is a plant nutrient that can cause the excessive growth of algae. In bodies of water polluted by phosphorus, algae can form large floating mats, called *algal blooms,* as shown in **Figure 18.** As the algae die and decompose, most of the dissolved oxygen is used and fish and other organisms suffocate in the oxygen-depleted water.

Figure 18 ▶ In an effort to limit artificial eutrophication, some states have either banned phosphate detergents or limited the amount of phosphates in detergents.

Figure 19 ▶ Fish kills, such as this one in Brazil, can result from thermal pollution.

Thermal Pollution

If you look at **Figure 19,** you might assume that a toxic chemical caused the massive fish kill in the photo. But the fish were not killed by a chemical spill—they died because of thermal pollution. When the temperature of a body of water, such as a lake or stream, increases, **thermal pollution** can result. Thermal pollution can occur when power plants and other industries use water in their cooling systems and then discharge the warm water into a lake or river.

Thermal pollution can cause large fish kills if the discharged water is too warm for the fish to survive. But most thermal pollution is more subtle. If the temperature of a body of water rises even a few degrees, the amount of oxygen the water can hold decreases significantly. As oxygen levels drop, aquatic organisms may suffocate and die. If the flow of warm water into a lake or stream is constant, it may cause the total disruption of an aquatic ecosystem.

Groundwater Pollution

Pollutants usually enter groundwater when polluted surface water percolates down from the Earth's surface. Any pollution of the surface water in an area can affect the groundwater. Pesticides, herbicides, chemical fertilizers, and petroleum products are common groundwater pollutants. Leaking underground storage tanks are another major source of groundwater pollution. It is estimated that there are millions of underground storage tanks in the United States. Most of the tanks—located beneath gas stations, farms, and homes—hold petroleum products, such as gasoline and heating fuel. As underground storage tanks age, they may develop leaks, which allow pollutants to seep into the groundwater.

Connection to Chemistry

Dissolved Oxygen One of the most important measures of the health of a body of water is the amount of dissolved oxygen in the water. Gaseous oxygen enters water by diffusion from the surrounding air, as a byproduct of photosynthesis, and as a result of the rapid movement (aeration) of water. The amount of oxygen that water can hold is determined by the water's temperature, pressure, and salinity. Slow-moving water tends to have low levels of dissolved oxygen, while rapidly flowing streams have higher levels. Artificial eutrophication and thermal pollution also reduce levels of dissolved oxygen. When dissolved oxygen levels remain below 2 mg/L for several hours, fish and other organisms suffocate, and massive fish kills can result.

MATHPRACTICE

Parts per Million Water contamination is often measured in parts per million (ppm). If the concentration of a pollutant is 5 ppm, there are 5 parts of the pollutant in 1 million parts of water. If the concentration of gasoline is 3 ppm in 650,000 L of water, how many liters of gasoline are in the water?

The location of aging underground storage tanks is not always known, so the tanks often cannot be repaired or replaced until after they have leaked enough pollutants to be located. Modern underground storage tanks are contained in concrete and have many features to prevent leaks. Other sources of groundwater pollution include septic tanks, unlined landfills, and industrial wastewater lagoons, as shown in **Figure 20**.

Cleaning Up Groundwater Pollution Groundwater pollution is one of the most challenging environmental problems that the world faces. Even if groundwater pollution could be stopped tomorrow, some groundwater would remain polluted for generations to come. As you have learned, groundwater recharges very slowly. The process for some aquifers to recycle water and purge contaminants can take hundreds or thousands of years. Groundwater is also difficult to decontaminate because the water is dispersed throughout large areas of rock and sand. Pollution can cling to the materials that make up an aquifer, so even if all of the water in an aquifer were pumped out and replaced with clean water, the groundwater could still become polluted.

Figure 20 ▶ This diagram shows some of the major sources of groundwater pollution. Runoff and percolation transport contaminants to the groundwater.

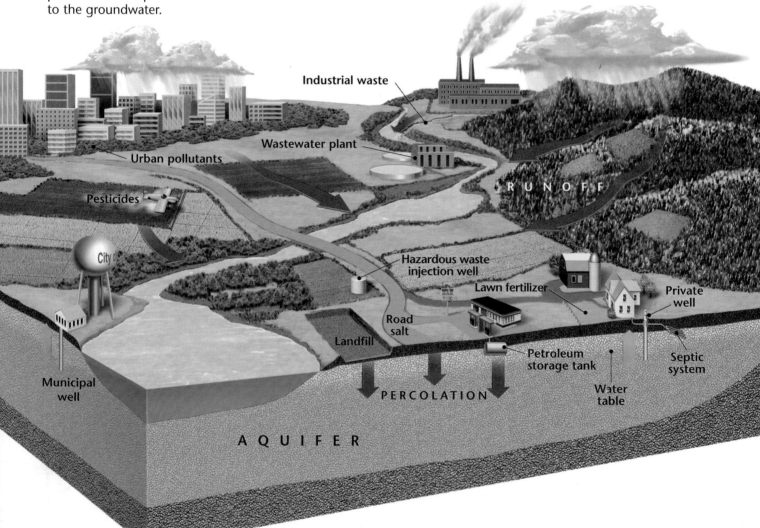

Figure 21 ▶ Major North American Oil Spills

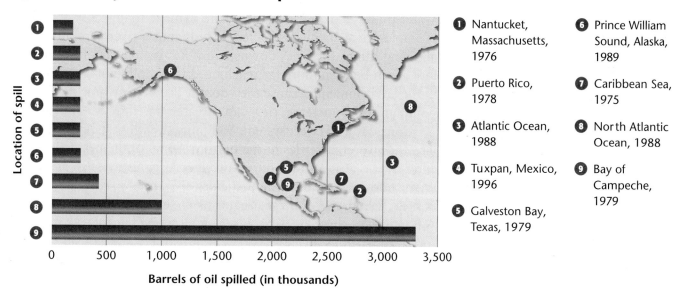

Location of spill (vertical axis)
Barrels of oil spilled (in thousands) — 0, 500, 1,000, 1,500, 2,000, 2,500, 3,000, 3,500

❶ Nantucket, Massachusetts, 1976

❷ Puerto Rico, 1978

❸ Atlantic Ocean, 1988

❹ Tuxpan, Mexico, 1996

❺ Galveston Bay, Texas, 1979

❻ Prince William Sound, Alaska, 1989

❼ Caribbean Sea, 1975

❽ North Atlantic Ocean, 1988

❾ Bay of Campeche, 1979

Ocean Pollution

Pollutants are often dumped directly into the oceans. For example, ships can legally dump wastewater and garbage overboard in some parts of the ocean. But at least 85 percent of ocean pollution—including pollutants such as oil, toxic wastes, and medical wastes—comes from activities on land. If polluted runoff enters rivers, for example, the rivers may carry the polluted water to the ocean. Most activities that pollute oceans occur near the coasts, where much of the world's human population lives. As you might imagine, sensitive coastal ecosystems, such as coral reefs, estuaries, and coastal marshes, are the most affected by pollution.

Oil Spills Ocean water is also polluted by accidental oil spills. Disasters such as the 1989 *Exxon Valdez* oil spill in Prince William Sound, Alaska, make front-page news around the world. In 2001, a fuel-oil spill off the coast of the Galápagos Islands captured public attention. Each year, approximately 37 million gallons of oil from tanker accidents are spilled into the oceans. **Figure 21** shows some of the major oil spills that have occurred off the coast of North America in the last 30 years.

Oil spills have dramatic effects, but they account for only about 5 percent of oil pollution in the oceans. Most of the oil that pollutes the oceans comes from cities and towns. Every year, as many as 200 million to 300 million gallons of oil enter the oceans from nonpoint sources on land. That's almost 10 times the amount of oil spilled by tankers. Limiting these nonpoint sources of oil pollution would go a long way toward keeping the oceans clean.

Reading Check How can limiting nonpoint sources of oil pollution help to keep the oceans clean?

Ecofact

Cruise Ship Discharges In one year, ships dump almost 7 billion kilograms of trash into the oceans. About 75 percent of all ship waste comes from cruise ships. According to most international law, cruise ships are allowed to dump nonplastic waste—including untreated sewage—into the oceans. Increasing public pressure has begun to cause the cruise-ship industry to change this practice, however.

SCINKS.
www.scilinks.org
Topic: Water Pollution
Code: HE81629

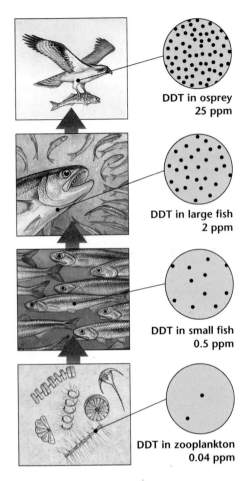

DDT in osprey
25 ppm

DDT in large fish
2 ppm

DDT in small fish
0.5 ppm

DDT in zooplankton
0.04 ppm

Figure 22 ▶ The accumulation of pollutants at successive levels of the food chain is called biomagnification.

Figure 23 ▶ The Cuyahoga River was so polluted with petroleum and petroleum byproducts that it caught on fire and burned in 1969.

Water Pollution and Ecosystems

Water pollution can cause immediate damage to an ecosystem. For example, toxic chemicals spilled directly into a river can kill nearly all living things for miles downstream. But the effects of water pollution can be even more far reaching. Many pollutants accumulate in the environment because they do not decompose quickly. As the pollutant levels increase, they can threaten an entire ecosystem.

Consider a river ecosystem. Soil tainted with pesticides washes into the river and settles to the bottom. Some of the pesticides enter the bodies of tiny, bottom-dwelling organisms, such as insect larvae and crustaceans. The pesticides are stored in their body tissues. A hundred of these organisms are eaten by one small fish. A hundred of these small fish are eaten by one big fish. A predatory bird, such as an eagle, eats 10 big fish. Each organism stores the pesticide in its tissues, so at each step along the food chain, the concentration of the pesticide passed on to the next organism increases. This buildup of pollutants at higher levels of the food chain is called **biomagnification.** Biomagnification, which is shown for the pesticide DDT in **Figure 22**, has alarming consequences for organisms at the top of the food chain. Many U.S. states limit the amount of fish that people can eat from certain bodies of water because of biomagnification.

Cleaning Up Water Pollution

In 1969, the Cuyahoga River in Cleveland, Ohio, was so polluted that the river caught on fire and burned for several days, as shown in **Figure 23**. This shocking event was a major factor in the passage of the Clean Water Act of 1972. The stated purpose of the act was to "restore and maintain the chemical, physical, and biological integrity of the nation's waters." The goal of the act was to make all surface water clean enough for fishing and swimming by 1983. This goal was not achieved; however, much progress has been made since the act was passed. The percentage of lakes and rivers that are fit for swimming and fishing has increased by about 30 percent, and many states have passed stricter water-quality standards of their own. Many toxic metals are now removed from wastewater before the water is discharged.

The Clean Water Act opened the door for other water-quality legislation, some of which is described in **Table 6**. For example, the Marine Protection, Research, and Sanctuaries Act of 1972 strengthened the laws against ocean dumping.

The Oil Pollution Act of 1990 requires all oil tankers traveling in U.S. waters to

Table 6 ▼

Federal Laws Designed to Improve Water Quality in the United States
1972 Clean Water Act (CWA) The CWA set a national goal of making all natural surface water fit for fishing and swimming by 1983 and banned pollutant discharge into surface water after 1985. The act also required that metals be removed from wastewater.
1972 Marine Protection, Research, and Sanctuaries Act, amended 1988 This act empowered the EPA to control the dumping of sewage wastes and toxic chemicals in U.S. waters.
1975 Safe Drinking Water Act (SDWA), amended 1996 This act introduced programs to protect groundwater and surface water from pollution. The act emphasized sound science and risk-based standards for water quality. The act also empowered communities in the protection of source water, strengthened public right-to-know laws, and provided water system infrastructure assistance.
1980 Comprehensive Environmental Response Compensation and Liability Act (CERCLA) This act is also known as the Superfund Act. The act makes owners, operators, and customers of hazardous waste sites responsible for the cleanup of the sites. The act has reduced the pollution of groundwater by toxic substances leached from hazardous waste dumps.
1987 Water Quality Act This act was written to support state and local efforts to clean polluted runoff. It also established loan funds to pay for new wastewater treatment plants and created programs to protect major estuaries.
1990 Oil Pollution Act This act attempts to protect U.S. waterways from oil pollution by requiring that oil tankers in U.S. waters be double-hulled by 2015.

FIELD ACTIVITY

Coastal Cleanups You can be a part of a coastal cleanup. Every September, people from all over the world set aside one day to help clean up debris from beaches. You can join this international effort by writing to The Center for Marine Conservation.

If you do participate in a coastal cleanup, keep a record of the types of trash you find in your *EcoLog*.

have double hulls by 2015 as an added protection against oil spills. Legislation has improved water quality in the United States, but the cooperation of individuals, businesses, and the government will be essential to maintaining a clean water supply in the future.

SECTION 3 Review

1. **Explain** why point-source pollution is easier to control than nonpoint-source pollution.

2. **List** the major types of water pollutants. Suggest ways to reduce the levels of each type of pollutant in a water supply.

3. **Describe** the unique problems of cleaning up groundwater pollution.

4. **Describe** the source of most ocean pollution. Is it point-source pollution or nonpoint-source pollution?

CRITICAL THINKING

5. **Interpreting Graphics** Read the description of biomagnification. Draw a diagram that shows the biomagnification of a pollutant in an ecosystem. **READING SKILLS**

6. **Applying Ideas** What can individuals do to decrease ocean pollution? Write and illustrate a guide that gives at least three examples. **WRITING SKILLS**

1 Water Resources

Key Terms

surface water, 290
river system, 291
watershed, 291
groundwater, 292
aquifer, 293
porosity, 293
permeability, 293
recharge zone, 294

Main Ideas

▶ Only a small fraction of Earth's water supply is fresh water. The two main sources of fresh water are surface water and groundwater.

▶ River systems drain the land that makes up a watershed. The amount of water in a river system can vary in different seasons and from year to year.

▶ Groundwater accumulates in underground formations called *aquifers*. Surface water enters an aquifer through the aquifer's recharge zone.

▶ If the water in an aquifer is pumped out faster than it is replenished, the water table drops, which can affect humans and animals that depend on the groundwater.

2 Water Use and Management

Key Terms

potable, 297
pathogen, 297
dam, 300
reservoir, 300
desalination, 303

Main Ideas

▶ There are three main types of water use: residential, industrial, and agricultural. Worldwide, most water use is agricultural.

▶ Dams and water diversion projects are built to manage surface-water resources. Damming and diverting rivers can have environmental and social consequences.

▶ Water conservation is necessary to maintain an adequate supply of fresh water. Desalination and transporting water are options to supplement local water supplies.

3 Water Pollution

Key Terms

water pollution, 304
point-source pollution, 305
nonpoint-source pollution, 305
wastewater, 306
artificial eutrophication, 308
thermal pollution, 309
biomagnification, 312

Main Ideas

▶ Water can become polluted by chemical, physical, or biological agents. Most water pollution in the United States is caused by nonpoint-source pollutants.

▶ Groundwater pollution is difficult to clean up because aquifers recharge slowly and because pollutants cling to the materials that make up an aquifer.

▶ Ocean pollution is mainly caused by coastal, nonpoint-source pollutants.

▶ Government legislation, such as the Clean Water Act of 1972, has succeeded in reducing surface-water pollution. Future challenges include reducing nonpoint-source pollution and groundwater pollution.

Using Key Terms

Use each of the following terms in a separate sentence.

1. *aquifer*
2. *recharge zone*
3. *reservoir*
4. *wastewater*
5. *biomagnification*

For each pair of terms, explain how the meanings of the terms differ.

6. *surface water* and *groundwater*
7. *porosity* and *permeability*
8. *watershed* and *river system*
9. *point-source pollution* and *nonpoint-source pollution*

✔ **STUDY TIP**

Root Words To practice vocabulary, write the key terms and definitions on a piece of paper and fold the paper lengthwise so that the definitions are covered. First, see how many definitions you already know. Then, write the definitions you do not know on another piece of paper, and practice until you know all of the terms.

Understanding Key Ideas

10. Which of the following processes is *not* a part of the water cycle?
    a. evaporation
    b. condensation
    c. biomagnification
    d. precipitation

11. Most of the fresh water on Earth is
    a. located underground in aquifers.
    b. frozen in the polar icecaps.
    c. located in rivers, lakes, streams, and wetlands.
    d. found in Earth's atmosphere.

12. Which of the following processes is *not* used in a conventional method of water treatment?
    a. filtration
    b. coagulation
    c. aeration
    d. percolation

13. Which of the following is *not* an example of point-source pollution?
    a. oil that is escaping from a damaged tanker
    b. heavy metals that are leaching out of an underground mine
    c. water runoff from residential lawns
    d. untreated sewage that is accidentally released from a wastewater treatment plant

14. Which of the following pollutants causes artificial eutrophication?
    a. heavy metals from unlined landfills
    b. inorganic plant nutrients from wastewater and fertilizer runoff
    c. toxic chemicals from factories
    d. radioactive waste from nuclear power plants

15. Pumping large amounts of water from an aquifer may cause the
    a. water table to rise.
    b. recharge zone to shrink.
    c. wells in an area to run dry.
    d. percolation of groundwater to stop.

16. Oil pollution in the ocean is mostly caused by
    a. major oil spills, such as the 1989 *Exxon Valdez* oil spill.
    b. the cumulative effect of small oil spills and leaks on land.
    c. decomposed plastic materials.
    d. intentional dumping of excess oil.

17. Thermal pollution has a harmful effect on aquatic environments because
    a. water has been circulated around power-plant generators.
    b. it increases the number of disease-causing organisms in aquatic environments.
    c. it reduces the amount of dissolved oxygen in aquatic environments.
    d. it decreases the nutrient levels in aquatic environments.

Short Answer

18. What effect can buildings and parking lots have on an aquifer's recharge zone?

19. Why is the use of overhead sprinklers for irrigation inefficient? What is a more efficient method of irrigation?

20. List three advantages and three disadvantages of dams.

21. What is the process of eutrophication, and how do human activities accelerate it?

22. Describe the steps that are involved in the primary and secondary treatment of wastewater.

Interpreting Graphics

The graph below shows the annual flow, or discharge, of the Yakima River in Washington. Use the graph to answer questions 23–25.

23. In which months is the river's discharge highest? What might explain these discharge rates?

24. What might cause the peaks in river discharge between November and March?

25. How might the data be different if the hydrograph readings were taken below a large dam on the Yakima River?

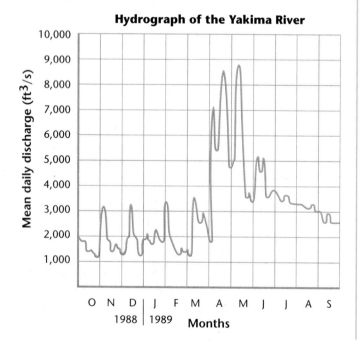

Hydrograph of the Yakima River

Concept Mapping

26. Use the following terms to create a concept map: *Earth's surface, rivers, underground, fresh water, water table, 3 percent,* and *icecaps.*

Critical Thinking

27. **Making Comparisons** Read the description of artificial eutrophication in this chapter. Do you think artificial eutrophication is more disturbing to the stability of a water ecosystem than natural eutrophication is? **READING SKILLS**

28. **Analyzing Relationships** Water resources are often shared by several countries. A river, for example, might flow through five countries before it reaches an ocean. When water resources are shared, how should countries determine water rights and environmental responsibility?

29. **Making Inferences** Explain why it takes 36 gallons of water to produce a single serving of rice, but it takes more than 2,000 gallons of water to produce a single serving of steak. What do you think the water is used for in each case?

30. **Making Inferences** Why is there so little fresh water in the world? Do you think that there would have been more fresh water at a different time in Earth's history?

Cross-Disciplinary Connection

31. **Social Studies** Find out how freshwater resources affected the development of one culture in history. Use at least five key terms from this chapter to write a two-paragraph description of how the availability of fresh water affected the culture you chose. **WRITING SKILLS**

Portfolio Project

32. **Investigation** Find out about the source of the tap water in your home. Where does the tap water come from, and where does your wastewater go? Does the water complete a cycle? Make a poster to illustrate your findings. You may want to work with several classmates and visit the sites you discover.

The graph below illustrates the pumping rates for a set of wells that provide water to a small community. Use the graph to answer question 33.

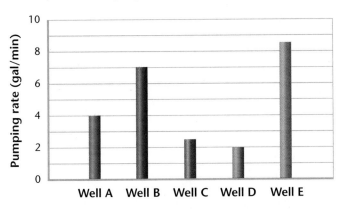

33. **Analyzing Data** How many gallons does Well B pump per day? What is the average pump rate for all of the wells? In one hour, how many more gallons of water will Well A pump than Well C?

34. **Making Calculations** If placing a container of water in your toilet tank reduces the amount of water per flush by 2 L, how much water would be saved each day if this were done in 80 million toilets? (Assume that each toilet is flushed five times per day.) Convert your answer into gallons (1 L = .26 Gal).

 WRITING SKILLS

35. **Communicating Main Ideas** Why is water pollution a serious problem?

36. **Writing Persuasively** Write a letter to a senator in which you voice your support or criticism of a hypothetical water diversion project.

 READING SKILLS

Read the passage below, and then answer the questions that follow.

Water use is measured in two ways: by withdrawal and by consumption. Withdrawal is the removal and transfer of water from its source to a point of use, such as a home, business, or industry. Most of the water that is withdrawn is eventually returned to its source. For example, much of the water used in industries and homes is treated and returned to the river or lake it came from. When water is withdrawn and is not returned to its source, the water is consumed. For example, when a potted plant is watered, almost all of the water eventually enters the atmosphere by *evapotranspiration* through the leaves of the plant. The evaporated water was consumed because it was not directly returned to its source.

1. According to the passage, which of the following statements is true?
   a. Water that is consumed was never withdrawn.
   b. Water that is withdrawn cannot be consumed.
   c. A fraction of the water withdrawn is usually consumed.
   d. All of the water withdrawn is consumed.

2. Which phrase best describes the meaning of the term *evapotranspiration*?
   a. the absorption of water by plant leaves
   b. the process by which potted plants transpire their leaves by evaporation
   c. the process by which the atmosphere maintains water levels in plant leaves
   d. the process by which water evaporates from plant leaves

3. Which of the following statements is an example of consumption?
   a. A river is diverted to irrigate crops.
   b. A power plant takes in cool water from a lake and returns the water to the lake.
   c. A dam forms a reservoir on a river.
   d. An aquifer is recharged by surface water.

Standardized Test Prep

Understanding Concepts

Directions (1–4): For *each* question, write on a separate sheet of paper the letter of the correct answer.

1 Why are the oceans important to the water cycle?
   A. Oceans contain saltwater.
   B. The four major oceans are all joined.
   C. Most of Earth's water is contained in the oceans.
   D. Oceans cover more of Earth's surface area.

2 Where do we find most of the water that is available for human use?
   F. groundwater
   G. the ocean
   H. polar ice caps
   I. rivers and streams

3 Which of the following is an example of a nonpoint-source of pollution?
   A. chemical factory
   B. livestock feedlot
   C. oil spill
   D. wastewater treatment plant

4 How does heat act as a water pollutant?
   F. It slows down the flow of water.
   G. It speeds up chemical reactions.
   H. It increases the nutrients in the water.
   I. It decreases oxygen in the water.

Directions (5–6): For *each* question, write a short response.

5 Economic forces influence how people use natural resources. One rule of economics is the law of supply and demand. This law states that the greater demand for a resource, the more that resource is worth. How do economic forces affect the use of water resources in developing countries?

6 People often live in areas where water resources are inadequate. Justify the use of water management projects, such as dams, in these areas.

Reading Skills

Directions (7–9): Read the passage below. Then answer the questions.

In 1969, the Cuyahoga River in Ohio was so polluted that the river caught fire and burned for several days. This event was a major factor in the passage of the Clean Water Act of 1972. The stated purpose of the act was to "restore and maintain the chemical, physical, and biological integrity of the nation's waters." Although the goal of the act was not achieved, much progress has been made since the act was passed. The percentage of lakes and rivers that are fit for swimming and fishing has increased by about 30 percent.

Additional water-quality legislation has been enacted, both by the federal government and individual states. Many toxic metals are now removed from wastewater before the water is discharged.

7 What was a major factor in passing the Clean Water Act?
   A. All the lakes in the United States were heavily polluted.
   B. The Cuyahoga River was so polluted that it caught fire and burned for several days.
   C. People could not swim or fish in any lakes or rivers.
   D. Previous laws were never passed.

8 What was achieved through the Clean Water Act?
   F. About 30 percent more lakes and rivers are now fit for swimming and fishing.
   G. The chemical, physical, and biological integrity of the nation's waters has been restored.
   H. All of Ohio's bodies of fresh water are now in good condition.
   I. Wastewater with toxic metals is stored, not dumped.

9 Infer three reasons why the goal of the Clean Water Act was not achieved.

Interpreting Graphics

Directions (10–12): For *each* question below, record the correct answer on a separate sheet of paper.

The map below shows the water resources of Canada. Use this map to answer questions 10 through 12.

Canada's Water

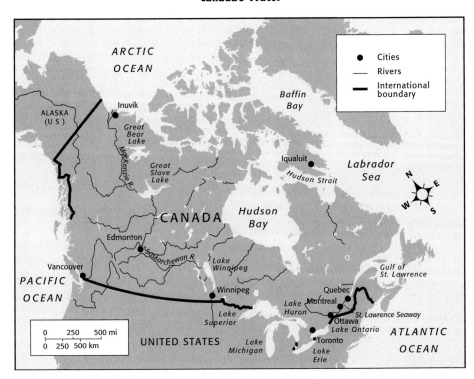

10 What can be inferred about the human population of Canada?
  A. Most people live in the southeast part of Canada.
  B. The greatest number of people live along the west coast.
  C. The Hudson Bay area is the most populous part of Canada.
  D. More people live around the Great Lakes than along the Saskatchewan River.

11 Which of the following is the northernmost source of fresh water?
  F. Baffin Bay
  G. Great Bear Lake
  H. Hudson Strait
  I. MacKenzie River

12 What is the relationship between cities and water resources?
  A. Cities are always located near rivers.
  B. Cities are always located near lakes.
  C. Cities are never located near salt water.
  D. Cities are usually located near water resources.

Test TIP

When analyzing relationships, look for the answer that is not only true but that also best describes the relationship as a whole.

Exploration Lab: MODELING

Objectives

▶ **Construct** a model of the Earth's natural groundwater filtering system.

▶ **USING SCIENTIFIC METHODS** **Test** the ability of your groundwater filters to filter contaminants out of different solutions.

Materials

beakers, 750 mL (5)
glucose solution
glucose test paper
graduated cylinder
gravel
metric ruler
soda bottles, 2 to 3 L (4)
red food coloring
sand
soil
stirring rod
wax pencil

optional contaminants:
cooking oil, detergent, fertilizer, vinegar, soda

optional filter materials:
alum, charcoal

▶ **Filter Apparatus** Your ground filtration models should be layered as shown here.

Groundwater Filters

As surface water travels downward through rock and soil, the water is filtered and purified. As a result, the water in aquifers is generally cleaner than surface water. In this investigation, you will work in small teams to explore how layers of the Earth act as a filter for groundwater. You will make models of the Earth's natural filtration system and test them to see how well they filter various substances.

Procedure

1. Label four beakers as follows: "Contaminant: glucose," "Contaminant: soil," "Contaminant: food coloring," and "Water (control)."

2. Fill these beakers two-thirds full with clean tap water. Then add to each beaker the contaminant listed on its label. (The table on the next page shows how much of each contaminant you should use.) Stir each mixture thoroughly.

3. Copy the data table into your notebook. Carefully observe each beaker, and record your observations. Use some of the glucose test paper to test the glucose level in the glucose beaker.

4. Make four separate filtration systems similar to the one shown below. Your teacher will provide you with bottle caps that have holes poked through them. Fasten each cap to a bottle. Cut the bottom off of each soda bottle, and fill each bottle with layers of gravel, sand, and soil. Consider using the optional filter materials, such as alum or charcoal, but be sure to make all four of your systems identical.

Soil

Sand

Gravel

Observations of Substances in Surface Water		
Contaminant	Before filtration	After filtration
Glucose (15 mL)		
Soil (15 mL)		
Food coloring (15 drops)		
Water (control)		

DO NOT WRITE IN THIS BOOK

5. You are now going to pour each mixture through a filtration system. But first predict how well the filters will clean each water sample. Write your predictions in your notebook.

6. Stir a contaminant mixture in its beaker, and immediately pour the mixture through a filtration system into a clean beaker. Observe the resulting "groundwater," and record your observations in the table you created. CAUTION: Do not taste any of the substances you are testing.

7. Repeat step 6 for each mixture. Clean and relabel the contaminant beakers as you go along.

Analysis

1. **Analyzing Results** Test the glucose-water mixture for the presence of glucose. Can you see the glucose?

2. **Analyzing Results** Was the soil removed from the water by filtering? Was the food coloring removed? How do you know?

Conclusions

3. **Drawing Conclusions** How accurate were your predictions?

4. **Drawing Conclusions** What conclusions can you draw about the filtration model and the materials you used?

▶ **Step 6** Pour each sample of contaminated surface water through a filter.

Extension

1. **Making Predictions** Choose a substance from the materials list that has not been tested. Predict what will happen if you mix this substance in the water supply.

2. **Evaluating Results** Now test your prediction. Use the filter that was the control in the earlier experiment. How did your results compare with your prediction?

3. **Analyzing Results** Compare your results with the results of other teams. What precautions do you recommend for keeping groundwater clean?

>POINTS >of view

THE THREE GORGES DAM

China's Yangtze River is the third-longest river in the world after the Nile and the Amazon. The Yangtze River flows through the Three Gorges region of central China, which is famous for its natural beauty and historical sites. For thousands of years, the area's sheer cliffs have inspired paintings and poems. This idyllic region seems like the sort of place that would be protected as a park or reserve. But in fact, it is the construction site for the Three Gorges Dam—the largest hydroelectric dam project in the world. When the dam is fully operational, the Yangtze River will rise to form a reservoir that is 595 km (370 mi) long—as long as Lake Superior. In other words, the reservoir will be about as long as the distance between Los Angeles and San Francisco!

Benefits of the Dam

The dam has several purposes. It will control the water level of the Yangtze River to prevent flooding. About 1 million people died in the last century from flooding along the river. The damage caused by a severe flood in 1998 is estimated to have cost as much as the entire dam project. The dam will also provide millions of people with hydroelectric power. China now burns air-polluting coal to meet 75 percent of the country's energy needs. Engineers project that when the dam is completed, its turbines will provide enough electrical energy to power a city that is 10 times the size of Los Angeles. When the Yangtze's flow is controlled, the river will be deep enough for large ships to navigate on it, so the dam will also increase trade in a relatively poor region of China.

Some Disadvantages

The project has many drawbacks, however. The reservoir behind the dam will flood an enormous area.

▶ **The Three Gorges Dam** is named for the beautiful canyons it will flood. When completed, the dam may meet 20 percent of China's energy needs with hydroelectric power.

Almost 2 million people living in the affected areas must be relocated—there are 13 cities and hundreds of villages in the area of the proposed reservoir. As the reservoir's waters rise, they will also destroy fragile ecosystems and valuable archeological sites.

Opponents of the project claim that the dam has already increased pollution levels in the Yangtze River. Most of the cities and factories along the river dump untreated wastes directly into the water. Some people think the reservoir will become the world's largest sewer when 1 billion tons of sewage flow into the reservoir every year.

Long-Term Concerns

People have also raised long-term concerns about the project. The dam is being built over a fault line. Scientists question whether the dam would be able to withstand earthquakes that may occur along the

▶ The reservoir that will form behind the Three Gorges Dam is shown in yellow.

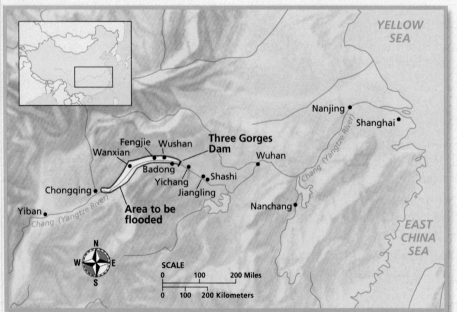

fault. If the dam burst, towns and cities downstream would be flooded. Another concern is that the reservoir may quickly fill with sediment. The Yangtze picks up enormous amounts of yellowish soil and sediment as it flows across China. When the river is slowed by the dam, much of the silt will be deposited in the new reservoir. As sediment builds up behind the dam, the deposited sediment will reduce the size of the reservoir—limiting the flood-prevention capacity of the dam. In addition, productive farming regions below the dam will be deprived of the fertile sediment that is deposited every year when the river floods.

The enormous reservoir may also cause disease among the local population. The potential heath risks include an increase in encephalitis and malaria. The most deadly disease spread by the Three Gorges Dam could be a parasitic disease called schistosomiasis.

Hidden Costs?

Supporters of the dam claim that the project will cost $25 billion, while opponents claim that the cost will be closer to $75 billion. The true cost of the dam may never be known because corruption and inefficiency have plagued the project from the start. Controversy over the dam has prompted the U.S. government and the World Bank to withhold money for the project. Public opposition to the project has been silenced since the Tiananmen Square crackdown. But with help from private investment companies from the United States, the Chinese government is continuing with the project, and the dam is slowly being built. The world's third-longest river will soon swell in the middle, and China will change along with it.

▶ When the dam waters rise, these ancient temples will be flooded.

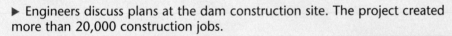

▶ Engineers discuss plans at the dam construction site. The project created more than 20,000 construction jobs.

What Do You Think?

Hundreds of dams in the western United States provide electrical energy, drinking water, and water for crops. Unfortunately, these dams flooded scenic canyons and destroyed ecosystems. Now that the environmental consequences of large dams are known, do you think that China should reconsider the Three Gorges Dam project?

Air

PRE-READING ACTIVITY

FOLDNOTES

Booklet
Before you read this chapter, create the **FoldNote** entitled "Booklet" described in the Reading and Study Skills section of the Appendix. Label each page of the booklet with a main idea from the chapter. As you read the chapter, write what you learn about each main idea on the appropriate page of the booklet.

Nagano, Japan, is just one of many cities around the world that suffers from unhealthy levels of air pollution.

SECTION 1
What Causes Air Pollution?

In Mexico City, children rarely use the color blue when they make paintings of the sky. This metropolitan area of 20 million people is known as the most dangerous city in the world for children because of its very polluted air.

Clean air consists mostly of nitrogen and oxygen gas, as well as very small amounts of argon, carbon dioxide, and water vapor. When harmful substances build up in the air to unhealthy levels, the result is **air pollution.**

Most air pollution is the result of human activities, but pollutants can also come from natural sources. A volcano, for example, can spew clouds of particles and sulfur dioxide, SO_2, into the atmosphere. Natural pollutants also include dust, pollen, and spores.

Primary and Secondary Pollutants

A pollutant that is put directly into the air by human activity is called a **primary pollutant.** An example of a primary pollutant is soot from smoke. **Figure 1** shows some sources of primary air pollutants. **Secondary pollutants** form when primary pollutants react with other primary pollutants or with naturally occurring substances such as water vapor. An example of a secondary pollutant is ground-level ozone. Ground-level ozone forms when the ultraviolet rays of the sun cause emissions from cars, trucks, and natural sources to react with oxygen in the atmosphere.

✓ **Reading Check** Why is ground-level ozone an example of a secondary pollutant? (See the Appendix for answers to Reading Checks.)

Objectives

▶ Name five primary air pollutants, and give sources for each.

▶ Name the two major sources of air pollution in urban areas.

▶ Describe the way in which smog forms.

▶ Explain the way in which a thermal inversion traps air pollution.

Key Terms

air pollution
primary pollutant
secondary pollutant
smog
temperature inversion

Figure 1 ▶ Each day in the United States, hundreds of thousands of tons of polluting emissions that result from human activity enter the air.

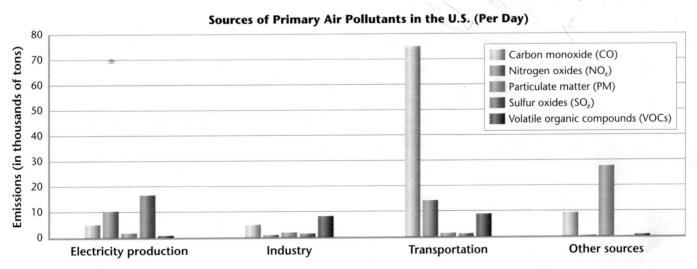

Sources of Primary Air Pollutants in the U.S. (Per Day)

Source: U.S. Environmental Protection Agency.

Table 1 ▼

		Primary Air Pollutants	
Pollutant	**Description**	**Primary Sources**	**Effects**
Carbon monoxide (CO)	CO is an odorless, colorless, poisonous gas. It is produced by the incomplete burning of fossil fuels.	Sources of CO are cars, trucks, buses, small engines, and some industrial processes.	CO interferes with the blood's ability to carry oxygen, slowing reflexes and causing drowsiness. In high concentrations, CO can cause death.
Nitrogen oxides (NO_x)	When combustion (burning) temperatures exceed 538°C, nitrogen and oxygen combine to form nitrogen oxides.	NO_x comes from burning fuels in vehicles, power plants, and industrial boilers.	NO_x can make the body vulnerable to respiratory infections, lung diseases, and cancer. NO_x contributes to the brownish haze seen over cities and to acid precipitation.
Sulfur dioxide (SO_2)	SO_2 is produced by chemical interactions between sulfur and oxygen.	SO_2 comes mostly from burning fossil fuels.	SO_2 contributes to acid precipitation as sulfuric acid. Secondary pollutants that result from reactions with SO_2 can harm plant life and irritate the respiratory systems of humans.
Volatile organic compounds (VOCs)	VOCs are organic chemicals that vaporize readily and form toxic fumes.	VOCs come from burning fuels. Vehicles are a major source of VOCs.	VOCs contribute to smog formation and can cause serious health problems, such as cancer. They may also harm plants.
Particulate matter (particulates or PM)	Particulates are tiny particles of liquid or solid matter.	Most particulates come from construction, agriculture, forestry, and fires. Vehicles and industrial processes also contribute particulates.	Particulates can form clouds that reduce visibility and cause a variety of respiratory problems. Particulates have also been linked to cancer. As well, they may corrode metals and erode buildings and sculptures.

SCLINKS.
www.scilinks.org
Topic: Air Pollution
Code: HE80033

Sources of Primary Air Pollutants As shown in **Table 1** above, household products, power plants, and motor vehicles are sources of primary air pollutants such as carbon monoxide, nitrogen oxide, sulfur dioxide, and chemicals called *volatile organic compounds* (VOCs). Carbon monoxide gas is an important component of the exhaust from vehicles. Vehicles are also a major source of emissions of nitrogen oxides. Coal-burning power plants are another source of nitrogen oxides. Sulfur dioxide gases are formed when coal and oil, which contain sulfur, are burned. Power plants, refineries, and metal smelters contribute much of the sulfur dioxide emissions to the air. Vehicles and gas station spillage make up most of the human-made emissions of volatile organic compounds. VOCs are also found in many household products.

Particulate matter can also pollute the air and is usually divided into fine and coarse particles. Fine particles enter the air from fuel burned by vehicles and coal-burning power plants. Sources of coarse particles are cement plants, mining operations, incinerators, wood-burning fireplaces, fields, and roads.

The History of Air Pollution

Air pollution is not a new phenomenon. Whenever something burns, pollutants enter the air. Two thousand years ago, Seneca, a Roman philosopher and writer, complained about the foul air in Rome. In 1273, England's King Edward I ordered that burning a particularly dirty kind of coal called sea-coal was illegal. One man was even hanged for disobeying this medieval "clean air act."

The world air-quality problem is much worse today because modern industrial societies burn large amounts of fossil fuels. As shown in **Figure 2**, most air pollution comes from motor vehicles and industry.

Motor Vehicle Emissions

Almost one-third of our air pollution comes from gasoline burned by vehicles. According to the U.S. Department of Transportation, Americans drove their vehicles over 2.6 trillion miles in 1998. Over 90 percent of that mileage was driven by passenger vehicles. The rest was driven by trucks and buses.

Controlling Vehicle Emissions

The Clean Air Act, passed in 1970 and strengthened in 1990, gives the Environmental Protection Agency (EPA) the authority to regulate vehicle emissions in the United States. The EPA required the gradual elimination of lead in gasoline, and as a result, lead pollution has been reduced by more than 90 percent in the United States. In addition, catalytic converters, which are required in automobiles, clean exhaust gases of pollutants before the pollutants are able to exit the tailpipe. The EPA estimates that cars and trucks today burn fuel 35 percent more efficiently and with 95 percent fewer emissions of pollutants, excluding carbon dioxide, than they did 30 years ago.

Geofact

Sea-Coal In 12th-century London, wood was becoming too scarce and too expensive to use as a fuel source. Large deposits of coal called *sea-coal* that are found off the northeast coast of England provided a plentiful alternative. However, this soft coal did not burn efficiently. The sea-coal produced mostly smoke and not much heat. The smoke from the coal emanated from London homes and factories and combined with fog to produce smog.

Connection to **Law**

Off with His Head! Around 1300 CE, King Edward II of England forbade the burning of coal while Parliament was in session. "Be it known to all within the sound of my voice," King Edward II said, "whosoever shall be found burning coal shall suffer the loss of his head."

Figure 2 ▶ The refinery shown in this photograph is a source of volatile organic compounds. The tanker truck in the foreground is emitting nitrous oxide into the atmosphere.

California Zero-Emission Vehicle Program

A catalytic converter, as shown in **Figure 3**, is a device that is used to control emissions from most American vehicles. In California, motor vehicles account for more than half of the ozone and particulate matter that pollutes the air. To improve air quality, the state's Air Resources Board established the Zero-Emission Vehicle (ZEV) program in 1990 to encourage the development of less-polluting vehicles. ZEV programs have also been adopted in Maine, Massachusetts, New York, and Vermont.

Zero-emission vehicles have no tailpipe emissions, no emissions from gasoline, and no emission-control systems, which deteriorate over time. Battery-powered electric vehicles are the only true ZEVs at the moment, but there are two types of partial ZEVs. One type is clean, fuel-efficient hybrid cars, which are powered by both batteries and gasoline engines. Hybrid cars are already in use today and are very popular. The other type is vehicles powered by methanol fuel cells. Many automobile manufacturers have built these vehicles, but they are still in the prototype stage of development.

Figure 3 ▶ The catalyst material in a catalytic converter (top) causes a chemical reaction that changes exhaust emissions to less harmful substances. The bottom illustration shows a car's contribution to air pollution.

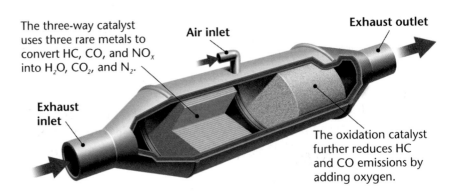

The three-way catalyst uses three rare metals to convert HC, CO, and NO_x into H_2O, CO_2, and N_2.

Air inlet

Exhaust outlet

Exhaust inlet

The oxidation catalyst further reduces HC and CO emissions by adding oxygen.

Interior
▶ Car seats may be covered in plastic that contains a volatile organic compound called *vinyl chloride*.

Body and Frame
▶ Steel smelters send thousands of metric tons of sulfur dioxide into the air each year.

▶ Many auto factories in Mexico, Eastern Europe, and some Asian countries lack pollution-control devices.

Fuel Tank
▶ When filling the car with gasoline, VOCs escape into the atmosphere.

Exhaust
▶ Car exhaust is a major source of nitrogen oxides, carbon monoxide, and hydrocarbons.

▶ In developing countries, car exhaust may contain over a thousand poisonous substances.

▶ Each car on average releases 4.5 metric tons (5 tons) of carbon dioxide every year.

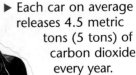

Figure 4 ▶ In 1996, the federal government established standards to reduce emissions of VOC-producing chemicals used in dry cleaning.

Ecofact

Air Pollution's Impact on Birds
Scientists in Finland have documented the effects of harmful emissions from a copper smelter in Finland on two species of birds that live nearby. The two species of birds respond differently to the pollutants containing heavy metals and acidic substances. One species appears to suffer directly from the toxic effects of the pollutants. The other species suffers because the amount of insect food for its nestlings has been reduced. When heavy metal emissions from the smelter decreased, a rapid improvement in breeding success and decrease in the heavy metal found in the bones of nestlings was observed.

Industrial Air Pollution

Many industries, as well as power plants that generate electricity, burn fuel to produce energy. They usually burn fossil fuels. Burning fossil fuels releases sulfur dioxide and nitrogen oxides into the air. Power plants that produce electricity emit at least two-thirds of all sulfur dioxide and more than one-third of all nitrogen oxides that pollute the air.

Some industries, such as the drying cleaning industry shown in **Figure 4,** also produce VOCs. VOCs are chemical compounds that form toxic fumes. Oil refineries, chemical manufacturing plants, furniture refinishers, and automobile repair shops also contribute to the VOCs in the air.

Regulating Air Pollution From Industry The Clean Air Act requires many industries to use scrubbers or other pollution-control devices. Scrubbers remove some of the more harmful substances that would otherwise pollute the air. A *scrubber,* as shown in **Figure 5,** is a machine that moves gases through a spray of water that dissolves many pollutants.

Electrostatic precipitators are machines used in cement factories and coal-burning power plants to remove dust particles from smoke-stacks. In an electrostatic precipitator, gas containing dust particles is blown through a charged chamber. An electrical charge is transferred to the dust particles, which causes them to stick to one another and the sides of the chamber. The clean gas is released from the chamber, and the concentrated dust particles can then be collected and removed. Electrostatic precipitators remove 22 million metric tons (20 million tons) of ash generated by coal-burning power plants from the air each year in the United States.

✓ **Reading Check** Name two pollution-control devices. State how they help to limit the amount of pollutants in air.

Figure 5 ▶ Scrubbers work by spraying gases with water, which removes many pollutants.

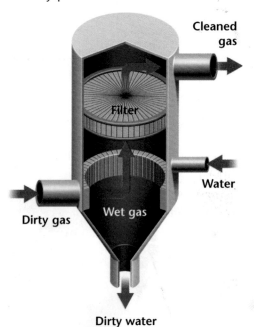

Cleaned gas

Filter

Water

Dirty gas

Wet gas

Dirty water

Figure 6 ▶ The diagram below shows how smog is formed. Large cities with dry, sunny climates and millions of automobiles often suffer from smog.

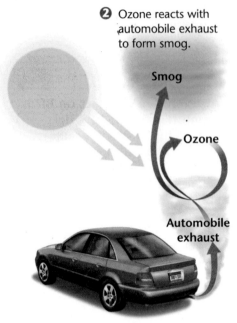

❷ Ozone reacts with automobile exhaust to form smog.

Smog

Ozone

Automobile exhaust

❶ In sunlight, automobile exhaust reacts with air to form ozone.

Figure 7 ▶ Normal air circulation is shown at left, whereas a temperature inversion, in which pollutants are trapped near the Earth's surface, is shown at right.

Smog When air pollution hangs over urban areas and reduces visibility, it is called **smog.** As you can see in **Figure 6,** smog results from chemical reactions that involve sunlight, air, automobile exhaust, and ozone. Pollutants released by vehicles and industries are the main causes of smog.

Temperature Inversions The circulation of air in the atmosphere usually keeps air pollution from reaching dangerous levels. During the day, the sun heats the surface of the Earth and the air near the Earth. The warm air rises through the cooler air above and carries pollutants away from the ground and into the atmosphere.

Sometimes, however, pollution is trapped near the Earth's surface. Usually, air temperatures decrease with altitude, but sometimes a **temperature inversion** occurs when the air above is warmer than the air below. **Figure 7** shows how a temperature inversion traps pollutants near the Earth's surface. The warmer air above keeps the cooler air at the surface from moving upward. So, pollutants are trapped below with the cooler air. If a city is located in a valley, the city has a greater chance of experiencing temperature inversions. Los Angeles, which is surrounded on three sides by mountains, often has temperature inversions that trap smog in the city.

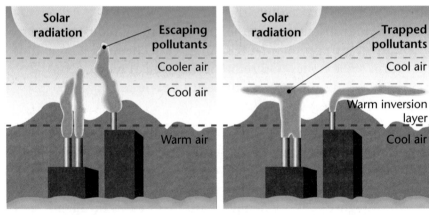

Normal situation

Solar radiation
Escaping pollutants
Cooler air
Cool air
Warm air

Temperature inversion

Solar radiation
Trapped pollutants
Cool air
Warm inversion layer
Cool air

SECTION 1 **Review**

1. **Name** five primary air pollutants, and give important sources for each.

2. **Name** the two major sources of air pollution in urban areas.

3. **Describe** the way in which smog forms.

4. **Define** the term *temperature inversion*. Explain how temperature inversion traps pollutants near Earth's surface.

CRITICAL THINKING

5. **Making Decisions** Read the passage on the California Zero-Emission Vehicle Program. Should automobile makers be made to adhere to quotas of zero-emission vehicles set by states, even if the quota causes automakers to lose revenue? `READING SKILLS`

6. **Analyzing Relationships** Can you think of any other possible type of pollution-control device that could be used to remove particulates from smokestacks in a manner similar to an electrostatic precipitator?

Air, Noise, and Light Pollution

People who are very young or very old and people who have heart or lung problems are most affected by air pollutants. Decades of research have linked air pollution to disease. But because pollution adds to the effects of existing diseases, no death certificates list the cause of death as air pollution. Instead, diseases such as emphysema, heart disease, and lung cancer are cited as causes of death. The American Lung Association has estimated that Americans pay tens of billions of dollars a year in health costs to treat respiratory diseases caused by air pollution.

Short-Term Effects of Air Pollution on Health

Many of the effects of air pollution on people's health are short-term and are reversible if their exposure to air pollution decreases. The short-term effects of air pollution on people's health include headache; nausea; irritation to the eyes, nose, and throat; tightness in the chest; coughing; and upper respiratory infections, such as bronchitis and pneumonia. Pollution can also make the condition of individuals who suffer from asthma and emphysema worse.

Long-Term Health Effects of Air Pollution

Long-term effects on health that have been linked to air pollution include emphysema, lung cancer, and heart disease. Long-term exposure to air pollution may worsen medical conditions suffered by older people and may damage the lungs of children.

Objectives

▶ Describe three short-term effects and three long-term effects of air pollution on human health.

▶ Explain what causes indoor air pollution and how it can be prevented.

▶ Describe three human health problems caused by noise pollution.

▶ Describe solutions to energy waste caused by light pollution.

Key Terms

sick-building syndrome
asbestos
decibel (dB)

www.scilinks.org
Topic: Respiratory Disorders
Code: HE81306

Figure 8 ▶ This police officer wears a smog mask as he directs traffic in Bangkok, Thailand.

Formaldehyde Formaldehyde is a colorless gas that has a strong odor. It is a very common industrial and commercial chemical that is used to make building materials and household products. In the home, significant amounts of formaldehyde are found in adhesives in plywood, particle board, furniture, and carpet. Other sources of formaldehyde may be foam insulation, gas stoves, tobacco smoke, and dry-cleaned clothing. The health effects of formaldehyde may include eye irritation, burning sensations in the throat, nausea, and difficulty breathing.

Indoor Air Pollution

The quality of air inside a home or a building is sometimes worse than the quality of the air outside. Chemicals that are used to make carpets, building materials, paints, and furniture are major sources of pollutants in buildings. **Figure 9** shows examples of some indoor air pollutants.

Buildings that have very poor air quality have a condition called **sick-building syndrome.** Sick-building syndrome is most common in hot places where buildings are tightly sealed to keep out the heat. In Florida, for example, a new, tightly sealed county courthouse had to be abandoned. Half of the people who worked there developed allergic reactions to fungi that were growing in the air-conditioning ducts, ceiling tiles, carpets, and furniture.

Identifying and removing the sources of indoor air pollution is the most effective way to maintain good indoor air quality. Ventilation, or mixing outdoor air with indoor air, is also necessary for good air quality. Activities such as renovation and painting, which cause indoor air pollution, require good ventilation.

✔ **Reading Check** Why is sick-building syndrome most common in hot places?

CASE STUDY

The Health Effects of Ground-Level Ozone

You have learned that the ozone layer in the stratosphere shields the Earth from the harmful effects of ultraviolet radiation from the sun. At the surface of the Earth, however, ozone is a human-made air pollutant that at certain concentrations damages human health.

Ozone forms from the reaction of volatile organic compounds (VOCs) and nitrogen oxides (NO_x) in the presence of heat and sunlight. High concentrations of ozone form in the atmosphere on sunny days that have high temperatures. The sources of VOCs and NO_x emissions are largely motor vehicles, power plants, gasoline vapors, and chemical solvents. Most ozone pollution forms in urban and suburban areas. However, ozone-

▶ Children who engage in vigorous outdoor activities where pollutant concentrations are often high may have a greater risk of developing asthma or other respiratory illnesses.

producing chemicals may be transported hundreds of kilometers from their source.

As ozone concentrations in the atmosphere increase, greater numbers of people may experience harmful health effects of ozone on the lungs. Some of the short-term effects of ozone on health include irritation of the respiratory system, a reduction in lung function, the aggravation of asthma, and inflammation to the lining of the lungs. Scientists believe that ozone may

have other damaging effects on human health. Lung diseases such as bronchitis and emphysema may be aggravated by ozone. Scientists

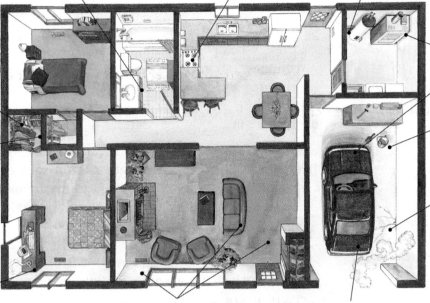

Bleach, sodium hydroxide, and hydrochloric acid from household cleaners

Nitrogen oxides from unvented gas stove, wood stove, or kerosene heater

Fungi and bacteria from dirty heating and air conditioning ducts

Carbon monoxide from faulty furnace and car left running

Tetrachloro-ethylene from dry-cleaning fluid

Paradichloro-benzene from moth-ball crystals and air fresheners

Methylene chloride from paint strippers and thinners

Radon-222 from uranium-containing rocks under the house

Tobacco smoke from cigarettes and pipes

Formaldehyde from furniture, carpeting, particleboard, and foam insulation

Gasoline from car and lawn mower

Figure 9 ▶ Some indoor air pollutants and their sources are shown here.

▶ A therapist performs a lung-function test on a patient by using a machine that measures various aspects of lung function.

EARTH SCIENCE CONNECTION

Those who are most at risk from ozone include children, adults who exercise or work outdoors, older people, and people who suffer from respiratory diseases. In addition, there are some healthy individuals who have unusually high susceptibility to ozone.

CRITICAL THINKING

1. Making Decisions Write a brief paragraph explaining whether or not lung-function tests should be mandatory for children who live in urban areas where high concentrations of ozone are frequent. **WRITING SKILLS**

2. Making Decisions If lung-function tests become mandatory, who will pay for these tests, and who will provide the equipment? Would these tests be performed at school, in a doctor's office, or at a hospital?

believe that permanent lung injury may result from repeated short-term exposure to ozone pollution. Children who are regularly exposed to high concentrations of ozone may have reduced lung function as adults. Exposure to ozone may also accelerate the natural decline in lung function that is part of the aging process.

Radon Gas Radon is a colorless, tasteless, odorless gas. It is also radioactive. *Radon* is one of the elements produced by the decay of uranium, a radioactive element that occurs naturally in the Earth's crust. Radon can seep through cracks and holes in foundations into homes, offices, and schools, where it adheres to dust particles. When people inhale the dust, radon enters their lungs. In the lungs, radon can destroy the genetic material in cells that line the air passages. Such damage can lead to cancer, especially among people who smoke. Radon is the second-leading cause of lung cancer in the United States.

Asbestos Several minerals that form in long, thin fibers and that are valued for their strength and resistance to heat are called **asbestos.** Asbestos is primarily used as an insulator and as a fire retardant, and it was used extensively in building materials. The U.S. government banned the use of most asbestos products in the early 1970s. Exposure to asbestos in the air is dangerous. Asbestos fibers that are inhaled can cut and scar the lungs, which causes the disease asbestosis. Victims of the disease have more and more difficulty breathing and may eventually die of heart failure. Schools in the United States have taken this threat seriously. Billions of dollars have been spent to remove asbestos from school buildings. **Figure 10** shows asbestos fibers and asbestos removal from a building.

Figure 10 ▶
Asbestos (right) forms in long, thin fibers. The worker above is removing debris from a structure that was built with asbestos.

Table 2 ▼

Intensity of Common Noises	
Noise	**Intensity (dB)**
Rocket engine	180
Jet engine	140
Rock concert	120
Car horn	110
Chainsaw	100
Portable CD player	90–120
Lawnmower	90
Conversation	60
Whisper	30
Faintest sound heard by the human ear	0

Noise Pollution

Unwanted sound is noise pollution, and it is one of the prices we pay for modern living. It is irritating, and it damages our hearing by destroying cells in our ears. Hearing loss has doubled in the United States in the last 30 years. About 12 percent of teens have permanent hearing loss, likely due to the prevalence of portable listening devices. One study found that people living in a quiet environment in Africa had better hearing at the age of 80 than most Americans do at 30.

The intensity of sound is measured in units called **decibels** (dB). **Table 2** shows the intensity of some common noises. For each 10-fold increase in decibel intensity, the decibel level is 10 times higher than the previous level. For example, 20 dB is 10 times the intensity of 10 dB. A sound of 120 dB is at the threshold of pain. Noise pollution can be controlled by devices such as mufflers on vehicles and lawn mowers, and by insulation. In Europe, MP3 players must produce no more than 100 dB of noise. According to the National Institutes of Health, the safe threshold for personal listening devices is 85 dB for 8 hours. Personal listening devices are not regulated in the United States.

Light Pollution

Unlike air or water pollution, light pollution does not present a direct hazard to human health. However, light pollution does negatively affect our environment. Light pollution in urban areas diminishes our view of the night sky, as shown in **Figure 11.**

A more important environmental concern of lighting is energy waste. For example, energy is wasted when light is directed upward into the night sky and lost to space. Examples of light pollution are billboards and other signs that are lit from below, the lighting of building exteriors, and poor-quality street lights. One solution to energy waste includes shielding light so it is directed downward. Using time controls so that light is used only when needed and using low-pressure sodium sources—the most energy-efficient source of light—where possible are two other solutions.

✔ **Reading Check** What are three sources of light pollution in a city?

Figure 11 ▶ This view of Seattle shows how lighting in urban areas can cause skyglow, which is an effect of light that can dramatically reduce our view of the night sky.

FIELD ACTIVITY

Light Pollution At night, in your neighborhood or from your front porch, note any efficient or inefficient uses of light that you see, and write down your observations in your *EcoLog.*

SECTION 2 Review

1. **Describe** the long-term effects and the short-term effects of air pollution on health.

2. **Describe** two ways in which indoor air pollution can be prevented.

3. **Describe** some of the human health problems caused by noise pollution.

4. **Describe** several solutions to the energy waste associated with light pollution.

CRITICAL THINKING

5. **Making Comparisons** Read the descriptions of noise and light pollution in this section. Explain ways in which noise pollution and light pollution are similar and ways they are different. **READING SKILLS**

6. **Analyzing Relationships** Molds can grow in new, tightly sealed buildings where the humidity is high and the ventilation is poor. Explain how you would control the growth of mold in this type of environment.

Acid Precipitation

 SEV.5.e

EARTH SCIENCE CONNECTION

Objectives

▶ Explain the causes of acid precipitation.

▶ Explain how acid precipitation affects plants, soils, and aquatic ecosystems.

▶ Describe three ways that acid precipitation affects humans.

▶ Describe ways that countries are working together to solve the problem of acid precipitation.

Key Terms

acid precipitation
pH
acid shock

Imagine that you are hiking through the forests of the Adirondack Mountains in New York. You come to a lake and sit down to rest. You are amazed at how clear the water is; it is so clear that you can see the bottom of the lake. But after a few minutes you feel uneasy. Something is wrong. What is it? Suddenly, you realize that the lake has no fish.

What Causes Acid Precipitation?

This lake and thousands of lakes throughout the world are victims of acid precipitation, which is also known as acid rain. **Acid precipitation** is precipitation such as rain, sleet, or snow that contains a high concentration of acids. When fossil fuels are burned, they release oxides of sulfur and nitrogen. When the oxides combine with water in the atmosphere, they form sulfuric acid and nitric acid, which fall as acid precipitation. This acidic water flows over and through the ground, and into lakes, rivers, and streams. Acid precipitation can kill living things, and can result in the decline or loss of some local animal and plant populations.

A **pH** (power of hydrogen) number is a measure of how acidic or basic a substance is. A pH scale is shown in **Figure 12.** As you can see from the scale, the lower the pH number is, the more acidic a substance is; the higher a pH number is, the more basic a substance is. Each whole number on the pH scale indicates a tenfold change in acidity.

Figure 12 ▶ The pH scale measures how basic or how acidic a substance is. Below are the pH measurements of some common substances.

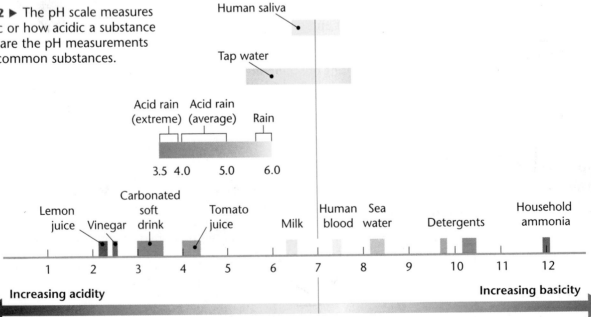

Pure water has a pH of 7.0. Normal precipitation is slightly acidic, because atmospheric carbon dioxide dissolves into the precipitation and forms carbonic acid. Normal precipitation has a pH of about 5.6. Acid precipitation has a pH of less than 5.0. **Figure 13** shows how acid precipitation forms.

The pH of precipitation varies between different geographic areas. For example, Eastern Europe and parts of Scandinavia have precipitation with a pH of 4.3 to 4.5, whereas the remainder of Europe has precipitation with pH values of 4.5 to 5.1. The pH of precipitation in the eastern United States and Canada ranges from 4.2 to 4.8. The most acidic precipitation in North America occurs around Lake Erie and Lake Ontario. It has a pH of 4.2.

How Acid Precipitation Affects Soils and Plants

Acid precipitation can cause a drop in the pH of soil and water. This increase in the concentration of acid is called *acidification*. Acidification changes the balance of a soil's chemistry in several ways. When the acidity of soil increases, some nutrients are dissolved and washed away by rainwater. Increased acidity causes aluminum and other toxic metals to be released and possibly absorbed by the roots of plants. Aluminum also causes root damage. Sulfur dioxide dissolved in water vapor clogs the openings on the surfaces of plants. **Figure 14** shows the harmful effects of acid precipitation on trees.

Reading Check How does the pH of pure water compare with that of acid precipitation?

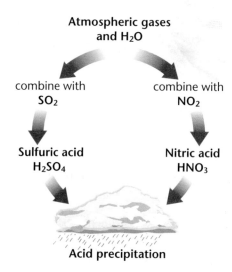

Figure 13 ▶ Sulfur oxides and nitrogen oxides combine with water in the atmosphere to form sulfuric and nitric acids. Rainfall that contains these acids is called *acid precipitation*.

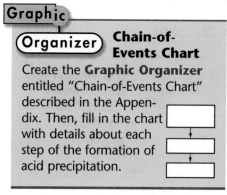

Graphic Organizer Chain-of-Events Chart
Create the **Graphic Organizer** entitled "Chain-of-Events Chart" described in the Appendix. Then, fill in the chart with details about each step of the formation of acid precipitation.

Figure 14 ▶ The trees in this forest in Poland show the dramatic effect that acid precipitation can have on plants.

Acid Precipitation and Aquatic Ecosystems

Aquatic animals are adapted to live in an environment with a particular pH range. If acid precipitation falls on a lake and changes the water's pH, acid can kill fish and other aquatic animals. The change in pH is not the only thing that kills fish. Acid precipitation causes aluminum to leach out of the soil surrounding a lake. The aluminum accumulates in the gills of fish and interferes with oxygen and salt exchange. As a result, fish are slowly suffocated.

The effects of acid precipitation are worst in the spring, when acidic snow that accumulated in the winter melts and rushes into lakes and other bodies of water. This sudden influx of acidic water that causes a rapid change in the water's pH is called **acid shock.** This phenomenon may kill large numbers of fish, as shown in **Figure 15.** Acid shock also affects the reproduction of fish and amphibians. They produce fewer eggs, and these eggs often do not hatch. The offspring that do survive often have birth defects and cannot reproduce.

Acid Precipitation and Humans

Acid precipitation can affect humans in a variety of ways. Toxic metals such as aluminum and mercury can be released into the environment when soil acidity increases. These toxic metals can find their way into crops, water, and fish. The toxins then poison the human body.

Acid precipitation can lead to other human health problems. Research has indicated that there may be a correlation between large amounts of acid precipitation received by a community and an increase in respiratory problems in the community's children.

The standard of living of some people is affected by acid precipitation. Decreases in numbers of fish caused by the acidification of lakes and streams can influence the livelihood of commercial fishers and people involved in the sport-fishing industry. Forestry is also affected when trees are damaged by acid precipitation.

Acid precipitation can dissolve the calcium carbonate in common building materials, such as concrete, marble, and limestone. Some of the world's most important monuments are being dissolved by acid precipitation. These monuments include the Acropolis in Greece, the Taj Mahal in India, ancient temples and pyramids in Egypt and in the rain forests of Central America, and the Lincoln Memorial in Washington, DC.

International Conflict and Cooperation

One problem in controlling acid precipitation is that pollutants may be released in one area and fall to the ground hundreds of kilometers away. For example, almost half of the acid precipitation that falls in southeastern Canada results from pollution produced in the northeastern United States. **Figure 16** shows areas of

Figure 15 ▶ Acid shock can cause the death of many fish.

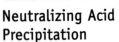

Neutralizing Acid Precipitation

Procedure
1. Pour 1/2 Tbsp of **vinegar** into one cup of **distilled water,** and stir the mixture well. Check the pH of the mixture by using **pH paper.** The pH should be about 4.
2. Crush one stick of **blackboard chalk** into a powder. Pour the powder into the vinegar and water mixture. Check the pH of the mixture.

Analysis
1. Did the vinegar and water mixture become more or less acidic after the powdered chalk was poured in?

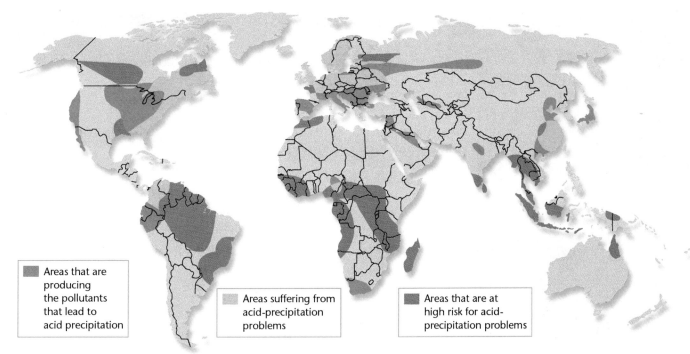

Areas that are producing the pollutants that lead to acid precipitation

Areas suffering from acid-precipitation problems

Areas that are at high risk for acid-precipitation problems

Figure 16 ▶ Acid precipitation is a global problem.

the world that produce pollutants and areas which are then affected by acid precipitation. Acid precipitation is an international problem. In the spirit of cooperation, Canada and the United States signed the Canada–U.S. Air Quality Agreement in 1991. Both countries agreed to reduce emissions that flow across the Canada–U.S. boundary.

As a result of this agreement, sulfur dioxide emissions in the United States and Canada have been reduced dramatically since the 1970s. In Europe, similar agreements have reduced sulfur dioxide emissions by about 40 percent since 1980, although reductions in emissions of nitrogen oxides have been offset by vehicle exhaust from increased road traffic. Meanwhile, China still burns large amounts of high-sulfur coal without pollution controls. The polluted air that results produces acid precipitation in other parts of Asia that are far from the coal-burning plants in China.

www.scilinks.org
Topic: Acid Rain
Code: HE80008

✓ **Reading Check** How can pollutants from the United States cause acid precipitation in Canada?

SECTION 3 **Review**

1. **Explain** how acid precipitation forms.

2. **Describe** the harmful effects that acid precipitation can have on plants, soils, and aquatic ecosystems.

3. **Describe** three ways in which acid precipitation can affect humans.

4. **Describe** a way in which countries are working together to solve the problem of acid precipitation.

CRITICAL THINKING

5. **Inferring Relationships** In addition to negatively affecting forestry and the fishing industry, how might acid precipitation affect local economies?

6. **Analyzing Viewpoints** Write a short essay in which you discuss whether or not a country that releases significant amounts of pollutants into the air that fall as acid precipitation in another country should be expected to pay some of the costs of cleanup. **WRITING SKILLS**

1 What Causes Air Pollution?

Key Terms

air pollution, 325
primary pollutant, 325
secondary pollutant, 325
smog, 330
temperature inversion, 330

Main Ideas

▶ Primary pollutants are pollutants put directly in the air by human activity.

▶ Secondary pollutants are formed when a primary pollutant comes into contact with other primary pollutants or with naturally occurring substances and a chemical reaction takes place.

▶ Most air pollution comes from vehicles and industry.

▶ Air pollution that hangs over cities and reduces visibility is called *smog*.

▶ Pollution can be trapped near the surface of the Earth by a temperature inversion.

2 Air, Noise, and Light Pollution

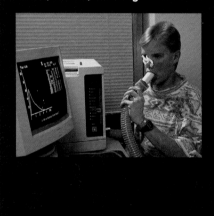

sick-building syndrome, 332
asbestos, 334
decibel (dB), 334

▶ Air pollution may have both long- and short-term effects on human health.

▶ The air indoors may be more polluted than the air outside. Plastics, cleaning chemicals, and building materials are major sources of indoor air pollution.

▶ Noise is a pollutant that affects human health and the quality of life.

▶ Inefficient lighting diminishes our view of the night sky and wastes energy.

3 Acid Precipitation

acid precipitation, 336
pH, 336
acid shock, 338

▶ Acid precipitation is precipitation such as rain, sleet, or snow that contains a high concentration of acids.

▶ Acid shock occurs when a sudden influx of acidic water enters a lake or stream and causes a rapid change in pH that harms aquatic life.

▶ Pollutants released in one geographical area may fall to the ground hundreds of kilometers away as acid precipitation—sometimes in another country.

Using Key Terms

Use each of the following terms in a sentence.

1. *air pollution*
2. *smog*
3. *temperature inversion*
4. *sick-building syndrome*
5. *pH*

For each pair of terms, explain how the meanings of the terms differ.

6. *primary pollutant* and *secondary pollutant*
7. *asbestos* and *radon*
8. *pH* and *acid precipitation*
9. *acidification* and *acid shock*

✔ **STUDY TIP**

Predicting Exam Questions Before you take a test, do you ever attempt to predict what the questions will be? For example, of the 10 multiple-choice questions that appear on this page, how many would you have predicted to be asked in a review of this chapter? Before your next test, predict and answer possible exam questions.

Understanding Key Ideas

10. Which of the following air pollutants is *not* a primary pollutant?
    a. particulate matter
    b. ozone
    c. sulfur dioxide
    d. volatile organic compounds

11. A device used to clean exhaust gases before they exit an automobile's tailpipe is called a(n)
    a. electrostatic precipitator.
    b. catalytic converter.
    c. scrubber.
    d. None of the above

12. The majority of sulfur dioxide produced by industry comes from
    a. oil refineries.
    b. dry cleaners.
    c. chemical plants.
    d. coal-burning power plants.

13. Which of the following substances is *not* involved in the chemical reaction that produces smog?
    a. sunlight
    b. particulate matter
    c. automotive exhaust
    d. ozone

14. Which of the following respiratory diseases is considered a long-term effect of air pollution on human health?
    a. emphysema
    b. bronchitis
    c. pneumonia
    d. all of the above

15. Which of the following substances is a colorless, tasteless, and odorless radioactive gas?
    a. asbestos
    b. carbon monoxide
    c. radon
    d. ozone

16. A sound measuring 40 dB has how many times the intensity of a sound that measures 10 dB?
    a. 4 times
    b. 30 times
    c. 400 times
    d. 1,000 times

17. Which of the following choices is *not* an effective solution to the energy waste related to inefficient lighting?
    a. using low-pressure sodium lighting sources
    b. pointing lights on billboards and street signs upward
    c. placing light sources on time controls
    d. shielding light to direct it downward

18. Which of the following numbers on the pH scale would indicate that a substance is acidic?
    a. 5.0
    b. 7.0
    c. 9.0
    d. none of the above

19. Normal precipitation has a pH of
    a. 7.0.
    b. 5.6.
    c. 5.1.
    d. 4.5.

Short Answer

20. Define the term *zero-emission vehicle*. What types of vehicles qualify as zero-emission vehicles?

21. Identify five indoor air pollutants and examples of sources of each pollutant.

22. Explain the health hazards that radon gas poses for humans.

23. Why does acid precipitation damage monuments such as the Acropolis, the Taj Mahal, and the Lincoln Memorial?

24. Explain why acid precipitation is a source of international conflict and why international cooperation is necessary to resolve the problem.

Interpreting Graphics

The map below shows the pH of precipitation that has been measured at field stations in the northeastern United States. Use the map and legend to answer questions 25–26.

25. Which area(s) of the northeastern United States have the most-acid precipitation?

26. Are the areas that have the highest pH located close to or far from major cities?

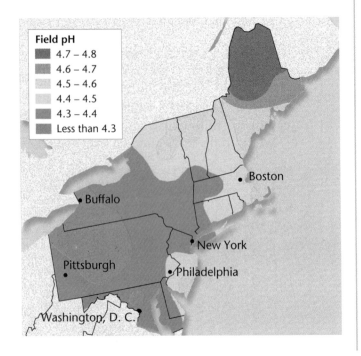

Field pH
- 4.7 – 4.8
- 4.6 – 4.7
- 4.5 – 4.6
- 4.4 – 4.5
- 4.3 – 4.4
- Less than 4.3

Boston
Buffalo
New York
Pittsburgh
Philadelphia
Washington, D. C.

Concept Mapping

27. Use the following terms to create a concept map: *air pollution, primary pollutant, volatile organic compound, scrubber, secondary pollutant, smog,* and *temperature inversion.*

Critical Thinking

28. **Making Decisions** Five states now have zero-emission vehicle programs in place that will help decrease some primary pollutants. What would be the advantages or disadvantages of a federal program that required automobile makers to produce a set number of ZEVs nationwide?

29. **Making Decisions** In some cities, noise-pollution laws, such as restrictions placed on the use of leaf blowers, have been put in place. Do you think the benefits of noise reduction outweigh the costs of enforcing the law?

30. **Inferring Relationships** As you read under the head "International Conflict and Cooperation," about half of the acid precipitation that falls in southeastern Canada is produced by pollutants from the United States. How do the acid pollutants get from their sources to southeastern Canada? **READING SKILLS**

Cross-Disciplinary Connection

31. **Health** Asbestos, lead paint, tobacco, and many other products have been linked to adverse effects on human health. Research one such case that has been brought into the courts. Describe the allegations and the outcome of the trial and write a paragraph that explains whether you agree or disagree with the decision. **WRITING SKILLS**

Portfolio Project

32. **Make a Poster** Create a poster similar to the diagram that appears in Figure 9. This diagram may be of your home, your garage, a portion of your school, or a particular classroom in your school. Use the diagram to identify and label potential sources of indoor air pollutants. Photographs may be used to document these sources.

Use the graph below to answer questions 33 and 34.

33. **Analyzing Data** The graph below shows the change in air-pollution emissions in the United States between 1970 and 1997. Excluding NO_x, which emissions category experienced the greatest decrease over this period of time?

34. **Interpreting Graphics** Why is lead, Pb, shown separately from the other air pollutants?

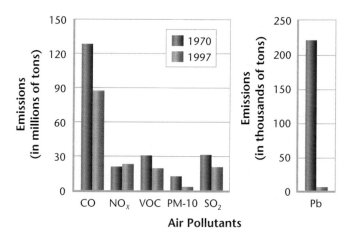

Air Pollutants

35. **Outlining Topics** Outline the major sources of air pollution in the United States. Include information about pollution sources and pollution types.

36. **Writing Persuasively** Write a letter to a legislator that expresses your concern about a particular aspect of air, noise, or light pollution that is important to you.

Read the passage below, and then answer the questions that follow.

Lichens are unique organisms that consist of a fungus and microscopic alga that live together and function as a single organism. The alga is the photosynthetic partner, whereas the fungus absorbs water and minerals and anchors the plant. Lichens form crusts or leafy growths on rocks, trees, and bare ground. Lichens do not have roots. Instead, they absorb the nutrients they need directly from rain. Lichens grow very slowly and can live for centuries. Species of lichens have adapted to almost every environment in the world.

Lichens are sensitive to air pollution, particularly sulfur dioxide. When lichens are exposed to high levels of sulfur dioxide, the sulfur destroys chlorophyll and inhibits photosynthesis. So, lichens are good indicators of air pollution. Lichens usually disappear from areas where sulfur dioxide levels are high. Where the air is free of pollutants, a greater number of lichens will usually be present. In areas where sulfur dioxide pollution is decreasing, lichens will slowly return and colonize the area.

1. Which of the following statements about lichens is true?
   a. Lichens are present when sulfur dioxide levels are high.
   b. Lichens absorb nutrients through their root systems.
   c. Lichens photosynthesize.
   d. Lichens grow only where the climate is moderate.

2. Where would you be most likely to see the greatest number of lichens?
   a. in areas where sulfur dioxide levels are high
   b. in areas where sulfur dioxide levels are low
   c. in areas where sulfur dioxide levels are decreasing
   d. in areas where sulfur dioxide is absent

Understanding Concepts

Directions (1–4): For *each* question, write on a separate sheet of paper the letter of the correct answer.

1 What is the biggest cause of air pollution?
A. dust particles
B. forest fires
C. human activities
D. volcanic eruptions

2 Which of the following releases the most primary pollutants into the air?
F. electric power plants
G. manufacturing plants
H. mining operations
I. transportation industry

3 Which of the following is a long-term health effect of air pollution?
A. blindness
B. diabetes
C. emphysema
D. hepatitis

4 Which of the following statements is true?
F. Ground-level ozone is harmless to children.
G. Noise pollution occurs at low decibel levels.
H. Light pollution is a direct hazard to human health.
I. Sick-building syndrome is caused by poor air quality.

Directions (5–6): For *each* question, write a short response.

5 Plant communities have adapted over long periods of time to the acidity of the soil in which they grow. Acid precipitation can cause a drop in the pH of soil. Analyze the changes to soil that are caused by acidification.

6 Clean air consists mostly of nitrogen and oxygen gas, as well as very small amounts of argon, carbon dioxide, and water vapor. Substances that pollute the air can be in the form of solids, liquids, or gases. Differentiate between primary and secondary air pollutants.

Reading Skills

Directions (7–8): Read the passage below. Then answer the questions.

Power plants that generate our nation's electricity must burn fuel to get the energy they need. They usually burn fossil fuels, but fossil fuels release huge quantities of sulfur dioxide and nitrogen oxide into the air. The Clean Air Act requires many industries to use pollution-control devices, such as scrubbers.

Scrubbers remove some of the more harmful substances that would otherwise pollute the air. A scrubber is a machine that moves gases through a spray of water which dissolves many pollutants. In electrostatic precipitators, gas containing dust particles is blown through a charged chamber. An electrical charge is transferred to the dust particles, which causes them to stick to one another and the sides of the chamber. The clean gas is released from the chamber, and the concentrated dust particles can then be collected and removed.

7 Where would you most likely find an electrostatic precipitator being used?
A. car factory
B. bakery
C. gas station
D. power plant

8 How do pollution-control devices affect acid precipitation?

Directions (9): Read the passage below. Then answer the question.

The Environmental Protection Agency set up an allowance trading system designed to reduce sulfur-dioxide emissions. In this system, one ton of sulfur dioxide emission is equivalent to one allowance. Sulfur dioxide allowances are inexpensive and can be bought from the EPA. There are a limited number of allowances allocated each year.

9 How does a company use the allowance trading system to comply with the Clean Air Act?

Interpreting Graphics

Directions (10–13): For *each* question below, record the correct answer on a separate sheet of paper.

The illustration below shows the formation of acid precipitation in the atmosphere. Use it to answer questions 10 through 12.

Formation of Acid Precipitation

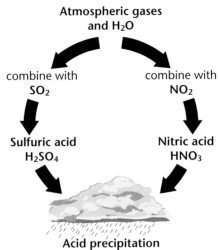

Atmospheric gases
and H_2O

combine with
SO_2

combine with
NO_2

Sulfuric acid
H_2SO_4

Nitric acid
HNO_3

Acid precipitation

10 What is the relationship between sulfur dioxide (SO_2) and sulfuric acid (H_2SO_4)?
  F. Sulfur dioxide combines with oxygen to form nitric acid.
  G. Sulfur dioxide is the main pollutant that forms nitric acid.
  H. Sulfur dioxide is the main pollutant that forms sulfuric acid.
  I. Sulfur dioxide combines with nitrogen dioxide to form ozone.

11 What are the two main polluting components in acid precipitation?
  A. ozone and oxygen atoms   **C.** sulfuric acid and nitric acid
  B. ozone and water   **D.** sulfuric acid and water

12 What is the relationship between nitrogen dioxide (NO_2) and nitric acid (HNO_3)?
  F. Nitrogen dioxide combines with ozone to form oxygen.
  G. Nitrogen dioxide is the main pollutant that forms nitric acid.
  H. Nitrogen dioxide combines with oxygen to form ozone.
  I. There is no relationship between nitrogen dioxide and nitric acid.

13 What is the main cause of acid precipitation?
  A. the ozone hole
  B. oxygen atoms
  C. sulfur atoms
  D. nitrogen dioxide and sulfur dioxide

Test TIP

For questions involving chemical reactions, write out the chemical formulas to better visualize the entire reaction.

Exploration Lab: MODELING

Objectives

▶ **Perform** a chemical reaction that produces sulfur dioxide, a component of acid precipitation.

▶ **USING SCIENTIFIC METHODS**
Hypothesize what the effects of acids that contain sulfur on plants will be.

Materials

beaker, 50 mL
clear plastic bags, large (2)
houseplants of the same type, potted (2)
sodium nitrite (2 g)
sulfuric acid, 1 M (2 mL)
twist tie or tape

▶ **Step 1** Place a plant and a beaker that contains sodium nitrite into a plastic bag. Do not seal the bag.

The Acid Test

Acid precipitation is one of the effects of air pollution. When pollutants that contain nitrogen or sulfur react with water vapor in clouds, dilute acid forms. These acids fall to Earth as acid precipitation.

Often, acid precipitation does not occur in the same place where the pollutants are released. The acid precipitation usually falls some distance downwind—sometimes hundreds of kilometers away. Thus, the sites where pollutants that cause acid precipitation are released may not suffer the effects of acid precipitation.

Coal-burning power plants are one source of air pollution. These power plants release sulfur dioxide into the air. Sulfur dioxide reacts with the water vapor in air to produce acid that contains sulfur. This acid later falls to Earth as acid precipitation.

In this investigation, you will create a chemical reaction that produces sulfur dioxide. The same acids that result from coal-burning power plants will form. You will see the effects of acid precipitation on living things—in this case, plants.

Procedure

1. Place 2 g of sodium nitrite in a beaker. Place a plant and the beaker inside a plastic bag. Do not seal the bag.
   CAUTION: Steps 2–4 should be carried out *only* under a fume hood or outdoors.

2. Carefully add 2 mL of a 1 M solution of sulfuric acid to the beaker. Immediately seal the bag tightly, and secure the bag with a twist tie or tape. CAUTION: Because this reaction produces sulfur dioxide, a toxic gas, the bag should have no leaks. If a leak occurs, move away from the bag until the reaction is complete and the gas has dissipated.

3. Seal the same type of plant in an identical bag that does not contain sodium nitrite or sulfuric acid.

Day	Control Plant	Experimental Plant
1		
2	DO NOT WRITE IN THIS BOOK	
3		

4. After 10 minutes, cut both bags open. Stay at least 5 m from the bags as the sulfur dioxide gas dissipates. Keep the plants and bags under the fume hood.

5. Predict the effects of the experiment on each plant over the next few days. Record your predictions.

6. Observe both plants over the next three days. Record your observations below.

Analysis

1. **Examining Data** How closely did your predictions about the effects of the experiment on each plant match your observations?

2. **Explaining Events** What does this experiment suggest about the effects of acid precipitation on plants?

Conclusions

3. **Drawing Conclusions** In what ways is this a realistic model of acid precipitation?

4. **Drawing Conclusions** In what ways is this experiment *not* a realistic simulation of acid precipitation?

Extension

1. **Analyzing Models** Would you expect to see similar effects occur as rapidly, more rapidly, or less rapidly in the environment? Explain your answer.

2. **Building Models** Acid precipitation is damaging to plants because it clogs the openings on the surfaces of plants and interferes with photosynthesis. What kind of a safe model would demonstrate the damaging effects of acid precipitation on plant photosynthesis? Would this model be a realistic simulation of acid precipitation?

LIGHT SOURCES

MAP SKILLS

This map of what the Earth looks like from space at night shows light sources that are human in origin. The map is a composite image made from hundreds of images taken by orbiting satellites. Use the map of light sources on Earth to answer the questions below.

1. **Inferring Relationships** Using the brightness of the light sources on the map as a key, can you estimate the locations of some of the most densely populated areas on Earth? Where are some of these areas?

2. **Inferring Relationships** Some climatic conditions on Earth, such as extreme cold, heat, wetness, or a thin atmosphere, make parts of our planet less

habitable than others. Examples of areas on our planet that do not support large populations include deserts, high mountains, polar regions, and tropical rain forests. From the map, can you identify regions of the Earth where climatic conditions may not be able to support large human populations? What are some of these places?

3. **Finding Locations** Many large cities are seaports that are located along the coastlines of the world's oceans. From the map, can you pick out light sources along coastlines that might indicate the sites of large ports? Identify some of these cities by name.

4. **Inferring Relationships** From the differences in the density of the light sources, can you pick out any international borders?

THE DONORA, PENNSYLVANIA, KILLER SMOG

For the residents of the small Monongahela Valley town of Donora, Pennsylvania, living with the smoke that billowed from the local zinc smelter was an everyday occurrence—until October 26, 1948. On that night, a temperature inversion and an absence of wind began to trap a deadly mixture of sulfur dioxide, carbon monoxide, and metal dust that would hang in the valley air for five days. Over that period of time, 20 residents lost their lives and 7,000 other residents—about half of the town's population—suffered some form of respiratory problems.

The Weekend of the Killer Smog

By Saturday afternoon, October 29, 1948, the yellowish smog had become so thick that spectators in the stands at a local high-school football game could not see the players on the field. Only the whistles of the referees could be heard. By nightfall, driving was unsafe. This proved to be catastrophic because doctors recommended that any residents who suffered from respiratory ailments be evacuated from town. In an attempt to alleviate the suffering of people who were struggling to breathe, several local firemen carried oxygen tanks through the streets to different homes. Because of the low visibility, the firemen had to feel their way along buildings and fences. Because the supply of oxygen was limited, only a few breaths of oxygen could be given to each person. Eleven people died that night. A makeshift morgue was set up in the local community center.

Even as the killer smog choked the valley, the zinc smelter continued production throughout the night. The smelter continued sending more gases and dust into the air over Donora. The smelter was shut down only when the magnitude of the problem became apparent—6:00 A.M. on Sunday, October 30, 1948.

Later that day, a drizzling rain began to fall and washed the pollutants from the sky. By the time the rain fell, 20 people ages 52 to 85, who suffered from respiratory ailments, were dead. Thousands of other people were at home in bed or were filling the corridors and examining rooms of the two area hospitals. People who were less affected by the smog suffered from nausea and vomiting, headaches, and abdominal cramps. Some victims were choking or coughing up blood. The zinc smelter resumed operation on Monday morning, October 31.

The Aftermath

The smog of Donora was one of the United States' most serious environmental disasters. Shortly after the incident, investigations were undertaken by the Pennsylvania Department of Health, the U.S. Public Health Service, and other agencies. This was the first time an organized attempt was made to document the effects of air pollution on health in the United States. The knowledge that air pollution could be linked directly to the deaths of individuals resulted in legislation at the local, regional, state, and federal levels. These laws were set to limit emissions of sulfur dioxide, carbon monoxide, particulate matter, and other pollutants. The greatest legacy of the Donora tragedy was passage of the Clean Air Act of 1970.

▶ This historical photo from the *Pittsburgh Gazette* captures the town of Donora, Pennsylvania, as it is enveloped in smog at noon on Saturday, October 28, 1948.

What Do You Think?

Who do you think should be held responsible for the Donora, Pennsylvania, disaster? Explain your answer. Given what you know about the regulation of industrial pollutants under the Clean Air Act, do you think another incident such as the Donora killer smog could happen in the United States today?

Atmosphere and Climate Change

PRE-READING ACTIVITY

Tri-Fold
Before you read this chapter, create the **FoldNote** entitled "Tri-Fold" described in the Reading and Study Skills section of the Appendix. Write what you know about climate change in the column labeled "Know." Then, write what you want to know in the column labeled "Want." As you read the chapter, write what you learn about climate change in the column labeled "Learn."

The climate on Earth can be very extreme. This satellite image of Hurricane Fran was taken before it struck the coastline of North Carolina in early September 1996.

Climate and Climate Change

 SCSh.2.a; SCSh.2.b; SCSh.3.c; SCSh.4.a;
SCSh.6.a; SCSh.6.d

EARTH SCIENCE CONNECTION

Weather is the state of the atmosphere at a particular place at a particular moment. **Climate** is the long-term prevailing weather conditions at a particular place based upon records taken. To understand the difference between weather and climate, consider Seattle, Washington, and Phoenix, Arizona. These two cities may have the same weather on a particular day. For example, it may be raining, warm, or windy in both places. But their climates are quite different. Seattle's climate is cool and moist, whereas Phoenix's climate is hot and dry.

What Factors Determine Climate?

Climate is determined by a variety of factors. These factors include latitude, atmospheric circulation patterns, oceanic circulation patterns, the local geography of an area, solar activity, and volcanic activity. The most important of these factors is distance from the equator. For example, the two locations shown in **Figure 1** have different climates mostly because they are at different distances from the equator.

Objectives

► Explain the difference between weather and climate.

► Identify four factors that determine climate.

► Explain why different parts of the Earth have different climates.

► Explain what causes the seasons.

Key Terms

climate
latitude
El Niño
La Niña

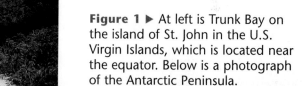

Figure 1 ► At left is Trunk Bay on the island of St. John in the U.S. Virgin Islands, which is located near the equator. Below is a photograph of the Antarctic Peninsula.

Figure 2 ▶ At the equator, sunlight hits the Earth vertically. The sunlight is concentrated on a smaller surface area at the equator. Away from the equator, sunlight hits the Earth at an oblique angle and spreads over a larger surface area.

Latitude

The distance from the equator measured in degrees north or south of the equator is called **latitude.** The equator is located at 0° latitude. The most northerly latitude is the North Pole, at 90° north, whereas the most southerly latitude is the South Pole, at 90° south.

Low Latitudes Latitude influences climate because the amount of solar energy an area of Earth receives depends on its latitude. More solar energy falls on areas that are near the equator than on areas that are closer to the poles, as shown in **Figure 2.** The incoming solar energy is concentrated on a relatively small surface area at the equator.

In regions near the equator, night and day are both about 12 hours long throughout the year. In addition, temperatures are high year-round, and there are no summers or winters.

High Latitudes In regions closer to the poles, the amount of energy arriving at the surface is reduced. In the northern and southern latitudes, sunlight hits the Earth at an oblique angle and spreads over a larger surface area than it does at the equator. Yearly average temperatures near the poles are therefore lower than they are at the equator. The hours of daylight also vary. At 45° north and south latitude, there is as much as 16 hours of daylight each day in summer and as little as 8 hours of sunlight each day in winter. Near the poles, the sun sets for only a few hours each day in summer and rises for only a few hours each day in winter.

✓ Reading Check How is the amount of energy received in northern and southern latitudes different from the amount received at the equator? (See the Appendix for answers to Reading Checks.)

North Pole

Oblique rays

Vertical rays

Vertical rays

Oblique rays

South Pole

Atmospheric Circulation

Three important properties of air illustrate how air circulation affects climate. First, cold air sinks because it is denser than warm air. As cold air sinks, it compresses and warms. Second, warm air rises. It expands and cools at it rises. Third, warm air can hold more water vapor than cold air can. Therefore, when warm air cools, the water vapor it contains may condense into liquid water to form rain, snow, or fog.

Solar energy heats the ground, which warms the air above it. The warm air rises, and cooler air moves in to replace it. This movement of air within the atmosphere is called *wind.* Because the Earth rotates, and because different latitudes receive different amounts of solar energy, the pattern of global atmospheric circulation shown in **Figure 3** results. This circulation pattern determines Earth's precipitation pattern. For example, the intense solar energy striking the Earth's surface at the equator causes the surface as well as the air above the equator to become very warm. The warm air can hold large amounts of water that evaporate from the equatorial oceans and land. As the warm air rises, however, it cools, which reduces some of its ability to hold water. Thus, areas near the equator receive large amounts of rain.

SC*i*LINKS®

www.scilinks.org
Topic: Winds
Code: HE81670

Ecofact

Deserts Air that is warmed at the equator rises and flows northward and southward to 30° north and south latitude, where it sinks. The sinking air is compressed and its temperature increases. As the temperature of the air increases, the air is able to hold a larger quantity of water vapor. Evaporation from the land surface is so great beneath these sinking warm air masses that little water returns to Earth in the form of precipitation. Thus, most of the Earth's deserts lie at 30° north and south latitude.

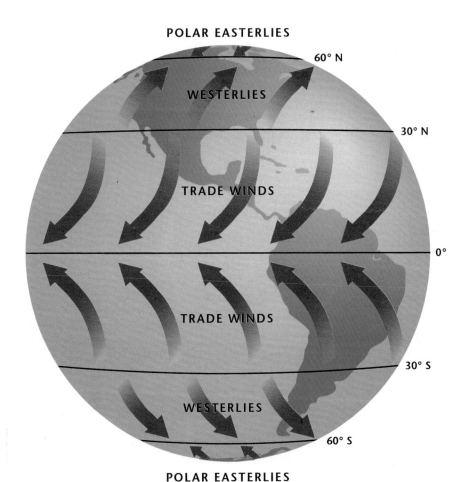

POLAR EASTERLIES

60° N

WESTERLIES

30° N

TRADE WINDS

0°

TRADE WINDS

30° S

WESTERLIES

60° S

POLAR EASTERLIES

Figure 3 ▶ Three belts of prevailing winds occur in each hemisphere.

Investigating Prevailing Winds

Procedure

1. Cut a 20 cm diameter disk out of **cardboard**.

2. Insert a **pencil** through the center of the disk. Place the tip of the eraser on a table so that the cardboard is tilted slightly.

3. Place a few drops of **water** near the center of the cardboard, and spin the cardboard on the pencil tip. What happens?

Analysis

1. How is the motion of the water related to the prevailing winds?

Global Circulation Patterns Cool air normally sinks, but cool air over the equator cannot sink because hot air is rising below the cool air. As a result, the cool air rises and is forced away from the equator toward the North and South Poles. At about 30° north latitude and 30° south latitude, some of this cool air sinks back down to the Earth's surface. The air becomes warmer as it descends. The warm, dry air moves across the surface of the Earth and causes water to evaporate from the land below, which creates dry conditions.

Air descending at 30° north latitude and 30° south latitude either moves toward the equator or toward the poles. Air moving toward the poles warms while it is near Earth's surface. At about 60° north latitude and 60° south latitude, this air collides with cold air traveling from the poles. The warm air rises. When this rising air reaches the top of the troposphere, a small amount of the air returns back to the circulation pattern between 60° and 30° north latitude and 60° and 30° south latitude. However, most of this uplifted air is forced toward the poles. Cold, dry air descends at the poles, which are essentially very cold deserts.

EARTH SCIENCE CONNECTION

CASE STUDY

Ice Cores: Reconstructing Past Climates

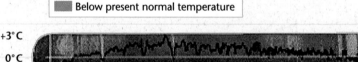

■ Above present normal temperature
■ Below present normal temperature

Source: National Glaciological Program.

▶ With the help of ice cores, scientists are beginning to reconstruct Earth's climate history over hundreds of thousands of years.

Imagine having at your fingertips a record of Earth's climate that extends back several thousand years. Today, ice cores are providing scientists an indirect glimpse of Earth's climate history. These ice cores have been drilled out of ice sheets thousands of meters thick in Canada, Greenland, and Antarctica.

How do scientists reconstruct the climate history of our planet from ice cores? As snow falls to Earth, the snow carries substances that are in the air at the time. If snow falls in a cold climate where it does not melt, the snow turns to ice because of the weight of the snow above it. The substances contained in snow, such as soot, dust, volcanic ash, and chemical compounds, are buried year after

year, one layer on top of another. Air between snowflakes and grains becomes trapped in bubbles when the snow is compacted. These bubbles of air can provide information about the composition of the atmosphere over time.

How do scientists date ice cores? Scientists have learned that differences exist between snow lay-

ers that are deposited in the winter and in the summer. Knowing these differences allows scientists to count and place dates with the annual layers of ice.

Scientists can discover important events in Earth's climate history by studying ice cores. For example, volcanoes produce large quantities of dust, so a history of volcanic

Prevailing Winds Winds that blow predominantly in one direction throughout the year are called *prevailing winds*. Because of the rotation of the Earth, these winds do not blow directly northward or southward. Instead these winds are deflected to the right in the Northern Hemisphere. They are deflected to the left in the Southern Hemisphere.

Belts of prevailing winds blow most of the time in both hemispheres between 30° north and south latitudes and the equator. These belts of wind are called the *trade winds*. The trade winds blow from the northeast in the Northern Hemisphere and from the southeast in the Southern Hemisphere.

Prevailing winds known as the westerlies are produced between 30° and 60° north latitudes and 30° and 60° south latitudes. In the Northern Hemisphere, these westerlies are southwest winds. In the Southern Hemisphere, these westerlies are northwest winds, as shown in **Figure 4**. The polar easterlies blow from the poles to 60° north and south latitudes.

Figure 4 ▶ The red areas indicate fires around Sydney, Australia, at about 32° south. The smoke is blown by the prevailing westerly winds.

▶ Whether scientists work on ice cores in the field or in the laboratory, all ice cores must be handled in such a way that the cores do not become contaminated by atmospheric pollutants.

activity is preserved in ice cores. Most important, a record of concentrations of carbon dioxide, an important greenhouse gas, has been preserved in air bubbles trapped in the ice. Some scientists who study ice cores have come to believe that rapid, global climate change may be more the norm than the exception. Evidence of increases in global temperature of several Celsius degrees over several decades has been discovered in ice cores from thousands of years ago.

CRITICAL THINKING

1. Expressing Viewpoints How might information about past carbon dioxide concentrations on Earth contribute to scientists' understanding of present carbon dioxide concentrations?

2. Applying Ideas What information, besides what is mentioned in this Case Study, might scientists learn about Earth's climatic history from ice cores?

Figure 5 ▶ The El Niño-Southern Oscillation (ENSO) is a periodic change in the location of warm and cold water masses in the Pacific Ocean. The phase of ENSO in which the eastern Pacific surface water is warm is called *El Niño,* and the phase in which it is cool is called *La Niña.*

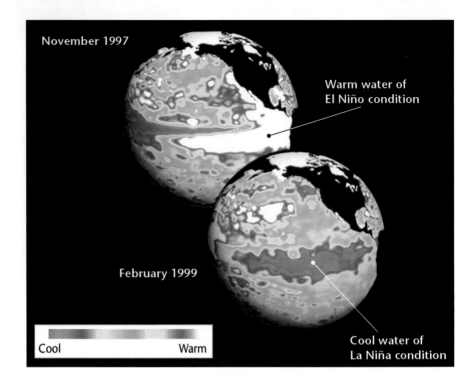

November 1997

Warm water of El Niño condition

February 1999

Cool | Warm

Cool water of La Niña condition

Oceanic Circulation Patterns

Ocean currents have a great effect on climate because water holds large amounts of heat. The movement of surface ocean currents is caused mostly by winds and the rotation of the Earth. These surface currents redistribute warm and cool masses of water around the planet. Some surface currents warm or cool coastal areas year-round.

Surface currents affect the climate in many parts of the world. Here, we will only discuss surface currents that change their pattern of circulation over time.

El Niño—Southern Oscillation **El Niño** (el NEEN yoh) is the name given to the short-term (generally 6- to 18-month), periodic change in the location of warm and cold water masses in the Pacific Ocean. During an El Niño, winds in the western Pacific Ocean, which are usually weak, strengthen and push warm water eastward. Rainfall follows this warm water eastward and produces increased rainfall in the southern half of the United States and in equatorial South America. El Niño causes drought in Indonesia and Australia. During **La Niña** (lah NEEN yah), on the other hand, the water in the eastern Pacific Ocean is cooler than usual. El Niño and La Niña are opposite phases of the *El Niño–Southern Oscillation* (ENSO) cycle. El Niño is the warm phase of the cycle, and La Niña is the cold phase, as illustrated in **Figure 5.**

Pacific Decadal Oscillation The *Pacific Decadal Oscillation* (PDO), shown in **Figure 6,** is a long-term, 20- to 30-year change in the location of warm and cold water masses in the Pacific Ocean. PDO influences the climate in the northern Pacific Ocean and North America. It affects ocean surface temperatures, air temperatures, and precipitation patterns.

Figure 6 ▶ This satellite image shows the cool phase of the Pacific Decadal Oscillation. During the cool phase, cooler water (purple and blue) can be seen in the eastern Pacific Ocean. During the warm phase, the situation is reversed.

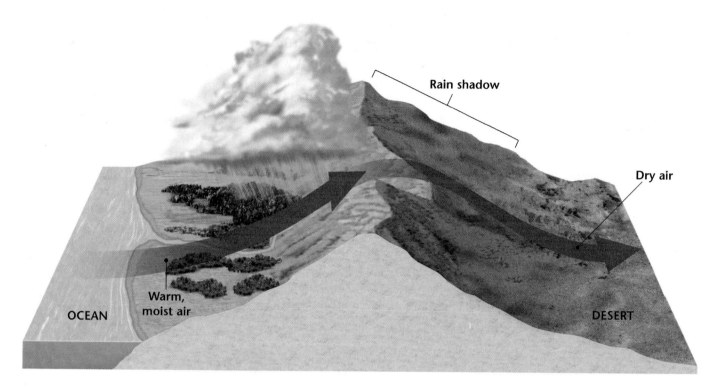

Topography

Mount Kilimanjaro, a 5,896 m extinct volcano in Tanzania, is about 3° south of the equator, but snow covers its peak year-round. Kilimanjaro illustrates the important effect of height above sea level (elevation) on climate. Temperatures fall by about 6°C (about 11°F) for every 1,000 m increase in elevation.

Mountains and mountain ranges also influence the distribution of precipitation. For example, consider the Sierra Nevada mountains of California. Warm air from the Pacific Ocean blows east, hits the mountains, and rises. As the air rises, it cools, which causes it to rain on the western side of the mountains. By the time the air reaches the eastern side of the mountains, it is dry. This effect is known as a rain shadow, as shown in **Figure 7**.

Other Influences on Earth's Climate

Both the sun and volcanic eruptions influence Earth's climate. At a *solar maximum*, shown in **Figure 8**, the sun emits an increased amount of ultraviolet (UV) radiation. UV radiation produces more ozone, warming the stratosphere. The increased radiation can also warm the lower atmosphere and surface of the Earth a little.

In large-scale volcanic eruptions, sulfur dioxide gas can reach the upper atmosphere. The sulfur dioxide gas reacts with smaller amounts of water vapor and dust in the stratosphere. This reaction forms a bright layer of haze that reflects enough sunlight to cause the global temperature to decrease.

✔ Reading Check How do large-scale volcanic eruptions influence Earth's climate?

Figure 7 ▶ Moist ocean air moves up the coastal side of a mountain range. The air cools and releases its moisture as rain or snow. Air then becomes drier as it crosses the range. When the dry air descends on the inland side of the mountains, the air warms and draws up moisture from the surface.

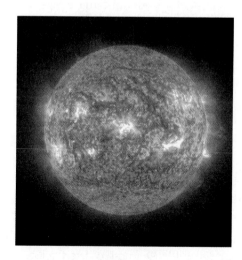

Figure 8 ▶ The sun has an 11-year cycle in which it goes from a maximum of activity to a minimum.

Seasonal Changes in Climate

You know that temperature and precipitation change with the seasons. But do you know what causes the seasons? As shown in **Figure 9**, the seasons result from the tilt of Earth's axis (about 23.5° relative to the plane of its orbit). Because of this tilt, the angle at which the sun's rays strike the Earth changes as the Earth moves around the sun.

During summer in the Northern Hemisphere, the Northern Hemisphere tilts toward the sun and receives direct sunlight. The number of hours of daylight is greatest in the summer. Therefore, the amount of time available for the sun to heat the Earth becomes greater. During summer in the Northern Hemisphere, the Southern Hemisphere tilts away from the sun and receives less direct sunlight. During summer in the Southern Hemisphere, the situation is reversed. The Southern Hemisphere is tilted toward the sun, whereas the Northern Hemisphere is tilted away.

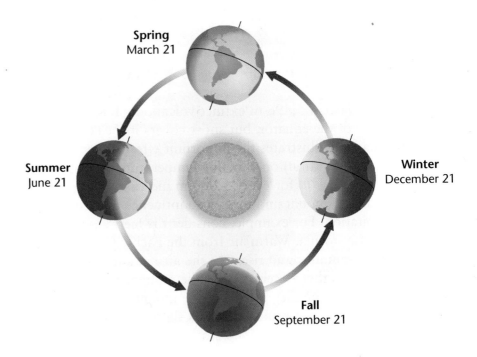

Figure 9 ▶ Because of the Earth's tilt, the angle at which the sun's rays strike the Earth changes as the Earth orbits the sun. This change in angle accounts for seasonal climate differences around the world. The seasons for the Northern Hemisphere are shown here.

SECTION 1 Review

1. **Explain** the difference between weather and climate.

2. **Name** four factors that determine climate.

3. **Explain** why different parts of the Earth have different climates.

4. **Explain** what causes the seasons.

CRITICAL THINKING

5. **Making Comparisons** At the equator, there are no summers or winters, only wet and dry seasons. Based on what you have learned about atmospheric circulation patterns, why do you think there are no seasons? Write a paragraph that explains your answer. **WRITING SKILLS**

6. **Analyzing Processes** If the Earth were not tilted in its orbit, how would the climates and seasons be affected at the equator and between 30° north and south latitudes?

The **ozone layer** is an area in the stratosphere where ozone is highly concentrated. *Ozone* is a molecule made of three oxygen atoms. The ozone layer absorbs most of the ultraviolet (UV) light from the sun. Ultraviolet light is harmful to organisms because it can damage the genetic material in living cells. By shielding the Earth's surface from most of the sun's ultraviolet light, the ozone in the stratosphere acts like a sunscreen for the Earth's inhabitants.

Chemicals That Cause Ozone Depletion

During the 1970s, scientists began to worry that a class of human-made chemicals called **chlorofluorocarbons (CFCs)** might be damaging the ozone layer. For many years CFCs were thought to be miracle chemicals. They are nonpoisonous and nonflammable, and they do not corrode metals. CFCs quickly became popular as coolants in refrigerators and air conditioners. They were also used as a gassy "fizz" for making plastic foams and as a propellant in spray cans of everyday products such as deodorants, insecticides, and paint.

At the Earth's surface, CFCs are chemically stable. So, they do not combine with other chemicals or break down into other substances. But CFC molecules break apart high in the stratosphere, where UV radiation, a powerful energy source, is absorbed. Once CFC molecules break apart, parts of the CFC molecules destroy protective ozone.

Over a period of 10 to 20 years, CFC molecules released at the Earth's surface make their way into the stratosphere. **Figure 10** shows how the CFCs destroy ozone in the stratosphere. Each CFC molecule contains from one to four chlorine atoms, and scientists have estimated that a single chlorine atom from CFC can destroy 100,000 ozone molecules.

Objectives

▶ Explain how the ozone layer shields the Earth from much of the sun's harmful radiation.

▶ Explain how chlorofluorocarbons damage the ozone layer.

▶ Explain the process by which the ozone hole forms.

▶ Describe the damaging effects of ultraviolet radiation.

▶ Explain why the threat to the ozone layer is still continuing today.

Key Terms

ozone layer
chlorofluorocarbons (CFCs)
ozone hole
polar stratospheric clouds

Figure 10 ▶ The CFC molecule in this illustration contains a single chlorine atom. This chlorine atom continues to enter the cycle and repeatedly destroys ozone molecules.

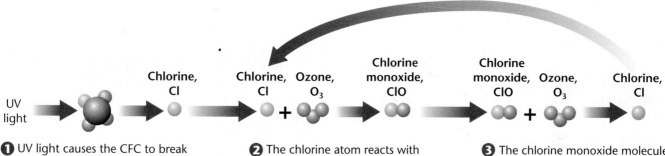

❶ UV light causes the CFC to break down, releasing a chlorine atom.

❷ The chlorine atom reacts with an ozone molecule to create an oxygen molecule and a chlorine monoxide molecule.

❸ The chlorine monoxide molecule then reacts with another ozone molecule, creating two molecules of oxygen and one chlorine atom.

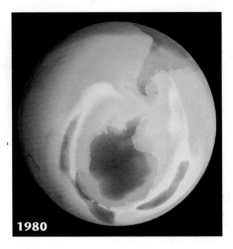

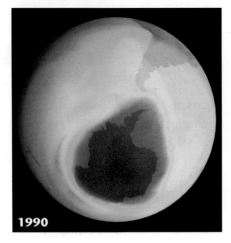

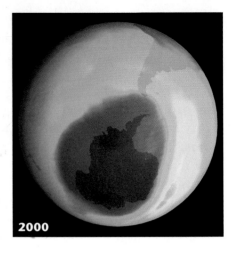

1980

1990

2000

Figure 11 ▶ These satellite images show the growth of the ozone hole, which appears purple, over the past two decades.

Connection to Meteorology

Polar Stratospheric Clouds
Because the stratosphere is extremely dry, clouds normally do not form in this layer of the atmosphere. However, during polar winters, temperatures become low enough to cause condensation and cloud formation. These clouds, which occur at altitudes of about 21,000 m, are known as polar stratospheric clouds, or PSCs. Because of their iridescence, PSCs are called mother-of-pearl or nacreous clouds. Outside of the poles, the stratosphere is too warm for these clouds to form. Because these clouds are required for the breakdown of CFCs, ozone holes are confined to the Antarctic and Arctic regions.

The Ozone Hole

In 1985, an article in the scientific journal *Nature* reported the results of studies by scientists working in Antarctica. The studies revealed that the ozone layer above the South Pole had thinned by 50 to 98 percent. This was the first news of the **ozone hole,** a thinning of stratospheric ozone that occurs over the poles during the spring.

After the results were published, NASA scientists reviewed data that had been sent to Earth by the *Nimbus 7* weather satellite since the satellite's launch in 1978. They were able to see the first signs of ozone thinning in the data from 1979. Although the concentration of ozone fluctuates during the year, the data showed a growing ozone hole, as shown in **Figure 11.** Ozone levels over the Arctic have decreased as well.

How Does the Ozone Hole Form? During the dark polar winter, strong circulating winds over Antarctica, called the *polar vortex,* isolate cold air from surrounding warmer air. The air within the vortex grows extremely cold. When temperatures fall below about −80°C, high-altitude clouds made of water and nitric acid, called **polar stratospheric clouds,** begin to form.

On the surfaces of polar stratospheric clouds, the products of CFCs are converted to molecular chlorine. When sunlight returns to the South Pole in spring, molecular chlorine is split into two chlorine atoms by ultraviolet radiation. The chlorine atoms rapidly destroy ozone. This causes a thin spot, or ozone hole, which lasts for several months. Some scientists estimate that as much as 70 percent of the ozone layer can be destroyed during the spring.

Because ozone is also being produced as air pollution, you may wonder why this ozone does not repair the ozone hole in the stratosphere. The answer is that ozone is very chemically reactive. Ozone produced by pollution breaks down or combines with other substances in the troposphere long before it can reach the stratosphere to replace the ozone that is being destroyed.

✓ Reading Check What evidence showed that a hole had formed in the ozone layer?

Effects of Ozone Thinning on Humans As the amount of ozone in the stratosphere decreases, more ultraviolet light is able to pass through the atmosphere and reach Earth's surface, as shown in **Figure 12.** UV light is dangerous to living things because it damages DNA. DNA is the genetic material that contains the information that determines inherited characteristics. Exposure to UV light makes the body more susceptible to skin cancer, and may cause certain other damaging effects to the human body.

Effects of Ozone Thinning on Animals and Plants High levels of UV light can kill single-celled organisms called *phytoplankton* that live near the surface of the ocean. The loss of phytoplankton could disrupt ocean food chains and reduce fish harvests. In addition, a reduction in the number of phytoplankton would cause an increase in the amount of carbon dioxide (CO_2) in the atmosphere.

Some scientists believe that increased UV light could be especially damaging for amphibians, such as toads and salamanders. Amphibians lay eggs that lack shells in the shallow water of ponds and streams. UV light at natural levels kills many eggs of some species by damaging unprotected DNA. Higher UV levels might kill more eggs and put amphibian populations at risk. Ecologists often use the health of amphibian populations as an indicator of environmental change due to the environmental sensitivity of these creatures.

UV light can damage plants by interfering with photosynthesis. This damage can result in lower crop yields. The damaging effects of UV light are summarized in **Table 1.**

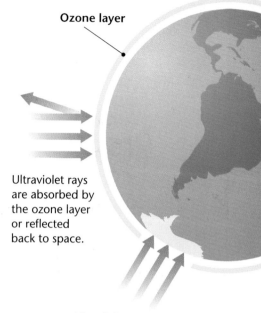

Ozone layer

Ultraviolet rays are absorbed by the ozone layer or reflected back to space.

Ultraviolet rays penetrate to the Earth's surface through the ozone hole.

Figure 12 ▶ Depletion of the ozone layer allows more ultraviolet (UV) radiation to reach the surface of the Earth.

Table 1 ▼

Damaging Effects of UV Light	
Humans	• increased incidence of skin cancer • premature aging of the skin • increased incidence of cataracts • weakened immune response
Amphibians	• death of eggs • genetic mutations among survivors • reduction of populations
Marine Life	• death of phytoplankton in surface water • disruption of food chain • reduction in the number of photosynthesizers
Land Plants	• interference with photosynthesis • reduced crop yields

Protecting the Ozone Layer

In 1987, a group of nations met in Canada and agreed to take action against ozone depletion. Under an agreement called the Montreal Protocol, these nations agreed to sharply limit their production of CFCs. A second conference on the problem was held in Copenhagen, Denmark, in 1992. Developed countries agreed to eliminate most CFCs by 1995. The United States pledged to ban all substances that pose a significant danger to the ozone layer by 2000.

After developed countries banned most uses of CFCs, chemical companies developed CFC replacements. Aerosol cans no longer use CFCs as propellants, and air conditioners are becoming CFC-free. Because many countries were involved and decided to control CFCs, many people consider ozone protection an international environmental success story. **Figure 13** illustrates the decline in world CFC production since the 1987 Montreal Protocol.

The battle to protect the ozone layer is not over. CFC molecules remain active in the stratosphere for 60 to 120 years.

www.scilinks.org
Topic: Ozone Shield
Code: HE81100

Figure 13 ▶ Chlorofluorocarbon production has declined greatly since developed countries agreed to ban CFCs in 1987.

✓ **Reading Check** How did the Montreal Protocol help to protect the ozone layer?

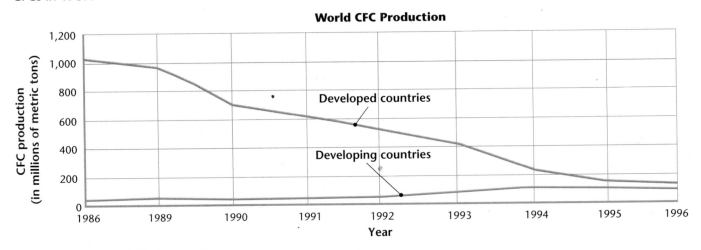

World CFC Production

Source: UN Environment Programme.

SECTION 2 Review

1. **Describe** the process by which chlorofluorocarbons destroy ozone molecules in the stratosphere.

2. **Describe** the process by which the ozone hole forms over Antarctica in spring.

3. **List** five harmful effects that UV radiation could have on plants or animals as a result of ozone thinning.

4. **Explain** why it will take years for the ozone layer to recover, even though the use of CFCs has declined significantly. Write a paragraph that explains your answer. **WRITING SKILLS**

CRITICAL THINKING

5. **Making Decisions** If the ozone layer gets significantly thinner during your lifetime, what changes might you need to make in your lifestyle?

6. **Analyzing Relationships** CFCs were thought to be miracle chemicals when they were first introduced. What kinds of tests could be performed on any future miracle chemical to make sure serious environmental problems do not result from its use?

SECTION 3
Global Warming

Have you ever gotten into a car that has been sitting in the sun for a while with all its windows closed? Even if the day is cool, the air inside the car is much warmer than the air outside. On a hot summer day, opening the door of a car can seem like opening the door of an oven.

The reason heat builds up inside a car is that the sun's energy streams into the car through the clear glass windows in the form of sunlight. The carpets and upholstery in the car absorb the light and change it into heat energy. Heat energy does not pass through glass as easily as light energy does. Sunlight continues to stream into the car through the glass, but heat cannot get out. The heat continues to build up and is trapped inside the car. A greenhouse works the same way. By building a house of glass, gardeners trap the sun's energy and grow delicate plants in the warm air inside the greenhouse even when there is snow on the ground outside.

The Greenhouse Effect

The Earth is similar to a greenhouse. The Earth's atmosphere acts like the glass in a greenhouse. As shown in **Figure 14,** sunlight streams through the atmosphere and heats the Earth. As this heat radiates up from Earth's surface, some of it escapes into space. The rest of the heat is absorbed by gases in the troposphere and warms the air. This process of heat absorption is called the *greenhouse effect.*

Not every gas in our atmosphere absorbs heat in this way. The gases that do absorb and radiate heat are called **greenhouse gases.** The major greenhouse gases are water vapor, carbon dioxide, chlorofluorocarbons, methane, and nitrous oxide. Of these, water vapor and carbon dioxide account for most of the absorption of heat that occurs in the atmosphere.

Objectives

▶ Explain why Earth's atmosphere is like the glass in a greenhouse.

▶ Explain why the carbon dioxide content of the atmosphere is increasing.

▶ Identify one possible explanation for the increase in average global temperature.

▶ Describe what a warmer Earth might be like.

Key Terms

greenhouse gases
global warming
Kyoto Protocol

Figure 14 ▶ **How the Greenhouse Effect Works**

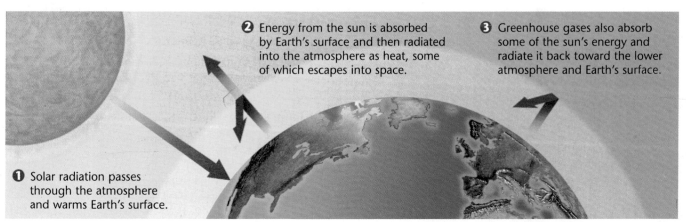

❷ Energy from the sun is absorbed by Earth's surface and then radiated into the atmosphere as heat, some of which escapes into space.

❸ Greenhouse gases also absorb some of the sun's energy and radiate it back toward the lower atmosphere and Earth's surface.

❶ Solar radiation passes through the atmosphere and warms Earth's surface.

Measuring Carbon Dioxide in the Atmosphere In 1958, a geochemist named Charles Keeling installed an instrument at the top of a tall tower on the volcano Mauna Loa in Hawaii. Keeling wanted to measure the amount of CO_2 in the air, far from forests and cities where CO_2 levels vary every day. The winds that blow steadily over Mauna Loa have come thousands of miles across the Pacific Ocean, mixing as they traveled. Keeling reasoned that at Mauna Loa, the average CO_2 levels in the air could be measured for the entire Earth.

Most of the CO_2 that is released into the air dissolves in the ocean or is used by plants for photosynthesis. As a result, the levels of CO_2 in the air vary with the seasons. During the summer, growing plants use more CO_2 for photosynthesis than they release in respiration. This causes CO_2 levels in the air to decrease in the summer. In the winter, dying grasses and fallen leaves decay and release the carbon that was stored in them during the summer. As a result, CO_2 levels naturally rise.

Rising Carbon Dioxide Levels After only a few years of measuring CO_2 levels, it became obvious that they were changing in ways other than just the seasonal fluctuations. **Figure 15** shows that CO_2 levels in the atmosphere have increased by over 20 percent in less than 50 years. This increase is due largely to the CO_2 released into the air when fossil fuels are burned.

The data in Figure 15 provide a record of changes in CO_2 levels since 1958. Levels of CO_2 in the atmosphere thousands of years ago can be determined by analyzing ice cores drilled from ice sheets. These measurements show that CO_2 levels in the atmosphere today are higher than they have been for the last 420,000 years, and probably for the last 20 million years.

Reading Check What are two advantages of setting up instruments for measuring carbon dioxide on top of Mauna Loa?

Figure 15 ▶ The graph shows that the average yearly concentration of carbon dioxide in the atmosphere has increased since 1958.

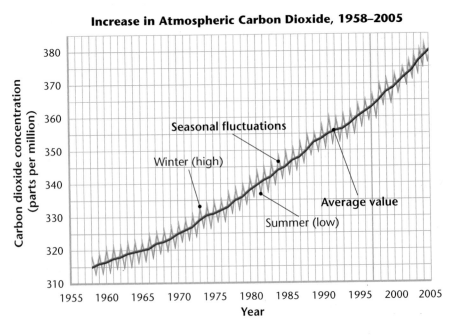

Increase in Atmospheric Carbon Dioxide, 1958–2005

Greenhouse Gases and the Earth's Temperature Many scientists think that because greenhouse gases trap heat near the Earth's surface, more greenhouse gases in the atmosphere will result in an increase in global temperature. A comparison of carbon dioxide in the atmosphere and average global temperatures for the past 400,000 years supports this view.

Today, we are releasing more carbon dioxide than any other greenhouse gas into the atmosphere. Millions of tons of carbon dioxide are released into the atmosphere each year from power plants that burn coal or oil and from cars that burn gasoline. Millions of trees are burned in tropical rain forests to clear the land for farming. Thus, the amount of carbon dioxide in the atmosphere is increasing. We are also releasing other greenhouse gases, such as CFCs, methane, and nitrous oxide, in significant amounts. **Table 2** shows the sources of some major greenhouse gases.

Global Warming

Figure 16 shows that the average temperature at Earth's surface increased during the twentieth century. This increase is known as **global warming.** Because the temperature is rising at a similar rate to the increase in greenhouse gases in the atmosphere, many scientists have hypothesized that the increase in greenhouse gases has caused the increase in temperature. Thousands of experiments and computer models support this hypothesis. The increase in temperature is predicted to continue throughout the 21st century. This does not mean that temperatures are rising at a constant rate, or that they are rising in all parts of the world. It is not possible to rule out natural climatic variability. For example, we know that fluctuations in temperatures on Earth occur naturally over the centuries.

Table 2 ▼

Major Greenhouse Gases and Their Sources
Carbon dioxide, CO_2: burning fossil fuels and deforestation
Chlorofluorocarbons (CFCs): refrigerants, aerosols, foams, propellants, and solvents
Methane, CH_4: animal waste, biomass burning, fossil fuels, landfills, livestock, rice paddies, sewage, and wetlands
Nitrous oxide, N_2O: biomass burning, deforestation, burning of fossil fuels, and microbial activity on fertilizers in the soil
Water vapor, H_2O: evaporation, plant respiration

Figure 16 ▶ This graph shows that the average surface temperature of Earth warmed during the 20th century. For example, the average global surface temperature in the year 2005 was 0.61°C above the 20th-century average temperature.

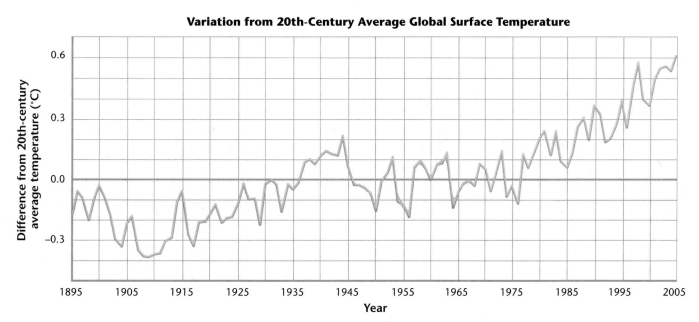

Variation from 20th-Century Average Global Surface Temperature

Source: National Climatic Data Center.

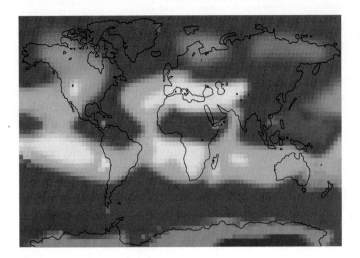

Average rate of heat gain (watts per square meter)

−1 0 1 2 3

Figure 17 ▶ These maps were developed from computer models. The map on the left shows the effect of greenhouse gases on the Earth before sulfur pollution was added. The map on the right shows how the addition of the sulfur pollution variable causes a cooling effect.

Connection to **Biology**

Ocean Warming Commercial fishing in the northern Atlantic Ocean depends heavily on a fish called a *cod*. In recent years, the numbers of cod in the North Atlantic have greatly decreased. In 2001, English scientists embarked on a research project to find out if the decline in the numbers of cod was linked to the changing global climate. They sailed the ocean waters between Greenland and Iceland collecting samples of zooplankton. The scientists found that zooplankton levels have drastically decreased since 1963, the date of the last survey. The scientists believe that slowly warming ocean-water temperatures have in some way affected zooplankton in the North Atlantic Ocean, which has in turn impacted animals such as cod that rely on the zooplankton for food.

Modeling Global Warming Predictions about future changes in climate are based on computer models. Scientists write equations that represent the atmosphere and oceans. Then they enter data about CO_2 levels, prevailing winds, and many other variables. The resulting models can be used to predict how factors such as temperature and sea level will be affected, as shown in **Figure 17.**

Weather forecasters use programs similar to those used by climate scientists. You have probably been rained on when a forecaster predicted dry weather, so you know that the programs and the models they produce are not always accurate. Computer models are becoming more reliable, however, as more data are available and additional variables are included.

The Consequences of a Warmer Earth

In North America, tree swallows, Baltimore orioles, and robins are nesting about 11 days earlier than they did 50 years ago. These are birds that winter in the south and return north to breed in the spring. In Britain, at least 200 species of plants are flowering up to 55 days earlier in the year than they did 40 years ago. There is no evidence that these changes are caused by global warming. Scientists know, however, that the time at which birds nest and the time at which plants flower are both strongly influenced by temperature.

Scientists are not sure how quickly the Earth will warm or how severe the effects will be. Different computer models give different predictions. The possible effects of global warming include a number of potentially serious environmental problems. These problems include changes in weather patterns and rising sea levels. The possible effects of a warmer Earth will not be the same everywhere. For instance, some ecosystems are less sensitive to changes in climate than others are. Countries, too, will vary in their ability to respond to problems caused by changes in climate.

Melting Ice and Rising Sea Levels Ice melts as global temperatures increase, causing the amount of ice near the poles to decrease, as shown in **Figure 18.** The melting of ice and snow from polar landmasses, such as Greenland and Antarctica, causes sea levels around the world to rise. The rise in sea levels could affect coastal areas in several ways. Coastal wetlands and other low-lying areas could be flooded. Enormous numbers of people who live near coastlines could lose their homes and sources of income. Beaches could be extensively eroded. The salinity of bays and estuaries might increase, which could adversely affect marine fisheries. Also, coastal freshwater aquifers could become too salty to be used as sources of fresh water.

Global Weather Patterns If the Earth warms up significantly, the surface of the oceans will absorb more heat, which may make hurricanes and typhoons more common. Some scientists are concerned that global warming will also cause a change in ocean current patterns, such as shutting off the Gulf Stream. Such a change could significantly affect the world's weather. For instance, some regions might have more rainfall than normal, whereas other regions might have less. Severe flooding could occur in some regions at the same time that droughts devastate other regions.

Human Health Problems Warmer average global temperatures pose potential threats to human health. Greater numbers of heat-related deaths could occur. Very young and very old city dwellers are at greatest risk during heat waves. Since trees and flowering plants, such as grasses, would flower earlier and for longer than they do now, people who are allergic to pollen would suffer from allergies for more of the year. As well, warmer temperatures could enable mosquitoes—vectors of diseases such as malaria, dengue fever, and encephalitis—to establish themselves in areas that are too cold for them at the moment.

Figure 18 ▶ This is a satellite map of an 11,000 km² iceberg—the size of Connecticut!—that split off from the Ross Ice Shelf in Antarctica in March of 2000.

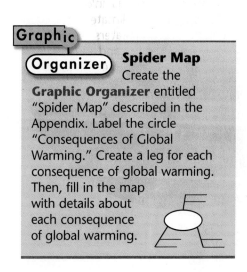

Graphic Organizer **Spider Map** Create the **Graphic Organizer** entitled "Spider Map" described in the Appendix. Label the circle "Consequences of Global Warming." Create a leg for each consequence of global warming. Then, fill in the map with details about each consequence of global warming.

Figure 19 ▶ These corn plants died from a lack of water.

www.scilinks.org
Topic: Global Warming
Code: HE80681

Figure 20 ▶ In spite of its name, the crabeater seal actually feeds on zooplankton. This seal is a resident of Antarctica.

Agriculture Agriculture would be most severely impacted by global warming if extreme weather events, such as droughts, became more frequent. The effects of drought are shown in **Figure 19.** Higher temperatures could result in decreased crop yields. The demand for irrigation could increase, which would further deplete aquifers that have already been overused.

Effects on Plants and Animals Climate change could alter both the range of plant species and the composition of plant communities. Trees could colonize cooler areas. Forests could shrink in the warmer part of their range and lose diversity.

Global warming may cause a shift in the geographical range of some animals. For example, birds in the Northern Hemisphere may not have to migrate as far south for winter. Warming in the surface waters of the ocean might cause a reduction of zooplankton, which many marine animals depend on for food. The crabeater seal, shown in **Figure 20,** would be just one of the animals affected by fewer zooplankton. Warming in tropical waters may kill the algae that nourish corals, thus destroying coral reefs.

Recent Findings

The Intergovernmental Panel on Climate Change (IPCC) is a network of approximately 2,500 of the world's leading climatologists from 70 countries. In 2001, the IPCC issued its Third Assessment Report (TAR). TAR describes what is currently known about the global climate system and provides future estimates about the state of the global climate system. Some of the findings of the IPCC included that the average global surface temperature increased by 0.6°C during the 20th century, that snow cover and ice extent have decreased, and that the average global sea level has risen. The IPCC has also reported that concentrations of atmospheric greenhouse gases have continued to increase as a result of human activities. It has also predicted that human influences will continue to change the composition of the Earth's atmosphere throughout the 21st century.

✔ Reading Check What are two ways that drought could affect agriculture on a warmer Earth?

Reducing the Risk

In 1997, representatives from 160 countries met and set timetables for reducing emissions of greenhouse gases. These timetables will go into effect when a treaty called the *Kyoto Protocol* is ratified by 55 percent of the attending nations. The **Kyoto Protocol** requires developed countries to decrease emissions of carbon dioxide and other greenhouse gases by an average of 5 percent below their 1990 levels by 2012. In March of 2001, the United States decided not to ratify the Kyoto Protocol. Most developed nations are going ahead with the treaty.

The need to slow global warming has been recognized by the global community. Some nations and organizations have engaged in reforestation projects to reduce CO_2, such as the project shown in **Figure 21**. However, the attempt to slow global warming is made difficult by the economic, political, and social factors faced by different countries. Conflict has already arisen between developed and developing countries over future CO_2 emissions, the projections of which are shown in **Figure 22**.

Figure 21 ▶ Because plants take in carbon dioxide during photosynthesis, reforestation projects such as this project in Haiti help to offset a portion of global carbon dioxide emissions.

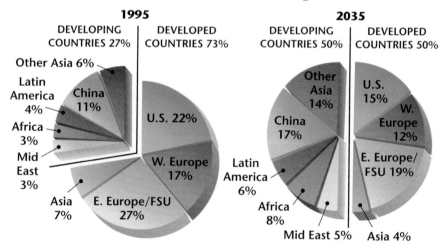

Total World Emissions of CO₂

1995

DEVELOPING COUNTRIES 27% | DEVELOPED COUNTRIES 73%

Other Asia 6%
Latin America 4%
China 11%
Africa 3%
U.S. 22%
Mid East 3%
Asia 7%
E. Europe/FSU 27%
W. Europe 17%

2035

DEVELOPING COUNTRIES 50% | DEVELOPED COUNTRIES 50%

Other Asia 14%
China 17%
U.S. 15%
W. Europe 12%
E. Europe/FSU 19%
Latin America 6%
Africa 8%
Mid East 5%
Asia 4%

Source: U.S. Environmental Protection Agency.

Figure 22 ▶ Developing countries are projected to make up half of all CO_2 emissions by 2035. In 1995, total carbon released as CO_2 was 6.46 billion tons (5.86 billion metric tons). In 2035, total carbon emissions are projected to be 11.71 billion tons (10.62 billion metric tons).

SECTION 3 Review

1. **Explain** why Earth's atmosphere is like the glass in a greenhouse.

2. **Explain** why carbon dioxide in the atmosphere is increasing.

3. **Explain** one theory for why Earth's climate is becoming warmer.

4. **Name** some of the possible consequences of a warmer Earth.

CRITICAL THINKING

5. **Making Predictions** Read the text under the heading "Modeling Global Warming." What difficulties do scientists face when they attempt to construct models that accurately predict the rate of global warming? `READING SKILLS`

6. **Analyzing Relationships** How could environmental problems in developing countries that result from global climate change affect the economies of developed countries, such as the United States?

Highlights

1 Climate and Climate Change

Key Terms

climate, 351
latitude, 352
El Niño, 356
La Niña, 356

Main Ideas

▶ Climate is the long-term prevailing weather conditions at a particular place.

▶ Factors that determine climate include latitude, atmospheric and oceanic circulation patterns, local geography, and solar and volcanic activity. Latitude is the most important determining factor of climate.

▶ The angle at which the sun's rays strike the Earth changes as the Earth moves around the sun. This change in angle is what causes the seasons to change.

2 The Ozone Shield

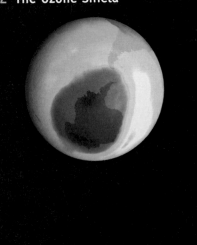

Key Terms

ozone layer, 359
chlorofluorocarbons (CFCs), 359
ozone hole, 360
polar stratospheric clouds, 360

Main Ideas

▶ The ozone layer in Earth's stratosphere absorbs most of the ultraviolet (UV) light from the sun.

▶ Chlorofluorocarbons are human-made chemicals that destroy ozone molecules and damage the ozone layer.

▶ Ozone levels measured over the polar regions have been decreasing over the past several decades.

▶ Thinning of the ozone layer increases the amount of ultraviolet light that reaches Earth's surface.

3 Global Warming

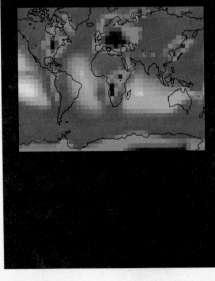

Key Terms

greenhouse gases, 363
global warming, 365
Kyoto Protocol, 369

Main Ideas

▶ Gases that absorb and radiate heat in the atmosphere are called *greenhouse gases*. The important greenhouse gases are water vapor, carbon dioxide, CFCs, methane, and nitrous oxide.

▶ The predicted increase in global temperature that occurs as a result of increasing greenhouse gases in the atmosphere is called *global warming*.

▶ Because climate patterns are complex, scientists use computer models to attempt to predict the rate of global warming.

▶ Global warming could produce a number of potentially serious environmental problems.

▶ In 1997, representatives from 160 countries ratified the Kyoto Protocol, which set timetables for reducing emissions of greenhouse gases.

Using Key Terms

Use each of the following terms in a separate sentence.

1. *latitude*
2. *El Niño*
3. *chlorofluorocarbons*
4. *polar stratospheric clouds*
5. *Kyoto Protocol*

For each pair of terms, explain how the meanings of the terms differ.

6. *weather* and *climate*
7. *El Niño* and *La Niña*
8. *ozone layer* and *ozone hole*
9. *greenhouse gases* and *global warming*

✔ STUDY TIP

Qualifiers When taking a test, locate qualifiers in the sentences. Qualifiers are words that modify or limit the meaning of another word or group of words. *Never, always, all, some, none, greatest,* and *least* are examples of qualifiers.

Understanding Key Ideas

10. The belt of prevailing winds that is produced between 30° and 60° north latitudes and 30° and 60° south latitudes is called the
    a. doldrums.
    b. westerlies.
    c. polar easterlies.
    d. trade winds.

11. Which of the following statements about El Niño is true?
    a. El Niño is the cold phase of the El Niño–Southern Oscillation cycle.
    b. El Niño is a long-term change in the location of warm and cold water masses in the Pacific Ocean.
    c. El Niño produces storms in the northern Pacific Ocean.
    d. El Niño produces winds in the western Pacific Ocean that push warm water eastward.

12. Polar stratospheric clouds convert the products of CFCs into
    a. carbon dioxide.
    b. hydrochloric acid.
    c. nitric acid.
    d. molecular chlorine.

13. Which of the following is *not* an adverse effect of high levels of ultraviolet light?
    a. disruption of photosynthesis
    b. disruption of ocean food chains
    c. premature aging of the skin
    d. increased amount of carbon dioxide in the atmosphere

14. In which season (in the Northern Hemisphere) does carbon dioxide in the atmosphere decrease as a result of natural processes?
    a. fall
    b. winter
    c. summer
    d. spring

15. Which of the following gases is a greenhouse gas?
    a. carbon dioxide
    b. water vapor
    c. methane
    d. all of the above

16. Which of the following substances is *not* a source of methane?
    a. fossil fuels
    b. sewage
    c. fertilizer
    d. rice

17. The average global temperature increased by how many Celsius degrees during the 20th century?
    a. 0.4°C
    b. 0.6°C
    c. 0.8°C
    d. 1.0°C

18. Which of the following countries decided not to ratify the Kyoto Protocol?
    a. Russia
    b. United States
    c. Canada
    d. Finland

Short Answer

19. Name three properties of air that are important for understanding how air circulation affects global climate.

20. Explain how local geography can influence the local pattern of precipitation.

21. Describe the properties chlorofluorocarbons possess that made them seem like miracle chemicals when they were discovered.

22. Explain why stratospheric ozone protection has been considered an environmental success story.

23. Explain the general process scientists use to make computer models of global warming.

24. Describe some of the environmental problems that rising sea level might cause.

25. Describe what is currently known about the state of the climate system as reported in the Third Assessment Report of the Intergovernmental Panel on Climate Change.

Interpreting Graphics

The graph below shows the average monthly temperature of two locations that are at the same latitude but are in different parts of the United States. Use the graph to answer questions 26–27.

26. Which location has the smallest temperature range between summer and winter?

27. What factors could cause the difference in climate between the two locations?

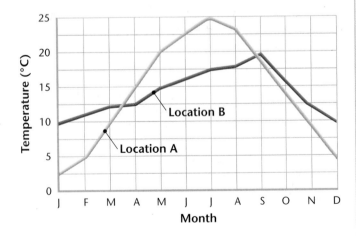

Concept Mapping

28. Use the following terms to create a concept map: *ozone layer, ultraviolet (UV) light, chlorofluorocarbons, polar vortex, polar stratospheric clouds,* and *ozone hole.*

Critical Thinking

29. **Making Predictions** Over a long period of time, how might living things adapt to increased carbon dioxide levels and global warming? Do you think most species will adapt, or are many species likely to go extinct? Write a short essay that explains your answers. **WRITING SKILLS**

30. **Analyzing Relationships** Read about the harmful effects that ultraviolet light can have on humans as a result of ozone thinning under the heading "Effects of Ozone Thinning on Humans." However, ultraviolet light serves an extremely important function that benefits life on Earth. What is this function and how does it help make life on Earth possible? **READING SKILLS**

Cross-Disciplinary Connection

31. **Economics** Insurance companies set some of their rates by estimating the number of destructive natural events, such as hurricanes and floods, that will occur in the next 20 years. Explain why insurance companies would be interested in knowing scientists' predictions about global warming for the next two decades.

Portfolio Project

32. **Designing a Pamphlet** Design a pamphlet that documents the harmful effects of ultraviolet light on living things. Table 1 can be used as a source of information. You might also collect information by checking out the Web sites of the American Cancer Society and the Environmental Protection Agency. Distribute the pamphlet to your classmates, and include it in your portfolio.

MATH SKILLS

33. **Making Calculations** In 1958, the carbon dioxide level measured in Earth's atmosphere was approximately 315 parts per million. In 2000, the carbon dioxide level in the atmosphere had increased to approximately 368 ppm. What was the average annual increase in carbon dioxide in the atmosphere between 1958 and 2000 measured in parts per million?

WRITING SKILLS

34. **Communicating Main Ideas** Imagine that you are a scientist who is studying the effects of chlorofluorocarbons on stratospheric ozone. Follow the path of a chlorine atom from the time it is released into the atmosphere from a CFC source through the time it has destroyed ozone molecules. Summarize your findings in a brief essay.

35. **Writing Persuasively** Imagine you are a scientist who has been studying the subject of global warming. You have been asked by the President of the United States to write a recommendation for his environmental policy on the subject. The President has asked you to provide important facts that can be used to promote the proposed policies. Summarize your recommendations in a brief letter.

36. **Writing Persuasively** You are the mayor of a low-lying coastal town. Write a plan of expansion for your town. The plan should take global warming into account. Report your plan of expansion in front of the class.

READING SKILLS

Read the passage below, and then answer the questions that follow.

During photosynthesis, a plant takes in carbon dioxide from the air. Some of the carbon in the carbon dioxide becomes part of the plant's body. That carbon is not returned to the air until the leaves fall or the plant dies and decays.

Some plants, however, never completely decay. Instead, they are covered by sediments. After millions of years of being buried, the plants become coal, oil, and natural gas, which are fossil fuels. When fossil fuels are burned, they release the stored carbon as carbon dioxide. Millions of tons of carbon dioxide are released into the atmosphere each year from power plants that burn coal or oil and from cars that burn gasoline.

The burning of living plants also releases carbon dioxide. This process increases the carbon dioxide in the air in two ways. First, a burning plant gives off carbon dioxide. Second, when a living plant is burned, there is one less plant to remove carbon dioxide from the air by photosynthesis. As millions of trees are burned in tropical rain forests to clear the land for farming, the amount of carbon dioxide in the atmosphere increases.

1. According to the above passage, plants give off carbon dioxide
   a. when they are buried under sediments.
   b. when they die and decay.
   c. when they are burned.
   d. Both (b) and (c)

2. According to the passage above, which of the following is a process that does *not* add carbon dioxide to the atmosphere?
   a. the decay of plants
   b. photosynthesis
   c. burning trees in tropical rain forests
   d. burning coal in power plants

Understanding Concepts

Directions (1–4): For *each* question, write on a separate sheet of paper the letter of the correct answer.

1 Which of the following is the most important factor in determining climate?
 A. volcanic activity
 B. nearness to an ocean
 C. distance from the equator
 D. atmospheric circulation patterns

2 What causes the changes of seasons on Earth?
 F. the relatively constant flow of oceanic currents
 G. the tilt of Earth's axis as Earth moves around the sun
 H. the distribution of precipitation influenced by topography
 I. the changes in prevailing wind patterns at different latitudes

3 The development and widespread use of CFCs led to what scientific discovery?
 A. CFC molecules are chemically stable.
 B. CFC molecules contain chlorine atoms.
 C. CFC molecules are destroying the ozone layer.
 D. CFC molecules are protecting the ozone layer.

4 Why would global warming have an effect on sea levels?
 F. The warmth would cause polar icecaps to melt.
 G. There would be widespread beach erosion.
 H. Rainfall would increase all around the globe.
 I. There would be increased cloud cover blocking the sunlight.

Directions (5): Write a short response for the queston below.

5 The Earth's atmosphere acts like the glass in a greenhouse. Predict what would happen to life on Earth if Earth did not have a greenhouse effect.

Reading Skills

Directions (6–7): **Read the passage below. Then answer the questions.**

Many scientists hypothesize that the increasing greenhouse gases in our atmosphere will result in increasing average temperatures on Earth. Scientists are currently unable to make accurate predictions about the rate of global warming because climatic patterns are complex and too many variables must be taken into account to be solved even using today's fastest computers. The computer models predict how phenomena such as temperature, rainfall patterns, and sea level, will be affected by carbon dioxide levels, prevailing winds, and other variables.

Computer modeling is complicated by Earth's feedback systems which sometimes make it necessary to use different equations under changing simulated environments.

6 How could faster computers influence the predictions of climate change?
 A. Faster computers could produce more data.
 B. Faster computers could solve more complex equations.
 C. Faster computers could reduce the number of variables needed.
 D. Faster computers could increase the degree of certainty over a prediction.

7 Assess the information needed by scientists to build computer models that can predict climate change.

Directions (8): **Read the passage below. Then answer the question.**

El Niño is the name given to the periodic change in the location of warm and cold water masses in the Pacific Ocean. During an El Niño, winds in the western Pacific Ocean, which are usually weak, strengthen and push warm water eastward.

8 How would you expect El Niño to affect climate in the United States?

Interpreting Graphics

Directions (9–11): For *each* question below, record the correct answer on a separate sheet of paper.

The map below shows wind patterns across the Earth. Use this map to answer questions 9 through 11.

Global Wind Patterns

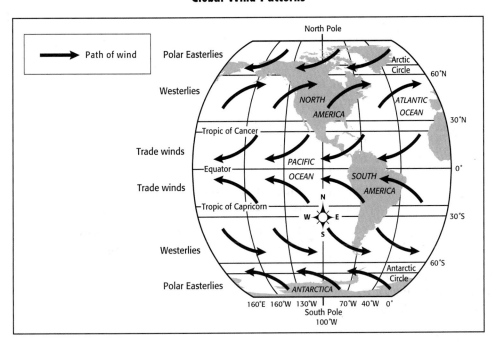

9 Which of the following characteristics has the **largest** effect on wind movement?

F. cardinal direction
G. latitude
H. longitude
I. seasonal change

10 Central America is located in the western hemisphere, linking North and South America. Which way does the wind blow in Central America?

A. northeast to southwest
B. southeast to northwest
C. northwest to southeast
D. southwest to northeast

11 If you were sailing from North America to Europe, in which range of latitudes would you sail?

F. 0° to 30°N
G. 30°N to 60°N
H. 0° to 30°S
I. 30°S to 60°S

Test TIP

Before looking at the answer choices for a question, try to answer the question yourself.

Inquiry Lab: MODELING

Objectives

▶ **Examine** a model that shows how the movement of air creates a system of wind currents on Earth.

▶ **USING SCIENTIFIC METHODS**
Hypothesize why the closed system of an aquarium is like the Earth and its atmosphere.

Materials

aquarium, 15 gal, glass, with cover
goose-neck lamp, adjustable, with a 100 W incandescent bulb
ice cubes, large (24)
incense stick
masking tape
matches
thermometers, outdoor (2)

Build a Model of Global Air Movement

Warm air rises and cools, and cold air sinks and warms. This is true whether we are observing the temperature and air circulation in a room or around the globe. On Earth, this movement of air creates a system of wind currents that you will demonstrate by building a model. You will build a closed system in which ice represents the polar regions and a lamp represents the equator. You will follow the movement of the air over these regions by watching a trail of smoke as it traces the path of air. (Remember that in the global circulation pattern, warm air moving toward the poles collides with cold air that is traveling from the poles. This collision, which takes place at about 60° north latitude and 60° south latitude, causes the warm air to rise.)

Procedure

1. Stack the ice cubes on the bottom of the aquarium against one end of it. Place the lamp outside the other end of the aquarium, and direct the bulb at the bottom half of that end. Use masking tape to attach one thermometer to each end inside of the aquarium. Make sure the thermometers can be read from the outside of the aquarium. Place the cover on the aquarium.

2. Wait 5 minutes. Then read and record the temperature at each end of the aquarium.

3. Light the end of the incense stick so that it produces a steady plume of smoke.

▶ **Step 1** Attach a thermometer to each end of the aquarium, making certain that the thermometers can be read from the outside of the aquarium.

4. Lift the aquarium cover very slightly so that you can insert the incense stick. Hold it steadily in place over the ice about 5 cm from the cover, and observe the smoke.

5. Observe the movement of the smoke. How does the smoke behave? Draw a diagram of the aquarium. Use arrows to indicate the movement of the smoke in the aquarium.

6. Remove several ice cubes and record your observations.

7. Remove all of the ice cubes and record your observations.

Analysis

1. **Explaining Events** Did the air movement pattern change after some ice was removed? Explain your answer.

2. **Explaining Events** Did the air movement pattern change after all of the ice was removed? Explain your answer.

Conclusions

3. **Drawing Conclusions** Why is the difference between temperatures at the two ends of the aquarium an important factor in the flow of heat through the aquarium?

4. **Making Predictions** Predict how air movement patterns will change if polar ice begins to thaw because of global warming.

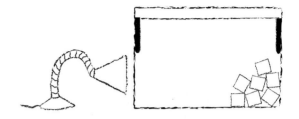

▶ **Diagramming Smoke Flow**
Make a simple diagram of the aquarium showing the position of the light source and the ice cubes. Draw arrows to indicate the movement of the smoke in the aquarium.

Extension

1. **Analyzing Models** A closed system is a collection of elements that nothing can escape from or enter. Your aquarium is an example of a closed system. Convection is the movement of warm air relative to cooler air. Discuss your observations of convection in the closed system of the aquarium. How can you apply this information to the movement of air over the Earth?

2. **Analyzing Models** How is the Earth and its atmosphere like the closed system of your aquarium? What factors that affect air movement, climate, and weather exist on Earth but not in your model?

Making a difference

OZONE SCIENTIST

Susan Solomon will not soon forget crawling across the roof of an Antarctic field station in windchill temperatures of –62°C (–80°F), moving heavy equipment, and adjusting mirrors while the winds howled and whipped about her. Sounds like an adventure, right? It sure was! But it is just part of what Solomon has done to establish herself as one of the world's leading authorities on ozone destruction.

Q: Is it true that you have traveled to the ends of the Earth to get information about the ozone layer?
A: Yes, I guess it is. My colleagues and I have studied the ozone hole in Antarctica, and we've measured and documented ozone chemistry above Greenland. But it's not all adventure. When I'm not visiting one of the poles, I run computer simulations of the atmosphere and study data at the National Oceanic and Atmospheric Administration (NOAA) in Boulder, Colorado.

Q: What is the significance of discoveries regarding the ozone hole?
A: Before British scientists discovered the ozone hole in Antarctica, no one was sure about ozone changes in the atmosphere. The popular belief was that in 100 years there might be 5 percent less ozone. So there were questions about whether it was a serious environmental problem. But when the British researchers released data that showed 50 percent less ozone over Antarctica in 1985 than was present 20 years earlier, the research raised our awareness that the problem was far more serious than previously thought.

Q: How have you contributed to the study of ozone?
A: Well, when the British data was first released, no one had much of an explanation about what was causing the destruction of the ozone layer. I thought about the problem a lot. Later that year, I sat in on a lecture about types of clouds called *polar stratospheric clouds*. These are beautifully colored clouds that are known for their iridescence. While I was looking at these clouds, which are common in the Antarctic but rare elsewhere, it occurred to me that they may have something to do with ozone depletion. Perhaps they provide a surface for chemical reactions that activate reactive chlorine from CFCs (human-made chlorofluorocarbons). If so, once activated, the chlorine could contribute to reactions that destroy ozone.

Q: Did you get the chance to test your hypothesis?
A: Yes, the next year the National Science Foundation chose me to lead a group of 16 scientists for a nine-week expedition in Antarctica. We were the first team of scientists from the United States sent to the Antarctic to study the ozone hole. Within one month we could see that unnaturally high levels of chlorine dioxide did occur in the stratosphere during ozone depletion. This discovery was very exciting because it seemed that we were on the right track. We kept collecting data that year and collected more data during a second trip the next year. Pretty soon, the evidence seemed to support my hypothesis that CFCs and ozone depletion are linked.

▶ The ozone hole can be seen in this satellite image. The hole is the pale blue and black region immediately above Solomon's shoulder.

▶ Polar stratospheric clouds like these led Susan Solomon to make important discoveries about the cause of ozone depletion.

▶ Solomon has braved freezing polar temperatures to gather data about the ozone hole.

Q: How did this discovery make you feel?
A: On the one hand, it's very exciting scientifically to be involved in something like this. On the other hand, sometimes I think it's a little depressing. It would be nice to be involved in something more positive, to bring people good news. So far, we've brought nothing but bad news. We were hoping that we wouldn't find the same ozone chemistry in the Arctic that we found in the Antarctic. Unfortunately, we did. We hope for a positive result for the planet, but we don't always get it.

Q: How has your research helped to make a difference in our world?
A: Since our findings and others were announced, many of the world's countries have agreed to restrict or ban the use of CFCs. As a result, the ozone hole will eventually go away, but it will take a

very long time. So although most countries have slowed their use of CFCs, CFCs from years past will still be hanging around in our atmosphere for the next 50 to 100 years. But I think our work has led in a small way to the realization that our actions do have consequences, and this realization should bring positive change.

Dr. Solomon has received international recognition for her work on the ozone hole over the Antarctic. She is a member of the U.S. National Academy of Sciences, the European Academy of Sciences, and the Académie des Sciences de France. In 2000, Dr. Solomon was awarded the National Medal of Science and the American Meteorological Society's Carl-Gustav Rossby Medal. In April 2002, she was nominated co-chair of the United Nations Climate Change Working Panel.

For More Information
If you would like free information about the ozone layer and what you can do to protect it, contact the Environmental Protection Agency, Public Outreach, 401 M St. SW, Washington, DC 20460.

What Do You Think?
If Susan Solomon had not sat in on the lecture about polar stratospheric clouds and had not realized the role that these clouds play in ozone destruction, where do you think our current understanding of the ozone hole would be? How does this reinforce the idea that a single person can make a tremendous contribution to humankind?

Land

PRE-READING ACTIVITY

FOLDNOTES

Layered Book

Before you read this chapter, create the **FoldNote** entitled "Layered Book" described in the Reading and Study Skills section of the Appendix. Label the tabs of the layered book with "Rural Land Use," "Urban Land Use," "Land Management," and "Conservation." As you read the chapter, write information you learn about each category under the appropriate flap.

On the edge of Palm Springs, California, suburban housing has been built on what was once a desert ecosystem.

SECTION 1
How We Use Land

Some years ago, officials in California decided to find out how land was being used in the state. Measurements were made using maps, aerial photographs, field surveys, and a computerized mapping system. The results were startling. Between 1984 and 1992, nearly 84,000 hectares (about 210,000 acres) of farmland, rangeland, and woodland had been converted into suburbs and cities. This change is happening all over the world.

Land Use and Land Cover

We use land for many purposes, including farming, mining, recreation, and building cities and highways. Land cover is what you find on a patch of land, and it often depends on how the land is used. For example, land cover might be a forest, a field of grain, or a parking lot. There are different types of land cover and different human uses for each cover type, as shown in **Table 1**.

Land that is covered mainly with buildings and roads is called **urban** land. The U.S. Census Bureau defines an urban area as an area that contains 2,500 or more people and usually has a governing body, such as a city council. Any area not classified as urban is considered rural. Land that contains relatively few people and large areas of open space is a **rural** area. **Figure 1** shows the relative proportion of each of the types of land cover defined in **Table 1**. As the table shows, most land provides one or more resources that humans consume. These resources include wood in forests, crops in farmland, and mineral resources.

✔ **Reading Check** What are two different types of land cover? (See the Appendix for answers to Reading Checks.)

Table 1 ▼

Primary Land-Use Categories	
Land cover type	**Human use of land**
Rangeland	land used to graze livestock and wildlife
Forest land	land used for harvesting wood, wildlife, fish, nuts, and other resources
Cropland	land used to grow plants for food and fiber
Parks and preserves	land used for recreation and scenic enjoyment and for preserving native animal and plant communities and ecosystems
Wetlands, mountains, deserts, and other	land that is difficult to use for human purposes
Urban land	land used for houses, businesses, industry, and roads

Objectives

▶ Distinguish between urban and rural land.

▶ Describe three major ways in which humans use land.

▶ Explain the concept of ecosystem services.

Key Terms

urban
rural
ecosystem services

Land Use in the United States

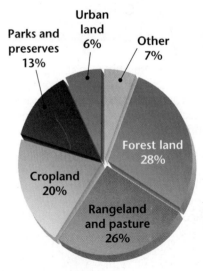

Source: Natural Resources Conservation Service.

Figure 1 ▶ The graph above shows the percentage of each land cover type in the United States.

Section 1   How We Use Land   **381**

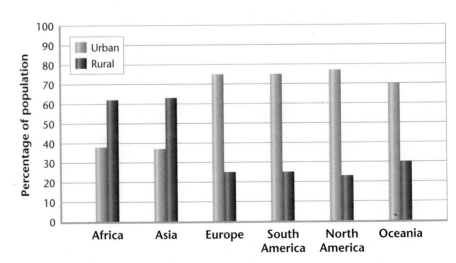

Figure 2 ▶ The photo on the left, of New York City, shows a typical urban scene. The photo on the right, of the Connecticut River Valley, shows a typical rural scene.

Where We Live

Until about 1850, most people lived in rural areas. Many of them were farmers, who grew crops and raised livestock for food, clothing, and manufacturing. Other people managed the forests, worked in local mines or mills, or manufactured the necessities of life for a town.

The Industrial Revolution changed this pattern. Machinery was built that made it possible for fewer people to operate a farm or a grain mill. In addition, better transportation allowed manufacturers to be located far from their customers. So thousands of jobs in rural areas were eliminated. Many people had to move to cities to find jobs. As a result, urban areas grew rapidly during the 20th century and spread over more land. **Figure 3** shows that today, most people throughout the world live in urban areas. The movement of people from rural areas to urban areas happened rapidly in developed countries between about 1880 and 1950. Now, this movement is occurring rapidly in developing countries.

Figure 3 ▶ This graph shows the proportion of people living in urban areas and rural areas in different parts of the world.

Source: Population Reference Bureau.

The Urban-Rural Connection

Whether people live in cities or in the countryside, they are dependent on the resources produced in rural areas. These resources include clean drinking water, fertile soil and land for crops, trees for wood and paper, and much of the oxygen we breathe, which is produced by plants. The resources that are produced by natural and artificial ecosystems are called **ecosystem services.** Some examples of ecosystem services are listed in **Table 2.**

Supporting Urban Areas The area of rural land needed to support one person depends on many factors, such as the climate, the standard of living, and how efficiently resources are used. Each person in a developed country uses the ecosystem services provided by about 8 hectares of land and water. In the United States each person uses the ecosystem services from more than 12 hectares, whereas each person in Germany uses about 6 hectares' worth. Many people in developing nations do not have access to all the resources for a healthy life. They may use ecosystem services from less than a hectare of land per person.

✓ **Reading Check** How does each person's use of ecosystem services in the United States compare with each person's use in Germany?

MATHPRACTICE

Ecosystem Services
Earth contains about 12.4 billion hectares of productive land—cropland, grazing land, forest, fresh water, and fisheries. In 1996, the world population was about 5.7 billion people, for a mean of 2.18 hectares of productive land per person. The world population in 2010 is projected to be 6.8 billion. On average, how much productive land per person will there be in 2010?

SC*L*INKS.

www.scilinks.org
Topic: Ecosystem
Services
Code: HE80465

Table 2 ▼

Examples of Ecosystem Services
purification of air and water
preservation of soil and renewal of soil fertility
prevention of flood and drought
regulation of climate
maintenance of biodiversity
movement and cycling of nutrients
detoxification and decomposition of wastes
aesthetic beauty

SECTION 1 Review

1. **Explain** how ecosystem services link rural lands with urban lands.

2. **Describe** three main ways in which humans use land. Write a paragraph to explain your answer.
   WRITING SKILLS

3. **Distinguish** between rural lands and urban lands, and provide an example of each.

CRITICAL THINKING

4. **Making Decisions** What could individuals do to reduce the loss of ecosystem services per person as the human population grows?

5. **Making Inferences** How does the movement of people from rural lands to urban lands affect people's relationship with natural resources?

Urban Land Use

 SEV.1.c; SEV.5.d

Objectives

▶ Describe the urban crisis, and explain what people are doing to deal with it.

▶ Explain how urban sprawl affects the environment.

▶ Explain how open spaces provide urban areas with environmental benefits.

▶ Explain the heat-island effect.

▶ Describe how people use the geographic information system as a tool for land-use planning.

Key Terms

urbanization
infrastructure
urban sprawl
heat island
land-use planning
geographic information system (GIS)

People live where they can find the things that they need and want, such as jobs, schools, and recreational areas. For most people today, this means living in an urban area.

Urbanization

The movement of people from rural areas to cities is known as **urbanization.** People usually leave rural areas for more plentiful and better paying jobs in towns and cities. In developed countries, urbanization slowed in the second half of the 20th century. In 1960, 70 percent of the U.S. population was classified as urban. By 1980, this percentage had increased only slightly to 75 percent. As urban populations have grown, many small towns have grown together and formed larger urban areas. The U.S. Census Bureau calls these complexes metropolitan areas. Some examples are Denver-Boulder in Colorado and Boston-Worcester-Lawrence in Massachusetts. **Figure 5** shows the expansion of the Washington, D.C.–Baltimore metropolitan area over the years. These maps were created using data from the U.S. Census Bureau.

Urban areas that have grown slowly are often relatively pleasant places to live. Roads and public transportation in these areas have been built to handle the growth, so that traffic flows freely. Buildings, roads, and parking lots are mixed in with green spaces and recreational areas. These green spaces may provide these urban areas with much needed ecosystem services such as moderation of temperature, infiltration of rainwater runoff, and aesthetic value.

Figure 5 ▶ The Washington, D.C.–Baltimore area has grown larger and more densely populated over the years. Red areas indicate urban development.

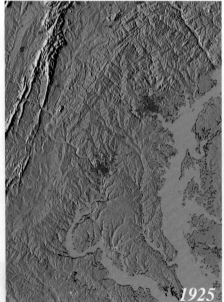

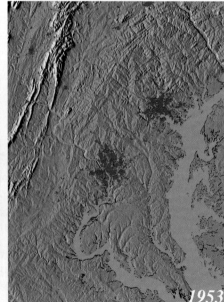

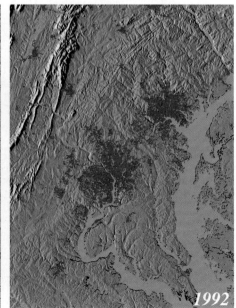

1925

1953

1992

The Urban Crisis When urban areas grow rapidly, they often run into trouble. A rapidly growing population can overwhelm the infrastructure and lead to traffic jams, substandard housing, and polluted air and water. **Infrastructure** is all of the things that a society builds for public use. Infrastructure includes roads, sewers, railroads, bridges, canals, fire and police stations, schools, libraries, hospitals, water mains, and power lines. When more people live in a city than its infrastructure can support, the living conditions deteriorate. This growth problem has become so widespread throughout the world that the term *urban crisis* was coined to describe the problem. **Figure 6** shows an example of urban crisis in Hong Kong. The hillside is covered with substandard housing in an area that lacks the necessary infrastructure for people to live in healthy conditions.

Urban Sprawl Rapid expansion of a city into the countryside around the city is called **urban sprawl.** Much of this expansion results from building suburbs or housing and associated commercial buildings on the boundary of a larger town. People living in the suburbs generally commute to work in the city by car. Many of these suburbs are built on land that was previously used for food production, as shown in **Figure 7.** In 2000, more Americans lived in suburbs than in cities and the countryside combined. Each year suburbs spread over another 1 million hectares (2.5 million acres) of land in the United States.

Figure 6 ▶ Rapid urban growth has led to substandard housing on the hillsides above Hong Kong.

FIELD ACTIVITY

Local Urban Sprawl On your way home from school, observe your surroundings. In your *EcoLog*, write down any signs of urban sprawl that you observed. What criteria did you use for making this assessment?

Figure 7 ▶ This photograph shows suburban development spreading out around Maui, Hawaii.

Figure 8 ▶ The search for ocean views lead people to build these homes on the California coastline, which is giving way as a result of erosion.

Figure 9 ▶ The urban heat island over Atlanta is shown in this computer-enhanced satellite image. Areas with higher temperatures appear red.

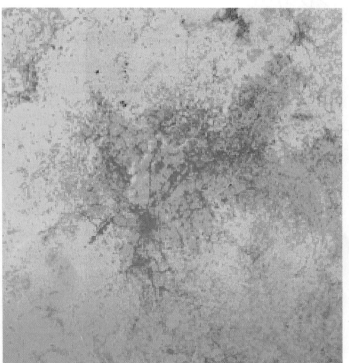

Development on Marginal Lands Many cities were first built where there was little room for expansion. As the cities grew, suburbs were often built on *marginal land*—land that is poorly suited for building. For example, Los Angeles and Mexico City are built in basins. These cities have expanded up into the surrounding mountains where the slopes are prone to landslides. The houses shown in **Figure 8** were built on land that is unsuitable for development because of the natural processes of erosion along the coastline. Structures built on marginal land can become difficult or impossible to repair and can be expensive to insure.

Other Impacts of Urbanization Environmental conditions in a city are different from those of the surrounding countryside. Cities both generate and trap more heat. Roads and buildings absorb more heat than vegetation does. They also retain heat longer. The increased temperature in a city is called a **heat island.** Atlanta, Georgia, is an example of a city that has a significant heat island, as shown in **Figure 9.**

Heat islands can affect local weather patterns. Hot air rises over a city, cooling as it rises, and eventually produces rain clouds. In Atlanta and many other cities, increased rainfall is a side effect of the heat island. The heat-island effect may be moderated by planting trees for shade and by installing rooftops that reflect rather than retain heat.

✓ **Reading Check** How do heat islands affect the local rainfall?

Urban Planning

Land-use planning is determining in advance how land will be used—where houses, businesses, and factories will be built, where land will be protected for recreation, and so on. Land-use planners determine the best locations for shopping malls, sewers, electrical lines, and other infrastructure.

In practice, making land-use plans is complex and often controversial. The federal, state, and local governments require developers to prepare detailed reports assessing the environmental impact of many projects. And the public has a right to comment on these reports. Developers, city governments, local businesses, and citizens often disagree about land-use plans. Projects that affect large or environmentally sensitive areas are often studied carefully and even bitterly debated.

Technological Tools Land-use planners have sophisticated methods and tools available to them today. One important technological tool for land-use planning involves using the geographic information system.

A **geographic information system** (GIS) is a computerized system for storing, manipulating, and viewing geographic data. GIS software allows a user to enter different types of data about an area, such as the location of sewer lines, roads, and parks, and then create maps. **Figure 10** shows several images of Seattle, Washington, created from GIS data. Each image corresponds to a different combination of information. The power of GIS is that it allows a user to display layers of information about an area and to overlay these layers, like overhead transparencies, on top of one another.

Connection to **History**

Ancient Urban Planning
People have practiced urban planning for thousands of years. The ancient Mexican city of Teotihuacan was a marvel of urban planning. The city had a grid plan oriented to 15 degrees, 25 minutes east of true north. It had two central avenues that divided the city into four quadrants. About 2,000 homes and apartment compounds lined the main avenue, which also had a channel running under it that gathered rainwater. Teotihuacan had all this—before 750 CE.

Figure 10 ▶ The images below are of Seattle, Washington. Each image represents a different GIS layer, each with specific information.

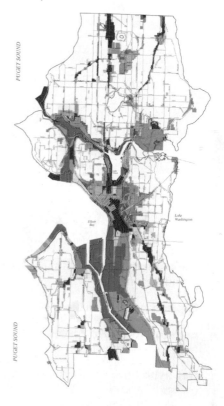

Figure 11 ▶ This mass transit system in California's San Francisco Bay Area moves thousands of people a day with much less environmental impact than if the people drove their own cars.

Transportation Most cities in the United States are difficult to travel in without a car. Many U.S. cities were constructed after the invention of the automobile. In addition, availability of land was not a limiting issue, so many American cities sprawl over large areas. By contrast, most cities in Europe were built before cars, have narrow roads, and are compact.

In many cities, *mass transit systems* have been constructed to get people where they want to go. Mass transit systems, such as the one shown in **Figure 11**, use buses and trains to move many people at one time. Mass transit systems save energy, reduce highway congestion, reduce air pollution, and limit the loss of land to roadways and parking lots. Where the construction of mass transit systems is not reasonable, carpooling is an important alternative.

Open Space *Open space* is land within urban areas that is set aside for scenic and recreational enjoyment. Open spaces include parks, public gardens, and bicycle and hiking trails. Open spaces left in their natural condition are often called *greenbelts*. These greenbelts provide important ecological services.

Open spaces have numerous environmental benefits and provide valuable functions. The plants in open spaces absorb carbon dioxide, produce oxygen, and filter out pollutants from air and water. The plants even help keep a city cooler in the summer. Open spaces, especially those with vegetation, also reduce drainage problems by absorbing more of the rainwater runoff from building roofs, asphalt, and concrete. This ecological service results in less flooding after a heavy rain. As well, open spaces provide urban dwellers with much-needed places for exercise and relaxation.

✓ **Reading Check** What are three benefits that are provided by open spaces in urban areas?

SECTION 2 Review

1. **Describe** the urban crisis, and explain how people are addressing it.

2. **Explain** how urban areas create heat islands.

3. **Explain** how open spaces provide environmental benefits to urban areas.

4. **Describe** how a GIS system can be used as a land-use tool.

CRITICAL THINKING

5. **Identifying Relationships** Write a short paragraph in which you describe the benefits of using a geographic information system for land-use planning. **WRITING SKILLS**

6. **Making Decisions** Describe the environmental implications of urban sprawl.

Land Management and Conservation

SEV.1.c; SEV.5.c; SEV.5.d

EARTH SCIENCE · CONNECTION

As the human population grows, the resources of more rural land are needed to support the population. The main categories of rural land are farmland, rangeland, forest land, national and state parks, and wilderness. Throughout our history, we have sometimes managed these lands sustainably so that they will provide resources indefinitely. We have also sometimes reduced their productivity by overusing or polluting them. The condition of rural land is important because of the ecological services that it provides. These services are especially important for the urban areas that rely on the productivity of rural land.

Farmlands

Farmland, such as that shown in **Figure 12,** is land that is used to grow crops and fruit. The United States contains more than 100 million hectares of prime farmland. However, in some places, urban development threatens some of the most productive farmland. Examples of places where farmland is threatened are parts of North Carolina's Piedmont region and the Twin Cities area of Minnesota. In 1996, the U.S. government established a national Farmland Protection Program to help state, county, and local governments protect farmland in danger of being paved over or otherwise developed.

Objectives

▶ Explain the benefits of preserving farmland.

▶ Describe two ways that rangeland can be managed sustainably.

▶ Describe the environmental effects of deforestation.

▶ Explain the function of parks and of wilderness areas.

Key Terms

overgrazing
deforestation
reforestation
wilderness

Hedgerows Farmland forms an important habitat for wildlife in Great Britain, which has relatively few remaining natural areas. Fields are separated by rows of bushes called hedgerows, which provide shelter for a variety of birds, mammals, reptiles, and insects.

Figure 12 ▶ This farmland next to the suburbs of Mililani, Hawaii, is used to grow a variety of crops.

Rangelands

Land that supports different vegetation types like grasslands, shrublands, and deserts and that is not used for farming or timber production is called *rangeland*. Rangelands can be arid, like rangelands in the desert Southwest, or relatively wet, like the rangelands of Florida. The most common human use of rangeland is for the grazing of livestock, as shown in **Figure 13**. The most common livestock are cattle, sheep, and goats, which are valued for their meat, milk, wool, and hides. Native wildlife species also graze these lands. Like farmland, rangeland is essential for maintaining the world's food supply. World population growth may require a 40 percent increase in the food production of rangeland from 1977 to 2030.

Problems on the Range Some rangelands in the United States have become degraded by poor land management strategies. Most damage to rangeland comes from **overgrazing,** or allowing more animals to graze in an area than the range can support. When animals overgraze, too many of the plants are eaten, and the land can become degraded. Overgrazing often results in changes in the plant community. Less desirable plant species may invade the area and replace more-desirable plant species. In severe cases, all the vegetation is eaten. Once the plants are gone, there is nothing to keep the soil from eroding.

Maintaining the Range Much of the rangeland in the United States is public land managed by the federal government, which leases the rangeland to ranchers. Much of it is degraded. The Public Rangelands Improvement Act of 1978 was enacted to reverse this trend and improve land management practices.

Sustaining the productivity of rangeland generally means reducing overgrazing by limiting herds to sizes that do not degrade the land. Rangeland may also be left unused for periods of time so that the vegetation can recover. Improving rangeland that has been degraded by overgrazing often includes methods such as killing invasive plants, planting native vegetation, and fencing areas to let them recover to the state they were in before they were overgrazed. As well, ranchers control grazing by digging several small water holes so that livestock do not overgraze the vegetation around a single water hole.

✔ **Reading Check** How does rangeland become degraded?

Graphic Organizer **Venn Diagram** Create the **Graphic Organizer** entitled "Venn Diagram" described in the Appendix. Label the circles with "Rangelands Land Management" and "Forest Land Management." Then, fill in the diagram with characteristics that each type of land management shares with the other.

Figure 13 ▶ The photo below shows productive rangeland in the western United States.

Figure 14 ▶ Methods for harvesting trees include clear-cutting (top) and selective cutting (bottom).

Forest Lands

Trees are harvested to provide products we use everyday, such as paper, furniture, and lumber and plywood for our homes. In addition to wood and paper, we value forest products such as maple syrup and turpentine. There are many ecosystem services provided by forests; however, one of the most important is the removal of CO_2 from the air.

Harvesting Trees People use enormous amounts of wood. The worldwide average is 1,800 cm³ of wood used per person each day. However, on average, each person in the United States uses about 3.5 times this amount. This is the equivalent of each person in the United States cutting down a tree that is 30 m tall every year. About 1.5 billion people in developing countries depend on firewood as their main source of fuel.

The timber industry classifies forest lands into three categories—virgin forest, which is forest that has never been cut; native forest, which is forest that is planted and managed; and tree farms, which are areas where trees are planted in rows and harvested like other crops. The two most widely used methods of harvesting trees are clear-cutting and selective cutting. These methods are shown in **Figure 14.** *Clear-cutting* is the process of removing all of the trees from an area of land. Clear-cutting large areas destroys established wildlife habitat and may cause soil erosion. The main alternative is selective cutting, which is usually practiced on smaller areas owned by individuals. *Selective cutting* is the process of cutting and removing only middle-aged or mature trees. Selective cutting is more expensive than clear-cutting, but selective cutting is usually much less destructive.

QuickLAB

Measuring Soil Depth and Compaction

Procedure

1. Find a plot of **undisturbed soil** in a forest, meadow, park, or other undisturbed area near your school.
2. Press a **meterstick** down into the undisturbed soil as far as it will go. Record how deep the meterstick went into the soil. Record how soft the soil was and how easy it was to press the meterstick into the soil. Repeat this five times in the same plot of undisturbed soil.
3. Pour 1 L of **water** onto the undisturbed soil. Use a **stopwatch** to record how long it takes for the soil to fully absorb the water.
4. Repeat this procedure at a plot of **disturbed soil** in a bike path, dirt road, or other area where the soil is bare and vegetation has been cleared or trampled.

Analysis

1. How did the soil depth and hardness in the plot of undisturbed soil differ from that in the plot of disturbed soil?
2. Which plot absorbed water faster?
3. How might grazing cattle affect the depth and compaction of an undisturbed plot of land?
4. How might clear-cutting affect an undisturbed plot of land?

Deforestation The clearing of trees from an area without replacing them is called **deforestation.** Most countries become severely deforested as populations expand and the demand for forest products increases. Forests are cleared to convert the land into farmland. People also clear forests to make space for roads, homes, factories, and office buildings.

Deforestation reduces wildlife habitat, but it has other impacts, too. For example, when forests are cleared from a hillside, soil erosion usually results if the area is not quickly planted with a cover crop. Without tree roots to hold the soil in place, soil is easily washed or blown into the valley below. In New York, forests on hillsides were cleared for farmland during the 19th century. Plowing also increased the rate of erosion, and as much as 90 percent of the soil eroded. Then, during the Great Depression, which was in the 1930s, hundreds of farmers in this area went bankrupt. The state bought many of the abandoned farms, and let the forests regenerate. Today, many of the hillsides are covered with state forest, which is used for recreation.

The rate of deforestation is especially high in tropical rain forests, where the soil is relatively thin. Farmers who clear forests in these areas must always move from one plot of land to another and clear more forest each time they move. Whether forests are cleared for farming or wood, if trees are not replanted, natural resources are steadily depleted.

CASE STUDY

California's Wilderness Corridors

California has an extraordinary range of habitats, from coastal islands, where elephant seals breed, to mountains where salmon, cougars, bobcats, and badgers are found. Many of these animals live on wildlife preserves and other public lands or on private land.

Animals do not know that they are safest if they stay on preserves. Many animals naturally migrate at different times of the year. Young animals are often evicted from their territories by their parents and must search for territories of their own to survive. Many animals also leave their territories in search of mates from other populations. This process is important because if animals reproduce only with members of the species that live nearby, the population becomes inbred and genetic defects become more common.

As California becomes more urbanized, however, migration routes between one population of animals and another population are increasingly blocked by highways and housing developments.

A possible solution is the acquisition of conservation corridors—thin strips of protected land that connect one preserve with another preserve. Conservation biologists have argued for years over whether such corridors are

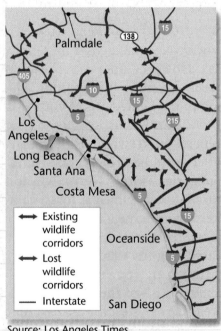

Source: Los Angeles Times

▶ This diagram shows suspected wildlife corridors around Los Angeles, California.

Reforestation Clear-cut forest can be replanted or allowed to regrow naturally, without human intervention. **Reforestation** is the process by which trees are planted to re-establish trees that have been cut down in a forest land. In some places, reforestation is happening faster than trees are being cut down. New England, for example, now contains more forest than it did a century ago. Much of the original forest had been cleared for farming, but the land was unable to sustain productive crops over a long period. As farming in this area became less economical, farms were abandoned and the forest regenerated. The same process has happened in places where steep hillsides were deforested for farming or development. The cost of deforestation, which caused soil erosion, landslides, and flooding, was too high. So forest has now been allowed to regenerate or has been replanted.

Some governments require reforestation after timber has been harvested from public land. A reforestation project is shown in **Figure 15**. Worldwide, more than 90 percent of all timber comes from forests that are not managed by an agency that monitors the health of forest ecosystems. Many governments are currently working to improve reforestation efforts and to promote less destructive logging methods. Private organizations have also established tree-planting programs on roadsides and in cities.

Figure 15 ▶ Tree seedlings have been planted to reforest this hillside as part of a reforestation project in the Fiji Islands.

▶ Cougars may need wildlife corridors in order to survive in parts of California.

effective in linking habitats and protecting animals.

One such corridor in California is the Tenaja corridor, which connects the Santa Rosa Plateau Ecological Preserve and the larger Cleveland National Forest in the Santa Ana Mountains southeast of Los Angeles. Biologist Paul Beir studied the movements of a population of cougars in the Santa Ana Mountains by putting radio collars on more than 30 animals to track their movements. He found that the animals used the Tenaja corridor and avoided urban areas.

Now there is public pressure to preserve 232 of the corridors that link critical habitats. Voters have approved bond measures that will supply the money to buy some of the land, and the Nature Conservancy is also contributing land. The question of whether wildlife corridors preserve species may finally be answered by California's initiative.

CRITICAL THINKING

1. Applying Ideas California's state emblem is a grizzly bear, which is a species no longer found in the state. Why do you think the bears disappeared?

2. Expressing Viewpoints Should California spend state money to preserve habitats? Explain your answer.

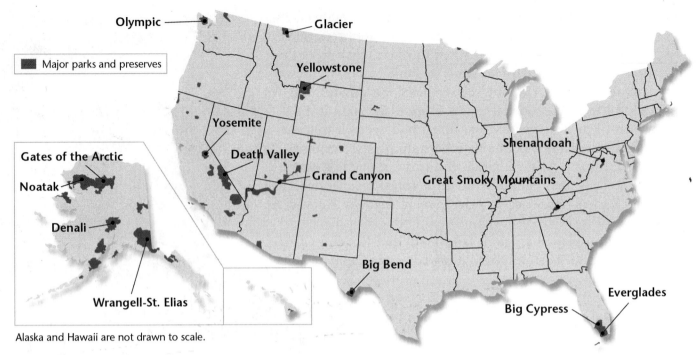

Major parks and preserves

Olympic

Glacier

Yellowstone

Yosemite

Death Valley

Grand Canyon

Shenandoah

Great Smoky Mountains

Gates of the Arctic

Noatak

Denali

Wrangell-St. Elias

Big Bend

Big Cypress

Everglades

Alaska and Hawaii are not drawn to scale.

Figure 16 ▶ National parks in the United States are concentrated in the West.

Figure 17 ▶ Biosphere reserves are places where human populations and wildlife live side by side.

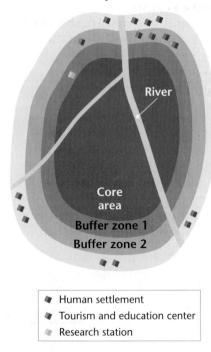

River

Core area

Buffer zone 1

Buffer zone 2

Human settlement
Tourism and education center
Research station

Parks and Preserves

In the 1870s, a group of explorers brought news to Congress of a magnificent expanse of land in Wyoming and Montana. The explorers expressed their concern that the land would be damaged by the development that had changed the northeastern United States. Congress agreed to protect the land, and the first national park—Yellowstone—was created. Today, the United States has about 50 national parks, as shown in **Figure 16.**

Public lands in the United States have many purposes. Most public lands are not as protected as the national parks are. Some public lands are leased to private companies for logging, mining, and ranching. Other public lands are maintained for hunting and fishing, as wildlife refuges, or for protecting endangered species.

International efforts include the United Nations's Man and the Biosphere Program. This program has set up several hundred preserves throughout the world since 1976. These preserves are called *biosphere reserves* and are unusual in that they include people in the management plan of the reserves, as shown in **Figure 17.**

Wilderness The U.S. Wilderness Act, which was passed in 1964, designated certain lands as wilderness areas. **Wilderness** is an area in which the land and the ecosystems it supports are protected from all exploitation. So far, 474 regions covering almost 13 million hectares (32 million acres) have been designated as wilderness in the United States. **Figure 18** shows an example of a wilderness area. Wilderness areas are open to hiking, fishing, boating (without motors), and camping. Building roads or structures and using motorized equipment are not allowed in these areas.

✓ **Reading Check** What are three uses of public lands in the United States?

Benefits of Protected Areas Without national and private parks and preserves around the world, many more species would now be extinct. In a crowded world, these protected areas often provide the only place where unspoiled forests, deserts, or prairies remain. Without these areas, the plants and animals that can survive only in these ecosystems would disappear. These protected areas also provide recreation for people. People can camp, hike, fish, and watch birds and other wildlife in these areas. Wilderness areas also serve as outdoor classrooms and research laboratories where people can learn more about the natural world.

Threats to Protected Areas There is a constant battle in our world between our conservation efforts and the growing and increasingly mobile population. Around the world, more people visit national parks and wilderness areas each year and leave their mark on the land. Litter and traffic jams that have plagued our cities now plague many of our national parks. Rangelands, mining and logging sites, oil and gas drilling operations, factories, power plants, and urban areas are often close enough to the parks to affect the parks. In addition, preserved areas are affected by climate change and by air and water pollution, as are most other parts of the world.

In attempts to protect wilderness from damage, limits have been set on the number of people permitted in some areas at any given time. Other areas are completely closed to visitors to allow wild animals to breed. In addition, volunteer programs are now active in many wilderness areas. Volunteers help pick up trash, build trails, control invading or exotic species, and educate the visiting public.

Figure 18 ▶ In the United States, wilderness areas, such as the High Uintas Wilderness area shown here, are supposed to be preserved untouched for our own and future generations.

SECTION 3 **Review**

1. **Explain** what reforestation is and why it is important.

2. **List** and explain two methods of managing rangelands sustainably.

3. **Describe** the function of parks and of wilderness.

4. **Describe** the environmental effects of deforestation.

CRITICAL THINKING

5. **Recognizing Relationships** Read the first paragraph under the head "Threats to Protected Areas." Why do you suppose that some of our nation's national parks and wilderness areas are degraded? **READING SKILLS**

6. **Recognizing Relationships** What are the benefits of preserving farmland?

1 How We Use Land

Key Terms

urban, 381
rural, 381
ecosystem services, 383

Main Ideas

▶ Land is covered with forest, farm fields and pastures, roads, and towns.

▶ Urban areas are mostly covered with houses, roads, businesses, and industrial and municipal structures. Rural areas have less dense human populations and include forest land, cropland, rangeland, and other land cover types.

▶ Urban areas need very large areas of rural ecosystems to supply them with water, food, wood, and other ecosystem services.

2 Urban Land Use

Key Terms

urbanization, 384
infrastructure, 385
urban sprawl, 385
heat island, 386
land-use planning, 387
geographic information system (GIS), 387

Main Ideas

▶ Urbanization is the migration of people from rural to urban areas.

▶ When cities grow more rapidly than infrastructure can be built, they tend to suffer from substandard housing and traffic problems.

▶ Unplanned growth of a city results in urban sprawl, as low-density development spreads into the surrounding countryside.

▶ Land-use planning is essential if urban areas are to be pleasant places to live.

3 Land Management and Conservation

Key Terms

overgrazing, 390
deforestation, 392
reforestation, 393
wilderness, 394

Main Ideas

▶ Farmland is used to raise crops and livestock.

▶ Rangeland is land used primarily for grazing livestock. Rangeland is easily degraded by overgrazing.

▶ Trees are harvested for many purposes. Deforestation can cause soil erosion and may threaten forest plants and animals with extinction.

▶ National lands are used for many purposes, including lumber, mining, and recreation. Wilderness is national land that is protected from all exploitation for the benefit of future generations.

Using Key Terms

Use each of the following terms in a separate sentence.

1. *rangeland*
2. *infrastructure*
3. *urbanization*
4. *ecosystem services*
5. *geographic information system*

For each pair of terms, explain how the meanings of the terms differ.

6. *heat island* and *urban sprawl*
7. *overgrazing* and *deforestation*
8. *urban* and *rural*
9. *selective cutting* and *clear-cutting*

✓ **STUDY TIP**

Flash Cards With a partner, make flash cards for the key words and most important ideas in the chapter. Take turns quizzing each other about the content of the course. Do another round, and this time the person being asked questions should try to use each key word and idea in a complete sentence.

Understanding Key Ideas

10. Building a mass transit system is likely to have which of the following effects?
    a. increasing air pollution
    b. traffic congestion
    c. increasing the temperature of the urban heat island
    d. none of the above

11. National parks and wilderness areas are designed to do which of the following?
    a. provide recreation
    b. protect wildlife
    c. preserve natural areas
    d. all of the above

12. Which of the following is *not* an example of urbanization?
    a. Immigrants settle in New York City.
    b. A farmer who can no longer afford to lease farmland moves to a city.
    c. A drop in timber prices in Oregon causes a lumberjack to lose his job and he moves to Portland.
    d. An Indian family moves to the city of Calcutta after a landslide destroys their village.

13. Which of the following is *not* an example of infrastructure?
    a. a railroad
    b. a school
    c. a telephone line
    d. a dairy farm

14. Which of the following is a likely result of deforestation?
    a. The amount of carbon dioxide removed from the atmosphere is reduced.
    b. Wind blows soil away because the plant cover has been removed.
    c. Water runs off the land more rapidly and causes floods.
    d. all of the above

15. Which of the following is *not* likely to cause the degradation of rangeland?
    a. adding more animals to a herd grazing on rangeland
    b. a drought in which rainfall is lower than usual for three years
    c. planting grass seed on the land
    d. driving a vehicle off-road

16. Which of the following is an example of reforestation?
    a. replanting forest land that has been clear-cut
    b. planting a cherry tree in your backyard
    c. planting oak trees in a city
    d. all of the above

17. Which of the following is *not* an ecosystem service provided by rural lands?
    a. oxygen in the air
    b. plastic for making bottles
    c. aesthetic beauty
    d. wood for making paper

Short Answer

18. Explain one way rangeland can be degraded.
19. Do national parks and forests in the United States protect ecosystems from human activities? Explain your answer.
20. What is the difference between a U.S. wilderness area and a national park?
21. Are national parks located only in the United States?
22. How can building a mass transit system improve living standards in an urban area?

Interpreting Graphics

The map below shows a typical UN Biosphere Reserve. Use the map to answer questions 23–25.

23. Where is the reserve's research station located, and why has it been placed there rather than anywhere else in the reserve?
24. What indicators can you see that this reserve might be an ecotourism destination?
25. What does the map tell you about the function of buffer zone 2?

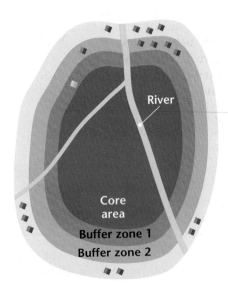

- ◢ Human settlement
- ◢ Tourism and education center
- ◢ Research station

Concept Mapping

26. Use the following terms to create a concept map: *geographic information system, land-use planning, infrastructure, population,* and *urban area.*

Critical Thinking

27. **Recognizing Relationships** Read about clear-cutting under the head "Harvesting Trees." What effects does clear-cutting a hillside have on the environment? **READING SKILLS**
28. **Drawing Inferences** If we see many invasive plant species and large areas of bare soil on rangeland, what conclusions can we draw about the land management practices on this rangeland? Explain your answer.
29. **Evaluating Assumptions** We tend to think that the main use of livestock is for meat. However, the Masai herders of Africa do not slaughter their cattle. They use the milk. They also bleed the cattle and use the blood to make a protein-rich sausage. What other uses for livestock can you think of that do not involve killing the animals?

Cross-Disciplinary Connection

30. **History** Find out how deforestation has affected a community. If you live in a forest biome, you can document the effects of deforestation on local rivers and farmland. If not, you will probably have to find an example on the Internet or in a magazine. Write a paragraph for your answer, using at least three key terms from this chapter. **WRITING SKILLS**

Portfolio Project

31. **Research** Diagram the growth of your community over the last 100 years. Express this as a graph that shows the growth of the population and a map that shows the area of ground the community covers. There are various possible sources for the data you will need. If there is a local historical society, this is probably the best source. Otherwise, city hall or the local newspaper will probably have the information.

The graph below shows land cover in the United States in 1997. Use the graph below to answer questions 32–33.

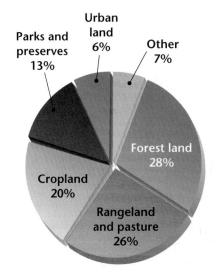

Parks and preserves 13%

Urban land 6%

Other 7%

Forest land 28%

Cropland 20%

Rangeland and pasture 26%

32. **Analyzing Data** If the percentage of cropland increased to 25 percent, and all other land cover categories except for rangeland and pasture remained the same, what percentage would rangeland and pasture be?

33. **Making Calculations** What percentage of the United States is planted in crops if 11 percent of cropland is idle (unplanted) at any one time?

34. **Communicating Main Ideas** In what ways does urban sprawl reduce the quality of life for people in the suburbs as well as in the town or city?

Read the passage below, and then answer the questions that follow.

When more people live in a city than its infrastructure can support, living conditions deteriorate. For example, many people do not have access to clean water for drinking and washing. In addition, overcrowding causes the prices of existing houses and apartments to rise above the reach of many workers. Increasing numbers of people become homeless. These problems have become so widespread throughout the developed and developing world, that the term *urban crisis* was coined to describe the problem. According to the United Nations, the crisis is so bad that almost one-fourth of the world's city dwellers could be homeless by the year 2020.

1. According to the passage, which of the following statements is true?
   a. Cities have grown so rapidly that the rural areas that supply the cities with food and fuel cannot do so fast enough.
   b. Overcrowded cities lead to unaffordable housing and homelessness.
   c. The urban crisis does not usually involve water pollution.
   d. Living conditions usually improve when the population of a city increases.

2. Which of the following is an example of the urban crisis, according to the passage?
   a. To make space for more cars, roads into and through a city are widened.
   b. Deforestation in the countryside surrounding a city causes the water level in a river that flows through the city to increase when it rains.
   c. Homelessness is increasing rapidly in cities in both developed and developing countries.
   d. Inadequate planning for a growing number of commuters results in traffic jams on roads leading into the city in rush hour.

Understanding Concepts

Directions (1–5): For *each* question, write on a separate sheet of paper the letter of the correct answer.

1 What is the term for the movement of people from rural areas to cities?
  A. land-use planning
  B. infrastructure
  C. urban sprawl
  D. urbanization

2 Unplanned, rapid urban growth can create what problem?
  F. degradation of the ecosystem
  G. elimination of invasive vegetation
  H. infrastructure that can not adequately support the population
  I. rangeland damaged from overgrazing

3 Which of the following statements generalizes population distribution changes over the last 200 years?
  A. Urban areas have doubled in size in 200 years.
  B. More people lived in rural areas 200 years ago.
  C. Population distribution has not significantly changed in 200 years.
  D. Undeveloped countries have seen the most changes in 200 years.

4 Which of the following is an important aspect of land management?
  F. increasing the overall size of the herds
  G. leasing public lands from the federal government
  H. reducing damage to land caused by overgrazing
  I. removing fences from rangeland to allow livestock more grazing area

5 Which of the following is an environmental benefit of open space?
  A. Open space leads to a reduction in traffic flow.
  B. Open space helps filter pollutants from air and water.
  C. Open space means more land is available for planting.
  D. Open space results in lower temperatures in the wintertime.

Directions (6–7): For *each* question, write a short response.

6 As the human population grows, more land resources are needed to support the population. Describe two ways that human activities make rural lands less productive.

7 Analyze the relationship between protecting rangeland and ensuring the world's food supply.

Reading Skills

Directions (8–10): Read the passage below. Then answer the questions.

People use enormous amounts of wood. The worldwide average is 1,800 cm³ of wood per person each day. However, each person in the United States uses about 3.5 times this amount, the equivalent of cutting down a 30 m tall tree every year.

The timber industry classifies forest lands into three categories—virgin forests, which is forest that has never been cut; native forest, which is forest that is planted and managed; and tree farms, which are areas where trees are planted in rows and harvested like other crops. The two most widely used methods of harvesting trees are clear-cutting and selective cutting. Clear-cutting is the process of removing all trees from an area of land. Clear-cutting large areas destroys wildlife habitat and causes soil erosion. Selective cutting is the process of cutting and removing only middle-aged or mature trees. Selective cutting is more expensive than clear-cutting but selective cutting is usually much less destructive.

8 The forest land classification that can be deduced as the most rare is
  F. deciduous forest
  G. evergreen forest
  H. native forest
  I. virgin forest

9 Compare clear-cutting with selective logging.

10 What is the most effective way to help a forest recover from tree harvesting?

Interpreting Graphics

Directions (11–14): For *each* question below, record the correct answer on a separate sheet of paper.

The map below shows land use in the United States. Use this map to answer questions 11 through 14.

Land Use in the United States

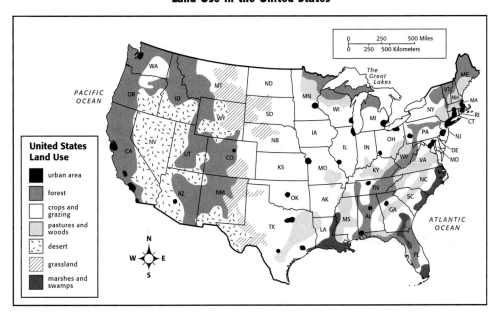

11 Which land-use designation has the **greatest** potential for growth?
A. forest
B. desert
C. urban areas
D. pasture lands

12 What is the **most** prevalent land use in the continental United States?
F. crops and grazing
G. desert
H. pastures and woods
I. urban areas

13 Which of the following conclusions is suggested by the map?
A. Most farmers live west of the Rocky Mountains.
B. There are more rural lands in the U.S. than there are urban lands.
C. Manufacturing plants are concentrated along the Mississippi River.
D. Industries dependent on wood and wood products are located mostly in the Midwest.

14 What percentage of states in the continental United States have some land available for crops and grazing?
F. 10%
G. 50%
H. 80%
I. 100%

Test TIP

Try to picture in your mind the terrain and buildings that would be present in the various land-use designations.

Inquiry Lab: DESIGN YOUR OWN

Objectives

▶ **Create** a simulated land-use model.

▶ **Recognize** conflicts of interest that arise during a negotiation.

▶ **USING SCIENTIFIC METHODS** **Analyze** and draw conclusions about the effect of compromise on the desired outcome for each interested party in a land-use plan.

Materials

colored pencils
graph paper
pens

Laws

- At least 10 percent of each type of habitat must be preserved.

- Landfills must be at least two acres away from all housing, wetlands and freshwater sites.

- Roads and bridges may cross rivers and wetlands but they must go around large natural areas.

- Roads must be connected to all developed areas of the city.

- There must be no building over wetlands, slopes and fresh water. Only parks may partially cover these habitats. Roads and bridges may cross them.

Creating a Land-Use Model

Land-use plans are drawn up by planners, but they are created with the combined input of various members of a community. Along with three other people, you are meeting to plan the development of 400 acres of land for your growing city. Your team is composed of the following four members:

Team Members

- The **Planner** is concerned with creating a plan that encourages the sort of growth that will attract businesses and new citizens to the area.

- The **Developer** bought the land from the city and is interested in the right to build housing and a shopping center.

- The **Conservationist** is interested in preserving open space and natural areas from further development.

- The **Law Enforcer** ensures that all of the laws and regulations are met for any new development project.

Procedure

1. Have each team member select one of the four jobs above.

2. Use all or part of a large piece of graph paper as your map. Mark off an area that will represent 400 acres. Determine the approximate scale, and label the sides of your area accordingly.

3. The planner will color in the map as follows:
   a. 40 acres will be fresh water (rivers and/or lakes) and will be colored light blue.
   b. 80 acres will be wetlands that are right next to some of the fresh water and will be colored light purple or lavender.
   c. 40 acres will be land that is too sloped for building and will be colored tan.
   d. 240 acres is land that is good for development and will be colored light green.

4. Once the land is colored in, it cannot be altered. That will be the land you work with.

5. After the area is colored in, the group must discuss how and where to put the following items:
   a. 40 acres for a landfill
   b. 20 acres for utilities such as power plants and water treatment facilities.
   c. 40 acres for parks and wildlife
   d. 40 acres for housing. Try to put the houses near a beautiful area.

e. 40 acres for shopping

f. 20 acres for anything that the group agrees to add. For example, you could add a few acres for community gardens or for sports and playing fields. The law enforcer cannot suggest anything, but if the group can't agree on what to add, the law enforcer may cast the deciding vote.

g. 40 acres of roads and bridges (you can divide an acre up so that you can build long, thin roads rather than create short, fat roads that are an entire acre thick). Make sure at least one road goes into and out of town.

6. The law enforcer should make sure that the plans abide by the planning regulations by checking the map for violations.

7. Use the key under the map to mark which areas are which. For example, an R denotes a road or bridge. Use a pencil and write in the things softly at first in case changes are to be made. You may need a second copy of the map in case you make mistakes the first time.

Analysis

1. Describing Events Did everyone on your team agree on the plan, or were there conflicts of interest? Explain.

2. Describing Events Were you able to get everything your team wanted into the plan or did you face any problems? Describe what happened.

3. Identifying Patterns How did the features of the land constrain the plan that you made? Did you encounter any problems?

Conclusions

4. Evaluating Results Does the plan your group created meet the needs of all of the group members? Does it allow for development while preserving the environment?

5. Evaluating Models How do you think this land planning "simulation" compares to the real-life process of land-use planning?

Extension

1. Research and Communications Look in the newspaper or on the Internet for a story about a land-use controversy in your area. Identify the different members involved. Role-play with your team to see what forces will bear on this controversy.

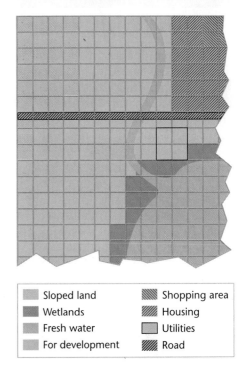

Sloped land	Shopping area
Wetlands	Housing
Fresh water	Utilities
For development	Road

▶ **Example Map** This is an example of what your land-use model might look like.

RESTORING THE RANGE

When Ohioan J. David Bamberger first moved to San Antonio, Texas as a vacuum cleaner sales representative, he was charmed by the dry, grass-covered rangeland of the Texas Hill Country. But much of the land was degraded. It had been overgrazed by cattle and was left with thin soil and dried-up creeks.

Bamberger became intrigued by the idea of restoring some of the range to its original beauty. He was inspired by a book his mother gave him called *Pleasant Valley,* by Louis Bromfield. Long before it was popular, Bromfield had theories about how degraded habitats could be restored and how they could then be managed in a sustainable manner. Bamberger was intrigued by the idea of putting Bromfield's theories into action.

The Bamberger Ranch

In 1959, David Bamberger bought his first plot of land near Johnson City. Since then, David and Margaret Bamberger have expanded the ranch to nearly 2,300 hectares (5,500 acres). It is one of the largest habitat restoration projects in Texas, and shows the beauty of this area before it was damaged by human activities.

In its natural state, the ranch should have been grassland, with woody shrubs only near creeks. Instead, it had become overgrown with juniper shrubs and trees (often called cedar, *Juniperus ashei*), which can grow in poor soil and choke out other plants.

Bamberger read everything he could find on the degradation and restoration of rangeland. He found that two main things destroy the range: overgrazing and the suppression of wildfires.

Overgrazing causes soil erosion. The lack of fires permits the growth of shrubs that shade out grasses and wildflowers.

The Bambergers set to work to restore the property. They cleared most of the junipers, which left more water in the soil. They planted native trees, wildflowers, and grasses, and they controlled the grazing.

Grazing is necessary for healthy grassland. The American prairies were home to huge herds of bison (buffalo), which cropped the grass and fertilized the soil with their droppings. The Bambergers combined the grazing they needed with the preservation of an endangered species. San Antonio Zoo asked the Bambergers if they could help preserve the endangered scimitar-horned oryx, an antelope with thin, curved horns that is native to North Africa. Only a few small herds of this species remained, and the zoo feared that the oryx were becoming inbred, with too little genetic diversity. The Bambergers agreed, and the ranch is now home to a large herd of oryx.

The Effects of Restoration

The change in the ranch since Bamberger first bought it is most obvious at the fence line bordering the ranch. Beyond the fence there is a small forest of junipers and little other vegetation. On Bamberger's side, the main plants are grasses and wildflowers, with shrubs and trees in canyons and gullies beside the creeks. When the Bambergers first arrived, they counted only 48 species of birds on the ranch. Now, there are more than 150 species because there are many more different plants on the ranch. In the early

▶ David Bamberger, founder of the Bamberger Ranch Preserve.

days, deer on the ranch weighed only about 20 kg. Now they weigh about 40 kg, thanks to the improved grazing.

In addition to deer and oryx, cattle and goats live on the ranch. Some of these are used for experiments on the effects of domestic animals on rangeland. Students and faculty from nearby universities are studying this question by using exclosures. These are fences that keep large animals out of an area. The vegetation inside an exclosure is invariably taller than that outside because grazing animals are excluded. But in addition, the plant mix inside the exclosure is different from that outside. This is because grazing mammals eat only a few nutritious species and leave the others.

The Distribution of Water

One important change in the ranch under the Bambergers' management has been the change in water distribution. Water is very important in rangeland, which naturally gets little rainfall. Many of the creeks dry up between rainy periods, but water remains in the soil and underground. Grasses have spreading root systems that absorb water from a wide area. Poor management changes this balance by allowing junipers to take over the land. A juniper can take up 10 L of water a day from the soil, leaving too little for nearby grasses and wildflowers to survive. Then, when it rains heavily, the junipers cannot absorb all the water and it runs off the land. With no grass roots to hold the soil in place, the soil erodes into the creeks.

When the Bambergers arrived at the ranch, it was degraded rangeland. They drilled wells 150 m deep (500 ft) and did not reach the water table. Now, with the restoration of grassland, soil erosion has been reduced and much more water remains in the soil. Creeks and lakes contain water for most of the year, and a dry spell is not a disaster. The water in the creeks and lakes is clear and full of fish, instead of muddy because it is full of soil.

Sustainability

The Bamberger Ranch is a working ranch, raising and selling livestock, but it is also home to dozens of other projects. Bamberger consultants advise others who are interested in managing rangeland in a sustainable fashion. Volunteers help by building and repairing nature trails and performing all kinds of maintenance work. The ranch hosts research on grasslands and range management, conferences on habitat restoration, educational workshops, as well as vacations for those interested in all aspects of nature.

▶ At nearly 2,300 hectares, the Bamberger Ranch is one of the largest habitat restoration projects in Texas. This is a photo of a portion of the Bamberger Ranch used for sustainable ranching.

What Do You Think?

Habitat restoration shows us what the land was like before the settlers arrived. It also shows us how much the land has changed under human management. Can you think of any habitat in your area that could be restored? How would you go about trying to restore it? What do you think it would look like after restoration?

Food and Agriculture

1 Feeding the World
2 Crops and Soil
3 Animals and Agriculture

PRE-READING ACTIVITY

Key-Term Fold

Before you read this chapter, create the **FoldNote** entitled "Key-Term Fold" described in the Reading and Study Skills section of the Appendix. Write a key term from the chapter on each tab of the key-term fold. Under each tab, write the definition of the key term.

This farmland in rural Pennsylvania is used to grow alfalfa, corn, and soybeans. Agriculture can be thought of as one of the most important relationships people have with the environment.

SECTION 1
Feeding the World

In 1985, lack of rain, loss of soil, and war caused crops to fail in Ethiopia. This resulted in **famine,** widespread starvation caused by a shortage of food. Events like the famine in Ethiopia present a frightening picture of the difficulty of feeding the Earth's growing population. By 2050, the world's farmers will need to feed about 9 billion people. That is 50 percent more than they feed today. In this chapter, you will learn why feeding all the world's people a nutritious diet is difficult, and how food production can be increased without irreversibly damaging the environment.

Humans and Nutrition

The human body uses food both as a source of energy and as a source of materials for building and maintaining body tissues. The amount of energy that is available in food is expressed in *Calories*. One Calorie (Cal) is equal to 1,000 calories, or one kilocalorie. As shown in **Table 1,** the major nutrients we get from food are carbohydrates, proteins, and lipids. Our bodies need smaller amounts of vitamins and minerals to remain healthy.

Malnutrition is a condition that occurs when people do not consume enough Calories or do not eat a sufficient variety of foods to fulfill all of the body's needs. There are many forms of malnutrition. For example, humans need to get eight essential amino acids from proteins. This is easily done if a variety of foods are eaten. However, in some parts of the world, the only sources of food may be corn or rice. Both corn and rice contain proteins, but they lack some essential amino acids, vitamins, and minerals. Protein-energy malnutrition results, affecting the normal physical and mental development of children.

Objectives

▶ Identify the major causes of malnutrition.

▶ Compare the environmental costs of producing different types of food.

▶ Explain how poverty is a major cause of malnutrition.

▶ Explain the importance of the green revolution.

Key Terms

famine
malnutrition
diet
yield

SCILINKS
www.scilinks.org
Topic: Food and Diet
Code: HE80590

Table 1 ▼

Major Nutrients in Human Foods				
Nutrient	Composition	Sources	Energy yield	Function
Carbohydrates	sugars	wheat, corn, and rice	4 Cal/g	is the main source of the body's energy
Lipids (oils and fats)	fatty acids and fatty alcohols	olives, nuts, and animal fats	9 Cal/g	helps form membranes and hormones
Proteins	amino acids	animal food and smaller amounts from plants	about 4 Cal/g	helps build and maintain all body structures

Connection to Biology

Essential Amino Acids Animals make their own proteins from amino acids. Essential amino acids are those that must be supplied in the diet because the body needs them but cannot make them from other amino acids. A lack of essential amino acids in the diet can lead to the human diseases kwashiorkor and marasmus, which can cause brain damage in children.

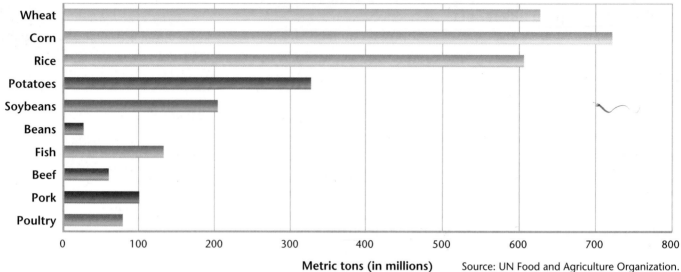

World Food Production, 2004

Metric tons (in millions)   Source: UN Food and Agriculture Organization.

Figure 1 ▶ This bar graph shows that in 2004, more grains (wheat, corn, and rice) were produced than any other food. Wheat and corn are eaten by humans and are fed to farm animals.

Sources of Nutrition A person's **diet** is the type and amount of food that he or she eats. A healthy diet is one that maintains a balance of the right amounts of nutrients, minerals, and vitamins. In most parts of the world, people eat large amounts of food that is high in carbohydrates, such as rice, potatoes, and bread. As shown in **Figure 1,** the foods produced in the greatest amounts worldwide are *grains*, plants of the grass family whose seeds are rich in carbohydrates. Besides eating grains, most people eat fruits, vegetables, and smaller amounts of meats, nuts, and other foods that are rich in fats and proteins.

Diets Around the World People worldwide generally consume the same major nutrients and eat the same basic kinds of food. But diets vary by region, as shown in **Figure 2.** People in more-developed countries tend to eat more food and a larger proportion of proteins and fats than people eat in less developed countries. For example, in the United States, almost half of all Calories people consume come from meat, fish, and oil.

✓ Reading Check In general, how do the diets of people in developed countries compare with the diets of people in developing countries? (See the Appendix for answers to Reading Checks.)

Figure 2 ▶ People in developed countries generally eat more food and more proteins and fats than people in less developed countries eat.

Total Calorie Supply, per Person, per Day

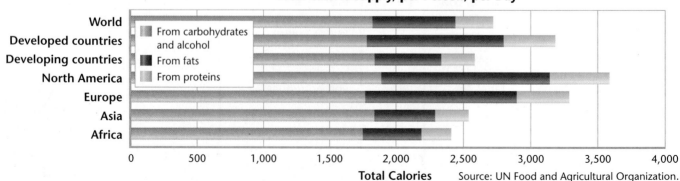

Total Calories   Source: UN Food and Agricultural Organization.

The Ecology of Food

As the human population grows, farmland and suburbs replace forests and grasslands. Feeding everyone while maintaining natural ecosystems becomes more difficult. Different kinds of agriculture have different environmental impacts and different levels of efficiency.

Food Efficiency The *efficiency* of a given type of agriculture is a measure of the quantity of food produced on a given area of land with limited inputs of energy and resources. An ideal food crop is one that efficiently produces a large amount of food with little negative impact on the environment.

On average, more energy, water, and land are used to produce a Calorie of food from animals than to produce a Calorie of food from plants. Animals that are raised for human use are usually fed plant matter. Because less energy is available at each higher level on a food chain, only about 10 percent of the energy from the plants gets stored in the animals. Thus, a given area of land can usually produce more food for humans when it is used to grow plants than when it is used to raise animals. The efficiency of raising plants for food is one reason why diets around the world are largely based on plants. However, meat generally provides more nutrients per gram than most food from plants.

Old and New Foods Researchers hope to improve the efficiency of food production by studying plants and other organisms that have high **yield**—the amount of food that can be produced in a given area. Researchers are interested in organisms that can thrive in various climates and that do not require large amounts of fertilizer, pesticides, or fresh water. As shown in **Figure 3**, some organisms have been a source of food for centuries, while other sources are just being discovered.

Figure 3 ▶ Glasswort (top) is a salad green that may become an important food source in the future because it can grow in salty soil. Seaweed (bottom) has been harvested and eaten by humans for centuries.

Figure 4 ▶ Malnourished citizens in Bangladesh (an impoverished country in Asia) wait for food assistance.

World Food Problems

The world's farmers produce enough grain to feed up to 10 billion people an adequate vegetarian diet. However, no one is satisfied with having just enough to eat. Many of us consume about a third of our calories from animals, not grain.

Poverty As shown in **Figure 4,** malnutrition today is almost entirely a result of poverty. No one with enough money, anywhere in the world, needs to be hungry. The world's hungry are nearly all farm workers and *subsistence farmers*—farmers who grow only enough food for local use. They work tiny plots of land, trying to produce enough food for their families, with something left over to sell. They generally do not have access to enough water for irrigation, which would increase the productivity of their land. Most of them live in extreme poverty, defined as an income of less than $1 a day. The world's hungry live mainly in Africa, Asia, and the mountains of South America.

More Income and More Food The number of people living in extreme poverty has declined by nearly half a billion since 1980. This achievement is largely the result of rapid economic development in East Asia, especially in China and India. **Figure 5** shows, however, that although the world's grain production has increased for 50 years, it has not grown as fast as the world's population. To feed the people of the world in 2050, we will need to produce more food. As well, we will need to abolish poverty, particularly among rural people. Increasing the productivity of the world's subsistence farmers will go a long way toward achieving both goals.

✔ **Reading Check** What could be done to increase the productivity of the land worked by subsistence farmers?

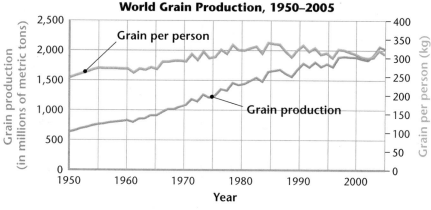

World Grain Production, 1950–2005

Source: U.S. Department of Agriculture.

Figure 5 ▶ Worldwide grain production has increased steadily, but not as rapidly as the population has grown.

The Green Revolution

Between 1950 and 1970, Mexico increased its production of wheat eight-fold and India doubled its production of rice, without increasing the area of farmland used. These spectacular increases were called *the green revolution*. They resulted from new varieties of grain, as shown in **Figure 6.** The new varieties produce large yields if they are supplied with enough water, fertilizer, and pesticides. The green revolution reduced the price of food and improved the lives of millions of people.

The green revolution had limitations, however. Most of the increases that resulted from the green revolution came from large farms, which continue to increase their productivity. Because subsistence farmers often live in extreme poverty, they do not have the money to acquire the water and chemicals that the new crop varieties need.

As well, subsistence farmers cannot use much machinery because their farms generally consist of less than 2 acres. Subsistence farmers need small-scale irrigation systems and high-value crops, such as vegetables and fruits, that they can sell. Much research today is devoted to developing plant varieties that produce high yields of nutritious food on poor soil, using as little water and expensive chemicals as possible. Distributing the seeds and technology to scattered rural farms remains a problem to be solved.

Figure 6 ▶ New rice varieties and farming methods developed during the green revolution are used to increase yield in this experimental farm in China.

SECTION 1 Review

1. **Identify** the major causes of malnutrition.

2. **Compare** the environmental costs of producing different types of food.

3. **Explain** how malnutrition today is linked to poverty.

4. **Describe** the importance and effects of the green revolution.

CRITICAL THINKING

5. **Identifying Relationships** Study the graph in Figure 5. World grain production increased during the 1990s. Why did the amount of grain per person decline during that decade?

6. **Inferring Relationships** Write a short paragraph that explains how a decrease in the production of grain worldwide could lead to a shortage of other food sources. **WRITING SKILLS**

Crops and Soil

SEV.4.a; SEV.4.b; SEV.4.c

EARTH SCIENCE · CONNECTION

Objectives

▶ Distinguish between traditional and modern agricultural techniques.

▶ Describe fertile soil.

▶ Describe the need for soil conservation.

▶ Explain the benefits and environmental impacts of pesticide use.

▶ Explain what is involved in integrated pest management.

▶ Explain how genetic engineering is used in agriculture.

Key Terms

arable land
topsoil
erosion
desertification
compost
salinization
pesticide
biological pest control
genetic engineering

Much of the Earth's surface cannot be farmed. Only about 10 percent of the Earth's surface is **arable land,** land that can be used to grow crops. Urban areas occupy about 3 percent of the Earth's land surface and are expanding, often into arable land. We need to use our remaining arable land as efficiently as possible, for it to continue to grow enough food for the world.

Agriculture: Traditional and Modern

The basic processes of farming include plowing, fertilization, irrigation, and pest control. In traditional agriculture, plows are pushed by the farmer or pulled by livestock. Plowing helps crops grow by mixing soil nutrients, loosening soil particles, and uprooting weeds. Organic fertilizers, such as manure, are used to enrich the soil so that plants grow strong and healthy. Fields are irrigated by water flowing through ditches. Weeds are removed by hand or machine. These traditional techniques have been used since the earliest days of farming, centuries before tractors and pesticides were invented.

In industrialized countries, the basic processes of farming are now carried out using modern agricultural methods. Machinery powered by fossil fuels is now used to plow the soil and harvest crops, as shown in **Figure 7.** Synthetic chemical fertilizers are now used instead of manure and plant wastes to fertilize soil. A variety of overhead sprinklers and drip systems may be used for irrigation. And synthetic chemicals are used to kill pests.

Figure 7 ▶ In modern agriculture, machinery is used to do much of the work previously performed by humans and animals.

Fertile Soil: The Living Earth

Soil that can support the growth of healthy plants is called *fertile soil*. Plant roots grow in **topsoil**, the surface layer of soil, which is usually richer in organic matter than the subsoil is. Fertile topsoil is composed of living organisms, rock particles, water, air, and organic matter, such as dead and decomposing organisms.

Most soil forms when rock is broken down into smaller and smaller fragments by wind, water, and chemical weathering. *Chemical weathering* happens when the minerals in the rock react chemically with substances such as water to form new materials. Temperature changes and moisture cause rock to crack and break apart, which creates smaller particles on which the seeds of pioneer plants fall and take root. It can take hundreds or even thousands of years to form a few centimeters of soil.

Other processes also help to produce fertile topsoil. The rock particles supply mineral nutrients to the soil. Fungi and bacteria live in the soil. They decompose dead plants and organic debris, and add more nutrients to the soil. Earthworms, insects, and other small animals help plants grow by breaking up the soil and allowing air and water into it. **Table 2** lists some of the organisms that live in fertile soil.

As you can see in **Figure 8**, several layers of soil lie under the topsoil. The bottom layer is bedrock, which is the solid rock from which most soil originally forms.

Reading Check Name two processes that help to make soil fertile.

Table 2 ▼

Numbers of Organisms in Average Farm Soil	
Organisms	**Quantity**
Insects	23 million per hectare
All arthropods (including insects)	725 million per hectare
Bacteria	2.5 billion per gram
Algae	50,000 per gram
Earthworms	6 million per hectare

Note: One hectare equals about 2.47 acres.
Source: US Department of Agriculture.

Figure 8 ▶ Soil is made of rock particles, air, water, and dead and living organisms. The number and characteristics of the soil layers may be different in different types of soil.

Ants and earthworms break up and aerate the soil.

Bacteria and fungi decompose organic matter.

Rhizobium bacteria produce fixed nitrogen.

Surface litter fallen leaves and partially decomposed organic matter

Topsoil organic matter, living organisms, and rock particles

Zone of leaching dissolved or suspended materials moving downward

Subsoil larger rock particles with organic matter, and inorganic compounds

Rock particles rock that has undergone weathering

Bedrock solid rock layer

Section 2 Crops and Soil **413**

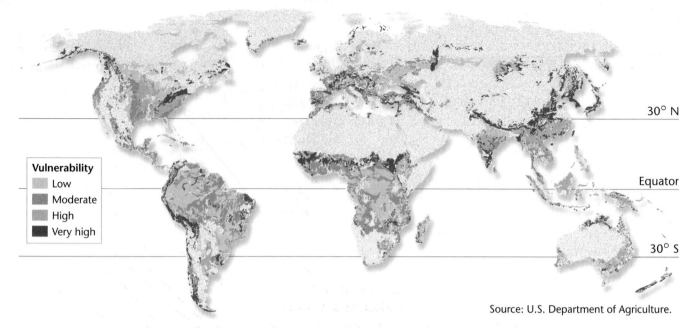

30° N

Equator

30° S

Vulnerability
- Low
- Moderate
- High
- Very high

Source: U.S. Department of Agriculture.

Figure 9 ▶ Soil erosion is one of the most serious environmental problems the world faces. This map shows the vulnerability of soils worldwide to erosion by water.

QuickLAB

Preventing Soil Erosion

Procedure

1. Obtain three **trays**, and fill one with **sod**, one with **topsoil**, and one with a type of mulch, such as **hay**.

2. Place each tray at an angle by creating a surface that resembles a hill by using **doorstoppers** and **textbooks**. Place a **large bowl** at the bottom of each tray to catch the runoff.

3. Sprinkle **2 L of water** slowly on each tray to simulate heavy rainfall.

4. Use a **scale** to weigh the runoff of soil and water that collected in each bowl.

Analysis

1. Which tray had the most soil erosion and water runoff? Which tray had the least? Why? What does this lab demonstrate about soil erosion?

Soil Erosion: A Global Problem

Erosion is the movement of rock and soil by wind and water. Eroded soil washes into nearby rivers or is blown away in clouds of dust. In the United States, about half of the original topsoil has been lost to erosion in the past 200 years. **Figure 9** shows potential soil erosion worldwide. Without topsoil, crops cannot be grown.

Most farming methods increase the rate of soil erosion. Plowing loosens the soil and removes plants that hold the soil in place. When water from irrigation runs off the land, it carries some of the soil with it.

Land Degradation

Land degradation happens when human activity or natural processes damage the land so that it can no longer support the local ecosystem. In areas with dry climates, desertification can result. **Desertification** is the process by which land in arid or semiarid areas becomes more desertlike.

Desertification has happened in the Sahel region of northern Africa. In the past, people who lived in the drier parts of the Sahel grazed animals. People who lived in parts of the Sahel with more rainfall planted crops. The grazing animals were moved from place to place to find food. The cropland was planted for only a few years, and then the land was allowed to lie *fallow,* or to remain unplanted, for several years. These practices allowed the land to support the people in the Sahel. But the population in the region has grown, and the land is being farmed, grazed, and deforested faster than it can regenerate. Now, too many crops are planted too frequently, and fallow periods are being shortened or eliminated. As a result, the soil is losing its fertility and productivity. Because of overgrazing, the land has fewer plants to hold the topsoil in place. So, large areas have become desert and can no longer produce food.

Soil Conservation

There are many ways of protecting and managing topsoil to reduce erosion. Soil usually erodes downhill, and many soil conservation methods are designed to prevent downhill erosion, as shown in **Figure 10.** Building soil-retaining terraces across a hillside may be cost-effective for producers of valuable crops, such as wine grapes and coffee. On gentler slopes, *contour plowing* is used. This method includes plowing across the slope of a hill instead of up and down the slope. An even more effective method of plowing is leaving strips of vegetation across the hillside instead of plowing the entire slope. These strips catch soil and water that run down the hill. Overhead irrigation tends to wash away soil. Soil (and water) can be conserved by using drip irrigation instead.

In traditional farming, after a crop is harvested, the soil is plowed to turn it over and bury the remains of the harvested plants. In *no-till farming,* shown in **Figure 11,** a crop is harvested without turning over the soil. Later, the seeds of the next crop are planted among the remains of the previous crop. The remains of the first crop hold the soil in place while the new crop develops. No-till farming saves time compared with conventional methods. It can also reduce soil erosion to one-tenth of the erosion caused by traditional methods. However, no-till farming may not be suitable for some crops. Other disadvantages can include soil that is too densely packed and lower crop yields over time.

Figure 10 ▶ Terracing (left) keeps soil in multiple, small, level fields. Contour plowing (right) follows the natural contours of the land. Both methods prevent soil erosion by keeping water from running directly downhill.

SC**LINKS**®
www.scilinks.org
Topic: Soil Erosion
Code: HE81410

Figure 11 ▶ This farmer is practicing no-till farming. The tractor plants a new crop by poking seeds into the soil through the remains of the old crop.

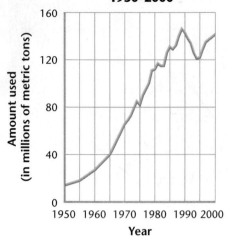

World Fertilizer Use, 1950–2000

Source: UN Food and Agriculture Organization.

Figure 12 ▶ The use of inorganic fertilizers has increased dramatically worldwide since 1950.

Connection to Geology

Soil Formation Over Time
Most rock breaks down into finer particles over time and changes from gravel to sand to clay. You can tell the age of soil by looking at its rock particles. Young soil is sandy or gravelly, and it falls apart when you squeeze it in your hand. Older soil contains clay, and damp clay stays together in lumps when you squeeze it in your hand.

Enriching the Soil

In traditional farming, the soil is enriched by adding organic matter, such as manure and leaves, to the soil. As the organic matter decomposes, it adds nutrients to the soil and improves the texture of the soil. However, inorganic fertilizers that contain nitrogen, phosphorus, and potassium have changed farming methods. Without these fertilizers, world food production would be less than half of what it is today. Over the past 50 years, the use of such fertilizers has increased rapidly, as shown in **Figure 12**.

A modern method of enriching the soil is to use both organic and inorganic fertilizers by adding compost and chemical fertilizers to the soil. **Compost** is partly decomposed organic material. Compost comes from many sources. For example, you can buy composted cow manure in a garden store. Also, many cities and industries now compost yard waste and crop wastes. This compost is sold to farmers and gardeners, and the process is saving costly landfill space.

Salinization

The accumulation of salts in the soil is known as **salinization** (SAL uh nie ZAY shuhn). Salinization is a major problem in places such as California and Arizona, which have low rainfall and naturally salty soil. In these areas, irrigation water comes from rivers or groundwater, which is saltier than rainwater. When water evaporates from irrigated land, salts are left behind. Eventually, the soil may become so salty that plants cannot grow.

Irrigation can also cause salinization by raising the groundwater level temporarily. Once groundwater comes near the surface, the groundwater is drawn up through the soil like water is drawn up through a sponge. When the water reaches the surface, the water evaporates and leaves salts in the soil. Salinization can be slowed if irrigation canals are lined to prevent water from seeping into the soil, or if the soil is watered heavily to wash out salts.

✓ Reading Check Why is salinization a problem in California and Arizona?

SECTION 2 Mid-Section Review

1. **Explain** the differences between traditional and modern farming methods.

2. **Describe** the structure and composition of fertile soil.

3. **Explain** why the presence of plants helps prevent soil erosion.

4. **Explain** why soil conservation is an important agricultural practice.

CRITICAL THINKING

5. **Inferring Relationships** Study the graph in Figure 12. What do you think might have happened to food production between 1990 and 1995?

6. **Applying Ideas** Erosion is a natural process. Why has it become such a serious environmental problem? Write a paragraph that explains your reasoning.
   WRITING SKILLS

Figure 13 ▶ **Examples of major crop pests** include ❶ weeds, ❷ plant-eating insects, and ❸ fungi.

Pest Control

In North America, insects eat about 13 percent of all crops. Crops in tropical climates suffer even greater insect damage because the insects grow and reproduce faster in these climates. In Kenya, for example, insects destroy more than 25 percent of the nation's crops. Worldwide, pests destroy about 33 percent of the world's potential food harvest.

As shown in **Figure 13**, insects are one of several types of organisms considered pests. A *pest* is any organism that occurs where it is not wanted or that occurs in large enough numbers to cause economic damage. Humans try to control populations of many types of pests, including many plants, fungi, and microorganisms.

Wild plants often have more protection from pests than crop plants do. Wild plants grow throughout a landscape, so pests have a harder time finding and feeding on a specific plant. Crop plants, however, are usually grown together in large fields, which provides pests with a one-stop source of food. Wild plants are also protected from pests by a variety of pest predators that live on or near the plants. Some wild plants have even evolved defenses to many pests, such as poisonous chemicals that repel pests.

Pesticides

Many farmers rely on pesticides to produce their crops. **Pesticides** are chemicals used to kill insects, weeds, and other crop pests. During the last 50 years, scientists invented many new pesticides. The pesticides were so effective that farmers began to rely on them almost completely to protect their crops from pests. However, pesticides can also harm beneficial plants and insects, wildlife, and even people.

Crop Rotation Farmers and gardeners have known for centuries that you get higher yields and less pest damage if you plant different crops each year on a piece of land. This method works because most pests are specialists and will only eat one or a few types of plants. The tomato hornworm is an example of one of these pests. If you plant tomatoes in one place every year, the hornworm population grows rapidly and will destroy the crop. If beans are planted in place of the tomatoes in alternate years, the hornworms cannot find food and will die.

Figure 14 ▶ A cropduster sprays pesticide on a field of pineapples in Hawaii. Cropdusting is an easy way to apply pesticide to a large area.

Pesticide Resistance You might think that the most effective way to get rid of pests is to spray often with large amounts of pesticides, as shown in **Figure 14.** However, over time, this approach usually makes the pest problem worse. Pest populations may evolve *resistance,* the ability to survive exposure to a particular pesticide. More than 500 species of insects have developed resistance to pesticides since the 1940s.

Human Health Concerns Pesticides are designed to kill organisms, so they may also be dangerous to humans. For example, in some areas fruit and vegetable farmers use large amounts of pesticides on their crops. Cancer rates among children in these areas are sometimes higher than the national average, and nervous system disorders may be common. Workers in pesticide factories may also become ill. And people who live near these factories may be endangered by accidental chemical leaks. People who apply pesticides need to follow safety guidelines to protect themselves.

Pollution and Persistence The problem of pesticides harming people and other organisms is especially serious with pesticides that are persistent. *Persistent* pesticides do not break down rapidly into harmless chemicals when they enter the environment. As a result, they accumulate in the water and soil. Some persistent pesticides have been banned in the United States, but many of them remain in the environment for many years. DDT, a persistent pesticide banned in the United States in the 1970s, can still be detected in the environment and has even been found in women's breast milk.

✓ Reading Check Why can spraying pests with large amounts of pesticides become ineffective over time?

Connection to ▶ Law

Pesticide Regulation The only pesticides that are fully regulated in the United States are newly introduced pesticides designed for use on some food crops. Many older pesticides in use have not been adequately tested for toxicity and are not effectively regulated. According to the National Academy of Sciences, much of the cancer risk from pesticides in our diet comes from older pesticides used on foods such as tomatoes, potatoes, and oranges.

Figure 15 ▶ A parasitic wasp injects its eggs into an aphid (left). A predatory mite is attacked by another species of mite (right).

Biological Pest Control

Most farmers practice some form of *pest management*. **Biological pest control** is the use of living organisms to control pests. Every pest has enemies in the wild, and these enemies can sometimes be used to control pest populations, as shown in **Figure 15**. One of the first recorded examples of biological control was in India in the mid-1800s. American prickly pear cactus had been introduced into India to feed insects that are used to make a valuable red dye. Because the cactus had no natural enemies in India, the cactus grew and spread. The plants were finally controlled by the introduction of an American beetle that eats the cactus.

Pathogens Organisms that cause disease, called *pathogens* (PATH uh juhnz), can also be used to control pests. One of the most common pathogens used to control pests is the bacterium *Bacillus thuringiensis* (buh SIL uhs THUHR in JIEN sis), often abbreviated *Bt*. This bacterium can kill the caterpillars of moths and butterflies that we consider to be pests.

Plant Defenses Scientists and farmers have bred plant varieties that have defenses against pests. For example, if you buy tomato plants or seeds, you may see that they are labeled "VNT." This label means they are resistant to certain fungi, worms, and viruses. Examples of plant defenses include chemical compounds that repel pests and physical barriers, such as tougher skin.

Chemicals from Plants Another type of biological pest control also makes use of plants' defensive chemicals. For example, chemicals found in chrysanthemum plants are now sold as pesticides. Most insect sprays that contain these chemicals are designed for use in the home because they are less harmful to humans and pets. These products are biodegradable, which means that they are broken down by bacteria and other decomposers.

FIELD ACTIVITY

Pest Search Make a list of the pests you can find in your area. Look for weeds and insects. What evidence can you find that these organisms are pests? You will not be able to see pests in the soil or microscopic bacteria, fungi, or viruses, but you may be able to see the damage the microscopic pests cause—black spots or dead patches on leaves. Can you think of a way to decrease the damage that is caused by these pests that involves the use of biological pest control? Record your observations in your *EcoLog*.

Organic Chemistry All food contains organic chemicals, but the term *organic* is used differently in the field of chemistry than in agriculture. The term generally means "of or pertaining to living organisms." In chemistry, an *organic chemical* is any chemical compound that contains carbon. Most organic chemicals are derived from living organisms, but chemists can now synthesize organic chemicals—and even invent new ones—in the lab. In contrast, *organic agriculture* is the practice of raising crops or livestock without using synthetic chemicals. Foods labeled as organic in the grocery store have been raised using organic methods.

Disrupting Insect Breeding If you have a dog, you may feed it a pill once a month to keep it free of fleas. The pill contains a *growth regulator,* a chemical that interferes with some stage of a pest's life cycle. When a flea sucks the dog's blood, the flea ingests the growth regulator. The regulator stops the flea's eggs from developing into adult fleas.

Pheromones (FER uh MOHNZ), chemicals produced by one organism that affect the behavior of another organism, can also be used in pest control. For example, female moths release pheromones that attract males from miles away. By treating crops with pheromones, farmers can confuse the male moths and interfere with the mating of the moths. Another way to prevent insects from reproducing is to make it physically impossible for the males to reproduce. For example, male insects are treated with X rays to make them sterile and then are released. When they mate with females, the females produce eggs that do not develop.

Integrated Pest Management

Integrated pest management is a modern method of controlling pests on crops. The steps involved in integrated pest management are shown in **Figure 16.** The goal of integrated pest management is to reduce pest damage to a level that causes minimal economic damage. A different management program is developed for each crop. The program can include a mix of farming methods, biological pest control, and chemical pest control. Each of these methods is used at the appropriate time in the growing season. Fields are monitored from the time the crops are planted. When significant pest damage is found, the pest is identified. Then a program to control the pest is created.

✔ Reading Check Describe one strategy that can be used to control insect pests.

Figure 16 ▶ This flow diagram shows the steps involved in integrated pest management.

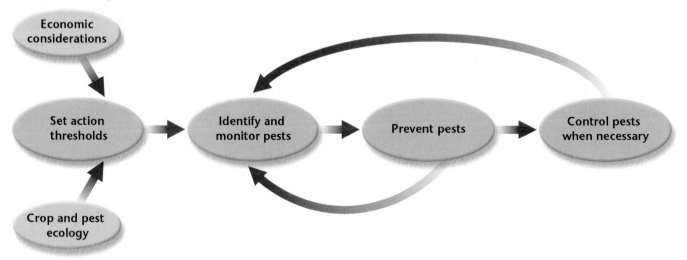

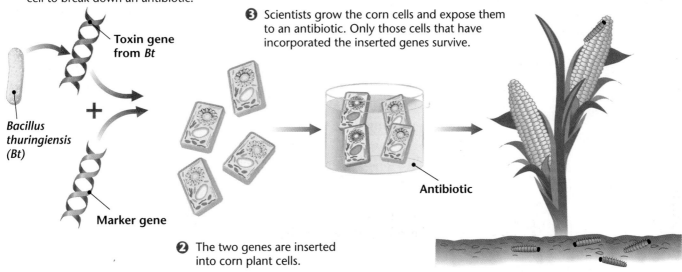

❶ Scientists isolate the gene from *Bt* that directs a cell to produce a toxin. The *Bt* gene is then joined to a "marker gene" that enables a cell to break down an antibiotic.

Toxin gene from *Bt*

Bacillus thuringiensis (Bt)

Marker gene

❷ The two genes are inserted into corn plant cells.

❸ Scientists grow the corn cells and expose them to an antibiotic. Only those cells that have incorporated the inserted genes survive.

Antibiotic

❹ The surviving cells grow into corn plants. These plants produce the *Bt* toxin, which kills caterpillars.

Figure 17 ▶ Genetic Engineering
This diagram shows the main steps used to produce a genetically modified plant—in this case, corn that produces its own insecticide.

Biological methods are the first methods used to control a pest. So, natural predators, pathogens, and parasites of the pest may be introduced. Cultivation controls, such as vacuuming insects off the plants, can also be used. As a last resort, small amounts of insecticides may be used. The insecticides are changed over time to reduce the ability of pests to evolve resistance.

Engineering a Better Crop

Plant breeding has been used since agriculture began. Farmers select the plants that have the tastiest tomatoes and the least pest damage. They save seeds from these plants to use in planting the next crop. The selected seeds are more likely to contain the genes for large, tasty fruits and for pest resistance than seeds from other plants are.

A faster way of creating the same result is to use **genetic engineering,** the technology in which genetic material in a living cell is modified for medical or industrial use. Genetic engineering involves isolating genes from one organism and implanting them into another. Scientists may use genetic engineering to transfer desirable traits, such as resistance to certain pests. The plants that result from genetic engineering are called *genetically modified* (GM) plants.

Figure 17 shows an example of the steps used to produce a GM plant. In this case, the gene introduced into the plant is not a plant gene. It is an insecticide gene from *Bt,* a bacterium that produces a chemical that kills plant-eating caterpillars but does not harm other insects. Plants that have the *Bt* gene make this insecticide within their leaves. Hundreds of gene transfers have now been performed to create many other GM crops.

www.scilinks.org
Topic: Genetic Engineering
Code: HE80654

Implications of Genetic Engineering In the United States, we now eat and use genetically engineered agricultural products every day. Many of these products have not been fully tested for their environmental impacts, and some scientists warn that these products will cause problems in the future. For example, genes are sometimes transferred from one species to another in the wild. Suppose a corn plant that was genetically engineered to be resistant to a pesticide were to pass the resistance genes to a wild plant. That wild plant might be a pest that could not be killed by that pesticide.

Sustainable Agriculture

Farming that conserves natural resources and helps keep the land productive indefinitely is called *sustainable agriculture*. Also called *low-input farming*, sustainable agriculture minimizes the use of energy, water, pesticides, and fertilizers. This method involves planting productive, pest-resistant crop varieties that require little energy, pesticides, fertilizers, and water. **Figure 18** shows an experimental farm where new sustainable agriculture techniques are being researched.

Figure 18 ▶ At the Land Institute in Salina, Kansas, sustainable agriculture techniques are being used to increase seed quantity in wheatgrass (background) and to increase yield in young sunflowers (foreground).

SECTION 2 **Review**

1. **Define** the term *pest*.

2. **Compare** the benefits and environmental impacts of pesticide use.

3. **Describe** how biological pest control is part of integrated pest management.

4. **Describe** how genetic engineering is used in agriculture.

CRITICAL THINKING

5. **Inferring Relationships** Write a paragraph to explain the similarities and differences between traditional plant breeding and genetic engineering. **WRITING SKILLS**

6. **Predicting Consequences** Read the description of integrated pest control in this section. Why do you think this pest control technique is not practiced everywhere? **READING SKILLS**

Animals and Agriculture

SCSh.9.d; SEV.4.c

We have seen that the total energy needed to grow plants for food is much less than the energy needed to raise animals as food. However, most animal proteins contain more essential amino acids than proteins found in plants do and most humans include some animal products in their diet. Food from animals has been the basis of life for some human populations for centuries.

Our ancestors obtained animal proteins by hunting and fishing, but today most people get animal proteins from domesticated species. About 50 animal species have been **domesticated,** which means that they are bred and managed for human use. Domesticated animals include chicken, sheep, cattle, honey bees, silkworms, fish, and shellfish. In many parts of the world, goats, pigs, and water buffalo are also important domesticated animals.

Food from Water

Because fish are an important food source for humans, the harvesting of fish has become an important industry worldwide. However, as shown in **Figure 19,** when too many fish are harvested over a long period of time, ecological systems can be damaged.

Overharvesting Catching or removing from a population more organisms than the population can replace is called **overharvesting.** Many governments are now trying to stop overharvesting. They have created no-fishing zones, so that fish populations can recover. Research shows that fishing in areas surrounding no-fishing zones improves after no-fishing zones have existed for a few years. In some areas of the world, such restrictions are necessary if fish markets, such as the one shown in **Figure 20,** are to prosper.

✓ **Reading Check** Describe one way governments try to prevent overharvesting.

Objectives

▶ Explain how overharvesting affects the supply of aquatic organisms used for food.

▶ Describe the current role of aquaculture in providing seafood.

▶ Describe the importance of livestock in providing food and other products.

Key Terms

domesticated
overharvesting
aquaculture
livestock
ruminant

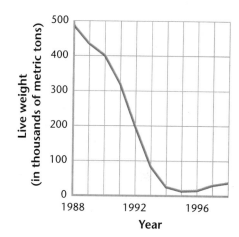

Source: Department of Fisheries and Oceans, Canada.

Figure 19 ▶ The North Atlantic cod fishery has collapsed because of overharvesting.

Figure 20 ▶ Whole, fresh tuna are one of the many types of seafood for sale at the Tokyo fish market, the largest fish market in the world.

Aquaculture

Fish and other aquatic organisms provide up to 20 percent of the animal protein consumed worldwide. But overharvesting is reducing the amount of fish and other organisms in the world's oceans. One solution to this problem may be a rapid increase in **aquaculture** (AK wuh KUHL chuhr), the raising of aquatic organisms for human use or consumption.

Aquaculture is not a new idea. This practice probably began in China about 4,000 years ago. Today, China leads the world in using aquaculture to produce freshwater fish.

There are a number of different methods of aquaculture. The oyster farm shown in **Figure 21** represents one such method. The most common method is known as a fish farm. Fish farms generally consist of many individual ponds that each contain fish at a specific stage of development. Clean water is circulated through the ponds and brings in oxygen while sweeping away carbon dioxide and fecal wastes. The fish grow to maturity in the ponds and then are harvested.

Another type of aquaculture operation is known as a ranch. In this method, fish such as salmon are raised until they reach a

Figure 21 ▶ This oyster farm in Washington State shows how aquaculture concentrates seafood production.

CASE STUDY

Menhaden: The Fish Behind the Farm

One of the largest commercial catches in the United States each year is of a fish that most people have never heard of—the menhaden (men HAYD 'n). Menhaden are small, silver, oily fish in the herring family and are found in the Atlantic Ocean from Maine to Florida. Menhaden make up more than one-third of the weight of commercial fish caught on the East Coast each year. But menhaden are so full of bones that they are inedible. So why are they so important?

When the first colonists arrived in the area we now call New England, local Indians showed them how to fertilize their crops with menhaden. This is where the legend that the best corn is grown by planting a fish with each seed came from. Later, menhaden oil was used

in oil lamps, and ground menhaden were added to cattle feed.

The menhaden catch is processed to produce fishmeal and fish oil. The oil is used in cooking oils and margarine. The fishmeal has a high protein content, and it is added to the feed of pets, chickens, turkey, hogs, cattle, and farm fish. Menhaden are also used by recreational fishers as bait for fish such as bluefin, striped bass, shark, and tuna.

Menhaden spawn in the ocean. The eggs hatch into larvae, which are carried into estuaries where they spend their first year. After the menhaden mature, they return to the ocean and usually live within 50 km of the coast. The Chesapeake Bay is one of the most important nurseries for menhaden.

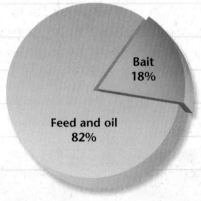

Source: Menhaden Resource Council.

▶ The enormous menhaden catch is used entirely to produce feed and oil and as bait for catching other fish.

Menhaden live in large schools near the surface, so they are easily caught with *purse seine* nets, nets that hang down from the surface. Boats towing the nets encircle the

certain age and then are released. The salmon, for example, migrate downstream to the ocean, where they live until adulthood. When they are mature, the fish return to their birthplace to reproduce. When they return, they are captured and harvested.

Today, most of the catfish, oysters, salmon, crayfish, and rainbow trout eaten in the United States are the products of aquaculture. In the 1980s, domestic production of these species quadrupled, and imports of these species increased even faster. Worldwide, about 23 percent of seafood now comes from aquaculture.

However, as with other methods of food production, aquaculture can cause environmental damage if not managed properly. For example, the aquatic organisms can create a large amount of waste, which can be a source of pollution. Also, because aquaculture requires so much water, the process can deplete local water supplies. In a few cases, sensitive wetlands have been damaged when large aquaculture operations were located within the wetland. Despite these problems, aquaculture will continue to be an important source of protein for the human diet.

Graphic
Organizer **Comparison Table**

Create the **Graphic Organizer** entitled "Comparison Table" described in the Appendix. Label the columns with "Aquaculture Farming" and "Aquaculture Ranching." Label the rows with "Advantages" and "Disadvantages." Then, fill in the table with details about the advantages and disadvantages of each type of aquaculture.

▶ A menhaden catch is unloaded from purse seine nets in Chesapeake Bay, Virginia.

fish, which are pumped out of the ocean into refrigerated containers.

An adult menhaden is an important member of the marine ecosystem. The fish are filter feeders that scoop up large mouthfuls of water and filter out the plankton for food. An adult menhaden can filter a million gallons of water in six months.

The Chesapeake Bay Ecological Foundation estimates that the menhaden population removes up to one-fourth of the nitrogen pollutants dumped into the Chesapeake Bay each year. Because nitrogen runoff from lawns and farms is a major pollutant of the Chesapeake Bay, this function of the fish is important. Sport fishers also value menhaden as bait because they are the natural food of many sportfish.

Both environmentalists and the sport fishing industry were worried when the menhaden catch declined during the 1990s. The catch in 2000 was the second-lowest catch

on record. Both groups believe that overharvesting by commercial fishing boats was the reason for the reduced catch. As a result, the Atlantic Menhaden Management Board, which manages the menhaden fishery, has been restructured to have fewer members who represent the commercial fisheries.

CRITICAL THINKING

1. Applying Ideas Many different groups have potentially conflicting interests in the future of the menhaden fishery. Write a paragraph that explains the opposing points of view of two of these groups. **WRITING SKILLS**

2. Expressing Viewpoints If you were on the Atlantic Menhaden Management Board, what changes would you suggest to prevent the fishery from declining? Write a paragraph that explains these changes. **WRITING SKILLS**

Figure 22 ▶ Modern livestock operations, such as this pig farm in North Carolina, are large and efficient.

Table 3 ▼

UN FAO Estimates of Animal Populations			
	Global Livestock Populations		
Species	**1961**	**2004**	**Increase**
Chickens	3.9 billion	16.4 billion	320%
Sheep	1 billion	1.1 billion	10%
Cattle	942 million	1.3 billion	38%
Pigs	406 million	945 million	132%
Goats	349 million	708 million	123%
Horses, donkeys, and mules	110 million	109 million	−0.9%

Livestock

Domesticated animals, such as those listed in **Table 3,** that are raised to be used on a farm or ranch or to be sold for profit are called **livestock.** Large livestock operations, such as the pig farm shown in **Figure 22,** produce most of the meat that is consumed in developed countries. Meat production per person has increased worldwide since 1950, as shown in **Figure 23.** Livestock are also important in developing countries. In these countries, livestock provide leather, wool, eggs, and meat, and serve many other functions. Some are used as draft animals to pull carts and plows. Other livestock provide manure, which is used for fertilizer or as a fuel for cooking.

Ruminants Cattle, sheep, and goats are **ruminants** (ROO muh nuhnts), cud-chewing mammals that have three- or four-chambered stomachs. *Cud* is the food that these animals regurgitate from the first chamber of their stomachs and chew again to aid digestion. Ruminants have microorganisms in their intestines, which allow the animals to digest plant materials that humans cannot digest. When we eat the meat of ruminants, we are using them to convert plant material, such as grass stems and woody shrubs, into food that we can digest—such as beef.

Humans have created hundreds of breeds of cattle that are suited to life in different climates. Cattle are most common in North America, India, and Africa. But the cattle are not always slaughtered for meat. In Africa for example, traditional Masai herders drink milk and blood from their cattle. India has almost one-fifth of the world's cattle. However, many of these cattle are not killed or eaten because cows are sacred to Hindus, who make up a large part of India's population. These cattle instead produce milk and dung, and are used as draft animals.

✔ **Reading Check** How are livestock important in developed and in developing countries?

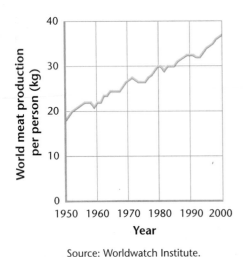

Source: Worldwatch Institute.

Figure 23 ▶ Worldwide meat production per person has increased significantly since 1950.

Poultry Since 1961, the population of chickens worldwide has increased by a greater percentage than the population of any other livestock, as shown in **Table 3.** Chickens are a type of *poultry,* domesticated birds raised for meat and eggs, which are good sources of essential amino acids. In more-developed countries, chickens and turkeys are usually raised in factory farms, as shown in **Figure 24.** Some people have criticized this industry because the animals live in cramped, artificial environments.

Fewer ducks and geese are raised worldwide than chickens, but in some areas ducks and geese are economically important. For example, the Chinese use ducks not only for meat, but also as part of an integrated system that produces several types of food at one time. The ducks' droppings are used to fertilize fields of rice called *rice paddies.* The rice paddies are flooded several times per year with water from nearby ponds. Mulberry trees, which feed silkworms, are also irrigated by the ponds. Plant materials and filtered sewage are dumped in the ponds and serve as food for carp and other fish. The integrated system uses little fresh water, recycles waste, and produces ducks, silk, rice, and fish.

Figure 24 ▶ Modern chicken farms, such as this one, are often huge, industrial-scale operations.

SECTION 3 **Review**

1. **Explain** why the percentage of seafood produced by aquaculture is increasing so rapidly.

2. **Explain** how overharvesting affects the supply of fish such as salmon.

3. **Describe** the importance of livestock to cultures that consume no meat.

CRITICAL THINKING

4. **Inferring Relationships** Read the description of poultry above and explain why chickens are such an important source of food for humans. **READING SKILLS**

5. **Applying Ideas** Look at the graph in Figure 23. Write a short paragraph explaining why meat production has increased so rapidly. **WRITING SKILLS**

1 Feeding the World

Key Terms

famine, 407
malnutrition, 407
diet, 408
yield, 409

Main Ideas

▶ The foods produced in the greatest amounts worlwide are grains, the seeds of grass plants.

▶ Malnutrition is a condition that occurs when people do not consume enough Calories or do not eat a sufficient variety of foods to fulfill all of the body's needs.

▶ More food is needed each year to feed the world's growing population. Poverty is the main reason for hunger in the world today.

▶ The green revolution introduced new crop varieties with increased yields through the application of modern agricultural techniques.

2 Crops and Soils

arable land, 412
topsoil, 413
erosion, 414
desertification, 414
compost, 416
salinization, 416
pesticide, 417
biological pest control, 419
genetic engineering, 421

▶ The basic processes of farming are plowing, fertilization, irrigation, and pest control. Modern agricultural methods have replaced traditional methods in much of the world.

▶ Fertile soil is soil that can support the growth of healthy plants. Soil conservation methods are important for protecting and managing topsoil and reducing erosion.

▶ Pests cause considerable crop damage. The use of pesticides has both positive and negative effects on the environment. Integrated pest management can minimize the use of chemical pesticides.

▶ Genetic engineering is the process of transferring genes from one organism to another. Plants that result from genetic engineering are called genetically modified plants.

3 Animals and Agriculture

domesticated, 423
overharvesting, 423
aquaculture, 424
livestock, 426
ruminant, 426

▶ Overharvesting has reduced the populations of many aquatic organisms worldwide.

▶ Aquaculture, the raising of aquatic animals, may be a solution to the problem of overharvesting.

▶ Livestock are important for the production of food and other products. Worldwide meat production per person has increased greatly over the past several decades.

Using Key Terms

Use each of the following terms in a separate sentence.

1. *overharvesting*
2. *erosion*
3. *livestock*
4. *yield*
5. *genetic engineering*

For each pair of terms, explain how the meanings of the terms differ.

6. *pesticide* and *biological pest control*
7. *arable land* and *topsoil*
8. *livestock* and *ruminant*
9. *malnutrition* and *famine*
10. *salinization* and *desertification*

✔ **STUDY TIP**

Making It a Habit Many people find that developing a routine helps them to study more effectively. Decide which time of day you feel most alert, and set it aside for studying. Make sure that any distractions around you will be minimal. When you regularly follow through with your study plan, you may find that you begin to learn more in less time.

Understanding Key Ideas

11. Malnutrition can be caused by
    a. a lack of enough Calories.
    b. a lack of carbohydrates.
    c. a lack of essential amino acids.
    d. All of the above

12. Humans need which of the following nutrients?
    a. carbohydrates and minerals
    b. lipids and vitamins
    c. proteins
    d. all of the above

13. Which of the following is *not* one the six most produced foods worldwide each year?
    a. potatoes
    b. beef
    c. rice
    d. wheat

14. Which of the following statements about human diets in all parts of the world is true?
    a. Most people eat pork.
    b. An adequate diet includes carbohydrates, proteins, and fats.
    c. Most people do not have protein in their diets.
    d. Most people are obese.

15. Malnutrition is largely a result of
    a. war.
    b. soil erosion.
    c. poverty.
    d. salinization.

16. Which of the following is *not* found in fertile soil?
    a. rock particles
    b. worms
    c. high concentrations of salts
    d. high concentrations of organic matter

17. Which of the following is *not* a soil conservation method?
    a. contour plowing
    b. salinization
    c. no-till farming
    d. terracing

18. Which of the following statements is a disadvantage of using chemical pesticides?
    a. Pesticides can pollute waterways.
    b. Pests evolve resistance to pesticides.
    c. Pesticides kill beneficial insects.
    d. all of the above

19. How do pesticides that are growth regulators work?
    a. They kill fleas.
    b. They disrupt the pest's life cycle.
    c. They attract predators of the pest.
    d. They prevent the pest from attacking the plant by poisoning its nervous system.

Short Answer

20. Why does it cost more to produce a kilogram of meat than to produce a kilogram of plants?

21. How does plowing soil increase soil erosion?

22. Why are biological controls for killing pests sometimes more effective than chemical pesticides are?

23. Why are ruminants valuable livestock?

24. Explain how soil degradation leads to loss of arable land.

Interpreting Graphics

Use the graph below to answer questions 25–27.

25. In which year was the most corn planted? In which year was the least corn harvested?

26. How many acres were planted with corn in 1991?

27. According to the graph, more acres of corn are planted than are harvested each year. Why?

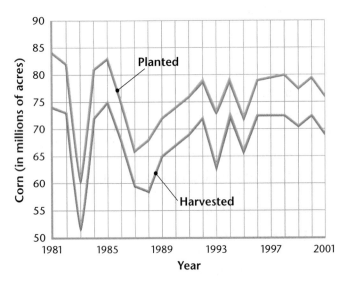

Source: U.S. Department of Agriculture.

Concept Mapping

28. Use the following terms to create a concept map: *contour plowing, no-till farming, organic farming, careful irrigation, soil erosion, nutrient depletion,* and *salinization.*

Critical Thinking

29. Making Predictions Reread the text under the heading "World Food Problems." Write a paragraph to predict how increasing the productivity of the world's subsistence farmers would affect poverty and food production. **WRITING SKILLS**

30. Analyzing Ideas What incentives to conserve soil do farmers in developed nations have?

31. Inferring Relationships Read the text in this chapter under the heading, "Disrupting Insect Breeding." Are pheromones a type of pesticide? Explain your reasoning. **READING SKILLS**

Cross-Disciplinary Connection

32. Social Studies Thousands of tons of dead fish are shoveled back into the ocean each year from fishing vessels because the fish are species that consumers do not want to buy. Identify some ways that humans might be able to reuse this protein.

33. Economics Hundreds of thousands of people starve to death every year. How is this problem related to the problem of poverty? Explain your answer.

Portfolio Project

34. Prepare a Report Environmental degradation caused by farming is not a new problem. The Dust Bowl of the 1930s is an example of an environmental disaster caused by farming practices that we would now consider to be damaging. Investigate the Dust Bowl, and write a report about it. Include information about the farming practices, laws, and regulations that were introduced in the United States as a result of the lessons learned during the 1930s. **WRITING SKILLS**

MATH SKILLS

Use the table below to answer questions 35–38.

World Food Production (in millions of tons)			
Food	1990	1995	1999
Total grains	1,700	1,800	1,900
Wheat	590	540	590
Rice	350	370	400
Legumes	58	55	59
Poultry	37	51	58
Milk	441	381	387

35. Analyzing Data Which foods had increased production in 1995 and 1999?

36. Analyzing Data Which foods had lower production in 1995 than in 1990?

37. Analyzing Data Taking into account the 1999 data, can you think of any possible reasons for the answer to question 36?

38. Analyzing Data The human population of the world grew by 15 percent between 1990 and 1999. By what percentage did total grain production increase during this time?

WRITING SKILLS

39. Communicating Ideas Explain how the way in which insects reproduce allows them to evolve pesticide resistance very rapidly.

40. Analyzing Ideas Explain why the pesticide DDT can still be detected in the environment even though its use was banned decades ago.

READING SKILLS

Read the passage below, and then answer the questions that follow.

A large amount of energy is needed to produce food. In all parts of the world, the energy used to process, distribute, and cook food is greater than the energy used to grow it. In the United States, it is estimated that every Calorie of food on our dinner tables has required 9 Calories of energy to get there. Half a Calorie accounts for the energy used on the farm. The other 8.5 Calories account for the energy used to process, package, distribute, and cook the food. In rural India, twice as much energy goes into cooking a kilogram of rice as was invested in producing it. Energy shortages, such as a shortage of wood for cooking, have caused environmental problems such as deforestation. In poor countries, cooking may require more energy than is used by transportation, heating, and all other energy uses combined.

1. According to the passage, which of the following statements about food is true?
   a. Most of the energy invested in food production goes into distributing the food.
   b. More energy is used to grow food on the farm than is used to cook the food.
   c. Most energy used to produce food goes into processing, distributing, and cooking the food.
   d. In developing countries only, cooking food requires more energy than growing food does.

2. Which of the following points is not discussed in this passage?
   a. Packaging is the least costly part of preparing food for sale to the customer.
   b. It takes more energy to cook a kilogram of rice than to grow a kilogram of rice.
   c. In some countries, cooking requires more energy than all other processes that use energy combined.
   d. Gathering sufficient wood to cook food has led to deforestation.

Understanding Concepts

Directions (1–4): For *each* question, write on a separate sheet of paper the letter of the correct answer.

1 Which of the following is a major cause of malnutrition in the world today?
A. food efficiency
B. improved yield
C. poverty
D. no-till farming

2 What is the main difference between fertile and infertile soil?
F. Fertile soil supports plant life; infertile soil cannot.
G. Infertile soil supports plant life; fertile soil cannot.
H. Fertile soil supports insect life; infertile soil cannot.
I. Infertile soil supports insect life; fertile soil cannot.

3 What is the eventual result of land degradation?
A. desertification
B. fertilization
C. integration
D. salinization

4 Which of the following is an effect of soil erosion?
F. increased crop yields
G. increase in land fertility
H. decrease in desertification
I. decrease in the amount of topsoil

Directions (5–6): For *each* question, write a short response.

5 Over time, controlling pests with pesticides can make a pest problem worse if pest populations develop resistance. Resistance is the ability to survive exposure to a particular pesticide. Why are subsequent generations of resistant pest populations more likely to be resistant?

6 Evaluate the practice of biological pest control.

Reading Skills

Directions (7–8): Read the passage below. Then answer the questions.

Plant breeding has been used since agriculture began. Farmers select the plants that have the most desirable characteristics. They save seeds from these plants to use in planting the next crop. The selected seeds are more likely to contain the genes for the desired traits. The same result is achieved with genetic engineering, the technology in which genetic material in a living cell is modified for medical or industrial use.

Genetic engineering involves isolating genes from one organism and implanting them into another. The plants that result from genetic engineering are called genetically modified plants. Sometimes genes introduced into plants are not plant genes. An insecticide gene from a bacterium that produces a chemical that kills plant-eating caterpillars can be implanted into crop plants. Hundreds of gene transfers have now been performed to create many genetically modified crops. In the United States, we now eat and use genetically engineered agricultural products every day.

7 What impact has the technology of genetic engineering had on the agricultural community?
A. The technology of genetic engineering has increased the efficiency of the agricultural community.
B. The technology of genetic engineering has decreased the efficiency of the agricultural community.
C. The technology of genetic engineering has increased cultivation within the agricultural community.
D. The technology of genetic engineering has decreased cultivation within the agricultural community.

8 What effect could introducing insecticide genes into crops have on insecticide resistance?

Interpreting Graphics

Directions (9–11): For *each* question below, record the correct answer on a separate sheet of paper.

The graph below shows world grain production over a 55-year period. Use this graph to answer questions 9 through 11.

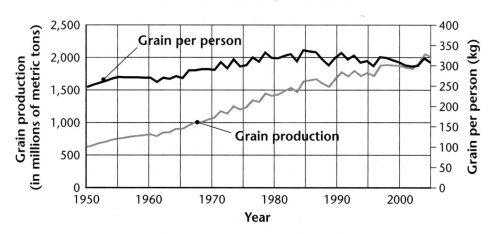

World Grain Production, 1950–2005

9 In what year did the total amount of grain production equal the average amount of grain per person?

F. 1980
G. 1983
H. 2003
I. The two amounts were never equal.

10 What is the main reason that, while total grain production has increased each year, the amount of grain per person has been relatively steady?

A. Much of the grain produced could not be distributed efficiently.
B. The world's population has grown faster than grain production.
C. The world's population has remained roughly the same for the last 35 years.
D. Much of the grain produced in the world was used to feed livestock or as seed.

11 If the trend that was in place from 1990–1995 continued through 2005, what would have been the average amount of grain available per person in 2005?

F. 200 kg
G. 250 kg
H. 300 kg
I. 350 kg

Test TIP

Slow, deep breathing may help you relax. If you suffer from test anxiety, focus on your breathing in order to calm down.

CHAPTER 15

Inquiry Lab: MODELING

Objectives

▶ **USING SCIENTIFIC METHODS**
Hypothesize how to reduce the amount of water a garden needs.

▶ **Compare** the amount of water different soil samples can hold.

▶ **Explain** how adding materials to a soil sample can help increase the sample's ability to hold water.

Materials

beaker, 250 mL
compost, 5 g
crucible (or other heat-safe container)
dry chopped grass clippings, 5 g
eyedropper
filter paper
funnel
heat source (hot plate or oven)
metric balance
sawdust, 5 g
soil sample, 50 g
stirring rod
tongs
watch (or clock)
water

Managing the Moisture in Garden Soil

You work as a soil specialist with the Smith County Soil Conservation District. You are trying to help Mrs. Latisha Norton, a local resident, solve an agricultural problem. Mrs. Norton has found that she must water her vegetable garden very often to keep it healthy. As a result, her family's water bills have skyrocketed! Mrs. Norton and her family may have to give up their garden project because of the added expense.

You realize that the water is probably draining out of the garden soil too quickly. To solve this problem, you need to find out how much water the soil can hold. You visit her garden and collect several soil samples. (Your teacher will provide you with soil samples.)

Procedure

1. Dry your soil sample without burning any of the organic matter. To do this, place about 50 g of soil in a crucible or other heat-safe container. Using tongs, gently heat the sample over a hot plate or put the sample in an oven. Stir the sample occasionally with a stirring rod to ensure that the sample becomes completely dry.

2. After the sample is completely dry, weigh about 10 g of dry soil. Record the mass in a data table.

3. Dampen a circle of filter paper until it is thoroughly moist, but not dripping. Weigh the moist filter paper, and record its mass in a data table.

4. As shown below, fold the moist filter paper into quarters. Next, open the filter paper to form a cup that fits in a funnel. Place the cup-shaped filter paper in the funnel.

5. Place the dry soil sample on the filter paper in the funnel. Place the funnel in the beaker.

6. Add water to the soil sample one drop at a time until all of the soil is moist and water begins to drip out of the funnel. Stop adding water, and let the funnel sit for 5 min.

▶ **Step 4** Fold the moist filter paper into quarters, and then open it to form a cup that fits in a funnel.

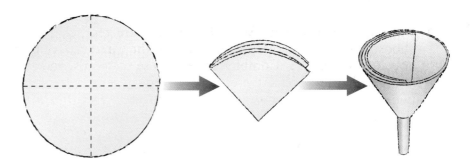

7. After 5 min, remove the filter paper and moist soil from the funnel, and weigh the paper and soil together. Record their mass in a data table.

8. Calculate the mass of the moistened soil sample by subtracting the mass of the damp filter paper from the mass of the completely moistened sample and the filter paper. Record the mass in a data table.

9. Calculate the amount of water that your soil sample can hold by subtracting the mass of the dry soil sample from the mass of the moistened soil sample. Record the result in a data table.

10. Calculate the percentage of water that your sample held. Divide the mass of water the soil held by the mass of the moistened soil sample, and multiply by 100. The higher the percentage is, the more water the soil can hold. Record the percentage in a data table.

11. Divide the remaining dry soil sample into three 5 g portions. To the first soil sample, add 5 g of dry compost. To the second soil sample, add 5 g of dry chopped grass clippings. To the third soil sample, add 5 g of dry sawdust. Weigh each mixed soil sample, and record the masses of the three samples in a data table.

12. Perform steps 3–10 for each of your mixed soil samples. Record your results in a data table.

▶ **Step 6** When adding water to the soil sample, add one drop at a time until all of the soil is moist and water begins to drip out of the funnel.

Analysis

1. **Organizing Data** Compare your results with the results of your classmates. Which soil samples held water the best? Why?

2. **Analyzing Data** Which of the additional materials improved the soil's ability to hold water?

Conclusions

3. **Evaluating Methods** Based on your results as well as your research, what could you recommend to Mrs. Norton to reduce the amount of water her garden needs?

Extension

1. **Designing Experiments** With the help of your teacher, choose one more material in addition to the three materials you used in step 11. Combine two of these materials, and mix them with a soil sample. Combine the remaining two materials with another soil sample. Perform steps 3–10 for these two mixed soil samples. Compare your results with the results you gathered earlier in the lab. Which combination of materials in the soil samples held water the best?

GENETICALLY ENGINEERED FOODS

Genetically engineered foods are now on sale in the world's supermarkets, and we do not recognize them because they are not labeled as such.

As the world's population continues to increase, food production must try to keep pace with the increase. Genetic engineering provides one way to develop new foods. Biotechnologists develop desirable characteristics in an organism by altering its genes or by inserting new genes into the organism's cells. For example, a gene that makes one plant species resistant to pests might be transferred to another plant species. The second plant species would then have the same resistance to pests.

In 1994, the first genetically modified food was offered for sale. It was a tomato called the Flavr Savr™ which softens slowly, so it can remain on grocery shelves longer before becoming soft and overripe. Biotechnologists developed the tomato by altering the gene that causes ripe tomatoes to soften. The Food and Drug Administration (FDA) said it was as safe as other tomatoes and cleared it for sale. Here are two points of view on genetically engineered foods.

The Benefits Outweigh the Risks

Scientists who support the development of genetically engineered foods view the process as simply an extension of previous plant-breeding techniques. Traditionally, farmers altered the genetic makeup of plants by crossbreeding different strains to combine the best traits of both plants. However, the direct manipulation of genes makes it possible to control genetic changes more precisely and efficiently.

▶ A scientist examines experimental samples of genetically modified fruit trees.

Biotechnologists say that their new products are as safe for consumers as plants developed through crossbreeding. Why shouldn't genetically engineered foods sit beside other foods on grocery store shelves?

The benefits of creating genetically engineered fruits and vegetables include keeping produce fresh longer, adding nutrients, and creating more-successful crops. For example, by inserting a gene that gives virus resistance to squash plants, scientists could boost the plants' resistance to viral infection. These resistant squash could produce five times the amount of squash per harvest as other squash do. Or scientists could increase the amino acids in a food product to give it more nutritional value.

Crops could be developed to grow faster and have higher yields. To combat world hunger, scientists may be able to develop seeds that can grow well in areas that have poor soil or poor water conditions. For more immediate relief, genetically engineered foods that would not spoil as quickly could be shipped to needy nations.

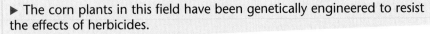

▶ The corn plants in this field have been genetically engineered to resist the effects of herbicides.

The Risks Outweigh the Benefits

Critics of genetically engineered foods believe that these products are significantly different from foods developed through traditional methods. Genetic engineering allows genes from any living organism, including genes from animals or bacteria, to be placed into crops. Opponents are concerned about the safety of foods that contain these "foreign" genes.

Another safety concern is the possibility of allergic reactions. Some foods, such as peanuts and shellfish, cause allergic reactions in many people. If genes from these foods are placed in entirely different products, people who eat these new products and do not know that the new products contain the foreign genes may have allergic reactions.

Other critics object because of religious or ethical reasons. Certain religions prohibit eating pork and other foods. People may object to the insertion of genes from pigs or other prohibited foods into foods they normally eat. Similarly, vegetarians might object to eating foods containing animal genes.

Some scientists are concerned that genetically engineered plant species may be accidentally introduced into the wild. Genetic engineering may give a new species an advantage over an existing wild species. If the new species thrives at the expense of the wild species, the wild species could become extinct.

▶ This farmer from Oaxaca, Mexico, holds up ears of traditional corn varieties. Some people fear that genes from genetically engineered varieties could accidentally be introduced into native varieties.

▶ These people in Montreal, Quebec, are protesting the importation of genetically modified organisms (GMOs). Many countries have not accepted genetically engineered crops as much as the United States has.

What Do You Think?

Some people propose that genetically engineered foods should have labels that identify them as such. Could such a measure decrease criticism about the safety of genetically engineered foods? Based on what you have read, decide whether you would buy genetically engineered foods at the grocery store. Explain your reasoning.

MINERAL AND ENERGY RESOURCES

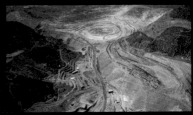

CHAPTER 16
Mining and Mineral Resources

CHAPTER 17
Nonrenewable Energy

CHAPTER 18
Renewable Energy

CHAPTER 19
Waste

This pit in Brazil is one of the world's largest iron ore mines. Mineral and energy resources are essential to human societies, but extracting and using these resources has environmental consequences.

439

Mining and Mineral Resources

1 Minerals and Mineral Resources

2 Mineral Exploration and Mining

3 Mining Regulations and Mine Reclamation

PRE-READING ACTIVITY

FOLDNOTES

Three-Panel Flip Chart
Before you read this chapter, create the **FoldNote** entitled "Three-Panel Flip Chart" described in the Reading and Study Skills section of the Appendix. Label the flaps of the chart with "Mineral Resources," "Mining," and "Mining Regulations and Reclamation." As you read the chapter, write information you learn about each category under the appropriate panel.

Obtaining the minerals humans need requires removing large amounts of rock at mines like this open-pit copper mine in Arizona. The challenge is to satisfy the increasing demand for mineral resources while minimizing the cost to the environment.

Minerals and Mineral Resources

 SEV.4.a; SEV.4.c; SEV.4.e

EARTH SCIENCE CONNECTION

Take a look at the human-made objects that surround you. Almost every solid object you see is made of minerals. As shown in **Figure 1,** we depend on the use of mineral resources in almost every aspect of our daily lives. The current challenge is to obtain minerals at minimal cost to the environment. In this chapter you will learn about minerals and the environmental effects of mining.

What Is a Mineral?

A **mineral** is a naturally occurring, usually inorganic solid that has a characteristic chemical composition, an orderly internal structure, and a characteristic set of physical properties. Minerals are made up of atoms of a single element, or of *compounds*—atoms of two or more elements chemically bonded together. The atoms that make up minerals are arranged in regular, repeating geometric patterns. The arrangement of the atoms, along with the strength of the chemical bonds between them, determine the physical properties of minerals.

The elements gold, silver, and copper are considered minerals. These types of minerals are called *native elements.* However, most minerals are compounds. For example, the mineral quartz is made up of silica, a compound consisting of one silicon atom and two oxygen atoms. When combined with other elements, silica forms most of the minerals that make up Earth's crust.

✓ **Reading Check** **List three characteristics of all minerals. (See the Appendix for answers to Reading Checks.)**

Objectives

▶ Define the term *mineral.*

▶ Explain the difference between a metal and a nonmetal, and give two examples of each.

▶ Describe three processes by which ore minerals form.

Key Terms

mineral
ore mineral

FIELD ACTIVITY

Identifying Objects Made of Minerals Take a walk around your neighborhood or through your home with a notebook and pencil. Pick an object such as a car, an appliance, or a computer. List as many materials that make up that object as you can. Be as specific as possible. Repeat the procedure for several other objects. Which of these objects do you think are made from minerals? Write to the company that made one of your objects, and ask what materials are used to make the object. Record your observations, along with the company's response, in your *EcoLog.*

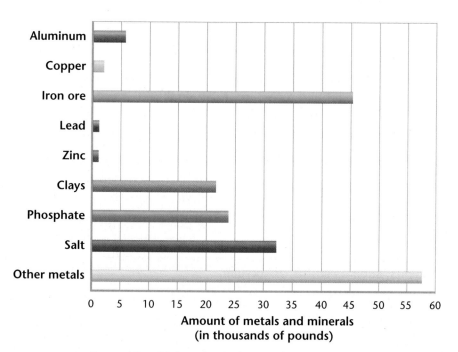

Amount of metals and minerals
(in thousands of pounds)

Source: Mineral Information Institute.

Figure 1 ▶ Mineral consumption is greatest in developed countries, such as the United States. This graph shows the average amount of minerals a person in the U.S. will consume over his or her lifetime.

Figure 2 ▶ Certain minerals are mined because of the valuable metals they contain, as shown in the table. Wulfenite (above) is a minor ore of lead. Nice specimens of wulfenite are much sought after by mineral collectors.

www.scilinks.org
Topic: Minerals
Code: HE80966

Table 1 ▼

Selected Elements and Their Ore Minerals	
Element	**Important ore minerals**
Aluminum (Al)	gibbsite, boehmite, diaspore (bauxite)
Beryllium (Be)	beryl
Chromium (Cr)	chromite
Copper (Cu)	bornite, cuprite, chalcocite, chalcopyrite
Iron (Fe)	goethite, hematite, magnetite, siderite
Lead (Pb)	galena
Manganese (Mn)	psilomelane, pyrolusite
Mercury (Hg)	cinnabar
Molybdenum (Mo)	molybdenite
Nickel (Ni)	pentlandite
Silver (Ag)	acanthite
Tin (Sn)	cassiterite
Titanium (Ti)	ilmenite, rutile
Uranium (U)	carnotite, uraninite
Zinc (Zn)	sphalerite

Ore Minerals

Minerals that are valuable and economical to extract are known as **ore minerals.** As shown in **Table 1,** ore minerals contain elements, many of which are economically valuable. During the mining process, ore minerals, along with minerals that have no commercial value, or *gangue* (GANG) *minerals,* are extracted from the host rock. After extraction, mining companies use various methods to separate ore minerals from the gangue minerals. The ore minerals are then further refined to extract the valuable elements they contain. For mining to be profitable, the price of the final product must be greater than the costs of extraction and refining.

Metallic Minerals Ore minerals are either metallic or nonmetallic. Metals conduct electricity, have shiny surfaces, and are opaque. Many valuable metallic minerals are native elements such as gold, shown in **Figure 3.** Silver and copper are also important native elements. Other important ore minerals are compounds in which metallic elements combine with nonmetallic elements, such as sulfur or oxygen.

Nonmetallic Minerals Nonmetals tend to be good insulators, may have shiny or dull surfaces, and may allow light to pass through them. Nonmetallic minerals can also be native elements or compounds.

Figure 3 ▶ Gold is one of the most economically important metallic minerals.

How Do Ore Minerals Form?

As shown in **Figure 4**, economically important ore deposits form in a variety of ways. The types of minerals that form depend on the environment in which they form. For example, metallic minerals form below ground when magma cools and hardens. The metallic minerals tend to form early in the cooling process and sink to the lower part of the magma body because they are denser. This process concentrates important ore minerals that can be extracted economically.

Hydrothermal Solutions Hot, subsurface waters that contain dissolved minerals are called *hydrothermal solutions*. As hydrothermal solutions flow through cracks in rocks, they dissolve minerals they come in contact with. New minerals crystallize out of these solutions and then fill fractures to form ore deposits called *veins*.

Evaporites As rivers and streams wash over land surfaces, they dissolve salts and carry them into the sea or inland lakes. When the water in these seas or lakes evaporates, deposits of these salts, called *evaporites*, are left behind. Evaporites form in arid regions where rates of evaporation are high. Important evaporite minerals include halite (rock salt) and gypsum.

✔ **Reading Check** How do evaporites form?

Figure 4 ▶ Mineral Environments
Ore deposits form in different ways upon and beneath Earth's surface, and at the bottom of lakes and oceans.

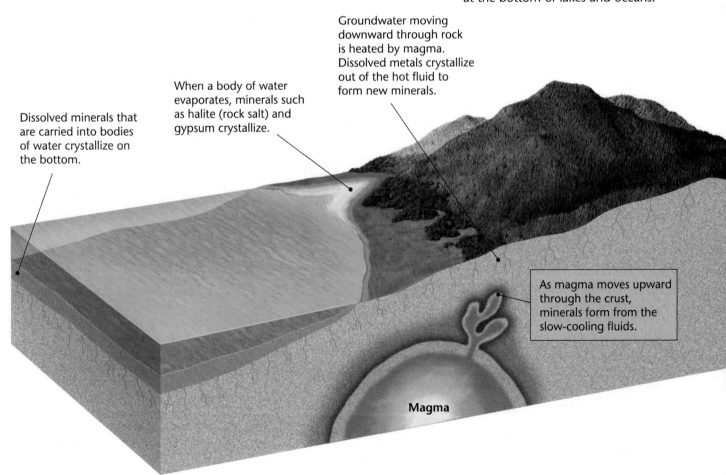

Dissolved minerals that are carried into bodies of water crystallize on the bottom.

When a body of water evaporates, minerals such as halite (rock salt) and gypsum crystallize.

Groundwater moving downward through rock is heated by magma. Dissolved metals crystallize out of the hot fluid to form new minerals.

As magma moves upward through the crust, minerals form from the slow-cooling fluids.

Magma

Table 2 ▼

Uses of Important Metallic and Nonmetallic Elements
Aluminum: cans, foil; windows, doors, siding; appliances, cooking utensils; automobiles, aircraft
Copper: cables, wires; electrical and electronic products; plumbing, heating; alloys; coinage
Gold: computers; communications equipment; spacecraft; dentistry, medicine; jewelry
Iron: steel making
Lead: batteries; ammunition; glass; ceramics
Silicon: computer chips; glass; ceramics
Silver: photography; electrical and electronic products; mirrors; chemistry
Sulfur: sulfuric acid; gunpowder; rubber; fungicides
Titanium: jet engines, aircraft bodies, spacecraft, missiles; pigments
Zinc: coatings on steel; brass; chemical compounds in rubber and paints

Mineral Resources and Their Uses

Certain metals are of major economic and industrial importance, as shown in **Table 2.** Some metals can be pounded or pressed into various shapes or stretched very thinly without breaking. Other metals are good conductors of heat and electricity, or are prized for their durability and resistance to corrosion. Often, two or more metals are combined to form *alloys*. Alloys are important because they often combine the most desirable properties of the metals used to make them. As shown in **Figure 5,** many new technologies depend on the mining of metallic minerals.

Nonmetals are among the most widely used minerals in the world. For example, gypsum has many applications in the construction industry. It is used to make Sheetrock™, or wallboard, for homes and commercial buildings. It is also a major component of concrete, which is used to build roads, buildings, and other structures. Industrial sand and gravel have uses that range from glassmaking to the manufacture of computer chips. Some nonmetallic minerals, called *gemstones*, are prized purely for their beauty, rarity, or durability. Important gemstones include diamond, ruby, sapphire, emerald, aquamarine, topaz, and tourmaline.

Figure 5 ▶ The mineral ilmenite (inset) is an important source of titanium. Because titanium is both strong and lightweight, it is used in aircraft such as this stealth fighter.

SECTION 1 Review

1. **Define** the term *mineral.*

2. **Explain** the difference between a metal and a nonmetal, and give examples of each.

3. **Describe** three processes by which minerals form.

4. **List** five properties that make metals economically and industrially important.

CRITICAL THINKING

5. **Analyzing Relationships** A mineral is a naturally occurring substance. Are synthetic minerals produced in laboratories minerals? Explain your answer.

6. **Making Comparisons** Unlike metals, nonmetals are not good conductors of heat and electricity. How might these properties influence the use of nonmetals in industry? Write a paragraph to explain your answer. **WRITING SKILLS**

Mineral Exploration and Mining

SEV.4.a; SEV.4.b; SEV.4.e

EARTH SCIENCE   **CONNECTION**

The rate of technological change in the mining industry is increasing rapidly. Computers are commonly used to make models that show the location of ore within a deposit. Mineral exploration data are now obtained from orbiting satellites or from airplanes that carry sophisticated instruments. These instruments help scientists find new ore deposits.

Mineral Exploration

Through mineral exploration, mining companies can identify areas where there is a high likelihood of finding valuable mineral resources in quantities that are worth mining. Usually, a mineral deposit has 100 to 1,000 times the concentration of the mineral than ordinary rocks do and enough material to justify opening a mine.

Exploring rock for mineralization is the first step in finding an ore deposit. Planes carrying instruments that identify patterns in gravity, magnetism, or radioactivity fly over and collect these data, as well as images and photographs of an area. When used with satellite images, these data and aerial photographs can be used to create a geological map of the surface. As shown in **Figure 6,** rock samples are then taken from the area. The samples are analyzed to determine ore grade—the metal content of an ore. If the ore grade is high enough, the companies will drill test holes that help them estimate the three-dimensional extent of the ore. If the ore grade is high enough and the deposit extensive enough, the cost to open a mine may be warranted.

Reading Check   **How are planes used to find rich ore deposits?**

Objectives

▶ Describe the manner in which mining companies explore for new mineral deposits.

▶ Describe three methods of subsurface mining.

▶ Describe two methods of surface mining.

▶ Define *placer deposit,* and explain how placer deposits form.

▶ Describe the steps that take place in smelting an ore.

Key Terms

subsurface mining
surface mining
placer deposit
smelting

Figure 6 ▶ A geologist takes ore samples across the freshly blasted tunnel of a Canadian gold mine.

www.scilinks.org
Topic: Mining Minerals
Code: HE80968

Subsurface Mining

Ore deposits that are usually found 50 m or more beneath Earth's surface are mined by using **subsurface mining** methods. A common method of subsurface mining that is used to extract coal and salt is known as *room-and-pillar mining*. In coal mines, a network of entries, called *rooms,* are cut into a seam, a horizontal layer of coal. Between the rooms, pillars of coal are left standing to support the roof. When the mining of rooms is completed, the pillars are then removed, beginning with pillars at the farthest point in the mine. A room in a German salt mine, along with mining equipment, is shown in **Figure 7**.

Longwall Mining A more efficient way to remove coal from a subsurface seam is to use a method called *longwall mining*. In longwall mining, a machine called a shearer moves back and forth across the face of a coal seam. A shearer that is used in longwall mining is shown in **Figure 8**. The wall of the seam, called the *longwall,* may be more than 300 m long. As coal is sheared from the face, it falls onto a conveyor. The conveyor transports the coal out of the mine. A row of hydraulic roof supports protects the miners and the equipment. As the shearer advances forward through the coal seam, the mine roof behind the hydraulic supports collapses.

Figure 8 ▶ Heavy equipment, like the rotating shearer of the longwall mining system shown here, is used to remove coal in subsurface mines.

Solution Mining For underground deposits of soluble mineral ores such as potash, salt, and sulfur, solution mining is an economical mining method. In solution mining, hot water is injected into the ore and dissolves it. Compressed air is then pumped into the dissolved ore, and air bubbles lift it to the surface.

Surface Mining

Surface mining methods are used when ore deposits are located close to Earth's surface. *Open-pit mining* is a method that is often used to mine large quantities of near-surface ore. Coal and metals such as copper are mined using the open-pit method.

In an open-pit mine, the ore is mined downward, layer by layer. First, explosives are used, if needed, to break up the ore. Then, the ore is loaded into haul trucks. The haul trucks transport the ore from the mine. Some ores, such as gold ore, are taken to heap leaching pads, such as the pads shown in **Figure 9.** There, the gold is extracted from the ore using chemicals.

Figure 9 ▶ Cyanide heap leaching is being used to extract gold from ore at this open-pit mine in Idaho.

Surface Coal Mining In the 19th-century American Midwest, horse- or mule-drawn plows were used to remove the rock, called *overburden*, that covered near-surface coal seams. Today, some of the largest machines in the world are used to strip the overburden that covers shallow coal deposits.

The first step in surface coal mining is to remove and set aside the soil that covers the area to be mined. Next, the overburden is removed by heavy equipment in cuts that may be up to 50 m wide and over a kilometer long. The overburden is piled alongside the cut. Loaders enter the pit and remove the exposed coal seam. Once the coal is taken out, the pit is refilled with the overburden and contoured. The soil that has been set aside is now laid on top of the overburden.

Quarrying Building stones such as granite and marble are mined in quarries like the one shown in **Figure 10.** Sand, gravel, and crushed rock, known as *aggregates*, are the main products of quarrying. Quarries also produce clay, gypsum, and talc.

> ✔ **Reading Check** Describe what happens to the overburden once all the coal has been taken out of a surface coal mine.

Connection to Chemistry

Cyanide Heap Leaching
Sodium cyanide, NaCN, has been used to extract gold from low-grade ore deposits since the cyanide heap-leaching process was pioneered in the United States in the early 1970s. Crushed ore from a mine is placed on pads that have bottoms of asphalt or on impervious plastic sheets. A solution of dilute cyanide is sprayed on the ore. The cyanide percolates down through the ore for several weeks to months and leaches out the gold. The gold, which is now in solution, drains off the pad into a pond. From the pond, the gold-bearing solution is pumped to a recovery plant, where the gold is removed from solution.

Figure 10 ▶ Open pits called *quarries* are used to mine near-surface materials such as building stone, crushed rock, sand, and gravel.

Figure 11 ▶ This is an aerial view of solar evaporation ponds that are used to produce salt on San Francisco Bay.

Solar Evaporation The solar evaporation process consists of placing sea water, which is about 2.7 percent sodium chloride, into enormous, shallow ponds. The sun evaporates the sea water, which causes the sodium chloride concentration to increase. When the concentration of sodium chloride in the sea water reaches a little over 25 percent, salt crystals begin to form. With further evaporation, layers of crystalline salt, or halite, build up. When these layers reach the desired thickness, the salt is harvested. Salt harvesting generally occurs once a year.

Solar evaporation is a method of salt production that is used in areas that receive little rainfall and that have high evaporation rates. Along the Mediterranean Sea, on San Francisco Bay, and particularly in Australia, solar evaporation is practical because evaporation far exceeds rainfall. Steady prevailing winds, which increase the rate of evaporation, are also important to solar evaporation. **Figure 11** shows solar evaporation ponds on San Francisco Bay.

The solar evaporation process has been used to produce salt for thousands of years. Today, solar evaporation is used largely in developing countries. About 30 percent of the world's salt comes from the solar evaporation process.

EARTH SCIENCE  **CONNECTION**

CASE STUDY

Hydraulic Mining in the California Goldfields

About 50 million years ago, rivers bearing gold flowed across present-day northern California. Over time, the geologic processes that formed the Sierra Nevada Mountains buried the gold-bearing river gravels beneath as much as 60 m of soil. A method was needed to remove this soil and recover the gold from the gravels of the ancient riverbeds.

The technology to perform this task, called *hydraulic mining,* was developed in the early 1850s. Hydraulic miners used huge 4 to 5.5 m long water cannons, called *monitors,* to send high-pressure streams of water into the Sierra Nevada mountainsides. The sediments that were blasted from the mountainsides mixed with the water to form a slurry, which was washed through a series of long, inclined

▶ By 1874, giant water monitors worked 24 hours a day, 7 days a week, at the Malakoff mine and processed about 50,000 tons of gravel a day. The resulting canyon was more than 2,000 m long, 900 m wide, and 180 m deep.

Placer Mining

When rock weathers and disintegrates, minerals within the rock are released. These minerals are concentrated by wind and water into surface deposits called **placer deposits.** The most important placer deposits are stream placers. Streams transport mineral grains to a point where they fall to the streambed and are concentrated. Concentration occurs at places where currents are weak and the dense mineral grains can no longer be carried in the water. These stream placers often occur at bends in rivers, where the current slows.

Placer deposits may form along coastlines from heavy minerals that wash down to the ocean in streams. These heavy minerals are concentrated by wave action.

Placer gold, diamonds, and other heavy minerals are mined by dredging. As shown in **Figure 12,** a dredge consists of a floating barge on which buckets fixed on a conveyor are used to excavate sediments in front of the dredge. Gold, diamonds, or heavy minerals are separated from the sediments within the dredge housing. The processed sediments are discharged via a conveyor that is located behind the dredge.

Figure 12 ▶ This dredge is mining gold from placer deposits along a river on New Zealand's South Island.

▶ To this day, the mountainsides in the Sierra Nevada bear the scars of hydraulic mining.

troughs called *sluices.* The sluices were lined with a series of devices known as *riffles* to catch the gold. Mercury was also added to the riffles to help capture the gold. The muddy water and processed sediments were then discharged into adjacent rivers.

Hydraulic mining proved to be an environmental disaster. Muddy water and sediments polluted rivers and caused them to fill with silt. The silt from the hydraulic mines traveled as far downstream as San Francisco and into the Pacific Ocean. As much as 1.4 to 3.6 million kilograms of mercury may have been released downstream, which poisoned fish, amphibians, and invertebrates. Farmers in California's central valley sustained millions of dollars in damage as their fields were flooded when the sediment-choked Sacramento

River overflowed its banks. But the farmers fought back. In January 1884, Judge Lorenzo Sawyer ruled that mine tailings could no longer be discharged into the rivers. The Sawyer decision was the first environmental ruling to be handed down in the United States. This ruling closed the door on hydraulic mining in the Sierra Nevada goldfields, where 2 billion cubic meters of soil and rocks had been carved from the mountainsides in slightly over 30 years.

CRITICAL THINKING

1. Making Inferences What do you think were other environmental effects of hydraulic mining that were not mentioned in this article?

2. Analyzing Relationships Write a paragraph about how the mercury that was lost during hydraulic mining may still be affecting the environment today. **WRITING SKILLS**

Figure 13 ▶ At a smelter, such as this aluminum smelter in Venezuela, ore is melted at high temperatures in a furnace to obtain a desired metal.

QuickLAB

Surface Coal Mining

Procedure

1. Cut off the top part of a **2 L plastic soda bottle** to make a container that has an open end.
2. Spread a 5 cm layer of **soil** on the bottom of the bottle.
3. Spread a 0.75 cm layer of **rice** on top of the soil to represent a coal seam.
4. Spread a 12.5 cm layer of soil on top of the coal.
5. To excavate the coal, dig out the top layer of soil with a **spoon,** and place it in a **bowl.** Measure the volume of this soil by using a **graduated cylinder.** Record the volume.
6. Dig out the layer of coal, and place it in a second bowl. Measure and record the volume.

Analysis

1. What is the ratio of overburden to coal?
2. What are some factors that you would need to consider if you were going to surface-mine coal economically?

Smelting

In the process called **smelting,** crushed ore is melted at high temperatures in furnaces to separate impurities from molten metal. In the furnace, material called a *flux* bonds with impurities and separates them from the molten metal. The molten metal, which is desired, falls to the bottom of the furnace and is recovered. The flux and impurities, which are less dense, form a layer called *slag* on top of the molten metal. Gases such as sulfur dioxide form within the furnace and are captured, so they do not enter the environment. **Figure 13** shows a smelter in Venezuela.

Undersea Mining

The ocean floor contains significant mineral resources, which include diamonds, precious metals such as gold and silver, mineral ores, and sand and gravel. Since the late 1950s, several attempts have been made to mine the ocean. These attempts met with varying degrees of success. Competition with land-based companies that can mine minerals more cheaply and the great water depths at which some mineral deposits are found are two of the reasons undersea mining has been largely unsuccessful to date.

SECTION 2 Review

1. **List** the steps in mineral exploration.
2. **Describe** three methods of subsurface mining.
3. **Describe** two methods of surface mining.
4. **Describe** the steps involved in smelting ore.
5. **Define** the term *placer deposit,* and explain how placer deposits form.

CRITICAL THINKING

6. **Making Comparisons** Read about surface and subsurface mining techniques. What are some of the advantages and disadvantages of each technique? **READING SKILLS**

7. **Understanding Relationships** If a mining company were exploring a river for potential placer deposits, where are some likely places they would focus their exploration?

Mining Regulations and Mine Reclamation

SCSh.2.b; SCSh.3.c; SCSh.3.e; SCSh.4.b;
SCSh.4.c; SCSh.6.a; SEV.4.a; SEV.4.c

EARTH SCIENCE CONNECTION

With an increase in U.S. energy requirements, particularly the demand for coal to fuel power plants that produce electricity, the scale of surface mining has grown. So, too, have the potential environmental effects of mining. For example, surface coal mining requires the removal of enormous amounts of soil and rock to reach near-surface coal seams.

Because of the environmental impacts of mining on such a large scale, mining has become one of the most heavily regulated industries in the United States. Mining companies now spend large amounts of money to preserve the environment. Reclaiming the land, or returning the land to its original condition after mining is completed, is part of every surface coal mining operation. Before mining, companies develop a plan to reclaim the land. Even before mining is complete, this plan is put into action. With environmental preservation now a clear goal of mining companies, future generations of Americans will not have to view scars in the Earth, such as the one shown in **Figure 14**.

The Environmental Impacts of Mining

There are many environmental impacts of mining. In the United States, the federal and state governments and mining companies are spending billions of dollars to clean up abandoned mines. Much of this legacy has been left to U.S. citizens from a time when there was little regulation of mining and mineral processing.

Objectives

▶ Describe seven important potential environmental consequences of mining.

▶ Name four federal laws that relate to mining and reclaiming mined land.

▶ Define the term *reclamation*.

▶ Describe two ways in which state governments regulate mining.

Key Terms

subsidence
reclamation

Figure 14 ▶ At 215 m deep and 1.6 km in circumference, the "Big Hole" at the Kimberley Mine in South Africa is the largest hand-dug excavation in the world. By the time the mine closed in 1914, 22.5 million tons of rock had yielded almost 3,000 kg of diamonds.

Air and Noise Pollution Surface mining can cause both air pollution and noise pollution. At surface coal mines, removing, loading, hauling, and dumping soil and overburden produce dust. Winds that blow across unreclaimed soil and overburden storage areas also produce dust. Loading, hauling, and unloading ore create dust emissions at open-pit mines. As well, dust is created in open-pit mines when the ore is blasted apart.

Noise is created by the equipment that is used in a mine as well as by blasting. Whereas equipment noise may be a nuisance, blasting can cause physical damage to nearby structures.

Because of air and noise pollution, most surface mines are not located near urban populations. More important, regulations in the U.S. forbid mining operations to allow dust or noise to exit the area that is being mined.

Water Contamination Water resources can be negatively impacted by mining. Water that seeps into mines or through piles of excess rock can pick up or dissolve toxic substances like arsenic. These contaminants can wash into streams, where they can harm or kill aquatic life.

Coal or minerals that contain a lot of sulfur can cause a similar problem. When these materials react with oxygen and water, they form dilute sulfuric acid. This acid can dissolve toxic minerals that remain in mines and excess rock. The contaminated water that results from this process is known as *acid mine drainage,* or AMD. An example of AMD is shown in **Figure 15**. Mining regulation in the U.S. requires companies to dispose of acid-producing rock in such a way that water is not contaminated.

Figure 15 ▶ Copper mines have polluted the Queen River in Tasmania with acid mine drainage. This photo shows the river flowing past residential housing.

Displacement of Wildlife Removing soil from a surface mine site strips away all plant life. With their natural habitat removed, animals will leave the area. In addition, when mining is completed and the soil is returned to the mine site, different plants and animals may establish themselves, which creates an entirely new ecosystem. However, a good development plan to reclaim a mine site can ensure that the displacement of wildlife is merely temporary.

Dredging can negatively affect aquatic ecosystems and physically change the bottoms of rivers. Dredging disturbs river bottoms and destroys aquatic plant life in the dredged portion of the river. The disturbance of a riverbed can cause sediments to contaminate a river for up to 10 km.

✔ **Reading Check** Why does surface mining cause animals to leave an area?

Erosion and Sedimentation Excess rock from mines is sometimes dumped into large piles called *dumps*. Running water erodes unprotected dumps and transports sediments into nearby streams. The sediments may harm water quality and aquatic life.

Soil Degradation Soil at a mine site is removed from the uppermost layer downward. When this soil is stored for later reuse, care must be taken to ensure that the upper soil layers are not buried beneath soil layers that were originally below them. In this way, the soil layers that are richest in important nutrients are not covered. If soil is not removed and stored in separate layers, the soil may be nutrient poor when it is reclaimed.

Minerals that contain sulfur may be found in deeper soil layers. If these minerals are exposed to water and oxygen in the atmosphere, chemical reactions result in the release of acid, which then acidifies the soil. When the acidified soil is returned to the mine site, it may be difficult for plants to grow.

Subsidence The sinking of regions of the ground with little or no horizontal movement is called **subsidence** (suhb SIED'ns). Subsidence occurs when pillars that have been left standing in mines collapse or the mine roof or floor fails.

Buildings, houses, roads, bridges, underground pipelines, and utilities that are built over abandoned mines could be damaged if the ground below them subsides. In November and December 2000, underground limestone mines that were several hundred years old collapsed in Edinburgh, Scotland. The collapse caused property damage and forced people to evacuate their homes. **Figure 16** shows the potential effects of mine subsidence.

Reading Check How might exposing deep soil layers to the air prevent plants from growing?

Figure 16 ▶ A hole created by the subsidence of a gold mine has swallowed this house in New Zealand.

Figure 17 ▶ This photo shows a coal seam that is on fire in a surface coal mine in China.

Ecofact

Bats and Mines Over the past century, human disturbance of traditional bat roosting sites, such as caves and trees, has caused bats to move into abandoned mines. At present, 30 of the 45 species of bats in the United States live in mines. Some of the largest populations of endangered bat species now live in abandoned mines.

Graphic

Organizer **Spider Map** Create the **Graphic Organizer** entitled "Spider Map" described in the Appendix. Label the circle "Mining Regulations." Create a leg for each type of mining regulation. Then, fill in the map with details about each type of mining regulation.

Underground Mine Fires Fires that start in underground coal seams are one of the most serious environmental consequences of coal mining. Lightning, forest fires, and burning trash can all cause coal-seam fires. In addition, fires can start by themselves when minerals in the coal that contain sulfur are exposed to oxygen. These fires are hard to put out and are often left to burn themselves out, which may take decades or even centuries. For example, a fire that has been burning through an underground coal seam in an Australian mountain is estimated to be 2,000 years old! Underground fires that burn their way to the surface release smoke and gases that can cause respiratory problems. A fire in a coal seam is shown in **Figure 17.**

Mining Regulation and Reclamation

Mines on land in the United States are regulated by federal and state laws. To ensure that contaminants from mines do not threaten water quality, mining companies must comply with regulations of the Clean Water Act and the Safe Drinking Water Act. The release of hazardous substances into the air, soil, and water by mining is regulated by the Comprehensive Response Compensation and Liability Act. In addition, all mining operations must comply with the Endangered Species Act. This act ensures that mining activities will not affect threatened or endangered species and their habitats.

Reclamation The process of returning land to its original or better condition after mining is completed is called **reclamation.** The Surface Mining Control and Reclamation Act of 1977 (SMCRA) created a program for the regulation of surface coal mining on public and private land. The act set standards that would minimize the surface effects of coal mining on the environment. SMCRA also established a fund that is administered by the federal government and is used to reclaim land and water resources that have been adversely affected by past coal-mining activities.

State Regulation of Mining States have created programs to regulate mining on state and private lands. Mining companies must obtain permits from state environmental agencies before mining a site. These permits specify certain standards for mine design and reclamation. In addition, some states have bond forfeiture programs. In a bond forfeiture program, a mining company must post funds, called a *bond*, before a mining project begins. If the company does not mine and reclaim a site according to the standards required by its permits, the company must give these funds to the state. The state then uses the funds to reclaim the site. A reclaimed surface coal mine is shown in **Figure 18.**

State agencies are also responsible for inspecting mines to ensure compliance with environmental regulations. Agencies issue violations to companies that do not comply with environmental regulations and assess fines for noncompliance. In addition, states such as Pennsylvania have begun large projects to reclaim abandoned mine lands. Acid mine drainage, mine fires, mine subsidence, and hazards related to open shafts and abandoned mining structures are all problems that these projects will attempt to correct.

Connection to **History**

Jihlava Jihlava is an ancient town in the Czech Republic. In the 1200s, silver was discovered in Jihlava. The rush that followed brought miners, merchants, and traders from all over Europe. As a result, Jihlava became very prosperous. In addition to creating municipal laws, the town passed its own mining laws. Jihlava's mining laws served as an example for other mining towns in central Europe.

Figure 18 ▶ Reclamation often includes seeding, planting, and irrigating to return the land to its original state.

SECTION 3 **Review**

1. **List** seven potential environmental impacts of mining.

2. **Name** four federal laws that regulate mining activities in the United States.

3. **Define** the term *reclamation*.

4. **Describe** two ways in which state governments regulate mining.

CRITICAL THINKING

5. **Making Decisions** Give examples of environmental concerns that would be taken into account by a mining company when it created a reclamation plan for a mine site.

6. **Making Decisions** Read about how topsoil is removed and stored for later reclamation under the heading "Soil Degradation." How can this process be implemented to keep soils from degrading?
   READING SKILLS

1 Minerals and Mineral Resources

Key Terms

mineral, 441
ore mineral, 442

Main Ideas

▶ A mineral is a naturally occurring, usually inorganic solid that has a characteristic chemical composition, an orderly physical structure, and a characteristic set of physical properties.

▶ Minerals that are valuable and economical to extract are known as *ore minerals*.

▶ Ore minerals may form from the cooling of magma, the circulation of hot-water solutions through rocks, and the evaporation of water that contains salts.

▶ Metals are important economically because of their electrical and thermal conductivity, durability, and heat and corrosion resistance.

2 Mineral Exploration and Mining

Key Terms

subsurface mining, 446
surface mining, 447
placer deposit, 449
smelting, 450

Main Ideas

▶ Mining companies conduct mineral exploration to identify areas where there is a high likelihood of finding valuable mineral resources in quantities worth mining.

▶ Room-and-pillar mining, longwall mining, and solution mining are subsurface mining methods.

▶ Open-pit mining, surface coal mining, quarrying, and solar evaporation are surface-mining methods.

▶ Minerals are concentrated by wind and water into surface deposits called *placer deposits*.

▶ Smelting is the process in which ore is melted at high temperatures to separate impurities from the molten metal.

3 Mining Regulations and Mine Reclamation

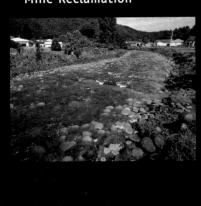

Key Terms

subsidence, 453
reclamation, 454

Main Ideas

▶ Some of the environmental consequences of mining may include air and noise pollution, water contamination, displacement of wildlife, erosion and sedimentation, soil degradation, subsidence, and underground mine fires.

▶ The U.S. government has enacted legislation that regulates mining and attempts to minimize the impact of mining on the environment.

▶ Federal and state agencies issue permits to mining companies, issue violations and assess penalties when mining companies do not comply with standards set by their permits, and ensure that abandoned mine lands are reclaimed.

Using Key Terms

Use each of the following terms in a separate sentence.

1. *mineral*
2. *placer deposit*
3. *smelting*
4. *subsidence*
5. *reclamation*

For each pair of terms, explain how the meanings of the terms differ.

6. *element* and *mineral*
7. *ore mineral* and *gangue mineral*
8. *placer deposit* and *dredging*
9. *subsurface mining* and *surface mining*

> ✓ **STUDY TIP**
>
> **Using Terms** Work together with a study partner. Learn the definitions of both the boldfaced and italicized words that appear in this chapter. When both you and your partner feel confident in having learned the meanings of these terms, take out a piece of paper. On this paper, you and your partner will each write a one-page essay in which you use as many of these terms as possible. When you both are finished, exchange essays and review them for accuracy.

Understanding Key Ideas

10. Which of the following statements does *not* correctly describe a mineral?
    a. A mineral is a naturally occurring substance.
    b. A mineral is an organic substance.
    c. A mineral is a solid substance.
    d. A mineral has a characteristic chemical composition.

11. Gold, silver, and copper are
    a. nonmetallic minerals.
    b. native elements.
    c. compounds.
    d. gangue minerals.

12. Ore deposits form from
    a. the cooling of magma.
    b. the evaporation of water that contains salts.
    c. the circulation of hot-water solutions in rocks.
    d. All of the above

13. Which of the following economically important elements is *not* a metal?
    a. zinc
    b. titanium
    c. copper
    d. sulfur

14. Which of the following methods is *not* a subsurface mining method?
    a. quarrying
    b. solution mining
    c. longwall mining
    d. room-and-pillar mining

15. Which of the following mining methods would most likely be used to mine salt?
    a. solution mining
    b. open-pit mining
    c. solar evaporation
    d. both (a) and (c)

16. Dredging would *not* be used to mine
    a. diamonds.
    b. salt.
    c. heavy minerals.
    d. gold.

17. Which of the following elements in minerals causes soil to become acidified?
    a. potassium
    b. calcium
    c. sulfur
    d. barium

18. Which of the following pieces of federal legislation established a program for regulating coal mining on public and private lands?
    a. the Comprehensive Response and Liability Act
    b. the Clean Air Act
    c. the Clean Water Act
    d. the Surface Mining Control and Reclamation Act of 1977

Short Answer

19. What is the difference between native elements and compounds?

20. Describe the solar evaporation process.

21. What are the surface and subsurface methods by which coal is commonly mined?

22. Explain why undersea mining has been largely unsuccessful to date.

23. Describe how reclaimed soil may become degraded.

24. Explain the purpose of a state bond forfeiture program.

Interpreting Graphics

The graph below shows total U.S. mineral production from 1995 to 1999. Use the graph to answer questions 25–26.

25. In 1995, metals accounted for $14 billion of the $39 billion total U.S. production of minerals. Metals accounted for what percentage of the total U.S. production of minerals?

26. In 1999, metals accounted for only $10 billion of the $39 billion total U.S. production of minerals. Metals accounted for what percentage of the total U.S. production of minerals?

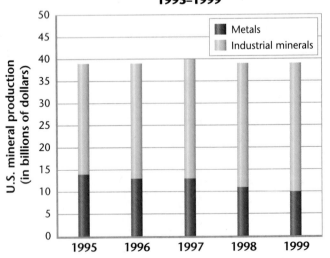

Changes in U.S. Mineral Production 1995–1999

U.S. mineral production (in billions of dollars)

■ Metals
■ Industrial minerals

Source: U.S. Geological Survey.

Concept Mapping

27. Use the following terms to create a concept map: *subsurface mining, surface mining, room-and-pillar mining, longwall mining, solution mining, open-pit mining, surface coal mining, and quarrying.*

Critical Thinking

28. **Analyzing Relationships** Read about the technological changes in the mining industry that are discussed in the introduction to Section 2. What method or methods of mining seem well suited for automation, particularly robotics? **READING SKILLS**

29. **Making Decisions** Mining companies use computer models to show them where high- and low-grade ores are located in the deposit that they are mining. If the price of the ore mineral that a company is mining suddenly increases, how would computer modeling help the company economically exploit the mineral deposit to take advantage of the increase in price?

Cross-Disciplinary Connection

30. **Social Studies** Fifteen to 20 miles southwest of Santa Fe, New Mexico, are a series of low hills known as Los Cerrillos. Native Americans mined the blue-green gemstone turquoise from narrow veins in rock from these hills for more than 1,000 years, beginning in about the year 875. Research Native American mining at Los Cerrillos, New Mexico. Write a short report about your findings. **WRITING SKILLS**

Portfolio Project

31. **Debate** A mining company has applied for permits to establish a surface mine on land that is located near a stretch of river in which an endangered species of fish lives. Assume that the ore to be mined is rare and has important new applications in cancer treatment. Weighing both sides of the argument, would you issue the permits? Make your case for or against issuing the mining permits in a debate with your classmates.

MATH SKILLS

32. Making Calculations Some low-grade gold ores that have been mined economically average about 0.1 oz of gold per ton of ore. Five tons of rock must be removed to obtain one ton of ore. How many tons of rock must be mined to obtain 1 oz of gold? How many pounds of ore must be processed to obtain 1 oz of gold?

WRITING SKILLS

33. Communicating Main Ideas One of the main ideas of this chapter is that the human need for minerals requires mining companies to continually find new deposits of minerals that can be extracted inexpensively. Extraction must be done in such a way that the environment is not severely affected. Using surface coal mining or open-pit mining as an example, explain why it is difficult to mine large ore deposits without affecting the environment.

34. Writing Persuasively A mining company is applying for permits to establish an open-pit mine near your home. Do research to determine what impact, if any, the operation will have on your quality of life, the environment, and the economics of your community. Summarize your findings in a concise one-page paper.

35. Outlining Topics You are an exploration geologist who works for a mining company. You are searching for a new deposit of an ore mineral. Outline the steps you would take to find a deposit and to determine whether that deposit would be economical to mine.

READING SKILLS

Read the passage below, and then answer the questions that follow.

One of the only two rocks in which diamonds have been found is called *kimberlite*. Kimberlite is an uncommon kind of rock that forms cylindrical subsurface bodies called *kimberlite pipes*. Kimberlite pipes look very much like the vents that bring lava to the surface in volcanoes. Diamonds form deep in the Earth's mantle under enormous temperatures and pressures. Diamonds are believed to be carried to the surface in kimberlite pipes in very rapid, explosive events. However, not all kimberlite pipes contain diamonds.

Kimberlite is a soft, black, blue, or green rock that weathers rapidly when it reaches Earth's surface. Because kimberlite decomposes rapidly, it does not form rock outcrops. Instead, it forms circular depressions several feet below the surface of the ground. These depressions may be covered with a bluish kimberlite soil called *blue ground*. Iron-stained soils may also cover depressions. These soils are referred to as *yellow ground*.

1. Which of the following statements about kimberlite is *not* true?
   a. Diamonds are found in kimberlite.
   b. All kimberlite contains diamonds.
   c. Kimberlite weathers rapidly at Earth's surface.
   d. Kimberlite is an uncommon kind of rock.

2. If you were an exploration geologist searching for a deposit of diamonds, which of the following would *not* be a good surface indicator of the existence of a kimberlite pipe?
   a. a circular depression
   b. a bluish soil that fills a depression
   c. an iron-stained soil that fills a depression
   d. a large rock outcrop

Understanding Concepts

Directions (1–4): For *each* question, write on a separate sheet of paper the letter of the correct answer.

1 Which of the following statements is true?
 A. Minerals are found both on and beneath Earth's surface.
 B. Minerals are metallic compounds of economic importance.
 C. Minerals are limited resources easily extracted from the ground.
 D. Minerals are unlimited resources extracted from the ground at little cost.

2 Which of these nonmetallic minerals has many uses in the construction industry?
 F. gypsum
 G. quartz
 H. silicon
 I. tourmaline

3 Salt is mined underground using what technique?
 A. longwall mining
 B. open-pit mining
 C. solution mining
 D. surface mining

4 What distinguishes native elements from most other minerals?
 F. Native elements are not compounds.
 G. Native elements are always non-metallic.
 H. Native elements are mined by solar evaporation.
 I. Native elements are essentially the minerals that make up Earth's crust.

Directions (5–6): For *each* question, write a short response.

5 Excess rock from mines is sometimes dumped into large piles. Running water erodes these unprotected dumps, transporting the rocks and sediment into nearby streams. What effect does the resulting sedimentation have on a stream's ecosystem?

6 The ocean floor contains significant mineral resources. Assess the environmental impact of mining on the ocean floor.

Reading Skills

Directions (7–9): **Read the passage below. Then answer the questions.**

The process of returning land to its original or better condition after mining is completed is called reclamation. In the United States billions of dollars are spent to clean up abandoned mines. The Surface Mining Control and Reclamation Act of 1977 (SMCRA) created a program for the regulation of surface coal mining on public and private lands. The act set standards that would minimize the surface effects of coal mining on the environment. SMCRA also established a fund that is used to reclaim land and water resources that have been adversely affected by past coal-mining activities.

States also have programs to regulate mining activities. Mining companies must obtain permits from state environmental agencies before mining a site.

7 Reclamation is
 A. a program for the regulation of surface coal mining on public and private lands.
 B. a program to regulate mining activities.
 C. the process of returning land to its original or better condition before mining.
 D. the process of returning land to its original or better condition after mining.

8 What is the focus of the SMCRA?
 F. maximizing profits from surface coal mines
 G. decreasing air pollution from surface coal mines
 H. minimizing harm to the environment caused by surface coal mining
 I. ensuring safe conditions for people who work in coal mines

9 Before mining a site, coal-mining companies must
 A. reclaim land and water resources.
 B. return land to its original or better condition.
 C. obtain permits from state environmental agencies.
 D. set standards to minimize the effects of mining on the environment.

Interpreting Graphics

Directions (10–13): For *each* question below, record the correct answer on a separate sheet of paper.

The table below shows the properties for some minerals. Use this table to answer questions 10 through 12.

Properties of Selected Minerals

Mineral	Luster	Color	Streak	Hardness	Specific Gravity
Bauxite (a mixture of several minerals)	varies	brownish yellow, brown, red, gray	varies	varies	varies
Beryl ($Be_3Al_2Si_6O_{18}$)	vitreous	blue, green, yellow, pink	white	$7\frac{1}{2}$–8	2.6–2.8
Chromite ($FeCr_2O_4$)	metallic to sub-metallic	black to brownish black	dark brown	$5\frac{1}{2}$	4.5–4.8
Cinnabar	adamantine (diamond-like)	scarlet red to brownish red	vermillion (vivid red to red orange)	2–$2\frac{1}{2}$	8.0–8.2
Cuprite (Cu_2O)	adamantine or submetallic	red, sometimes very dark red	brownish red	$3\frac{1}{2}$–4	5.8–6.1

10 If a mineral sample has an adamantine luster, what test could be used to **most** accurately identify the specific mineral?
- **F.** color
- **G.** hardness
- **H.** specific gravity
- **I.** streak

11 Using the table, what conclusion can be reached about beryl?
- **A.** It is a soft mineral.
- **B.** Its color varies greatly.
- **C.** It has a metallic luster.
- **D.** It is seven times heavier than water.

12 What properties can a scientist observe **most** easily in the field?
- **F.** color and luster
- **G.** hardness and streak
- **H.** specific gravity and hardness
- **I.** streak and specific gravity

13 Bauxite is the major ore mineral of what element?
- **A.** aluminum
- **B.** copper
- **C.** manganese
- **D.** titanium

Test TIP

Take time to read each question completely, including all of the answer choices. Consider each answer choice before determining which one is correct.

Skills Practice Lab: OBSERVATION

Objectives

▶ **Extract** copper from copper carbonate in much the same way that copper is extracted from malachite ore.

▶ **USING SCIENTIFIC METHODS**
Hypothesize how this process can be applied to extract other metallic elements from ores.

Materials

Bunsen burner
copper (cupric) carbonate
funnel
iron filings
sulfuric acid, dilute
test-tube holder
test-tube rack
test tubes, 13 mm x 100 mm (2)
water

Extraction of Copper from Its Ore

Most metals are combined with other elements in the Earth's crust. A material in the crust that is a profitable source of an element is called an *ore*. Malachite (MAL uh KIET) is the basic carbonate of copper. The green corrosion that forms on copper because of weathering has the same composition that malachite does. The reactions of malachite are similar to those of copper carbonate.

In this investigation, you will extract copper from copper carbonate using heat and dilute sulfuric acid. The process you will be using will be similar to the process in which copper is extracted from malachite ore.

Procedure

1. CAUTION: Wear your laboratory apron, gloves, and safety goggles throughout the investigation. Fill one of the test tubes about one-fourth full of copper carbonate. Record the color of the copper carbonate.

2. Light the Bunsen burner, and adjust the flame.

3. Heat the copper carbonate by holding the tube over the flame with a test-tube holder, as shown in the figure on the next page. CAUTION: When heating a test tube, point it away from yourself and other students. To prevent the test tube from breaking, heat it slowly by gently moving the test tube over the flame. As you heat the copper carbonate, observe any changes in color.

4. Continue heating the tube over the flame for 5 min.

5. Allow the test tube to cool. Observe any change in the volume of the material in the test tube. Then, place the test tube in the test-tube rack. Insert a funnel in the test tube, and add

▶ **Copper Ore** Malachite is a carbonate of copper that commonly forms in copper deposits. It is sometimes used as an ore of copper.

dilute sulfuric acid until the test tube is three-fourths full. CAUTION: Avoid touching the sides of the test tube, which may be hot. If any of the acid gets on your skin or clothing, rinse immediately with cool water and alert your teacher.

6. Allow the test tube to stand until some of the substance at the bottom of the test tube dissolves. After the sulfuric acid has dissolved some of the solid substance, note the color of the solution.

7. Use a second test tube to add more sulfuric acid to the first test tube until the first test tube is nearly full. Allow the first test tube to stand until more of the substance at the bottom of the test tube dissolves. Pour this solution (copper sulfate) into the second test tube.

8. Add a small number of iron filings to the second test tube. Observe what happens.

9. Clean all of the laboratory equipment, and dispose of the sulfuric acid as directed by your teacher.

Analysis

1. **Explaining Events** Disregarding any condensed water on the test-tube walls, what do you call the substance formed in the first test tube? Explain any change in the volume of the new substance relative to the volume of the copper carbonate.

2. **Explaining Events** When the iron filings were added to the second test tube, what indicated that a chemical reaction was taking place? Explain any change to the iron filings. Explain any change in the solution.

▶ **Step 3** To heat the copper carbonate, hold the tube over the flame with a test-tube holder. Point the test tube away from yourself and other students.

Conclusions

3. **Drawing Conclusions** Why was sulfuric acid used to extract copper from copper carbonate?

Extension

1. **Analyzing Data** Suppose that a certain deposit of copper ore contains a minimum of 1 percent copper by mass and that copper sells for $0.30 per kilogram. Approximately how much could you spend to mine and process the copper from 100 kg of copper ore and remain profitable?

2. **Making Comparisons** How is the process used in this experiment similar to the cyanide heap-leaching process used to extract gold from low-grade ore?

MINERAL PRODUCTION IN THE UNITED STATES

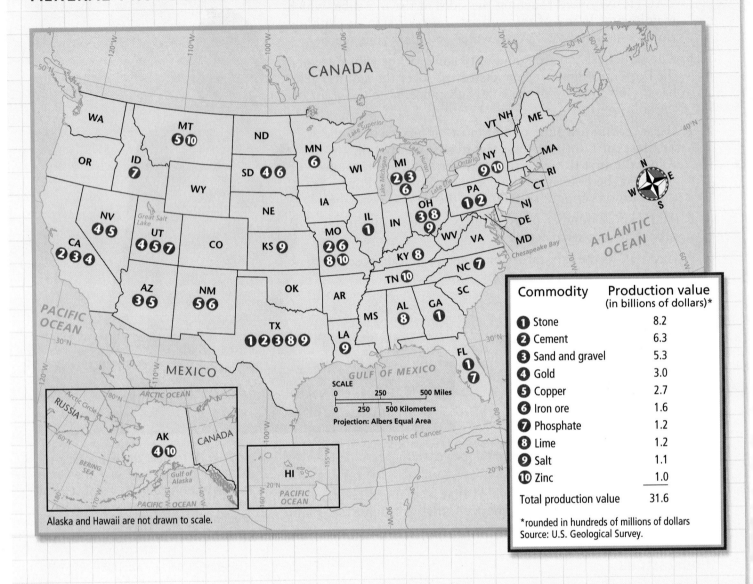

Commodity	Production value (in billions of dollars)*
❶ Stone	8.2
❷ Cement	6.3
❸ Sand and gravel	5.3
❹ Gold	3.0
❺ Copper	2.7
❻ Iron ore	1.6
❼ Phosphate	1.2
❽ Lime	1.2
❾ Salt	1.1
❿ Zinc	1.0
Total production value	31.6

*rounded in hundreds of millions of dollars
Source: U.S. Geological Survey.

Alaska and Hawaii are not drawn to scale.

MAP SKILLS

In 1999, the top 10 mineral commodities produced in the United States had a total value of about $31.6 billion. Over half of this production value came from the top three commodities: stone, cement, and sand and gravel. The map above shows the distribution of the production of these commodities by state. Use the map above to answer the following questions.

1. **Using a Key** Find your state on the map of mineral production. Which of the top 10 mineral commodities, if any, were produced in your state in 1999?

2. **Evaluating Data** Gold, copper, iron ore, and zinc are metals in the top 10 mineral commodities produced in 1999. What percentage of total 1999 production value do these metals represent? Which states were the producers of these metals in 1999?

3. **Evaluating Data** Stone, sand, and gravel are collectively known as *aggregates*. What percentage of total 1999 production value do aggregates represent? Which states were the major producers of aggregates in 1999?

4. **Using a Key** Which states produced salt in 1999?

COLTAN AND THE WAR IN THE CONGO

If you purchase a mobile phone, pager, or laptop computer, you may not be aware of the connection between these devices and politics in central Africa. Each of these products requires tantalum in its manufacture. Tantalum is a heat-resistant metal that can hold a high electric charge. Tantalum is ideal for the production of capacitors, which are used to regulate voltage in many of the electronic products in use today.

The main ore of tantalum is columbite-tantalite, which is often shortened to coltan. Eighty percent of the world's coltan reserves are found in the mountains of the eastern part of the Democratic Republic of the Congo (DRC). From the DRC, coltan makes its way into the world market, much of it illegally.

The 1996 Civil War

In 1996, hostilities between ethnic peoples caused civil war to break out in the DRC. Two years later, neighbors Rwanda and Uganda entered the conflict and backed two Congolese rebel movements. Shortly thereafter, Angola, Namibia, and Zimbabwe lent their support to the government of the DRC. Today, the Rwandan- and Ugandan-backed rebels have primary control of the coltan ore in the eastern DRC.

The war in the DRC is as much an economic war as an ethnic war. The price of coltan has reached prices as high as $400 per kilogram. Forces from neighboring Rwanda, Uganda, and Burundi have been accused of smuggling coltan out of the DRC and making enormous profits. This money is being used to help finance the continuing war efforts of these countries.

The Consequences of Civil War

Since 1998, almost 2.5 million people have died in the fighting in the

▶ Cell phones are just one of the electronic products in common use today that require tantalum in their production.

DRC. Government and rebel forces have attacked, killed, and tortured innocent civilians to maintain their rule. Almost half of the population of the DRC lacks safe drinking water. Access to health care is limited, and an estimated 2 million people suffer from HIV/AIDS.

Meanwhile, coltan mining has moved into coltan-rich national parks and reserves. Wildlife is being lost at an alarming rate as miners kill animals for food and elephants for ivory.

▶ Columbite-tantalite miners in the Democratic Republic of the Congo can earn from $10 to $50 a week, whereas the average Congolese worker earns around $10 a month.

What Do You Think?

Many electronics companies have stopped buying columbite-tantalite ore from central African countries. What effect, if any, do you think this action will have on present conditions in the DRC?

Nonrenewable Energy

PRE-READING ACTIVITY

FOLDNOTES

Booklet
Before you read this chapter, create the **FoldNote** entitled "Booklet" described in the Reading and Study Skills section of the Appendix. Label each page of the booklet with a main idea from the chapter. As you read the chapter, write what you learn about each main idea on the appropriate page of the booklet.

At this petroleum refinery in Germany, crude oil pumped from the Earth is changed into fuels, such as gasoline, and other products.

SECTION 1
Energy Resources and Fossil Fuels

How does a sunny day 200 million years ago relate to your life today? Chances are that if you traveled to school today or used a product made of plastic, you used some of the energy from sunlight that fell on Earth several hundred million years ago. Life as we know it would be very different without the fuels or products formed from plants and animals that lived alongside the dinosaurs.

The fuels we use to run cars, ships, planes, and factories and to produce electricity are natural resources. Most of the energy we use comes from a group of natural resources called *fossil fuels*. **Fossil fuels** are the remains of ancient organisms that changed into coal, oil, or natural gas. Fossil fuels are central to life in modern societies, yet there are two main problems with fossil fuels. First, the supply of fossil fuels is limited. Second, obtaining and using them causes environmental problems. In the 21st century, societies will continue to explore alternatives to fossil fuels but will also focus on developing more-efficient ways to use these fuels.

Fuels for Different Uses

Fuels are used for five main purposes: for cooking, transportation, manufacturing, heating and cooling buildings, and generating electricity to run machines and appliances. The suitability of a fuel for each application depends on the fuel's energy content, cost, availability, and safety, and the byproducts of the fuel's use. For example, it is hard to imagine an airplane, such as the one shown in **Figure 1**, running on coal. Although coal is readily available and inexpensive, to power an airplane using coal would require hundreds of tons of coal. Likewise, the people shown around the campfire are not warming themselves by burning airplane fuel, they are burning wood, which is a perfect fuel for their needs.

Objectives

▶ List five factors that influence the value of a fuel.

▶ Explain how fuels are used to generate electricity in an electric power plant.

▶ Identify patterns of energy consumption and production in the world and in the United States.

▶ Explain how fossil fuels form and how they are used.

▶ Compare the advantages and disadvantages of fossil-fuel use.

▶ List three factors that influence predictions of fossil-fuel production.

Key Terms

fossil fuels
electric generator
petroleum
oil reserves

Figure 1 ▶ Different Fuels, Different Purposes The airplane (left) is being refueled with a highly refined liquid fuel. Airplane fuel must have a high ratio of energy to weight. The campers (below) are keeping warm by burning wood in an open fire.

Electricity—Power on Demand

The energy in fuels is often converted into electrical energy in order to power machines, because electricity is more convenient to use. Computers, for example, run on electricity rather than oil. Electricity can be transported quickly across great distances, such as an entire state, or across tiny distances, such as inside a computer chip. The electricity that powers the lights in your school was generated in a power plant and then carried to users through a distribution grid like the one shown in **Figure 2**. Two disadvantages of electricity are that it is difficult to store and other energy sources have to be used to generate it.

How Is Electricity Generated? An **electric generator** is a machine that converts mechanical energy, or motion, into electrical energy. Generators produce electrical energy by moving an electrically conductive material within a magnetic field. Most commercial electric generators convert the movement of a turbine into electrical energy, as shown in **Figure 3**. A *turbine* is a wheel that changes the force of a moving gas or liquid into energy that can do work. In most power plants, water is boiled to produce the steam that turns the turbine. The water is heated by burning a fuel in coal-fired and gas-fired plants or is heated from the fission of uranium in nuclear plants. The turbine spins a generator to produce electricity.

Figure 2 ▶ These pylons and wires are part of an electricity distribution grid in upstate New York.

Figure 3 ▶ How a Coal-Fired Power Plant Works

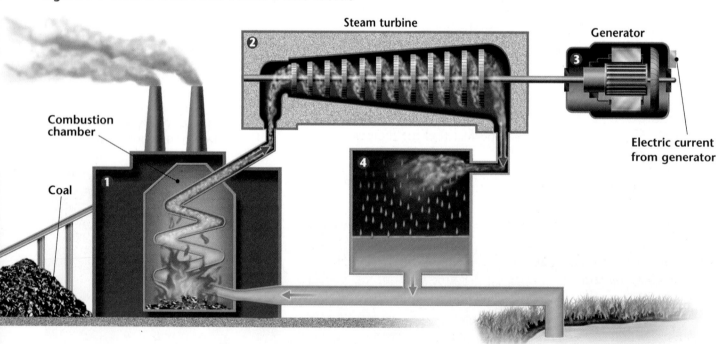

❶ Burning fossil fuels release energy in the form of heat, which is used to boil water and produce high-pressure steam.

❷ The steam is directed against the blades of a turbine, which is set into motion.

❸ The turbine is connected to an electric generator. The turbine sets the generator in motion, generating electricity.

❹ Steam from the turbine is directed to a condenser where it cools and becomes liquid water to be cycled again.

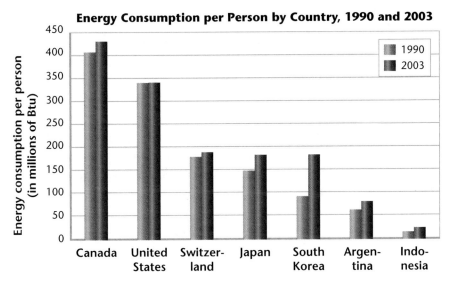

Energy Consumption per Person by Country, 1990 and 2003

Source: U.S. Department of Energy.

Figure 4 ▶ During this fourteen-year period, energy use per person stayed about the same in Switzerland and in the United States. Energy use per person in South Korea increased by almost 50 percent.

Energy Use

Every product requires energy to produce. And the price of most products and services that you use reflects the cost of energy. Buying a plane ticket, for example, includes the cost of the fuel.

World Patterns People in developed societies use much more energy than people in developing countries do. However, energy use in some developing countries is growing rapidly. Even within the developed world there are striking differences in energy use. For example, **Figure 4** shows that a person in Canada or the United States uses more than twice as much energy as a person in Japan or Switzerland does. Yet personal income in Japan and Switzerland is higher than personal income in Canada and the United States. One reason for this difference lies in how energy is generated and used in those countries.

Energy Use in the United States The United States uses more energy per person than any other country in the world except Canada and the United Arab Emirates. Part of the reason that the United States uses so much energy is that, as **Figure 5** shows, the United States uses more than 25 percent of its energy resources to transport goods and people, mainly by trucks and personal vehicles. In contrast, Japan and Switzerland have extensive rail systems and they are relatively small, compact countries. The availability and cost of fuels also influence fuel use. Residents of the United States and Canada enjoy some of the lowest gasoline taxes in the world. There is little incentive to conserve gasoline when its cost is so low. Japan and Switzerland, which have minimal fossil-fuel resources, supplement a greater percentage of their energy needs with other energy sources, such as hydroelectric or nuclear power.

✔ **Reading Check** Give two reasons why the United States uses more energy per person compared with most other countries. (See the Appendix for answers to Reading Checks.)

QuickLAB

Generating Electricity

Procedure

1. Tightly wrap 100 cm of **fine-gauge copper wire** around a small **cardboard tube.**
2. Attach a **galvanometer** or a **battery tester** to the ends of the wire.
3. Pass a **bar magnet** through the cardboard tube, and observe the galvanometer.

Analysis

1. What did you observe?
2. How could you increase the current you detected?
3. How does this lab model an electric power plant?

How Energy Is Used in the United States

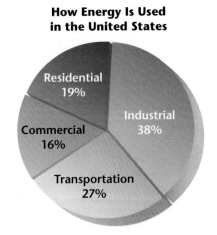

Source: International Energy Agency.

Figure 5 ▶ This graph shows the percentages of total energy use in the United States for different purposes.

How Fossil-Fuel Deposits Form

Fossil fuels are not distributed evenly, as shown in **Figure 6.** For example, why is there an abundance of oil in Texas and Alaska but very little in Maine? Why does the eastern United States produce so much coal? The answers to these questions lie in the geologic history of the areas.

Coal Formation Coal forms from the remains of plants that lived in swamps hundreds of millions of years ago. Much of the coal in the eastern United States formed about 320 million to 300 million years ago, when vast areas of swampland covered the eastern United States. As ocean levels rose and fell, these swamps were repeatedly covered with sediment. Layers of sediment compressed the plant remains, and heat and pressure within the Earth's crust caused coal to form. Coal deposits in the western United States also formed from ancient swamps, but those deposits are much younger. The abundant coal deposits in states such as Wyoming formed between 100 million and 40 million years ago.

Oil and Natural Gas Formation Oil and natural gas result from the decay of tiny marine organisms that accumulated on the bottom of the ocean millions of years ago. After these remains were buried by sediments, they were heated until they became complex energy-rich carbon-based molecules. Over time, the molecules migrated into the porous rocks that now contain them. Much of the oil and natural gas in the United States is located in Alaska, Texas, California, and the Gulf of Mexico.

Graphic Organizer) Chain-of-Events Chart

Create the **Graphic Organizer** entitled "Chain-of-Events Chart" described in the Appendix. Then, fill in the chart with details about each step of the formation of fossil fuels.

Figure 6 ▶ This map shows coal, oil, and natural gas deposits in the United States.

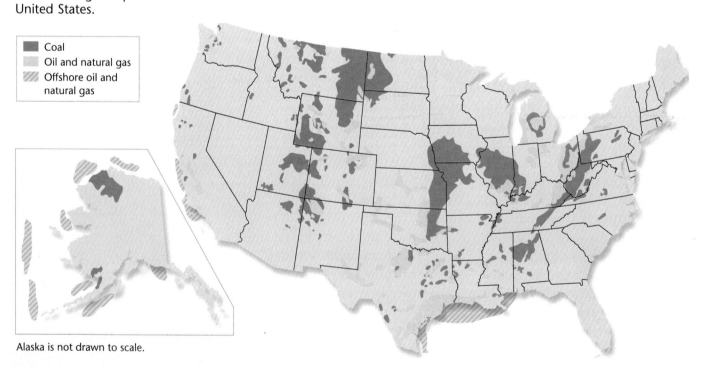

Coal
Oil and natural gas
Offshore oil and natural gas

Alaska is not drawn to scale.

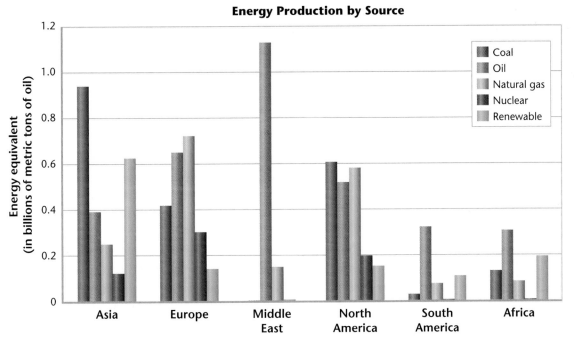

Energy Production by Source

Energy equivalent (in billions of metric tons of oil)

Legend:
- Coal
- Oil
- Natural gas
- Nuclear
- Renewable

Regions: Asia, Europe, Middle East, North America, South America, Africa

Source: International Energy Agency.

Figure 7 ▶ The Middle East produces the majority of the world's oil. Asia, however, produces the most coal.

Coal

Most of the world's fossil-fuel reserves are made up of coal. Asia and North America are particularly rich in coal deposits, as shown in **Figure 7.** Two major advantages of coal are that it is relatively inexpensive and that it needs little refining after it has been mined. About half of the electricity generated in the United States comes from coal-fired power plants, as shown in **Figure 8.**

Coal Mining and the Environment

The environmental effects of coal mining vary. Underground mines can have a minimal effect on the environment at the surface. However, surface coal-mining operations sometimes remove the top of an entire mountain to reach the coal deposit. In addition, if waste rock from coal mines is not properly contained, toxic chemicals can leach into nearby streams. A lot of research focuses on developing better methods of locating the most productive, clean-burning coal deposits and developing less damaging methods of mining coal.

Air Pollution

The quality of coal varies. Higher-grade coals, such as bituminous coal, produce more heat and less pollution than a lower-grade coal, such as lignite. Sulfur, which is found in all grades of coal, can be a major source of pollution when coal is burned. When high-sulfur, low-grade coal is burned, it releases much more pollution than a low-sulfur bituminous coal does. The air pollution and acid precipitation that result from burning high-sulfur coal without adequate pollution controls are serious problems in countries such as China. However, clean-burning coal technology has dramatically reduced air pollution in countries such as the United States.

Figure 8 ▶ About half of the electricity generated in the United States comes from burning coal. This power plant (bottom) in West Virginia is located close to the abundant coal deposits in that state.

How Electricity Is Generated in the United States

- Natural gas 18%
- Hydroelectricity 7%
- Oil 3%
- Other 2%
- Nuclear 20%
- Coal 50%

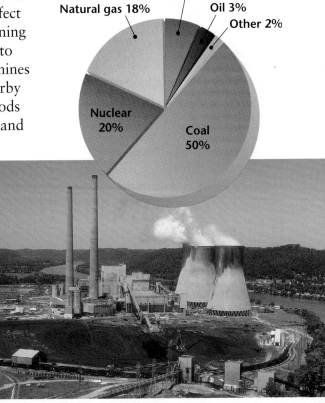

Catalytic Converters Catalytic converters are one of the most important emission-control features on cars. These devices use two separate catalysts—a *reduction catalyst* and an *oxidation catalyst*. The reduction catalyst uses platinum and rhodium to separate nitrous oxides, forming nitrogen and oxygen molecules. The oxidation catalyst uses platinum and palladium to burn—or oxidize—hydrocarbons and carbon monoxide, forming carbon dioxide, which is less harmful.

Petroleum

Oil that is pumped from the ground is also known as *crude oil*, or **petroleum.** Anything that is made from crude oil, such as fuels, chemicals, and plastics, is called a *petroleum product*. Much of the world's energy needs are met by petroleum products. In fact, petroleum accounts for 45 percent of the world's commercial energy use.

Locating Oil Deposits Oil is found in and around major geologic features, such as folds, faults, and salt domes, that tend to trap oil as it moves in the Earth's crust. These features are bound by impermeable layers of rock, which prevent the oil from escaping. Most of the world's oil reserves are in the Middle East. Large oil deposits also exist in the United States, Venezuela, the North Sea, Siberia, and Nigeria. When geologists have gathered all of the data that they can from the Earth's surface, exploration wells are drilled to determine the volume and availability of the oil deposit. If oil can be extracted at a profitable rate, wells are drilled and the oil is pumped or flows to the surface. After the oil is removed from a well, it is transported to a refinery to be converted into fuels and other petroleum products.

Reading Check What is the purpose of drilling exploration wells for oil?

Methane Hydrates— Fossil Fuel of the Future?

Deep under the waves in the Gulf of Mexico lies an untapped resource that could be the fuel of the future. It looks like ice, but it burns with a bright fire. This strange compound is called methane hydrate.

A methane hydrate is a cagelike lattice of ice that contains trapped molecules of methane. Methane is a natural gas made up of carbon and hydrogen. The methane in methane hydrates results from the bacterial decomposition of organic matter.

Methane hydrates have been known to exist since 1890. However, nobody knew that the hydrates formed in nature until 1964, when a large deposit was discovered by a Soviet crew that was

drilling for oil in Siberia. Today, huge deposits of this "solid" natural gas have been discovered around the edges of most continents. The deposits are often several hundred meters thick.

Methane hydrates form in geologic situations in which temperatures are stable and low and pressure is high. In places such as Siberia and Alaska, methane hydrates form below the tundra where permafrost extends down into shallow sediments. They also form under the ocean in water that is deeper than 500 m. In the United States, there are deposits of methane hydrates off the shores of Alaska, Washington, California, and

the Carolinas and in the Gulf of Mexico. If we could recover just one percent of the methane hydrates around the United States we could more than double our supply of natural gas, a clean-burning fuel that produces little pollution except for carbon dioxide.

Natural gas is in increasing demand for use in new electric power stations. These power stations are cheaper to build than other power stations and produce little air pollution. Natural gas is also used to fuel low-pollution vehicles.

Natural gas will become an increasingly important substitute for coal and petroleum as countries limit their emissions of the greenhouse

The Environmental Effects of Using Oil When petroleum fuels are burned, they release pollutants. Internal combustion engines in vehicles that burn gasoline pollute the air in many cities. These pollutants contribute to the formation of smog and cause health problems. Emissions regulations and technology such as catalytic converters have reduced air pollution in many areas. However, in developing countries, cars are generally older, and the gasoline that they burn contains significantly more sulfur, a pollutant that contributes to acid precipitation. As well, the carbon dioxide released from burning petroleum fuels may contribute to global warming.

Oil spills, such as the one shown in **Figure 9**, are another potential environmental problem of oil use. In recent years, new measures have been taken to prevent oil spills from tankers. These measures include requiring that new tankers be double-hulled so that puncturing the outer hull does not allow the oil to leak out. Also, response times to clean up oil spills have improved. While oil spills are dramatic, much more oil pollution comes from everyday sources, such as leaking cars. However, measures to reduce everyday contamination of our waterways from oil lag far behind the efforts made to prevent large spills.

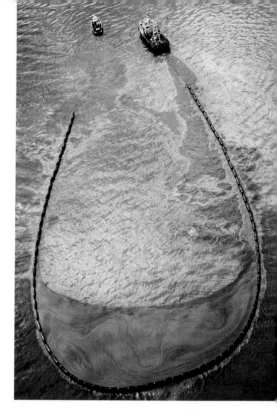

Figure 9 ▶ This ship is attempting to contain the oil spilled from the *Sea Empress* in 1996.

EARTH SCIENCE **CONNECTION**

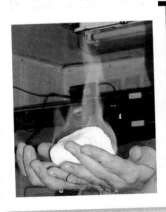 

▶ A researcher holds a chunk of burning methane hydrate (far left). A methane hydrate mound in the Gulf of Mexico (left).

gas carbon dioxide to reduce global warming. The use of fuel-cell technology in vehicles will also increase. Fuel cells need hydrogen as a power source, and natural gas is a convenient source of hydrogen. The first fuel-cell vehicles will probably be fueled at a gas station that also has a natural gas pump.

So far, we have no technology to recover or use this strange mixture of ice and methane. One potential idea is to pump heated water into a methane hydrate deposit to melt the ice and release the methane gas. The gas would then have to be pumped to a processing plant.

CRITICAL THINKING

1. Applying Processes What are the differences between the geologic processes by which petroleum and natural gas form and the way methane hydrates form?

2. Analyzing Relationships Methane is a very effective greenhouse gas. How might this factor into the extraction or use of methane hydrates in the future?

Figure 10 ▶ Except when it is refueling, a vehicle that runs on natural gas looks like one that runs on gasoline.

Natural Gas About 20 percent of the world's nonrenewable energy comes from natural gas. Natural gas, or methane (CH_4), is a good example of how advances in technology can make a fuel more common. In the past, when natural gas was encountered in an oil well, it was burned off because it was considered a nuisance. As technology improved, transporting natural gas in pipelines and storing it compressed in tanks became more practical. Now, many more oil wells recover natural gas. Because burning natural gas produces fewer pollutants than burning other fossil fuels, vehicles that run on natural gas, such as the one in **Figure 10**, require fewer pollution controls. Electric power plants can also use this clean-burning fuel.

Fossil Fuels and the Future

Today, fossil fuels supply about 90 percent of the energy used in developed countries. Some projections suggest that by 2050 world energy demand will have doubled, mainly as a result of increased population and industry in developing countries. As the demand for energy resources increases, the cost of fossil fuels will likely increase enough to make other energy sources more attractive. Planning now for the energy we will use in the future is important because it takes many years for a new source of energy to make a significant contribution to our energy supply.

Predicting Oil Production Oil production is still increasing, but it is increasing much more slowly than it has in the past, as shown in **Figure 11**. Many different factors must be considered when predicting oil production. **Oil reserves** are oil deposits that can be extracted profitably at current prices using current technology. In contrast, some oil deposits are yet to be discovered or to become commercial. Predictions must also take into account changes in technology that would allow more oil to be extracted in the future.

MATHPRACTICE

World Energy Use
In 1980, worldwide production of petroleum was 59.6 million barrels per day. In 1998, petroleum production was 66.9 million barrels a day. Calculate the percent increase in oil production during this period.

Figure 11 ▶ This graph shows past oil production and one prediction for the future.

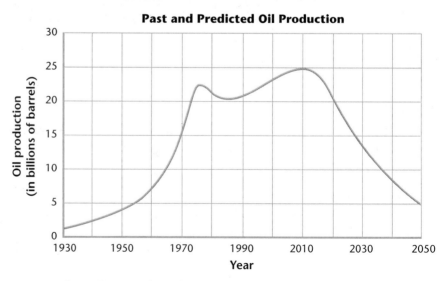

Source: Petroconsultants S.A.

Finally, all predictions of future oil production are guided by an important principle: the relative cost of obtaining fuels influences the amount of fossil fuels that we extract from the Earth. For example, as the supply of readily available oil decreases, we may begin to rely less on oil reserves and focus on using oil more selectively. At that time, oil will begin to be used more for applications in which it is essential. Cars and power plants, which can be powered in many ways, will begin to rely on other energy sources.

Future Oil Reserves No large oil reserves have been discovered in the past decade, and geologists predict that oil production from fields accessible from land will peak in about 2010. Additional oil reserves are under the ocean, but extracting oil from beneath the ocean floor is much more expensive. Currently, oil platforms can be built to drill for oil at depths greater than 1,800 m, but much of the oil in the deep ocean is currently inaccessible. Deep-ocean reserves may be tapped in the future, but unless oil-drilling technology improves, oil from the deep ocean will be much more expensive than oil produced on land.

Connection to Astronomy

Cosmic Oil Some scientists support a controversial hypothesis that some oil and natural gas deposits did not come from the remains of ancient life but were incorporated into the Earth during its formation from the solar nebula 4.5 billion years ago. Hydrocarbons are some of the most common compounds in the universe and large amounts of them could have been incorporated in the Earth as it formed. If this theory is correct, the Earth could contain vast reserves of "cosmic fossil fuels" that are not yet discovered.

Figure 12 ▶ This offshore oil rig is extracting petroleum from beneath the ocean floor.

SECTION 1 **Review**

1. **Describe** five factors that influence the value of a fuel.

2. **Describe** how fossil fuels are used to produce electricity, and explain how an electric generator works.

3. **Describe** how coal, oil, and natural gas form, how these fuels are used, and how using each fuel affects the environment.

CRITICAL THINKING

4. **Analyzing Relationships** What is the relationship between natural gas and petroleum?

5. **Making Comparisons** Read the description of how fossil-fuel deposits form. Are fossil fuels produced today by the same geologic processes as in the past?
   READING SKILLS

6. **Making Inferences** Examine Figure 11. What do you think accounts for the dramatic increase in the worldwide production of oil after 1950?

SECTION 2
Nuclear Energy

Objectives

▶ Describe nuclear fission.
▶ Describe how a nuclear power plant works.
▶ List three advantages and three disadvantages of nuclear energy.

Key Terms

nuclear energy
nuclear fission
nuclear fusion

SCLINKS.

www.scilinks.org
Topic: Nuclear Energy
Code: HE81047

In the 1950s and 1960s, nuclear power plants were seen as the power source of the future because the fuel they use is clean and plentiful. It was predicted that a nationwide network of nuclear power plants would provide electricity that was "too cheap to meter." But in the 1970s and 1980s, almost 120 planned nuclear power plants were canceled, and about 40 partially constructed nuclear plants were abandoned. What happened? In this section, you will learn how nuclear power works and why about 17 percent of the world's electricity comes from nuclear power today.

Fission: Splitting Atoms

Nuclear power plants get their power from **nuclear energy,** the energy within the nucleus of an atom. The forces that hold together the nucleus of an atom are more than 1 million times stronger than the chemical bonds between atoms. In nuclear power plants, atoms of the element uranium are used as the fuel.

The nuclei of uranium atoms are bombarded with atomic particles called *neutrons*. These collisions cause the nuclei to split in a process called **nuclear fission.** A fission reaction is shown in **Figure 13.** Nuclear fission releases a tremendous amount of energy and more neutrons, which in turn collide with more uranium nuclei. If a fission reaction is allowed to continue, this chain reaction will escalate quickly. One example of an uncontrolled fission reaction is the explosion of an atomic bomb. In contrast, nuclear power stations are designed so that the chain reaction produces a controllable level of energy.

Figure 13 ▶ Neutrons are released from the fission, or the splitting, of a uranium atom's nucleus. Some of these neutrons then cause other atoms to undergo nuclear fission in a process called a *chain reaction.*

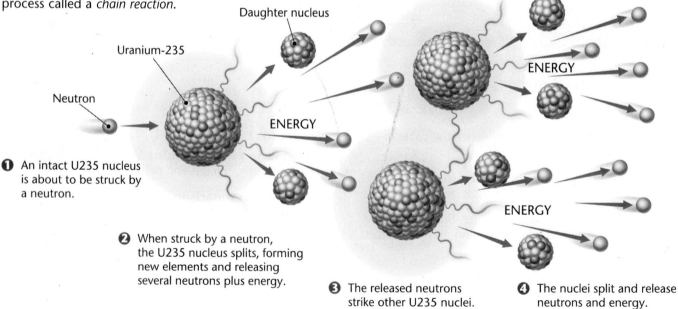

Daughter nucleus

Uranium-235

Neutron

ENERGY

ENERGY

ENERGY

❶ An intact U235 nucleus is about to be struck by a neutron.

❷ When struck by a neutron, the U235 nucleus splits, forming new elements and releasing several neutrons plus energy.

❸ The released neutrons strike other U235 nuclei.

❹ The nuclei split and release neutrons and energy.

How Nuclear Energy Works

A nuclear reactor is surrounded by a thick pressure vessel that is filled with a cooling fluid. The pressure vessel is designed to contain the fission products in case of an accident. Thick concrete walls also surround reactors as shown in **Figure 14**.

Inside a reactor, shown in **Figure 15**, metal fuel rods that contain solid uranium pellets are bombarded with neutrons. The chain reaction that results releases energy and produces more neutrons. The reactor core contains control rods that control the rate of fission in the reactor. They do this by absorbing neutrons, which prevents the neutrons from causing fission reactions in the uranium fuel.

The heat released during nuclear reactions is used to generate electricity in the same way that power plants burn fossil fuels to generate electricity. In a nuclear power plant, energy released from the fission reactions heats a closed loop of water that heats another body of water. As the water boils, it produces steam that drives a steam turbine, which is used to generate electricity.

✓ Reading Check What is the function of the pressure vessel of a nuclear reactor?

Figure 14 ▶ Every year, the Diablo Canyon nuclear plant generates enough energy for 2 million Californian households—the energy equivalent of burning 20 million barrels of oil.

Figure 15 ▶ How a Typical Nuclear Power Plant Works

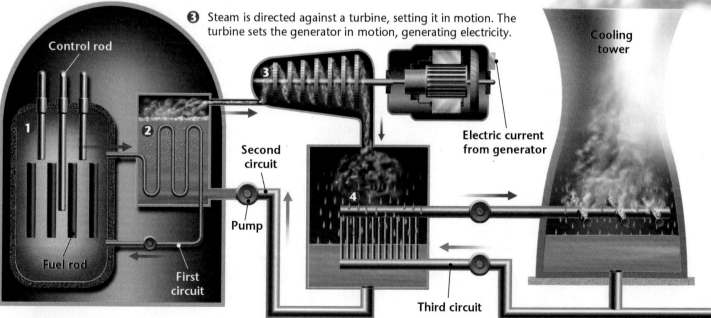

❷ The superheated water is pumped to a heat exchanger, which transfers the heat of the first circuit to the second circuit. Water in the second circuit flashes into high-pressure steam.

❸ Steam is directed against a turbine, setting it in motion. The turbine sets the generator in motion, generating electricity.

Cooling tower

Control rod

Electric current from generator

Second circuit

Pump

Fuel rod

First circuit

Third circuit

❶ Energy released by the nuclear reaction heats water in the pressurized first circuit to a very high temperature.

❹ A third circuit cools the steam from the turbine and the waste heat is released from the cooling tower in the form of steam.

The Advantages of Nuclear Energy

Nuclear energy has many advantages. Nuclear fuel is a very concentrated energy source, as shown in **Figure 16.** Furthermore, nuclear power plants do not produce greenhouse gases. When operated properly, nuclear plants release less radioactivity than coal-fired power plants do. Many countries with limited fossil-fuel reserves rely heavily on nuclear plants to supply electricity. France, for example, generates about three-fourths of its electricity from nuclear power. France produces less than one-fifth of the air pollutants per person than does the United States, which relies on fossil fuels for almost 70 percent of its electricity needs.

Why Aren't We Using More Nuclear Energy?

Building and maintaining a safe reactor is very expensive. The last 20 nuclear reactors built in the United States cost more than $3,000 per kilowatt of electrical capacity. In contrast, wind power is being installed at less than $1,000 per kilowatt. This cost will decrease as construction costs decrease. Natural gas power plants are also less expensive to build than nuclear power plants, costing less than $600 per kilowatt.

Storing Waste The difficulty of finding a safe place to store nuclear wastes is one of the greatest disadvantages of nuclear power. The fuel cycle of uranium produces fission products that remain dangerously radioactive for thousands of years. Uranium mining and fuel development produce radioactive wastes. In addition, the used fuel, liquids, and equipment from a reactor core are also considered hazardous wastes. Storage sites for nuclear wastes must be located in areas that are geologically stable for tens of thousands of years. The United States has spent over two decades studying a site called Yucca Mountain in southern Nevada as a place to store nuclear waste. Scientists are also researching a process called transmutation, which would recycle the radioactive elements in nuclear fuel.

Figure 16 ▶ Uranium is a very compact fuel. The uranium pellets (above) can generate as much electricity as the trainload full of coal does.

Safety Concerns In a poorly designed nuclear plant, the fission process can potentially get out of control. This is what happened during the world's worst nuclear reactor accident, which occurred at Chernobyl in the Ukraine in 1986. Engineers turned off most of the reactor's safety devices to conduct an unauthorized test. This test caused explosions that destroyed the reactor and released large amounts of radioactive materials into the air. Areas of northern Europe and the Ukraine are still contaminated. The Chernobyl reactor was an old design that, for safety reasons, is not used in the United States. The nuclear reactor had no containment building. In addition, the engineers at Chernobyl violated basic safety guidelines.

✔ Reading Check Why is it so difficult to find a place that can be used to store nuclear waste safely?

Radon Uranium occurs naturally in rock and soil. When uranium undergoes radioactive decay, it gives off a number of products, including an invisible and odorless radioactive gas called radon. Radon can seep into buildings from the surrounding rock and soil, and if buildings are not ventilated properly, dangerous levels of radon can build up. It is estimated that radon causes 5,000 to 20,000 people in the United States to die from lung cancer each year.

In the United States, the most serious nuclear accident occurred in 1979 at the Three Mile Island nuclear power plant in Pennsylvania. Human error, along with blocked valves and broken pumps, caused the accident. Fortunately, only a small amount of radioactive gas escaped. Since this accident, the U.S. Nuclear Regulatory Commission has required more than 300 safety improvements to nuclear power plants.

The Future of Nuclear Power

One possible future energy source is nuclear fusion. **Nuclear fusion** occurs when lightweight atomic nuclei combine to form a heavier nucleus and release tremendous amounts of energy. **Figure 17** illustrates the process of nuclear fusion. Nuclear fusion powers all of the stars, including our sun. Fusion is potentially a safer energy source than nuclear fission is because it creates less dangerous radioactive byproducts.

Unfortunately, although the potential of fusion is great, so is the technical difficulty of achieving it. For fusion to occur, atomic nuclei must be heated to extremely high temperatures (about 100,000,000°C, or 180,000,000°F). The nuclei must also be maintained at very high concentrations and properly confined. Achieving all three of these conditions simultaneously is extremely difficult. The technical problems are so complex that building a nuclear fusion plant may take decades or may never happen.

Connection to History

Three Mile Island The Three Mile Island accident was a wake-up call for the nuclear industry. Many reforms and safety measures were instituted throughout the industry after the accident occurred. In 1989, 10 years after the accident, the nuclear plant received the best INPO rating in the world. The rating was based on a measure of reliability, efficiency, and safety. In 1999, the plant set a world record after running continuously for 688 days.

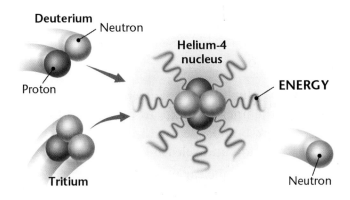

Figure 17 ▶ During nuclear fusion, the nuclei of two forms of hydrogen (deuterium and tritium in this case) join to form helium, which releases large amounts of energy.

SECTION 2 Review

1. **Compare** a power plant that burns fossil fuels with a nuclear power plant.

2. **Describe** two advantages and two disadvantages of nuclear power plants.

3. **Explain** the difference between nuclear fission and nuclear fusion.

CRITICAL THINKING

4. **Applying Ideas** Read about the advantages of nuclear energy. Explain why countries such as France and Japan rely heavily on nuclear power. **READING SKILLS**

5. **Making Decisions** Which poses more of an environmental threat: transporting spent nuclear fuel or transporting toxic chemicals? Write your opinion in the form of a short essay. **WRITING SKILLS**

1 Energy Resources and Fossil Fuels

Key Terms

fossil fuel, 467
electric generator, 468
petroleum, 472
oil reserves, 474

Main Ideas

▶ Most of the world's energy needs are met by fossil fuels, which are nonrenewable resources.

▶ Coal is abundant in North America and Asia. In the United States, coal is used primarily to produce electricity.

▶ Petroleum can be refined into fuels to power vehicles and machines. Petroleum can also be used to manufacture many other products.

▶ Natural gas is often found above oil deposits. In general, burning natural gas releases fewer pollutants than burning coal or oil.

▶ The extraction, transportation, and use of fossil fuels cause many environmental problems, including air and water pollution and habitat destruction.

▶ Calculations of fossil-fuel reserves predict that oil production will peak and then decline in the early 21st century.

2 Nuclear Energy

nuclear energy, 476
nuclear fission, 476
nuclear fusion, 479

▶ Nuclear energy is energy that exists within the nucleus of an atom. When uranium nuclei are bombarded with neutrons, they undergo fission and release large amounts of energy.

▶ In a nuclear power station, the heat generated by fission is used to heat water to form steam. The steam drives turbines that generate electricity.

▶ The main advantages of nuclear power are that the fuel is compact and the power stations generally do not pollute. The main disadvantage is that nuclear power produces radioactive waste, which will be dangerous for centuries.

Using Key Terms

Use each of the following terms in a separate sentence.

1. *fossil fuel*
2. *petroleum*
3. *oil reserves*
4. *nuclear fission*
5. *nuclear fusion*

For each pair of terms, explain how the meanings of the terms differ.

6. *petroleum* and *oil reserve*
7. *turbine* and *electric generator*
8. *nuclear fission* and *nuclear fusion*

✔ STUDY TIP

Get Organized Being organized can help make studying more efficient and less confusing. Start by reducing clutter and consolidating loose papers. Arrange your items by subject, and be sure to label your books, notebooks, and dividers. A planner, or agenda book, can help you balance schoolwork with other activities. It also can serve as reminder of upcoming deadlines and help you to prioritize multiple tasks.

Understanding Key Ideas

9. Which of the following statements provides a reason for the widespread use of fossil fuels?
   a. Fossil fuels are a renewable source of energy.
   b. Fossil fuels are readily available and inexpensive.
   c. Fossil fuels are not harmful to the environment.
   d. all of the above

10. Which of the following pairs are design features that nuclear power plants and coal-fired power plants share?
    a. fuel rods and containment buildings
    b. turbines and generators
    c. combustion chamber and reactor cores
    d. none of the above

11. The main reason for the worldwide slow-down in the construction of nuclear power plants is that
    a. we have run out of uranium fuel.
    b. the electricity from nuclear power is generally more expensive to produce than electricity from other sources.
    c. nuclear reactors are inherently unsafe.
    d. nuclear reactors release large quantities of greenhouse gases.

12. Which is an example of the direct use of fossil fuels?
    a. a nuclear reactor
    b. an oil-fired furnace
    c. a wind generator
    d. a wood-burning stove

13. Which of the following statements describes the process by which modern nuclear power plants use nuclear energy?
    a. Power plants use nuclear fusion to split uranium atoms and release nuclear energy.
    b. Power plants use nuclear fusion to combine atomic nuclei and release nuclear energy.
    c. Power plants use nuclear fission to split uranium atoms and release nuclear energy.
    d. Power plants use nuclear fission to combine atomic nuclei and release nuclear energy.

14. If fossil fuels are still forming today, why are they considered nonrenewable resources?
    a. Fossil fuels are broken down by natural processes faster than they form.
    b. We are depleting fossil fuels much faster than they form.
    c. The fossil fuels being formed today are deep under the ocean, where they cannot be reached.
    d. The only fossil fuels being produced are methane hydrates, which we cannot use yet.

15. Which of the following is *not* a disadvantage of nuclear energy?
    a. the difficulty of safe storage of nuclear waste
    b. the high levels of air pollution produced
    c. the use of natural gas to produce nuclear energy
    d. the possibility that a nuclear chain reaction can get out of control

Short Answer

16. Why have fossil fuels become our primary energy resource?

17. How did the Three Mile Island accident affect nuclear safety in the United States?

18. What factors make nuclear power expensive?

19. What is the difference between oil reserves and oil deposits?

Interpreting Graphics

The graph below shows the different contributions of various fuels to the U.S. energy supply since 1850. Use the graph to answer questions 20–24.

20. When did oil first become a more important energy source than coal?

21. Why do you think the use of coal increased so rapidly between 1850 and 1920?

22. The data for oil and natural gas are nearly parallel—they rise and fall together. Why do you think this pattern exists?

23. Why do you think the use of coal is on the rise after having fallen in the 1950s?

24. Why do you think that the use of wood as a fuel has not significantly increased or decreased since about 1850?

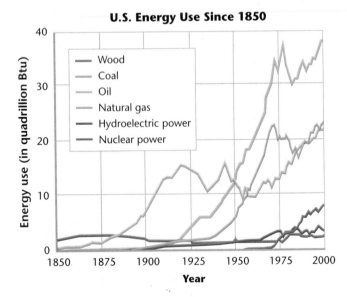

U.S. Energy Use Since 1850

Legend:
- Wood
- Coal
- Oil
- Natural gas
- Hydroelectric power
- Nuclear power

y-axis: Energy use (in quadrillion Btu)
x-axis: Year (1850, 1875, 1900, 1925, 1950, 1975, 2000)

Concept Mapping

25. Use the following terms to create a concept map: *oil well, petroleum, refinery, gasoline, natural gas, plastics,* and *oil reserve.*

Critical Thinking

26. **Demonstrating Reasoned Judgment** The invention of artificial plastics had a damaging effect on the environment because most plastics break down very slowly, so they remain in landfills and are dangerous to wildlife. However, the invention of plastics also affected the environment in many positive ways. List as many positive effects as you can.

27. **Analyzing Relationships** Read the description of how fossil-fuel deposits form. Explain why fossil fuels are a form of stored solar energy. **READING SKILLS**

28. **Analyzing Relationships** The United States currently imports about half of all the crude oil it uses. Why might this be a problem? Write a paragraph that describes the recommendations that you would make to U.S. lawmakers, manufacturers, and consumers to reduce the country's dependence on foreign oil. **WRITING SKILLS**

Cross-Disciplinary Connection

29. **Economics** What incentives could encourage automobile manufacturers in the United States to produce more fuel-efficient cars? The U.S. government could increase the requirements for fuel efficiency. However, at least two other strong forces are likely to change the types of vehicles that manufacturers produce. What do you think these forces are?

Portfolio Project

30. **Prepare a Display** Find out how petroleum, natural gas, coal, or uranium are extracted. For example, engineers have developed methods to drill sideways to reach oil deposits thousands of feet underground. Research one method and prepare a model or a posterboard display that communicates your findings. Be sure to include information about the environmental effects of the method you studied.

MATH SKILLS

The graph below compares the contribution of each world region to world oil production. Use the graph to answer question 31.

31. Analyzing Data If the total sales of oil in 2002 were $500 billion, what is the value of the oil produced by each region?

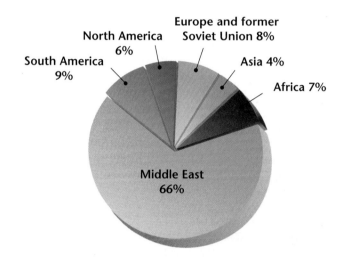

North America 6%

South America 9%

Europe and former Soviet Union 8%

Asia 4%

Africa 7%

Middle East 66%

WRITING SKILLS

32. Communicating Main Ideas How would our lives change if oil reserves became so depleted that gasoline was very expensive?

33. Recognizing Relationships Outline the major forms of environmental change that have resulted from fossil-fuel use. Include your thoughts on subjects such as habitat loss, pollution, and our use of land. Remember to include positive environmental changes.

READING SKILLS

Read the passage below, and then answer the questions that follow.

Paula Curtis became chief executive officer of Zaft Motors in 2002. She has a strong interest in the environment. Because she is chief executive of the country's second-largest auto manufacturer, she has an influence on the automobile industry. For instance, Zaft left the Global Climate Coalition, a group of companies that denied the scientific research proving global warming. Within four months, two other auto manufacturers also left. Zaft publishes a "corporate citizenship" report each year. In 2001, the report stated that Zaft's vehicles and factories emit 350 million metric tons of carbon dioxide annually and contribute to global warming. The report also stated that Zaft was committed to reducing this number.

However, Zaft has a long way to go to fulfill this goal. Zaft has failed to improve the fuel economy of its cars and trucks, so its new vehicles get fewer miles per gallon, on average, than the vehicles built in 1982. Modern technology for engines, transmissions, and aerodynamics could help Zaft achieve an average fuel economy of 40 mi/gal for its cars, pickups, and sport utility vehicles. As a result, the United States would save almost 1 million barrels of oil per day—over half as much as the country imports from Saudi Arabia.

1. Which of the following statements best describes the thesis of the article?
   a. Zaft Motors is jeopardizing its position as the country's second-largest auto manufacturer by enacting environmental controls.
   b. Zaft left the Global Climate Coalition because it acknowledged the scientific evidence for global warming.
   c. Although Zaft has taken some actions to be an environmentally responsible corporate citizen, the company still needs to improve the fuel efficiency of its vehicles.
   d. none of the above

Understanding Concepts

Directions (1–3): For *each* question, write on a separate sheet of paper the letter of the correct answer.

1 Where do coal, oil and natural gas come from?
   A. the melting of polar ice packs
   B. the remains of organisms
   C. the residue of volcanic eruptions
   D. the understory of forests

2 When fossil fuels are burned and converted to electricity, how does the total amount of usable energy change?
   F. The amount of usable energy remains the same.
   G. The amount of usable energy decreases during conversion.
   H. The amount of usable energy doubles during conversion.
   I. The amount of usable energy depends on how well the power plant is maintained.

3 Which of the following statements describes energy consumption trends today?
   A. Developed nations are using less energy per person.
   B. Developing nations are using less energy per person.
   C. Developed nations are using more energy than undeveloped nations.
   D. Developing nations are using more energy than developed nations.

Directions (4–5): For *each* question, write a short response.

4 The United States uses more than 25% of its energy to transport goods and people. This percentage of resources, used mostly by trucks and personal vehicles, is much higher than energy used for transportation in Japan or Switzerland. Why do these two developed countries use less energy for transportation than the United States?

5 Provide one reason why building and maintaining nuclear power plants is expensive.

Reading Skills

Directions (6–8): Read the passage below. Then answer the questions.

Today, fossil fuels supply about 90% of the energy used in developed countries. Oil production is increasing, but it is increasing much more slowly than it has in the past. Many different factors must be considered when predicting oil production. Oil reserves are oil deposits that can be extracted profitably at current prices using current technology. Some projections suggest that by 2050 world demand for fossil fuels will have doubled, mainly as a result of increased population and industry in developing nations. People in developed countries use much more energy than people in developing countries do. As the demand for energy resources increases, the cost of fossil fuels will likely increase enough to make other energy sources more attractive.

6 How would you assess the effect of technology on oil prices?
   F. Technology raises production and lowers prices.
   G. Technology lowers production and raises prices.
   H. Technology raises production and raises prices.
   I. Technology lowers production and lowers prices.

7 If oil prices continue to increase, what effect would this have on industries in developing countries?

8 Which of the following statements is false?
   A. Fossil fuels supply about 90% of the energy used in developed countries.
   B. World demand for fossil fuels will likely increase significantly by 2050.
   C. People in developed countries use more energy than people in developing countries use.
   D. The cost of fossil fuels will likely decrease in the future.

Interpreting Graphics

Directions (9–12): For *each* question below, record the correct answer on a separate sheet of paper.

The graph below shows past and predicted oil production. Use this graph to answer questions 9 through 12.

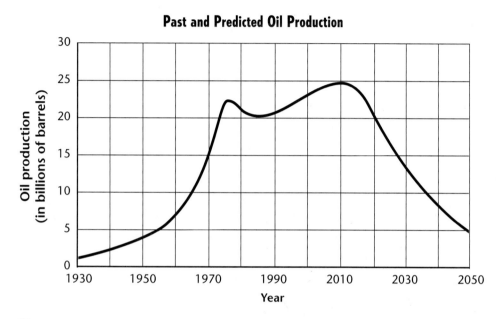

Past and Predicted Oil Production

9 If oil production after 2010 continues at the predicted rate, when will the oil reserves run out?
F. 2040
G. 2050
H. 2060
I. 2070

10 What can be concluded about oil production from the graph?
A. Oil production hit its peak in the mid 20th century.
B. Oil production saw a dramatic increase during the 1980s.
C. Oil production continued to increase throughout the 1900s.
D. Oil production more than doubled between 1965 and 1975.

11 What can be inferred about the cost of oil after 2010?
F. It will increase.
G. It will decrease steadily.
H. It will remain unchanged.
I. It will increase until 2030, then decrease.

12 What is the difference in billions of barrels produced in 1990 compared to 1970?
A. Production doubled.
B. Production fell by half.
C. Production hit a new low.
D. Production was up six billion barrels.

Test TIP

Sometimes, only a portion of a graph or table is needed to answer a question. Focus only on the necessary information to avoid confusion.

CHAPTER 17

Skills Practice Lab: CONSUMER

Objectives

▶ USING SCIENTIFIC METHODS **Identify** the ways in which electricity is consumed in your household.

▶ **Compute** the energy consumption of your household.

▶ **Interpret** an electric utility bill and an electric meter.

Materials

calculator
electric bill
notebook
pen or pencil

▶ **Keeping Track of Energy Use**

An electric meter (below) records the amount of electricity that a household uses. A utility bill (below) calculates the cost of the electricity used.

Your Household Energy Consumption

We use electricity for many activities at home, such as drying clothes, cooking food, and heating and cooling. The total amount of energy that we use depends both on how much energy each individual appliance consumes and on how long we use the appliance each day. In this lab, you will survey your household to determine how much electricity you consume and you will analyze an electric bill to calculate how much you pay for your electricity.

Procedure

1. Create a table similar to the one shown below. To determine daily energy consumption in kilowatt-hours, divide the wattage of an appliance by 1,000 and then multiply by the number of hours the item is used per day.

Appliance	Energy consumed in 1 hour (watts)	Hours used (per day)	Daily energy consumption (Kwh)

DO NOT WRITE IN THIS BOOK

2. Walk through your home, and identify all appliances and devices that use electricity. List each item in your table.

3. Fill in each column in your table. Determine the wattage of each item by referring to the table on the next page.

4. Find the electric meter. It may be on an outside wall of your house or apartment building. Record the current reading on the meter. The reading may change as you watch it. If so, electricity is currently being consumed in your household. If the reading is changing, write down an estimate of the current reading.

Electric Service	Meter#	Read Date		Reading
	141707	04/05/2002		87671.00
		03/07/2002		87503.00
		Read Difference		168.00
		Total Consumption in KWH		168

Billing Rate: Residential Service Winter

Customer Charge			$6.00
Energy Charge	168.00 @ $ .0355000 per KWH		$5.96
Fuel Charge	168.00 @ $ .0177400 per KWH		$2.98
Sales Tax			$0.15
TOTAL CURRENT CHARGES - Electric			**$15.09**

Analysis

1. **Organizing Data** Add up the energy consumption per day for all items. This number is the total energy consumed by your household in one day.

2. **Organizing Data** On your electric bill, find the total number of kilowatt-hours consumed during this time period. An electric bill usually lists a meter reading for the beginning of the time period and for the end of the time period. The difference is the energy consumption in kilowatt-hours.

3. **Analyzing Data** Divide the number of kilowatt-hours from your electric bill by the number of days in the time period. This number reflects the average daily energy consumption for this time period.

4. **Analyzing Results** Compare the daily energy consumption that you calculated from your home survey with the average calculated from your electric bill. Is there a difference? If so, what could explain the difference?

5. **Analyzing Data** Find the cost of electricity per kilowatt-hour on your electric bill. How much does washing your clothes in a washing machine cost?

Conclusions

6. **Drawing Conclusions** What can you conclude about energy consumption in your home? What activities consume the most energy? How could you reduce the energy consumption in your home?

7. **Evaluating Methods** How could the energy survey be refined to estimate more accurately your daily energy consumption?

Extension

1. **Communicating Ideas** Even when an appliance is turned off, it can still consume electricity. This type of electricity consumption is called a *phantom load*. Find out about phantom loads and prepare a booklet that shows how people can reduce this type of energy use.

Energy Consumption for Common Household Appliances	
Appliance	Energy consumed in 1 hour (watts)
Ceiling fan	120
Clock radio	10
Clothes washer	425
Clothes dryer (electric)	3,400
Coffee maker	1,050
Dishwasher	1,800
Window fan	150
Hair dryer	1,500
Heater (portable)	1,100
Iron	1,400
Light bulbs	60, 75, 100
Microwave oven	900
Personal computer	270
Refrigerator (frost free, 16 ft³)	725
Stereo	400
Television (color)	130
Toaster	1,100
Toaster oven	1,225
Vacuum cleaner	1,200
VCR/DVD	19/22
Water heater (40 gal)	5,000
Water pump (deep well)	650
Window fan	150

NUCLEAR POWER PLANTS IN THE UNITED STATES

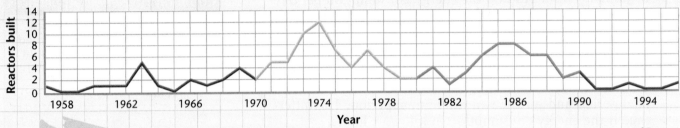

Source: U.S. Department of Energy.

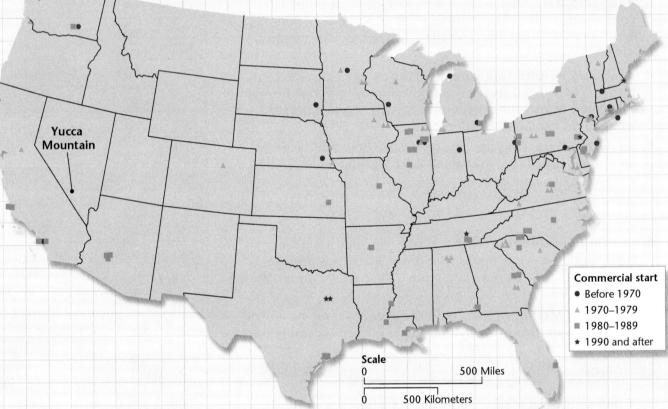

Yucca Mountain

Commercial start
- Before 1970
- 1970–1979
- 1980–1989
- ★ 1990 and after

Scale
0   500 Miles

0   500 Kilometers

MAP SKILLS

1. **Identifying Trends** During what time period did most of the nuclear plants in the United States begin operation?

2. **Using the Key** Use the symbols on the map to describe the history of nuclear power in the Northeast, the Southeast, the Great Plains states, and the western states.

3. **Comparing Areas** What region of the United States has the most nuclear power plants? What region has the fewest? Why?

4. **Identifying Relationships** Why do you think that many nuclear reactors are built close together?

5. **Calculating Problems** The U.S. government is considering storing most of its nuclear waste produced in the United States in a facility in Yucca Mountain in Nevada. This location is marked on the map. What are the average distances from the nuclear plants in California, Texas, Florida, and New York to this site?

FROM CRUDE OIL TO PLASTICS

Can you imagine using shampoo from a glass bottle? Your parents or grandparents might remember a time when a dropped shampoo bottle meant shards of glass on the shower floor. Today, plastic is in everything from shampoo bottles, car fenders, artificial limbs, refrigerators, and cameras, to snowboards. While these products are all vastly different, they started out in the same way, as petroleum, or crude oil.

Petroleum is the most common fuel used to power vehicles and heat homes. But you may not realize that this versatile fuel contains many different organic compounds, which are used to produce many other products and chemicals of modern society. However, before these compounds can be used, they must be separated from petroleum. At a refinery, petroleum is heated so that it separates into petroleum distillates during a process called fractional distillation. When petroleum is heated, petroleum distillates evaporate and condense at different temperatures. These different compounds are then used to make many products we use every day.

A Refined Resource

When the crude oil is heated, volatile compounds that have very low boiling points, such as those that make up gasoline and airplane fuel, evaporate first and are collected. Compounds that have very high boiling points are left behind. These compounds are used to make products such as diesel oil, heating oil, lubricants, asphalt, paraffin wax, and tar. Petroleum distillates are also used in pesticides, cleaning fluids, metal polishes, spot removers, lubricants, and many other products.

▶ A fractionation tower separates petroleum into its component compounds.

All petroleum distillates are toxic. When their vapors are breathed, they can cause chemical pneumonia, lung damage, or death. Therefore, all household products that contain 10 percent or more petroleum distillates are required to have hazard warnings. Products containing petroleum distillates should be used carefully.

Plastics

Plastic is one type of material that is manufactured from petroleum distillates. Before plastics can be made, however, the petroleum distillates must be processed. Ethane and propane, two petroleum distillates, are "cracked," or broken into smaller compounds called ethylene and propylene. These compounds are combined with a catalyst and other additives to create a powdered polymer. This polymer is melted and formed into small pellets. Manufacturers purchase the pellets, melt them, add color, and create many products with which you are familiar.

Plastics are also being used in ways you may not have thought of before. Scientists at Ohio State University recently developed a plastic that can withstand temperatures up to 800°F. Military aircraft may soon take advantage of this technology, and it may not be long before you find yourself in a car that has an engine made of plastic.

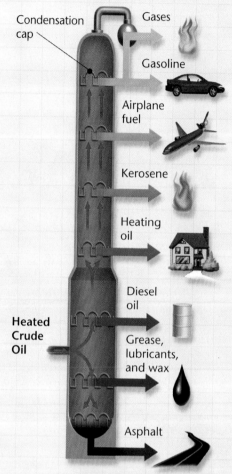

Lowest Boiling Point

Condensation cap

Gases

Gasoline

Airplane fuel

Kerosene

Heating oil

Heated Crude Oil

Diesel oil

Grease, lubricants, and wax

Asphalt

Highest Boiling Point

What Do You Think?

There are many possible substitutes for petroleum fuels to power vehicles and electric generators. However, finding substitutes for petroleum used as solvents and in other products is not easy. If petroleum supplies are limited, can you think of any substitutes for petroleum?

Renewable Energy

CHAPTER 18

1 Renewable Energy Today
2 Alternative Energy and Conservation

PRE-READING ACTIVITY

FOLDNOTES

Double-Door Fold
Before you read this chapter, create the **FoldNote** entitled "Double-Door Fold" described in the Reading and Study Skills section of the Appendix. Write "Advantages of renewable energies" on one flap of the double door and "Disadvantages of renewable energies" on the other flap. As you read the chapter, compare the two topics, and write characteristics of each type of renewable energy on the inside of the appropriate flap.

The power of the wind is one of the oldest energy resources used by humans. These Spanish windmills were built to grind grain hundreds of years ago. Today, wind energy is a rapidly growing industry.

Renewable Energy Today

GA SEV4b; SEV4d

EARTH SCIENCE **CONNECTION**

When someone mentions renewable energy, you may think of high-tech solar-powered cars, but life on Earth has always been powered by energy from the sun. **Renewable energy** is energy from sources that are constantly being formed. In addition to solar energy, renewable energy sources include wind energy, the power of moving water, and the Earth's heat.

Many governments plan to increase their use of renewable sources. For example, the European Union plans to produce 12 percent of their energy from renewable sources by 2010. Such a change will reduce the environmental problems caused by the use of nonrenewable energy. However, all sources of energy, including renewable sources, affect the environment.

Solar Energy—Power from the Sun

What does the space station shown in **Figure 1** have in common with a plant? Both are powered by energy from the sun. The sun is a medium-sized star that radiates energy from nuclear fusion reactions in its core. Only a small fraction of the sun's energy reaches the Earth. However, this energy is enough to power the wind, plant growth, and the water cycle. So nearly all renewable energy comes directly or indirectly from the sun. You use direct solar energy every day. When the sun shines on a window and heats a room, the room is being heated by solar power. Solar energy can also be used indirectly to generate electricity in solar cells.

Objectives

▶ List six forms of renewable energy, and compare their advantages and disadvantages.

▶ Describe the differences between passive solar heating, active solar heating, and photovoltaic energy.

▶ Describe the current state of wind energy technology.

▶ Explain the differences in biomass fuel use between developed and developing nations.

▶ Describe how hydroelectric energy, geothermal energy, and geothermal heat pumps work.

Key Terms

renewable energy
passive solar heating
active solar heating
biomass fuel
hydroelectric energy
geothermal energy

Figure 1 ▶ What does this plant have in common with a space station's solar panels? Both use energy from the sun.

Passive Solar Heating The cliff dwellings shown in **Figure 2** used passive solar heating, the simplest form of solar energy. **Passive solar heating** uses the sun's energy to heat something directly. In the Northern Hemisphere, south facing windows receive the most solar energy, so passive solar buildings have large windows that face south. Solar energy enters the windows and warms the house. At night, the heat is released slowly to help keep the house warm. Passive solar buildings must be well insulated with thick walls and floors in order to prevent heat loss.

Passive solar buildings are oriented according to the yearly movement of the sun. In summer, the sun's path is high in the sky and the overhang of the roof shades the building and keeps it cool. In winter, the sun's path is lower in the sky, so sunlight shines into the home and warms it. If there is reliable winter sunlight, an extremely efficient passive solar heating system can heat a house even in very cold weather without using any other source of energy. However, an average household could reduce its energy bills by using any of the passive solar features shown in **Figure 3.**

Figure 2 ▶ Seven hundred years ago, the Ancestral Puebloans, also called the Anasazi, lived in passive solar cliff dwellings in Mesa Verde, New Mexico.

CASE STUDY

A Super-Efficient Home

Imagine a home located deep in the Rocky Mountains, where winter temperatures can plunge to –40°C (–40°F). The home has no furnace, yet it manages to stay comfortably warm even in the coldest weather. This home, built by energy experts Hunter and Amory Lovins in Snowmass, Colorado, is a prime example of a new generation of super-efficient structures.

Efficiency without sacrifice was the goal in designing the Lovins's home, which also houses the Rocky Mountain Institute (RMI), an energy-research organization. The structure uses one-tenth the electricity and one-half the water of a similar-sized conventional building. The building

cost more to build than a conventional structure, but that extra cost was recovered through energy savings in only three years.

Solar energy is the most important energy source for RMI. An abundance of south-facing windows lets in plenty of sunshine. As a result, little daytime lighting is required. Artificial lighting is provided by compact fluorescent lamps that draw only 18 W but provide as much light as standard 75 W incandescent bulbs. These lamps also last 10 to 13 times longer than ordinary bulbs. Motion sensors turn the lights off when a room is empty and turn them back on when someone enters the room.

Much of the building's electricity is provided by solar cells. If the building did not have equipment such as copiers and computers, it might not require any outside electricity at all. RMI staffer Owen Bailey said, "When the copier is not running, we actually send power back to the utility company."

Solar energy, plus the heat from appliances and human bodies, meets 90 percent of the heating needs. The other 10 percent is provided by two wood-burning stoves. The walls and roof of RMI are heavily insulated, greatly reducing heat loss. Also, the walls and windows are airtight, eliminating another common source of heat loss.

Figure 3 ▶ A passive solar home is designed to reduce heating and cooling expenses.

Vent allows hot air to escape in summer.

Insulated drapes or window shades reduce nighttime heat loss in winter.

Ceilings are heavily insulated.

Summer sun

Shade trees help keep a home cool in the summer.

Winter sun

Thick walls and floors store heat in winter.

South-facing, double-paned windows let sunlight in but reduce heat loss on cold nights.

▶ **The Rocky Mountain Institute** uses the energy of the sun so efficiently that it can stay warm in the coldest Colorado winters.

During extended cloudy winter weather (with no solar heat input) the building loses only about 1°F per day. Nevertheless, the structure is well ventilated. It has specially designed air exchangers that vent stale air and warm the incoming fresh air.

The RMI structure shows that conservation does not require discomfort. The building is comfortable and spacious. As Amory Lovins said, "The main thing that the Institute demonstrates is that conservation . . . doesn't mean freezing in the dark."

EARTH SCIENCE CONNECTION

CRITICAL THINKING

1. Inferring Relationships Specially designed homes in Colorado are able to meet most of their heating needs using passive solar heating. But in parts of Canada and Alaska where winter weather can be similar to the weather in Colorado, solar-heating systems are often inadequate. Use what you know about latitude and solar radiation and write an explanation for this. **WRITING SKILLS**

2. Applying Ideas Currently, only about 1 percent of the homes built in this country have energy-efficient designs. What could be done to increase this percentage?

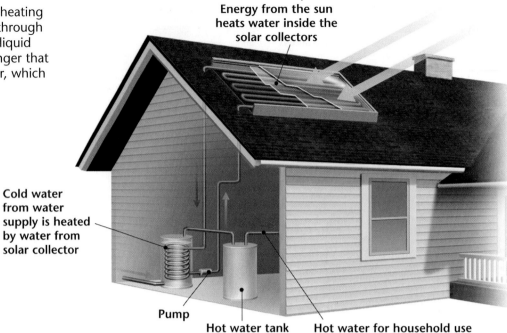

Figure 4 ▶ In a solar water heating system, a liquid is pumped through solar collectors. The heated liquid flows through a heat exchanger that transfers the energy to water, which is used in a household.

Energy from the sun heats water inside the solar collectors

Cold water from water supply is heated by water from solar collector

Pump

Hot water tank

Hot water for household use

Active Solar Heating

Active Solar Heating Energy from the sun can be gathered by collectors and used to heat water or to heat a building. This technology is known as **active solar heating.** More than 1 million homes in the United States use active solar energy to heat water. Solar collectors, usually mounted on a roof, capture the sun's energy, as shown in **Figure 4.** A liquid is heated by the sun as it flows through the solar collectors. The hot liquid is then pumped through a heat exchanger, which heats water for the building. About 8 percent of the energy used in the United States is used to heat water; therefore, active solar technology could save a lot of energy.

Photovoltaic Cells Solar cells, also called *photovoltaic* (FOHT oh vahl TAY ik) *cells,* convert the sun's energy into electricity, as shown in **Figure 5.** Solar cells have no moving parts, and they run on nonpolluting power from the sun. So why don't solar cells meet all of our energy needs? A solar cell produces a very small electrical current. So meeting the electricity needs of a small city would require covering hundreds of acres with solar panels. Solar cells also require extended periods of sunshine to produce electricity. This energy is stored in batteries, which supply electricity when the sun is not shining.

Despite these limitations, energy production from solar cells has doubled every four years since 1985. Solar cells have become increasingly efficient and less expensive. Solar cells have great potential for use in developing countries, where energy consumption is minimal and electricity distribution networks are limited. Currently, solar cells provide energy for more than 1 million households in the developing world.

✔ Reading Check How is liquid used in active solar heating? (See the Appendix for answers to Reading Checks.)

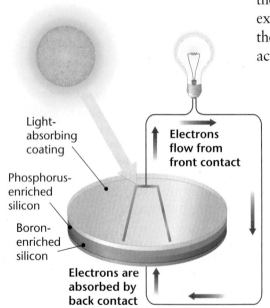

Light-absorbing coating

Phosphorus-enriched silicon

Boron-enriched silicon

Electrons flow from front contact

Electrons are absorbed by back contact

Figure 5 ▶ Sunlight falls on a semiconductor, causing it to release electrons. The electrons flow through a circuit that is completed when another semiconductor in the solar cell absorbs electrons and passes them on to the first semiconductor.

494 Chapter 18 **Renewable Energy**

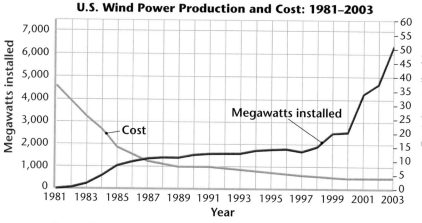

U.S. Wind Power Production and Cost: 1981–2003

Source: American Wind Energy Association.

Figure 6 ▶ The cost of wind power has been steadily falling as wind turbines have become more efficient.

Wind Power—Cheap and Abundant

Energy from the sun warms the Earth's surface unevenly, which causes air masses to flow in the atmosphere. We experience the movement of these air masses as wind. Wind power, which converts the movement of wind into electric energy, is the fastest-growing energy source in the world. New wind turbines are cost effective and can be erected in three months. As a result, the cost of wind power has declined dramatically, as shown in **Figure 6**. The world production of electricity from wind power quadrupled between 1985 and 2000.

Wind Farms Large arrays of wind turbines, like the one shown in **Figure 7**, are called *wind farms*. In California, large wind farms supply electricity to 280,000 homes. In windy rural areas, small wind farms with 20 or fewer turbines are also becoming common. Because wind turbines take up little space, some farmers can add wind turbines to their land and still use the land for other purposes. Farmers can then sell the electricity they generate to the local utility.

An Underdeveloped Resource Scientists estimate that the windiest spots on Earth could generate more than ten times the energy used worldwide. Today, all of the large energy companies are developing plans to use more wind power. Wind experts foresee a time when prospectors will travel the world looking for potential wind-farm sites, just as geologists prospect for oil reserves today. However, one of the problems of wind energy is transporting electricity from rural areas where it is generated to urban centers where it is needed. In the future, the electricity may be used on the wind farm to produce hydrogen from water. The hydrogen could then be trucked or piped to cities for use as a fuel.

Figure 7 ▶ California wind farms, such as this one in Altamont Pass, generate more than enough electricity to light a city the size of San Francisco.

495

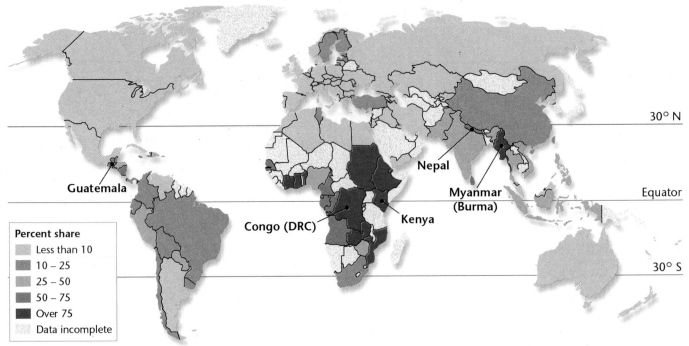

Share of Woodfuels in Energy Consumption

Guatemala

Nepal

Myanmar
(Burma)

Kenya

Congo (DRC)

30° N

Equator

30° S

Percent share
- Less than 10
- 10 – 25
- 25 – 50
- 50 – 75
- Over 75
- Data incomplete

Figure 8 ▶ The consumption of wood as an energy source has increased by nearly 80 percent since 1960. In developing countries such as Nepal, Burma, Guatemala, Congo (DRC), and Kenya, the use of fuelwood places an enormous burden on local environments.

FIELD ACTIVITY

Biomass Survey Walk around your neighborhood, and list as many sources of biomass fuel as you can find. Are any of these (such as a pile of firewood) large enough to be used as fuel sources? What do you think the advantages and disadvantages of using biomass as a fuel in your area would be? Record your observations in your *EcoLog*.

Biomass—Power from Living Things

Plant material, manure, and any other organic matter that is used as an energy source is called a **biomass fuel.** While fossil fuels are organic and can be thought of as biomass energy sources, fossil fuels are nonrenewable. Renewable biomass fuels, such as wood and dung, are major sources of energy in developing countries, as shown in **Figure 8.** More than half of all wood cut in the world is used as fuel for heating and cooking. Although wood is a renewable resource, if trees are cut down faster than they grow, the resulting habitat loss, deforestation, and soil erosion can be severe. In addition, harmful air pollution may result from burning wood and dung.

Methane When bacteria decompose organic wastes, one by-product is methane gas. Methane can be burned to generate heat or electricity. In China, more than 6 million households use bio-gas digesters to ferment manure and produce gas used for heating and cooking. In the developed world, biomass that was once thought of as waste is being used for energy. In 2002, Britain's first dung-fired power station started to produce electricity. This power station uses the methane given off by cow manure as fuel. Similarly, some landfills in the United States generate electricity by using the methane from the decomposition of trash.

Alcohol Liquid fuels can also be derived from biomass. For example, ethanol, an alcohol, can be made by fermenting fruit or agricultural waste. In the United States, corn is a major source of ethanol. Cars and trucks can run on ethanol or *gasohol,* a blend of gasoline and ethanol. Gasohol produces less air pollution than fossil fuels do. For this reason, some U.S. states require the use of gasohol in vehicles as a way to reduce air pollution.

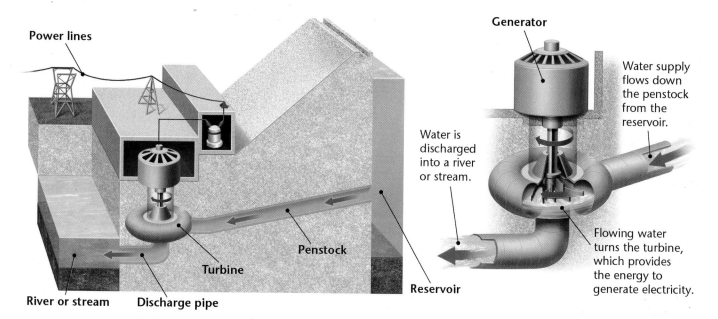

Power lines

Generator

Water supply flows down the penstock from the reservoir.

Water is discharged into a river or stream.

Penstock

Turbine

River or stream   Discharge pipe

Reservoir

Flowing water turns the turbine, which provides the energy to generate electricity.

Hydroelectricity—Power from Moving Water

Energy from the sun causes water to evaporate, condense in the atmosphere, and fall back to the Earth's surface as rain. As water flows across the land, the energy in its movement can be used to generate electricity. **Hydroelectric energy,** which is energy produced from moving water, is a renewable resource that accounts for about 20 percent of the world's electricity. The countries that lead the world in hydroelectric energy are, in decreasing order, Canada, the United States, Brazil, China, Russia, and Norway.

Figure 9 shows how a hydroelectric power plant works. Large hydroelectric power plants have a dam that is built across a river to hold back a reservoir of water. The water in the reservoir is released to turn a turbine, which generates electricity. The energy of this water is evident in **Figure 10,** which shows the spillway of the world's largest hydroelectric dam.

The Benefits of Hydroelectric Energy Although hydroelectric dams are expensive to build, they are relatively inexpensive to operate. Unlike fossil fuel plants, hydroelectric dams do not release air pollutants that cause acid precipitation. In addition, hydroelectric dams tend to last much longer than fossil fuel-powered plants. Dams also provide other benefits such as flood control and water for drinking, agriculture, industry, and recreation.

✔ **Reading Check** Explain how hydroelectric energy begins with the sun.

Figure 9 ▶ Hydroelectric dams convert the *potential energy,* or stored energy, of a reservoir into the *kinetic energy,* or moving energy, of a spinning turbine. The movement of the turbine is then used to generate electricity.

Figure 10 ▶ The Itaipu Dam in Paraguay supplies about 75 percent of the electricity used by Paraguay and 25 percent of the electricity used by Brazil.

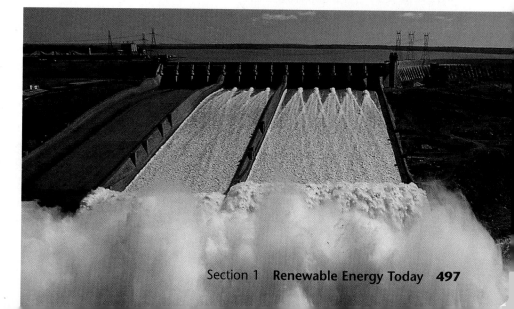

Disadvantages of Hydroelectric Energy A dam changes a river's flow, which can have far-reaching consequences. A reservoir floods large areas of habitat above the dam. The water flow below the dam is reduced, which disrupts ecosystems downstream. For example, many of the salmon fisheries of the northwestern United States have been destroyed by dams that prevent the salmon from swimming upriver to spawn. When the land behind a dam is flooded, people are often displaced. An estimated 50 million people around the world have been displaced by dam projects. Dam failure can be another problem—if a dam bursts, people living in areas below the dam can be killed.

Dams can also affect the land below them. As a river slows down, the river deposits some of the sediment it carries. This fertile sediment builds up behind a dam instead of enriching the land farther down the river. As a result, farmland below a dam can become less productive. Recent research has also shown that the decay of plant matter trapped in reservoirs can release large amounts of greenhouse gases—sometimes more than a fossil fuel-powered plant.

Modern Trends In the United States, the era of large dam construction is probably over. But in developing countries, such as Brazil, India, and China, the construction of large dams continues. A modern trend is *micro-hydropower*, which is electricity produced in a small stream without having to build a big dam. The turbine may even float in the water, not blocking the river at all. Micro-hydropower is much cheaper than large hydroelectric dam projects, and it permits energy to be generated from small streams in remote areas.

Geothermal Energy—Power from the Earth

In some areas, deposits of water in the Earth's crust are heated by energy within the Earth. Such places are sources of **geothermal energy**—the energy from heat in the Earth's crust. As **Figure 11** shows, this heat can be used to generate electricity. Geothermal power plants pump heated water or steam from rock formations and use the water or steam to power a turbine that generates electricity. Usually the water is returned to the Earth's crust where it can be heated and used again.

The United States is the world's largest producer of geothermal energy. The world's largest geothermal power plant is The Geysers, in California, which produces electricity for about

Figure 11 ▶ Geothermal power plants generate electricity using the following steps: ❶ steam rises through a well; ❷ steam drives turbines, which generate electricity; ❸ leftover liquid water is pumped back into the hot rock.

Heated water

Hot rock

The ground is warmer than the air in winter.

Heat is transferred from the ground to warm the house.

The ground is cooler than the air in summer.

Heat is transferred from the house to the ground to cool the house.

Figure 12 ▶ In the winter (left), the ground is warmer than the air is. A fluid is circulated underground to warm a house. In the summer (right), the ground is cooler than the air is, and the fluid is used to cool a house.

1.7 million households. Other countries that produce geothermal energy include the Philippines, Iceland, Japan, Mexico, Italy, and New Zealand. Although geothermal energy is considered a renewable resource, the water in geothermal formations must be managed carefully so that it is not depleted.

Geothermal Heat Pumps: Energy for Homes More than 600,000 homes in the United States are heated and cooled using geothermal heat pumps such as the one shown in **Figure 12.** Because the temperature of the ground is nearly constant year-round, a *geothermal heat pump* uses stable underground temperatures to warm and cool homes. A heat pump is simply a loop of piping that circulates a fluid underground. In warm summer months, the ground is cooler than the air, and the fluid is used to cool a home. In the winter, the ground is warmer than the air, and the fluid is used to warm the home.

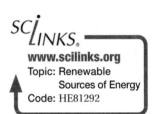

SECTION 1 Review

1. **List** six forms of renewable energy, and compare the advantages and disadvantages of each.

2. **Describe** the differences between passive solar heating, active solar heating, and photovoltaic energy.

3. **Describe** how hydroelectric energy, geothermal energy, and geothermal heat pumps work.

4. **Explain** whether all renewable energy sources have their origin in energy from the sun.

CRITICAL THINKING

5. **Making Decisions** Which renewable energy source would be best suited to your region? Write a paragraph that explains your reasoning. **WRITING SKILLS**

6. **Identifying Trends** Identify a modern trend in hydroelectric power and in wind energy.

7. **Analyzing Relationships** Write an explanation of the differences in biomass fuel use between developed and developing countries. **WRITING SKILLS**

Alternative Energy and Conservation

SCSh.2.b; SCSh.3.c; SCSh.3.e; SCSh.4.a;
SCSh.4.b; SCSh.4.c; SCSh.6.a; SCSh.9.c;
SCSh.9.d

EARTH SCIENCE   CONNECTION

Objectives

▶ Describe three alternative energy technologies.

▶ Identify two ways that hydrogen could be used as a fuel source in the future.

▶ Explain the difference between energy efficiency and energy conservation.

▶ Describe two forms of energy-efficient transportation.

▶ Identify three ways that you can conserve energy in your daily life.

Key Terms

alternative energy
ocean thermal energy
  conversion (OTEC)
fuel cell
energy efficiency
energy conservation

To achieve a future where energy use is sustainable, we must make the most of the energy sources we already have and develop new sources of energy. **Alternative energy** describes energy sources that are still in development. Some renewable energy sources that we use now, such as geothermal power, were once considered alternative energy. For an alternative energy source to become a viable option for the future, the source must be proven to be cost effective. Also, the environmental effects of using the energy source must be acceptable. Government investment is often the only way to research some of these future energy possibilities.

Tidal Power

Tides are the movement of water in the oceans and seas caused by gravitational attraction between the sun, Earth, and moon. The tides, which happen twice each day, are marked by the rising and falling of the sea level. The energy of the tides was used nearly a thousand years ago to power mills in France and Britain. Today, tidal power is used to generate electricity in countries such as France, Russia, and Canada.

As **Figure 13** shows, a tidal power plant works much like a hydroelectric dam. As the tide rises, water flows behind a dam; when the sea level falls, the water is trapped behind the dam. When the water in the reservoir is released, it turns a turbine that generates electricity. Although tidal energy is renewable and non-polluting, it will not become a major energy source in the future. The cost of building and maintaining a tidal power plant is high, and there are few locations that are suitable.

Figure 13 ▶ As the tide rises, water enters a bay behind a dam. The gate then closes at high tide. At low tide, the gate opens and the water in the bay rushes through, spinning a turbine that generates electricity.

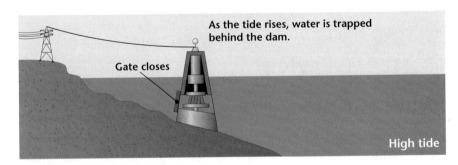

As the tide rises, water is trapped behind the dam.

Gate closes

High tide

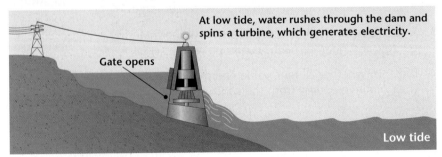

At low tide, water rushes through the dam and spins a turbine, which generates electricity.

Gate opens

Low tide

Ocean Thermal Energy Conversion

In the tropics, the temperature difference between the surface of the ocean, which is warmed by solar energy, and deep ocean waters can be as much as 24°C (43°F). An experimental power station off the shores of Hawaii uses this temperature difference to generate electricity. This technology, which is shown in **Figure 14,** is called **ocean thermal energy conversion (OTEC).** In this system, warm surface water is used to boil sea water. This is possible because water boils at low temperatures when it is at low pressure in a vacuum chamber. The boiling water turns into steam, which spins a turbine. The turbine runs an electric generator. Cold water from the deep ocean cools the steam, turning the steam into water that can be used again.

Japan has also experimented with OTEC power, but so far, no project has been able to generate electricity cost-effectively. One problem with OTEC is that the power needed to pump cold water up from the deep ocean uses about one-third of the electricity the plant produces. The environmental effects of pumping large amounts of cold water to the surface are also unknown.

Hydrogen—A Future Fuel Source?

Hydrogen, the most abundant element in the universe, can be burned as a fuel. Hydrogen is found in every molecule of living things, and it is found in water. Hydrogen does not release pollutants associated with burning fossil fuels and biomass. When hydrogen is burned, it combines with oxygen to produce water vapor, a harmless byproduct. Hydrogen gas (H_2) can be produced by using electricity to split molecules of water (H_2O). In the future, we may also be able to grow plants to produce hydrogen cost-effectively, as shown in **Figure 15.**

✓ Reading Check What are two advantages of using hydrogen as a fuel source?

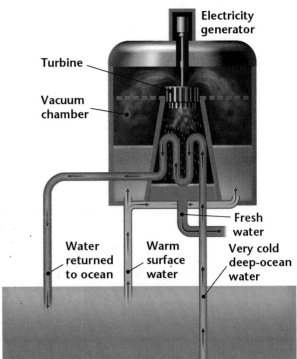

Figure 14 ▶ In an open cycle OTEC plant, warm surface water is brought to boil in a vacuum chamber. The boiling water produces steam to drive a turbine that generates electricity. Cold deep-ocean water is pumped in to condense the steam. Fresh water is a byproduct of this type of OTEC plant.

SCLINKS.
www.scilinks.org
Topic: Fuel Cells
Code: HE80625

Figure 15 ▶ Hydrogen fuel can be made from any material that contains a lot of hydrogen, including the experimental plot of switchgrass shown here.

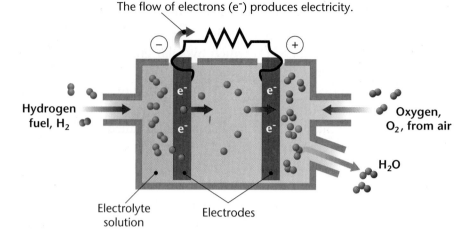

The flow of electrons (e^-) produces electricity.

Hydrogen fuel, H_2

Oxygen, O_2, from air

H_2O

Electrolyte solution

Electrodes

Figure 16 ▶ This diagram shows how a fuel cell produces electrical energy.

QuickLAB

Hydrolysis

Procedure

1. Coat a **9 V cell** with **petroleum jelly.** Be careful not to get any on the terminals.

2. Mix **1 Tbsp** of **salt** in a **600 mL beaker** of **water.**

3. Fill **two test tubes** with the saltwater solution, and invert them in the beaker, making sure to cover the ends of the test tubes. No air should be trapped in the test tubes.

4. Place the 9 V cell upright in the beaker. Position a battery terminal under the open mouth of each test tube. You will observe hydrogen gas collecting in the test tube located over the negative terminal and oxygen gas collecting over the positive terminal.

Analysis

1. Did you collect the same volume of hydrogen as oxygen? Explain why or why not.

The Challenge of Hydrogen Fuel Why is hydrogen the fuel of the future and not of today? There are two main problems. First, the current methods that are used to produce hydrogen are not very efficient. They require a lot of energy, are expensive, and cause pollution. In the future, this problem may be solved by producing hydrogen from water using solar power. Second, a lot of hydrogen is needed to produce the same amount of energy as a tank of gasoline. Therefore, the hydrogen must be compressed to fit into a vehicle. Tanks that hold hydrogen safely at high pressure are still being developed.

Fuel Cells Fuel cells, like the one in **Figure 16,** may be the engines of the future. Like a battery, a **fuel cell** produces electricity chemically, by combining hydrogen fuel with oxygen from the air. When hydrogen and oxygen are combined, electrical energy is produced and water is the only byproduct. Fuel cells can be fueled by anything that contains plenty of hydrogen, including natural gas, alcohol, or even gasoline. The space shuttles have used fuel cells for years. In the change from cars powered by internal combustion engines to those powered by fuel cells, vehicles may get hydrogen from gasoline so that they can be refueled at existing gas stations.

Energy Efficiency

Energy efficiency is the percentage of energy put into a system that does useful work. Energy efficiency can be determined using this simple equation: energy efficiency (in %) = useful energy out/energy in × 100. Thus, the efficiency of a light bulb is the proportion of electrical energy that reaches the bulb and is converted into light energy rather than into heat. The relationship between the transfer of energy to the work done and the heat transferred is known as the *first law of thermodynamics.* This law explains that the energy going in must equal the energy coming out of a system. Therefore any heat transfer reduces the energy available for work, thus affecting efficiency. This relationship holds true for biological systems as well as physical systems. Most of our devices are fairly inefficient. More than 40 percent of all commercial energy used in the United States is wasted. Most of it is lost from inefficient fuel-wasting vehicles, furnaces, and appliances and from leaky, poorly insulated buildings. We could save enormous amounts of energy by using fuel cells instead of internal combustion engines in cars, and by changing from incandescent to fluorescent light bulbs, as shown in **Table 1.** However, many increases in efficiency involve sacrifices or investments in new technology.

Efficient Transportation   Nothing would increase the energy efficiency of American life more than developing efficient engines to power vehicles and increasing the use of public transportation systems. The internal combustion engines that power most vehicles use fuel inefficiently and produce air pollution. The design of these engines has hardly changed since 1900, but they may change radically in the next 50 years. However, in the United States, gasoline prices have been so low that there has been little demand for fuel-efficient vehicles, which are more common in other countries.

Hybrid Cars   Hybrid cars, such as the one shown in **Figure 17,** are examples of energy-efficient vehicles. Hybrid cars use a small, efficient gasoline engine most of the time, but they also use an electric motor when extra power is needed. Hybrid cars feature other efficient technologies. They convert some of the energy of braking into electricity and they store this energy in the battery. To save fuel, hybrid cars sometimes shut off the gasoline engine, such as when the car is idling. Hybrid cars are also designed to be aerodynamic, and they are made of lightweight materials so they need less energy to accelerate. Hybrid cars cost less to refuel than conventional vehicles, and they produce less harmful emissions. These benefits are leading auto makers to design many hybrid car models, including hybrid trucks and SUVs.

✔ **Reading Check**   Identify three ways that hybrid cars are energy efficient.

Table 1 ▼

Energy Efficiency of Common Conversion Devices	
Device	**Efficiency**
Incandescent light bulb	5%
Fluorescent light bulb	22%
Internal combustion engine (gasoline)	10%–15%
Human body	20%–25%
Steam turbine	45%
Fuel cell	60%

www.scilinks.org
Topic: Mass Transit
Code: HE80919
Topic: Energy
      Conservation
Code: HE80510

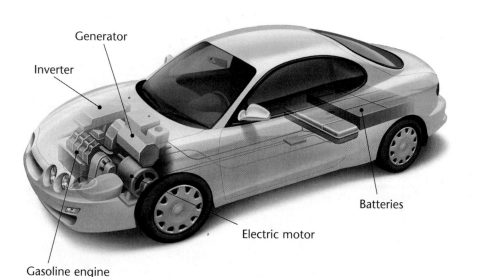

Generator

Inverter

Gasoline engine

Electric motor

Batteries

Figure 17 ▶ A hybrid car has a gasoline engine and an electric motor.

MATHPRACTICE

Energy Efficiency In the
United States, each person
uses an average of 459 gallons
of gasoline per year. In Germany,
each person uses an average of 140
gallons a year. Auto manufacturers
estimate that vehicles would use 2
percent less gasoline if everyone
kept their tires inflated to the correct
pressure. How much gasoline would
a person in the United States save
and a person in Germany save each
year if their tires were kept inflated
to the correct pressure?

Cogeneration

One way to use fuel more efficiently is *cogeneration*, the production of two useful forms of energy from the same fuel source. For
example, the waste heat from an industrial furnace can power a
steam turbine that produces electricity. The industry may use the
electricity or sell it to a utility company. Small cogeneration systems have been used for years to supply heat and electricity to multiple buildings at specific sites. Small units suitable for single
buildings are now available in the United States.

Energy Conservation

Energy conservation means saving energy. It can occur in many
ways, including using energy-efficient devices and wasting less
energy. The people in **Figure 18** are conserving energy by bicy-
cling instead of driving. Between 1975 and 1985, conservation
made more energy available in the United States than all alternative energy sources combined did.

Cities and Towns Saving Energy The town of Osage, Iowa, numbers 3,600 people. You might not think that a town this small
could make much of a difference in energy conservation. Yet the
town adopted an energy conservation plan that saves more than
$1 million each year. The residents plugged the leaks around win-
dows and doors where much of the heat escapes from a house. In
addition, they replaced inefficient furnaces and insulated their hot
water heaters. Businesses in Osage also found ways to conserve
energy. In addition to saving energy, the town has greatly improved
its economy through energy conservation. Businesses have relocated to the area in order to take advantage of low energy costs.
Unemployment rates have also declined. This small town in Iowa is
just one example of the dramatic benefits of energy conservation.

Conservation Around the Home The average household in the
United States spends more than $1,500 on energy bills each year.
Unfortunately, much of that energy is wasted. Most of the energy
lost from homes is lost through poorly insulated windows, doors,

Figure 18 ▶ In Copenhagen,
Denmark, companies provide free
bicycles in exchange for publicity.
Anyone wishing to use a bike is free
to borrow one after paying a refund-
able deposit. The program helps cut
down on pollution and auto traffic.

walls, and the roof. So a good way to increase energy efficiency is to add to the insulation of a home. Replacing old windows with new high efficiency windows can reduce your energy bill by 15 percent. Two of the best places to look for ways to conserve energy are doors and windows. Much of the energy lost from a house escapes as hot air in winter or cold air in summer passes through gaps around doors and windows. Hold a ribbon up to the edges of doors and windows. If it flutters, you've found a leak. Sealing these leaks with caulk or weather stripping will help conserve energy. There are dozens of other ways to reduce energy use around the home. Some of these are shown in **Figure 19**.

Conservation in Daily Life There are many simple lifestyle changes that can help save energy. First, remember that using less of any resource usually translates into saving energy. For example, washing your clothes in cold water uses only 25 percent of the energy needed to wash your clothes in warm water. **Table 2** lists a few ways that you can conserve energy every day. Can you think of other ways?

Table 2 ▼

Energy Conservation Tips
• Walk or ride a bicycle for short trips.
• Carpool or use public transportation whenever possible.
• Drive a fuel-efficient automobile.
• Choose ENERGY STAR® products.
• Recycle and choose recycled products whenever possible.
• Set computers to "sleep" mode when they are not in use.

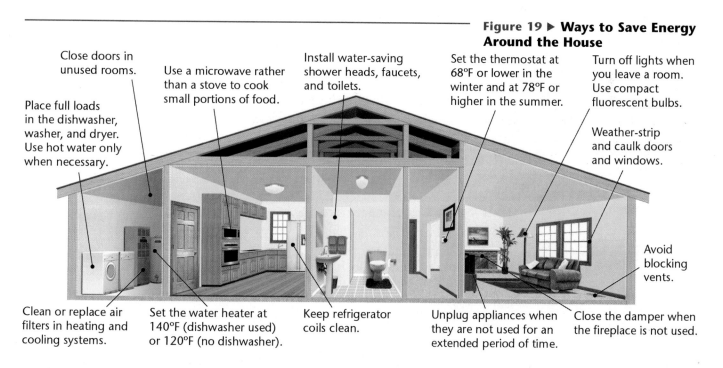

Figure 19 ▶ Ways to Save Energy Around the House

Close doors in unused rooms.

Use a microwave rather than a stove to cook small portions of food.

Install water-saving shower heads, faucets, and toilets.

Set the thermostat at 68°F or lower in the winter and at 78°F or higher in the summer.

Turn off lights when you leave a room. Use compact fluorescent bulbs.

Place full loads in the dishwasher, washer, and dryer. Use hot water only when necessary.

Weather-strip and caulk doors and windows.

Avoid blocking vents.

Clean or replace air filters in heating and cooling systems.

Set the water heater at 140°F (dishwasher used) or 120°F (no dishwasher).

Keep refrigerator coils clean.

Unplug appliances when they are not used for an extended period of time.

Close the damper when the fireplace is not used.

SECTION 2 Review

1. **Describe** three alternative energy technologies, and identify two ways that hydrogen could be used as a fuel source in the future.

2. **List** as many ways as you can for individuals and communities to conserve energy.

3. **Describe** the difference between energy conservation and energy efficiency.

CRITICAL THINKING

4. **Making Inferences** What factors influence a person's choice to conserve energy?

5. **Making Comparisons** Read the description of hydrogen fuel cells and explain why hydrolysis (splitting water molecules with electricity to produce hydrogen and oxygen) is the opposite of the reaction that occurs in a hydrogen fuel cell. **READING SKILLS**

1 Renewable Energy Today

Key Terms

renewable energy, 491

passive solar heating, 492

active solar heating, 494

biomass fuel, 496

hydroelectric energy, 497

geothermal energy, 498

Main Ideas

▶ Renewable energy is energy from sources that are constantly being formed.

▶ Solar energy can be used to heat a house directly or to heat another material, such as water, which can then be used to heat a house. Solar cells can also be used to generate electricity.

▶ Wind power is the fastest growing source of energy in the world.

▶ Many people in developing countries get most of their energy from biomass such as fuelwood. Biomass is increasingly used in developed countries to generate electricity.

▶ Hydroelectric energy is electricity generated by the energy of moving water.

▶ Geothermal energy, the heat within the Earth, can be used to generate electricity.

2 Alternative Energy and Conservation

Key Terms

alternative energy, 500

ocean thermal energy conversion (OTEC), 501

fuel cell, 502

energy efficiency, 502

energy conservation, 504

Main Ideas

▶ Alternative energy sources are energy sources that are still in development.

▶ Ocean thermal energy conversion (OTEC) uses the temperature difference between layers of ocean water to generate electricity.

▶ Hydrogen may be one of the fuels of the future. It can be made from any organic material and produces only water as a waste product when burned.

▶ Hydrogen fuel cells may be the engines of the future. Many experiments with them are now underway.

▶ Energy efficiency is the percentage of energy put into a system that does useful work. Energy conservation means saving energy.

Using Key Terms

Use the correct key term to complete each of the following sentences.

1. Much of the energy needs of the developing world are met by _____, such as fuel-wood.

2. A _____ converts the potential energy of a reservoir into the kinetic energy of a spinning turbine.

3. Turning off the lights when you leave a room is an example of _____.

Use each of the following terms in a separate sentence.

4. *renewable energy*

5. *geothermal energy*

6. *alternative energy*

7. *energy conservation*

✔ **STUDY TIP**

Get Some Exercise Ride a bike, go for a walk, or play Frisbee or basketball. Try to get at least a half hour of exercise before you begin studying. Then when you study you will be more relaxed and you will be able to focus on the subject you want to learn. As you study, take a moment to notice if the exercise helped. Scientists have proven that regular physical exercise helps fight memory loss.

Understanding Key Ideas

8. Which of the following forms of renewable energy uses the sun's energy most directly?
   a. biomass fuel
   b. passive solar heating
   c. geothermal energy
   d. a hydrogen fuel cell

9. Which of the following energy sources is useful in most parts of the world?
   a. tidal power
   b. OTEC
   c. geothermal energy
   d. active solar energy

10. A house that uses passive solar heating in the Northern Hemisphere will
    a. be built of a material such as concrete or adobe that stores heat well.
    b. have little insulation.
    c. have large north-facing windows.
    d. have an overhang to shade the house from direct winter sun.

11. A passive solar house in the Southern Hemisphere will face
    a. north.
    b. south.
    c. east.
    d. west.

12. Photovoltaic cells convert the sun's energy into
    a. heat.
    b. fuel.
    c. electricity.
    d. light.

13. In a developing country, you are most likely to find biomass used
    a. to generate electricity.
    b. for manufacturing.
    c. for heating and cooking.
    d. as a source of hydropower.

14. Which of the following is *not* true of fuel cells?
    a. They produce electricity.
    b. They will work with many different fuels.
    c. They are more energy efficient than most engines used today.
    d. They cannot be fueled by hydrogen.

15. Which renewable energy source is the fastest growing energy source in the world?
    a. oil
    b. wind
    c. biomass
    d. photovoltaic cells

16. Which statement describes why geothermal heat pumps work?
    a. They are located in areas with abundant geothermal energy.
    b. The ground is warmer than the air in summer and colder than the air in winter.
    c. The ground is colder than the air in summer and warmer than the air in winter.
    d. They run on hydrogen fuel cells.

Short Answer

17. Rivers are recharged by the water cycle, so what is the original source of hydroelectric energy?

18. Salt water corrodes metals rapidly. What effect is this likely to have on the cost of electricity produced from tidal power?

19. Why is it likely that hydroelectric energy will be generated increasingly by micro-hydropower plants rather than by large hydroelectric dams?

Interpreting Graphics

Use the information in the figure below to answer questions 20–22.

20. Describe the path of the water in the loop during winter. Where is the water warmed? Where is the water cooled?

21. Describe the path of the water in the loop during summer. Where is the water warmed? Where is the water cooled?

22. What is the difference in the temperature between the house, the closed loop, and the air in the summer? What is the temperature difference in the winter?

Concept Mapping

23. Use the following terms to create a concept map: *sun, hydroelectric energy, solar energy, passive solar heating, active solar heating, water cycle, biomass fuel, wind energy, photovoltaic cell,* and *electric current.*

Critical Thinking

24. **Making Comparisons** Read the description of energy efficiency and energy conservation in this chapter. How are the two concepts related? Give several examples. **READING SKILLS**

25. **Analyzing Ideas** Does the energy used by fuel cells come from the sun? Explain your answer.

26. **Analyzing Ideas** Explain whether you think the most important advances of the 21st century will be new sources of energy or more efficient use of sources that already exist.

27. **Drawing Inferences** Don Huberts of Shell Hydrogen said, "The Stone Age didn't end because the world ran out of stones." He was talking about the future of fossil fuels. Write a short essay that explains what he meant. **WRITING SKILLS**

Cross-Disciplinary Connection

28. **Geography** Create a world map that shows at least 10 renewable energy or alternative energy projects currently in operation. Annotate your map with details and photographs of each project.

Portfolio Project

29. **Energy Timeline** The first energy source used by human societies was human muscle. It was used to build houses, make clothing, and shape tools that could be used to dig up plants and kill animals for food. What was the next source of energy? Make a timeline of the energy sources that humans began to use at various times in history. Add interesting facts and images that relate to each energy source on your timeline. Continue your timeline into the future. What energy sources do you think we will use in the future?

MATH SKILLS

The pie graph below shows electric generating capacity from renewable sources in the United States in 1998. Use the data to answer questions 30–31.

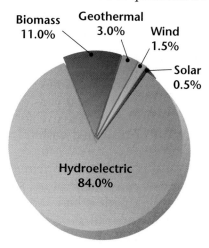

Biomass 11.0%
Geothermal 3.0%
Wind 1.5%
Solar 0.5%
Hydroelectric 84.0%

30. **Making Calculations** How much generating capacity came from biomass, geothermal, wind, and solar combined?

31. **Making Calculations** In 1998, the United States had a total of 94,822 MW of electric generating capacity from renewable energy. How much of that capacity came from biomass? How much came from wind power?

WRITING SKILLS

32. **Communicating Main Ideas** Explain why scientists are working to reduce the use of the two main sources of energy people use today—fossil fuels and biomass.

33. **Writing Persuasively** Write a guide that encourages people to conserve energy and offers practical tips to show them how.

READING SKILLS

Read the passage below, and then answer the questions that follow.

Aluminum is refined from the ore *bauxite,* which is deposited in a thin layer at the Earth's surface. Worldwide, bauxite strip mines cover more of the Earth's surface than any other type of metal ore mine. Aluminum production uses so much electrical energy that the metal has been referred to as "congealed electricity." Producing six aluminum cans takes the energy equivalent of 1 L of gasoline. For this reason, aluminum smelters are located close to cheap and reliable energy sources, such as hydroelectric dams in the Pacific Northwest, Quebec, and the Amazon. When the environmental effects of producing new aluminum are considered, the importance of recycling becomes clear. Recycling one aluminum can saves enough energy to run a television set for 4 hours! Currently, the United States obtains about 20 percent of its aluminum from recycling.

1. Why is aluminum referred to as "congealed electricity"?
   a. Smelting aluminum requires a different form of electrical energy.
   b. Aluminum has an electric charge.
   c. Like electrical energy, aluminum can also be recycled.
   d. So much electrical energy is required to produce aluminum that it is almost as if aluminum were solidified electricity.

2. Which of the following statements describes the author's main point?
   a. Hydroelectricity is a cheap, reliable source of energy.
   b. Recycling aluminum can make a significant contribution to energy conservation.
   c. Aluminum is available in many places, so there is no need to conserve it.
   d. The environmental effects of hydroelectric dams are not related to the consumption of aluminum.

Understanding Concepts

Directions (1–4): For *each* question, write on a separate sheet of paper the letter of the correct answer.

1 What is the ultimate source of all renewable energy?
  A. the biosphere
  B. the moon
  C. the ocean
  D. the sun

2 Which of the following is a renewable energy source?
  F. coal mine
  G. gas pipeline
  H. power plant
  I. wind farm

3 What is the most important factor in the development and implementation of alternative energy sources?
  A. The most important factor is the abundance of the source.
  B. The most important factor is its cost effectiveness.
  C. The most important factor is whether government approval can be obtained.
  D. The most important factor is if the source can gain social acceptance.

4 Why is hydrogen called the fuel of the future?
  F. It is very inexpensive to produce.
  G. It requires very little energy to produce.
  H. It is the most abundant element in the universe.
  I. It contains carbon which disperses in the atmosphere when burned.

Directions (5–6): For *each* question, write a short response.

5 Energy efficiency is the percentage of energy put into a system that does useful work. Why is energy efficiency always less than 100%?

6 Estimate the potential of wind power as an energy source.

Reading Skills

Directions (7–8): Read the passage below. Then answer the questions.

Ancient cliff dwellings contain elements of the simplest form of solar energy called passive solar heating. Passive solar heating uses the sun's energy to heat something directly. In the Northern Hemisphere, windows facing south receive the most solar energy, so passive solar buildings have large windows that face south. Solar energy enters the windows and warms the house. At night, the heat is released slowly to keep the house warm. Passive solar buildings must be insulated with thick walls and floors.

Passive solar buildings are oriented according to the yearly movement of the sun. In summer, the sun's path is high in the sky and the overhang of the roof shades the building and keeps it cool. If there is reliable winter light, an extremely efficient passive solar heating system can heat a house in very cold weather without using any other source of energy.

7 In the Northern Hemisphere, in what direction should the largest windows face in order for the house to be as cool as possible?
  A. north
  B. south
  C. east
  D. west

8 Why do passive solar houses require thick walls and insulation to be efficient at heating the house in winter?

Directions (9): Read the passage below. Then answer the question.

Energy conservation means saving energy. It can occur in many ways, including using energy-efficient devices and wasting less energy. Between 1975 and 1985, conservation made more energy available in the United States than all alternative energy sources combined did.

9 Describe two ways that a family could reduce the amount of energy wasted in their home by increasing energy efficiency.

Interpreting Graphics

Directions (10–12): For *each* question below, record the correct answer on a separate sheet of paper.

The map below shows hydroelectric power generation in the United States. Use this map to answer questions 10 and 11.

Hydroelectric Power

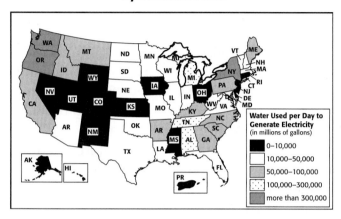

10 What can be inferred about the use of hydroelectric power in the United States?
  F. There are more dams in Oregon than in Kansas.
  G. There is more hydroelectric power used in New Mexico than in Alabama.
  H. The upper Midwest uses more water for hydroelectric power than New England.
  I. The biggest users of water for hydroelectricity are located along the Mississippi River.

11 How many states use 10,000 million gallons of water or less per day?
  A. 5   **C.** 15
  B. 10   **D.** 20

Use the diagram below to answer question 12.

The flow of electrons (e-) produces electricity.

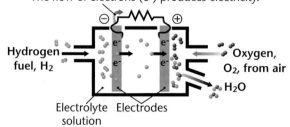

12 What type of electrical generation is depicted in the diagram?
  F. fuel cell
  G. geothermal plant
  H. ocean thermal energy
  I. tidal plant

Test *TIP*

Carefully read the instructions, the question, and the answer options before choosing an answer.

Objectives

▶ **USING SCIENTIFIC METHODS** **Prepare** a detailed sketch of your solution to the design problem.

▶ **Design and build** a functional windmill that lifts a specific weight as quickly as possible.

Materials

blow-dryer, 1,500 W
dowel or smooth rod
foam board
glue, white
paper clips, large (30)
paper cup, small (1)
spools of thread, empty (2)
string, 50 cm

optional materials for windmill blades: foam board, paper plates, paper cups, or any other lightweight materials

Blowing in the Wind

M E M O

To: Division of Research and Developers

Quixote Alternative Energy Systems is accepting design proposals to develop a windmill that can be used to lift window washers to the tops of buildings. As part of the design engineering team, your division has been asked to develop a working model of such a windmill. Your task is to design and build a prototype of a windmill that can capture energy from a 1,500 W blow-dryer. Your model must lift 30 large paper clips a vertical distance of 50 cm (approximately 2 ft) as quickly as possible.

Procedure

1. Build the base for your windmill (shown below). Begin by attaching the two spools to the foam board using the glue. Make sure the spools are parallel before you glue them.

2. Pass a dowel or a smooth rod through the center of the spools. The dowel should rotate freely. Attach one end of the string securely to the dowel between the two spools.

3. Poke a hole through the middle of the foam board to allow the string to pass through.

4. Attach the cup to the end of the string. You will use the cup to lift the paper clips.

5. Place your windmill base between two lab tables or in any other area that will allow the string to hang freely.

▶ **Windmill Base** Your windmill base should allow the dowel to spin as freely as possible. The pinwheel shown at the end of the dowel is a suggested design for your windmill blades.

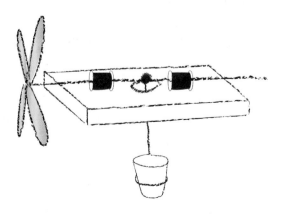

6. Prepare a sketch of your prototype windmill blades based on the objectives for this lab. Include a list of the materials that you will use and safety precautions (if necessary).

7. Have your teacher approve your design before you begin construction.

8. Construct a working prototype of your windmill blades. Test your model several times to collect data on the speed at which it lifts the paper clips. Record your data for each trial.

9. Vary the type of material used for construction of your windmill blades. Test the various blades to determine whether they improve the original plan.

10. Vary the number and size of the blades on your windmill. Test each design to determine whether the change improves the original plan.

Analysis

1. **Summarize Results** Create a data table that lists the speed for each lift for several trials. Include an average speed.

2. **Graphing Data** Prepare a bar graph that shows your results for each blade design.

Conclusions

3. **Evaluating Methods** After you observe all of the designs, decide which ones you think best solve the problem and explain why.

4. **Evaluating Models** Which change improved your windmill the most—varying the materials for the blades, varying the number of blades, or varying the size of the blades? Would you change your design further? If so, how?

Extension

1. **Research** Windmills have been used for more than 2,000 years. Research the three basic types of vertical-axis machines and the applications in which they are used. Prepare a report of your findings.

2. **Making Models** Adapt your design to make a water wheel. You'll find that water wheels can pull much more weight than a windmill can. Find designs on the Internet for micro-hydropower water wheels such as the Pelton wheel, and use the designs as inspiration for your models. You can even design your own dam and reservoir.

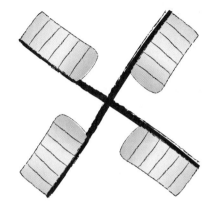

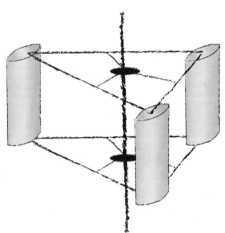

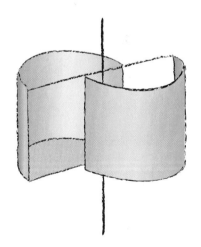

▶ **Sample Windmill Blade Designs**

MAPS in action

WIND POWER IN THE UNITED STATES

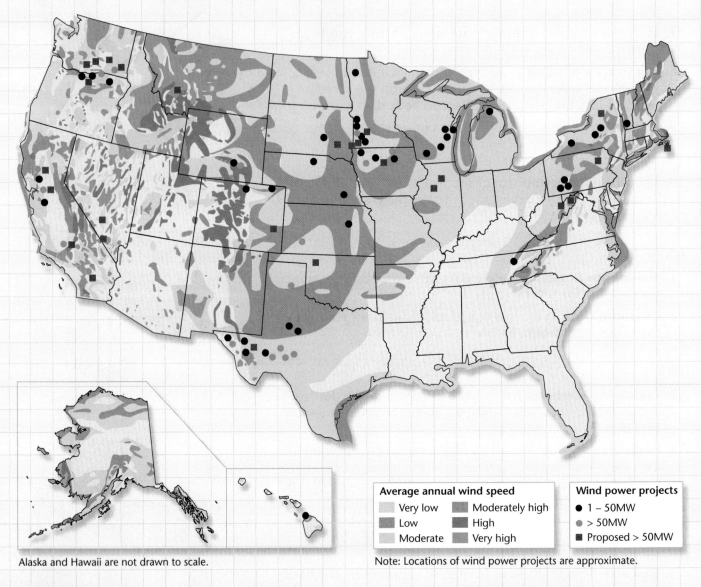

Average annual wind speed

Very low   Moderately high
Low   High
Moderate   Very high

Wind power projects

● 1 – 50MW
● > 50MW
■ Proposed > 50MW

Note: Locations of wind power projects are approximate.

Alaska and Hawaii are not drawn to scale.

MAP SKILLS

1. **Analyzing Data** Why are most of the wind farms located in the western and central United States and not in the eastern United States?

2. **Understanding Topography** Examine Idaho, Wyoming, Montana, and Colorado. What landscape feature might account for the strong winds in those states?

3. **Using the Key** Use the wind power key to locate where you would plan five wind power projects that are larger than 50 MW.

4. **Using the Key** The Great Plains states have been called the "Saudi Arabia of wind energy." Use the key to explain what this statement means.

5. **Finding Locations** The first offshore wind farm in the United States is proposed off the East Coast. Find where the proposed wind farm will be located, and describe the wind conditions in that area.

6. **Using the Key** Use the map to determine which state has the greatest unused potential for wind energy. Explain your reasoning.

BACK TO MUSCLE POWER

In 2001, U.S. forces dropped radios into remote parts of Afghanistan so that people could hear news broadcasts. The radios did not contain batteries, and there are few electrical outlets in rural Afghanistan. So how were people supposed to power the radios? The answer is surprisingly simple. The radios use our oldest form of energy—human muscle. Thirty seconds of cranking a handle on one of these radios stores enough energy for an hour of listening.

All Wound Up

The windup radios were invented by Trevor Bayliss in a London garden shed. They were first marketed in 1995 by Freeplay Energy. Now there are also flashlights and electric generators powered by cranks. Some people use them for boating and camping trips and for times when the power goes out. In developing countries, these devices are used in areas where there is no power supply.

These windup devices have several advantages over battery-powered devices. One main advantage is that there is no hazardous waste to dispose of in the form of used batteries. Also, batteries are heavy. Replacing batteries with longer-lasting, lighter sources of electricity has long been a goal of inventors.

The Secret Is in the Design

The first Freeplay radios worked like clockwork toys. The user would turn the handle, winding up a long spring, which then slowly unwound, releasing energy. In a newer model, cranking drives an alternator that charges a tiny battery.

How are these devices different from older clockwork devices, such as the first record players? They are much lighter and much easier to crank. The secret, says Freeplay, is enormously strong, lightweight components that survive for a long time.

An Inspiring Invention

This new technology has captured the imagination of many groups with different goals. There are dozens of experiments going on all over the world. A new line of windup generators will power everything from computers and mobile phones to land-mine detectors and water purification systems.

Watchmakers have developed watches whose batteries never need to be changed. These watches are powered by movement of the wrist. Typing your term paper or playing volleyball powers your watch. Another watch is powered by the heat of your body.

A shoe company is investigating ways to charge small batteries by walking. One design contains a material that generates electricity every time your heel hits the ground.

Defense agencies are studying ways to convert mechanical energy and heat energy into electricity. The goal is to make lighter versions of equipment that has to be carried. Soldiers would no longer have to carry heavy batteries in their packs. The possible applications for these new energy technologies are almost endless.

▶ The Freeplay Radio (below) was invented in a London garden shed, and now the idea is being used all over the world. The flashlight (right) is powered by shaking.

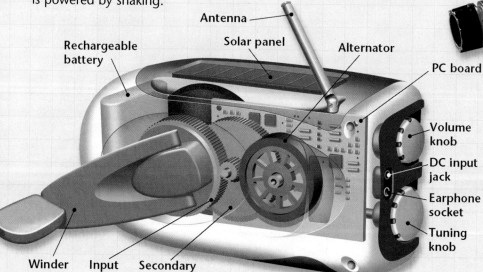

Antenna

Solar panel

Alternator

Rechargeable battery

PC board

Volume knob

DC input jack

Earphone socket

Tuning knob

Winder handle

Input gear

Secondary gear

What Do You Think?

Can you think of any other lightweight gadgets that could be powered by human muscle or body heat instead of by batteries? In what ways are the devices described here more environmentally friendly than the devices they replace?

Waste

PRE-READING ACTIVITY

FOLDNOTES

Three-Panel Flip Chart
Before you read this chapter, create the **FoldNote** entitled "Three-Panel Flip Chart" described in the Reading and Study Skills section of the Appendix. Label the flaps of the chart with "Solid Waste," "Reducing Solid Waste," and "Hazardous Waste." As you read the chapter, write information you learn about each category under the appropriate panel.

This landfill in New Jersey stores municipal solid waste that people throw away on a day-to-day basis. Every year, the United States generates more than 210 million metric tons of municipal solid waste.

Solid Waste

 SCSh.6.d; SEV.5.e

It is lunchtime. You stop at a fast-food restaurant and buy a burger, fries, and a soda. Within minutes, the food is gone, and you toss your trash into the nearest wastebasket. **Figure 1** shows what might be in your trash: a paper bag, a polystyrene burger container, the cardboard carton that held the fries, a paper cup with a plastic lid, a plastic straw, a handful of paper napkins, and several ketchup and mustard packets. Once you throw away your trash, you probably do not give it a second thought. But where does the trash go?

The trash from the wastebasket probably will be picked up by a collection service and taken to a landfill, where the trash will be dumped with thousands of tons of other trash and covered with a layer of soil. A landfill provides a place to store trash, but the trash does not simply disappear. Where will your trash go when the landfill fills up? What would happen if rainwater ran down into the landfill, and leached a harmful chemical, such as paint thinner, and it seeped into the groundwater? Suddenly, the trash that was not bothering anyone is causing an environmental problem.

The Generation of Waste

Imagine multiplying the waste disposal problems that come with your lunch by the number of things that you and everyone else throw away each day. Every year, the United States generates more than 10 billion metric tons of solid waste. **Solid waste** is any discarded solid material. Solid waste includes everything from junk mail to coffee grounds to cars. Many products that we buy today are used once and then thrown away. As a result, the amount of solid waste each American produces every year has more than doubled since the 1960s.

Objectives

▶ Name one characteristic that makes a material biodegradable.
▶ Identify two types of solid waste.
▶ Describe how a modern landfill works.
▶ Name two environmental problems caused by landfills.

Key Terms

solid waste
biodegradable
municipal solid waste
landfill
leachate

SC*LINKS*
www.scilinks.org
Topic: Solid Waste
Code: HE81419

Figure 1 ▶ Where does your trash go when you throw it away?

Figure 2 ▶ The barge *Mobro* (right) from Islip, New York, sailed up and down the East Coast and to the Gulf of Mexico for five months looking for a place to dump its load of garbage. The map below shows its route.

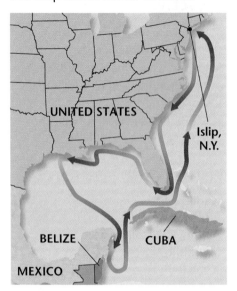

Space and Waste Today, many towns are running out of space to dispose of the amounts of waste that people create. For example, in 1987, the barge shown in **Figure 2** was loaded with 3,200 tons of garbage and left the town of Islip, New York, in search of a place to unload its waste. The barge sailed along the Atlantic coast to the Gulf of Mexico for more than five months in search of a state that would be willing to dispose of the waste. When no one would accept the garbage, it was finally burned in New York, and the 430 tons of ash was sent to Islip to be buried.

Population and Waste While the Earth's human population and the amount of waste we produce grows larger, the amount of land available per person becomes smaller. Thousands of years ago, in the time of hunter-gatherer societies, the human population was smaller and the waste created consisted mostly of animal and vegetable matter. This type of waste combined with a large amount of available land made disposing the waste much easier. However, today, the average person living in the United States produces 4.4 pounds of solid waste per day, as shown in **Figure 3**. Because the human population and the amount of waste we create is increasing and the amount of available land is decreasing, it is getting harder to dispose of the waste we create.

Figure 3 ▶ The total amount of municipal solid waste generated in the United States has more than doubled in the past 40 years.

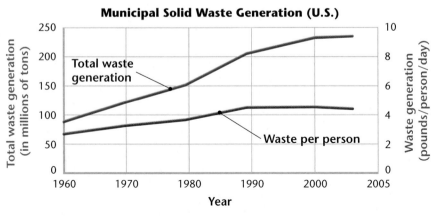

Source: U.S. Environmental Protection Agency.

Not All Wastes Are Equal

Problems are caused not only by the amount of solid waste but also by the type of solid waste. There are two main types of solid waste: biodegradable and nonbiodegradable. A material is **biodegradable** if it can be broken down by biological processes. Plant and animal matter are examples of biodegradable materials. Products made from natural materials are usually biodegradable. Examples of biodegradable products include newspapers, paper bags, cotton fibers, and leather.

Many products made from synthetic materials are not biodegradable. A *nonbiodegradable material* cannot be broken down by biological processes. Synthetic materials are made by combining chemicals to form compounds that do not form naturally. Polyester and plastic are examples of synthetic materials.

Plastic Problems Plastics illustrate how nonbiodegradable materials can cause problems. Plastics are made from petroleum or natural gas. Petroleum and natural gas consist mostly of carbon and hydrogen, which are the same elements that make up most molecules found in living things. But in plastics, these elements are put together in molecular chains that are not found in nature. Over millions of years, microorganisms have evolved the ability to break down nearly all biological molecules. However, microorganisms have not yet evolved ways to break down the molecular structures of most plastics. Therefore, some plastics that we throw away may accumulate and last for hundreds of years.

Types of Solid Waste

Most of what we throw out on a day-to-day basis is called municipal solid waste. Manufacturing waste, such as the computers shown in **Figure 4,** and mining waste make up about 70 percent of the other types of solid waste produced in the United States.

> ✔ **Reading Check** Is a product made of polyester biodegradable or nonbiodegradable?

Ecofact

Breaking Down Biodegradable Material Decomposers, such as fungi and bacteria, are examples of organisms that break down biodegradable material. Once these materials are broken down, they can be reused by other organisms. Scavengers, such as vultures, and insects, such as dung beetles, also help recycle organic waste.

Figure 4 ▶ These discarded computers have been exported from the United States and disposed of in China. Unwanted computers, televisions, audio equipment, and printers are types of electronic waste.

United States Municipal Solid Waste (Percentage by Weight)

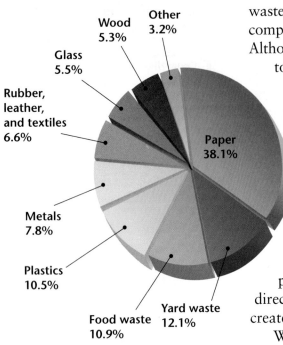

- Other 3.2%
- Wood 5.3%
- Glass 5.5%
- Rubber, leather, and textiles 6.6%
- Metals 7.8%
- Plastics 10.5%
- Food waste 10.9%
- Yard waste 12.1%
- Paper 38.1%

Source: U.S. Environmental Protection Agency.

Figure 5 ▶ Paper makes up most of the municipal solid waste in the United States. How much of the waste shown in this graph could be recycled?

MATHPRACTICE

Municipal Solid Waste
The United States generated approximately 236 million tons of municipal solid waste in 2003. In 1998, the United States generated approximately 223 million tons of municipal solid waste. What was the percent increase in municipal solid waste generation from 1998 to 2003?

Figure 6 ▶ Modern landfills are lined with clay and plastic and have a system for collecting and treating liquid that passes through the compacted solid waste.

Municipal Solid Waste About 2 percent of the total solid waste in the United States is made up of **municipal solid waste,** which is the waste produced by households and businesses. **Figure 5** shows the composition of municipal solid waste in the United States. Although municipal solid waste makes up only 2 percent of the total solid waste in the United States, this amounts to more than 236 million tons each year. That is enough waste to fill a convoy of garbage trucks that would stretch around the Earth about six times. Furthermore, the amount of municipal solid waste is growing much faster than the amount of mining or agricultural waste.

Solid Waste from Manufacturing, Mining, and Agriculture Solid waste from manufacturing, mining, and agriculture make up most of the rest of the total solid waste produced in the United States. Solid waste from manufacturing includes items such as scrap metal, plastics, paper, sludge, and ash. Although consumers do not directly produce waste from manufacturing, they indirectly create it by purchasing products that have been manufactured.

Waste from mining consists of the rock and minerals that are left over from excavation and processing. This waste is left exposed in large heaps, is dumped in oceans or rivers, or is disposed of by refilling and landscaping abandoned mines. Agricultural waste includes crop wastes and manure. Because agricultural waste is biodegradable, it can be broken down and returned to the soil. However, the increasing use of fertilizers and pesticides may cause agricultural waste to become more difficult to dispose of. If this waste is returned to the soil, it could harm plants and animals. It could also contaminate groundwater in the area.

Solid Waste Management

Most of our municipal waste in the United States is sent to landfills such as the one shown in **Figure 6.** However, some of our waste is incinerated, and more than 30 percent of our waste is recycled. By comparison, in 1970, we recycled only 6.6 percent of our waste.

Landfills More than 50 percent of the municipal and manufacturing solid waste created in the United States ends up in landfills as shown in **Table 1**. A **landfill** is a permanent waste-disposal facility where wastes are put in the ground and covered each day with a layer of soil, plastic, or both. The parts of a modern landfill are shown in **Figure 7**. The most important function of a landfill is to contain waste so that it does not pollute the environment. The waste must be prevented from leaching toxins into the soil and groundwater.

Problems with Landfills One problem with landfills is leachate. **Leachate** is a liquid that has passed through compacted solid waste in a landfill. Leachate forms when water seeps down through a landfill and collects dissolved chemicals from decomposing garbage. Leachate may contain chemicals from paints, pesticides, cleansers, cans, batteries, and appliances. Landfills typically have monitoring wells and storage tanks to measure and store leachate. Stored leachate can then be treated as waste water. However, if landfills are not monitored properly, leachate can flow into groundwater supplies and make water from nearby wells unsafe to drink.

Another problem with landfills is methane. Decomposing organic waste may produce methane, a highly flammable gas. Methane gas is usually pumped out of landfills and used as fuel. However, if methane gas production is not monitored safely, it may seep through the ground and into basements of homes up to 300 m from a landfill. If the methane is ignited by a spark, it can cause dangerous explosions.

Reading Check How can leachate in a landfill affect drinking water in nearby wells?

Table 1 ▼

Where Municipal Solid Waste in the United States Goes	
Waste-disposal method	Percentage of waste by weight
Stored in landfills	57
Recycled	28
Incinerated	15

Figure 7 ▶ This landfill generates electricity by burning methane gas that is produced by decomposing garbage.

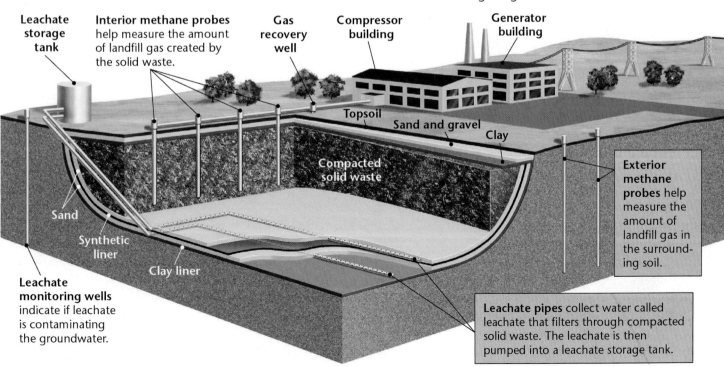

Leachate storage tank

Interior methane probes help measure the amount of landfill gas created by the solid waste.

Gas recovery well

Compressor building

Generator building

Topsoil

Sand and gravel

Clay

Compacted solid waste

Sand

Synthetic liner

Clay liner

Exterior methane probes help measure the amount of landfill gas in the surrounding soil.

Leachate monitoring wells indicate if leachate is contaminating the groundwater.

Leachate pipes collect water called leachate that filters through compacted solid waste. The leachate is then pumped into a leachate storage tank.

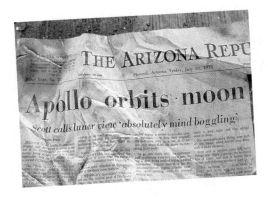

Figure 8 ▶ Biodegradable materials do not degrade quickly in modern landfills. This newspaper was put in a Tempe, Arizona landfill in 1971 and was removed in 1989.

Safeguarding Landfills The Resource Conservation and Recovery Act, passed in 1976 and updated in 1984, requires that new landfills be built with safeguards to reduce pollution problems. New landfills must be lined with clay and a plastic liner and must have systems for collecting and treating leachate. Vent pipes must be installed to carry methane out of the landfill, where the methane can be released into the air or burned to produce energy.

Adding these safeguards to landfills increases the cost of building them. Also, finding acceptable places to build landfills is difficult. The landfills must be close to the city producing the waste but must be far enough from residents who object to having a landfill near their homes. Any solution is likely to be expensive, either because of the legal fees a city must pay to fight residents' objections or because of the cost of transporting garbage to a distant site.

Building More Landfills Although we can build safer landfills, we are currently running out of space that we are willing to develop for new landfills. The materials we bury in landfills are not decomposing as fast as we can fill landfills. Even biodegradable materials, such as the newspaper in **Figure 8**, take several years to decompose. The total number of active landfills in the United States in 1988 was 8,000. By 2005, the total number of active landfills was less than 1,700 because many landfills had been filled to capacity. The U.S. Environmental Protection Agency (EPA) estimates that the active landfills in 20 states will be filled to capacity within 10 years as shown in **Figure 9**.

Figure 9 ▶ The map below shows the number of years until landfill capacity is reached in each state.

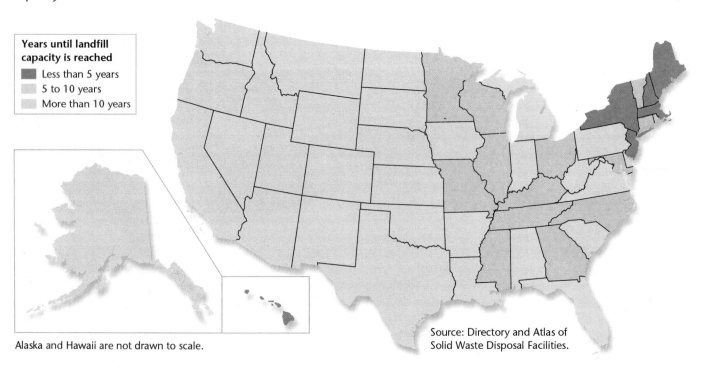

Years until landfill capacity is reached
- Less than 5 years
- 5 to 10 years
- More than 10 years

Alaska and Hawaii are not drawn to scale.

Source: Directory and Atlas of Solid Waste Disposal Facilities.

Incinerators One option for reducing the amount of solid waste sent to landfills is to burn it in incinerators, as shown in **Figure 10**. In 1999, the United States had 102 operational incinerators that were capable of burning up to 94,000 metric tons of municipal solid waste per day. However, the waste that is burned does not disappear. Although incinerators can reduce the weight of solid waste by 75 percent, they cannot separate materials that should not be incinerated before burning the waste. So, some materials that should not be burned, such as cleansers, batteries, and paints, end up in the air as polluting gases. The rest of the solid waste is converted into ash that must be disposed of in a landfill.

Incinerated material takes up less space in landfills, but the incinerated material can be more toxic than it was before being incinerated. Even incinerators that have special air pollution control devices release small amounts of poisonous gases and particles of toxic heavy metals into the air.

Figure 10 ▶ A solid-waste incinerator reduces the amount of trash that goes to landfills and can be used to generate electricity. However, the material that is created by the incinerator can be toxic.

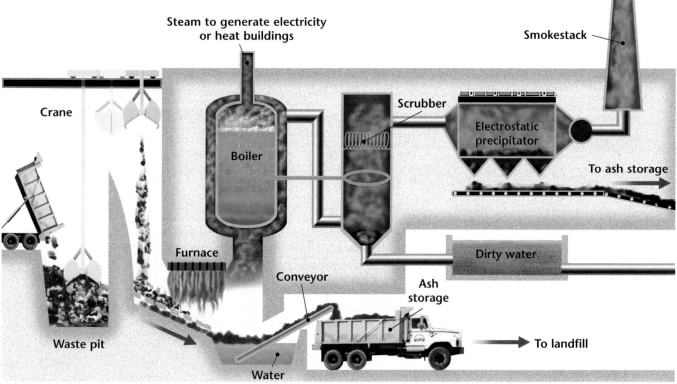

SECTION 1 **Review**

1. **Explain** what makes a material biodegradable.

2. **Compare** municipal solid waste and manufacturing solid waste.

3. **Describe** how a modern landfill works. Write a short paragraph to explain your answer. List two environmental problems that can be caused by landfills.
   WRITING SKILLS

4. **Describe** one advantage and one disadvantage of incinerating solid waste.

CRITICAL THINKING

5. **Identifying Relationships** Name two non-biodegradable products that you use. What makes these products nonbiodegradable? Name two biodegradable products that you can use instead.

6. **Identifying Alternatives** What can you do to help reduce the amount of solid waste that you throw away? What can you do to help people in your neighborhood reduce the amount of solid waste that is thrown away?

SECTION 2
Reducing Solid Waste

Objectives

▶ Identify three ways you can produce less waste.

▶ Describe how you can use your consumer buying power to reduce solid waste.

▶ List the steps that an item must go through to be recycled.

▶ List two benefits of composting.

▶ Name one advantage and one disadvantage to producing degradable plastic.

Key Terms

source reduction
recycling
compost

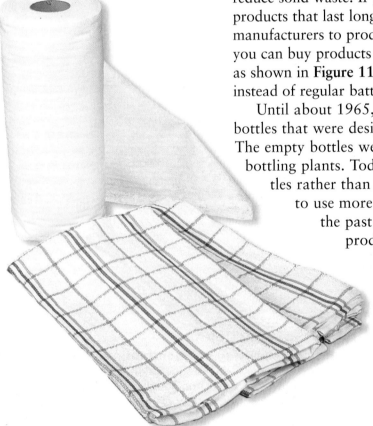

If landfills and incinerators can pollute the environment and are expensive to operate, what else can we do to safely reduce solid waste? This section examines ways to reduce solid waste through producing less waste, recycling, and changing the materials and products we use. All of these techniques help reduce waste before it is delivered to landfills or incinerators. This method of reducing solid waste is known as source reduction. **Source reduction** is any change in design, manufacture, purchase, or use of materials or products to reduce their amount or toxicity before they become municipal solid waste.

Reducing Solid Waste

If we produce less waste, we will reduce the expense and difficulty of collecting and disposing of it. Many ideas for reducing waste are common sense, such as using both sides of a sheet of paper and not using unneeded bags, napkins, or utensils at stores and restaurants.

Buying Less As a consumer, you can influence manufacturers to reduce solid waste. If you buy products that have less packaging, products that last longer, or reusable products, you will encourage manufacturers to produce more of those products. For example, you can buy products such as dish towels instead of paper towels, as shown in **Figure 11.** You can also buy rechargeable batteries instead of regular batteries to help reduce solid waste.

Until about 1965, nearly all bottled beverages were sold in bottles that were designed to be returned to stores when empty. The empty bottles were then collected, washed, and refilled at bottling plants. Today, there is a demand for disposable bottles rather than for refillable bottles. If consumers began to use more refillable bottles similar to those used in the past, beverage manufacturers would begin producing the refillable bottles.

Lasting Longer Manufacturers could also reduce waste and conserve resources by redesigning products to use less material. A return to products that last longer and that are designed to be easily repaired would both save resources and reduce waste disposal problems.

Figure 11 ▶ You can help reduce solid waste by purchasing items that have less packaging. Purchasing items that last longer, such as dish towels, can also reduce solid waste.

Recycling

In addition to reducing waste, we need to find ways to make the best use of all the materials we throw away. **Recycling** is the process of reusing materials or recovering valuable materials from waste or scrap. Making products from recycled materials usually saves energy, water, and other resources. For example, 95 percent less energy is needed to produce aluminum from recycled aluminum than from ore. About 70 percent less energy is needed to make paper from recycled paper than from trees.

Recycling: A Series of Steps When most people think about recycling, they probably think about only the first step — bringing their bottles, cans, and newspapers to a recycling center or putting these things at the curb. However, as shown in **Figure 12,** a series of steps is needed for recycling to work.

First, the discarded materials must be collected and sorted by type. Next, each type of material must be taken to a facility where it can be cleaned and made ready to be used again. For example, glass is sorted by color and is crushed, and paper is sorted by type and made into a pulp with water. Then the materials are used to manufacture new products. Finally, the new products are sold to consumers. If more people buy products made from recycled materials, there will be an increase in the demand for these products. This demand encourages manufacturers to build facilities to make recycled products. When such facilities are built, it becomes easier for communities to sell the materials they collect from residents for recycling.

Reading Check How can consumer demand influence the packaging of bottled beverages?

Figure 12 ▶ **The steps of recycling** include ❶ collecting and sorting discarded materials by type, ❷ taking the materials to a recycling facility, ❸ cleaning the discarded materials so that they can be shredded or crushed, and ❹ reusing the shredded or crushed materials to manufacture new products.

Table 2 ▼

Benefits of Composting

- keeps organic wastes out of landfills
- provides nutrients to the soil
- increases beneficial soil organisms, such as worms and centipedes
- suppresses some plant diseases
- reduces the need for fertilizers and pesticides
- protects soil from erosion

Composting Yard waste often makes up more than 15 percent of a community's solid waste. None of this waste has to go to a landfill. Because yard waste is biodegradable, it will decompose in a compost pile. Fruit and vegetable trimmings and table scraps will also decompose in a compost pile. The more oxygen and moisture there are in a compost pile, the more rapidly microorganisms will break down the biodegradable waste. Eventually the material becomes **compost,** a dark brown, crumbly material made from decomposed plant and animal matter that is spread on gardens and fields to enrich the soil. Compost is rich in the nutrients that help plants grow. More benefits of composting are listed in **Table 2.**

Some cities collect yard waste from homes and compost it at a large, central facility. Composting can also be an effective way of handling waste from food-processing plants and restaurants, manure from animal feedlots, and municipal sewage sludge. If all biodegradable wastes were composted, the amount of solid waste going to landfills could be reduced.

✔ **Reading Check** What conditions help biodegradable material break down rapidly?

CASE STUDY

Paper or Plastic?

The following question may sound familiar: Do you want paper or plastic? If you have ever stood in the checkout line of a grocery store, it probably is. Many grocery stores offer a choice between either paper or plastic bags for sacking grocery items. Many people make their choice based on convenience. But what is the best choice for someone who is concerned about the environment?

On the surface, it may seem that paper is the better choice. Paper comes from a renewable resource—trees—and is biodegradable. Plastic, on the other hand, comes from petroleum or natural gas, which are usually considered nonrenewable resources. In addition, plastic bags are not biodegradable.

Upon closer examination, however, the decision may not be as simple as it seems. Removing large numbers of trees from forests to manufacture paper can disrupt woodland ecosystems. Plus, a tremendous amount of energy is required to convert trees into pulp and then manufacture paper from the pulp.

To make the best decision about which product is better for the environment, the following questions should be considered.

- How much raw material, energy, and water is needed to manufacture each bag?
- What waste products will result from the manufacture of each bag, and what effect will those wastes have on water, the atmosphere, and the land?

▶ Making an educated decision at the grocery store will help reduce solid waste.

- Can recycled materials be used in the manufacture of the bag? If so, to what degree will the use of recycled materials reduce the amount of raw materials, energy,

Changing the Materials We Use

Simply changing the materials we use could eliminate much of the solid waste we produce. For example, single-serving drink boxes are made of a combination of foil, cardboard, and plastic. The drink boxes are hard to recycle because there is no easy way to separate the three components. More of our waste could be recycled if such products were no longer made and if all drinks came in recyclable glass, cardboard, or aluminum containers.

Recycling other common household products into new, useable products could also help eliminate solid waste. For example, newspapers can be recycled to make cardboard, egg cartons, and building materials. Telephone books, magazines, and catalogs can also be recycled to make building materials. Used aluminum beverage cans can be recycled to make new beverage cans, lawn chairs, aluminum siding for houses, and cookware. Used glass jars and bottles can be recycled to make new glass jars and bottles. Finally, plastic beverage containers can be recycled to make nonfood containers, insulation, carpet yarn, textiles, fiberfill, scouring pads, toys, plastic lumber, and crates.

SCiLINKS.
www.scilinks.org
Topic: Waste Prevention
Code: HE81623

EARTH SCIENCE CONNECTION

and water used and wastes produced in making the bag?

- How will the bag decompose, and what will the environmental impact be if it is incorrectly disposed of?

Although several studies have analyzed these questions, most have been conducted by parties with a vested interest, such as plastic or paper manufacturing companies. As you might expect, the studies done by plastic manufacturers conclude that plastic bags have the least environmental impact, while the studies done by paper producers conclude that paper bags have the least environmental impact. Often, the researchers fail to study all of the important factors listed above.

But the plastic versus paper debate has caused both industries to improve the way their products affect the environment. For example, paper bags recently outsold plastic bags because they were considered

▶ A reusable canvas shopping bag may be the best response to the paper-or-plastic question.

stronger, better for reusing or recycling, and less harmful in a landfill.

Then, new technology allowed the plastics industry to gain a larger market share. By incorporating recycled plastic into the bags, manufacturers improved the image of plastic bags.

Therefore, the debate continues and environmentally conscious people are still wondering which is better. Right now there seems to be no right answer. However, the following are environmentally sound options.

- Carry your groceries in bags brought from home (paper, plastic, or canvas bags).
- Choose the bag you are most likely to reuse in the future.
- If you have only one or two small items do not use a bag.

CRITICAL THINKING

1. Identifying Relationships
Explain how environmentally conscious shoppers have helped improve paper and plastic bag manufacturing in this country.

2. Understanding Concepts
Why should a person care which bag he or she is given at the grocery store?

Graphic

Organizer Chain-of-
Events Chart

Create the **Graphic Organizer**
entitled "Chain-of-Events Chart"
described in the Appen-
dix. Then, fill in the chart
with details about each
step of the degradation
of degradable plastics.

Degradable Plastics As you read earlier, most plastics are not biodegradable. To make plastic products more appealing to people who are concerned about the environment, several companies have developed new kinds of plastics that they say are degradable. One type, called *photodegradable plastic,* is made so that when it is left in the sun for many weeks, it becomes weak and brittle and eventually breaks into pieces.

Another type of degradable plastic, called *green plastic,* is made by blending the sugars in plants with a special chemical agent to make plastic. Green plastics are labeled as green because they are made from living things and are considered to be more environmentally friendly than other plastics. The production of green plastics requires 20 to 50 percent less fossil fuel than the production of regular plastics does. The fork in **Figure 13** is made of green plastic. This plastic has been engineered to degrade within 45 days of being thrown away. When this plastic is buried, the bacteria in the soil eat the sugars and leave the plastic weakened and full of microscopic holes. The chemical agent then gradually causes the long plastic molecules to break into shorter molecules. These two effects combine to cause the plastic to eventually fall apart into small pieces.

Problems with Degradable Plastics The main problem with these so-called degradable plastics is that although they do break apart and the organic parts can degrade, the plastic parts are only reduced to smaller pieces. This type of plastic can help reduce the harmful effects that plastic litter has on animals in the environment, because the plastic pieces will be too small to get caught in their throats or around their necks. However, the small pieces of plastic will not disappear completely. Instead, the pieces of plastic will be spread around. So, these biodegradable plastics can remain in landfills for many years, just as regular plastics can.

Figure 13 ▶ Green plastics made from living things are biodegradable. The plastic fork below has been engineered to degrade within 45 days of disposal.

DAY 0   DAY 12   DAY 33   DAY 45

SECTION 2 Review

1. **Name** three things you could do each day to produce less waste.

2. **Explain** how buying certain products can help reduce solid waste.

3. **Describe** the steps it takes to recycle a piece of plastic.

4. **List** two benefits of composting.

CRITICAL THINKING

5. **Analyzing Methods** What are the advantages and disadvantages to producing degradable plastics?

6. **Demonstrating Reasoned Judgement** Read the Case Study in this section and decide which type of bag you would choose the next time you go shopping. Explain why you made this choice. What are other uses of the bag you chose? **READING SKILLS**

SECTION 3
Hazardous Waste

Many of the products we use today, from laundry soap to computers, are produced in modern factories that use thousands of chemicals. Some of these chemicals make up parts of the products, while other chemicals are used as cleaners or for generating electricity for the factories. Large quantities of the chemicals used are often leftover as waste. Many of these chemicals are classified as **hazardous waste,** which is any waste that is a risk to the health of humans or other living things.

Types of Hazardous Waste

Hazardous wastes may be solids, liquids, or gases. Hazardous wastes often contain toxic, corrosive, or explosive materials. Some examples of hazardous wastes include substances such as cleansers used to disinfect surfaces or lubricants used to help machines run smoothly. More examples of hazardous wastes are listed in **Table 3.**

The methods used to dispose of hazardous wastes often are not as carefully planned as the manufacturing processes that produced them. One case of hazardous waste disposal that had horrifying results occurred at Love Canal, in Niagara Falls, New York. At Love Canal, homes and a school were built on land that a chemical company had used as a site to dump toxic waste. Problems started when the toxic waste began to leak from the site.

The events at Love Canal shocked people into paying more attention to how hazardous wastes were being disposed of and stored throughout the United States. In other places throughout the country, improperly stored or discarded wastes—such as those shown in **Figure 14**—were leaking into the air, soil, and groundwater. Federal laws were passed to clean up old waste sites and regulate future waste disposal.

Objectives

▶ Name two characteristics of hazardous waste.
▶ Describe one law that governs hazardous waste.
▶ Describe two ways to treat hazardous waste safely.

Key Terms

hazardous waste
deep-well injection
surface impoundment

Table 3 ▼

Types of Hazardous Waste
• dyes, cleansers, and solvents
• PCBs (polychlorinated biphenyls) from older electrical equipment, such as heating systems and television sets
• solvents, lubricants, and sealants
• toxic heavy metals, such as lead, mercury, cadmium, and zinc
• pesticides
• radioactive wastes from spent fuel that was used to generate electricity

Figure 14 ▶ An improperly maintained hazardous waste site can leak toxic wastes into the air, soil, and groundwater.

Resource Conservation and Recovery Act The Resource Conservation and Recovery Act (RCRA) was passed by Congress in 1976 and amended in 1984. The RCRA created the first significant role for federal government in waste management. The act was established to regulate solid and hazardous waste disposal and to protect humans and the environment from waste contamination.

The primary goals of the RCRA include protecting human health from the hazards of waste disposal, conserving energy and natural resources by recycling and recovering, reducing or eliminating waste, and cleaning up waste, which may have spilled, leaked, or been improperly disposed of.

Figure 15 ▶ This map shows the number of approved and proposed Superfund sites as of 2001. These sites are some of the most hazardous areas in the United States.

Resource Conservation and Recovery Act

The Resource Conservation and Recovery Act (RCRA) requires producers of hazardous waste to keep records of how their wastes are handled from the time the wastes are made to the time the wastes are placed in an approved disposal facility. If the wastes cause a problem in the future, the producer is legally responsible for the problem. RCRA also requires all hazardous waste treatment and disposal facilities to be built and operated according to standards that are designed to prevent the facilities from polluting the environment.

The Superfund Act

Because the safe disposal of hazardous wastes is expensive, companies that produce hazardous wastes may be tempted to illegally dump them to save money. In 1980, the U.S. Congress passed the Comprehensive Environmental Response, Compensation, and Liability Act, more commonly known as the Superfund Act. The Superfund Act gave the U.S. Environmental Protection Agency (EPA) the right to sue the owners of hazardous waste sites who had illegally dumped waste. Also, the EPA gained the right to force the owners to pay for the cleanup. The Superfund Act also created a fund of money to pay for cleaning up abandoned hazardous waste sites.

Cleaning up improperly discarded waste is difficult and extremely expensive. At Love Canal alone, $275 million was spent to put a clay cap on the site, to install a drainage system and treatment plant to handle the leaking wastes, and to relocate the residents. More than 20 years after Love Canal was evacuated, many Superfund sites still needed to be cleaned up, as shown in **Figure 15**. As of 2001, cleanup had been completed at only 75 of the roughly 1,200 approved or proposed Superfund sites.

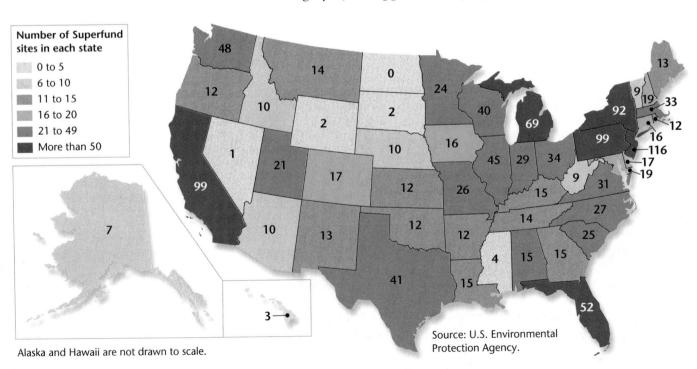

Number of Superfund sites in each state
- 0 to 5
- 6 to 10
- 11 to 15
- 16 to 20
- 21 to 49
- More than 50

Source: U.S. Environmental Protection Agency.

Alaska and Hawaii are not drawn to scale.

Figure 16 ▶ Safely transporting hazardous waste is an important part of hazardous waste management.

www.scilinks.org
Topic: Hazardous
Waste
Code: HE80717

Hazardous Waste Management

Each year, the United States produces about 252 million metric tons of hazardous waste, and this amount is growing. It is difficult to guarantee that the disposal techniques used today will not eventually pollute our air, food, or water.

Preventing Hazardous Waste One way to prevent hazardous waste is to produce less of it. In recent years, many manufacturers have discovered that they can redesign manufacturing methods to produce less or no hazardous waste. For example, some manufacturers who used chemicals to clean metal parts of machines have discovered that they can use tiny plastic beads instead. The beads act like a sandblaster to clean the parts, can be reused several times, and are not hazardous when disposed of. Often, such techniques save the manufacturers money by cutting the cost of materials as well as in cutting the cost of waste disposal.

Another way to deal with hazardous waste is to find a way to reuse it. In the United States, companies often work together to reduce waste. For example, a company that once would have thrown away a cleaning solvent after one use may instead sell it to another company that has a use for it.

Conversion into Nonhazardous Substances Some types of wastes can be treated with chemicals to make the wastes less hazardous. For example, lime, which is a base, can be added to acids to neutralize them. A base is a compound that can also react with acids to convert acids into salts, which are less harmful to the environment. Also, cyanides, which are extremely poisonous compounds, can be combined with oxygen to form carbon dioxide and nitrogen. In other cases, wastes can be treated biologically. Sludge from petroleum refineries, for example, may be converted by soil bacteria into less harmful substances.

✔ Reading Check How can cleaning machinery with plastic beads rather than solvents help to reduce hazardous waste?

QuickLAB

Neutralizing Hazardous Waste

Procedure

1. Using a **measuring spoon,** obtain about a teaspoon of **baking soda,** and place it in a **500 mL beaker.** The baking soda will act as the base which will neutralize the acid.
2. In a separate **500 mL beaker,** pour approximately **200 mL of vinegar.** The vinegar is a weak acid.
3. Add the vinegar (acid) to the baking soda (base).

Analysis

1. What happened when you added the vinegar to the baking soda?
2. How is this lab similar to the technique used to convert some hazardous wastes into nonhazardous substances?

Hazardous Chemical Reactions After a material is thrown away, it may become more hazardous as a result of a chemical reaction with other discarded wastes. For example, metallic mercury is considered to be toxic. Metallic mercury is often used in thermometers and computers. If it is buried in a landfill, the bacteria in a landfill can cause it to react with methane to form methyl mercury. Methyl mercury, which is more toxic than metallic mercury, can cause severe nerve damage.

Land Disposal Most of the hazardous waste produced in the United States is disposed of on land. One land disposal facility, illustrated in **Figure 17**, is called deep-well injection. During **deep-well injection,** wastes are pumped deep into the ground, where they are absorbed into a dry layer of rock below the level of groundwater. After the wastes are buried below the level of groundwater, the wastes are covered with cement to prevent contamination of the groundwater. Another common land disposal facility is a **surface impoundment,** which is basically a pond that has a sealed bottom. The wastes accumulate and settle to the bottom of the pond, while water evaporates from the pond and leaves room to add more wastes.

Hazardous wastes in concentrated or solid form are often put in barrels and buried in landfills. Hazardous waste landfills are similar to those used for ordinary solid waste, but these landfills have extra safety precautions to prevent leakage.

In theory, if all of these facilities are properly designed and built, they should provide safe ways to dispose of hazardous wastes. However, if they are not properly maintained, they can develop leaks that may result in contamination of the air, soil, or groundwater.

CASE STUDY

Green Chemistry

Walk into any pharmacy, and you will see a wide range of headache tablets for sale. Several popular brands contain ibuprofen as the active ingredient. But the production of ibuprofen used to create a headache itself.

When first developed and patented in the 1960s, the six-step process to make ibuprofen produced large quantities of unwanted byproducts. In fact, more waste was made than useful product. In the 1990s, a new three-step process was developed. This process uses millions of metric tons fewer chemicals as raw materials and prevents the formation of millions of metric tons of waste. Fewer chemicals used and less waste produced adds up to

a process that is better for the environment, and less expensive for the manufacturer. This is an example of green chemistry in action.

A set of principles guide green chemists. The first principle of the U.S. Green Chemistry Institute is that preventing pollution is better than trying to clean it up. Ideally, raw materials should be renewable, and the product should biodegrade into harmless substances when it is no longer needed. The ideal process would use little energy and convert all the raw materials into final product. Chemists are not usually able to develop processes that meet all of these guidelines. The closer they can get to an ideal process, however, the better it is for the environment.

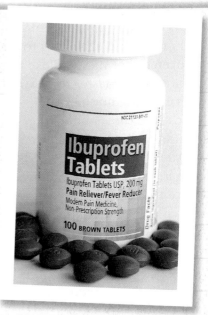

▶ The annual production of ibuprofen is about 14,000 metric tons, enough to make billions of painkiller tablets.

For example, the old process for the manufacture of ibuprofen used a substance called aluminum trichloride to increase the speed of one of the reactions. Unfortunately,

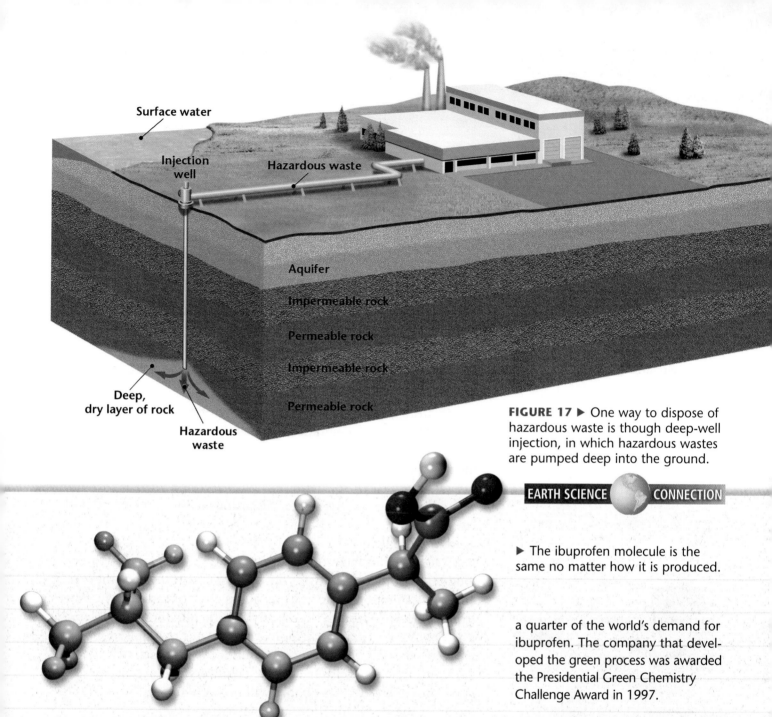

Surface water

Injection well

Hazardous waste

Aquifer

Impermeable rock

Permeable rock

Impermeable rock

Permeable rock

Deep, dry layer of rock

Hazardous waste

FIGURE 17 ▶ One way to dispose of hazardous waste is though deep-well injection, in which hazardous wastes are pumped deep into the ground.

EARTH SCIENCE CONNECTION

▶ The ibuprofen molecule is the same no matter how it is produced.

a quarter of the world's demand for ibuprofen. The company that developed the green process was awarded the Presidential Green Chemistry Challenge Award in 1997.

aluminum trichloride decayed during the reaction. It ended up as a waste product that usually went into landfills. In the new process, a different substance is used to speed up the reaction. This substance does not break down. It is the gas hydrogen fluoride, which is easily separated from the reactant mixture and reused.

In addition, the original process converted only 40 percent of the

weight of the raw materials used into ibuprofen. The new process raises this conversion to 77 percent and produces acetic acid (the acid in vinegar) as a useful byproduct.

In the fall of 1992, the largest plant in the world for the manufacture of ibuprofen opened in Bishop, Texas. This plant operates on the principles of green chemistry and is capable of producing about 6 billion tablets every year—about

CRITICAL THINKING

1. Making Decisions Think of a chemistry experiment you have done. Write a paragraph to explain how the experiment could have been "greener."

2. Expressing Opinions Should subsidies be given to companies to encourage them to develop and put into practice greener processes?

Figure 18 ▶ Chemicals can be used to clean up hazardous wastes. This tractor is applying chemicals to an oil spill to help absorb the oil.

Geofact

Biomining Bacteria are not only used to break down hazardous wastes, but they are also used to extract copper and gold from ore. This technique is called *biomining*. Currently, 25 percent of the world's copper is produced through bio-mining. Today, scientists are attempting to bioengineer bacterial strains that can mine poisonous heavy metals such as arsenic, cadmium, and mercury from ore.

Biologically Treating Hazardous Waste

Some hazardous wastes can be absorbed or broken down, or their toxicity can be reduced when they are treated with biological and chemical agents. Certain bacteria can be used to clean up an area in the environment that has been contaminated with hazardous substances, such as crude oil, PCBs, and cyanide. Scientists can grow bacteria in a lab and apply the bacteria to a contaminated area in the environment to break down the hazardous substances. Plants that absorb heavy metals can also be planted in contaminated areas. As shown in **Figure 18**, chemicals can be used to neutralize and absorb hazardous wastes.

Incinerating Hazardous Waste Some hazardous wastes are disposed of by burning, often in specially designed incinerators. Incinerators can be a safe way to dispose of waste, but they have several problems. Incineration is generally the most expensive form of waste disposal because they require a lot of energy to operate. Incinerators also need pollution-control devices and need to be carefully monitored so that hazardous gases and particles are not released into the air. Also, after hazardous waste is incinerated, the leftover ash needs to be buried. This ash is usually buried in a hazardous waste landfill.

When we put hazardous waste into disposal facilities for long-term storage the wastes do not disappear. Instead, they must be closely monitored. For example, disposal of radioactive wastes from nuclear reactors is an especially difficult storage problem. The only way to make the radioactive wastes nonhazardous is to let them sit for thousands of years until the radioactivity decreases to safe levels. Therefore, engineers and geologists search for disposal sites that probably will not be damaged by movements of the Earth for thousands of years.

Exporting Hazardous Waste Until recently, only local laws regulated waste disposal in the United States. Companies would often get rid of hazardous wastes by sending them to landfills in other states, especially the less populated southern states. In the 1980s, as southern populations grew, these southern states began to refuse hazardous wastes from other states.

Hazardous wastes are also exported through international trade agreements. Some hazardous wastes are exported to other countries because there may be a facility in another country that specializes in treating, disposing of, or recycling a particular hazardous waste.

✓ Reading Check What are two problems associated with using incinerators to dispose of hazardous waste?

Hazardous Wastes at Home

You may think of hazardous waste management as a problem that only big industries face. However, everyday household products can also create hazardous waste. Chemicals, including house paint, pesticides, and batteries all create hazardous waste and are used in homes, schools, and businesses. Additional hazardous household products are listed in **Table 4.** Hazardous materials poured down the drain or put in the trash end up in solid-waste landfills. These hazardous wastes should instead be disposed of in a specially designed hazardous waste landfill.

Disposing of Household Hazardous Waste To make sure that household hazardous waste is disposed of properly, more and more cities around the country have begun to provide collection for household hazardous waste. Some cities collect materials only once or twice a year, while other cities have permanent facilities where residents can drop off hazardous waste. Trained workers sort the hazardous materials and send some materials for recycling and pack other materials into barrels for disposal. Used batteries and motor oil are recycled. Paint may be blended and used for city park maintenance or to clean up graffiti.

Motor Oil If you have ever changed the oil in your car yourself, you have probably wondered what to do with the old, dirty oil. It is illegal to pour it on the ground or throw it in the trash. But, you may be surprised to find out that people in the United States throw away about 700 million liters (185 million gallons) of used motor oil every year. This amount does not include the oil disposed of by service stations and automobile repair shops.

So what can people do with the oil? One option is to take it to an automobile service station, where it will be turned in for recycling. Some cities have designated oil-collection receptacles as shown in **Figure 19.** These cities recycle the used oil turned in by citizens. If you do not know what services your community provides, you can call your local city government and find out.

Table 4 ▼

Common Hazardous Household Products	
• motor oil	• pesticides
• paints	• fertilizers
• batteries	• cleaners
• computers	• antifreeze
• mobile phones	

Figure 19 ▶ Used motor oil should be disposed of at an automobile service station or in an oil-collection receptacle.

SECTION 3 Review

1. **Name** two characteristics of hazardous waste.

2. **Identify** one law that governs hazardous waste.

3. **Describe** two common ways to dispose of hazardous waste in the United States. What is one advantage and one disadvantage of one of these methods?

4. **Describe** how bacteria could be used to degrade hazardous wastes. Write a short paragraph to explain your answer. **WRITING SKILLS**

CRITICAL THINKING

5. **Evaluating Ideas** Suppose that a surface impoundment site for hazardous waste is planned for your community. Would you oppose locating the site in your community? Explain your answer.

6. **Applying Ideas** Suppose someone dumped leftover motor oil on a driveway. Could this disposal method contaminate the air, water, or soil? Explain your answer.

1 Solid Waste

Key Terms

solid waste, 517
biodegradable, 519
municipal solid waste, 520
landfill, 521
leachate, 521

Main Ideas

▶ Every year, people in the United States generate more than 10 billion metric tons of soild waste.

▶ Materials that are biodegradable, such as newspapers and cotton fibers, can be broken down by biological processes. Materials that are not biodegradable such as plastics, are a major cause of disposal problems.

▶ Municipal solid waste makes up only a small fraction of the total solid waste generated, but it still amounts to over 236 million tons per year.

▶ Landfills and incinerators are two facilities used for disposing solid waste.

2 Reducing Solid Waste

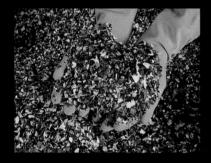

Key Terms

source reduction, 524
recycling, 525
compost, 526

Main Ideas

▶ Source reduction is a method by which we can produce less waste, recycle, and reuse materials.

▶ Recycling is the process of reusing materials or recovering valuable materials from waste or scrap.

▶ A compost pile made from plant and animal matter can be spread on gardens and fields to enrich the soil.

▶ Degradable plastic is a type of plastic that is partially made from living things.

3 Hazardous Waste

Key Terms

hazardous waste, 529
deep-well injection, 532
surface impoundment, 532

Main Ideas

▶ Hazardous waste is any waste that is a risk to the health of humans or other living things.

▶ The Resource Conservation and Recovery Act (RCRA) and the Superfund Act were established to regulate solid and hazardous waste disposal and to protect humans and the environment from waste contamination.

▶ Activities at home can create hazardous waste. Household hazardous wastes should be properly disposed of at designated collection sites.

Using Key Terms

Use each of the following terms in a separate sentence.

1. *source reduction*
2. *leachate*
3. *municipal solid waste*
4. *biodegradable*
5. *recycling*

Use the correct key term to complete each of the following sentences.

6. _____ is any waste that is a risk to the health of humans or other living things.

7. A dark brown, crumbly material made from decomposed vegetable and animal matter is called _____.

8. A _____ is a waste disposal facility where wastes are put in the ground and covered each day with a layer of dirt, plastic, or both.

✔ **STUDY TIP**

Increase Your Vocabulary To learn and remember vocabulary words, use a dictionary for words you do not understand and become familiar with the glossaries of your textbooks.

Understanding Key Ideas

9. Solid waste includes all of the following *except*
   a. newspaper and soda bottles.
   b. food scraps and yard clippings.
   c. ozone and carbon dioxide.
   d. junk mail and milk cartons.

10. If your shirt is made of 50 percent cotton and 50 percent polyester, what part is biodegradable?
    a. cotton
    b. polyester
    c. both (a) and (b)
    d. none of the above

11. Microorganisms are unable to break down plastics because plastics
    a. are made from oil.
    b. are too abundant.
    c. are made of elements not found in any other substance.
    d. do not occur in nature.

12. Municipal solid waste is approximately what percentage of all solid waste?
    a. 2 percent
    b. 20 percent
    c. 60 percent
    d. 90 percent

13. Leachate is a substance that
    a. is produced in a compost pile.
    b. is a byproduct of bacterial digestion.
    c. is produced by incinerators.
    d. contains dissolved toxic chemicals.

14. Which of the following is not a benefit of incinerating waste?
    a. It reduces the amount of material sent to landfills.
    b. It produces energy in the form of heat.
    c. It can be used to produce electricity.
    d. It neutralizes all of the toxic materials in the waste.

15. Manufacturers could reduce waste and conserve resources by making products that
    a. use more materials.
    b. are more durable.
    c. are difficult to repair.
    d. are disposable.

16. Which of the following is one way to reduce an over-supply of recyclable materials?
    a. build more recycling plants
    b. increase the amount of recyclable materials that can be collected
    c. increase the demand for products made from recycled materials
    d. put the excess materials in landfills

17. Most of the municipal solid waste in the United States is
    a. stored in landfills.
    b. recycled.
    c. incinerated.
    d. None of the above

Short Answer

18. Do you think incineration is an efficient disposal method for glass and metal wastes? Write a short paragraph that explains why or why not. **WRITING SKILLS**

19. How do plastic liners and layers of clay help protect the environment around a landfill?

20. What are the materials that make up compost? List at least three benefits of composting.

21. How does the Superfund Act allow the federal government to ensure proper disposal of hazardous waste?

Interpreting Graphics

The graph below shows the number of landfills in the United States from the year 1988 to the year 1998. Use the graph to answer questions 22–24.

22. Approximately how many landfills existed in 1988? in 1998?

23. During the span of 10 years, did the overall number of landfills increase or did the number decrease? What may have caused this change? Explain your answer.

24. If this trend continues, what might the graph look like for the year 2028?

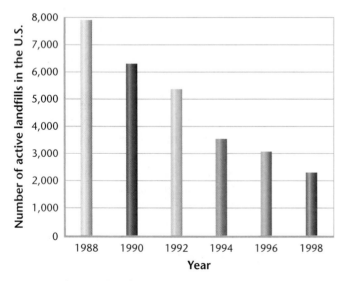

Source: *BioCycle.*

Concept Mapping

25. Use the following terms to create a concept map: *solid waste, hazardous waste, landfills, types of waste, surface impoundment, methods of waste disposal, incineration,* and *deep-well injection.*

Critical Thinking

26. **Understanding Concepts** During the 1970s, the production of municipal solid waste decreased. An economic recession was also occurring. How might the reduction in waste have been related to the recession?

27. **Making Comparisons** Read the description of recycling in this chapter and compare the benefits of buying a product that has been recycled to the benefits of buying a brand new product. Which product would you prefer to buy? Explain your answer. **READING SKILLS**

28. **Evaluating Information** How would a ban on the production of plastics affect both the environment and society?

29. **Identifying Relationships** When we purchase hazardous household products, such as motor oil, bleach, and pesticides, what happens to the containers when they are empty? What happens to the hazardous waste that these products create?

30. **Predicting Consequences** How might a person's current shopping habits affect the quality of the environment 100 years in the future?

Cross-Disciplinary Connection

31. **Social Studies** Use an almanac to determine which five states have the greatest number of hazardous waste sites. What factors do you think might account for the number of hazardous waste sites located in a state?

Portfolio Project

32. **Make a Display** Do a special project about recycling in your community. Determine what types of materials are collected, where they are taken for processing, how they are recycled, and what products are made from them. Display your findings on a poster.

MATH SKILLS

Use the table below to answer questions 33–35.

Paper Products in Municipal Solid Waste		
Product	Generation (tons)	Percentage recycled
Newspapers	13,620	56.4
Books	1,140	14.0
Magazines	2,260	20.8
Office papers	7,040	50.4

33. **Evaluating Data** How many tons of paper products were generated according to the table?

34. **Making Calculations** How many tons of newspapers were recycled? How many tons of newspapers were not recycled?

35. **Making Calculations** How many tons of office papers were recycled? How many tons of office papers were not recycled?

WRITING SKILLS

36. **Writing Persuasively** Pretend that you work for a company that sells degradable plastics. Write an advertising campaign that would persuade consumers to buy materials made from your company's brand of degradable plastic.

37. **Outlining Topics** Describe the various ways in which hazardous waste can be disposed of. List the advantages and disadvantages of each way.

READING SKILLS

Read the passage below, and then answer the questions that follow.

All organisms need nitrogen to make proteins and nucleic acids. The complex pathway that nitrogen follows within an ecosystem is called the nitrogen cycle. Most living things cannot use nitrogen gas directly from the atmosphere. The process of converting nitrogen gas to compounds that organisms can use is called nitrogen fixation. Organisms rely on the actions of bacteria that are able to transform and "fix" nitrogen gas into these compounds. Nitrogen-fixing bacteria convert nitrogen gas into ammonia, which plants can absorb and use to make proteins. Nitrogen-fixing bacteria live in the soil and in the roots of some kinds of plants, such as beans, peas, clover, and alfalfa.

Decomposers break down the wastes of organisms and release the nitrogen they contain as ammonia. This process is known as ammonification. Through ammonification, nitrogen that would otherwise be buried is reintroduced into the ecosystem.

1. After nitrogen-fixing bacteria convert nitrogen gas into ammonia,
   a. nitrogen fixation occurs.
   b. plants can absorb the ammonia to make proteins.
   c. nitrogen-fixing bacteria absorb the ammonia.
   d. decomposers absorb the ammonia.

2. If decomposers did not break down the waste that organisms create,
   a. nitrogen would be released into the atmosphere as ammonia.
   b. ammonification would occur.
   c. nitrogen-fixing bacteria would not convert nitrogen gas into ammonia.
   d. nitrogen would not be released into the soil as ammonia.

Understanding Concepts

Directions (1–4): For *each* question, write on a separate sheet of paper the letter of the correct answer.

1 Which of the following is biodegradable?
A. a nylon jacket
B. a plastic cup
C. a television set
D. a wool sweater

2 What is source reduction?
F. Source reduction is a method by which we can produce less waste.
G. Source reduction is a method of reducing recyclable materials.
H. Source reduction is a process that changes the number of landfills.
I. Source reduction is a process that allows manufacturers to make more products from plastics.

3 What is the relationship between packaging and solid waste?
A. Packaging made of plastic decreases the amount of solid waste.
B. Packaging has little effect on the amount of solid waste produced.
C. Packaging that can be recycled increases the amount of solid waste.
D. Packaging for single-serving items increases the amount of solid waste.

4 Which of the following statements is true?
F. There is little danger of hazardous waste entering groundwater if the waste is disposed of through deep-well injection.
G. During the 1990s the amount of waste generated per person remained almost constant, decreasing the total amount of waste generated.
H. Composting could reduce the amount of waste that restaurants, food-processing plants, and animal feedlots send to landfills.
I. Landfills are the safest way to dispose of solid waste because the materials buried in them decompose quickly.

Directions (5–6): For *each* question, write a short response.

5 How could the widespread use of compost affect water pollution that results from the use of chemical fertilizers?

6 If plastics are made from petroleum, why are plastic products nonbiodegradable?

Reading Skills

Directions (7–9): Read the passage below. Then answer the questions.

Many of the products in use today are produced in modern factories that use thousands of chemicals. Many of these chemicals are classified as hazardous waste, which is any waste that is a risk to the health of living things.

Each year, the United States produces about 252 metric tons of hazardous wastes, and this amount is growing. In recent years, many manufacturers have discovered that they can redesign manufacturing methods to produce less or no hazardous waste. For example, some manufacturers who used chemicals to clean metal parts of machines have discovered that they can use tiny plastic beads instead. The beads act like a sandblaster to clean the parts, can be reused several times, and are not hazardous when disposed of. Often, such techniques save the manufacturers money by cutting the cost of materials as well as in cutting the cost of waste disposal.

7 Which of the following items associated with an automobile is not considered hazardous waste?
A. motor oil
B. rubber tire
C. gasoline
D. antifreeze fluid

8 Is the United States increasing or decreasing its production of hazardous waste?

9 What extra benefits can result when a company finds ways to reduce hazardous waste?

Interpreting Graphics

Directions (10–13): For *each* question below, record the correct answer on a separate sheet of paper.

The graph below shows the composition (by weight) of municipal solid wastes in the United States. Use this graph to answer questions 10 through 12.

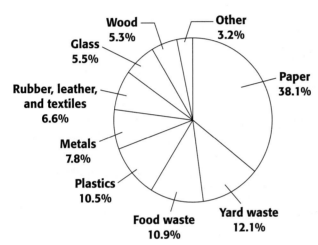

Municipal Solid Waste
(Percentage by Weight)

Wood 5.3%
Glass 5.5%
Rubber, leather, and textiles 6.6%
Metals 7.8%
Plastics 10.5%
Food waste 10.9%
Yard waste 12.1%
Other 3.2%
Paper 38.1%

10 If the most recyclable materials are paper, plastics, metal and glass, by what percentage would municipal solid waste be reduced if every person in the country recycled?
F. 38%
G. 43%
H. 54%
I. 62%

11 Which of the following is a type of waste you would likely find under the category of "Other" in this pie graph?
A. banana peels
B. glazed ceramics
C. grass clippings
D. industrial chemicals

12 By how much would the amount of municipal waste be reduced if every household in the country had a compost pile?
F. 12%
G. 23%
H. 35%
I. 41%

13 Where does municipal waste come from?
A. agriculture and mining
B. households and business
C. manufacturing and business
D. mining and households

Test TIP

For multiple-choice questions, try to eliminate any answer choices that are obviously incorrect, and then consider the remaining answer choices.

Objectives

▶ **Recognize** various categories and amounts of solid waste produced.

▶ **Compute** percentages of waste, by category, produced per person in a single meal.

▶ **Generalize** data from a small sample for a large population using calculations.

▶ **USING SCIENTIFIC METHODS** **Infer** from small data samples the impact that waste production has on a large population.

▶ **USING SCIENTIFIC METHODS** **Evaluate** how waste data can be used to communicate results and offer solutions.

Materials

balance, triple beam or
  electronic calculator
paper towels
plastic bags
ruler

Solid Waste in Your Lunch

Are you aware of how much waste you produce during one meal? Various government and private agencies study the amount and types of food waste we produce and are continuously working to solve the problems of waste disposal. In this lab activity, you will determine how much solid waste you produce during a typical lunch. You will also predict through calculations how much solid waste your school population produces during lunch.

Procedure

1. Collect all your lunch waste on the day of the lab activity or the day before the lab activity depending on whether your class meets before or after lunch. Put all of your lunch waste in a plastic bag, including leftover food items, wrappers, napkins, straws, unopened containers of condiments, and disposable trays.

2. Each lab group member should place his or her plastic bag of waste on the worktable. Each member should separate his or her waste on a paper towel into the following categories: paper and cardboard, plastic, metal, glass, wood, and food.

3. For each category of waste, determine the mass of waste produced by each person in the group. Create a data table similar to the one shown below and record the masses.

4. Detemine the total mass for each category for the lab group. Then, determine the average mass of solid waste per student for each category. Finally, determine the overall total amount of solid waste produced for each student.

Waste category	Student 1	Student 2	Student 3	Total mass of lab group	Average mass/student
Paper and cardboard					
Plastic					
Metal					
Glass					
Wood					
Food					
Total					

DO NOT WRITE IN THIS BOOK

Analysis

1. **Organizing Data** Use the equation below to determine the percentages for the waste categories that make up your total waste as an individual. Add another column to your data table to record this value.

$$\frac{\text{Mass (in grams) of waste category}}{\text{Mass (in grams) of total waste}} \times 100 = \begin{array}{l}\text{waste category's}\\\text{percentage of}\\\text{total waste}\end{array}$$

2. **Organizing Data** Use the equation above to determine the percentages for the waste categories that make up the total waste for your lab group. Divide the total waste for each category from the table on the previous page by the grand total and multiply by 100. Add another column to your data table to record these values.

3. **Examining Data** Compare your averages for the different categories and your total with other groups in the class. How and why are the data different or similar?

4. **Examining Data** Which category of waste makes up the greatest percentage of the total waste? Explain your answer.

Conclusions

5. **Making Predictions** How can you calculate the lunch waste produced in each category and overall by your entire school's student body in a day? Use your equation to make this calculation.

6. **Applying Conclusions** How can you use the knowledge you have acquired by doing this calculation exercise to reduce the amount of waste you produce?

Extension

1. **Research and Communications** Write a letter to the editor of your school newspaper, the editor of the local newspaper, or your school principal or cafeteria manager sharing the data your class has gathered and calculated. Offer creative solutions to eliminate and reduce some of the waste.

▶ **Step 4** Determine the mass of the waste produced in grams for each category of waste.

POINTS of view

SHOULD NUCLEAR WASTE BE STORED AT YUCCA MOUNTAIN?

Yucca Mountain, in Nevada, has been chosen as the location for the nation's first permanent storage site for nuclear waste. Nuclear fuel is used to generate electricity. Nuclear waste is created after nuclear fuel can no longer be used to generate electricity. This waste is called high-level radioactive waste. High-level radioactive waste includes solids, liquids, and gases that contain a high concentration of radioactive isotopes that take thousands of years to decay. The idea is to seal 77,000 tons of radioactive waste in steel canisters and store the canisters in underground tunnels designed to last 10,000 years. Yucca Mountain is scheduled to receive its first shipment of nuclear waste by 2010.

Construction of the facility has already begun. But the debate continues about whether it would be safer to store radioactive wastes at Yucca Mountain or to keep them where they are now—in temporary storage facilities at each nuclear power plant.

For the Yucca Mountain Site

Those who support construction of the facility point out that there are two major advantages to the plan. First, Yucca Mountain is located in a remote region that is far from large populations of people. Second, the climate is extremely dry. Yucca Mountain usually receives less than 20 cm of precipitation a year, most of which evaporates before it can soak into the ground. Therefore, this dry climate means that precipitation is unlikely to cause the water table to rise and come in contact

▶ Supporters of the Yucca Mountain storage facility think that this isolated spot in Nevada is a suitable place for permanent nuclear-waste disposal.

with the stored nuclear waste. Water is the primary way by which radioactive material could move from the storage facility.

Many opponents of the site worry that changes in the climate might cause the water table to rise. They say groundwater could then reach the stored nuclear waste and become contaminated. However, supporters of the site point to several scientific studies, which determined that no significant rise or fall of the water table has occurred in the past 100,000 years.

Operators of nuclear power plants are anxious for the Yucca Mountain facility to be completed. Currently, each power plant stores its nuclear waste near the plant. Many of these storage sites have been in use for decades and are approaching their maximum capacity.

Some people think that storing wastes in one location will be safer than storing them at the individual power plants. In addition, some of the nuclear waste containers are stored in pools of water rather than in surface or underground storage

areas. Some people fear that the hazardous wastes could leak into neighborhoods around the country.

Supporters of the Yucca Mountain storage facility think that this isolated location in Nevada is a suitable place for permanent nuclear-waste disposal.

Against the Yucca Mountain Site

Perhaps the fiercest outcry against the Yucca Mountain site comes from Nevada residents. They fear that if tons of highly toxic waste are stored in one place, some of it might eventually leak. Because some of this waste is so toxic that a tiny amount could be lethal, some people think a major environmental disaster could result if small quantities of waste reach the environment.

Some people are concerned that the radioactive waste might leak into the groundwater. The waste containers are expected to last 500 to 1,000 years, but they will have to remain isolated and not come into contact with water for 10,000 years. Opponents of the plan say

that nobody can guarantee that the containers will remain isolated for that long.

If radioactive waste leaked out of the facility, the waste could contaminate the water in wells, springs, and streams. In time, the contamination could spread from the site and into the environment.

Another worry is that transporting nuclear waste across vast distances to Yucca Mountain is riskier than leaving the material near the facilities where it is produced. Any accident along the way could release radioactivity into the environment.

Most opponents of the Yucca Mountain site agree that current methods of storing nuclear waste are dangerous and should be improved. They suggest that by transferring the waste to steel and concrete containers, the waste could be safely stored at each nuclear power facility for 75 to 100 years. By that time, they suggest, more will be known about how to store the wastes safely for thousands of years.

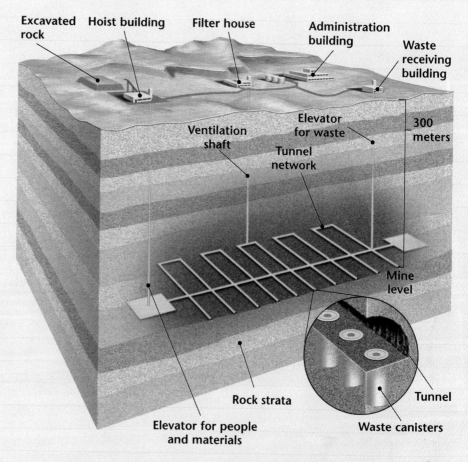

▶ The preliminary plan for the Yucca Mountain nuclear-waste storage facility shows radioactive materials carefully packaged and buried in tunnels deep underground.

▶ This map shows the nuclear power plants around the country that are possible sources of nuclear waste for the Yucca Mountain facility.

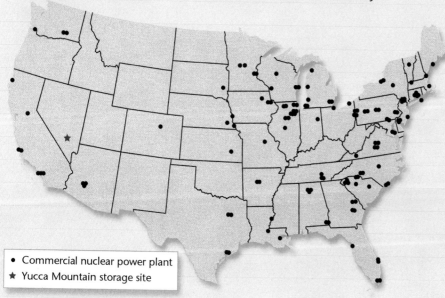

- Commercial nuclear power plant
- ★ Yucca Mountain storage site

What Do You Think?

There are over 100 nuclear power facilities in the United States. Using the Internet, research to find a nuclear power facility near your community. If there is not one near your community, how close is the nearest nuclear power facility? Is this facility still in operation? After researching, would you be for or against the Yucca Mountain site?

The casuarina tree is native to Australia and is one of the few pine trees that grow in nutrient-poor, sandy areas. This casuarina plantation on the coast of South Africa was established to hold sand dunes in place and to serve as a local source for wood fuel.

The Environment and Human Health

1 Pollution and Human Health

2 Biological Hazards

PRE-READING ACTIVITY

FOLDNOTES

Tri-Fold
Before you read this chapter, create the **FoldNote** entitled "Tri-Fold" described in the Reading and Study Skills section of the Appendix. Write what you know about environmental effects on human health in the column labeled "Know." Then, write what you want to know in the column labeled "Want." As you read the chapter, write what you learn about biodiversity in the column labeled "Learn."

This woman is washing a pot in a polluted river in Kathmandu, Nepal. Pollution is only one way the environment affects our health.

Pollution and Human Health

SCSh.2.b; SCSh.3.c; SCSh.3.e; SCSh.4.b;
SCSh.4.c; SCSh.6.a; SCSh.6.d; SEV.5.f

If you have ever coughed from breathing car exhaust, you have experienced a mild health effect of air pollution. Pollution of air, water, and soil is frequently in the news. Because people in the United States are so concerned about pollution, our country enjoys a relatively clean environment. But this situation is also due to the efforts of scientists who have studied the relationship between pollution and human health. Scientists are also beginning to understand the broader relationships between health and the environment.

Environmental Effects on Health

Pollution causes illnesses in two main ways. First, pollution may cause illnesses directly by poisoning, as in the cases of lead poisoning and lung cancer. Second, pollution may cause illnesses indirectly by infectious diseases that are spread in polluted environments. Examples of these diseases include cholera and river blindness, which are caused by organisms that inhabit polluted water.

The World Health Organization (WHO) has begun to collect data on how the environment affects human health. **Figure 1** shows the WHO's estimate of poor health by world region as a graph. Poor health is represented by the estimated number of days of healthy life that are lost to death and disease. The graph shows that, in general, people in developed countries suffer less from environmental causes of poor health. In developing countries, environmental causes of poor health are largely due to parasites and bacteria in polluted water and insect-borne diseases, such as malaria.

Objectives

▶ **List** five pollutants, their sources, and their possible effects on human health.

▶ **Explain** how scientists use toxicology and epidemiology.

▶ **Explain** how pollution can come from both natural sources and human activities.

▶ **Describe** the relationship between waste, pollution, and human health.

Key Terms

toxicology
dose
dose-response curve
epidemiology
risk assessment
particulates

Figure 1 ▶ This bar graph shows the environment's contribution to disease in different parts of the world.

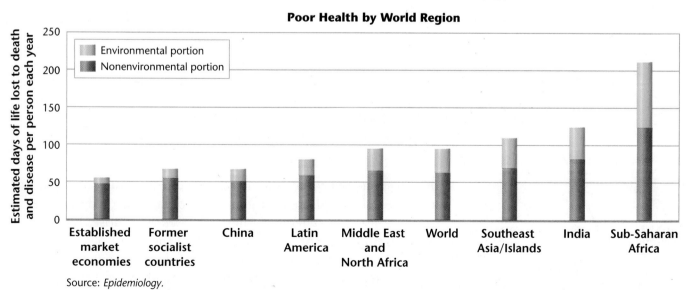

Poor Health by World Region

Estimated days of life lost to death and disease per person each year

- Environmental portion
- Nonenvironmental portion

Established market economies · Former socialist countries · China · Latin America · Middle East and North Africa · World · Southeast Asia/Islands · India · Sub-Saharan Africa

Source: *Epidemiology.*

Table 1 ▼

Types and Effects of Pollutants		
Pollutant	**Source**	**Possible effects**
Pesticides	use in agriculture and landscaping	nerve damage, birth defects, and cancer
Lead	lead paint and gasoline	brain damage and learning problems
Particulate matter	vehicle exhaust, burning waste, fires, and tobacco smoke	respiratory damage (asthma, bronchitis, cancer)
Coal dust	coal mining	black lung disease
Bacteria in food	poor sanitation and poor food handling	gastrointestinal infections

Toxicology

The word *toxic* means poisonous. **Toxicology** is the study of the harmful effects of substances on organisms. **Table 1** lists some important pollutants and their toxic effects.

Toxicity: How Dangerous Is It? We are exposed to small amounts of chemicals every day in food, in the air we breathe, and sometimes in the water we drink. Almost any chemical can be harmful if large enough amounts are taken in. The question is whether the concentration of any particular chemical in the environment is high enough to be harmful.

To determine the effect of a pollutant on health, we need to know how much of the pollutant is in the environment and how much gets into the body. Then we need to determine what concentration of the toxin damages the body. The amount of a harmful chemical to which a person is exposed is called the **dose** of that chemical. The damage to health that results from exposure to a given dose is called the *response.*

Whether a chemical has a toxic effect depends in part on the dose. The response also depends on the number of times a person is exposed, the person's size, and how well the person's body breaks down the chemical.

A *persistent chemical* is a chemical that breaks down slowly in the environment. The pesticide DDT is an example of a persistent chemical. Persistent chemicals are dangerous because more people are likely to come into contact with them, and these chemicals are more likely to remain in the body.

Dose-Response Curves The toxicity of a chemical can be expressed as a dose-response curve, as shown in **Figure 2**. A **dose-response curve** shows the relative effect of various doses of a drug or chemical on an organism or organisms as determined by experiments. Sometimes, there is a *threshold dose*. Exposure to any amount of the chemical less than the threshold dose has no adverse effect on health. Exposure to levels above the threshold dose usually leads to more or increased adverse effects.

Figure 2 ▶ A dose-response curve shows the response of an organism to different concentrations of a substance.

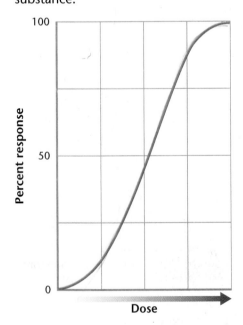

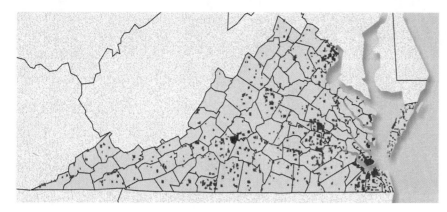

Source: Virginia Department of Health.

Figure 3 ▶ This map shows the location of cases of mercury poisoning in Virginia. Patterns point scientists toward areas of mercury pollution.

Epidemiology

When an epidemic occurs, such as a widespread flu infection, health officials use their knowledge of epidemiology to take action. **Epidemiology** (EP uh DEE mee AHL uh jee) is the study of the spread of diseases. Epidemiologists collect data from health workers on when and where cases of a disease have occurred. This information can be used to produce a map like the one in **Figure 3**.

Then scientists trace the disease to try to find its origin and how to prevent it from spreading. For example, in a case of mercury poisoning, health officials may ask questions such as: What did the people with mercury poisoning have in common? Were they all exposed to the same chemicals?

Risk Assessment In order to safeguard the public, health officials determine the risk posed by particular pollutants. Recall that risk is the probability of a negative outcome. In the case of human health, risk is the probability of suffering a disease, injury, or death.

Scientists and health officials work together on risk assessments for pollutants. A **risk assessment** is an estimate of the risk posed by an action or substance. During the process of risk assessment, scientists first compile and evaluate existing information on the substance. Then they determine how people might be exposed to it. **Figure 4** shows a diagram, created by a computer model, of how air pollutants might travel through a city area. The third step is determining the toxicity of the substance. Finally, scientists characterize the risk that the substance poses to the public. Risk assessments may lead to government regulations on how and where the substance can be used. In the United States, the Environmental Protection Agency (EPA) formulates these regulations.

Graphic Organizer **Spider Map** Create the **Graphic Organizer** entitled "Spider Map" described in the Appendix. Label the circle "Environmental Factors That Cause Disease." Create a leg for each type of environmental factor that causes disease. Then, fill in the map with details about each type of environmental factor that causes disease.

Figure 4 ▶ Air flow models like this one help scientists predict the path that air pollutants may follow through a city. The bright orange areas are receiving the most pollutants.

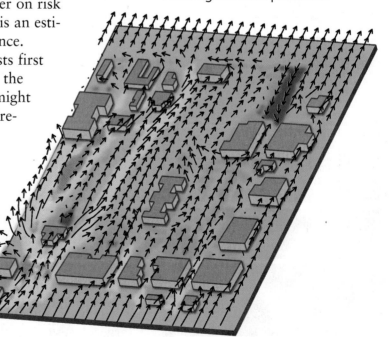

Figure 5 ▶ A dust storm descends upon Marrakesh, Morocco, in the photo above. Dust is perhaps the most common natural pollutant.

Figure 6 ▶ A town is coated with ash after the 1991 eruption of Mount Pinatubo, in the Philippines.

Pollution from Natural Sources

You may think of pollution as being entirely caused by people, but some pollutants occur naturally in the environment. Naturally occurring pollutants usually become hazardous to health when they are concentrated above their normal levels in the environment. One example is the radioactive gas radon. In some areas, radon from granite bedrock may seep into buildings, where it becomes concentrated. Because it is an odorless gas, people may unknowingly breathe it in. Radon causes an estimated 15,000 to 22,000 cancer deaths every year in the United States.

Particulates The most common pollutants from natural sources are dust, soot, and other particulates. **Particulates** (pahr TIK yoo lits) are particles in the air that are small enough to breathe into the lungs. These particles become trapped in the tiny air sacs in our lungs and cause irritation. This irritation can make lung conditions, such as chronic bronchitis and emphysema, worse. **Figure 5** shows particulate pollution from a dust storm, whereas **Figure 6** shows pollution from a volcanic eruption. Wildfires also produce large amounts of particulates.

Heavy Metals Another type of pollution from natural sources is caused by the so-called *heavy metals*. Dangerous heavy metals include the elements arsenic, cadmium, lead, and mercury. These metals occur naturally in rocks and soil. Most of these elements cause nerve damage when they are ingested beyond their threshold dose. Selenium, also found naturally in many soils, is actually a beneficial element when taken in very small quantities. But larger doses cause birth defects in birds and possibly humans.

Pollution from Human Activities

Human activities release thousands of types of chemicals into the environment, but we know surprisingly little about the health effects of most of them. Only about 10 percent of commercial chemicals have been tested for their toxicity, and about 1,000 new chemicals are introduced every year. **Figure 7** shows the introduction of pollutants into the environment by human activities.

Recent Improvements In the United States, regulations have helped reduce our exposure to pollutants. Most vehicles and factories now have pollution-control devices. As a result, people living in the United States contain lower levels of some toxic chemicals in their bodies, on average, than they did in the recent past. In 2001, 2003, and 2005, the U.S. Centers for Disease Control and Prevention (CDC) released studies on chemical residues in the U.S. population. Levels of nicotine (from smoking), mercury, and several other toxic chemicals were considerably lower in these peoples' tissues than they had been in 1991.

Because we know so little about the effects of chemicals on our health, new health risks are discovered frequently. For example, scientists now think that chemical pollution may be at least part of the cause of Parkinson's disease and Alzheimer's disease.

Burning Fuels Despite advances in public health resulting from pollution control, air pollution is still a major health problem. Burning fuels in vehicles, home furnaces, power plants, and factories introduces enormous amounts of pollutants into the air. These pollutants include the gas carbon monoxide and particulates. Gasoline and coal burning contribute to many premature deaths each year from asthma, heart disease, and lung disorders. A recent study found that long-term exposure to air contaminated with soot particles raises a person's risk of dying from lung and heart diseases.

✔ **Reading Check** Name a potential effect on human health of burning gasoline and coal. (See the Appendix for answers to Reading Checks.)

Figure 7 ▶ Human activities can pollute air and water. Paper mills contribute pollutants to rivers (above). Vehicle emissions cloud the air in urban areas worldwide (left).

MATHPRACTICE

Concentration Concentrations of chemicals in the environment are often expressed in parts per million (ppm) or parts per billion (ppb). One teaspoon of salt in two gallons of water produces a salt concentration of 1,000 ppm. What salt concentration, in ppm, would result from dissolving one teaspoon of salt in five gallons of water?

Pesticides *Pesticides* are chemicals designed to kill unwanted organisms such as insects, fungi, or weeds. Pesticides are beneficial in that they allow us to grow more food by reducing pest damage. Many of the increases in food production in the past 60 years are partly due to the development and use of more effective pesticides.

But because pesticides are designed to kill organisms, they are often dangerous to humans in large enough doses. Although we are exposed to pesticide residues on fruits and vegetables, the amounts consumed by most people pose little danger.

Most modern pesticides, such as most of those used in the United States, break down quickly in the environment into harmless substances. Widely used *organophosphate* pesticides have replaced more persistent pesticides, such as DDT. But organophosphates are very toxic, causing nerve damage and perhaps cancer. In 2004, U.S. poison centers reported nearly 7,200 cases of organophosphate poisoning. Most cases of pesticide poisoning affect the people applying the chemicals.

Persistent chemicals are still used in many developing countries. Such pesticides pose the greatest risk to children, whose internal organs are still developing and who eat and drink more in relation to their body weight than adults do.

CASE STUDY

Chemicals That Disrupt Hormones

In recent years, scientists have collected evidence that many pollutants disrupt the endocrine system. The glands that make up the human endocrine system produce hormones. *Hormones* are chemicals that circulate in the bloodstream and control many life processes, such as the development of muscles and sex organs.

Some pollutants, called *hormone mimics,* behave like natural hormones. Other pollutants are *hormone disrupters,* which prevent natural hormones from functioning normally. Even low levels of these kinds of pollutants can affect developing embryos and infants.

Hormone mimics were first discovered in fish in Europe. Researchers in England and France found that male trout and eels downstream from sewage treatment plants contained egg-yolk proteins usually produced only by females. Lab experiments showed that the water contained estrogen-like chemicals and that these chemicals induced the male fish to make proteins usually produced only by females. The chemicals are believed to have come from detergents and from the urine of women taking contraceptive pills.

Most hormone disrupters interfere with the sex hormones. They prevent normal production of testosterone in males or increase the chances of sexual abnormality in females. Examples of hormone disrupters include phthalates, which are widely used in cosmetics, such as hair dyes and fingernail polish. Polychlorinated biphenyls (PCBs),

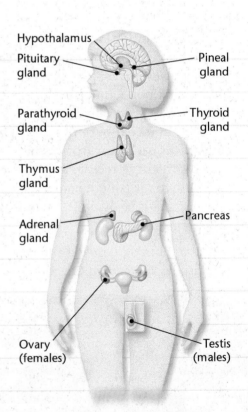

▶ The diagram above shows the major organs and glands of the human endocrine system.

Industrial Chemicals Railroad tankers carrying industrial solvents overturned near Rochester, New York, in 2001. Two solvents reacted to cause a fire that destroyed several houses. Several people were treated for breathing the fumes.

We are exposed to low levels of industrial chemicals every day, particularly inside new buildings that have new furnishings. Toxic chemicals are used to make building materials, carpets, cleaning fluids, and furniture. Older buildings, like the one shown in **Figure 8,** were often painted using lead-based paint. Lead is directly linked to brain damage and learning disabilities.

Often, industrial chemicals are not known to be toxic until they have been used for many years. For example, polychlorinated biphenyls (PCBs) are oily fluids that have been used for years as insulation in electrical transformers. PCBs break down very slowly in the environment. In 1996, studies showed that children exposed to PCBs in the womb can develop learning problems and IQ deficits. The waters of the Great Lakes are polluted by PCBs, and doctors warn pregnant women not to eat certain fish from these lakes. Studies have shown that adults with high concentrations of PCBs in their tissues have more memory problems than adults who do not.

Figure 8 ▶ Lead poisoning in children is most often due to direct exposure to lead-based paint.

▶ The fertility of American alligators, such as this one, has been reduced by their exposure to hormone disrupting pollutants.

some pesticides, lead, and mercury may also act as hormone disrupters.

Many cases of pollution by hormone disrupters have now been found in the United States. For example, alligators in a Florida lake that was polluted with local hazardous waste had such abnormally small penises and low testosterone levels that they could not reproduce. In 2002, scientists reported that even small amounts of the widely used herbicide atrazine disrupt the sexual development of frogs.

During the past 50 years, there has been a large increase in cancers of the prostate, testicles, ovaries, and breasts in most industrialized countries. All of these forms of cancer can be accelerated by abnormal levels of sex hormones. A recent analysis of sperm counts among men in industrialized countries shows that sperm counts have fallen by 50 percent in the last 50 years.

Scientists do not yet have concrete evidence that hormone disrupters in the environment are actually causing these human health problems. Research into this issue has accelerated since an international conference on hormone disrupters was held in 1996.

CRITICAL THINKING

1. Reading Comprehension Explain the difference between hormone mimics and hormone disrupters.

2. Analyzing Relationships If humans are increasingly exposed to these pollutants, what are some possible results?

Figure 9 ▶ Waste that is not disposed of properly can pollute beaches, where it can pose a threat to swimmers and sunbathers.

SCI **LINKS**
www.scilinks.org
Topic: Toxic Waste
Code: HE81540

Waste Disposal Much of the pollution in our environment is a byproduct of inadequate waste disposal. **Figure 9** shows the pollution of a beach with solid waste. Wastewater from cities can carry oil and dozens of toxic chemicals into our waterways. Waste incineration plants can emit toxic products into the air, and mining can release toxic contaminants into streams and rivers.

Methods of disposing of waste have improved. However, problems remain. Many old landfills are leaking. And many communities still have sewage treatment plants that release raw sewage into a river or the ocean after heavy rains. In addition, laws regulating waste disposal are not always enforced.

The United States government has not decided how it will dispose of radioactive waste from nuclear power plants. Meanwhile, the waste remains in barrels at or near the plants, and small quantities of radioactive iodine, cesium, and other elements leak into nearby waterways.

✔ **Reading Check** What are two examples of pollution related to inadequate waste disposal?

SECTION 1 Review

1. **List** five pollutants, their sources, and their possible effects on human health.

2. **Explain** how pollution can arise from both natural sources and from human activities.

3. **Describe** the relationship between waste, pollution, and human health.

CRITICAL THINKING

4. **Making Comparisons** Write a short paragraph that explains the relationship between toxicology and epidemiology. **WRITING SKILLS**

5. **Analyzing Relationships** In what ways do human activities increase the health risks from natural pollutants?

SECTION 2
Biological Hazards

Some of the damage to human health in which the environment plays a role is not caused by toxic chemicals but by organisms that carry disease. Today, we have outbreaks of diseases that did not exist or that few people had heard of 100 years ago, such as AIDS, Ebola, West Nile virus, hantavirus, and mad cow disease. In addition, diseases that have killed people for centuries, such as malaria, tuberculosis, yellow fever, and hookworm, kill many more people today than they did 50 years ago. All these diseases are caused by organisms. One of the reasons these diseases are now widespread is that we have altered our environment in ways that encourage them to spread.

The Environment's Role in Disease

Infectious diseases are caused by **pathogens,** organisms that cause disease. Some of these diseases, such as tuberculosis and whooping cough, are spread from person to person through the air. Other diseases are spread by drinking water that contains the pathogen. Still other diseases are transmitted by a secondary host, such as a mosquito. A **host** is an organism in which a pathogen lives all or part of its life. **Table 2** lists the most deadly infectious diseases worldwide.

Objectives

▶ Explain why the environment is an important factor in the spread of cholera.

▶ List two changes to the environment that can lead to the spread of infectious diseases.

▶ Explain what scientists mean when they say that certain viruses are emerging.

Key Terms

pathogen
host
vector

Table 2 ▼

Deaths from Diseases in 2000, Estimated by the World Health Organization		
Disease and examples	Cause	Estimated deaths per year (in millions)
Total infectious and parasitic diseases	bacteria, viruses, and parasites	10.5
Respiratory infections (pneumonia, influenza, and whooping cough)	bacteria, viruses	4.0
AIDS	virus	2.9
Diarrheal diseases (cholera, typhus, typhoid, and dysentery)	bacteria, viruses, parasites	2.1
Tuberculosis	bacteria	1.7
Childhood diseases (measles and diphtheria)	virus	1.5
Malaria	parasitic protist	1.1
Tetanus	bacteria	0.3
Tropical diseases (trypanosomiasis, Chagas' disease, schistosomiasis, and leishmaniasis)	bacteria, viruses, and parasites	0.1

QuickLAB

Simulating an Epidemic

Procedure

1. Obtain one **test tube** of **water** from your teacher. Your teacher has "contaminated" one of the test tubes with an invisible substance.

2. Pour half your water into the test tube of a classmate. Your classmate will then pour an equal amount back into your test tube. Exchange water with three classmates in this way.

3. Your teacher will now put a small amount of a **test chemical** into your test tube. If your water turns cloudy, you have been "contaminated."

Analysis

1. Who had the test tube that started the "infection"?

2. Name a disease that could be spread in this way. Explain your answer.

Waterborne Disease

Nearly three-fourths of infectious diseases are transmitted through water. In developing countries, where there is not enough water for basic needs, the local water supply is often used for drinking, washing, and sewage disposal. So, the water is usually very polluted and is a good breeding ground for pathogens. The pathogens breed in water and transfer diseases directly to humans through water, or organisms that carry the pathogens transfer them to humans through the water. Organisms, such as mosquitoes, that transmit diseases to people are called **vectors.** The construction of irrigation canals and dams, particularly in the tropics, has increased the habitat for vectors. For example, the Three Gorges Dam in China has created a huge freshwater lake. This lake is the habitat of the snail vector for schistosomiasis, an incurable disease that has become more common in the area since the dam was finished.

Cholera The deadliest waterborne diseases come from drinking water polluted by human feces. Pathogens, such as those that cause *cholera* and *dysentery*, enter the water in human feces. These diseases cause the body to lose water by diarrhea and vomiting. **Figure 10** shows a child being treated for dehydration. Cholera and dysentery cause most infant deaths around the world.

Malaria Another waterborne disease called *malaria* was once the world's leading cause of death. The disease is caused by parasitic protists and is transmitted by a bite from females of many species of mosquitoes. The mosquito vector lays her eggs in stagnant fresh water, which is where the mosquito larva develops. No effective vaccine for malaria exists, but preventative measures are used to control mosquitoes.

✓ **Reading Check** Why are local water supplies in developing countries often polluted?

Figure 10 ▶ This child is undergoing rehydration therapy during a cholera epidemic in South Africa.

Environmental Change and Disease

Many ways in which we alter the environment make the environment more suitable for pathogens to live and reproduce. For example, soil is often polluted with chemicals and pathogens. When soil erodes, these pollutants blow away and wash away with the soil and may contaminate areas thousands of miles away. Many parasites are spread through soil that is contaminated with feces. Hookworm, which causes acute exhaustion, was once common in the United States. People are infected by walking barefoot on soil that contains human and animal feces or by consuming contaminated food or water. **Figure 11** shows soil erosion in Nepal. In 1984, 87 percent of the population was found to be infected by parasitic worms. The high number of infections was most likely due to increased contaminated soil exposure caused by widespread erosion.

Figure 11 ▶ Soil erosion in Nepal (top) leads to the spread of parasites such as the hookworm (bottom).

Antibiotic Resistance Our actions cause pathogens to evolve resistance to antibiotics that are used to kill them. For example, in the United States, large quantities of antibiotics are fed to livestock each year to speed their growth. As a result, *Salmonella, Escherichia coli* (*E. coli*), and other bacteria that live in livestock evolve resistance to antibiotics. These bacteria now make thousands of U.S. citizens sick each year when they eat contaminated meat that has been improperly refrigerated or undercooked.

We also use enormous amounts of antibiotics to treat human illnesses. In 1979, 6 percent of European strains of pneumonia bacteria were resistant to antibiotics. Ten years later, 44 percent of the strains were resistant. Tuberculosis (TB) is another illness treated with antibiotics. The spread of TB in recent years is mostly due to the evolution of antibiotic resistance in the bacterium that causes TB.

Ecofact

Suburbs Spread Lyme Disease
Lyme disease is the most widespread vector-borne disease in the United States. It is caused by a bacterium similar to the one that causes the sexually transmitted disease syphilis. The vector is a tick found on white-tailed deer. The suburbs are a suitable place for deer to grow and reproduce, and their populations have exploded as suburbs have expanded. Lyme disease infects more than 13,000 people a year in the United States.

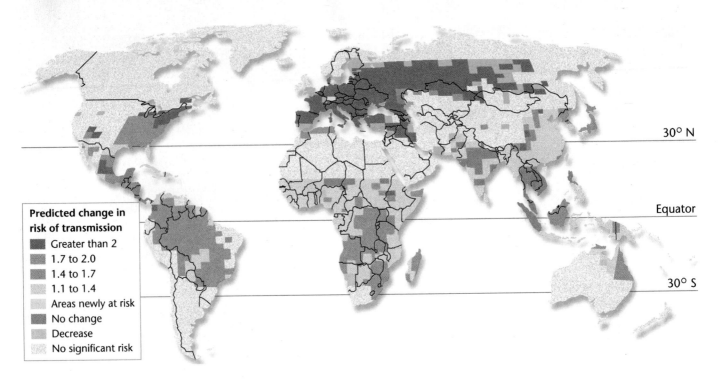

Predicted change in risk of transmission
- Greater than 2
- 1.7 to 2.0
- 1.4 to 1.7
- 1.1 to 1.4
- Areas newly at risk
- No change
- Decrease
- No significant risk

30° N

Equator

30° S

Figure 12 ▶ This computer model shows how malaria might spread under specific global warming conditions.

www.scilinks.org
Topic: Emerging Viruses
Code: HE80499

Malaria on the March Insects that breed in water are the secondary hosts that transmit malaria. The mosquitoes that transmit malaria are found in the warmer parts of the world. Epidemiologists believe that global warming may increase the areas where malaria occurs. **Figure 12** shows that malaria might spread across large areas of Central America, South America, Africa, and Asia.

Malaria was common in much of the United States and Europe before the days of mosquito control. Now, it is most common in tropical countries. Historically, malaria was controlled by draining marshes and rice paddies where the mosquitoes breed and by spraying with pesticides. Since the 1970s, however, mosquitoes have evolved resistance to most of the pesticides. Newer methods for controlling mosquitoes involve spreading growth regulators that prevent mosquito larvae from maturing into adults or that sterilize the female mosquitoes.

Emerging Viruses In recent years, medical scientists have been focusing on so-called emerging viruses that were unknown 100 years ago. One example is AIDS (acquired immune deficiency syndrome), which is caused by HIV (human immune deficiency virus). Most viral diseases spread directly from one person to another. Often, the virus invades the body through a cut or through mucus membranes. We do not have many effective drugs to treat viral diseases, and the drugs that we have are only effective against specific viruses. Our main defense against viral diseases is vaccination. The problem with vaccines is that they are very specific, and viruses evolve rapidly. When a new strain of a viral pathogen evolves, a new vaccine must be developed.

Reading Check Why was it necessary to develop new methods for controlling mosquitoes that transmit malaria?

Cross-Species Transfers In recent years, scientists have discovered an increasing number of pathogens that have made a *cross-species transfer,* or have moved from one species to another. For example, HIV and West Nile virus fall into this category. The pathogens that cause these diseases have lived for centuries in some species of wild animals and have done little damage. When the pathogens invade humans, the pathogens cause serious diseases. Some ecologists think that the ways in which we are altering the environment and destroying habitats ensure that diseases like these will become more common in the future.

Examples of Cross-Species Transfers One example of pathogens that made a cross-species transfer occurred in Argentina. Herbicides were sprayed on crops in Argentina. The herbicide killed the native grasses and allowed other plants to invade the farmland. These new plants attracted a species of rodent that feeds on them. The rodents were carrying viruses for a hemorrhagic fever, which infected many of the agricultural workers. Hemorrhagic fevers cause hemorrhages, or internal bleeding, by breaking blood vessels. Hantavirus is an example of a virus that causes hemorrhagic fever.

Influenza, or flu, is highly contagious. The flu virus passes from humans to animals (particularly birds) and back to humans again. Hong Kong flu gets its name from the fact that the virus was transmitted to humans from ducks bred in Hong Kong for food. **Figure 13** shows a poultry market, where the Hong Kong flu virus probably transferred from birds to people. Because flu is so easily spread from one person to another, epidemiologists predict that the greatest threat to human health may be the outbreak of a new, very virulent strain of influenza virus, which would spread rapidly through crowded urban populations.

Figure 13 ▶ Poultry markets, such as this one in Hong Kong, can contribute to the cross-species transfer of viruses from birds to humans.

SECTION 2 **Review**

1. **List** two changes to the environment that can lead to the spread of infectious diseases.
2. **Explain** why some diseases are likely to spread as a result of global warming.
3. **Explain** why the environment is an important factor in the spread of cholera.
4. **Explain** the term *emerging virus.*

CRITICAL THINKING

5. **Understanding Concepts** Read the information under the heading "Antibiotic Resistance." How is the use of antibiotics by humans increasing antibiotic resistance in pathogens? **READING SKILLS**

6. **Analyzing Relationships** How do human activities cause pathogens to move from one species to another? Give examples of cross-species transfer to help explain your answer.

1 Pollution and Human Health

Key Terms

toxicology, 550
dose, 550
dose-response curve, 550
epidemiology, 551
risk assessment, 551
particulates, 552

Main Ideas

▶ Toxic chemicals from both natural sources and human activities that pollute air, soil, water, and food may damage human health.

▶ Toxicology is used to determine how poisonous a substance is.

▶ After an outbreak of illness occurs, epidemiologists attempt to find its origin and try to find ways to prevent future epidemics.

▶ Most pollutants come from human activities, but some pollutants occur naturally.

▶ Improperly disposed of wastes may leak hazardous pollutants into the environment.

2 Biological Hazards

pathogen, 557
host, 557
vector, 558

▶ Most human diseases that have an environmental component are caused by pathogens.

▶ The environment provides breeding grounds for pathogens and for their secondary hosts and vectors.

▶ The transmission of many diseases involves water. We increase the areas where organisms that carry these diseases can reproduce when we create irrigation canals and inadequate sewage systems.

▶ Environmental changes that help spread infectious diseases include global warming and expanding suburbs and farmland.

▶ Many emerging diseases are caused by pathogens that have made cross-species transfers from animals to humans.

Using Key Terms

Use each of the following terms in a separate sentence.

1. *dose*
2. *vector*
3. *risk assessment*
4. *particulates*
5. *epidemiology*

For each pair of terms, explain how the meanings of the terms differ.

6. *pathogen* and *host*
7. *response* and *dose*
8. *toxicology* and *epidemiology*

✔ **STUDY TIP**

Vocabulary Practice To practice vocabulary, write the terms and definitions on a piece of paper and fold the paper lengthwise so that the definitions are covered. First, see how many definitions you already know. Then, write the definitions you don't know on another piece of paper, and practice again until you know all of them.

Understanding Key Ideas

9. Which of the following is *not* a true statement about the effects of pollution on health?
   a. It is difficult to determine how pollution affects health because many factors often contribute to a disease.
   b. The toxic effects of a pollutant depend upon the dose to which you are exposed.
   c. Many pollutants cause chronic diseases that result from exposure to the pollutant over the course of many years.
   d. Persistent chemicals are less toxic than chemicals that break down rapidly.

10. Which of the following is an emerging disease that was unknown 50 years ago?
    a. malaria
    b. dengue fever
    c. Lyme disease
    d. schistosomiasis

11. Cholera is usually transmitted from person to person by water because
    a. it is caused by a snail that breeds in water.
    b. it is usually contracted by someone drinking water polluted with human feces that contain the cholera pathogen.
    c. it is transmitted by mosquitoes.
    d. it is caused by a virus.

12. Tuberculosis (TB), which was once almost eradicated, is becoming more common, even in developed countries, because
    a. new varieties of the tuberculosis pathogen have evolved in rodents.
    b. livestock are given antibiotics.
    c. the pathogen that causes TB breeds in polluted water.
    d. some populations of the pathogen that causes TB are resistant to antibiotics.

13. Which of the following statements about environmental pollutants is true?
    a. Our environment contains fewer toxic chemicals than it did 50 years ago.
    b. Hormone mimics in our water supply pose no danger to humans
    c. There is no health risk from pollutants in indoor air.
    d. The bodies of people who live in the United States contain lower levels of some toxic chemicals than they did 20 years ago.

14. Which of the following actions is most likely to prevent yellow fever, which is transmitted by mosquitoes, from becoming epidemic?
    a. preventing dehydration in patients by treating them with oral rehydration therapy
    b. taking antibiotics
    c. encouraging people to empty water out of old cans, tires, plant saucers, and other areas that contain standing water
    d. spraying the area repeatedly with pesticides

Short Answer

15. How do scientists determine the toxicity of a chemical?

16. How can land use change contribute to the spread of infectious disease?

17. What role does the environment play in the transmission of infectious diseases?

18. Why would lung disease be more common in a large urban area than in a remote rural area?

Interpreting Graphics

The graph below shows the dose-response curves for two chemicals. Use the graph to answer questions 19–21.

19. Which chemical is more toxic at a lower dose?

20. Which chemical is more toxic at a very large dose?

21. Can you tell from the graph which chemical is more likely to be a problem if it persists in the environment?

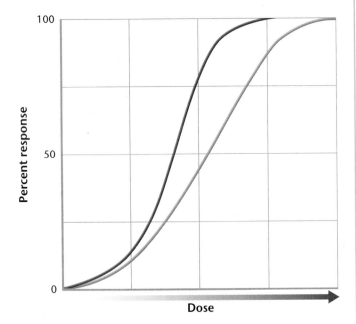

Concept Mapping

22. Use the following terms to create a concept map: *habitat destruction, pathogen, animal, vector,* and *human disease.*

Critical Thinking

23. Making Comparisons In what ways does a disease such as lung cancer, which is caused by breathing pollutants over a long period of time, differ from a disease such as malaria, which is caused by a pathogen?

Cross-Disciplinary Connection

24. History In 1775, Percival Pott noted that chimney sweeps had a high rate of cancer of the scrotum. What further investigations might be performed to find out what occupational hazard might be causing the cancer? How many of these would have been possible at the time, and how many require modern technology?

25. Economics Write a proposal to reduce the mosquito population of an area. How might you encourage the public to assist in this effort? **WRITING SKILLS**

26. Biology Read about mosquitoes under the heading "Malaria." How would you design an irrigation system to minimize the chances that mosquitoes would breed in it? **READING SKILLS**

Portfolio Project

27. Collect half a dozen pesticide containers that still have their labels. Make a table that has three columns. List the names of the pesticides in one column. Then read the label on each container. Use this information to decide which pesticide is the most dangerous and which pesticide is the least dangerous. In the second column, label the pesticides as most to least dangerous. In the third column, list the most important safety precautions required of anyone who uses the pesticides. **CAUTION:** Do not get pesticides on your face, and wash your hands thoroughly after handling the pesticide cans.

MATH SKILLS

The table below shows four diseases and the number of cases of each disease that were reported to the United States Centers for Disease Control in 1990 and 1998. Use the table below to answer questions 28–29.

Disease	1990	1998
Cryptosporidiosis	2	3,793
Lyme disease	2	16,801
Malaria	1,292	1,611
Typhoid fever	552	375

28. **Analyzing Data** Malaria cases increased between 1990 and 1998. What other facts would you want to know before deciding that the United States has a growing malaria problem?

29. **Making Calculations** By what percentage did the number of typhoid fever cases decline between 1990 and 1998?

WRITING SKILLS

30. **Communicating Main Ideas** Why do sewage systems that overflow when it rains need to be replaced with modern systems that do not overflow?

31. **Writing Persuasively** Write a letter to a newspaper. In the letter, argue either for or against homeowners' use of pesticides on their lawns and gardens.

READING SKILLS

Read the passage below, and then answer the questions that follow.

Dehydration is a serious threat to human survival—as dangerous as a high fever. However, as any athlete knows, drinking water alone is often not an adequate cure for dehydration. Sports drinks contain sugar and electrolytes (minerals) as well as water. This principle also underlies oral rehydration therapy, which is used to treat people suffering from diseases such as cholera and dysentery. These diseases cause water loss from diarrhea and vomiting. Severe dehydration often causes death, particularly in small children. Patients being treated for dehydration are fed a solution of salt, sugar, and water. The sugar and salt help the body absorb the water from the stomach. Sugar and salt also add electrolytes to the body fluids so that the fluids are not diluted. Millions of lives have been saved by rehydration therapy.

1. According to the passage, which of the following statements about oral rehydration therapy is *not* true?
   a. A solution containing sugars and salts is absorbed by the stomach more rapidly than water alone.
   b. The salts replace electrolytes in the bloodstream so that the blood is not diluted by the water.
   c. Any source of water is adequate to make up the solution of salts and sugar.
   d. Millions of lives have been saved by oral rehydration therapy.

2. According to the passage, which of the following statements about dehydration is *not* true?
   a. It may be fatal.
   b. It is especially dangerous to small children.
   c. It may be caused by diarrhea and vomiting from diseases such as cholera.
   d. It is not often caused by exercising on a hot day without drinking.

Standardized Test Prep

Understanding Concepts

Directions (1–4): For *each* question, write on a separate sheet of paper the letter of the correct answer.

1 Which of the following is a naturally occurring pollutant?
  A. pesticides
  B. radon
  C. sewage
  D. vectors

2 What is the study of the spread of disease called?
  F. antibiology
  G. epidemiology
  H. pathogenology
  I. toxicology

3 What is the difference between pollution from natural sources and pollution from human activities?
  A. Naturally occurring pollutants are less toxic.
  B. Pollution from human activities has not been researched.
  C. Pollution from human activities can be predicted and controlled.
  D. Naturally occurring pollutants are only hazardous in small dosages.

4 How has the construction of irrigation canals and dams enabled the spread of infectious disease?
  F. The construction allows viruses to evolve.
  G. Canals and dams provide sites for waste disposal.
  H. Canals and dams provide increased habitats for vectors.
  I. The construction eliminates the natural predators of pathogens.

Directions (5–6): For *each* question, write a short response.

5 Analyze how communal water sources transmit pollution and disease when residents use them for drinking, bathing, and sewage disposal.

6 Identify how naturally-occuring heavy metals can act as pollutants.

Reading Skills

Directions (7–9): Read the passage below. Then, answer the questions.

Some of the damage to human health in which the environment plays a role is not caused by toxic chemicals but by organisms that carry disease. Today we have outbreaks of diseases that did not exist one hundred years ago. And diseases that have killed people for centuries are killing as many or more people today. One of the reasons these diseases are now widespread is that we have altered our environment in ways that encourage their spread.

In recent years, scientists have discovered an increasing number of pathogens that have made a cross-species transfer, or have moved from one species to another. When the pathogens invade humans, the pathogens cause serious disease. One example of cross-species transfer occurred in Argentina. Herbicides were sprayed on crops in Argentina. The herbicides killed the native grasses and allowed other plants to invade the farmland. These new plants attracted a species of rodent that feeds on them. The rodents were carrying viruses for a hemorrhagic fever, which infected many of the agricultural workers.

7 A cross-species transfer involves
  A. pathogens moving from one species to another
  B. one species infecting a pathogen
  C. rodents feeding on otherwise healthy plants
  D. pathogens that infect native grasses

8 Describe the relationship between cross-species transfers and environmental change.

9 Herbicides were used in Argentina likely
  F. because invading species were taking over native grasses.
  G. to prevent weeds from growing among crops.
  H. because poisonous plants were endangering local people.
  I. to keep rodent populations under control.

Interpreting Graphics

Directions (10–13): **For *each* question below, record the correct answer on a separate sheet of paper.**

The graph below shows the environment's contribution to poor health in different regions of the world. Use the graph to answer questions 10 and 11.

Poor Health by World Region

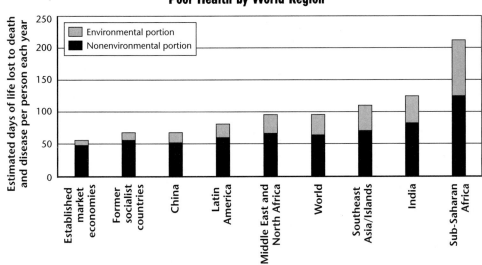

10 In which of these regions are nonenvironmental causes of poor health the largest percentage of the total?
A. China
B. India
C. Latin America
D. Sub-Saharan Africa

11 In which of these regions are nonenvironmental causes of poor health the smallest percentage of the total?
F. China
G. India
H. Latin America
I. Sub-Saharan Africa

12 What is the main factor in the poor health of developing countries?
A. too few doctors
B. infectious disease
C. industrial pollution
D. more imports than exports

13 The average person in the world will lose 95 days a year to death and disease. In years, approximately how much time will be lost to death and disease by the average person after 20 years?
F. 3
G. 5
H. 7
I. 9

Test TIP

When making comparisons from a graph, analyze each component separately, comparing the fraction to the total for each component. Then compare the components to each other.

Objectives

▶ **USING SCIENTIFIC METHODS** **Analyze** the relationship between lead poisoning and children's IQ.

▶ **Graph** experimental data.

▶ **Interpret** graphical data.

Materials

notebook
pen or pencil

▶ **Effects of Lead** Lead smelters, such as the one below in former Yugoslavia, can cause air pollution and lead poisoning.

Lead Poisoning and Mental Ability

People are usually exposed to lead in old buildings that were painted with lead paint. The lead can enter the body in dust that is breathed in and can permanently damage the brain and nervous system. Lead poisoning can cause aggressive behavior, hyperactivity, headaches, and hearing loss. At high levels, it can cause seizures, coma, and even death. The Centers for Disease Control and Prevention (CDC) state that a lead level of only 10 micrograms per deciliter in the blood can be harmful. (A microgram is one-millionth of a gram, and a deciliter is one-tenth of a liter.) In this lab, you will explore the effect of lead poisoning on the mental ability of children. The children all grew up near a lead smelter, a factory where raw lead ore is processed. Scientists measured the concentration of lead in the children's blood over time. Psychologists also performed tests on the children to determine their IQ. You will analyze the data to see if you can find a pattern.

Procedure

1. Design a hypothesis for the relationship between the lead concentration in the blood, the IQs, and the ages of the children. As the blood-lead concentration increases, how would you expect the person's IQ to change? How do you think this relationship would change as the children grow older?

2. The table on the next page lists the blood-lead concentration and IQ data for a group of 494 children. The children were measured five times as they grew up. The first measurement was made when they were six months old, and the last measurement was made when they were seven years old. The children were divided into four groups according to the amount of lead in their blood. Group 1 had the lowest concentration of lead, and group 4 had the highest concentration of lead. Prepare a graph for the data in the table. Plot lead concentration on the *x*-axis and IQ on the *y*-axis. Label each axis with the correct units. Choose an appropriate scale for each axis so that the entire range of data in the table will fit on the graph.

3. Plot the data from the table on your graph. Connect all data points for each age group with a single line. You should have five lines of data on your graph.

Group of children		Average blood-lead concentration (micrograms per deciliter)	Average IQ score
6 mo	1	8.3	109.4
	2	12.6	104.7
	3	16.8	102.9
	4	24.2	100.0
15 mo	1	11.8	109.3
	2	18.6	106.5
	3	24.4	102.9
	4	34.4	101.3
3 yr	1	11.6	110.2
	2	17.4	106.5
	3	22.4	102.2
	4	30.2	100.0
5 yr	1	8.3	109.3
	2	12.6	106.1
	3	17.2	104.1
	4	23.6	98.8
7 yr	1	6.6	109.6
	2	10.1	107.7
	3	13.7	102.7
	4	20.0	98.7

▶ **Lead Paint** Dust from lead paint peelings can cause lead poisoning.

Analysis

1. **Analyzing Data** For a single age group, how does IQ vary with lead concentration? Is this true for all age groups?

2. **Analyzing Data** How does the relationship between lead concentration and IQ change as a child grows older?

Conclusions

3. **Drawing Conclusions** What conclusions can you draw from your analysis about the effect of lead on IQ?

4. **Applying Conclusions** Based on your conclusions, what long-term effects might lead poisoning have on a community?

Extension

1. **Analyzing a Viewpoint** Based on the data presented in this lab, do you think the CDC's limit of 10 micrograms per deciliter is reasonable? Explain your answer.

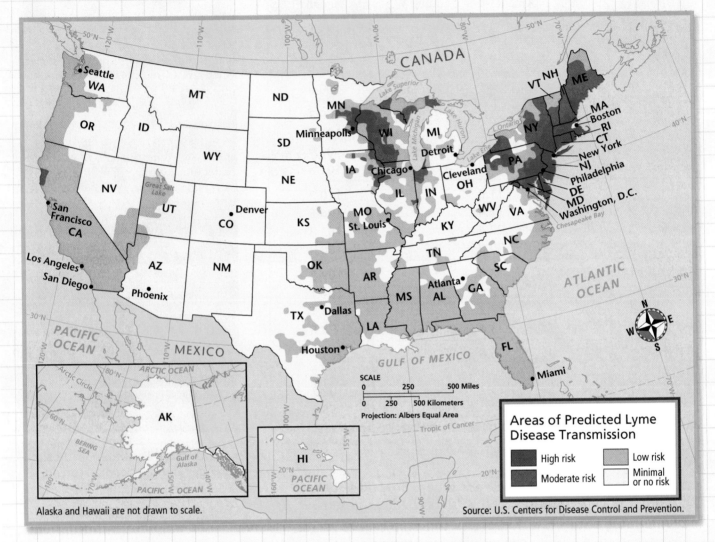

MAPS in action

LYME DISEASE RISK

Areas of Predicted Lyme Disease Transmission

- High risk
- Moderate risk
- Low risk
- Minimal or no risk

SCALE

| 0 | 250 | 500 Miles |

| 0 | 250 | 500 Kilometers |

Projection: Albers Equal Area

Alaska and Hawaii are not drawn to scale.

Source: U.S. Centers for Disease Control and Prevention.

▶ The map above shows the risk of contracting Lyme disease by geographic location in the United States.

MAP SKILLS

Use the Lyme disease risk map for the United States to answer the questions below.

1. **Using a Key** Using the map above, determine the risk of contracting Lyme disease in your city or town.

2. **Using a Key** In what general region of the United States is the risk of contracting Lyme disease greatest?

3. **Analyzing Relationships** Can you determine the relationship between the risk of contracting Lyme

disease and the concentration of ticks that act as vectors for the disease? Explain your answer.

4. **Analyzing Data** What is the difference between the risk of contracting Lyme disease in rural Massachussetts and the risk of contracting Lyme disease in rural Nevada?

5. **Forming a Hypothesis** What factors might account for the relatively high risk of contracting Lyme disease in the Northeast?

TOXIC MOLD

You may have seen stories in the news with titles such as "Mold Closes Schools" or "Homes Infested with Toxic Mold." In the past 10 years, news stories have reported on school evacuations, strange illnesses, and multimillion dollar lawsuits, all due to mold. What is toxic mold, and why is it a problem?

"Toxic mold" is a popular term for molds that grow indoors and are suspected of making people who are exposed to them sick.

▶ The mold pictured below, *Stachybotrys,* is commonly implicated in toxic building cases.

Recall that molds are fungi and are found almost everywhere on Earth. In buildings, molds tend to grow on damp surfaces, especially damp wood, where they appear as a black or dark green fuzzy layer.

Are Molds Toxic?

Some species of mold produce toxins that they use mainly to compete with other molds. These toxins can also harm people. The toxins become airborne attached to spores, the mold's reproductive particles, or on tiny mold fragments. Once the toxins are airborne, people can breathe them in.

The most commonly mentioned toxic mold is *Stachybotrys chartarum.* This mold produces several potent toxins that affect the immune system and cause hemorrhaging in toxicology tests on mice.

People handling material contaminated with *Stachybotrys* report coughing and burning sensations of

▶ This health worker is spraying portions of a house infested with mold that may be toxic.

the throat and nose. Some people have also reported memory loss and bleeding in the lungs. But scientists have not found a firm link between indoor mold and these more serious health problems.

Molds and Buildings

Molds are especially common in areas with high rainfall. If wood or paper stays damp for any length of time, odds are that mold spores will land on it and begin to grow.

Most of the problems with indoor mold occur in areas between walls or in other rarely seen places. The solution is to fix leaks as soon as possible and improve air circulation so that damp areas dry out.

Scientific Uncertainty

There are only a small number of well-studied cases of toxic mold poisoning, and even in these there exists the possibility of other causes for the illnesses. Scientists see toxic mold as an example of the difficulty of linking environmental exposure with human health. "You can't prove causation from epidemiological studies," notes one doctor. "All you can do is show that there is a correlation."

What Do You Think?

School districts and homeowners have spent millions of dollars replacing moldy parts of buildings. But in many cases the mold had not caused health problems. Should the government require schools and homeowners to repair moldy buildings? Who should pay for it?

Economics, Policy, and the Future

PRE-READING ACTIVITY

FOLDNOTES

Four-Corner Fold
Before you read this chapter, create the **FoldNote** entitled "Four-Corner Fold" described in the Reading and Study Skills section of the Appendix. Label each flap of the four-corner fold with a topic. Write what you know about each topic under the appropriate flap. As you read the chapter, add other information that you learn.

These people are using old tires to insulate a new community center in Ivory Park, South Africa. Community members are creating a sustainable eco-village here through cooperation with local and international governments and organizations.

Economics and International Cooperation

GA SCSh.5.e

Over six billion people live on Earth. They are supported by unprecedented levels of human resource use, productivity, and scientific knowledge. On average, people live longer and have more education than they did 50 years ago. They are also less likely to live in acute poverty. But Earth still faces many problems. Our goal must be to live in a sustainable way worldwide. **Sustainability** is the condition in which human society can go on indefinitely and future generations can have a standard of living as high as our own.

To live in a sustainable way, we need to look for new ways to solve problems. For example, fresh water and energy are becoming scarce and expensive in many parts of the world. We need to develop sustainable solutions. Suppose that we developed cheap, renewable, non-polluting sources of energy. We could then make all the fresh water we needed by desalinating sea water, solving both problems. By approaching problems with sustainability in mind, each new solution builds a better world.

International Development and Cooperation

We live in a time of *globalization*. Environmental and economic conditions are linked across political borders around the world. People cross these borders in search of economic opportunities and a better quality of life. Increasingly, governments, organizations, and businesses around the world must work together. Despite having different opinions, world leaders meet to identify common goals and to address worldwide problems, as shown in **Figure 1**.

> **Reading Check** What does it mean to live in a sustainable way? (See the Appendix for answers to Reading Checks.)

Objectives

▶ Describe some of the challenges to achieving sustainability.

▶ Describe several major international meetings and agreements relating to the environment.

▶ Explain how economics and environmental science are related.

▶ Compare two ways that governments influence economics.

▶ Give an example of a private effort to address environmental problems.

Key Terms

sustainability
economics

Figure 1 ▶ At the 2000 Millennium Summit in New York, world leaders agreed on principles to guide the United Nations in the 21st century. Sustainable development is a shared goal among most nations.

Table 1 ▼

International Organizations, Meetings, and Agreements	
Related to Sustainable Development	
The World Conservation Union (IUCN), established 1948	a worldwide partnership of States, government agencies, private and nonprofit organizations, and scientists and experts from 140 countries; encourages and assists in conservation as well as equitable and sustainable use of natural resources
UN Conference on Human Environment, Stockholm, 1972	first international meeting to consider global environment and development needs; led to the formation of the UN Environment Programme (UNEP)
UN Conference on Environment and Development (UNCED or Earth Summit), Rio de Janeiro, 1992	meeting that produced Agenda 21 and the Rio Declaration (Earth Charter), which outlined key policies for sustainable development; established the UN Commission on Sustainable Development (UNCSD)
World Summit on Sustainable Development, Johannesburg, 2002	meeting to review 10-year progress of Agenda 21 and to consider several major treaties
Related to Climate and Atmosphere	
Intergovernmental Panel on Climate Change (IPCC), established 1988	group of scientists from around the world that studies the scientific, social, and economic aspects of human-induced climate change
Framework Convention on Climate Change, Rio de Janeiro, 1992	agreement that established international recognition of the problems of climate change; proposed strategies to limit greenhouse gases
Montreal Protocol on Substances That Deplete the Ozone Layer, 1987	agreement by many countries to eliminate substances, such as CFCs, that damage the atmosphere's protective ozone layer
Kyoto Protocol on Climate Change, 1997	agreement to reduce worldwide emissions of greenhouse gases; requires larger reductions by developed countries; allows trading of permitted levels of emissions; promotes pollution-free development

Sustainable Development Many meetings and agreements among international governments have dealt with environmental concerns along with economic and political concerns. Some important examples are listed in **Table 1**. The Earth Summit of 1992 in Rio de Janeiro, Brazil, was a sign of new levels of international environmental awareness and cooperation. Representatives from around the world drew up several agreements. One of these was Agenda 21, a general plan to address a range of environmental problems while allowing continued economic development.

Climate and Atmosphere International organizations and agreements related to climate and the atmosphere are also listed in **Table 1**. One treaty, the Montreal Protocol, successfully reduced the amount of ozone-destroying chemicals in the atmosphere. However, not all agreements are successful. Any country may choose not to sign, enforce, or provide funding to implement an agreement.

For example, the Kyoto Protocol attempts to avoid or slow down global warming by reducing greenhouse-gas emissions around the world. Most of the developed countries have promised to reduce their emissions by about 5 percent by 2012. However, an argument against the Kyoto Protocol is that it would be costly to implement, even though it does not guarantee a stable climate. Another argument is that the treaty allows developing countries to continue to increase their use of fossil fuels, while it requires reductions in use of fossil fuels by the developed countries. Mainly for these reasons, the United States did not sign the treaty. However, U.S. corporations doing business in other parts of the world may still be subject to the treaty's requirements.

Other Agreements Hundreds of other international agreements have been made as new environmental issues have emerged. Sometimes, the results make news. For example, you may hear on the news that a cruise line was barred from a port or fined millions of dollars for dumping garbage at sea. The ship would be fined because its actions violate an agreement commonly known as MARPOL. (MARPOL refers to *marine pollution*.) Under MARPOL, large ships cannot dump garbage close to shore. MARPOL also regulates the practice of oil tankers washing out their tanks. As a result, beaches around the world are less polluted with tar despite the increasing volume of oil carried by tankers.

SCLINKS.

www.scilinks.org
Topic: Sustainable
Development
Code: HE81485
Topic: United Nations
Code: HE81579

Table 2 ▼

Other International Organizations, Meetings, and Agreements Related to the Environment	
Antarctic Treaty and Convention, 1959	agreement to use Antarctica solely for peaceful purposes "in the interest of all mankind" and to cooperate in scientific research there
International Convention for the Prevention of Pollution from Ships (MARPOL), 1973; modified 1978	agreement that regulates disposal of wastes by ships on the ocean: specifies where and how different types of garbage, oil, sewage, and toxic wastes may be dumped
Convention on International Trade in Endangered Species (CITES), 1973	agreement that classifies endangered and threatened species worldwide and monitors international trade of these species; widely adopted and successful for many listed species
Convention on Migratory Species (CMS), 1979	agreement that protects wild animal species that migrate across international borders
Law of the Sea, 1982	agreement that addresses ocean pollution from land runoff, ocean dumping, hazardous materials, oil exploration, mining, and air pollution; designates deep-sea resources as "the common heritage of mankind"
Basel Convention, 1989	agreement that regulates transportation and disposal of hazardous wastes
Convention on Biological Diversity (CBD), 1992	agreement to inventory and protect endangered and threatened species; nations compensate each other for use of organisms in products
Intergovernmental Forum on Chemical Safety (IFCS), 1994	panel that facilitates cooperation among governments for environmentally sound management of chemicals
Cartagena Protocol on Biosafety, 2000	agreement that addresses transportation and use of genetically modified organisms
UN Forum on Forests (UNFF), 2001	panel that promotes the management, conservation, and sustainable development of all types of forests

Economics and the Environment

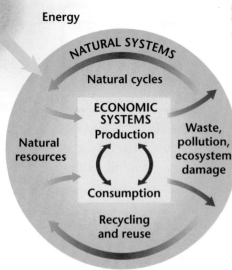

Figure 2 ▶ A complete economic model shows that economic systems operate within natural systems.

Economics is the study of the choices people make as they use and distribute limited resources. In the traditional model of economics, *markets* are seen as self-contained economic systems, in which money and products flow in cycles. People within a market will decide the *value* of something by comparing the costs and benefits from their own perspective. For example, people decide how much they will pay for a product or how much they must be paid to do a certain job. These values change over time as people see changes in the costs or benefits of their actions.

Economists say that an economic system is successful when there is *economic growth*, an increase in the flow of money and products within a market. However, economic systems may not account for external factors that do not have a direct economic value, such as air or wildlife. As the fields of economics and various sciences share knowledge, economists develop more complex and realistic models of resource use. The example in **Figure 2** shows that economic systems are contained within and dependent upon the environment.

✔ **Reading Check** How do people decide the value of a product?

International Whaling: Conflict and Cooperation

Because no country controls the open ocean, the ocean has been treated as if the resources it contains are free for anyone to take. However, people around the world have noticed the disappearance of species and the pollution of their shores. The history of agreements between countries to regulate whaling illustrates both the problems and successes of international cooperation.

Whales were once hunted for their fat, which was used for lamp oil, and they are still hunted for meat. By the 20th century, most large whale species were endangered. So, countries have had to negotiate with each other to hunt for whales and to save whales from extinction.

In 1949, the International Whaling Commission (IWC) voted to limit commercial whaling to a nation's territorial waters. France objected and used a special provision to opt out of IWC rules. France was the first of many countries to use this loophole, which weakens the IWC's ability to create regulations.

The 1949 agreement also established quotas to limit the number of whales a nation could harvest. However, because the quotas specified the number of whales but not the type of whales, the quotas did not prevent the killing of endangered whale species. As a result, blue whales, fin whales, humpback whales, and sei whales were hunted nearly to extinction. Then in 1960,

the IWC suspended quotas entirely. What followed was the largest whale catch in the history of the IWC.

Whales are intelligent mammals, and many people have an emotional desire to save whales from extinction. Because of public pressure to save the whales, the IWC reestablished a quota in 1967. And in 1972, the IWC allowed observers from member nations to monitor the whale harvest of other member nations. In 1977, the IWC created more restrictions on whaling, and passed a resolution urging nations to stop importing whale products. Finally, the IWC called for a total ban on whaling that was to begin in 1984. However, three countries with large whaling industries opted out

Economists see environmental problems as *market failures*. The market has failed if the price of something does not reflect its true cost. For example, the price of gasoline does not reflect the other expenses caused by auto emissions. Illnesses caused by air pollution cost society billions of dollars a year. In a balanced economic system, the price of gasoline should reflect these costs. One difficulty in pricing is that sometimes we do not know environmental costs. An economic system can include only those costs that are understood at the time people make decisions.

Regulation and Economic Incentives
Governments influence economic systems. Governments may do this by creating regulations or punishing people with fines and jail sentences. Governments may also create *economic incentives* by paying out money for actions that benefit society or charging taxes on actions that have a social cost. For example, some governments offer rebates to people who purchase energy-saving appliances.

Governments have tried many ways to regulate environmental damage such as pollution. However, regulations are criticized when they are difficult to enforce, do not distribute costs evenly, or do not control environmental damage. Governments and economists continue to work on ways to link economic decisions with environmental effects.

Eco fact

Environmental Ratings Each year, the World Economic Forum ranks countries on an Environmental Sustainability Index. In 2005, the top five countries were Finland, Norway, Uruguay, Sweden, and Iceland. The United States ranked 45th of 146 countries studied. The study concluded that no country is on a truly sustainable path.

► This Icelandic whaling ship (left) is harvesting fin whales. Sperm whales (right) are among the many endangered whale species.

CRITICAL THINKING

1. Expressing Opinions Write a paragraph describing your views about the issue of whaling. **WRITING SKILLS**

2. Predicting Outcomes Demand for whale meat in Japan has been decreasing in recent years. Why might this change be happening, and what might be the results of this change?

of this agreement—Norway, Japan, and the former Soviet Union.

International debate over these issues has continued. Populations of a few whale species have recovered since whaling was restricted. Other species, such as the right whale, breed so slowly and have such small populations that they may not survive.

In the 1990s, Norway and Japan continued to claim exceptions to the IWC's rules. Both countries harvested hundreds of minke whales each year, claiming that the minke population was large enough to survive limited hunting. Norway and Japan have also hunted in the IWC's designated whale sanctuary in the Antarctic Ocean. Japan has claimed that the IWC rules allow the country to harvest whales for research, although the meat is then sold as food in Japan.

Private Efforts Businesses and private organizations also play a role in addressing environmental problems. Businesses may donate land for parks or preserves or donate money to environmental causes. Many businesses have found that recycling their wastes saves money and improves their public image.

Private organizations often cooperate with each other and with governments. Such cooperation may include conducting research or creating plans for environmental management. **Figure 3** shows an area of Africa that several governments and private organizations are working together to manage. Local residents are also included in the process of planning for the area.

The Nature Conservancy is a nonprofit organization that uses a simple economic strategy to preserve ecosystems. This organization collects donations of money and land. If the donated land is not targeted for preservation, the organization trades or sells the land. Large preserves are put together by a combination of donations, exchanges, and purchases of land. The organization has created preserves in all 50 states and in 28 other countries.

Figure 3 ▶ The area around Mount Kilimanjaro in Kenya is an important home to wildlife such as elephants and giraffes. Several governments and organizations are working with local residents to manage the area for both wildlife preservation and sustainable economic development.

SECTION 1 Review

1. **Describe** some of the challenges to achieving sustainability.

2. **Describe** three major international meetings or agreements relating to the environment.

3. **Compare** two ways that governments influence economics.

4. **Give an example** of a private effort to address environmental problems.

CRITICAL THINKING

5. **Analyzing Processes** Write a paragraph that explains why a local government might use tax money to purchase park lands. **WRITING SKILLS**

6. **Applying Ideas** Read about interactions of economics and the environment. List some ways that both governments and organizations could encourage people to conserve resources. **READING SKILLS**

Environmental Policies in the United States

Many people in the United States have demonstrated a concern about environmental problems. In both local and national elections in the United States, candidates often talk about environmental issues in their campaigns. Each year, millions of dollars are donated to environmental causes by U.S. citizens and businesses, and billions of federal tax dollars are spent to uphold environmental policies and to manage resources. In recent decades, the United States has reduced many types of pollution and improved water quality in many places. But the United States is still struggling to use its resources in a sustainable way and to preserve its unique ecosystems.

History of U.S. Environmental Policy

During the 1800s, people in the United States made use of the country's vast resources. Prairies were turned into cropland, ancient forests were cut down, and several species of animals were hunted to extinction. By the 1900s, citizens began to realize the consequences of these actions, and the citizens' attitudes started to change. Leaders such as President Theodore Roosevelt and conservationist John Muir, shown in **Figure 4,** called for increased protection and management of the nation's resources. Many national forests and parks, and agencies to manage them, were established around the early 1900s.

Objectives

▶ **Describe** two major developments in U.S. environmental history.

▶ **Give** examples of three federal agencies that have environmental responsibilities.

▶ **Explain** the purpose of Environmental Impact Statements.

▶ **Give** an example of how citizens can affect environmental policy at each level of government—local, state, and national.

▶ **Evaluate** the media as a source of information about the environment.

Key Terms

Environmental Impact Statement
lobbying

SC*LINKS*.

www.scilinks.org
Topic: U.S. National
Parks
Code: HE81575

Figure 4 ▶ In the late 1800s and early 1900s, President Theodore Roosevelt (on left) and naturalist John Muir (on right) were leaders in the conservation of natural areas. They are shown here at Yosemite National Park, one of the first national parks.

Inherited Laws In parts of the United States that were previously under the control of European countries, some of the old laws regarding property and land use are still in effect. In Texas and California, many provisions of Spanish land law still apply to the states' water sources. Most rivers and creeks in these states are public property. Also, Texas has ownership of coastal areas stretching 10.4 mi from its shores. This gives Texas the ownership of many offshore oil deposits. Other coastal states own only 3 mi, as established by English common law in those states.

Environmental Agencies and Laws Throughout the 1900s, U.S. citizens became more aware of environmental problems. Widespread crop disasters in the 1930s showed the country that poor farming practices were causing soil erosion and poverty. Policies to encourage soil conservation were adopted. People objected to living near smelly garbage dumps, so research on better methods of waste disposal began. The public began to complain about pollution. The first Earth Day, celebrated around the world in 1970, was a sign of widespread environmental awareness. In the same year, the U.S. Environmental Protection Agency (EPA) was created.

U.S. lawmakers have created many policies and federal agencies to manage environmental affairs, as shown in **Table 3**. For example, the EPA enforces the Clean Air Act and the Clean Water Act. These acts set standards for acceptable levels of pollutants in air and water. The EPA uses regulations and economic incentives to encourage individuals and businesses to meet the standards. Environmental laws change as we learn more and draw different conclusions about how much to spend on preserving the environment. Deciding when to spend money to preserve the environment is equally important. Usually, anticipating and solving a possible problem before it occurs costs less than solving the problem after.

Table 3 ▼

U.S. Federal Agencies and Their Environmental Responsibilities	
Department or Agency	**Responsibilities**
Environmental Protection Agency	enforces National Environmental Policy Act; Clean Water Act; Clean Air Act; Solid Waste Disposal Act; Superfund; Federal Insecticide, Fungicide, and Rodenticide Control Act; Waste Reduction Act; Toxic Substances Control Act; Resource Conservation and Recovery Act
Department of the Interior	enforces Wild and Scenic Rivers Act (managed across several agencies)
U.S. Fish and Wildlife Service	enforces Endangered Species Act, National Wildlife Refuge System Act, Alaska National Interest Lands Conservation Act, Species Conservation Act, Fish and Wildlife Improvement Act, Fish and Wildlife Conservation Act
Bureau of Land Management	enforces Federal Land Policy and Management Act, Taylor Grazing Act
National Parks Service	manages national parks
Office of Surface Mining Reclamation and Enforcement	enforces Surface Mining Control and Reclamation Act
Department of Agriculture	enforces Soil and Water Conservation Act, National Forests Management Act
Department of Commerce	
National Oceanic and Atmospheric Administration	monitors international atmosphere, climate, and oceans
National Marine Fisheries Service	enforces Marine Mammal Protection Act
Nuclear Regulatory Commission	regulates nuclear power stations and nuclear waste
Department of Energy	enforces National Energy Act, Public Utility Regulatory Policies Act

Environmental Impact Statements Most government agencies are required to file an **Environmental Impact Statement** (EIS) for any proposed project or policy that would have a significant effect on the environment. Proposals for the construction of dams, highways, airports, and other projects that the federal government controls or funds must be evaluated with an EIS.

An EIS states the need for a project, the project's impact on the environment, and how any negative impact can be minimized. The public can comment on an EIS. For example, if a new dam is proposed, scientists and citizens may comment on any problems they foresee. Although public comment on an EIS rarely stops a project, the feedback may cause changes in the project's plans.

Federal agencies may also conduct an EIS when they plan changes in the regulation of public resources. Usually, several alternative actions are evaluated. For example, an EIS was conducted in the 1980s to evaluate alternative ways to release water from Glen Canyon Dam. Federal agencies were looking for ways to restore natural conditions downstream in the Grand Canyon, shown in **Figure 5**.

Figure 5 ▶ The Grand Canyon ecosystem was changed when the Glen Canyon Dam was built upstream in 1962. An Environmental Impact Statement in the 1980s evaluated alternative ways to operate the dam.

U.S. Public Lands Twenty-eight percent of the area of the United States is publicly owned. This means that local, state, or federal governments hold the land in the public interest. Most of this public land is federally controlled and is in the western states. 80 percent of Nevada is publicly owned, and more than 60 percent of Alaska, Utah, and Idaho are publicly owned.

Unfunded Mandates and Economic Impacts Some limits have been placed on federal government's power to pass environmental laws. In 1995, Congress passed a law to prevent *unfunded mandates*, which are federal regulations that do not provide funds for state or local governments to implement the regulations. The federal government must now provide funding for any new laws that will cost more than 50 million dollars to implement. Congress can no longer pass laws such as the Clean Water Act, which requires local communities to conduct their own tests of public water supplies. Another limit being placed on many federal agencies requires the agencies to evaluate both the economic and environmental impacts of their policies.

FIELD ACTIVITY

Local Policies Use newspapers, TV, or the Internet to find out about a local environmental issue or policy that is currently being debated. Write a short newspaper article about this issue. Make sure to describe the problem, give some factual information, and state both sides of the debate or argument. Complete the article with your own opinion about what should be done. Write the article in your *EcoLog.* Make sure to consider what individuals should do as well as what the government, businesses, and the legal system should do. You might want to send the article to your school newspaper or to a local newspaper for publication.

Figure 6 ▶ Many environmental decisions are made at the local level. Citizens can participate in local government at public meetings (below). Some communities set aside local wildlife habitat and green spaces, such as the Barton Creek Greenbelt in Austin, Texas (right).

Influencing Environmental Policy

You can influence environmental policy. For example, as a citizen, you can contact your elected representatives to tell them your opinion on issues. There are also many other ways that consumers, businesses, the media, and organizations can influence policy at all levels of government.

Many laws related to the environment are created at the national level. However, there are also many state and local laws that affect the environment. It is easier for an individual to influence policy at the local level than at the national level. It is also usually easier for citizens to organize and contact their representatives at the local level.

Local Governments Local governments make many decisions for their communities. City councils and governmental agencies hold public meetings, such as the meeting shown in **Figure 6.** Local governments can decide how land may be used and developed, and where businesses and housing may be located. Local governments and agencies also create plans for public facilities, for waste disposal and recycling, and for many other facets of local life.

One problem with local environmental planning is that communities often do not coordinate their plans. For example, your community may plan for clean air or water, but a neighboring community may allow development that pollutes your area. On the other hand, sometimes local communities do work together. For example, towns along the Hudson River in New York are cooperating to provide a "greenway" of natural areas for public use that stretch hundreds of miles along the river.

✓ Reading Check What is one way that people can influence environmental policy at the local level?

State Governments Environmental policy is also strongly influenced at the state level. The federal government passes laws that set environmental standards, but often these laws are minimum standards. Individual states may create laws that set higher standards. California's vehicle emission standards are higher than the federal standards because that state wants to control its problems with air pollution caused by traffic. States also have a lot of independent control over how to implement laws and manage public resources. For example, Ohio's Department of Natural Resources has used the state's endangered plant law to acquire habitats and to educate the public about the state's 350 endangered plant species.

Lobbying Lawmakers are heavily influenced by lobbying on many sides of issues. **Lobbying** is an organized attempt to influence the decisions of lawmakers. Both environmental and industry groups hire lobbyists to provide information to lawmakers and urge them to vote a certain way. One way to influence policy is to support an organization that lobbies for the policies that you agree with.

The Media and Sources of Information The media, especially television news, as shown in **Figure 7**, is the main source of information about environmental topics for most of us. Popular TV, radio, and newspapers tell us, for example, when Congress is debating about oil drilling in the Arctic National Wildlife Refuge or when our local government is planning to build a new sewage plant. However, media reports are usually brief and leave out information.

If you want to understand environmental problems, you will want to find information from sources other than popular media. Many other sources are available, and you should evaluate all sources for bias and accuracy. Scientists and others who are familiar with environmental issues produce reports, magazines, and Web sites that contain in-depth information. Local organizations hold public meetings and produce newsletters. And through the Internet, you can get first-hand information from people all over the world.

Figure 7 ▶ A news broadcast may be the only way that many people learn about an environmental problem. From what other sources can people get information?

✓ Reading Check Why should you look for information about environmental topics in sources other than the popular media?

SECTION 2 Review

1. **Describe** two major developments in U.S. environmental history from each of the past two centuries.

2. **Give examples** of at least three federal agencies with environmental responsibilities.

3. **Explain** the purpose of Environmental Impact Statements. In what ways are citizens allowed to respond to an Environmental Impact Statement?

CRITICAL THINKING

4. **Relating Concepts** Describe three environmental issues that are important to your community.

5. **Expressing Viewpoints** Read about the ways of influencing environmental policy. Explain which of these ways you think is most effective. **READING SKILLS**

6. **Evaluating Information** Write a paragraph that evaluates an environmental news story from a newspaper, the radio, or TV. **WRITING SKILLS**

The Importance of the Individual

Objectives

▶ Give examples of individuals who have influenced environmental history.

▶ Identify ways in which the choices that you make as an individual may affect the environment.

It is easy to feel that one person does not make much difference to the environment, but we all affect the environment with our daily actions. By learning about environmental problems and solutions, we are able to make responsible decisions. In addition, history has shown that one individual can have an influence on many others.

Influential Individuals

Some individuals who have influenced thinking about the environment in the United States are listed in **Table 4**. These people are famous because they brought attention to problems or convinced many people to think about new ideas. Many of these individuals wrote best-selling books about the subjects they knew well. These books were easy to understand and inspired people to think about environmental problems in a new way.

The 1960s Decade During the 1960s, environmental issues became widely known. It was then that biologists such as Paul Ehrlich, Barry Commoner, Rachel Carson, and Garrett Hardin drew public attention to environmental problems such as pollution, rapid population growth, and resource depletion.

Table 4 ▼

Some People Who Influenced Environmental Thinking in the United States	
Henry D. Thoreau (1817–1862) was a conservationist and writer who is best known for his essays about his stay in a cabin at Walden Pond in Massachusetts.	**Paul Ehrlich (1932–)** is a Stanford ecologist who warned of the dangers of rapid population growth with his 1968 book, *The Population Bomb*.
John Muir (1838–1914) was a Scottish-born naturalist and writer who founded the Sierra Club, explored the American West, and was a famous advocate for preserving western lands as wilderness.	**Jane Goodall (1934–)** studied chimpanzees in Tanzania's Gombe Stream National Park. Her books raised awareness of the plight of several endangered species and prompted new thinking about primate behavior.
Theodore "Teddy" Roosevelt (1858–1919) was the first American president to strongly support conservation. He founded the Forest Service, expanded national forests by 400 percent, and created the first National Monuments.	**Marion Stoddart (1928–)** led efforts to save the Nashua River in Massachusetts from pollution and development. *A River Ran Wild* is a book about her efforts. She is still active in protecting the Nashua River.
Alice Hamilton (1869–1970) was the first American expert on diseases caused by working with chemicals. In the early 1900s, she warned workers about exposure hazards and opposed the addition of lead to gasoline.	**Jacques Cousteau (1910–1997)** was a world-famous French oceanographer who produced many popular books, films, and TV programs that documented over four decades of his undersea explorations.
Rachel Carson (1907–1964) was a biologist with the U.S. Fish and Wildlife Service who raised awareness of toxic pesticides with her 1962 book, *Silent Spring*.	**Garrett Hardin (1915–2003)** was a distinguished professor of human ecology who is best known for his 1968 essay "The Tragedy of the Commons."

In *Silent Spring*, Rachel Carson argued that many public lands and resources were not adequately protected. She argued that resources such as water had to be protected and kept in natural, unpolluted conditions. Partly as a result of Carson's book, in 1964 Congress passed the Wilderness Act. This allowed the government to designate some federal lands as wilderness areas. These areas may only be used for low-impact recreation such as hiking and camping, and the number of visitors is limited.

Rising Awareness Also in the 1960s, several environmental disasters made headlines. Air pollution in New York City was blamed for 300 deaths. The bald eagle became endangered as a result of the widespread use of DDT. There was a massive oil spill near Santa Barbara. Lake Erie became so polluted that many of its beaches had to be closed. Eventually, pressure from the public led to new laws and efforts to reduce environmental damage. The first Earth Day, in 1970, was a historic demonstration of public concern for environmental issues.

Connection to History

Historical Writers Americans have been influenced by descriptions of America written by early explorers. An example is this passage written in 1805 by Meriwether Lewis, from his journal of the famous Lewis and Clark expedition:

"I beheld the Rocky Mountains for the first time . . . these points of the Rocky Mountains were covered with snow and the sun shone on it in such manner as to give me the most plain and satisfactory view. While I viewed these mountains I felt a secret pleasure in finding myself so near the head of the heretofore conceived boundless Missouri."

Figure 8 ▶ Examples of individuals who have brought attention to environmental issues: ❶ Rachel Carson, ❷ Marion Stoddart, and ❸ Jacques Cousteau.

Making a Decision

Procedure

1. Apply the following decision-making model to an environmental issue that interests you. After choosing an issue, find sources of information and opinions on different sides of the issue. Make notes about the ideas that you consider.

2. Consider which values apply to the issue. Consider scientific, economic, health, ethical, and cultural values. Which value is most important to you? to your community? Who else is involved, and how might they feel?

3. Explore the consequences of different actions. What are some possible outcomes? What are the pros and cons of each? How reliably can the outcomes be predicted?

4. Make your decision. Explain your reasoning in terms of the above considerations.

Analysis

1. Share your decision with a partner or group. Do not debate the issue; try to understand each others' reasoning, and give each other feedback about how carefully you applied the decision-making process.

Applying Your Knowledge

What will you be in the future? At the very least, you can expect to be a citizen who has the right to vote, a consumer who has choices of how to spend your money, and a member of the human race who has a role in the global environment. To make the decisions you will face, you can draw on your knowledge of environmental science.

Voting One of the most important decisions you may make is in the act of voting, as shown in **Figure 9**. The people we elect will make decisions that affect our environmental future. You have the right to support the candidates and laws that you think are best in both local and national elections. You can easily find out what a candidate thinks about environmental issues before an election. You can find information about candidates through the media, voter organizations, and Web sites.

One way to take action on environmental problems is as part of a group of people who share your concerns and interests. You can find many groups in your community asking for volunteers for activities such as planting trees, picking up trash, or maintaining trails. Many large nonprofit organizations hold meetings, educational activities, and trips to natural areas all over the country.

Weighing the Evidence A popular environmental slogan is to "think globally, act locally." This slogan reminds us that our everyday actions have broader effects. Being aware of the effects of our actions is an important step in making decisions that affect the environment. What choices of action could you make today that will affect your environment?

Each of us has the responsibility to educate ourselves as we make the decisions that affect the world around us. There is a wealth of information about environmental issues on the Internet, in libraries, and in the media. When you research a topic, use reliable sources for statistics and information. Do not be misled by information that may look convincing but that has no supporting evidence.

Figure 9 ▶ Voting is an opportunity to make a decision that affects the environment.

Consumer Choices An environmental slogan you may have heard is "reduce, reuse, recycle." As consumers, we can reduce the amount of things we buy and use, we can reuse things that are often used only once, and we can recycle many materials. How many ways can you think of to apply these ideas in your everyday life?

As a consumer, you may choose to buy products that are produced sustainably or that do less damage to the environment. It is not always easy to tell which products meet this standard. But as you learn more about environmental science, you'll be prepared to make decisions that guarantee that your impact on the environment will be a positive one.

✓ **Reading Check** What is an example of a consumer choice that benefits the environment?

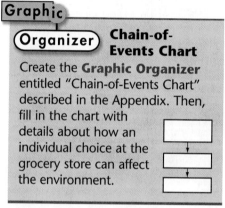
Graphic

Organizer **Chain-of-Events Chart**
Create the **Graphic Organizer** entitled "Chain-of-Events Chart" described in the Appendix. Then, fill in the chart with details about how an individual choice at the grocery store can affect the environment.

Figure 10 ▶ As consumers, we make many choices that affect the environment. What choices could you make today that will affect your environment?

SECTION 3 Review

1. **Give examples** of at least three individuals in history who have had an impact on environmental thinking. What do they have in common?

2. **Identify** at least three ways individual citizens can influence their environment.

3. **List** five choices that you could make today that would have some kind of effect on the environment.

CRITICAL THINKING

4. **Identifying Relationships** Think of one activity that you do often. Write a paragraph explaining all the environmental effects, positive or negative, that this activity might have over time. **WRITING SKILLS**

5. **Predicting Consequences** Choose one environmental issue that you have learned about in this book and describe all the ways that you could make a difference on this issue.

CHAPTER 21

1 Economics and International Cooperation

Key Terms

sustainability, 573
economics, 576

Main Ideas

▶ To achieve sustainability will require co-operation and communication at many levels of society.

▶ Some goals of international agreements on the environment have been achieved and successfully implemented. Other goals have been set but not yet achieved.

▶ Economic systems operate within the environment by using resources and by returning both desired and undesired results. Economic systems sometimes fail to balance all the costs and benefits of people's actions.

2 Environmental Policies in the United States

Environmental Impact Statement, 581
lobbying, 583

▶ In the last century, the U.S. government has developed policies to address environmental problems and has established agencies to implement those policies.

▶ Citizens can influence policy at all levels of government but especially at the local level.

▶ Lobbying and the media also influence policy and public opinion.

3 The Importance of the Individual

▶ Individuals can have an effect on environmental interactions through leadership and education. Many environmental problems were brought to the public's attention by a few individuals.

▶ You make important decisions about the environment every day. How you choose to spend money, vote, and use resources will have an impact on the environment.

▶ You can apply scientific thinking and knowledge to any decisions that you may face.

Using Key Terms

Use each of the following terms in a separate sentence.

1. *sustainability*
2. *economics*

Use the correct key term to complete each of the following sentences.

3. Every federal project must complete a(n) _____.

4. Many groups try to influence government policies through _____.

Understanding Key Ideas

5. Which of the following trends is *not* a challenge to achieving sustainability?
   a. the increasing human population
   b. the decreasing supply of fresh water in the world
   c. disagreement among governments
   d. advancement of scientific understanding

6. At the 1992 Earth Summit, representatives from around the world
   a. created the Kyoto Protocol.
   b. tried to balance economic development with environmental sustainability.
   c. could not reach agreement on anything important.
   d. talked about environmental problems for the first time ever.

7. International environmental agreements include
   a. the Montreal Protocol on Ozone.
   b. Earth Day.
   c. the World Trade Organization.
   d. the Wilderness Act of 1964.

8. Economic systems
   a. do not depend on limited natural resources.
   b. rarely balance the costs and benefits of every action.
   c. should not include the costs of pollution with the costs of an action.
   d. must operate within the environment.

9. Which of the following statements about U.S. environmental policy is *not* true?
   a. During most of the 19th century, most Americans were not concerned about environmental consequences.
   b. During the 1960s, several individuals had strong effects on public thinking about environmental issues.
   c. Before Earth Day 1970, no one in the United States cared about the environment.
   d. The Environmental Protection Agency was established at a time of increasing public awareness of environmental problems.

10. State and local environmental regulations
    a. cannot be influenced by individuals.
    b. simply enforce federal standards.
    c. do not have to follow federal standards.
    d. are often more strict than federal standards.

11. The main function of an Environmental Impact Statement is
    a. to predict the effect a federal project might have on the environment.
    b. to produce a record of environmental change throughout history.
    c. to satisfy the requirements of international agreements.
    d. to limit real estate development and the activities of businesses.

12. Local governments do not regulate
    a. recycling.
    b. sewage treatment.
    c. garbage disposal.
    d. Environmental Impact Statements.

Short Answer

13. What do world leaders do at gatherings such as the Earth Summit?

14. Why are some treaties not successful?

15. In what ways do state or local regulations differ from federal regulations?

16. Describe several ways that citizens can influence environmental policy.

17. How can a consumer affect the environment?

Interpreting Graphics

The figures below show a type of label that is required by law to be placed on all new appliances. Use the figures to answer questions 18–21.

18. What is the most likely reason that the tag on the right has an "energy star" symbol?

19. Which quantity on the tags is the most important piece of information about these appliances?

20. Why do you think the government has required such labels to be placed on all new appliances?

21. There are two types of refrigerators represented on these labels: top-freezer and side-by-side. Which type is generally more efficient? How can you tell?

Concept Mapping

22. Use the following terms to create a concept map: *groups, individuals, lobbying, state laws, federal laws,* and *voting.*

Critical Thinking

23. **Expressing a Viewpoint** Read the section about influential individuals in this chapter. Describe at least one effect that one of these individuals may have had on your life. **READING SKILLS**

24. **Making Predictions** What might the effects be if the United States doubled the tax on gasoline over the next 10 years?

Cross-Disciplinary Connection

25. **History** Some people argue that developing nations should be allowed to create polluting industries in order to develop economically, just as the developed nations did in the past. Explain your opinion of this argument.

Portfolio Project

26. **An International Treaty** Write a proposal for a new international treaty that would address a pressing environmental problem and that you think could be agreed upon by many nations. **WRITING SKILLS**

Based on standard U.S. Government tests

ENERGYGUIDE

Side-by-Side Refrigerators
Capacity: 21.6 Cubic Feet

Brand: Energy Beater
Model #: QWERTY

Compare the Energy Use of this Refrigerator with Others Before You Buy

This Model uses
759 kWh/year ▼

This Model's energy use ranks 8.5 on the scale

Energy use (kWh/year) range, on a scale of 1 (Least Use) to 10 (Most Use) of all similar models

Uses Least Energy	Uses Most Energy
714	767

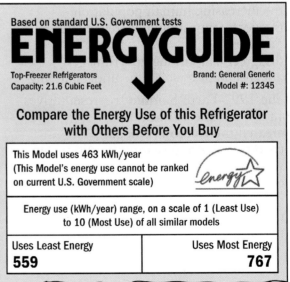

Based on standard U.S. Government tests

ENERGYGUIDE

Top-Freezer Refrigerators
Capacity: 21.6 Cubic Feet

Brand: General Generic
Model #: 12345

Compare the Energy Use of this Refrigerator with Others Before You Buy

This Model uses 463 kWh/year
(This Model's energy use cannot be ranked on current U.S. Government scale)

energy ⭐

Energy use (kWh/year) range, on a scale of 1 (Least Use) to 10 (Most Use) of all similar models

Uses Least Energy	Uses Most Energy
559	767

MATH SKILLS

Use the graphs below to answer question 27.

27. Analyzing Data The graph on the left shows the proportions of federal money that the public thinks should be spent on different types of research and development, based on a 1993 poll. The graph on the right shows how the money was actually spent. Which types of spending show close agreement between government spending and public opinion? Which types show the greatest difference?

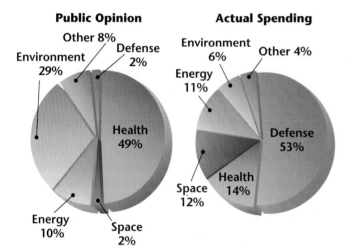

Public Opinion

Other 8%
Defense 2%
Environment 29%
Health 49%
Energy 10%
Space 2%

Actual Spending

Environment 6%
Other 4%
Energy 11%
Defense 53%
Space 12%
Health 14%

WRITING SKILLS

28. Communicating Main ideas Describe some signs that the world may be progressing toward a sustainable future. What are some likely challenges ahead?

29. Expressing Original Ideas Describe your vision of a sustainable future. Consider lifestyles, technology, forms of government, economic systems, and social organizations.

READING SKILLS

Read the passage below, and then answer the questions that follow.

Theodore Roosevelt was a unique and memorable president. A 1902 photograph shows him riding a moose across a river. Roosevelt thought of public lands as economic assets, to be used for timber harvesting, mining, and recreation. He felt that natural resources should be regulated and managed for the public benefit. He did not see these lands as refuges for threatened plants and animals. Roosevelt was considered to be the first conservationist president.

Roosevelt had some conflicts with preservationists such as John Muir. Preservationists believe in preserving public lands as untouched wilderness for future generations to study and enjoy. These conflicting views over how to use U.S. public lands continue today.

1. According to the passage, what is meant by the term *conservationist*?
   a. the same thing as *preservationist*
   b. one who believes in managing natural resources for the public benefit
   c. one who believes nature should be preserved untouched
   d. the same thing as *environmentalist*

2. According to the passage, which of these ideas about the uses of U.S. public lands was debated about 100 years ago?
   a. Mining should be legal.
   b. Wolves should be reintroduced into Yellowstone.
   c. Motors should be allowed in parks.
   d. Public lands should be preserved.

3. With which of the following opinions did both Roosevelt and Muir most likely agree?
   a. Public lands should not be used for mining or timber harvesting.
   b. The United States should own and regulate public lands.
   c. Wolves should be exterminated.
   d. Roosevelt was a preservationist.

Understanding Concepts

Directions (1–3): For *each* question, write on a separate sheet of paper the letter of the correct answer.

1 If you wanted to buy stock in a company with a sustainability policy, what would you look for?
A. You would look for a company that uses offshore labor.
B. You would look for a company that uses renewable resources.
C. You would look for a company that offers high quality products.
D. You would look for a company that has implemented a global marketing strategy.

2 What kind of information is contained in an Environmental Impact Statement?
F. An Environmental Impact Statement contains public comment on the proposed project.
G. An Environmental Impact Statement tells where funds for the project are coming from.
H. An Environmental Impact Statement predicts the project's expected impact on the environment.
I. An Environmental Impact Statement contains the total price of all construction materials and labor.

3 How can an individual have an effect on global environmental problems?
A. Buy things that provide only a single use.
B. Buy paper goods at the local discount store.
C. Structure daily activities around convenience.
D. Purchase vegetables that are organically grown.

Directions (4–5): For *each* question, write a short response.

4 Unfunded mandates are regulations that do not provide funds to implement the regulations. What was one effect of the ban on unfunded mandates in 1995?

5 What does the slogan, think globally, act locally, mean?

Reading Skills

Directions (6–8): Read the passage below. Then answer the questions.

During the 1960s, biologists such as Paul Ehrlich, Barry Commoner, and Rachel Carson drew public attention to environmental problems such as pollution, rapid population growth, and resource depletion. In the book *Silent Spring*, Rachel Carson argued that resources such as water had to be protected and kept in natural, unpolluted conditions. Partly as a result of this book, Congress passed the Wilderness Act in 1964. This allowed the government to designate some federal lands as wilderness areas.

Also in the 1960s, several environmental disasters made headlines. Air pollution in New York City was blamed for 300 deaths. The bald eagle became endangered as a result of the widespread use of DDT. There was a massive oil spill near Santa Barbara. Lake Erie became so polluted that many of its beaches had to be closed. Eventually, pressure from the public led to new laws and efforts to reduce environmental damage.

6 Predict how a lack of public interest in environmental issues could affect federal legislation.
F. Congress would hold more committee hearings.
G. States would take the lead in passing regulations.
H. New federal laws would be passed more quickly.
I. The federal government would stop enforcing existing laws.

7 What was a result of the highly-publicized environmental disasters in the 1960s?
A. Biologists began drawing attention to environmental problems.
B. Congress passed the Wilderness Act.
C. Rachel Carson wrote *Silent Spring*.
D. The public pressured the government to protect the environment.

8 How did the work of biologists affect public policy in the 1960s?

Interpreting Graphics

Directions (9–11): For *each* question below, record the correct answer on a separate sheet of paper.

The map below shows the location of national parks in Central America. Use this map to answer questions 9 through 11.

National Parks

Country	Population	Number of National Parks
Costa Rica	3,834,934	17
Nicaragua	5,023,818	2
Panama	2,882,329	11
Honduras	6,560,608	17
El Salvador	6,353,681	5
Belize	262,999	11
Guatemala	13,314,079	16

9 What percentage of national parks in Guatemala are located within 50 kilometers of the coast?
F. less than 15%
G. more than 25%
H. exactly 50%
I. almost 75%

10 Which country has the largest number of national parks per capita in Central America?
A. Belize
B. El Salvador
C. Guatemala
D. Nicaragua

11 How is the number of national parks related to the size of a country?
F. The bigger countries have more national parks.
G. The smaller countries have more national parks.
H. The countries with the most coastline have more national parks.
I. There is no correlation between a country's size and its national parks.

Test TIP

Per capita means per unit of population.

Inquiry Lab: RESEARCH

Objectives

▶ **USING SCIENTIFIC METHODS** Research a current environmental issue that requires an informed policy decision.

▶ **USING SCIENTIFIC METHODS** Prepare and present a report that is intended to inform the appropriate policy decision makers.

Materials

file folders
markers or colored pencils
note cards
posterboard
paper

optional materials: computer for word processing, graphing, or making a presentation

▶ **Scientific Reports** Scientists often present their findings in reports that can be reviewed by other scientists and by the public. Try to give your report a style and organization like that used by professional scientists.

Be an Environmental Scientist

Are you ready to put your knowledge of environmental science to work? Environmental scientists are often asked to help decision makers in government when there is a policy decision to be made that may affect the environment. Decision makers often want to make an informed decision based on a scientific analysis of a situation. Environmental scientists may be asked to study a situation or predict the results of an action and present their findings to the interested decision makers.

In this lab, you will be an environmental scientist who has been asked to prepare a report. The purpose of the report is to inform a group of decision makers of the possible results of their choices. You are expected to prepare an unbiased, thorough, and accurate report. And like a professional scientist's report, your report will be reviewed by your peers.

Procedure

1. Choose a current environmental issue that requires an informed policy decision. You might research legislation that is being considered in national or state governments. Or find out if any local projects or laws that have environmental effects are being debated in your community.

2. Do some simple beginning research to become familiar with the issue. Start in the library and then also try to find information from government agencies, scientific publications, and any private groups that are involved with the issue.

3. Write a brief description of the issue or proposal and a plan of how you will research and present your findings. Get your teacher's approval before proceeding.

4. Carry out your research. Don't forget to get help from librarians. Be sure to keep track of your sources of information, and check that they are reliable sources. Keep your teacher informed of your progress, and ask for help if you need it.

5. Create an outline of your report. Get your teacher's approval before proceeding.

6. Create the report. Be sure to do the following:

   a. Present the major options or different opinions being considered and the main arguments or reasons for each.

   b. For each option or potential action, explain the effects or consequences that might result.

   c. Create diagrams, tables, graphs, or other representations of the science involved.

   d. Provide citations of sources in a bibliography or other format, as approved by your teacher.

   e. Give a citation for each fact you present. Think critically about all sources of information you use. Try to find more than one source for information that seems doubtful.

   f. Be clear about how much data is available. Explain when there does not seem to be enough data to make a conclusion or establish a fact.

7. Present your report to your classmates and teacher.

▶ **Further Research** Like a real scientist, your research may lead you to new questions. You may wish to propose or conduct further research into the issue you have studied.

Analysis

1. **Analyzing Results** Read and listen to your classmates' reports, and evaluate them as described below.

Conclusions

2. **Evaluating Results** Evaluate your classmates' reports or presentations. Use the following criteria:

   a. What evidence or research did the scientist present to support his or her facts and conclusions?

   b. Was every conclusion supported by data or by scientific opinion?

   c. Was every fact or piece of data documented and supported by other sources?

   d. Were the concepts presented clearly? Did the report/presentation flow logically?

   e. Did the diagrams help you understand ideas?

   f. Was the report unbiased, or did the presenter show his or her opinion on the subject?

Extension

1. **Communications** Present or submit your report to a group that is making decisions about the issue you studied.

STUDENT CLUB SAVES EAGLES AND MORE

Not many people get to see a bald eagle up close, and most people never get to hold one. When Jeremy had the chance to care for an injured bald eagle and then return it to the wild, he felt "it was a life experience." Jeremy is just one of the hundreds of current and former members of the Southwestern High School Conservation Club (SWCC) in Somerset, Kentucky.

This club is unique in many ways. The SWCC's core mission is to help students understand the natural world through hands-on activities. In many ways, the club is an extension of a variety of environmental science classes offered at the school. However, the club is very busy and is involved in a wide variety of activities. Most important, the club members all feel that they are learning responsibility and important skills while making a difference in their environment.

Hands-On Science

Students at Southwestern High School (SWHS) can choose from six different environmental science courses, such as raptor biology or greenhouse management. In all of these classes, students spend more time getting their hands dirty than they spend using pencils and paper.

One SWHS science teacher said, "Biology is out there, beyond the classroom; you have to get outside to fully study it." Thanks to the hard work and leadership of students and teachers, the science facilities at SWHS now include a working greenhouse, native plant landscapes, a nature trail, an outdoor amphitheater, computer labs, and a weather station. The most exciting and unique facility at the school is the Raptor Rehabilitation Center, where SWCC members work every afternoon.

A Second Chance for Raptors

Raptors are birds of prey, such as owls, hawks, vultures, and eagles. Raptors in the United States have suffered many threats to their existence, from pollution to injury by cars or gunshots. Several federal and state laws are intended to protect raptors from such threats, but at least 300 raptors have been rescued from these threats by the students of SWHS.

Injured birds and orphaned fledglings are brought to the Raptor Rehabilitation Center from across the United States. The school has a special license to keep and care for raptors. The rehabilitation program requires veterinary equipment and supplies, specially designed cages, and a professional level of knowledge and training.

SWHS teacher and club sponsor Frances Carter started the rehabilitation program when the high school opened in 1993. She had previous experience with raptors and knew professionals in the field of wildlife management. These professionals asked her to help care for some of the birds that were being found because there were no other raptor facilities in the area.

A typical day in a raptor biology class involves about 30 min of instruction and an hour of bird maintenance. Additional bird care is done by SWCC members during nonschool hours. For example, club members Jeremy, Ben, and Grant spent hours each day for months—including holidays—working with two bald eagles.

Maintenance on a live bird usually involves grinding down excess growth on the beak, trimming the talons, exercising the bird, conducting a physical exam, and giving medications. Cages have to be cleaned weekly. Special diets have to be prepared. All of these tasks can be dangerous and messy. Handling the large birds requires training and skill.

They Say the Birds Choose You

The first goal of raptor rehabilitation is to be able to return the birds to the wild. This goal involves a tricky balance between building trust with each bird and

▶ **An eagle named Justice** was the first bald eagle to be rehabilitated and released in Kentucky, thanks to the SWCC. "I got chills," said one of the club members who was present, "It was gorgeous. That's a feeling you only get a few times in your life."

preserving its wild instincts. The raptor program has succeeded in releasing more than 30 percent of its birds. Yet for many students, letting the birds go is the hardest part of the work.

Imagine being handed three fuzzy, softball-sized baby owls, squawking for their lost mother. You might guess that these young great horned owls stole the hearts of the students at Southwestern. The students named them Bert, Ernie, and Elmo. Club members Amy and Valerie virtually adopted these baby owls and even took the birds home over vacations and gave them round-the-clock care. Amy recalls 3 A.M. feedings of dead mice or chicken livers rolled in calcium. "Killing mice by myself—nasty stuff. I thought it was the grossest thing I ever had to do in my life," she said.

However, Amy learned that the owls depended on her, "and that was the only thing that mattered." Eventually, the three owls grew to be healthy adults and were released. Amy reflected, "It was hard to watch the 'babies' fly off, never to be seen again."

Responsibility and Reward

In addition to the news-making events when the club releases another raptor into the wild, the club makes many efforts to educate their community. Presentations in which live raptors are perched on a student's hand are popular events at other schools, community fairs, and teacher training workshops. These presentations are also opportunities to educate people about wildlife and environmental issues. The school provides leadership, resources, and workshops for over 40 other schools in Kentucky. Also, club

▶ **Students in SWCC** are multitalented. They do everything from cleaning birdcages to making presentations around the nation and from picking up litter to competing in the national Envirothon competition. The Club's latest plan is to build a nature center.

members participate in a yearly environmental science competition called the *Envirothon*. The club advanced to national level in 2001.

The raptor rehabilitation program, greenhouse, nature trail, weather stations, and computer lab sound like a lot of fun, but most club members say that responsibility and making a difference are the important reasons to be in the club. Everyone in the club has a job title, from Club Reporter to Greenhouse Manager to Webmaster.

What Will They Do Next?

For the club and the teachers at SWHS, there is always more to be done. Club members do most of the planning, fundraising, and manual labor in a variety of projects. Recent projects include landscaping the school grounds with native plants, creating composting and recycling centers, and expanding the school's facilities. The school hopes to unite these facilities into a complete nature center that would educate tourists,

students, and scientists from around the nation.

Club members have developed career interests in veterinary medicine, wildlife biology, conservation, or environmental science fields. Jeremy may be a firefighter or a civil engineer. Amy and Cara may go into journalism. They all say that the club has given them unique opportunities and that they will never forget the experience.

What Do You Think?

Are there any groups like the SWCC in your area? Would you like to be like these students? What other ways can students make a difference for the environment? Explain your answers.

Answers to Appendix Practice Questions

Reading and Study Skills

How to Make Power Notes

1. Sample answer:

The Experimental Method

Power 1: observing

    Power 2: observation

Power 1: hypothesizing and predicting

    Power 2: hypothesis

    Power 2: prediction

Power 1: experimenting

    Power 2: experiment

        Power 3: variable

        Power 3: experimental group

        Power 3: control group

Power 1: organizing and analyzing data

    Power 2: data

Power 1: drawing conclusions

Power 1: repeating experiments

Power 1: communicating results

How to Make KWL Notes

1. a. The first step is observing.
   b. A hypothesis is more than a guess. It must be based on observations and testable by experiment.
   c. A good experiment has a single variable and a control group.

How to Make a Concept Map

1. a. core
   b. mesosphere
   c. inner core
2. Sample answers:
   - Earth is divided into layers.
   - The layers are categorized based on composition or structure.
   - The composition layers are the crust, the mantle, and the core.
3. a. concept
   b. linking words
   c. linking words
   d. concept

Math Skills Refresher

Geometry

1. 225,000 m^2
2. 1,230 cm^3 (rounded to three significant figures)
3. 96 cm^2

Exponents

1. a. 9
   b. 14,348,907
   c. 537,824
   d. 1

Order of Operations

1. 24
2. 7

Algebraic Rearrangements

1. a. $x = 20$
   b. $a = -1.75$
   c. $y = -6.3$
   d. $m = -4$
   e. $z = 2$
   f. $b = 5$

Scientific Notation

1. a. 1.23×10^7 m/s
   b. 4.5×10^{-12} kg
   c. 6.53×10^{-5} m
   d. 5.5432×10^{13} s
   e. 2.7315×10^2 K
   f. 6.2714×10^{-4} kg

Significant Digits

1. a. 4
   b. 5
   c. 4
   d. 3
2. a. 0.129 dm
   b. 2700 m/s
   c. 9.84 m^2
   d. 0.98 g

Appendix

CONTENTS

Lab Safety

General Guidelines For Laboratory Safety

In the laboratory, you can engage in hands-on explorations, test your scientific hypotheses, and build practical laboratory skills. However, while working in the laboratory or in the field, it is your responsibility to protect yourself and other students by conducting yourself in a safe manner. You will avoid accidents in the laboratory by following directions, handling materials carefully, and taking your work seriously. Read the following general safety guidelines and review the descriptions of the safety symbols on pp. xviii–xix before working in the laboratory.

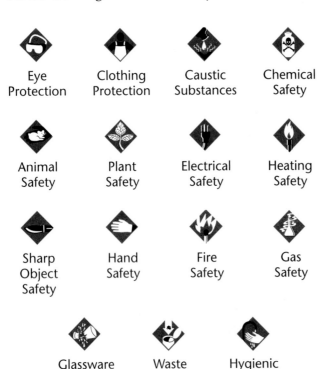

Eye Protection

Clothing Protection

Caustic Substances

Chemical Safety

Animal Safety

Plant Safety

Electrical Safety

Heating Safety

Sharp Object Safety

Hand Safety

Fire Safety

Gas Safety

Glassware Safety

Waste Disposal

Hygienic Care/ Clean Hands

Before You Begin...

◆ Be prepared. Study assigned experiments before class. Resolve any questions about procedures before starting work.

◆ Keep your work area uncluttered. Store books, backpacks, jackets, or other items you do not need out of the way.

◆ Arrange the materials you are using for an experiment in an orderly fashion on your work surface. Keep laboratory materials away from the edge of the work surface.

◆ Tie back long hair and remove dangling jewelry. Roll up sleeves and secure loose clothing.

◆ Do not wear contact lenses in the laboratory. Chemicals could get between the contact lenses and your eyes and cause irreparable eye damage. If your doctor requires that you wear contact lenses instead of glasses, then you should wear eyecup safety goggles—similar to goggles that are worn for underwater swimming—in the laboratory.

◆ Do not wear open-toed shoes, sandals, or canvas shoes in the laboratory because they will not protect your feet if any chemical, glassware, or other object is dropped on them.

◆ Know the location of the nearest phone. Find out where emergency telephone numbers, such as the number for the nearest poison control center, can be found.

◆ Know the location of safety equipment such as eyewash stations and fire extinguishers. Know how to operate this equipment.

◆ Know the fire evacuation routes established by your school.

◆ Before you begin the experiment, review the supplies you will be using and the safety issues you should be concerned about. Be on the alert for the safety symbols shown on this page and those that appear in your experiment.

While You Are Working...

◆ Do not play in the lab. Take your lab work seriously, and behave appropriately in the laboratory. Be aware of your classmates' safety as well as your own at all times.

◆ Never perform an experiment not authorized by your teacher.

◆ Never work alone in the laboratory.

◆ Always wear safety goggles and a lab apron when you are working in the lab.

Laboratories contain chemicals that can damage your clothing, skin, and eyes.

◆ Wear protective gloves when working with an open flame, chemicals, solutions, wild or unknown plants, or other items as directed by your teacher.

◆ Never look directly at the sun through any optical device or use direct sunlight to illuminate a microscope. The focused light can seriously damage your eyes.

◆ When heating substances in a test tube, always point the test tube away from yourself and others.

◆ Keep your hands away from the sharp or pointed ends of scalpels, scissors, and other sharp instruments.

◆ Observe all of the safety symbols that accompany the procedural steps of the experiment. Be sure to follow the safety practices that are called for in the experiment.

◆ Never put anything in your mouth, and never touch or taste substances in the laboratory unless your teacher instructs you to do so.

◆ If your teacher instructs you to smell a chemical in the laboratory, follow the correct procedure. The correct method is to gently fan your hand over the substance, waving its vapors toward your nose. Do not put your nose directly over the substance.

◆ Never eat, drink, chew gum, or apply cosmetics in the laboratory. Do not store food or beverages in the lab area.

◆ Report any accident, chemical spill, or unsafe incident to your teacher immediately.

◆ Check labels on containers of chemicals to be certain you are using the right material.

◆ When diluting an acid or base with water, always add the acid or base to water. Do NOT add water to the acid or base.

◆ Dispose of chemicals according to your teacher's instructions.

◆ Never return unused chemicals to the containers you obtained them from. Do not put any object into a bottle containing a laboratory chemical.

Emergency Procedures

Don't panic. In the event of a laboratory emergency follow these instructions.

◆ In the event of a fire, alert the teacher and leave the laboratory immediately.

◆ If your clothes catch fire, STOP, DROP, and ROLL! The quickest way to smother a fire is to stop immediately, drop to the floor, and roll.

◆ If your lab partner's clothes or hair catches fire, grab the nearest fire blanket and use it to extinguish the flames. Inform your teacher immediately.

◆ If a chemical spills on your skin or clothing, wash it off immediately with plenty of water, and notify your teacher.

Lab Safety

- If a chemical gets into your eyes or on your face, go to an eyewash station immediately, and flush your eyes (including under the eyelids) with running water for at least 15 minutes. Hold your eyelids open with your thumb and fingers, and roll your eyeball around. While doing this, have another student notify your teacher.

- If a chemical spills on the floor, do not clean it up yourself. Keep your classmates away from the area, and alert your teacher immediately.

- If you receive a cut, even if it is just a small one, notify your teacher.

Safety With Animals in the Laboratory

Observing and experimenting with animals can enrich your understanding of environmental science. However, you must use extreme caution to assure your own safety as well as the safety and comfort of animals you work with. When working with animals in the laboratory be sure to follow these guidelines.

- Do not touch or approach any animal unless your teacher specifically gives you permission.

- Handle animals only as your teacher directs. Mishandling or abusing any animal will not be tolerated.

- Do not bring any animal into the laboratory without your teacher's permission.

- Wear gloves or other appropriate protective gear when working with animals.

- Wash your hands after touching any animal.

- Inform your teacher immediately if you are scratched, bitten, stung, or otherwise harmed by an animal.

- Always follow your teacher's instructions regarding the care of laboratory animals. Ask questions if you do not clearly understand what you are supposed to do.

- Keep each laboratory animal in a suitable, escape-proof container in a location where the animal will not be frequently disturbed.

Animal containers should provide adequate ventilation, warmth, and light.

- Keep each laboratory animal's container clean. Clean cages of small birds and mammals daily.

- Provide each laboratory animal with water at all times.

- Feed animals regularly, according to their individual needs.

- If you are responsible for the care or feeding of animals, arrange for necessary care on weekends, holidays, and during vacations.

- No study that involves inflicting pain on a vertebrate animal should ever be conducted.

- Vertebrate animals must not be exposed to excessive noise, exhausting exercise, overcrowding, or other distressing stimuli.

- When an animal must be removed from the laboratory, your teacher will provide a suitable method.

Safety With Plants in the Laboratory

Some plants or plant parts are poisonous to the point of fatality, depending on the weight of the person and the amount of plant material ingested. Therefore, many plants or plant parts can present a safety hazard to you. When working with plants in the laboratory be sure to follow these guidelines.

- Never place any part of any plant in your mouth unless instructed to do so by your teacher. Seeds obtained from commercial growers can be particularly dangerous because such seeds may be coated with hormones, fungicides, or insecticides.

- Do not rub sap or juice of fruits on your skin or into an open wound.

- Never inhale or expose your skin or eyes to the smoke of any burning plant or plant parts.

- Do not bring unknown wild or cultivated plants into the laboratory.

- Do not eat, drink, or apply cosmetics after handling plants without first washing your hands.
- Provide adequate light and water and appropriate soil and temperature for plants growing in the laboratory.
- If you are responsible for plants, make necessary arrangements for their care on weekends, holidays, and during vacations.

Finishing up in the Laboratory...

- Broken glass, chemicals, and other laboratory waste products should be disposed of in separate special containers. Dispose of waste materials as directed by your teacher.
- Clean tables and sinks as directed by your teacher.
- Make sure all water faucets, gas jets, burners, and electrical appliances are turned off.
- Return all laboratory materials and equipment to their proper places.
- Wash your hands thoroughly with soap and water after completing each experiment.

Safe and Successful Fieldwork

Environmental scientists conduct much of their research in the field. For environmental scientists—and environmental science students such as you—there are three important issues to consider when working in the field. One issue is your personal safety. Another issue is the successful completion of the scientific work you set out to do. The third consideration is protection of the environment you have come to study. The following guidelines will help you address these three issues.

- Dress in a manner that will keep you comfortable, warm, and dry. Wear long pants rather than shorts or a skirt. Wear sturdy shoes that have closed toes. Do not wear sandals or heels. Wear waterproof shoes if you will be working in wetlands.
- Bring rain gear if there is any possibility of rain.
- Bring sunglasses, sunscreen, and insect repellent as needed.
- Do not go alone beyond where you can be seen or heard; travel with a partner at all times.
- Do not approach wild mammals, snakes, snapping turtles, or other animals that may sting, bite, scratch, or otherwise cause injury.
- Do not touch any animal in the wild without specific permission from your teacher.
- Find out whether poisonous plants or dangerous animals are likely to be where you will be going. Learn how to identify any hazardous species.
- Do not pick wildflowers or touch plants or plant parts unless your teacher gives you permission. Do not eat wild plants.
- Immediately report any hazard or injury to your teacher.
- Be sure you understand the purpose of your field trip and any assignments you have been given. Bring all needed school supplies, and keep them organized in a binder, backpack, or other container.
- Be aware of the impact you are having on the environments you visit. Just walking over fragile areas can harm them, so stay on trails unless your teacher gives you permission to do otherwise.
- Sketching, photographing, and writing field notes are generally more appropriate than collecting specimens for observation. Collecting from a field site may be permitted in certain cases, but always obtain your teacher's permission first.
- Do not leave garbage at the field site. Strive to leave natural areas just as you found them.

Reading and Study Skills

How to Make Power Notes

Power notes help you organize the environmental science concepts you are studying by distinguishing main ideas from details. Similar to outlines, power notes are linear in form and provide you with a framework of important concepts. To make power notes, you assign a *power* of 1 to each main idea and a 2, 3, or 4 to each detail. You can use power notes to organize ideas while reading your text or to restructure your class notes for studying purposes. Practice first by using simple concepts. For example, start with a few headers or boldfaced vocabulary terms from this book. Later you can strengthen your notes by expanding these simple words into more-detailed phrases and sentences. Use the following general format.

<u>Power 1</u>: Main idea
    <u>Power 2</u>: Detail or support for Power 1 idea
        <u>Power 3</u>: Detail or support for Power 2 concept
        <u>Power 4</u>: Detail or support for Power 3 concept

1 Pick a Power 1 word or phrase from the text

The text you choose does not have to come from your environmental science textbook. You may make power notes from your lecture notes or from another source. We'll use the term *environmental problems* as an example of a main idea.

<u>Power 1</u>: environmental problems

2 Using the text, select some Power 2 words to support your Power 1 word

We'll use the terms *resource depletion*, *pollution*, and *extinction*, which are the three main types of environmental problems.

<u>Power 1</u>: environmental problems
    <u>Power 2</u>: resource depletion
    <u>Power 2</u>: pollution
    <u>Power 2</u>: extinction

3 Select some Power 3 words to support your Power 2 words

We'll use the terms *renewable resources* and *nonrenewable resources*. These two terms are types of *resource depletion*, which is one of the Power 2 concepts.

<u>Power 1</u>: environmental problems
    <u>Power 2</u>: resource depletion
        <u>Power 3</u>: renewable resources
        <u>Power 3</u>: nonrenewable resources
    <u>Power 2</u>: pollution
    <u>Power 2</u>: extinction

4 Continue to add powers to support and detail the main idea as necessary

There are no restrictions on how many power numbers you can add to help you extend and organize your ideas. Words having the same power number should have a similar relationship to the power above, but do not have to be related to each other.

<u>Power 1</u>: environmental problems
    <u>Power 2</u>: resource depletion
        <u>Power 3</u>: renewable resources
        <u>Power 3</u>: nonrenewable resources
    <u>Power 2</u>: pollution
        <u>Power 3</u>: degradable pollutants
        <u>Power 3</u>: nondegradable pollutants
    <u>Power 2</u>: extinction
        <u>Power 3</u>: pollution
        <u>Power 3</u>: habitat loss

Practice

1. Use this book's lesson on the experimental method and power notes structure to organize the following terms: *observing, hypothesizing and predicting, experimenting, organizing and analyzing data, drawing conclusions, repeating experiments, communicating results, observation, hypothesis, prediction, experiment, variable, experimental group, control group,* and *data.*

Reading and Study Skills

How to Make KWL Notes

KWL stands for "what I Know—what I Want to know—what I Learned," The KWL strategy is somewhat different from other learning strategies because it prompts you to brainstorm about the subject matter before reading the assigned material. Relating new ideas and concepts with those that you have learned will help you to understand and apply the knowledge you obtain in this course. The section objectives throughout your text are ideal for using the KWL strategy. Read the objectives before reading each section, and follow the instructions in the example below.

1 **Read the section objectives.**

You may also want to scan headings, boldfaced terms, and illustrations in the section. We'll use a few of the objectives from a section of this book as examples.
- List and describe the steps of the scientific method.
- Describe why a good hypothesis is not simply a guess.
- Describe the two essential parts of a good experiment.

2 **Divide a sheet of paper into three columns. Label the columns "What I know," "What I want to know," and "What I learned".**

Here is an example table:

What I know	What I want to know	What I learned

3 **Brainstorm about what you know about the information in the objectives, and write these ideas in the first column.**

Because this table is designed to help you blend your own knowledge with new information, it is not necessary to write complete sentences.

4 **Think about what you want to know about the information in the objectives. Write these ideas in the second column.**

You'll want to know the information you will be tested on, so include information from both the section objectives and any other objectives your teacher has given you.

5 **Use the third column to write down the information you learned. Do this while you read the section, or just after reading.**

While you read, pay close attention to any information about the topics you wrote in the "What I want to know" column. If you do not find all of the answers you are looking for, you may need to reread the section or reference a second source. Be sure to ask your teacher if you still cannot find the information after reading the section a second time.

When you have completed reading the section, review the ideas you brainstormed. Compare your ideas in the first column with the information you wrote down in the third column. If you find that some of the ideas are incorrect, cross them out. Before you begin studying for your test, identify and correct any misconceptions you had prior to reading.

Here is an example of what your notes might look like after using the KWL strategy:

What I know	What I want to know	What I learned
• The experimental method is: predict, test, and conclude.	• What are the steps of the experimental method?	• The steps of the experimental method are: observing, hypothesizing, experimenting, organizing and analyzing data, drawing conclusions, communicating results, and repeating experiments.
• A hypothesis is like a guess, but you have an idea of what might happen.	• Why is a hypothesis not a guess?	• A hypothesis is more than a guess. You have to base it on observations and really think about what you are trying to prove. You should also design an experiment that can test if your hypothesis is wrong, but you cannot prove that it is correct.
• A good experiment includes a hypothesis and a lot of equipment.	• What are the two important parts of a good experiment?	• The two important parts of a good experiment are a single variable and a control group.

Practice

1. Use the third column from the table above to identify and correct any misconceptions in the following list of ideas.
   a. The first step of the experimental method is to predict.
   b. A hypothesis is like a guess.
   c. A good experiment includes a lot of equipment.

How to Make Two-Column Notes

Two-column notes can be used to learn and review definitions of vocabulary terms, examples of multiple-step processes, or details of specific concepts. The two-column-note strategy is simple: write the term, main idea, step-by-step process, or concept in the left-hand column, and the definition, example, or detail on the right.

One strategy for using two-column notes is to organize main ideas and their details. The main ideas from your reading are written in the left-hand column of your paper and can be written as questions, key words, or a combination of both. Details describing these main ideas are then written in the right-hand column of your paper.

1 Identify the main ideas.

The main ideas for a chapter are listed in the section objectives. However, you decide which ideas to include in your notes. The example below shows some main ideas from the objectives in a section of this book.

- Define environmental science and compare environmental science with ecology.
- List the six major fields of study that contribute to environmental science.

2 Divide a blank sheet of paper into two columns, and write the main ideas in the left-hand column.

Remind yourself that your two-column notes are precisely that—notes. Do not copy whole phrases out of the book or waste your time writing ideas in complete sentences. Summarize your ideas using quick phrases that are easy for you to understand and remember. Decide how many details you need for each main idea, and write that number in parentheses under the main idea.

Main idea	Detail notes
Environmental science (two definitions)	
Goals of environmental science (one main goal)	
What is studied (two main areas)	
Related fields of study (four major fields)	

3 Write the detail notes in the right-hand column

List as many details as you designated in the main-idea column.

Main idea	Detail notes
Environmental science (two definitions)	the <u>environment</u> is everything around us • includes the natural world and things produced by humans • is a complex web of connections <u>environmental science</u> is the study of how humans interact with the environment
Goals of environmental science (one main goal)	to understand and solve environmental problems
What is studied (two main areas)	interactions between humans and their environment • the ways we use natural resources, such as water and plants • how our actions alter our environment
Related fields of study (four major fields)	<u>biology</u> is the study of living organisms • includes zoology, botany, microbiology, ecology <u>earth science</u> is the study of the Earth's nonliving systems and the planet as a whole • includes geology, climatology, paleontology, hydrology <u>chemistry</u> is the study of chemicals and their interactions • includes biochemistry <u>social sciences</u> are the study of human populations • include geography, anthropology, sociology and demographics

You can use two-column notes to study for a short quiz or for a test on the material in an entire chapter. Cover the information in the right-hand column with a sheet of paper. Recite what you know and then uncover the notes to check your answers. Then, ask yourself what else you know about that topic. Linking ideas in this way will help you gain a more complete picture of environmental science.

Reading and Study Skills

How to Make a Concept Map

Making concept maps can help you understand new ideas and decide what is important as you read. A concept map is a simple drawing that shows how concepts are connected to each other. Making your own concept maps is a good way to study and to test your understanding of what you have learned. Concept maps are especially helpful if you have a visual learning style, because you can literally draw connections between words and ideas.

To make a concept map, you write main ideas in a few words, and draw lines to show relationships between them. Concept maps can be based on key vocabulary terms from a text. These terms are usually nouns, which make good labels for major concepts. You may add linking words to explain relationships. A group of connected words and lines together show a proposition. A proposition is another way of stating a main idea or explaining a concept. For example, "matter is changed by energy" is a proposition.

1 | List all the important concepts

We will use some of the terms from a chapter in this book as an example.

Earth	layers
composition	structure
crust	mantle
core	lithosphere
aesthenosphere	mesosphere
outer core	inner core

2 | Select a main concept for the map

We will use Earth as the main concept for this map.

3 | Build the map by placing the concepts under the main concept, according to their importance

One way of arranging the concepts is shown in the following map.

4 | Add linking words to give meaning to the arrangement of the concepts

When adding the links, be sure that each proposition makes sense. To distinguish concepts from links, place your concepts in circles, ovals, or rectangles. Then add cross-links with lines connecting concepts across the map. Note how the following map has represented the ideas found in step 1.

Chain-of-Events-Chart

1. Draw a box. In the box, write the first step of a process or the first event of a timeline.

2. Under the box, draw another box, and use an arrow to connect the two boxes. In the second box, write the next step of the process or the next event in the timeline.

3. Continue adding boxes until the process or timeline is finished.

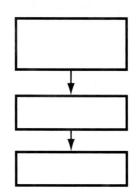

Venn Diagram

1. Draw a diagram like the one shown. You may have two or three circles depending on the number of topics. Make sure the circles overlap with each other.

2. In each circle, write a topic that you want to compare with a topic in another circle.

3. In the areas of the diagram where circles overlap, fill in characteristics that the topics in the overlapping circles share.

4. In the areas of the diagram where circles do not overlap, fill in characteristics that are unique to the topic of the particular circle.

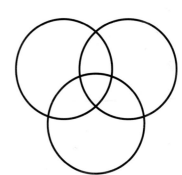

Cause-and-Effect Map

1. Draw a box and write a cause in the box. You can have as many cause boxes as you want. The diagram shown here is one example of a cause-and-effect map.

2. Draw another box to represent an effect of the cause. You can have as many effect boxes as you want. Draw a line from each cause to the effect(s).

3. In the cause boxes, write a description, explanation, or details about the cause. In the effect boxes, explain the effects that result from the process or factor identified in the cause box.

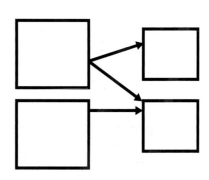

Reading and Study Skills

Analyzing Science Terms

You can often unlock the meaning of an unfamiliar science term by analyzing its word parts. Many parts of scientific word carry a meaning that derives from Latin or Greek. The parts of words listed below provide clues to the meanings of many science terms.

Word part	Meaning	Example
a-	not, without	abiotic
acr-, agr-	field	agriculture, acre
amphi-	both	amphibian
anti-	against	antibiotic
atmos-	vapor	atmosphere
auto-	self, same	autotrophic
benth-	depth	benthic, benthos
bio-	life	biology, biosphere, biotic
chloro-	green	chlorophyll
-cide	kill	insecticide, fungicide
co-, con-	with, together	coevolution, cooperation, commensalism
dem-, demo-	people	demography, epidemic
-duct-	to lead, draw	reproduction
e-, ec-, ex-	out, away from, outside	extinction, experiment
eco-	home, environment	ecology, ecosystem, economics
eu-	good, well	eutrophic
evolu-	to unroll	evolution
gen-	to give birth, produce	genetic, generation, genus
geo-	earth	geology, geosphere
hetero-	different	heterotroph
hydro-	water	hydrosphere, hydroelectric
im-, in-, ir-	not, without or in, into	invertebrate, immigration, irrigation
-ion	the act of	pollution, destruction
lith-	stone	lithosphere
-log-	to study	ecology, geology
-lu-, -lue-	dirt, impurity	pollution
mar-	sea	marine
micro-	small	microscopic, microorganisms
nutri-	food, nourishment	nutrient
organ-	tool, instrument	organic, organism
per-	through	permeable
photo-	light	photosynthesis
phyto-, -phyte	plant	phytoplankton, epiphyte
pre-	before, in front of	predator, prey, precipitation
pro-	forward	reproduction
re-	back, again	recycle, reproduce
spec-	appearance or shape	species, spectrum
-sphere	ball, globe	geosphere, ecosphere
stat-	position, standing	statistics, status
strati-, strato-	spread, layer	stratosphere
temper-	to measure or regulate	temperate, temperature
terra-, terre-	earth, land	terrain, terrestrial
thermo-	heat	thermosphere, thermal
-troph-	to feed, gather	eutrophic, autotroph

Math Skills Refresher

Geometry

A useful way to model the objects and substances studied in science is to consider them in terms of their shapes. For example, many of the properties of a wheel can be understood by pretending that the wheel is a perfect circle.

When using shapes as models, your ability to calculate the area or volume of shapes is a useful skill. The table below provides equations for the area and volume of several geometric shapes.

Geometric Areas and Volumes		
Geometric shape		**Useful equations**
Rectangle		Area $= lw$
Circle		Area $= \pi r^2$ Circumference $= 2\pi r$
Triangle		Area $= \frac{1}{2}bh$
Sphere		Surface area $= 4\pi r^2$ Volume $= \frac{4}{3}\pi r^3$
Cylinder		Volume $= \pi r^2 h$
Rectangular box		Surface area $= 2(lh + lw + hw)$ Volume $= lwh$

Practice

1. Calculate the area of a triangle that has a base of 900.0 m and a height of 500.0 m.
2. What is the volume of a cylinder that has a diameter of 14 cm and a height of 8 cm?
3. Calculate the surface area of a 4 cm cube.

Exponents

An exponent is a number that is superscripted to the right of another number. The best way to explain how an exponent works is with an example. In the value 5^4, the 4 is the exponent of the 5. The number with its exponent means that 5 is multiplied by itself 4 times:

$$5^4 = 5 \times 5 \times 5 \times 5 = 625$$

You will frequently hear exponents referred to as *powers*. Using this terminology, the above equation could be read as "five to the fourth power equals 625," or "five to the power of four equals 625." Keep in mind that any number raised to the power of 0 is equal to 1: $5^0 = 1$. Also, any number raised to the power of 1 is equal to itself: $5^1 = 5$.

A scientific calculator is a must for solving most problems involving exponents. Many calculators have dedicated keys for squares and square roots, but scientific calculators usually have a special key shaped like a caret, ^, for entering exponents. If you type in "5^4" and then hit the "=" key or the "Enter" key, the calculator will determine that 5^4 = 625 and display that answer.

Exponents		
	Rule	**Example**
Zero power	$x^0 = 1$	$7^0 = 1$
First power	$x^1 = x$	$6^1 = 6$
Multiplication	$(x^n)(x^m) = (x^{n+m})$	$(x^2)(x^4) =$ $x^{(2+4)} = x^6$
Division	$\dfrac{x^n}{x^m} = x^{(n-m)}$	$\dfrac{x^8}{x^2} = x^{(8-2)} = x^6$
Exponents raised to a power	$(x^n)^m = x^{nm}$	$(5^2)^3 =$ $5^6 = 15{,}625$

Practice

1. Perform the following calculations:
   a. $9^1 =$
   b. $(3^3)^5 =$
   c. $(14^2)(14^3) =$
   d. $11^0 =$

Math Skills Refresher

Order of Operations

Use this phrase to remember the correct order for long mathematical problems: "Please Excuse My Dear Aunt Sally" (some people just remember the acronym "PEMDAS"). This acronym stands for **p**arentheses, **e**xponents, **m**ultiplication, **d**ivision, **a**ddition, and **s**ubtraction. This is the correct order in which to complete operations. These rules are summarized in the table below.

Order of Operations

1 Simplify groups inside parentheses. Start with the innermost group and work out.

2 Simplify all exponents.

3 Perform multiplication and division in order from left to right.

4 Perform addition and subtraction in order from left to right.

Look at the following example.

$$4^3 + 2 \times [8 - (3 - 1)] = ?$$

First, simplify the operations inside parentheses. Begin with the innermost parentheses:

$$(3 - 1) = 2$$
$$4^3 + 2 \times [8 - 2] = ?$$

Then, move on to the next-outer parentheses:

$$[8 - 2] = 6$$
$$4^3 + 2 \times 6 = ?$$

Now, simplify all exponents:

$$4^3 = 64$$
$$64 + 2 \times 6 = ?$$

Next, perform the remaining multiplication:

$$2 \times 6 = 12$$
$$64 + 12 = ?$$

Finally, perform the addition:

$$64 + 12 = 76$$

Practice

1. $2^3 \div 2 + 4 \times (9 - 2^2) =$

2. $\dfrac{2 \times (6 - 3) + 8}{4 \times 2 - 6} =$

Algebraic Rearrangements

Algebraic equations contain *constants* and *variables*. Constants are simply numbers, such as 2, 5, and 7. Variables are represented by letters such as x, y, z, a, b, and c. Variables are unspecified quantities and are also called the *unknowns*. Often, you will need to determine the value of a variable in an equation that contains algebraic expressions.

An algebraic expression contains one or more of the four basic mathematical operations: addition, subtraction, multiplication, and division. Constants, variables, or terms made up of both constants and variables can be involved in the basic operations.

The key to finding the value of a variable in an algebraic equation is that the total quantity on one side of the equals sign is equal to the quantity on the other side. If you do the same operation on either side of the equation, the results will still be equal. To determine the value of a variable in an algebraic expression, you try to reduce the equation into a simple one that tells you exactly what x (or some other variable) equals.

Look at the simple problem below.

$$8x = 32$$

If we wish to solve for x, we can multiply or divide each side of the equation by the same factor. You can perform any operation on one side of an equation as long as you do the same thing to the other side of the equation. In this example, if we divide both sides of the equation by 8, we have:

$$\frac{8x}{8} = \frac{32}{8}$$

The 8s on the left side of the equation cancel each other out, and the fraction $\frac{32}{8}$ can be reduced to give the whole number, 4. Therefore, $x = 4$.

Next, consider the following equation.

$$2x + 4 = 16$$

If we divide each side by 2, we are left with $x + 2$ on the left and 8 on the right:

$$x + 2 = 8$$

Now, we can subtract 2 from each side of the equation to find that $x = 6$. In all cases, whatever operation is performed on the left side of the equals sign must also be performed on the right side.

Practice

1. Rearrange each of the following equations to give the value of the variable indicated with a letter.
   a. $8x - 32 = 128$
   b. $6 - 5(4a + 3) = 26$
   c. $-3(y - 2) + 4 = 29$
   d. $-2(3m + 5) = 14$
   e. $\left[8 \frac{(8 + 2z)}{3z}\right] + 2 = 5$
   f. $\frac{(6b + 3)}{3} - 9 = 2$

Scientific Notation

Many quantities that scientists deal with are very large or very small values. For example, light travels at about 300,000,000 meters per second, and an electron has a mass of about 0.000 000 000 000 000 000 000 000 000 9 g. Obviously, it is difficult to read, write, and keep track of numbers like these. We avoid this problem by using a method dealing with powers of the number 10.

Study the positive powers of 10 shown in the following table. You should be able to check these numbers using what you know about exponents. The number of zeros in the equivalent number corresponds to the exponent of the 10, or the power to which the 10 is raised. The equivalent of 10^4 is 10,000, so the number has four zeros.

But how can we use the powers of 10 to simplify large numbers such as the speed of light? The speed of light is equal to $3 \times 100,000,000$ m/s. The factor of 10 in this number has 8 zeros, so it can be rewritten as 10^8. So, 300,000,000 can be expressed as 3×10^8.

Negative exponents can be used to simplify numbers that are less than 1. Study the negative powers of 10 in the table. In these cases,

Powers of 10

Power of 10	Decimal Equivalent
10^4	10,000
10^3	1,000
10^2	100
10^1	10
10^0	1
10^{-1}	0.1
10^{-2}	0.01
10^{-3}	0.001

the exponent of 10 equals the number of decimal places you must move the decimal point to the right so that there is one digit just to the left of the decimal point. In the case of the mass of an electron, the decimal point has to be moved 28 decimal places to the right for the numeral 9 to be just to the left of the decimal point. The mass of the electron, about 0.000 000 000 000 000 000 000 000 000 9 g, can be rewritten as about 9×10^{-28} g.

Scientific notation is a way to express numbers as a power of 10 multiplied by another number that has only one digit to the left of the decimal point. For example, 5,943,000,000 is 5.943×10^9 when expressed in scientific notation. The number 0.000 083 2 is 8.32×10^{-5} when expressed in scientific notation.

Practice

1. Rewrite the following values using scientific notation.
   a. 12,300,000 m/s
   b. 0.000 000 000 004 5 kg
   c. 0.000 065 3 m
   d. 55,432,000,000,000 s
   e. 273.15 K
   f. 0.000 627 14 kg

Math Skills Refresher

Significant Digits

The following list can be used to review how to determine the number of *significant digits* (also called *significant figures*) in a given value or measurement.

Rules for Significant Digits:

1. All nonzero digits are significant. For example, 1,246 has four significant digits (shown in red).

2. Any zeros between significant digits are also significant. For example, 1,206 has four significant digits.

3. If the value does not contain a decimal point, any zeros to the right of a nonzero digit are not significant. For example, 1,200 has only two significant digits.

4. Any zeros to the right of a significant digit and to the left of a decimal point are significant. For example, 1,200. has four significant digits.

5. If a value has no significant digits to the left of a decimal point, any zeros to the right of the decimal point and also to the left of a significant digit are not significant. For example, 0.0012 has only two significant digits.

6. If a value ends with zeros to the right of a decimal point, those zeros are significant. For example, 0.1200 has four significant digits.

After you have reviewed the rules, use the following table to check your understanding of the rules. Cover up the second column of the table, and try to determine how many significant digits each number in the first column has. If you get confused, refer to the rule given.

When performing mathematical operations with measurements, you must remember to keep track of significant digits. If you are adding or

Significant Digits		
Measurement	Number of significant digits	Rule
12,345	5	1
2,400 cm	2	3
305 kg	3	2
2,350. cm	4	4
234.005 K	6	2
12.340	5	6
0.001	1	5
0.002 450	4	5 and 6

subtracting two measurements, your answer can only have as many decimal positions as the value that has the fewest number of decimal places. When multiplying or dividing measurements, your answer can only have as many significant digits as the value with the fewest number of significant digits.

Practice

1. Determine the number of significant digits in each of the following measurements:
   a. 65.04 mL   c. 0.007 504 kg
   b. 564.00 m   d. 1,210 K

2. Perform each of the following calculations, and report your answer with the correct number of significant digits and units:
   a. 0.004 dm + 0.12508 dm
   b. 340 m ÷ 0.1257 s
   c. 40.1 m × 0.2453 m
   d. 1.03 g − 0.0456 g

Graphing Skills

Line Graphs

In laboratory experiments, you will usually be controlling one variable and seeing how it affects another variable. Line graphs can show these relations clearly. For example, you might perform an experiment in which you measure the growth of a plant over time to determine the rate of the plant's growth. In this experiment, you are controlling the time intervals at which the plant height is measured. Therefore, time is the independent variable. The height of the plant is the dependent variable. The table below gives some sample data for an experiment that measures the rate of plant growth.

The independent variable is plotted on the x-axis. This axis will be labeled "Time (days)" and will have a range from 0 to 35 days. Be sure to properly label each axis, including the units.

The dependent variable is plotted on the y-axis. This axis will be labeled "Plant Height (cm)" and will have a range from 0 to 5 cm.

Experimental Data for Plant Growth Vs. Time	
Time (days)	Plant height (cm)
0	1.43
7	2.16
14	2.67
21	3.25
28	4.04
35	4.67

Think of your graph as a grid with lines running horizontally from the y-axis and vertically from the x-axis. To plot a point, find the x value on the x-axis. For the example above, plot each value for time on the x-axis. Follow the vertical line from the x-axis until it intersects the horizontal line from the y-axis at the corresponding y value. For the example, each time value has a corresponding height value. Place your point at the intersection of these two lines.

The line graph below shows how the data in the table might be graphed.

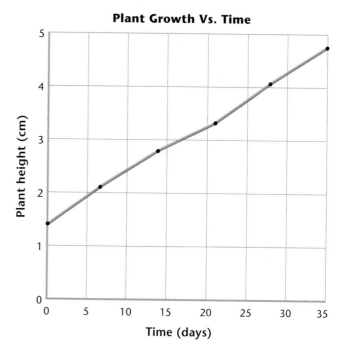

Plant Growth Vs. Time

Bar Graphs

Bar graphs are useful for comparing data values. If you wanted to compare the area or depth of the major oceans, you might use a bar graph. The table below gives the data for each of these quantities.

Depth of the Major Oceans	
Ocean	Depth (m)
Pacific Ocean	4,028
Atlantic Ocean	3,926
Indian Ocean	3,963
Arctic Ocean	1,205

To create a bar graph from the data in the table, begin on the x-axis by labeling four bar positions with the names of the four oceans. Label the y-axis "Depth (m)." Be sure the range on your y-axis encompasses 1,205 m and 4,028 m. Then, draw the bars to represent the area of each ocean, with a bar height on the *y*-axis that matches each ocean's area value, as shown in the bar graph below.

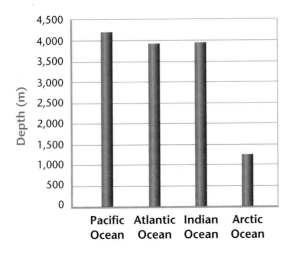

Pie Graphs

Pie graphs are an easy way to visualize how many parts make up a whole. Frequently, pie graphs are made from percentage data. For example, you could create a pie graph showing percentage of different materials that make up the waste generated in cities of the United States. Study the example data in the table below.

United States Municipal Solid Waste	
Material	**Percentage of total waste**
Paper	38.1%
Yard waste	12.1%
Food waste	10.9%
Plastics	10.5%
Metals	7.8%
Rubber, leather, and textiles	6.6%
Glass	5.5%
Wood	5.3%
Other	3.2%

To create a pie graph from the data in the table, begin by drawing a circle to represent the whole, or total. Then, imagine dividing the circle into 100 equal sections, to represent 100 percent. Shade in 38 consecutive sections, and label that area "Paper." Continue to shade sections with other colors until the entire pie graph has been filled in and until each type of waste has a corresponding area in the circle, as shown in the pie graph below.

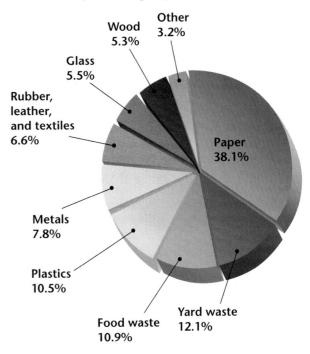

United States Municipal Solid Waste (Percentage by Weight)

Chemistry Refresher

Atoms and Elements

Every object in the universe is made up of particles of matter. Matter is anything that has mass and takes up space. An element is a substance that cannot be separated into simpler substances by chemical means. Elements cannot be separated in this way because each element consists of only one kind of atom. An atom is the smallest unit of an element that maintains the properties of that element.

Atomic Structure Atoms are made up of small particles called *subatomic particles*. The three major types of subatomic particles are **electrons, protons,** and **neutrons.** Electrons have a negative electrical charge, protons have a positive charge, and neutrons have no electrical charge. The protons and neutrons are packed close to one another and form the **nucleus.** The protons give the nucleus a positive charge. The electrons of an atom are located in a region around the nucleus known as an **electron cloud.** The negatively charged electrons are attracted to the positively charged nucleus. An atom may have several energy levels in which electrons are located.

Atomic Number To help in the identification of elements, scientists have assigned an **atomic number** to each kind of atom. The atomic number is equal to the number of protons in the atom. Atoms with the same number of protons are all of the same element. In an uncharged, or electrically neutral, atom there are an equal number of protons and electrons. Therefore, the atomic number also equals the number of electrons in an uncharged atom. The number of neutrons, however, can vary for a given element. Atoms that have different numbers of neutrons but are of the same element are called **isotopes.**

Periodic Table of the Elements A periodic table of the elements is shown on the next page. In a periodic table, the elements are arranged in order of increasing atomic number. Each element in the table is found in a separate box. In each horizontal row of the table, each element has one more

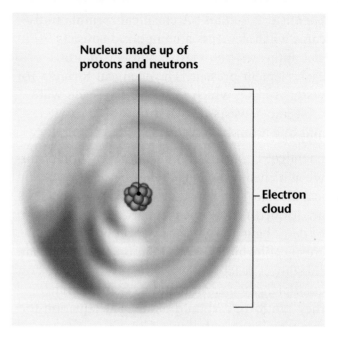

Nucleus made up of protons and neutrons

Electron cloud

▶ The nucleus of the atom contains the protons and neutrons. The protons give the nucleus a positive charge. The negatively charged electrons are in the electron cloud surrounding the nucleus.

electron and one more proton than the element to its left. Each row of the table is called a **period.** Changes in chemical properties across a period correspond to changes in the elements' electron arrangements. Each vertical column of the table, known as a **group,** contains elements that have similar properties. The elements in a group have similar chemical properties because they have the same number of electrons in their outer energy level. For example, the elements helium, neon, argon, krypton, xenon, and radon all have similar properties and are known as the noble gases.

Molecules and Compounds When the atoms of two or more elements are joined chemically, the resulting substance is called a **compound.** A compound is a new substance with properties different from those of the elements that compose it. For example, water (H_2O) is a compound formed when atoms of hydrogen (H) and oxygen (O) combine. The smallest complete unit of a compound that has all of the properties of that compound is called a **molecule.**

Chemistry Refresher

Chemical Formulas A chemical formula indicates what elements a compound consists of. It also indicates the relative number of atoms of each element present. The chemical formula for water is H_2O, which indicates that each water molecule consists of two atoms of hydrogen and one atom of oxygen.

Chemical Equations A chemical reaction occurs when a chemical change takes place. (In a chemical change, new substances with new properties are formed.) A chemical equation is a useful way of describing a chemical reaction by means of chemical formulas. The equation indicates what substances react and what the products are. For example, when carbon and oxygen combine, they can form carbon dioxide. The equation for this reaction is as follows: $C + O_2 \rightarrow CO_2$.

Acids, Bases, and pH An ion is an atom or group of atoms that has an electrical charge because it has lost or gained one or more electrons. When an acid, such as hydrochloric acid (HCl), is mixed with water, it separates into ions. An **acid** is a compound that produces hydrogen ions (H^+) in water. The hydrogen ions then combine with a water molecule to form a hydronium ion (H_3O^+). A solution that contains hydronium ions is an acidic solution. A **base,** on the other hand, is a substance that produces hydroxide ions (OH^-) in water.

To determine whether a solution is acidic or basic, scientists measure pH. **pH** is a measure of how many hydronium ions are in solution. The pH scale ranges from 0 to 14. The middle point, pH = 7, is neutral, neither acidic nor basic. Acids have a pH of less than 7; bases have a pH of more than 7. The lower the number, the stronger the acid. The higher the number, the stronger the base. A pH scale is shown in Figure 12, on page 336.

internet connect

Topic: Periodic Table
Go To: go.hrw.com
Keyword: Holt Periodic

Visit the HRW Web site for updates on the periodic table

THE PERIODIC TABLE OF THE ELEMENTS

| 1 H Hydrogen | | | | | | | | | | | | | | | | | Group 18 2 He Helium |

Metals
- Alkali metals
- Alkaline-earth metals
- Transition metals
- Other metals

Nonmetals
- Hydrogen
- Semiconductors
- Halogens
- Noble Gases
- Other nonmetals

6 — Atomic number
C — Symbol
Carbon — Name

Group 1	Group 2											Group 13	Group 14	Group 15	Group 16	Group 17	
3 Li Lithium	4 Be Beryllium											5 B Boron	6 C Carbon	7 N Nitrogen	8 O Oxygen	9 F Fluorine	10 Ne Neon
11 Na Sodium	12 Mg Magnesium	Group 3	Group 4	Group 5	Group 6	Group 7	Group 8	Group 9	Group 10	Group 11	Group 12	13 Al Aluminum	14 Si Silicon	15 P Phosphorus	16 S Sulfur	17 Cl Chlorine	18 Ar Argon
19 K Potassium	20 Ca Calcium	21 Sc Scandium	22 Ti Titanium	23 V Vanadium	24 Cr Chromium	25 Mn Manganese	26 Fe Iron	27 Co Cobalt	28 Ni Nickel	29 Cu Copper	30 Zn Zinc	31 Ga Gallium	32 Ge Germanium	33 As Arsenic	34 Se Selenium	35 Br Bromine	36 Kr Krypton
37 Rb Rubidium	38 Sr Strontium	39 Y Yttrium	40 Zr Zirconium	41 Nb Niobium	42 Mo Molybdenum	43 Tc Technetium	44 Ru Ruthenium	45 Rh Rhodium	46 Pd Palladium	47 Ag Silver	48 Cd Cadmium	49 In Indium	50 Sn Tin	51 Sb Antimony	52 Te Tellurium	53 I Iodine	54 Xe Xenon
55 Cs Cesium	56 Ba Barium	57 La Lanthanum	72 Hf Hafnium	73 Ta Tantalum	74 W Tungsten	75 Re Rhenium	76 Os Osmium	77 Ir Iridium	78 Pt Platinum	79 Au Gold	80 Hg Mercury	81 Tl Thallium	82 Pb Lead	83 Bi Bismuth	84 Po Polonium	85 At Astatine	86 Rn Radon
87 Fr Francium	88 Ra Radium	89 Ac Actinium	104 Rf Rutherfordium	105 Db Dubnium	106 Sg Seaborgium	107 Bh Bohrium	108 Hs Hassium	109 Mt Meitnerium	110 Ds Darmstadtium	111 Uuu* Unununium	112 Uub* Ununbium	113 Uut* Ununtrium	114 Uuq* Ununquadium	115 Uup* Ununpentium			

A team at Lawrence Berkeley National Laboratories reported the discovery of elements 116 and 118 in June 1999. The same team retracted the discovery in July 2001. The discovery of elements 113, 114, and 115 has been reported but not confirmed.

* The systematic names and symbols for elements greater than 110 will be used until the approval of trivial names by IUPAC.

58 Ce Cerium	59 Pr Praseodymium	60 Nd Neodymium	61 Pm Promethium	62 Sm Samarium	63 Eu Europium	64 Gd Gadolinium	65 Tb Terbium	66 Dy Dysprosium	67 Ho Holmium	68 Er Erbium	69 Tm Thulium	70 Yb Ytterbium	71 Lu Lutetium
90 Th Thorium	91 Pa Protactinium	92 U Uranium	93 Np Neptunium	94 Pu Plutonium	95 Am Americium	96 Cm Curium	97 Bk Berkelium	98 Cf Californium	99 Es Einsteinium	100 Fm Fermium	101 Md Mendelevium	102 No Nobelium	103 Lr Lawrencium

Economics Concepts

You may think that economics is about the complicated numbers of stock markets and interest rates, but the field of economics is based on simple concepts. *Economics* is the study of how people make decisions about the production, distribution, and consumption of limited resources as they attempt to fulfill their needs and wants. While economics can be a complex subject to study, it is a key part of understanding the relationship of humans and their environment. Here we will present some of the most basic concepts of economics.

Resources and Value

Resources that people use to create useful and desirable products are called *economic resources* or *capital*. Products and capital may exist in the form of *goods* or *services*. There are three general types of capital: natural, manufactured, and human. *Natural resources,* sometimes called *earth capital,* are resources such as land, fertile soil, air and water, oceans, wildlife, and minerals. *Manufactured capital* includes tools, machines, buildings, and other things that are made from natural resources and that are used to produce goods and services. *Human capital* includes the mental and physical abilities for which people may be paid wages or salaries.

A given resource or product has a specific *value* to a given group of people at a particular time. Generally, the *value* of something is the amount of money most people are willing to pay for it. For example, if many people are willing to pay $15 for a music CD, the value of that CD is $15. But value is not always the same as price. Some stores might sell the CD for $5. If the CD's price were lower than its value, an economist would say the CD is *undervalued.*

Economic activities that produce goods and services are called *industries.* A basic industry involves people using natural resources directly. The highest level of industry involves people working mostly with information instead of goods. The degree to which a single business or economic system has activities at multiple levels of industry is called *economic diversity.* For example, the United States has a high degree of economic diversity, but a small island that subsists on fishing and tourism has low economic diversity.

Economic Systems and Governments

Most societies use some type of *economic system* to decide what to produce, how to produce, and for whom to produce. The main difference between economic systems is in how much the government regulates the activities of businesses or controls access to resources.

In a *market economy* (also called a *capitalist, free-market,* or *free-enterprise system*), people own businesses and make their own decisions about what to make, sell, or buy. The theory of a market economy is that competition in open markets will result in the highest-quality goods being produced in the most efficient way and for the lowest price. In market theory, individuals acting in self-interest will efficiently decide what goods and services to buy or sell, so supply will be balanced with demand.

In a *command economy,* or a *centrally planned economy,* the government controls production and determines the amount and price of goods and services produced. Command economies are typically practiced by communist governments. A few countries and cultural groups still practice a *traditional economy,* which means they make economic decisions based on local customs or traditions.

However, economic systems are rarely practiced exactly according to theory. Most countries have a *mixed economy* in which a combination of government control and free markets exist. Governments may produce goods and services or may try to influence the flow of goods and services by charging taxes, paying out subsidies, or making regulations.

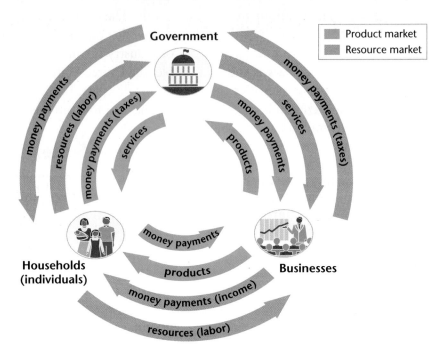

Product market
Resource market

Government

money payments
resources (labor)
money payments (taxes)
services

money payments (taxes)
services
money payments
products

Households (individuals)

money payments
products
money payments (income)
resources (labor)

Businesses

▶ **An Economic System Model** This *circular-flow model* illustrates the exchange of resources, products, and money payments in the economic system of nations such as the United States.

Economic Growth and Development

The economic growth within a country is usually measured by looking at the country's *gross domestic product* (GDP), or by looking at the *gross national product* (GNP). A country's GDP is the total value of all goods and services produced within the country in a year. The GNP is like the GDP, but the GNP includes income from outside of the country generated by individuals or companies based within the country. To represent each person's part in the economy, economists calculate the GNP or GDP *per capita,* which means the average GNP or GDP per person in the country.

Economists and social scientists often categorize countries based on indicators of their economic and social development. Countries that have high average incomes, slow population growth, diverse economies, and strong social support systems are considered to be *more devel-* *oped.* Countries that have low average incomes, simple economies, and rapid population growth are considered to be *less developed.* However, these categories are difficult to apply because countries may develop in different ways and because the economies of different countries are interconnected as people and goods move between countries.

The economies of the world are now so interconnected that economists often refer to the *global economy.* In the 20th century, most countries became more developed and tended toward market system economies. Also, international trade continued to increase. Many countries now work together to help manage the global economy. International organizations such as the World Bank, the World Trade Organization, or the European Union have become as influential as national governments.

ENVIRONMENTAL EDUCATOR

As a child who watched *The Underwater World of Jacques Cousteau* on public television every chance she had, **Niki Espy** dreamed of one day studying aquatic mammals for a living. She went to college with the intent of continuing on to graduate school to focus on behavioral studies in marine biology. But while pursuing a bachelor's degree in biology, she interned as a naturalist. Today, Niki works for the Milwaukee Public Museum. She provides educational programs for children, adults, and families and is responsible for developing and implementing school programs that focus on cultural and natural history. Niki also facilitates training for educators, including student teachers, active teachers, museum volunteers, and museum docents.

If we look at humans as a separate component of the world, we will not be able to truly reach sustainability.

Q: How does your current job relate to environmental education?

Niki Espy: I use the principles of environmental education to teach about natural and cultural history. The basics of awareness, appreciation, knowledge, and action assist me daily in my educational endeavors. I believe that if we don't have an understanding of the world, we can't begin to value or protect our resources. The museum's educational programs lead students to question, explore, analyze, evaluate, and discuss how the introductions of exotic plants and animals and the urbanization of the Milwaukee area have affected biodiversity. While interpreting the plant and animal changes, we don't forget the people and how indigenous groups used the land.

Q: What is the importance of including people in a discussion on biodiversity and environmental impact?

Niki Espy: If we look at humans as a separate component of the world, we will not be able to truly reach sustainability. By placing people in the equation, we can look at our behaviors and our impact on local and global ecoregions, economies, and social systems and can obtain the answers we need to create a sustainable future.

MORE ON THIS CAREER

Many museums have volunteer programs in which volunteers work directly with the public or in different administrative or scientific departments. For example, volunteers at the Milwaukee Public Museum may provide assistance at the information desk, give tours to the public through the exhibit galleries, demonstrate objects visitors can touch, help educate visitors about special exhibits, and work at special events. In addition, volunteers may work behind the scene in research areas such as anthropology, archeology, botany, geology, paleontology, and zoology. For more information on volunteer programs, contact a museum located near you.

▶ One of Niki Espy's goals as an environmental educator is to increase awareness and knowledge of the natural world.

ENVIRONMENTAL ENGINEER

John Roll began college studying chemistry and biology, and then halfway through his undergraduate degree he switched to agricultural engineering with a focus on water-quality issues. Roll completed his master's degree in agricultural engineering and expanded his environmental background to include livestock waste management. He spent the first three years after graduation on a project involving treated solids from a municipal wastewater treatment facility. For the next 14 years, John was manager of land reclamation and environmental permits for a surface coal mining company in Illinois. In 1990, Roll entered Oklahoma State University, where he studied groundwater transport of contaminants and received a Doctorate in Biosystems Engineering.

Q: What does an environmental engineer study in college?

John: First and foremost, a student must obtain an engineering degree. The individual must have a desire to study hard, and it helps to possess an aptitude for the math and hard-science courses (physics, chemistry, and mechanics) required by engineering programs. An environmental engineer can come from different engineering study areas, but all individuals should share a common desire to apply engineering principles to an aspect of the environment that is interesting to them. Agricultural engineering, chemical engineering, civil engineering, general engineering, geological engineering, and mechanical engineering programs routinely graduate individuals who work on environmental issues specific to their discipline.

Q: What kind of jobs does an environmental engineer do?

John: The range of jobs performed by an environmental engineer is extremely varied. A chemical engineer may develop new manufacturing methods that remove toxic contaminants from a product. A civil engineer may be involved in the design of water and wastewater treatment plants, the development of better methods to treat wastes, the development of road-building processes that

I have found out through firsthand experience that environmental issues require very careful communications skills.

▶ John Roll is shown conducting a survey of plant cover on reclaimed mined land.

are more environmentally friendly, and the design of groundwater treatment schemes. Mechanical and general engineering graduates may work on controlling air pollution from factories and producing changes in manufacturing methods to create less waste. Agricultural engineers often work on environmental issues involving livestock waste, runoff-water quality, erosion control, and application methods to lower the quantity of fertilizer, herbicides, and insecticides used to grow crops.

Q: What is the most important skill an environmental engineer should possess?

John: An environmental engineer must be skilled in the application of science and engineering principles to help solve a problem. Using a team approach to an environmental problem will yield a broader view on the issue. Team members usually have expertise in different environmental disciplines, and this results in multiple views on how to solve the problem at hand. Therefore, probably the least expected but the most important skill for an environmental engineer is the ability to communicate clearly through written and spoken words.

Q: Do you feel that environmental issues are often misunderstood?

John: I found out through first-hand experience that environmental issues require very careful communication skills. Environmental issues are often controversial. However, open communication between all interested parties, including those individuals who are against a project, can prevent misunderstanding. For example, the plans for the Industry Coal Mine were finalized after discussions with governmental agencies, local citizens, and authorities. The planning and public meetings lasted almost three years, and during this time everyone had a chance to question the coal company about its plans and to express their views. The public opinion ranged from very favorable to a few individuals who were totally against the project. By addressing the issues with good faith, a reclamation plan was developed that was ultimately approved by all state and federal agencies, local county officials, and zoning boards.

Q: What is the future need for environmental engineers?

John: My feeling is that the future will be a good one for environmental engineers. Since 1970, the environment has been an important focus for many people. Congress passed new laws and created new agencies such as the Environmental Protection Agency (EPA) to specifically address environmental problems. The agencies wrote regulations based on laws passed by Congress and approved by the President, and this resulted in new or additional permits, approvals, and public comment requirements for activities that might harm the environment. In order to enforce the regulations, new agencies were created in the states as well as the federal government. Industry and government currently hire many environmental engineers to meet regulatory requirements.

MORE ON THIS CAREER

For more information on environmental engineering as a career, contact the American Academy of Environmental Engineers, 130 Holiday Court, Suite 100, Annapolis, Maryland 21401, or call (410) 266-3311.

▶ John Roll managed the reclamation of this surface coal mine in Illinois. Land that has been reclaimed is seen to the right of the cut that is being mined.

ENVIRONMENTAL ARCHITECT

To **Michael Reynolds,** a house is not just a home, and old tires and empty soda cans are not just trash. For almost 30 years, this Taos, New Mexico, architect has been designing and building energy-efficient houses out of automobile tires, cans, and other discarded items. These houses, which Michael now calls "Earthships," not only provide a comfortable, affordable place for people to live but also contribute to a sustainable future for our planet.

The Origin of the Earthship Design

In 1970, a TV report about the growing number of beverage cans littering the streets and fields of America started Michael thinking about ways that trash could be used to build houses. Through many years of experimentation, he found that sturdy walls could be built by packing soil into old tires, stacking the tires like bricks, and covering them with cement or adobe, a heavy clay often used in buildings in the Southwest. Michael had this design tested by structural engineers to ensure that the walls would meet or surpass any existing building code requirements. One engineer even commented that the design could be used to construct dams!

Building an Earthship

The tire-stack design is used for three of the outside walls of an Earthship. These walls are approximately 1 m (3 ft) thick, and this large mass causes the walls to act like a battery, storing energy from the sun and releasing the energy when needed. Also, the base of the Earthship is built below the frost line (the deepest level to which the ground freezes). Below this line, the ground maintains a constant temperature—around 15°C (59°F)—and walls anchored below the frost line usually stay at that temperature, too. The fourth wall, which faces south, is constructed completely of glass to capture as much sunlight as possible. In the winter, the tire-stack walls hold in the sun's warmth. In the summer, cool air enters through windows in the front while warm air escapes through a skylight in the back.

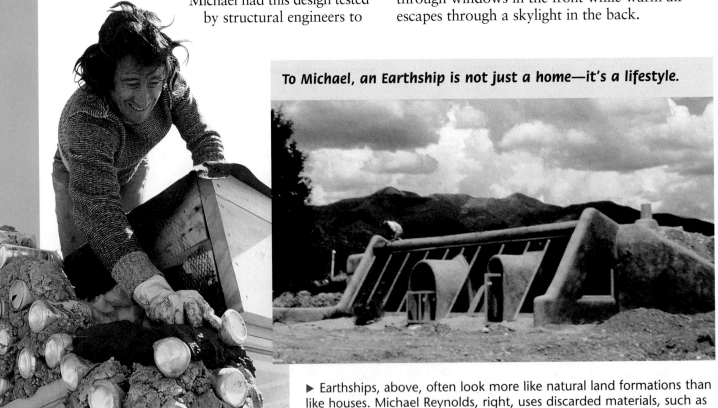

To Michael, an Earthship is not just a home—it's a lifestyle.

▶ Earthships, above, often look more like natural land formations than like houses. Michael Reynolds, right, uses discarded materials, such as used soda cans, to construct environmentally friendly houses.

▶ A greenhouse, built along the Earthship's southern glass wall, can provide residents with a sustainable food source.

Even the soil that is excavated for the site of the house is used to build the house. Some of the soil is pounded into the tires to construct the walls, and the remaining soil is piled against the outside of these walls and on top of the roof (constructed of beams) for further insulation. The most suitable location for this design is a south-facing slope of a hill, where the Earthship can simply be built into the hill. Often, Earthships look more like natural formations of land than houses.

Inside the house, walls between rooms are constructed by embedding empty beverage cans into mortar or mud. When these walls are covered with cement and then painted with latex paint or some other durable finish, they look just like walls constructed with conventional materials. Other inside surfaces, including stairs and even bathtubs, can be built using the beverage-can technique. Because the cans are so lightweight, this method can even be used to create dynamic interior structures such as arches and domes.

The Environmental Impact of the Earthship Design

Earthships are typically built to obtain electricity from photovoltaic cells that convert sunlight to electricity. All household water is supplied by rainwater that is collected on the roof. Wastewater from sinks, tubs, and the laundry room is recycled to nourish plants in the greenhouse, which can provide a sustainable source of food. With these features, people who live in Earthships use fewer of the Earth's resources and often have no utility bills.

Because Earthships are environmentally friendly and inexpensive to buy and maintain, more and more people are choosing them instead of conventional homes. More than 1,000 Earthships have already been built, mostly in the Southwest. However, the design can be used anywhere. In fact, Earthships have been built in Florida, Vermont, Canada, Mexico, Bolivia, and Japan. Wetter environments simply require that the house is built entirely above the ground and uses more cans and tires.

More tires in the design certainly wouldn't be a problem. According to the Environmental Protection Agency, more than 250 million tires are discarded in the United States every year. But most landfills do not accept tires because of their tendency to rise to the surface even when the landfill is covered over. Tire dealers usually pay to have used tires hauled away to stockpile areas, where they sit indefinitely. Earthships provide one way to diminish the stockpiles.

Michael enthusiastically shares his Earthship concept with others. To Michael, an Earthship is not just a home—it's a lifestyle. His dedication to designing Earth-friendly homes is a result of his commitment to "reducing the stress involved in living on the Earth, for both humans and the planet."

▶ The tire-stack design of the outer walls accounts for much of the Earthship's energy efficiency. These tire stacks will be covered with cement or adobe for a finished exterior.

MORE ON THIS CAREER

For more information on environmentally friendly, energy-efficient housing, use the Internet to locate government and nonprofit organizations that are involved in "green" building projects.

ENVIRONMENTAL FILMMAKER

Haroldo Castro considers himself a "citizen of the planet." It's easy to see why: he was born in Italy to a Brazilian father and a French mother, he was educated in France, he speaks five languages, and he has visited more than 80 countries. Furthermore, Haroldo has devoted his life to improving the planet's well-being. He has accomplished this by taking photographs, writing books and articles, and producing award-winning video documentaries. Haroldo works for Conservation International (CI), an environmental organization that establishes partnerships with countries all over the world to develop and implement ecosystem conservation projects.

Q: What do you do at CI?

Haroldo: I am the International Communications Project Director. What I do is make documentaries and take photographs of CI's conservation projects. These videos and photos are designed to teach people how to better interact with their local environment. Most of our work is done in countries that have tropical rain forests, such as those in Latin America, Asia, and Africa.

Q: Can you describe one of your documentaries?

Haroldo: Sure. We made a documentary in Guatemala about products that local people can sustainably harvest from the northern tropical forests.

After one year of production, we completed a half-hour documentary called *Between Two Futures*. CI then distributed the video to government officials, environmental organizations, university professors, and teachers. We also encouraged its broadcast on TV channels in Guatemala and other Latin American countries.

The film has been a real success story. I think our ability to be culturally sensitive to the Guatemalan people contributed in large part to the film's success. Each of us who worked on the project had a Latin American background. We worked closely with the Guatemalan people; we had a Guatemalan narrator, and we used only Guatemalan music. If you are trying to deliver an important message to people of a different culture, it's important to step into their shoes and deliver it from their point of view.

Q: What is your educational background and experience?

Haroldo: Although I do have a degree in economics, my best education and training has definitely come from traveling and other real-life experiences. I learn by studying the diverse cultures around the world.

Once I spent two years traveling around Latin America by van; another time I drove from Europe to India in six months. These experiences are my education. When my friends say that it is necessary to have a master's degree or doctorate to gain respect, I respond by saying that I have a Ph.D. in "Travelology." That's a degree I think my real-world experience on the road has earned me.

▶ Haroldo Castro, below left, is shown directing a video crew in Rio de Janeiro, Brazil.

If you are trying to deliver an important message to people of a different culture, it's important to step into their shoes and deliver it from their point of view.

Q: Do you ever have to deal with crisis situations?

Haroldo: [laughter] If there is not a crisis when I'm traveling, I'm worried—it usually means there will be a disaster later! Anyone who travels a lot has to deal with crises, such as getting sick on local food or getting robbed. I've had equipment stolen from Lebanon to Peru!

I would like to tell you a story. Several years ago we were working in a remote rain-forest region of Mexico for 10 days. When we were ready to leave, we boarded a small plane and set out for the nearest commercial airport, only to learn that it had been closed. We were forced to go to a nearby military airport instead.

When we landed and began to unload our large boxes of equipment, the military personnel got very nervous. We looked pretty grungy and unshaven and covered with mud. It was obvious that we'd been in the rain forest awhile. They thought we were terrorist guerrillas and surrounded us with machine guns. For three hours we pleaded our case, and finally they let us go. I think you might call that a crisis situation!

Q: If a high school student were to ask you what he or she could do to help the environment, what would your answer be?

Haroldo: I would say . . . Learn all you can, appreciate the world around you, and follow

▶ Haroldo Castro is filming slash-and-burn agriculture.

your passion. If you like photography, go out and take pictures of things that leave you with good and bad impressions. If you like gardening, start experimenting with seedlings. Whatever your interest, my advice is, just go for it!

MORE ON THIS CAREER

Many government offices, publishers, and environmental organizations have in-house communications departments for producing films or photographs. Have a librarian help you make a list of such places, and then call these places for more information and for possible volunteer or internship ideas.

While you're at the library, look through *The Guide to International Film and Video Festivals* for any mention of environmental film festivals in your area. Haroldo recommends attending a film festival if at all possible. "Doing so," he said, "would give you the invaluable opportunity to see some of the best films produced and to talk to the people who made them." If you can't find the guide or would like further information, contact the **Association of Independent Video & Filmmakers** at 304 Hudson Street, 6th Floor, New York, NY, 10013.

▶ For Haroldo, capturing images such as this Guatemalan girl holding a hummingbird on film allows him to recall rich travel experiences.

Environmental Careers 635

ENVIRONMENTAL LAWYER

Jana L. Walker used to be a nurse, but now she's showing her concern for individuals and their safety in a different way. She owns her own law practice that focuses on environmental protection and Native American issues.

Jana is a member of the Cherokee nation. She supports the "Great Law" of the Six Nations Iroquois Confederacy: "In our every deliberation, we must consider the impact of our decisions on the next seven generations." According to Jana, the Great Law is particularly relevant to environmental issues. She says the Great Law is relevant because it reflects the need to establish laws to protect our natural resources for future generations now, before lands and waters are permanently damaged and species are driven to extinction.

The environmental movement that took off in other parts of the country during the 1970s is only now reaching many Indian lands.

▶ The work Jana does in her New Mexico office is improving the quality of life for many tribal people.

Q: What inspired you to change from the nursing field to law?

Jana: Well, I'd always been interested in law, but I guess I never thought I'd be able to do it. But after seven years of nursing, I was really ready for a more independent career. So I made getting through law school my goal. Now I know that it's never too late to get additional education or to fulfill a personal goal.

After law school, I worked at a couple of different law firms—one large and one small. Then I decided that what I really wanted to do was practice law on my own. So I started a solo law practice to focus on Indian and environmental law issues. These issues are very important to me as an inhabitant of the planet, as an attorney, and as an Indian.

Q: What is the relationship between environmental law and the Indian nations?

Jana: Well, tribal lands have suffered from many environmental problems. You see, although the first federal environmental laws were enacted several decades ago, those laws did not address Indian tribes and reservations. And the tribes lacked the money to start these programs on their own. As a result, there are now over 53 million acres of tribal lands that have had little or no environmental protection for many years. So the environmental movement that took off in other parts of the country during the 1970s is only now reaching many Indian lands.

Q: What kinds of environmental problems do you encounter?

Jana: The problems range from leaking underground storage tanks to acid rain to radioactive contamination to water pollution to illegal, or "wildcat," dumping of trash.

Q: Those are tough problems. What can you do about them?

Jana: I help tribes set up regulatory programs to protect the wildlife, land, air, and water resources of the reservations. I also review environmental bills that could affect Indian lands to determine whether they would have a positive or negative impact. Then I lobby for those bills that would help tribal programs. It's an awful lot of reading and writing—definitely not what a television lawyer does!

Q: What are the most frustrating aspects of your work?

Jana: It's frustrating to see a tribe begin to move forward with environmental regulation and then have its efforts challenged by a neighboring community. For example, I know of a case in which the tribe wanted to establish water-quality standards for a large river that ran through its reservation. The river is listed as one of the 10 most endangered rivers in America because of severe pollution. The Environmental Protection Agency (EPA) approved of the tribal standards. Then officials for a large city upriver learned that the new standards would limit their use of the river for municipal waste discharge. So the city planners disputed the EPA's approval of the new standards. As a result, the improvements in water quality are again delayed for the tribal people as well as for other communities downstream from this city. This is frustrating! Persistence and the ability to cooperate with government authorities are necessary tools in such a situation.

Q: What personal qualities do you think are most important in your field?

Jana: Determination and self-motivation are musts. It's a long haul getting a law degree. Then, once you're a lawyer, the law is constantly changing. That means you must be willing to continue to learn and to study these changes. Creativity is also essential, because many times a law may not directly address your client's problem or need. As a result, you often have to weave together several legal theories to address a particular situation.

▶ Jana L. Walker, shown here next to the Río Grande in New Mexico, is working to improve the quality of river water that runs through tribal lands.

Q: What message would you like to send to high school students today?

Jana: I'd like to emphasize that protecting the Earth is everybody's job. But before we can tackle the work, we must become aware of the environment and how we fit into this world. And often that's not something you can learn from a book. It's only after we become truly conscious of nature and the environment that we can begin to see how our actions affect it and what steps must be taken to protect the Earth. So my advice is, go out and enjoy the natural world, and develop a real appreciation for it!

MORE ON THIS CAREER

If you're interested in learning more about a lawyer's work, check with your high school guidance counselor. You may be able to get a part-time or summer job in a law office. Or for more information, contact the American Bar Association, Law Student Division, 750 North Lake Shore Drive, Chicago, IL, 60611, or call (312) 988-5000.

▶ Jana hopes that actions taken because of her work and the work of others will increase awareness about and help solve serious environmental problems, such as water pollution.

CLIMATE RESEARCHER

One summer when **Dr. Richard Somerville** was just a child, he built a weather station in his backyard. His creation grew out of a fascination for the great power of weather—a phenomenon that affects everyone every day. So using instruments made out of coffee cans, balloons, and rubber bands, Richard began keeping track of daily weather conditions and questioning how the world's weather systems worked. As time went on, he began to question more than just the weather—he looked at clouds, oceans, and the world of living things as well. These pursuits led Richard to the prestigious Scripps Institution of Oceanography. Today he is a professor of meteorology at the Scripps Institution, which is part of the University of California at San Diego in La Jolla, California.

There are two general classes of technology that are most important to my work: satellites and computers.

Q: What exactly is meteorology?

Richard: Simply put, it is the science of the atmosphere—especially the study of weather and weather forecasting.

Q: What most appeals to you about your job?

Richard: Probably the most exciting aspect of any scientist's work involves those few, rare "Eureka!" moments when you realize that you've discovered something that no one else on Earth knows about. That's quite a feeling. It's also rewarding to know that you're adding to the knowledge of others, transferring important pieces of information to important people who can use that information to improve this world.

Q: What does your research involve?

Richard: Well, I do research on the greenhouse effect, on climate changes in general, and on the effects of long-range climate changes. I also study El Niño events and Indian monsoons. I see how these events and phenomena affect people—such as people involved in agriculture. The climate really affects the way people live!

I'm also researching whether the activities of humans are affecting the atmosphere. For example, each year, the world's growing population uses more and more energy by burning coal, oil, natural gas, and wood. When all of these substances are burned, they add carbon dioxide to the atmosphere. So I study the atmosphere to see how much the added carbon dioxide is intensifying the greenhouse effect. Then I try to determine how those changes will affect humans. You see, the more we know about the atmosphere, the better we can predict what will happen next.

Q: How is your research data used?

Richard: Many of my findings can affect public policy. For instance, How should the energy of the world be generated? I can help policymakers

▶ This computer simulation of increasing global temperatures allows Richard to study the possible effects of a changing climate on our planet.

This scientist uses state-of-the-art equipment to gather information about changes in ocean temperatures over time.

explore this question by providing them with data about the effects of fuels such as coal, oil, and gas on the atmosphere. Then I can recommend that they establish policies to reduce human reliance on those fuel sources. I can also encourage the use of resources such as solar, wind, and hydroelectric power.

Q: What tools do you use to obtain your data?

Richard: There are two general classes of technology that are most important to my work: satellites and computers. Together these two items have virtually revolutionized this field by hugely expanding what we've been able to observe and understand. Satellites, for example, can provide us with a whole different perspective of our world. The photographs generated by a satellite allow us to look at global temperatures as well as specific weather and sea conditions. Data are also collected on clouds, soil, and vegetation. By analyzing these observations, we can monitor changing conditions and identify possible problem areas.

Computers help us make sense of the data. Computer equipment in the satellites helps to answer our questions and helps us to better visualize the data. Personal computers help us record and summarize our findings. Then we have "super computers," which can simulate the motions of the atmosphere and the ocean, and thereby help us to answer questions and make predictions.

We also have access to ships and airplanes that are loaded with highly specialized equipment. These research platforms can be sent to specific areas of the world to gather more information about a situation or condition.

Q: What are the most frustrating aspects of your job?

Richard: Other demands that limit the time I spend doing research. There's a large fraction of time and energy that must be spent making research possible—you have to find money, so you spend lots of time writing proposals and doing other administrative work.

Q: What school subjects turned out to be the most important for your career?

Richard: You might be surprised. Math and science classes are essential, but in retrospect I value my English courses the most. Scientists are writers—the final products of their research are shown in published papers.

Q: What personal qualities do you think are most essential for a successful person in your field?

Richard: There are an enormous variety of scientists—some are sloppy, some are organized, some like to work alone, and some in teams. One thing all good scientists have in common, though, is dedication—they all want to do science above anything else. I think Thomas Edison's famous quotation, "Genius is 1 percent inspiration and 99 percent perspiration," is really on the mark. Not everyone can be born a genius, but anyone who is really dedicated can have a good career in science.

MORE ON THIS CAREER

If you are interested in learning more about a career in meteorology, contact the **American Meteorological Society,** 45 Beacon Street, Boston, MA, 02108.

RESEARCH WILDLIFE BIOLOGIST

Many people imagine wildlife biologists wrestling large game animals to the ground, slapping radio collars around their necks, and then creeping through the forest for weeks on end to study the creatures. According to **Mariko Yamasaki**, research wildlife biologist for the U.S. Department of Agriculture, Forest Service, there is a lot more to wildlife biology than that. To Mariko, "Nature is fascinating on many, many levels, from the tiniest ant all the way up to charismatic animals such as bears and wolves. We have to get away from the notion that animals with feathers or fur and big brown eyes are more important than slimy, scaly creatures with beady eyes. All organisms have a role—we must be sure that their contribution to the big picture is recognized."

Q: What is your educational background and experience?

Mariko: My background is basically a long and colorful stringing together of different experiences. I have bachelor's degrees in anthropology and zoology and a master's degree in natural resources (specific to wildlife). By the time I got out of school in the late 1970s, I came up against a surprising attitude—people in my home state really couldn't conceive of having female biologists supervising in the field. So I looked outside my home state. I ended up studying bald eagles for the Bureau of Land Management out West. This sort of snowballed into a permanent appointment in Washington as a wildlife biologist for the Bureau of Land Management. Today I work at the Northeastern Forest Experiment Station, where I do research in forested lands that cover a 200 mi radius, including parts of Maine and New Hampshire.

▶ To Mariko Yamasaki, every creature, no matter how small or seemingly insignificant, has an important role in this biosphere. She is shown here searching for salamanders in the wild.

Q: What organisms are you studying in the field right now?

Mariko: I'm studying small mammals, such as mice, shrews, voles, and squirrels. My colleagues and I also study insectivorous bats, migratory birds, and terrestrial salamanders. These are animals that we know something about, such as their basic biology, but we don't know how they respond to forest management. We're looking at these critters to get a sense of how they fit into the bigger picture.

Q: What types of questions are you trying to answer about these animals?

Mariko: One question my colleagues and I are trying to answer right now is how terrestrial salamanders respond to "even-aged management" of northern hardwoods. Even-aged management involves harvesting a large area of trees whose ages are within 20 years of each other.

We have to get away from the notion that animals with feathers or fur and big brown eyes are more important than slimy, scaly creatures with beady eyes.

▶ Mariko wants to know if the way in which trees are harvested from forested areas like this one affects the survival of terrestrial salamanders.

Foresters often use even-aged management because it is an efficient means of harvesting large amounts of timber at one time. My hypothesis is that when a large area of trees has been harvested, the ground temperature might change because the area is suddenly exposed to direct sunlight. This might affect the population and distribution of terrestrial salamanders in a negative way. I use the data I gather to make recommendations to forest managers about how they can manage tracts of forest to best support the needs of salamanders and other wildlife.

Q: Do you work with other people a lot?

Mariko: There's an old stereotype that a wildlife biologist leads a solitary life studying nature. This simply isn't true—it's important to know how to work with people and how to understand and deal with a variety of viewpoints. There is rarely a day that I sit alone in my office. But I will say that a wildlife biologist does have some control over the matter—generally, you can work with people as much or as little as you want.

Q: Do you ever have to deal with crisis situations?

Mariko: Not really, but I do see a lot of controversy, particularly related to wildlife and the use of natural resources. My work has often become the object of heated debate. Some people will support my findings wholeheartedly, while others call them worthless. There are any number of ways of dealing with this kind of pressure. I've found that it's real important to get my information together and analyze it as thoroughly as possible so that I can really stand behind what I'm saying. It's also important to realize that everyone is entitled to an opinion.

Q: What are the most interesting or exciting aspects of your work?

Mariko: Oh heavens! Being out and observing the natural world. Being able to test hypotheses. Being up real early on a bird survey. It's never the same twice. I also enjoy discovering something new—there's nothing any more special than that. There's a lot out there! The scale of things to observe and study is mind-boggling.

Q: What advice might you give to someone who is searching for a career?

Mariko: I think it's important to do something you are really interested in. My career, just like anybody else's, is not always a bed of roses. But if you really care about what you do, you can get beyond the problems and complications inherent to any job. It's also important to think that you've got something to contribute. I think that I can help contribute to the way people view wildlife, and that's important to me.

▶ This group of community leaders, politicians, and scientists is discussing how best to use the natural resources of a forested region in Maine.

MORE ON THIS CAREER

If you are interested in learning more about a career in wildlife biology, contact **The Wildlife Society**, 5410 Grosvenor Lane, Bethesda, MD 20814, or the **American Institute of Biological Sciences**, 1444 Eye Street NW, Suite 200, Washington, D.C., 20005.

ANY JOB CAN BE ENVIRONMENTAL

You don't have to be in an environmental career to make a positive impact on the environment. Gun Denhart is an excellent example of how you can make a difference through your career, even if your career doesn't directly involve the environment.

Hanna Andersson

Gun Denhart is the cofounder of Hanna Andersson, in Portland, Oregon. Hanna Andersson is a company that specializes in selling baby clothing and children's clothing through a mail-order catalog service. The company began in 1983 as an in-home enterprise, in which a spare room was used as the company office and the garage served as the warehouse. One-inch-square fabric samples were cut and pasted into each of the 75,000 catalogs that were mailed that first year. Hanna Andersson has grown enormously since 1983. An adult line of clothes has been added, several retail stores were opened, and a Web site was established.

The Used Clothing Recycling Program

As a parent, Gun Denhart realized that children outgrow their clothing very quickly and that clothing purchased at Hanna Andersson will last for more than a single child. Rather than waste clothing, she reasoned, why not pass these clothes on to children in need? So Gun instituted a program called Hannadowns®. The purpose of the program is to encourage the purchasers of Hanna Andersson clothing to recycle their used clothes. Gun says, *"You can make a critical difference. Most often, my clothes last for more than one child's use, and it's a great feeling to pass them on to younger children in your family, to your friends, or to charitable organizations. It is heartbreaking to realize how many children live at risk—an unbelievable 22 percent of children live below the poverty level in America. Providing them with nourishing food and warm clothing is a never-ending job. Fortunately, there are organizations that offer clothing and supportive services. To help them make a critical difference in children's lives, please send your outgrown children's clothes in good condition to these organizations."*

In the first 16 years of the company's existence, Hanna Andersson customers have donated over one million pieces of recycled clothes to children in need. These clothes could have ended up in landfills but have instead clothed kids all over the world.

In the first 16 years of the company's existence, Hanna Andersson customers have donated over one million pieces of recycled clothes to children in need.

▶ This clothing will be recycled because of an innovative program designed by Gun Denhart.

BOOSTING YOUR HOME'S
ENERGY EFFICIENCY

Many people don't realize the impact that energy production has on the environment. No matter what kind of energy plant serves your area, the production of that energy carries with it certain environmental risks. For example, when we burn coal to create electricity, many pollutants are released into the air. These pollutants may cause environmental problems such as global warming and acid rain. The more energy each of us uses, the more we contribute to these problems. So it makes environmental sense to conserve energy. Conservation is also a good way to save money—just a few energy-saving measures can substantially lower an energy bill.

Could the energy efficiency of your home be improved? Perform the following energy audit to find out.

The Wind Test

One day when it's windy outside, fasten a sheet of tissue paper onto a hanger with a piece of tape, as shown below. Next, hold the hanger in front of a window at the point where the window meets the wall. Hold the hanger still. If the paper moves, you've found a draft. Note the location of the draft in your *EcoLog*. Check all around the window, making comments about the drafts you find. Then examine all of the other windows, doors, electrical outlets, plumbing pipes, and baseboards that are on the outer walls of your home. Note every place where the tissue moves.

These drafts of air that you've discovered can add 20 to 35 percent to your heating and cooling bills. Fortunately, you can seal these air leaks with weatherstripping and caulk. Weatherstripping is for moving parts, such as doors and window frames. Caulk is for sealing cracks along joints and edges. These materials are relatively inexpensive, can be found at any hardware store, and can save 7 to 20 percent on your heating and cooling bills.

FOR MORE INFORMATION

Your local electric company can probably send you a packet of energy- and cost-saving ideas. In addition, your city may sponsor thorough in-house energy audits as well as rebates and loans for improving the energy efficiency of your home. Contact your city's electric utilities conservation department for more information.

Consult your library or bookstore for books on improving your home's energy efficiency. You might find these books helpful.

Consumer Guide to Home Efficiency, 7th ed., by Alex Wilson, Jennifer Thorne, and John Merrill, American Council for an Energy-Efficient Economy. White River Jct., VT: Chelsea Green Pub., 2000.

Energy Efficient Houses, by Fine Homebuilding Magazine. Newtown, CT: Taunton Press, 1993.

▶This simple device could help you improve the energy efficiency of your home.

ELIMINATING PESTS
NATURALLY

A huge cockroach is crawling across your floor. How will you get rid of it? Don't reach for an expensive store-bought chemical that could possibly contaminate the local water supply or even harm someone in your household. Instead, try a natural remedy!

Even the tidiest of homes can be bugged by insect pests. If this happens to your home, fight back—naturally!

Cockroaches Make a roach trap by putting honey in the bottom of a jar and setting it upright where the pests are most likely to visit. The sweet smell of the honey will lure roaches into the jar, but the stickiness of the substance will make it impossible for them to escape. You could also line the cracks where you think roaches are entering your home with bay leaves. The smell of bay leaves repels roaches. Prevent roaches from entering your home by keeping all food covered and stored and by cleaning dirty dishes. Seal cracks in walls, baseboards, and ducts with caulk so that roaches and other pests can't get in.

Ants Sealing cracks with caulk will also help keep ants out of your home. In the meantime, squeeze fresh lemon or lime juice into the holes or cracks. Then leave the peels where you've seen ants. Scatter mint around your shelves and cabinets, or pour a line of cream of tartar, red chili pepper, salt, paprika, dried peppermint, or talcum powder where ants enter your home. These substances either repel or kill the pests.

Another effective remedy for ridding your home of ants or cockroaches is to sprinkle a mixture of equal parts of boric acid and confectioners' sugar in dry areas where ants and cockroaches are found. The pests will eat the sugar and then die from the effects of the boric acid. Caution: If ingested, boric acid is acutely toxic to pets and small children. Use boric acid only in areas that are out of reach of kids and pets.

Ticks and Fleas If your pet has a problem with ticks or fleas, try feeding the animal brewer's yeast or vitamin B. Also wash your pet regularly with soap and water, then dry the animal and spray an herbal mixture of rosemary and water onto its coat. (You can make the mixture by steeping ½ cup of fresh or dried rosemary in one quart of boiling water. Let the liquid cool, pour it into a pump bottle, and then spray it onto your animal's coat.)

▶ You can help reduce the number of ticks and fleas that bother your pet by bathing it frequently and spraying an herbal mixture on its coat.

You can control the ticks and fleas in your yard by sprinkling the grass with diatomaceous earth, which is available at many nurseries. Diatomaceous earth consists of tiny glasslike skeletons of diatoms (a type of single-celled algae). These skeletons scratch the outer layer of an insect's body as it crawls along the ground. The insect eventually dies of dehydration. As well, bacteria can enter the insect's body through the open wounds, exposing the insect to disease. Caution: Diatomaceous earth can be harmful to your lungs if inhaled. Wear a protective mask when spreading the substance.

FOR MORE INFORMATION

Your city's environmental and conservation services department (if you have one) may have some other remedies for pests and some recipes for nontoxic household cleaners. Also check your local bookstore or library for books on natural pesticides, organic gardening, and chemical-free homes. You might find these books helpful.

The Good Earth Home and Garden Book, by Casey Kellar. Iola, WI: Krause Publications, 2002.

Natural Pest Control Alternatives to Chemicals for the Home and Garden, by A. Lopez. Austin, TX: Acres USA, 1990.

Environmental Shopping

Try to count how many products you've used today. It's probably not as easy as you think. In the first few minutes of your day, you may have used a dozen products.

All of those products and their packaging are made from valuable resources. More often than not, once those resources are used, they're tossed in a trash can and eventually hauled to the local landfill.

You can cut back on the amount of waste you send to the landfill and conserve resources in the process. On your next few shopping trips, think about the products you choose. If you're like most Americans, you'll probably be amazed at how many wasteful shopping habits you have. But after a while you'll begin to know instinctively which products are best for you and the environment.

Your Personal Shopping Guide

Read the information on the following page, and think of a way to reproduce it so that you (and other members of your household) have it handy when you set out on a shopping trip. For example, you may want to copy the questions and answers on the side of a brown paper bag. That way you'll have a shopper's guide, and you'll need one less sack at the checkout

On your next few shopping trips, think about the products you choose. If you're like most Americans, you'll probably be amazed at how many wasteful shopping habits you have.

stand. Another option is to write your guidelines on the back of an old grocery receipt and then adhere the receipt to the refrigerator with a magnet so that it will be handy for the other shoppers in your household. The options are limitless, so be creative, and try to incorporate recycled items into your design.

Before you create your personal shopping guide, you may want to review the section titled "Reducing Solid Waste" on pages 524 to 528 of your text.

FOR MORE INFORMATION

Consult your local library or a bookstore to find references that will help you with your environmental shopping. You might find one of the following books helpful.

Green Products by Design: Choices for a Cleaner Environment, by Gregory Eyring. Upland, PA: Diane Publications, 1992.

Mother Nature's Shopping List: A Buying Guide for Environmentally Concerned Consumers, by Michael D. Shook. New York: Carol Publishing Group, 1995.

An Environmental Shopper's Guide

Do I really need this product? Can I use something I already have?	Borrow or rent products you don't use often.
Is this a "throwaway" item that is designed to be used once or twice and then thrown away?	Avoid using disposable products whenever possible. Nondisposable alternatives may be more expensive initially, but in the long run they often save you money.
Does this product have more packaging than it really needs?	Look for alternatives with less packaging or wrapping. Purchase products in bulk or in a larger size so that in the long run you use less packaging (and save money!). Buy fresh vegetables and fruit instead of frozen or canned products.
Was this product's container or packaging made with recycled materials?	Choose products that have recycled paper, aluminum, glass, plastic, or other recycled materials in their packaging.
Is this product's container or packaging made from cardboard, aluminum, glass, or another material that I can easily recycle?	Find out which materials you can conveniently recycle, and then buy those sorts of containers. Also, think of ways to reuse old containers rather than throwing them out.
Does this product have bleaches, dyes, or fragrances added to it? Does it contain phosphates? Is it made from a petroleum-based synthetic fabric, such as polyester?	Phosphates and many other chemicals can pollute water sources. Look for natural, organic, and phosphate-free alternatives. When purchasing clothing, choose cotton or wool over synthetic fabrics.
Does the company that makes this product have a good environmental record?	You may have to do a little research to answer this one. Try the references listed on page 646.
Although this product has a "green" label, is it really good for me and the environment?	Don't be deceived by advertising and product labeling; carefully examine the contents of a product before you purchase it.
Do I really need a shopping bag to carry home the items I'm purchasing? If so, will I be more likely to recycle or reuse a plastic shopping bag or a paper one?	If you purchase just one or two items, tell the grocer that you don't need a bag to carry the products. For more items, bring old paper or plastic sacks with you when you go to the store, or use a canvas bag, which will last through many trips.
How much energy do I spend getting to the store?	If possible, ride your bike or walk to the store. If not, condense several short trips into one longer trip for a bigger supply of items.

MAKING YOUR OWN COMPOST HEAP

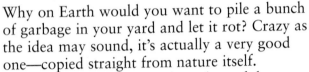

Why on Earth would you want to pile a bunch of garbage in your yard and let it rot? Crazy as the idea may sound, it's actually a very good one—copied straight from nature itself.

Compost is the natural product of the Earth's organic decaying process. When a dead organism decomposes, nutrients are returned to the soil. A compost heap is a collection of organic materials such as leaves, grass, and fruit peelings that will decompose over time to create rich, fertile soil. By making your own compost heap, you can reduce the amount of waste you send to the local landfill and create an excellent natural fertilizer for your garden.

There are many opinions on how to construct the best compost heap—it can be as basic or as fancy as you like. Either way, composting is easy, and it's almost impossible to foul up the process.

A compost heap can be placed just about anywhere in the yard. Either a sunny or a shady spot will be fine. You will want to keep it out of the way of normal activity, however.

Many people choose a spot on a concrete slab or a grassy area and then simply pile their materials there. (See the photo on this page.) This method is easy and effective.

A compost heap contains a mishmash of many different organic materials. Most of your heap will probably consist of grass clippings and leaves. You can also add raw vegetables, other uncooked food scraps, coffee grounds, tea bags, cotton, dust, discarded plants, and weeds. Avoid adding pet manure, cooked foods, and meat of any kind.

By making your own compost heap, you can reduce the amount of waste you send to the local landfill and create an excellent natural fertilizer for your garden.

▶ This is an easy and effective way to make your own compost heap.

Anatomy of a Compost Heap

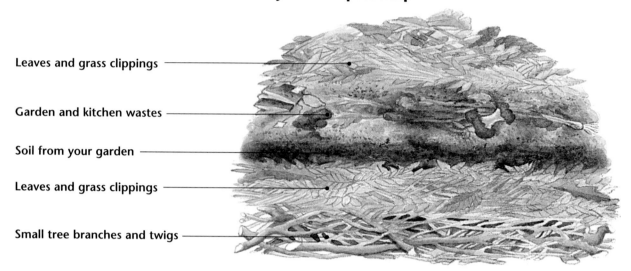

Leaves and grass clippings

Garden and kitchen wastes

Soil from your garden

Leaves and grass clippings

Small tree branches and twigs

If you add raw food wastes, cover them with leaves to keep away flies and to prevent an unpleasant odor.

Your heap will begin to decompose through the action of microorganisms. It's a good idea to shovel a couple of scoops of soil from your yard into the heap. The microorganisms in the soil will immediately begin decomposing the items in the heap.

Turn the heap at least once a month to keep it well aerated and active. Once the organic matter has broken down to the point that no single item is recognizable, it's ready to work into your garden's soil. The entire process can take anywhere from two months to one year, depending on the kinds of materials being decomposed and how often the heap is turned. Composting is more of an art than a science, so be prepared to experiment!

Compost Container

If you choose to contain your compost pile, you will be able to add more materials to a smaller area. You can buy a ready-made container from a hardware store, or you can build one yourself.

If you decide to build one, you may wish to use metal stakes and chicken wire to create a container like the one shown at right. Keep in mind, however, that as long as the container allows air to get in and out, the type of container you choose is limited only by your imagination!

Compost Heap Container

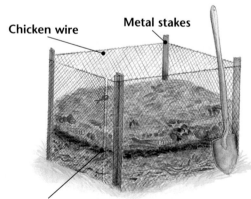

Chicken wire

Metal stakes

Loose wire can be twisted around two sections of chicken wire to create a "door" for easy turning.

▶ You can build this container for your compost heap with a few materials from your local hardware store.

FOR MORE INFORMATION

Consult your library for a manual on composting. You might find one of these helpful.

Let it Rot! The Home Gardener's Guide to Composting, 3d ed., by Stu Campbell. Pownal, VT: Storey Books, 1998.

Rodale Book of Composting, edited by Grace Gershuny and Deborah L. Martin. Emmaus, PA: Rodale Press, 1992.

Creating a Wildlife Garden

Manicured lawns and nonnative vegetation are not part of a natural ecosystem. Although these have been standard in urban and suburban neighborhoods for years, they usually require pesticides, fertilizers, water, and attention just to survive. In addition, they often exclude wildlife by removing some of their natural sources of food, water, and shelter.

To attract wildlife to your home, you simply need to provide native plants and the sorts of water sources and shelters naturally available to the wildlife in your area.

Plants

Plants are probably the most crucial element of your wildlife garden. Whether you have a lot of space for planting a wildflower meadow, a balcony on which you can create a container garden full of native plants, or a few windows to which you can attach boxes full of bright and cheery wildflowers, you will need a variety of native plants. Check with a local nursery, library, or bookstore for recommendations.

> To attract wildlife to your home, you simply need to provide native plants and the sorts of water sources and shelters naturally available to the wildlife in your area.

Water

People often overlook the need all animals have for water. Although some animals obtain enough water from the foods they eat, most require additional water for drinking and bathing.

Water sources are easy to provide. Many people purchase hanging or standing birdbaths from a nursery or hardware store. Others create ponds. You can make a simple pond by setting an old trash-can lid upside down in a corner of your yard and filling it with water. Surround your water source with plants, rocks, and other items so that the wildlife can find cover if necessary. In addition, make sure your pond or birdbath is at least partially shallow so that no animal is in danger of drowning, and keep the water clean.

Food and Shelter

Many different kinds of birdhouses and feeders are available at nature stores, hardware shops, and nurseries. Most of these can be hung on a balcony, and some can even be adhered to a window. Or, you could make your own birdhouse or feeder. A milk jug with a large hole cut in its side that is filled with seed and hung from a tree or balcony is an excellent way to feed many birds. If you would like to attract bats to your yard, use the Internet to find out how to make (or purchase) a bat house.

Woodpiles, rock piles, and brush piles are valuable sources of shelter for wildlife such as lizards and toads that might not frequent your backyard habitat otherwise. The most successful pile is one that incorporates different-sized spaces among the various components. You can make your pile attractive by planting vines in and around it.

Caution: *A shelter like the one described above may also attract poisonous snakes. Find out if any live in your area; if so, you may want to refrain from making a shelter pile.*

FOR MORE INFORMATION

Consult your library or bookstore for books on gardening with plants native to your area, gardening for the wildlife in your area, and xeriscape techniques. You might find these books helpful.

Noah's Garden: Restoring the Ecology of Our Own Back Yards, by Sara Bonnett Stein. Boston: Houghton Mifflin, 1995.

Your Backyard Wildlife Garden: How to Attract and Identify Wildlife in Your Yard, by Marcus Schneck. New York: St. Martin's Press, 1992.

Ecoskills

FLUSHING LESS WATER

A typical American uses over 100 gallons of water before he or she even leaves for work or school in the morning, and much of that water is wasted. You may wish to review Table 1 on page 297, which shows daily water use in the United States per person.

Many Americans are beginning to change their wasteful practices, however. One simple and inexpensive way you can waste less water is by making a water-displacement device for your toilet's tank. This device takes up space in the tank so that less water is required to fill the tank with every flush. It only takes about 10 minutes to make, and with it you can save 1–2 gallons of water every time you flush. This may not sound like much, but it adds up quickly. Most toilets use 5–7 gallons of water with every flush. If a toilet is flushed an average of eight times per day, it uses around 52 gallons of water per day, or 18,980 gallons per year. If you can save $1\frac{1}{2}$ gallons of water with every flush, you'll save 4,380 gallons of water each year. If just 250 other people take similar measures, over 1 million gallons of water could be saved each year.

Making a Quick and Easy Water Displacer

1. Remove the label from a plastic container. (Milk jugs, juice bottles, and dishwashing soap bottles work well. Be prepared to experiment with different-sized containers.) Drop a few rocks into the container to weigh it own, fill the container with water, and put the lid back on.
2. Place the container in the toilet tank, as shown at left.
3. Be certain that the container doesn't interfere with the flushing mechanism inside the tank.
4. Experiment with different containers. Your goal is to use the largest container that the tank will hold while still maintaining an effective flush.

ONE FINAL IMPORTANT NOTE

The more water you save, the less you pay for. No matter which water-saving device you install, your water bill should be noticeably lower.

SI Conversions

The metric system is used for making measurements in science. The official name of this system is the Système International d'Unités, or International System of Measurements (SI).

SI Units	From SI to English	From English to SI
Length		
kilometer (km) = 1,000 m	1 km = 0.62 mile	1 mile = 1.609 km
meter (m) = 100 cm	1 m = 3.28 feet	1 foot = 0.305 m
centimeter (cm) = 0.01 m	1 cm = 0.394 inch	1 inch = 2.54 cm
millimeter (mm) = 0.001 m	1 mm = 0.039 inch	
micrometer (μm) = 0.000 001 m		
nanometer (nm) = 0.000 000 001 m		
Area		
square kilometer (km²) = 100 hectares	1 km² = 0.386 square mile	1 square mile = 2.590 km²
hectare (ha) = 10,000 m²	1 ha = 2.471 acres	1 acre = 0.405 ha
square meter (m²) = 10,000 cm²	1 m² = 10.765 square feet	1 square foot = 0.093 m²
square centimeter (cm²) = 100 mm²	1 cm² = 0.155 square inch	1 square inch = 6.452 cm²
Volume		
liter (L) = 1,000 mL = 1 dm³	1 L = 1.06 fluid quarts	1 fluid quart = 0.946 L
milliliter (mL) = 0.001 L = 1 cm³	1 mL = 0.034 fluid ounce	1 fluid ounce = 29.577 mL
microliter (μL) = 0.000 001 L		
Mass		
kilogram (kg) = 1,000 g	1 kg = 2.205 pounds	1 pound = 0.454 kg
gram (g) = 1,000 mg	1 g = 0.035 ounce	1 ounce = 28.35 g
milligram (mg) = 0.001 g		
microgram (μg) = 0.000 001 g		
Energy		
British Thermal Units (BTU)	1 BTU = 1,055.056 joules	1 joule = 0.00095 BTU
Temperature		

°F   0   20   40   60   80   100   120   140   160   180   200   220

°C –20 –10   0   10   20   30   40   50   60   70   80   90   100

Freezing point of water   Normal human body temperature

Room temperature

Conversion of Fahrenheit to Celsius:

$$°C = \frac{5}{9}(°F - 32)$$

Conversion of Celsius to Fahrenheit:

$$°F = \frac{9}{5}(°C) + 32$$

Mineral Uses

	Mineral	Chemical formula	Identifying characteristics
Metallic Minerals	Chalcopyrite	$CuFeS_2$	brassy color; iridescent tarnish; soft for metal; brittle
	Chromite	$FeCr_2O_4$	iron-black color; weakly magnetic
	Galena	PbS	high density; perfect cleavage in four directions, which forms a cube; low hardness
	Gold	Au	golden color; low hardness; high density; malleable (can be pressed into various forms)
	Ilmenite	$FeTiO_3$	tabular crystals; no cleavage
	Magnetite	Fe_3O_4	8-sided crystals; magnetic
	Uraninite	UO_2	black to steel black color; dull luster; radioactive
Nonmetallic Minerals	Barite	$BaSO_4$	high density for nonmetal
	Borax	$Na_2B_4O_7 \bullet 10H_2O$	low hardness; low density; dissolves in water
	Calcite	$CaCO_3$	perfect cleavage in three directions; low hardness; fizzes in dilute hydrochloric acid
	Diamond	C	extreme hardness; transparency; perfect cleavage in four directions
	Fluorite	CaF_2	cubic or 8-sided crystals; perfect cleavage in four directions
	Gypsum	$CaSO_4 \bullet 2H_2O$	softness; perfect cleavage in one direction and good in two others
	Halite	$NaCl$	low hardness; perfect cleavage in three directions, which forms cubes; salty taste
	Sulfur	S	yellow color; low hardness; poor conductor of heat; odor
	Kaolinite	$Al_2Si_2O_5(OH)_4$	low hardness; white color; noncrystalline
	Quartz	SiO_2	hardness; conchoidal fracture; crystals form six-sided prisms
	Talc	$Mg_3Si_4O_{10}(OH)_2$	very low hardness; massive; perfect cleavage, which forms thin, flexible flakes; soapy or greasy feel

Explanation of Terms

cleavage: the splitting of a mineral along smooth, flat surfaces

fracture: the tendency of a mineral to break along curved or irregular surfaces; conchoidal fracture is a smooth, curved fracture

hardness: a measure of a mineral to resist scratching

luster: the way the surface of a mineral reflects light

Economically important deposits	Important Uses
Chile, USA, Indonesia	power transmission, electrical and electronic products, building wiring, telecommunications equipment, industrial machinery and equipment
South Africa, Kazahkstan, India	production of stainless steel, alloys, metalplating
Australia, China, USA	batteries, ammunition, glass and ceramics, x-ray shielding
South Africa, USA, Australia	computers, communications equipment, spacecraft, jet engines, dentistry, jewelry, coins
Australia, South Africa, Canada	jet engines; missile components; white pigment in paints, toothpaste, and candy
China, Brazil, Australia	steelmaking
Canada, Australia	fuel in nuclear power reactors, manufacture of radioisotopes
China, India, USA	weighting agent in oil well drilling fluids, automobile paint primer, x-ray diagnostic work
Turkey, USA, Russia	glass, soaps and detergents, agriculture, fire retardants, plastics and polymer additives
China, USA, Russia	cement, lime production, crushed stone, glassmaking, chemicals, optics
Australia, Democratic Republic of the Congo, Russia	jewelry, cutting tools, drill bits, computer chip production
China, Mexico, South Africa	hydrofluoric acid, steelmaking, water fluoridation, solvents, glass manufacture, enamels
USA, Iran, Canada	wallboard, building plasters, manufacture of cement
USA, China, Germany	chemical production, human and animal nutrition, highway deicer, water softener
Canada, USA, Russia	sulfuric acid, fertilizers, gunpowder, tires
USA, Uzbehkistan, Czech Republic	glossy paper, whitener and abrasive in toothpaste
USA, Germany, France	glass, computer chips, ceramics, abrasives, water filtration
China, USA, Republic of Korea	ceramics, plastics, paint, paper, rubber, cosmetics

Maps

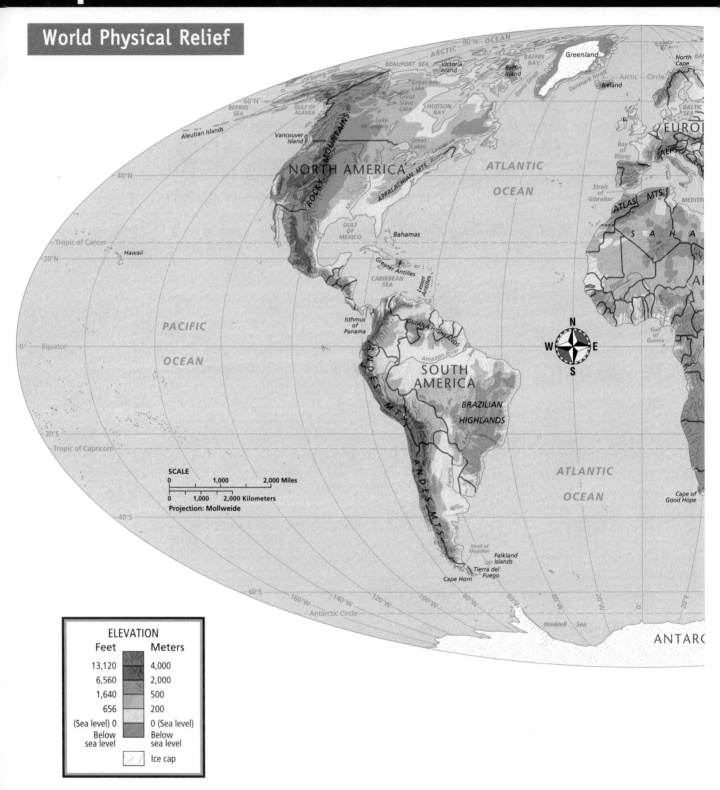

ELEVATION

Feet		Meters
13,120		4,000
6,560		2,000
1,640		500
656		200
(Sea level) 0		0 (Sea level)
Below sea level		Below sea level
	Ice cap	

Maps

World Climate Regions

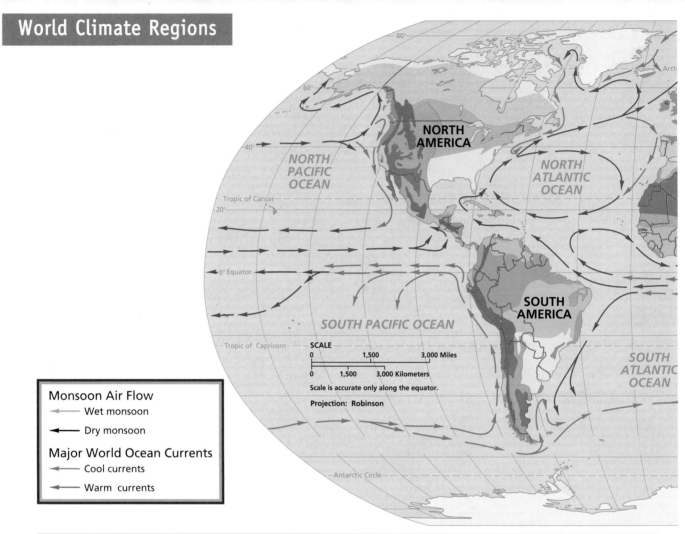

Monsoon Air Flow
— Wet monsoon
— Dry monsoon

Major World Ocean Currents
— Cool currents
— Warm currents

	Climate	Geographic Distribution	Major Weather Patterns	Vegetation
Tropical	**TROPICAL HUMID**	along equator; particularly equatorial South America, Congo Basin in Africa, Southeast Asia	warm and rainy year-round, with rain totaling anywhere from 65 to more than 450 in. (165–1,143 cm) annually; typical temperatures are 90°–95°F (32°–35°C) during the day and 65°–70°F (18°–21°C) at night	tropical rain forest
	TROPICAL WET AND DRY	between humid tropics and deserts; tropical regions of Africa, South and Central America, South and Southeast Asia, Australia	warm all year; distinct rainy and dry seasons; precipitation during the summer of at least 20 in. (51 cm); monsoon influences in some areas, such as South and Southeast Asia; summer temperatures average 90°F (32°C) during the day and 70°F (21°C) at night; typical winter temperatures are 75°–80°F (24°–27°C) during the day and 55°–60°F (13°–16°C) at night	tropical grassland with scattered trees
Dry	**ARID**	centered along 30° latitude; some middle-latitude deserts in interior of large continents and along western coasts; particularly Saharan Africa, Southwest Asia, central and western Australia, southwestern North America	arid; precipitation of less than 10 in. (25 cm) annually; sunny and hot in the tropics and sunny with great temperature ranges in middle latitudes; typical summer temperatures for lower-latitude deserts are 110°–115°F (43°–46°C) during the day and 60°–65°F (16°–18°C) at night, while winter temperatures average 80°F (27°C) during the day and 45°F (7°C) at night; in middle latitudes the hottest month averages 70°F (21°C)	sparse drought-resistant plants; many barren, rocky, or sandy areas
	SEMIARID	generally bordering deserts and interiors of large continents; particularly northern and southern Africa, interior western North America, central and interior Asia and Australia, southern South America	semiarid; about 10–20 in. (25–51 cm) of precipitation annually; hot summers and cooler winters with wide temperature ranges similar to desert temperatures	grassland; few trees
Middle Latitudes	**MEDITERRANEAN**	west coasts in middle latitudes near cool ocean currents; particularly southern Europe, part of Southwest Asia, northwestern Africa, California, southwestern Australia, central Chile, south-western South America	dry sunny warm summers and mild wetter winters; precipitation averages 14–35 in. (35–90 cm) annually; typical temperatures are 75°–80°F (24°–27°C) on summer days; the average winter temperature is 50°F (10°C)	scrub woodland and grassland
	HUMID SUBTROPICAL	east coasts in middle latitudes; particularly southeastern United States, eastern Asia, central southern Europe, southeastern parts of South America, South Africa, and Australia	hot humid summers and mild humid winters; precipitation year-round; coastal areas are in the paths of hurricanes and typhoons; precipitation averages 40 in. (102 cm) annually; typical temperatures are 75°–90°F (24°–32°C) in summer and 45°–50°F (7°–10°C) in winter	mixed forest

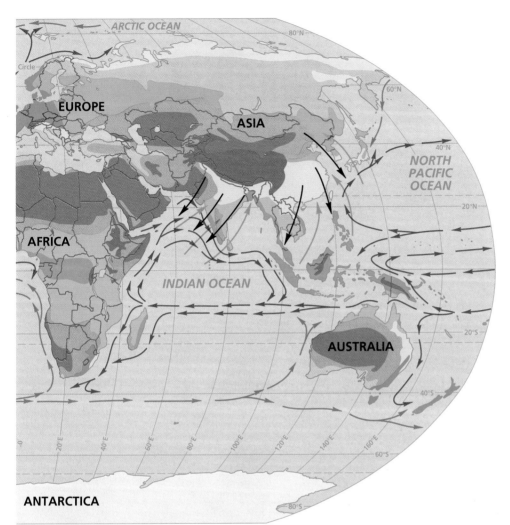

	Climate	Geographic Distribution	Major Weather Patterns	Vegetation
Middle Latitudes	**MARINE WEST COAST**	west coasts in upper-middle latitudes; particularly northwestern Europe and North America, southwestern South America, central southern South Africa, southeastern Australia, New Zealand	cloudy mild summers and cool rainy winters; strong ocean influence; precipitation averages 20–98 in. (51–250 cm) annually; westerlies bring storms and rain; average temperature in hottest month is usually between 60°F and 70°F (16°–21°C); average temperature in coolest month usually is above 32°F (0°C)	temperate evergreen forest
	HUMID CONTINENTAL	east coasts and interiors of upper-middle latitude continents; particularly northeastern North America, northern and eastern Europe, northeastern Asia	four distinct seasons; long cold winters and short warm summers; precipitation amounts vary, usually 20–50 in. (51–127 cm) or more annually; average summer temperature is 75°F (24°C); average winter temperature is below freezing	mixed forest
High Latitudes	**SUBARCTIC**	higher latitudes of interior and east coasts of continents; particularly northern parts of North America, Europe, and Asia	extremes of temperature; long cold winters and short mild summers; low precipitation amounts all year; precipitation averages 5–15 in. (13–38 cm) in summer; temperatures in warmest month average 60°F (16°C) but can warm to 77°F (25°C); winter temperatures average below 0°F (–18°C)	northern evergreen forest
	TUNDRA	high-latitude coasts; particularly far northern parts of North America, Europe, and Asia, Antarctic Peninsula, subantarctic islands	cold all year; very long cold winters and very short cool summers; low precipitation amounts; precipitation average is 5–15 in. (13–38 cm) annually; warmest month averages less than 50°F (10°C); coolest month averages a little below 0°F (–18°C)	moss, lichens, low shrubs; permafrost bogs in summer
	ICECAP	polar regions; particularly Antarctica, Greenland, Arctic Basin islands	freezing cold; snow and ice year-round; precipitation averages less than 10 in. (25 cm) annually; average temperatures in warmest month do not reach higher than freezing	no vegetation
	HIGHLAND	high mountain regions, particularly western parts of North and South America, eastern parts of Asia and Africa, southern and central Europe and Asia	greatly varied temperatures and precipitation amounts over short distances as elevation changes; prevailing wind patterns can affect rainfall on windward and leeward sides of highland areas	forest to tundra vegetation, depending on elevation

Maps

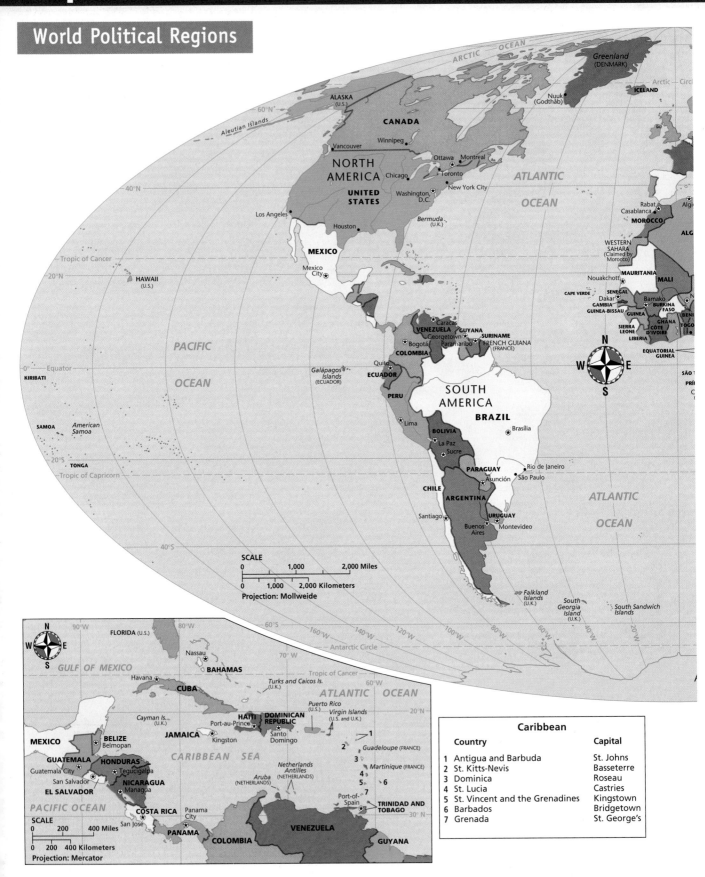

ARCTIC OCEAN

Greenland (DENMARK)

ALASKA (U.S.)

Nuuk (Godthåb)

ICELAND

Arctic Circle

CANADA

Vancouver Winnipeg

Ottawa Montreal

NORTH AMERICA Chicago Toronto

ATLANTIC OCEAN

UNITED STATES Washington D.C. New York City

60°N

Aleutian Islands

40°N

Los Angeles

Houston

Bermuda (U.K.)

Rabat

Casablanca

Algi

MOROCCO

ALG

Tropic of Cancer

20°N

HAWAII (U.S.)

MEXICO

Mexico City

WESTERN SAHARA (Claimed by Morocco)

MAURITANIA

Nouakchott MALI

CAPE VERDE SENEGAL

Dakar Bamako BURKINA FASO

GAMBIA GUINEA BENI

GUINEA-BISSAU GHANA TOGO

SIERRA CÔTE LEONE D'IVOIRE

LIBERIA

Caracas GUYANA SURINAME

VENEZUELA Georgetown FRENCH GUIANA (FRANCE)

Bogotá Paramaribo

COLOMBIA

EQUATORIAL GUINEA

PACIFIC

KIRIBATI

Quito

Galápagos Islands (ECUADOR) ECUADOR

PERU

0° Equator

OCEAN

SÃO

PRÍ

C

SOUTH AMERICA

BRAZIL

Lima

SAMOA

American Samoa

20°S

BOLIVIA Brasília

La Paz

Sucre

TONGA

Rio de Janeiro

PARAGUAY São Paulo

Tropic of Capricorn

Asunción

CHILE

ARGENTINA

Santiago

URUGUAY

Buenos Aires Montevideo

ATLANTIC

OCEAN

40°S

SCALE

0 1,000 2,000 Miles

0 1,000 2,000 Kilometers

Projection: Mollweide

Falkland Islands (U.K.)

South Georgia Island (U.K.)

South Sandwich Islands

N W E S

60°S

160°W 140°W 120°W 100°W 80°W 60°W 40°W 20°W

Antarctic Circle

N W E S

90°W 80°W

FLORIDA (U.S.)

70°W

60°W

Tropic of Cancer

ATLANTIC OCEAN

GULF OF MEXICO

Nassau

BAHAMAS

Turks and Caicos Is. (U.K.)

Puerto Rico (U.S.)

Virgin Islands (U.S. and U.K.)

20°N

Havana

CUBA

Cayman Is. (U.K.)

HAITI DOMINICAN REPUBLIC

1

2 Guadeloupe (FRANCE)

MEXICO BELIZE Belmopan

Port-au-Prince Santo Domingo

JAMAICA Kingston

3 Martinique (FRANCE)

GUATEMALA HONDURAS

CARIBBEAN SEA

4

Guatemala City Tegucigalpa

Netherlands Antilles (NETHERLANDS)

5 6

San Salvador NICARAGUA

Aruba (NETHERLANDS)

7

EL SALVADOR Managua

Port-of-Spain

TRINIDAD AND TOBAGO

PACIFIC OCEAN

COSTA RICA Panama City

30°N

SCALE

0 200 400 Miles

San Jose PANAMA

VENEZUELA

0 200 400 Kilometers

COLOMBIA

GUYANA

Projection: Mercator

Caribbean	
Country	Capital
1 Antigua and Barbuda	St. Johns
2 St. Kitts-Nevis	Basseterre
3 Dominica	Roseau
4 St. Lucia	Castries
5 St. Vincent and the Grenadines	Kingstown
6 Barbados	Bridgetown
7 Grenada	St. George's

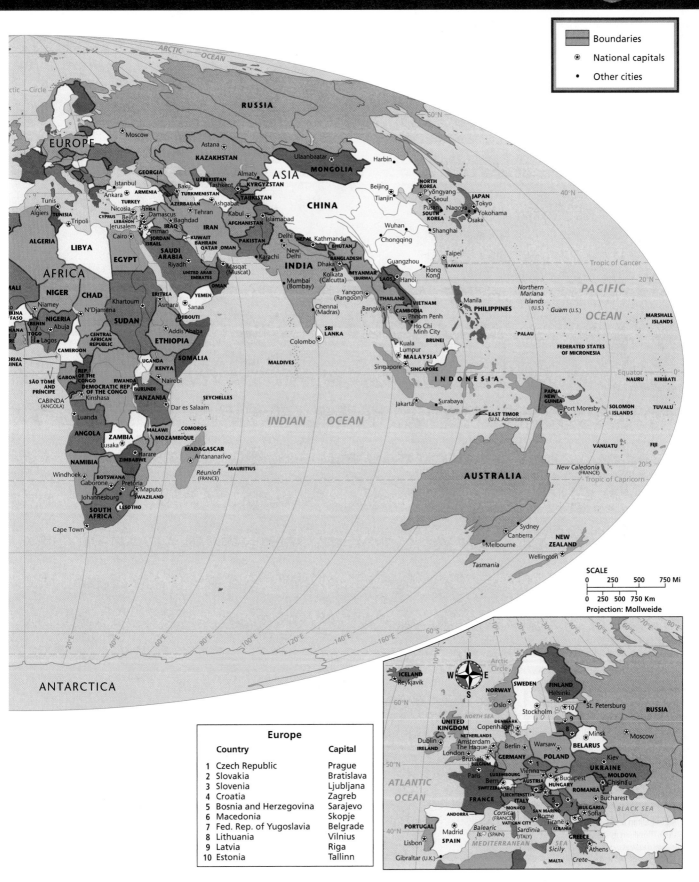

Boundaries
⊛ National capitals
• Other cities

ARCTIC OCEAN

RUSSIA

EUROPE

Moscow

Astana

KAZAKHSTAN

ASIA

Ulaanbaatar

MONGOLIA

Harbin

60°N

GEORGIA

Almaty

Istanbul

UZBEKISTAN

KYRGYZSTAN

Baku Tashkent

TAJIKISTAN

NORTH
KOREA

P'yŏngyang

JAPAN

40°N

Ankara ARMENIA

TURKEY

AZERBAIJAN

TURKMENISTAN

Ashgabat

CHINA

Beijing

Seoul SOUTH
Pusan KOREA

Tokyo
Nagoya Yokohama

Tunis

Nicosia

SYRIA

Tehran

Kabul

Tianjin

Osaka

Algiers

TUNISIA

CYPRUS
LEBANON

Damascus

AFGHANISTAN

Islamabad

Wuhan

Tripoli

Beirut

Baghdad

IRAN

PAKISTAN

Delhi

Chongqing

Shanghai

Jerusalem

JORDAN
ISRAEL

Amman

IRAQ

KUWAIT

New
Delhi

NEPAL Kathmandu

BHUTAN

Guangzhou

Taipei

ALGERIA

LIBYA

EGYPT

Cairo

SAUDI
ARABIA

BAHRAIN
QATAR

OMAN

Karachi

INDIA

Dhaka

BANGLADESH

Hong
Kong

TAIWAN

Tropic of Cancer

AFRICA

Riyadh

UNITED ARAB
EMIRATES

Masqat
(Muscat)

Mumbai
(Bombay)

Kolkata
(Calcutta)

MYANMAR
(BURMA)

LAOS

Hanoi

20°N

Northern
Mariana
Islands
(U.S.)

PACIFIC
OCEAN

MALI

NIGER

CHAD

Khartoum

ERITREA

Asmara

YEMEN

Sanaa

OMAN

Yangon
(Rangoon)

THAILAND

VIETNAM

CAMBODIA

Phnom Penh

Manila

PHILIPPINES

Guam (U.S.)

MARSHALL
ISLANDS

BURKINA
FASO

Niamey

N'Djamena

DJIBOUTI

Chennai
(Madras)

Bangkok

Ho Chi
Minh City

BRUNEI

PALAU

NIGERIA

Abuja

SUDAN

Addis Ababa

SRI
LANKA

FEDERATED STATES
OF MICRONESIA

GHANA

TOGO

BENIN

Lagos

CENTRAL
AFRICAN
REPUBLIC

ETHIOPIA

Colombo

Kuala
Lumpur

MALAYSIA

CAMEROON

UGANDA

KENYA

SOMALIA

MALDIVES

Singapore

SINGAPORE

NAURU

KIRIBATI

Equator

EQUATORIAL
GUINEA

SÃO TOMÉ
AND
PRÍNCIPE

GABON

REP.
OF THE
CONGO

DEMOCRATIC REP.
OF THE CONGO

RWANDA

BURUNDI

Nairobi

INDONESIA

PAPUA
NEW
GUINEA

SOLOMON
ISLANDS

TUVALU

CABINDA
(ANGOLA)

Kinshasa

TANZANIA

Dar es Salaam

SEYCHELLES

INDIAN   OCEAN

Jakarta

Surabaya

Port Moresby

Luanda

ANGOLA

ZAMBIA

MALAWI

MOZAMBIQUE

COMOROS

EAST TIMOR
(U.N. Administered)

VANUATU

FIJI

20°S

NAMIBIA

Lusaka

ZIMBABWE

Harare

MADAGASCAR

Antananarivo

Réunion
(FRANCE)

MAURITIUS

New Caledonia
(FRANCE)

Tropic of Capricorn

Windhoek

BOTSWANA

Gaborone

Pretoria

Maputo

SWAZILAND

AUSTRALIA

SOUTH
AFRICA

Johannesburg

LESOTHO

Sydney

Canberra

NEW
ZEALAND

Cape Town

Melbourne

Wellington

Tasmania

ANTARCTICA

SCALE

0   250   500   750 Mi

0 250 500 750 Km

Projection: Mollweide

Europe

ICELAND

Reykjavik

Arctic
Circle

SWEDEN

FINLAND

Helsinki

NORWAY

Oslo

Stockholm

10

St. Petersburg

RUSSIA

NORTH SEA

9

UNITED
KINGDOM

DENMARK

Copenhagen

8

Minsk

Moscow

Dublin

IRELAND

NETHERLANDS

Amsterdam

The Hague

Berlin

Warsaw

BELARUS

Kiev

London

BELGIUM

Brussels

GERMANY

POLAND

UKRAINE

Paris

LUXEMBOURG

1

Vienna

Budapest

MOLDOVA

Chisinau

FRANCE

Bern

SWITZERLAND

LIECHTENSTEIN

AUSTRIA

2

HUNGARY

4

ROMANIA

Bucharest

ITALY

3

7

BULGARIA

Sofia

BLACK SEA

MONACO

ANDORRA

Corsica
(FRANCE)

SAN MARINO

VATICAN CITY

Rome

5

Tirane

ALBANIA

6

PORTUGAL

Madrid

Balearic
Is. (SPAIN)

Sardinia
(ITALY)

GREECE

Athens

Lisbon

SPAIN

ATLANTIC

OCEAN

Gibraltar (U.K.)

MEDITERRANEAN

Sicily

SEA

MALTA

Crete

Maps

World Population Density

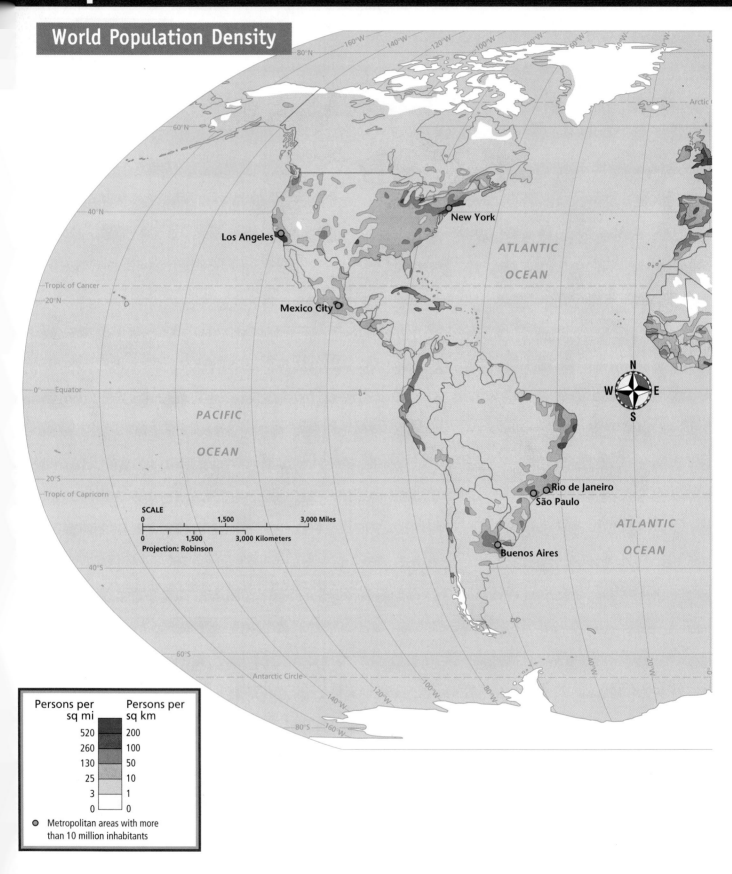

SCALE

0 — 1,500 — 3,000 Miles

0 — 1,500 — 3,000 Kilometers

Projection: Robinson

Persons per sq mi	**Persons per sq km**
520	200
260	100
130	50
25	10
3	1
0	0

● Metropolitan areas with more than 10 million inhabitants

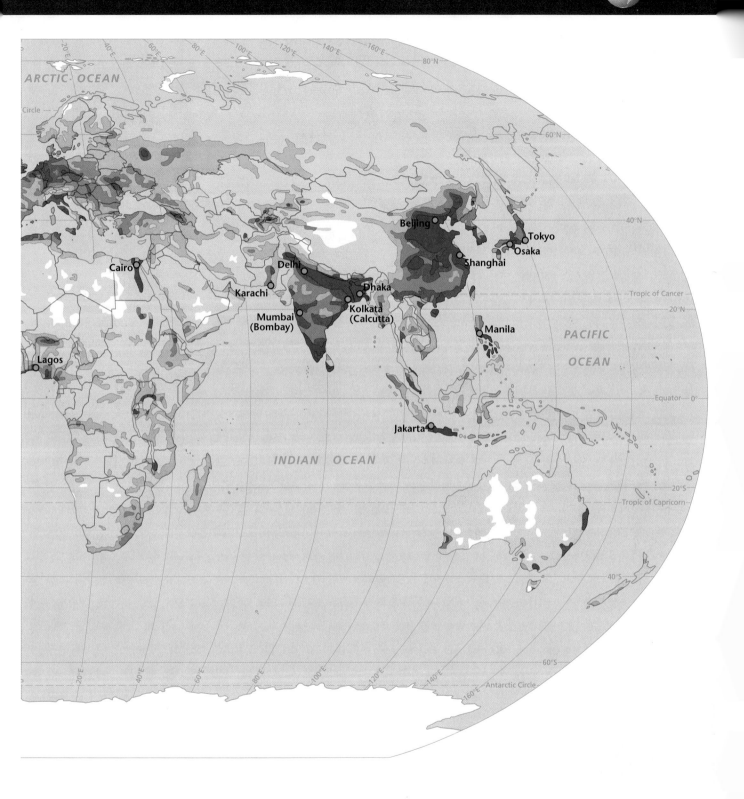

ARCTIC OCEAN

Circle

Cairo

Karachi

Delhi

Mumbai
(Bombay)

Dhaka

Kolkata
(Calcutta)

Beijing

Shanghai

Tokyo

Osaka

Lagos

Manila

PACIFIC

OCEAN

Jakarta

INDIAN OCEAN

Tropic of Cancer

Equator

Tropic of Capricorn

Antarctic Circle

Maps

World Carbon Dioxide Emissions Per Person

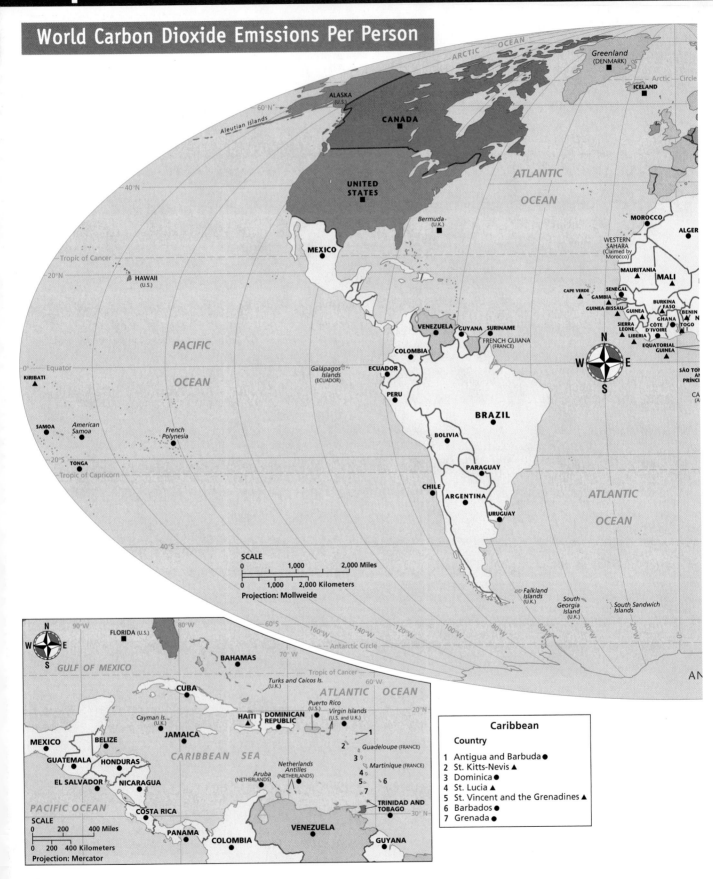

SCALE
0 — 1,000 — 2,000 Miles
0 — 1,000 — 2,000 Kilometers
Projection: Mollweide

SCALE
0 — 200 — 400 Miles
0 — 200 — 400 Kilometers
Projection: Mercator

Caribbean
Country

1 Antigua and Barbuda ●
2 St. Kitts-Nevis ▲
3 Dominica ●
4 St. Lucia ▲
5 St. Vincent and the Grenadines ▲
6 Barbados ●
7 Grenada ●

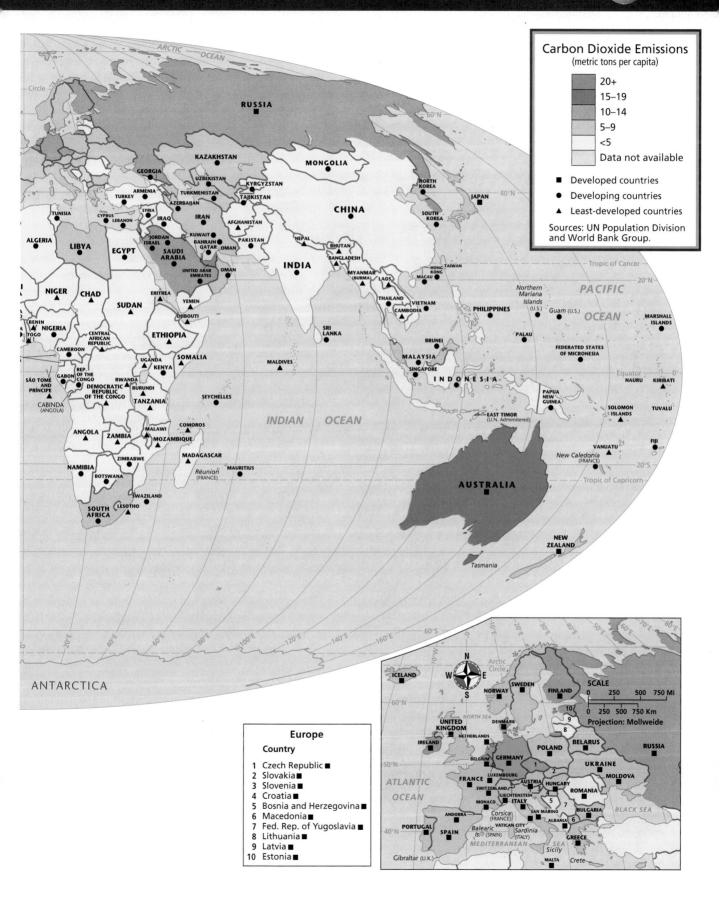

Carbon Dioxide Emissions
(metric tons per capita)

- 20+
- 15–19
- 10–14
- 5–9
- <5
- Data not available

- ■ Developed countries
- ● Developing countries
- ▲ Least-developed countries

Sources: UN Population Division and World Bank Group.

Europe

Country

1 Czech Republic ■
2 Slovakia ■
3 Slovenia ■
4 Croatia ■
5 Bosnia and Herzegovina ■
6 Macedonia ■
7 Fed. Rep. of Yugoslavia ■
8 Lithuania ■
9 Latvia ■
10 Estonia ■

Maps

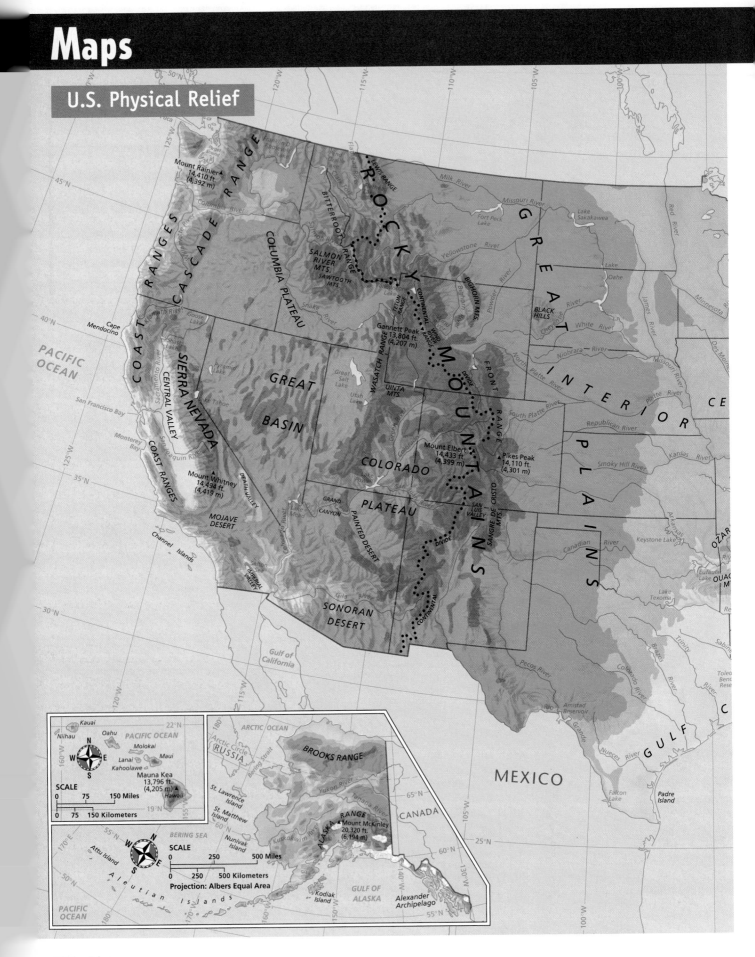

Map Labels

- PACIFIC OCEAN
- Cape Mendocino
- San Francisco Bay
- Monterey Bay
- COAST RANGES
- CASCADE RANGE
- Mount Rainier 14,410 ft. (4,392 m)
- Columbia River
- Puget Sound
- Franklin D. Roosevelt
- Flathead River
- LEWIS RANGE
- ROCKY
- BITTERROOT RANGE
- SALMON RIVER MTS.
- SAWTOOTH MTS.
- COLUMBIA PLATEAU
- Snake River
- Goose Lake
- Klamath River
- North River
- Shasta Lake
- Pyramid Lake
- SIERRA NEVADA
- CENTRAL VALLEY
- Sacramento River
- San Joaquin River
- Lake Tahoe
- GREAT BASIN
- Great Salt Lake
- Utah Lake
- WASATCH RANGE
- UINTA MTS.
- Mount Whitney 14,494 ft. (4,419 m)
- DEATH VALLEY
- COAST RANGES
- MOJAVE DESERT
- Channel Islands
- Salton Sea
- IMPERIAL VALLEY
- Colorado River
- Lake Mead
- GRAND CANYON
- Lake Powell
- COLORADO PLATEAU
- PAINTED DESERT
- SONORAN DESERT
- Gila River
- Gulf of California
- MOUNTAINS
- TETON RANGE
- CONTINENTAL DIVIDE
- Gannett Peak 13,804 ft. (4,207 m)
- WIND RIVER RANGE
- BIGHORN MTS.
- Bighorn River
- Powder River
- Yellowstone River
- Missouri River
- Fort Peck Lake
- Milk River
- GREAT
- BLACK HILLS
- Cheyenne River
- White River
- Niobrara River
- North Platte River
- South Platte River
- FRONT RANGE
- Mount Elbert 14,433 ft. (4,399 m)
- Pikes Peak 14,110 ft. (4,301 m)
- SAN LUIS VALLEY
- SANGRE DE CRISTO MTS.
- CONTINENTAL DIVIDE
- INTERIOR
- PLAINS
- Lake Sakakawea
- Lake Oahe
- Red River
- Minnesota
- James River
- Des Moines River
- Missouri River
- Republican River
- Smoky Hill River
- Kansas River
- Arkansas River
- Keystone Lake
- OZARK
- Eufaula Lake
- OUACHITA MTS.
- Canadian River
- Lake Texoma
- Pecos River
- Colorado River
- Brazos River
- Trinity River
- Sabine River
- Toledo Bend Reservoir
- Amistad Reservoir
- Rio Grande
- Nueces River
- Falcon Lake
- Padre Island
- GULF
- MEXICO

Hawaii Inset

- PACIFIC OCEAN
- Kauai
- Niihau
- Oahu
- Molokai
- Maui
- Lanai
- Kahoolawe
- Mauna Kea 13,796 ft. (4,205 m)
- Hawaii
- SCALE
- 0 — 75 — 150 Miles
- 0 — 75 — 150 Kilometers

Alaska Inset

- ARCTIC OCEAN
- Arctic Circle
- RUSSIA
- Bering Strait
- BROOKS RANGE
- Yukon River
- Tanana River
- Kuskokwim River
- ALASKA RANGE
- Mount McKinley 20,320 ft. (6,194 m)
- CANADA
- St. Lawrence Island
- St. Matthew Island
- Nunivak Island
- BERING SEA
- Attu Island
- Aleutian Islands
- PACIFIC OCEAN
- Kodiak Island
- GULF OF ALASKA
- Alexander Archipelago
- SCALE
- 0 — 250 — 500 Miles
- 0 — 250 — 500 Kilometers
- Projection: Albers Equal Area

CANADA

MESABI RANGE

Isle Royale

Lake Superior

Red River

Minnesota River

Mississippi River

Des Moines River

Lake Michigan

Lake Huron

Wisconsin River

CENTRAL LOWLAND

PLAINS

Missouri River

White River

Kansas River

Lake of the Ozarks

Illinois River

Wabash River

Ohio River

Lake Barkley

OZARK PLATEAU

OUACHITA MTS.

Eufaula Lake

Lake Texoma

White River

Kentucky Lake

Cumberland River

Cumberland Plateau

ALLEGHENY PLATEAU

Scioto River

Kanawha River

Monongahela River

Tennessee River

GREAT SMOKY MTS.

APPALACHIAN

BLUE RIDGE MOUNTAINS

MOUNTAINS

ADIRONDACK MTS.

CATSKILL MTS.

GREEN MTS.

WHITE MTS.

LONGFELLOW MTS.

Lake Champlain

St. Lawrence River

St. Lawrence Seaway

St. John River

Penobscot River

Connecticut River

Hudson R.

Delaware R.

Cape Cod

Long Island Sound

Long Island

Lake Ontario

Finger Lakes

Lake Erie

Allegheny River

Susquehanna River

Potomac River

James River

Roanoke River

Delaware Bay

Chesapeake Bay

PIEDMONT

ATLANTIC COASTAL PLAIN

ATLANTIC OCEAN

Pamlico Sound

Cape Hatteras

Sabine River

Red River

Trinity River

Brazos River

Toledo Bend Reservoir

Tombigbee River

Mississippi River

Coosa River

Alabama R.

Pearl River

Chattahoochee River

Oconee River

Altamaha River

Ocmulgee River

Savannah River

Sea Islands

COASTAL PLAIN

GULF

Padre Island

Chandeleur Islands

Mississippi Delta

Okefenokee Swamp

FLORIDA PENINSULA

Cape Canaveral

GULF OF MEXICO

The Everglades

Lake Okeechobee

Cape Sable

Florida Keys

Straits of Florida

BAHAMAS

CUBA

ELEVATION		
Feet		Meters
13,120		4,000
6,560		2,000
1,640		500
656		200
(Sea level) 0		0 (Sea level)
Below sea level		Below sea level
	Icecap	

SCALE

0 — 250 — 500 Miles

0 — 250 — 500 Kilometers

Projection: Albers Equal Area

N
W E
S

Maps

Legend:

- Tropical humid
- Tropical wet and dry
- Arid
- Semiarid
- Mediterranean
- Humid subtropical
- Marine west coast
- Humid continental
- Subarctic
- Tundra
- Icecap
- Highland

HAWAII

SCALE
0   100   200 Miles
0   100   200 Kilometers
Projection: Albers Equal Area

SCALE
0   250   500 Miles
0   250   500 Kilometers
Projection: Azimuthal Equal Area

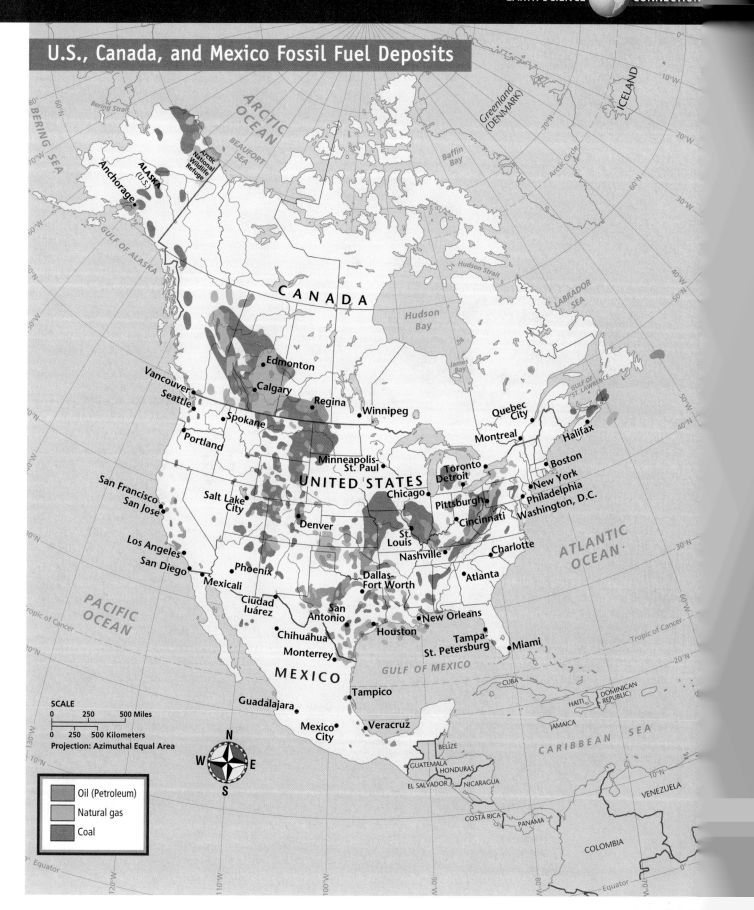

U.S., Canada, and Mexico Fossil Fuel Deposits

SCALE
0   250   500 Miles
0   250   500 Kilometers
Projection: Azimuthal Equal Area

Oil (Petroleum)
Natural gas
Coal

Maps

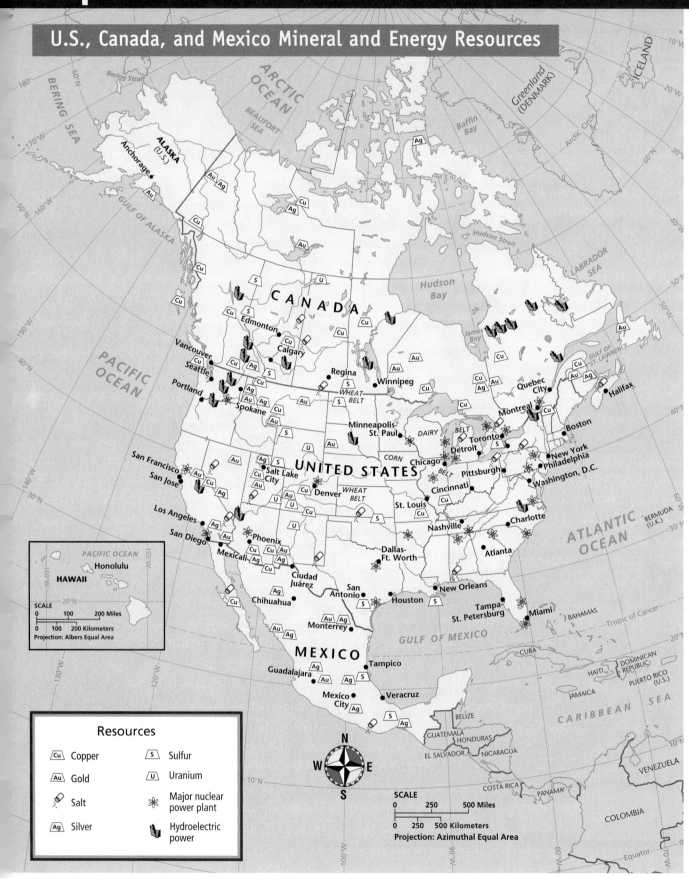

U.S., Canada, and Mexico Mineral and Energy Resources

Resources

- Cu Copper
- Au Gold
- Salt
- Ag Silver
- S Sulfur
- U Uranium
- ✳ Major nuclear power plant
- Hydroelectric power

SCALE
0   100   200 Miles
0   100   200 Kilometers
Projection: Albers Equal Area

SCALE
0   250   500 Miles
0   250   500 Kilometers
Projection: Azimuthal Equal Area

U.S., Canada, and Mexico Land Use

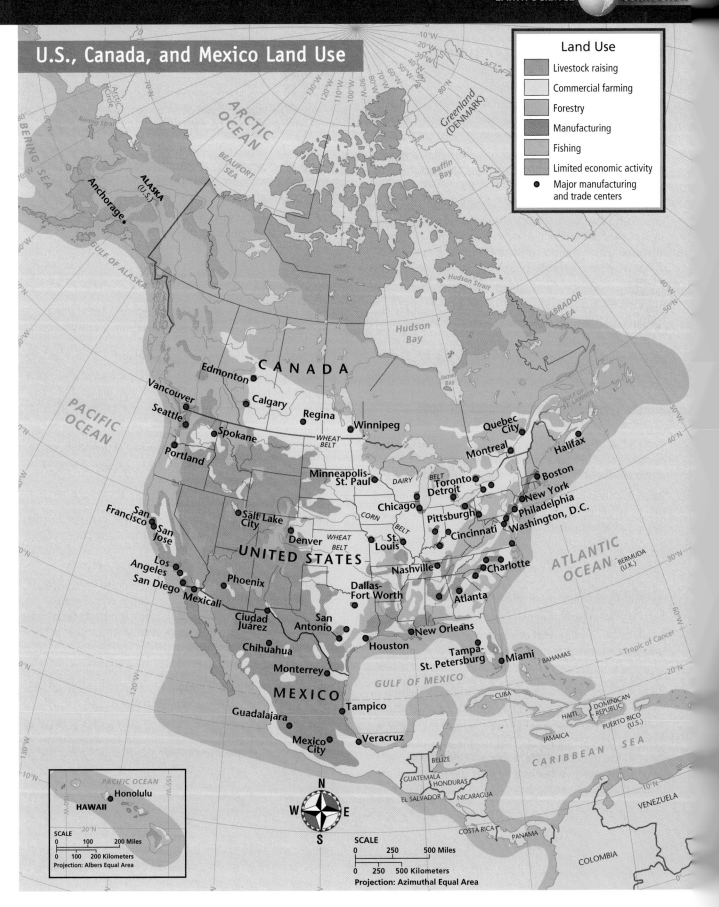

Land Use

- Livestock raising
- Commercial farming
- Forestry
- Manufacturing
- Fishing
- Limited economic activity
- • Major manufacturing and trade centers

ARCTIC OCEAN

BEAUFORT SEA

ALASKA (U.S.)

Anchorage

BERING SEA

GULF OF ALASKA

Greenland (DENMARK)

Baffin Bay

Hudson Strait

Hudson Bay

James Bay

LABRADOR SEA

PACIFIC OCEAN

CANADA

Edmonton

Vancouver
Seattle
Spokane
Portland

Calgary

Regina

Winnipeg

WHEAT BELT

GULF OF ST. LAWRENCE

Quebec City

Montreal

Halifax

Minneapolis-St. Paul

DAIRY BELT

Toronto
Detroit

Boston

New York

San Francisco
San Jose

Salt Lake City

Chicago

CORN BELT

Pittsburgh

Cincinnati

Philadelphia

Washington, D.C.

UNITED STATES

Denver

WHEAT BELT

St. Louis

ATLANTIC OCEAN

BERMUDA (U.K.)

Los Angeles
San Diego
Mexicali

Phoenix

Nashville

Charlotte

Ciudad Juárez

Dallas-Fort Worth

San Antonio

Atlanta

Chihuahua

Houston

New Orleans

Tampa-St. Petersburg

Miami

BAHAMAS

Tropic of Cancer

Monterrey

GULF OF MEXICO

CUBA

MEXICO

Tampico

HAITI
DOMINICAN REPUBLIC
PUERTO RICO (U.S.)

Guadalajara

JAMAICA

CARIBBEAN SEA

Mexico City

Veracruz

BELIZE

GUATEMALA
HONDURAS

EL SALVADOR   NICARAGUA

VENEZUELA

COSTA RICA   PANAMA

COLOMBIA

HAWAII

PACIFIC OCEAN

Honolulu

SCALE
0   100   200 Miles
0   100   200 Kilometers
Projection: Albers Equal Area

N
W   E
S

SCALE
0   250   500 Miles
0   250   500 Kilometers
Projection: Azimuthal Equal Area

Reading Check Answers

Chapter 1 Science and the Environment

Section 1
Page 6: Ecology is an important foundation of environmental science. The science of ecology helps environmental scientists to understand how human actions affect living things and their environment.

Page 9: Sample answer: Hunter-gatherers affected their environment by setting fires to prevent the growth of trees and by overhunting species to extinction.

Page 11: Sample answer: Switching from animal power to fossil fuels increased the efficiency of agriculture. Inventions such as the light bulb improved our quality of life. Our increased use of artificial substances such as plastics introduced new environmental problems.

Section 2
Page 17: The price of oil illustrates the law of supply and demand. In general, when the supply of oil decreases, the price of oil increases.

Page 21: In a sustainable world, human needs are met in such a way that a human population can survive indefinitely.

Chapter 2 Tools of Environmental Science

Section 1
Page 34: A hypothesis is a testable idea or explanation that leads to a scientific investigation. A prediction is a logical statement about what will happen if the hypothesis is correct.

Page 39: Snow's map helped him see that the homes of people who died from cholera were concentrated around the Broad Street pump.

Section 2
Page 41: The students calculated the mean length of the mussels by adding the lengths of the mussels and then dividing by the number of mussels.

Page 45: A conceptual model helps scientists to understand a system by showing what components the system contains, how they are arranged, and how they affect one another.

Section 3
Page 47: A decision-making model is helpful for making environmental decisions because it provides a systematic way of analyzing the issues and determining what is important.

Page 51: Michael found out that people are willing to pay more to live in counties with open spaces. He voted in favor of the preserve because he took this long-term economic benefit into account.

Chapter 3 The Dynamic Earth

Section 1
Page 65: Earth's outer core is a physical layer that is liquid.

Page 67: The magnitude of an earthquake is a measure of the energy released by the earthquake.

Section 2
Page 73: Ozone in the stratosphere protects life on Earth by reducing the amount of damaging UV radiation that reaches Earth's surface.

Page 75: Cool air sinks and warm air rises in the atmosphere because cool air is denser than warm air.

Section 3
Page 81: The ocean absorbs and releases heat more slowly than land does.

Page 84: Liquid water, moderate temperatures, and a source of energy make life possible in the biosphere.

Chapter 4 The Organization of Life

Section 1
Page 100: Biotic factors are the living or once-living parts of an ecosystem. Abiotic factors are the nonliving parts of an ecosystem.

Page 102: A habitat is important to an organism because it has the biotic and abiotic factors the organism needs to survive.

Section 2
Page 103: Natural selection is the survival and reproduction of organisms with particular traits. Over many generations, natural selection leads to a change in the genetic characteristics of a population. This change is called evolution.

Page 106: Humans use artificial selection to breed organisms with traits that humans want those organisms to have. Natural selection is not guided by human decisions but by an organism's chance of survival and reproduction in its environment.

Section 3
Page 109: Both bacteria and fungi cause diseases. Bacteria do not have nuclei, while fungi do have nuclei.

Page 111: Angiosperms depend on animals for pollination and dispersal of seeds. Animals depend on angiosperms for food, building materials, and fibers.

Chapter 5 How Ecosystems Work

Section 1

Page 126: A producer gets energy from the sun through photosynthesis. A consumer gets energy from the sun indirectly: by eating other organisms.

Page 130: A food chain shows the sequence in which energy is transferred from one organism to the next as each organism eats another. A food web shows many different feeding relationships and is made up of many interconnected food chains.

Section 2

Page 133: Car engines burn fossil fuels, releasing carbon dioxide into the atmosphere. Increased concentrations of carbon dioxide in the atmosphere may contribute to global warming.

Page 136: Algal blooms can harm aquatic ecosystems by depleting their nutrients, such as oxygen.

Section 3

Page 137: Primary succession occurs where no ecosystem existed before, while secondary succession occurs where an ecosystem previously existed.

Page 141: Sample answer: An example of primary succession in a city occurs when weeds grow through cracks in sidewalks.

Chapter 6 Biomes

Section 1

Page 153: Biomes are composed of many different ecosystems.

Page 154: Plants can live within only a certain range of temperatures, and they are affected by the length of the growing season.

Section 2

Page 158: Most of the animals that live in the rain forest live in the canopy.

Page 160: Sample answer: Two main threats to the organisms that live in tropical rain forests are habitat destruction and trading.

Section 3

Page 165: Sample answer: Savanna plants support herbivores such as antelopes and giraffes, as well as predators such as cheetahs and lions, which hunt the herbivores.

Page 169: Camouflage helps chaparral animals move through the brush without being noticed.

Chapter 7 Aquatic Ecosystems

Section 1

Page 187: Wetlands reduce the damage that is caused by flooding by absorbing extra water when rivers overflow.

Page 190: Runoff can maintain or improve the health of river organisms by washing nutrients from the surrounding land into the river. If runoff contains toxins from waste, it can damage the health of river organisms.

Section 2

Page 194: Both salt marshes and mangrove swamps are coastal wetlands. Both have been filled with waste and destroyed in many parts of the world.

Page 197: Coastal pollution and overfishing threaten organisms that live in the ocean.

Chapter 8 Understanding Populations

Section 1

Page 213: Exponential population growth takes place when the populations have plenty of food and space, and have little or no competition or predators.

Page 215: Sample answer: Plants grow over each other as they compete for light.

Section 2

Page 218: Species interactions are categorized based on whether each species causes harm or benefit to the other species in the relationship.

Page 222: The relationship between ants and ant acacia trees is mutualistic because it is beneficial to both species. The trees provide shelter and food for the ants, while the ants defend the trees against herbivores and other threats.

Chapter 9 The Human Population

Section 1

Page 236: A population pyramid helps demographers predict changes in a population over time by showing its age structure. If a population has more young people than older people, the population size likely will increase as the young people grow up and have children.

Page 239: The second stage of demographic transition is characterized by a high birth rate and a declining death rate.

Reading Check Answers

Section 2

Page 243: Rapid population growth means that people continue to build homes in the fertile Nile River valley, decreasing Egypt's available arable land.

Page 246: Sample answer: Governments could use public advertising or economic incentives to try to limit population growth.

Chapter 10 Biodiversity

Section 1

Page 259: A new species is considered known when it has been collected and described scientifically. Species that have not been collected and described scientifically are considered unknown.

Page 261: Genetic diversity increases the chance that some members of a population will survive environmental changes. Also, members of a population are less likely to inherit genetic diseases.

Section 2

Page 263: Scientists warn that a mass extinction is occurring now because the rate of extinction is estimated to have increased by a multiple of 50 since 1800.

Page 267: The biodiversity of coral reefs and coastal ecosystems is threatened because overfishing, pollution, and other human activities harm these ecosystems.

Section 3

Page 272: Protecting the habitat of threatened and endangered species involves large areas because a species confined to a small area could be wiped out by a single natural disaster. Also, some species require a large range to find food, find a mate, and rear their young.

Page 274: Sample answer: The IUCN protects species and habitats by working with groups like the World Wildlife Fund to sponsor conservation projects.

Chapter 11 Water

Section 1

Page 290: Most large cities depend on surface water for drinking water, water for growing crops, food such as fish, power for industry, and a means of transportation by boat.

Page 292: In wet regions, the water table may be at the Earth's surface. In deserts, the water table may be hundreds of meters beneath the Earth's surface.

Section 2

Page 298: Agriculture accounts for 67 percent of the water used in the world, while industry accounts for 19 percent.

Page 301: Industries help conserve water by recycling cooling water and by recycling wastewater.

Section 3

Page 307: It is expensive to dispose of sewage sludge because the volume of sludge that has to be disposed of every year is enormous.

Page 311: From nonpoint sources, 200 million to 300 million gallons of oil enter the ocean every year. Limiting these nonpoint sources would go a long way toward keeping the oceans clean.

Chapter 12 Air

Section 1

Page 325: Ground-level ozone is a secondary pollutant because it forms when primary pollutants react with oxygen in the presence of UV radiation.

Page 329: Sample answer: A scrubber reduces pollution by moving gases through a spray of water that dissolves many pollutants. An electrostatic precipitator reduces pollution by removing dust particles from smokestacks.

Section 2

Page 332: Sick-building syndrome is most common in hot places because buildings are tightly sealed against the heat. This type of environment encourages the growth of fungi that can cause allergic reactions.

Page 335: Three sources of light pollution in a city are billboards, the lighting of building exteriors, and poor-quality street lights.

Section 3

Page 337: Pure water has a pH of 7.0. Acid precipitation has a pH of less than 5.0.

Page 339: Pollutants from the United States can cause acid precipitation in Canada because pollutants may be released in one area and fall to the ground hundreds of kilometers away.

Chapter 13 Atmosphere and Climate Change

Section 1

Page 352: In northern latitudes and southern latitudes, the amount of energy arriving at Earth's surface is less than the amount received at the equator.

Page 357: Volcanic eruptions can decrease global temperatures by creating a haze that reflects sunlight.

Section 2

Page 360: Satellite images showed that a hole had formed in the ozone layer.

Page 362: The Montreal Protocol helped to protect the ozone layer because it was an agreement under which many nations pledged to limit their production of CFCs.

Section 3

Page 364: Mauna Loa is far from forests and cities. As well, the winds that blow across Mauna Loa have traveled thousands of miles across the Pacific Ocean, swirling and mixing as they traveled.

Page 368: Drought could result in decreased crop yields. As well, drought could increase the demand for irrigation, depleting aquifers.

Chapter 14 Land

Section 1

Page 381: Sample answer: A forest and a mountain are two types of land cover.

Page 383: Each person in the U.S. uses ecosystem services from more than 12 hectares, compared to 6 hectares for each person in Germany.

Section 2

Page 386: Heat islands can increase local rainfall.

Page 388: Sample answer: Plants in open spaces absorb carbon dioxide, produce oxygen, and filter out pollutants from air and water.

Section 3

Page 390: Rangeland becomes degraded when it is overgrazed.

Page 394: Sample answer: Public lands in the U.S. are used as national parks, leased to private companies, and maintained for protecting endangered species.

Chapter 15 Food and Agriculture

Section 1

Page 408: In general, people in developed countries tend to eat more food and a larger proportion of proteins and fats than people eat in developing countries.

Page 410: The productivity of land worked by subsistence farmers could be improved by providing access to water for irrigation.

Section 2

Page 413: Fungi and bacteria help make soil fertile by decomposing dead plants and organic debris. Small animals break up soil, allowing air and water into it.

Page 416: Salinization is a problem in Arizona and California because these regions have low rainfall and naturally salty soil.

Page 418: Pesticides become ineffective over time because pest populations may evolve resistance to the pesticides.

Page 420: Sample answer: Pheromones can be used to confuse insects such as moths and interfere with mating.

Section 3

Page 423: Governments try to stop overharvesting by creating no-fishing zones, so fish populations can recover.

Page 426: Livestock are important in developed countries mainly for the production of meat. Livestock are used in developing countries as sources of leather, wool, and food. They are also used as draft animals, and their manure is used as fertilizer and fuel.

Chapter 16 Mining and Mineral Resources

Section 1

Page 441: Sample answer: A mineral is naturally occurring, and has a characteristic chemical composition and an orderly internal structure.

Page 443: Dissolved salts are washed into seas or inland lakes. When the water in these seas or lakes evaporates, salt deposits called evaporites are left behind.

Section 2

Page 445: Planes carry instruments that identify patterns in gravity, magnetism or radioactivity. The planes fly over and collect data and images of an area.

Page 447: After mining is complete, the overburden is used to refill the pit. The soil that has been set aside is laid on top of the overburden.

Section 3

Page 452: Removing soil from a surface mine site strips away all plant life. With their natural habitat removed, animals will leave the area.

Page 453: Minerals that contain sulfur may be found in deeper soil layers. If these minerals are exposed to water and oxygen in the atmosphere, chemical reactions result in the release of acid. It is difficult for plants to grow in acidified soil.

Chapter 17 Nonrenewable Energy

Section 1

Page 469: The United States uses more energy per person than most other countries because over 25 percent of its energy resources are used to transport goods and people. In addition, the United States enjoys some of the lowest gasoline taxes in the world.

Page 472: Exploration wells are drilled to determine the volume and availability of an oil deposit.

Section 2

Page 477: The pressure vessel is used to contain the fission products in case of an accident

Page 478: It is difficult to find a place to store nuclear waste because the storage site must be located in an area that will be geologically stable for tens of thousands of years.

Reading Check Answers

Chapter 18 Renewable Energy

Section 1

Page 494: A liquid is heated by the sun as it flows through the solar collectors. The hot liquid is then pumped through a heat exchanger, which heats water for the building.

Page 497: Energy from the sun causes water to evaporate, condense in the atmosphere, and fall back to Earth's surface as rain. The movement of water across the land can be used to generate hydroelectricity.

Section 2

Page 501: Sample answer: Hydrogen is the most abundant element in the universe and does not release pollutants when burned.

Page 503: Sample answer: Hybrid cars use efficient gasoline engines, the cars can convert the energy of braking into electricity, and they are aerodynamically designed.

Chapter 19 Waste

Section 1

Page 519: A product made of polyester is nonbiodegradable.

Page 521: If landfills are not monitored properly, leachate can flow into groundwater supplies and make water from nearby wells unsafe to drink.

Section 2

Page 525: Consumer demand for packaging made from recycled materials encourages manufacturers to build facilities to make recycled packaging. As a result, it becomes easier for communities to sell the recycled materials they collect from residents.

Page 526: Biodegradable materials break down rapidly in moist, oxygen-rich conditions.

Section 3

Page 531: Cleaning machinery with plastic beads rather than solvents helps to reduce hazardous waste because the beads can be reused several times and are not hazardous when it is time to dispose of them.

Page 534: Sample answer: Incineration is generally the most expensive form of waste disposal because incinerators require a lot of energy to operate. Also, the leftover ash needs to be buried in a hazardous waste landfill.

Chapter 20 The Environment and Human Health

Section 1

Page 553: Sample answer: Burning gasoline and coal contributes to premature deaths from asthma and heart disease.

Page 556: Sample answer: Inadequate waste disposal can result in the buildup of solid waste on beaches and the release of toxic chemicals into waterways.

Section 2

Page 558: In developing countries, the local water supply is usually polluted because it is often used for drinking, washing, and sewage disposal.

Page 560: New methods for controlling malaria-carrying mosquitoes were needed because the mosquitoes evolved resistance to most of the pesticides.

Chapter 21 Economics, Policy, and the Future

Section 1

Page 573: Living in a sustainable way means looking for solutions to problems so that human society can go on indefinitely and future generations can have a standard of living as high as our own.

Page 576: People decide the value of a product by comparing the costs and benefits from their own perspective.

Section 2

Page 582: Sample answer: One way to influence environmental policy at the local level is to participate in public meetings held by city councils.

Page 583: It is important to look for information about environmental topics in sources other than the popular media because these sources are usually brief and leave out information.

Section 3

Page 587: Sample answer: A consumer can choose to buy products that are produced sustainably.

English and Spanish Glossary

abiotic (ay bie AHT ik) **factor** describes the non-living part of the environment, including water, rocks, light, and temperature (100)

factor abiótico un factor ambiental que no está asociado con las actividades de los seres vivos (100)

acid precipitation precipitation, such as rain, sleet, or snow, that contains a high concentration of acids, often because of the pollution of the atmosphere (336)

precipitación ácida precipitación tal como lluvia, aguanieve o nieve, que contiene una alta concentración de ácidos debido a la contaminación de la atmósfera (336)

acid shock the sudden runoff of large amounts of highly acidic water into lakes and streams when snow melts in the spring or when heavy rains follow a drought (338)

cambio brusco de la acidez entrada súbita de grandes cantidades de agua muy ácida a los lagos y arroyos cuando la nieve se derrite en la primavera o cuando llueve en abundancia después de una sequía (338)

active solar heating the gathering of solar energy by collectors that are used to heat water or heat a building (494)

calentamiento solar activo la recopilación de energía solar por medio de colectores que se usan para calentar agua o un edificio (494)

adaptation the process of becoming adapted to an environment; an anatomical, physiological, or behavioral change that improves a population's ability to survive (105)

adaptación el proceso de adaptarse a un ambiente; un cambio anatómico, fisiológico o en la conducta que mejora la capacidad de supervivencia de una población (105)

age structure the classification of members of a population into groups according to age or the distribution of members of a population in terms of age groups (236)

estructura de edades la clasificación en grupos de los miembros de una población en función de su edad, o bien, la distribución de los miembros de una población en función de grupos de edad (236)

agriculture the raising of crops and livestock for food or for other products that are useful to humans (10)

agricultura cultivar cosechas y criar ganado para usarlos como alimento o para producir productos útiles para los seres humanos (10)

air pollution the contamination of the atmosphere by the introduction of pollutants from human and natural sources (325)

contaminación del aire la contaminación de la atmósfera debido a la introducción de contaminantes provenientes de fuentes humanas y naturals (325)

alternative energy energy that does not come from fossil fuels and that is still in development (500)

energía alternativa energía que no proviene de los combustibles fósiles y que todavía se encuentra en desarrollo (500)

altitude the height of an object above a reference point, such as sea level or the Earth's surface (155)

altitud la altura de un objeto sobre un punto de referencia, tal como el nivel del mar o la superficie de la Tierra (155)

angiosperm (AN jee oh SPURM) a flowering plant that produces seeds within a fruit (111)

angiosperma una planta que da flores y que produce semillas dentro de la fruta (111)

aquaculture (AK wuh KUHL chur) the raising of aquatic plants and animals for human use or consumption (424)

acuacultura el cultivo de plantas y animales acuáticos para uso o consumo humano (424)

aquifer a body of rock or sediment that stores groundwater and allows the flow of groundwater (293)

acuífero un cuerpo rocoso o sedimento que almacena agua subterránea y permite que fluya (293)

arable land farmland that can be used to grow crops (243, 412)

tierra arable tierra agrícola que puede usarse para cosechar cultivos (243, 412)

English and Spanish Glossary

Archaebacteria a kingdom made up of prokaryotes (most of which are known to live in extreme environments) that are distinguished from other prokaryotes by differences in their genetics and in the makeup of their cell wall; currently, biologists prefer to classify members of this kingdom into the domain Archaea (108)

Archaebacteria un reino compuesto por procariotes (la mayoría de los cuales viven en ambientes extremos) que se distinguen de otros procariotes por diferencias genéticas y por la diferente composición de su pared celular; en la actualidad, los biólogos prefieren clasificar a los miembros de este reino dentro del dominio Archaea (108)

artificial eutrophication a process that increases the amount of nutrients in a body of water through human activities, such as waste disposal and land drainage (308)

eutrificación artificial un proceso que aumenta la cantidad de nutrientes en una masa de agua debido a actividades humanas, tales como el desecho de residuos y el drenaje de la tierra (308)

artificial selection the selective breeding of organisms (by humans) for specific desirable characteristics (106)

selección artificial la reproducción selectiva de organismos (por los seres humanos) para obtener características específicas deseables (106)

asbestos any of six silicate minerals that form bundles of minute fibers that are heat resistant, flexible, and durable (334)

asbesto cualquiera de seis minerales de silicato que forman montones de fibras diminutas que son resistentes al calor, flexibles y resistentes (334)

asthenosphere the solid, plastic layer of the mantle beneath the lithosphere; made of mantle rock that flows very slowly, which allows tectonic plates to move on top of it (65)

astenosfera la capa sólida y plástica del manto, que se encuentra debajo de la litosfera; está formada por roca del manto que fluye muy lentamente, lo cual permite que las placas tectónicas se muevan en su superficie (65)

atmosphere a mixture of gases that surrounds a planet, such as Earth (71)

atmósfera una mezcla de gases que rodea un planeta, tal como la Tierra (71)

B

bacteria extremely small, single-celled organisms that usually have a cell wall and reproduce by cell division (singular, *bacterium*) (108)

bacterias organismos extremadamente pequeños, unicelulares, que normalmente tienen pared celular y se reproducen por división celular (108)

barrier island a long ridge of sand or narrow island that lies parallel to the shore (194)

isla barrera un largo arrecife de arena o una isla angosta ubicada paralela a la costa (194)

benthic zone the bottom region of oceans and bodies of fresh water (186)

zona bentónica la región del fondo de los océanos y de las masas de agua dulce (186)

benthos organisms that live at the bottom of oceans or bodies of fresh water (185)

benthos organismos que viven en el fondo de los océanos o de las masas de agua dulce (185)

biodegradable material a material that can be broken down by biological processes (519)

material biodegradable un material que puede descomponerse por medio de procesos biológicos (519)

biodiversity the variety of organisms in a given area, the genetic variation within a population, the variety of species in a community, or the variety of communities in an ecosystem (15, 259)

biodiversidad la variedad de organismos que se encuentran en un área determinada, la variación genética dentro de una población, la variedad de especies en una comunidad o la variedad de comunidades en un ecosistema (15, 259)

Biodiversity Treaty an international agreement aimed at strengthening national control and preservation of biological resources; associated with the UN Conference on Environment and Development (UNCED or Earth summit) in 1992 (275)

Tratado de la Biodiversidad un acuerdo internacional cuyo objetivo es fortalecer el control y conservación nacional de los recursos biológicos; asociado con la Conferencia de las Naciones Unidas sobre el Medio Ambiente y el Desarrollo (UNCED o Cumbre de la Tierra) en 1992 (275)

biological pest control the use of certain organisms by humans to eliminate or control pests (419)

control biológico de plagas el uso de ciertos organismos por parte de los seres humanos para eliminar o controlar plagas (419)

biomagnification the accumulation of pollutants at successive levels of the food chain (312)

bioaumento la acumulación de contaminantes en niveles sucesivos de la cadena alimenticia (312)

biomass fuel plant material, manure, or any other organic matter that is used as an energy source (496)

combustible de biomasa material vegetal, abono o cualquier otra materia orgánica que se use como fuente de energía (496)

biome a large region characterized by a specific type of climate and certain types of plant and animal communities (153)

bioma una región extensa caracterizada por un tipo de clima específico y ciertos tipos de comunidades de plantas y animales (153)

biosphere the part of Earth where life exists (84)

biosfera la parte de la Tierra donde existe la vida (84)

biotic factor an environmental factor that is associated with or results from the activities of living organisms (100)

factor biótico un factor ambiental que está asociado con las actividades de los seres vivos o que resulta de ellas (100)

C

canopy the layers of treetops that shade the forest floor (158)

dosel vegetal las capas de las copas de los árboles que dan sombra al suelo del bosque (158)

carbon cycle the movement of carbon from the nonliving environment into living things and back (132)

ciclo del carbono el movimiento del carbono del ambiente sin vida a los seres vivos y de los seres vivos al ambiente (132)

carrying capacity the largest population that an environment can support at any given time (214)

capacidad de carga la población más grande que un ambiente puede sostener en cualquier momento dado (214)

cellular respiration the process by which cells produce energy from carbohydrates; atmospheric oxygen combines with glucose to form water and carbon dioxide (128)

respiración celular el proceso por medio del cual las células producen energía a partir de los carbohidratos; el oxígeno atmosférico se combina con la glucosa para formar agua y dióxido de carbono (128)

chaparral a type of vegetation that includes broadleafed evergreen shrubs and that is located in areas with hot, dry summers and mild, wet winters (168)

chaparral un tipo de vegetación que incluye arbustos de hoja perenne y ancha, y que se ubica en áreas donde los veranos son calientes y secos y los inviernos son templados y húmedos (168)

chlorofluorocarbons hydrocarbons in which some or all of the hydrogen atoms are replaced by chlorine and fluorine; used in coolants for refrigerators and air conditioners and in cleaning solvents; their use is restricted because they destroy ozone molecules in the stratosphere (abbreviation, CFCs) (359)

clorofluorocarbonos hidrocarburos en los que algunos o todos los átomos de hidrógeno son reemplazados por cloro y flúor; se usan en líquidos refrigerantes para refrigeradores y aires acondicionados y en solventes para limpieza; su uso está restringido porque destruyen las moléculas de ozono de la estratosfera (abreviatura: CFCs) (359)

climate the average weather conditions in an area over a long period of time (154, 351)

clima las condiciones promedio del tiempo en un área durante un largo período de tiempo (154, 351)

climax community a final, stable community in equilibrium with the environment (138)

comunidad clímax una comunidad final y estable, que está en equilibrio con el ambiente (138)

commensalism a relationship between two organisms in which one organism benefits and the other is unaffected (223)

comensalismo una relación entre dos organismos en la que uno se beneficia y el otro no es afectado (223)

English and Spanish Glossary

community a group of various species that live in the same habitat and interact with each other (102)

comunidad un grupo de varias especies que viven en el mismo hábitat e interactúan unas con otras (102)

competition the relationship between two species (or individuals) in which both species (or individuals) attempt to use the same limited resource such that both are negatively affected by the relationship (218)

competencia la relación entre dos especies (o individuos) en la que ambas especies (o individuos) intentan usar el mismo recurso limitado, de modo que ambas resultan afectadas negativamente por la relación (218)

compost a mixture of decomposing organic matter, such as manure and rotting plants, that is used as fertilizer and soil conditioner (416, 526)

composta una mezcla de materia orgánica en descomposición, como por ejemplo, estiércol y plantas en estado de putrefacción, que se usa como fertilizante y acondicionador del suelo (416, 526)

conceptual model a verbal or graphical explanation for how a system works or is organized (45)

modelo conceptual una explicación verbal o gráfica acerca de cómo funciona o está organizado un sistema (45)

condensation the change of state from a gas to a liquid (77)

condensación el cambio de estado de gas a líquido (77)

conduction the transfer of energy as heat through a material (74)

conducción la transferencia de energía en forma de calor a través de un material (74)

consumer an organism that eats other organisms or organic matter instead of producing its own nutrients or obtaining nutrients from inorganic sources (126)

consumidor un organismo que se alimenta de otros organismos o de materia orgánica, en lugar de producir sus propios nutrientes o de obtenerlos de fuentes inorgánicas (126)

control group in an experiment, a group that serves as a standard of comparison with another group to which the control group is identical except for one factor (35)

grupo de control en un experimento, un grupo que sirve como estándar de comparación con otro grupo, al cual el grupo de control es idéntico excepto por un factor (35)

convection the movement of matter due to differences in density that are caused by temperature variations; can result in the transfer of energy as heat (74)

convección el movimiento de la materia debido a diferencias en la densidad que se producen por variaciones en la temperatura; puede resultar en la transferencia de energía en forma de calor (74)

coral reef a limestone ridge found in tropical climates and composed of coral fragments that are deposited around organic remains (195)

arrecife de coral una cumbre de piedra caliza ubicada en climas tropicales, formada por fragmentos de coral depositados alrededor de restos orgánicos (195)

core the central part of the Earth below the mantle; also the center of the sun (65)

núcleo la parte central de la Tierra, debajo del manto; *también,* el centro del Sol (65)

correlation the linear dependence between two variables (37)

correlación la dependencia linear entre dos variables (37)

crust the thin and solid outermost layer of the Earth above the mantle (64)

corteza la capa externa, delgada y sólida de la Tierra, que se encuentra sobre el manto (64)

D

dam a structure that is built across a river to control a river's flow (300)

presa una estructura que se construye a través de un río para controlar el flujo del río (300)

data any pieces of information acquired through observation or experimentation (36)

datos cualquier parte de la información que se adquiere por medio de la observación o experimentación (36)

decibel the most common unit used to measure loudness (abbreviation, dB) (334)

decibel la unidad más común que se usa para medir el volumen del sonido (abreviatura: dB) (334)

decision-making model a conceptual model that provides a systematic process for making decisions (47)

modelo de toma de decisiones un modelo conceptual que brinda un proceso sistemático para tomar decisiones (47)

decomposer an organism that feeds by breaking down organic matter from dead organisms; examples include bacteria and fungi (127)

descomponedor un organismo que desintegra la materia orgánica de organismos muertos y se alimenta de ella; entre los ejemplos se encuentran las bacterias y los hongos (127)

deep-well injection deep-well disposal of hazardous waste (532)

inyección a pozo profundo método de desecho de residuos peligrosos por inyección a pozo (532)

deforestation the process of clearing forests (392)

deforestación el proceso de talar bosques (392)

demographic transition the general pattern of demographic change from high birth and death rates to low birth and death rates, as observed in the history of more-developed countries (239)

transición demográfica el patrón general de cambio demográfico de tasas de nacimiento y mortalidad altas a tasas de nacimiento y mortalidad bajas, tal como se observa en la historia de los países más desarrollados (239)

demography the study of the characteristics of populations, especially human populations (235)

demografía el estudio de las características de las poblaciones, sobre todo las poblaciones humanas (235)

density the number of individuals of the same species that live in a given unit of area (212)

densidad el número de individuos de la misma especie que viven en una unidad superficial determinada (212)

desalination (DEE SAL uh NAY shun) a process of removing salt from ocean water (303)

desalación (o desalinización) un proceso de remoción de sal del agua del océano (303)

desert a region that has little or no vegetation, long periods without rain, and extreme temperatures; usually found in warm climates (170)

desierto una región con poca vegetación o sin vegetación, largos períodos sin lluvia y temperaturas extremas; generalmente se ubica en climas calientes (170)

desertification the process by which human activities or climatic changes make arid or semiarid areas more desertlike (414)

desertificación el proceso por medio del cual las actividades humanas o los cambios climáticos hacen que un área árida o semiárida se vuelva más parecida a un desierto (414)

diet the type and amount of food that a person eats (408)

dieta el tipo y cantidad de alimento que come una persona (408)

dispersion in ecology, the pattern of distribution of organisms in a population (212)

dispersión en ecología, el patrón de distribución de organismos en una población (212)

distribution the relative arrangement of the members of a statistical population; usually shown in a graph (41)

distribución la organización relativa de los miembros de una población estadística; normalmente se muestra en una gráfica (41)

domesticated describes organisms that have been bred and managed for human use (423)

domesticado término que describe a organismos que han sido reproducidos y criados para uso humano (423)

dose the amount of a harmful substance to which a person is exposed; the quantity of medicine that needs to be taken over a period of time (550)

dosis la cantidad de medicina que se necesita tomar durante un período de tiempo; *también*, la cantidad de una sustancia dañina a la que está expuesta una persona (550)

English and Spanish Glossary

dose-response curve a graph that shows the relative effect of various doses of a drug or chemical on an organism or organisms (550)

curva de dosis-respuesta una gráfica que muestra el efecto relativo de varias dosis de un medicamento o substancia química en un organismo u organismos (550)

E

---

ecological footprint a calculation that shows the productive area of Earth needed to support one person in a particular country (19)

huella ecológica un cálculo que muestra el área productiva de la Tierra que se requiere para mantener a una persona en un cierto país (19)

ecological succession a gradual process of change and replacement in a community (137)

sucesión ecológica un proceso gradual de cambio y sustitución en una comunidad (137)

ecology the study of the interactions of living organisms with one another and with their environment (6)

ecología el estudio de las interacciones de los seres vivos entre sí mismos y entre sí mismos y su ambiente (6)

economics the study of how individuals and groups make decisions about the production, distribution, and consumption of limited resources as the individuals or groups attempt to fulfill their needs and wants (576)

economía el estudio de cómo los individuos y grupos toman decisiones acerca de la producción, distribución y consumo de recursos limitados, al mismo tiempo que estos individuos o grupos intentan satisfacer sus necesidades y deseos (576)

ecosystem (EE koh SIS tuhm) a community of organisms and their abiotic environment (99)

ecosistema una comunidad de organismos y su ambiente abiótico (99)

ecosystem services the role that organisms play in creating a healthful environment for humans (383)

servicios del ecosistema el papel que juegan los organismos en la creación de un ambiente saludable para los seres humanos (383)

ecotourism a form of tourism that supports the conservation and sustainable development of ecologically unique areas (262)

ecoturismo una forma de turismo que apoya la conservación y desarrollo sustentable de áreas ecológicamente únicas (262)

electric generator a device that converts mechanical energy into electrical energy (468)

descarga eléctrica la liberación de electricidad almacenada en una fuente (468)

El Niño (el NEEN yoh) the warm phase of the El Niño–Southern Oscillation; a periodic occurrence in the eastern Pacific Ocean in which the surface-water temperature becomes unusually warm (356)

El Niño la fase caliente de la Oscilación Sureña "El Niño"; un fenómeno periódico que ocurre en el océano Pacífico oriental en el que la temperatura del agua superficial se vuelve más caliente que de costumbre (356)

emergent layer the top foliage layer in a forest where the trees extend above surrounding trees (158)

capa emergente la capa superior de follaje en un bosque, en la que los árboles se extienden sobre los árboles circundantes (158)

endangered species a species that has been identified to be in danger of extinction throughout all or a significant part of its range, and that is thus under protection by regulations or conservation measures (263)

especie en peligro de extinción una especie que se ha identificado como en peligro de extinción en toda su zona de distribución o en una parte importante de ella, y que, por lo tanto, se encuentra protegida por normas y medidas de conservación (263)

Endangered Species Act an act that the U.S. Congress passed in 1973 to protect any plant or animal species in danger of extinction (273)

Ley de Especies en Peligro de Extinción una ley que el Congreso de los Estados Unidos emitió en 1973 cuyo fin es proteger las especies de animales o plantas que están en peligro de extinguirse (273)

endemic species a species that is native to a particular place and that is found only there (266)

especie endémica una especie que es nativa de un lugar particular y que únicamente se encuentra allí (266)

energy conservation the process of saving energy by reducing energy use and waste (504)

conservación de energía el proceso de ahorrar energía al reducir el uso y el gasto inútil de energía (504)

energy efficiency the percentage of energy put into a system that does useful work (502)

eficiencia energética el porcentaje de energía que se pone en un sistema que realiza un trabajo útil (502)

Environmental Impact Statement an assessment of the effect of a proposed project or law on the environment (581)

Evaluación del Impacto Ambiental una evaluación del efecto que una propuesta de proyecto o ley tendrá en el ambiente (581)

environmental science the study of the air, water, and land surrounding an organism or a community, which ranges from a small area to Earth's entire biosphere; it includes the study of the impact of humans on the environment (5)

ciencias ambientales el estudio del aire, agua y tierra circundantes en relación con un organismo o comunidad, desde un área pequeña de la Tierra hasta la biosfera completa; incluye el estudio del impacto que los seres humanos tienen en el ambiente (5)

epidemiology (EP uh DEE me AHL uh jee) the study of the distribution of diseases in populations and the study of factors that influence the occurrence and spread of disease (551)

epidemiología el estudio de la distribución de las enfermedades en poblaciones y el estudio de los factores que influyen en la incidencia y propagación de las enfermedades (551)

epiphyte a plant that uses another plant for support, but not for nourishment (158)

epifita una planta que utiliza otra planta para sostenerse pero no para alimentarse (158)

erosion a process in which the materials of Earth's surface are loosened, dissolved, or worn away and transported from one place to another by a natural agent, such as wind, water, ice, or gravity (70, 414)

erosión un proceso por medio del cual los materiales de la superficie de la Tierra se aflojan, disuelven o desgastan y son transportados de un lugar a otro por un agente natural, como el viento, el agua, el hielo o la gravedad (70, 414)

estuary an area where fresh water from rivers mixes with salt water from the ocean; the part of a river where the tides meet the river current (191)

estuario un área donde el agua dulce de los ríos se mezcla con el agua salada del océano; la parte de un río donde las mareas se encuentran con la corriente del río (191)

Eubacteria in a traditional taxonomic system, a kingdom made up of all prokaryotes except members of the kingdom Archaebacteria; currently, biologists prefer to classify members of this kingdom into the domain Bacteria (108)

Eubacteria en un sistema taxonómico tradicional, un reino que agrupa a todos los procariotes, excepto a los miembros del reino Archaebacteria; en la actualidad, los biólogos prefieren clasificar a los miembros de este reino dentro del dominio Bacteria (108)

eutrophication an increase in the amount of nutrients, such as nitrates, in a marine or aquatic ecosystem (187)

eutrofización un aumento en la cantidad de nutrientes, tales como nitratos, en un ecosistema marino o acuático (187)

evaporation the change of state from a liquid to a gas (77)

evaporación el cambio de estado de líquido a gas (77)

evolution a heritable change in the characteristics within a population from one generation to the next; the development of new types of organisms from preexisting types of organisms over time (103)

evolución un cambio hereditario en las características de una población que se produce de una generación a la siguiente; el desarrollo de nuevos tipos de organismos a partir de organismos preexistentes a lo largo del tiempo (103)

English and Spanish Glossary

exotic species a species that is not native to a particular region (265)

especie exótica una especie que no es originaria de una región en particular (265)

experiment a procedure that is carried out under controlled conditions to discover, demonstrate, or test a fact, theory, or general truth (35)

experimento un procedimiento que se lleva a cabo bajo condiciones controladas para descubrir, demostrar o probar un hecho, teoría o verdad general (35)

experimental group in an experiment, a group that is identical to a control group except for one factor and that is compared with the control group (35)

grupo experimental en un experimento, un grupo que es idéntico al grupo de control, excepto por un factor, y que es comparado con el grupo de control (35)

exponential growth logarithmic growth, or growth in which numbers increase by a certain factor in each successive time period (213)

crecimiento exponencial crecimiento logarítmico o crecimiento en el que los números aumentan en función de un cierto factor en cada período de tiempo sucesivo (213)

F

famine widespread malnutrition and starvation in an area due to a shortage of food, usually caused by a catastrophic event (407)

hambruna desnutrición e inanición generalizadas en un área debido a una escasez de alimento, normalmente causada por un suceso catastrófico (407)

fertility rate the number of births (usually per year) per 1,000 women of childbearing age (usually 15 to 44) (237)

tasa de fertilidad el número de nacimientos (normalmente por año) por cada 1,000 mujeres en edad de procrear (normalmente entre los 15 y 44 años de edad) (237)

food chain the pathway of energy transfer through various stages as a result of the feeding patterns of a series of organisms (130)

cadena alimenticia la vía de transferencia de energía través de varias etapas, que ocurre como resultado de los patrones de alimentación de una serie de organismos (130)

food web a diagram that shows the feeding relationships between organisms in an ecosystem (130)

red alimenticia un diagrama que muestra las relaciones de alimentación entre los organismos de un ecosistema (130)

fossil fuel a nonrenewable energy resource formed from the remains of organisms that lived long ago; examples include oil, coal, and natural gas (467)

combustible fósil un recurso energético no renovable formado a partir de los restos de organismos que vivieron hace mucho tiempo; algunos ejemplos incluyen el petróleo, el carbón y el gas natural (467)

fresh water water that contains insignificant amounts of salts, as in rivers and lakes (83)

agua dulce agua que contiene una cantidad insignificante de sales, como el agua de los ríos y lagos (83)

fuel cell a device that produces electricity chemically by combining hydrogen fuel with oxygen from the air (502)

pila de combustible un aparato que produce electricidad químicamente al combinar combustible de hidrógeno con oxígeno del aire (502)

fungus an organism whose cells have nuclei, rigid cell walls, and no chlorophyll and that belongs to the kingdom Fungi (109)

hongo un organismo que tiene células con núcleos y pared celular rígida, pero carece de clorofila, perteneciente al reino Fungi (109)

G

gene a segment of DNA that is located in a chromosome and that codes for a specific hereditary trait (260)

gene un segmento de ADN ubicado en un cromosoma, que codifica para un carácter hereditario específico (260)

genetic engineering a technology in which the genome of a living cell is modified for medical or industrial use (421)

ingeniería genética una tecnología en la que el genoma de una célula viva se modifica con fines médicos o industriales (421)

geographic information system an automated system for capturing, storing, retrieving, analyzing, manipulating, and displaying geographic data (abbreviation, GIS) (387)

sistema de información geográfica un sistema automatizado que sirve para capturar, almacenar, obtener, analizar, manipular y mostrar datos geográficos (abreviatura: SIG) (387)

geosphere the mostly solid, rocky part of Earth; extends from the center of the core to the surface of the crust (63)

geosfera la capa de la Tierra que es principalmente sólida y rocosa; se extiende desde el centro del núcleo hasta la superficie de la corteza terrestre (63)

geothermal energy the energy produced by heat within Earth (498)

energía geotérmica la energía producida por el calor del interior de la Tierra (498)

germ plasm hereditary material (chromosomes and genes) that is usually contained in the protoplasm of germ cells (270)

plasma germinal material hereditario (cromosomas y genes) que normalmente se encuentra contenido en el protoplasma de las células germinales (270)

global warming a gradual increase in average global temperature (365)

calentamiento global un aumento gradual de la temperatura global promedio (365)

greenhouse effect the warming of the surface and lower atmosphere of Earth that occurs when carbon dioxide, water vapor, and other gases in the air absorb and reradiate infrared radiation (76)

efecto de invernadero el calentamiento de la superficie terrestre y de la parte más baja de la atmósfera, el cual se produce cuando el dióxido de carbono, el vapor de agua y otros gases del aire absorben radiación infrarroja y la vuelven a irradiar (76)

greenhouse gas a gas composed of molecules that absorb and radiate infrared radiation from the sun (363)

gas de invernadero un gas compuesto de moléculas que absorben radiación infrarroja del Sol y la vuelven a irradiar (363)

groundwater the water that is beneath the Earth's surface (292)

agua subterránea el agua que está debajo de la superficie de la Tierra (292)

growth rate an expression of the increase in the size of an organism or population over a given period of time (212)

tasa de crecimiento una expresión del aumento en el tamaño de un organismo o población a lo largo de un cierto período de tiempo (212)

gymnosperm (JIM noh SPURM) a woody vascular seed plant whose seeds are not enclosed by an ovary or fruit (111)

gimnosperma una planta leñosa y vascular, la cual produce semillas que no están contenidas en un ovario o fruto (111)

habitat the place where an organism usually lives (102)

hábitat el lugar donde un organismo vive normalmente (102)

habitat conservation plan a land-use plan that attempts to protect threatened or endangered species across a given area by allowing some trade-offs between harm to the species and additional conservation commitments among cooperating parties (273)

plan de conservación del hábitat un plan de uso de la tierra que tiene como objetivo proteger a las especies amenazadas o en peligro de extinción en un área determinada, permitiendo algunas compensaciones entre el daño a las especies y compromisos adicionales de conservación entre las partes en cooperación (273)

hazardous wastes wastes that are a risk to the health of humans or other living organisms (529)

residuos peligrosos residuos que son un riesgo para la salud de los seres humano y otros seres vivos (529)

heat island an area in which the air temperature is generally higher than the temperature of surrounding rural areas (386)

isla de calor un área en la que la temperatura del aire es generalmente más alta que la temperatura de las áreas rurales circundantes (386)

English and Spanish Glossary

host an organism from which a parasite takes food or shelter (557)

huésped el organismo del cual un parásito obtiene alimento y refugio (557)

hydroelectric energy electrical energy produced by the flow of water (497)

energía hidroeléctrica energía eléctrica producida por el flujo del agua (497)

hypothesis (hie PATH uh sis) a testable idea or explanation that leads to scientific investigation (34)

hipótesis una idea o explicación que conlleva a la investigación científica y que se puede probar (34)

I

infrastructure the basic facilities of a country or region, such as roads, bridges, and sewers (241, 385)

infraestructura los servicios básicos de un país o región, tales como caminos, puentes y drenaje (241, 385)

invertebrate (in VUHR tuh brit) an animal that does not have a backbone (112)

invertebrado un animal que no tiene columna vertebral (112)

K

keystone species a species that is critical to the functioning of the ecosystem in which it lives because it affects the survival and abundance of many other species in its community (260)

especie clave una especie que es crítica para el funcionamiento del ecosistema en el que vive porque afecta la supervivencia y abundancia de muchas otras especies en su comunidad (260)

Kyoto Protocol an international treaty according to which developed countries that signed the treaty agree to reduce their emissions of carbon dioxide and other gases that may contribute to global warming by 2012 (369)

Protocolo de Kyoto un tratado internacional en función del cual los países desarrollados que lo firmaron acceden a reducir sus emisiones de dióxido de carbono y otros gases que pueden contribuir al calentamiento global para el año 2012 (369)

L

landfill an area of land or an excavation where wastes are placed for permanent disposal (521)

entierro de residuos un área de terreno o una excavación donde se colocan los residuos para deshacerse de ellos permanentemente (521)

land-use planning a set of policies and activities related to potential uses of land that is put in place before an area is developed (387)

planeación del uso de tierras un conjunto de políticas y actividades relacionadas con los usos potenciales de la tierra, que se establecen antes de desarrollar un área (387)

La Niña (la NEEN yah) the cool phase of the El Niño–Southern Oscillation; a periodic occurrence in the eastern Pacific Ocean in which the surface-water temperature becomes unusually cool (356)

La Niña la fase fría de la Oscilación Sureña "El Niño"; un fenómeno periódico que ocurre en el océano Pacífico oriental en el que la temperatura del agua superficial se vuelve más fría que de costumbre (356)

latitude the distance north or south from the equator; expressed in degrees (155, 352)

latitud la distancia hacia el norte o hacia el sur del ecuador; se expresa en grados (155, 352)

law of supply and demand a law of economics that states that as the demand for a good or service increases, the value of the good or service also increases (17)

ley de la oferta y la demanda una ley de economía que establece que al aumentar la demanda de un bien o servicio, el valor del bien o servicio también aumenta (17)

leachate a liquid that has passed through solid waste and has extracted dissolved or suspended materials from that waste, such as pesticides in the soil (521)

lechado un líquido que ha pasado a través de desechos sólidos y ha extraído materiales disueltos o suspendidos de los desechos, como por ejemplo, pesticidas en el suelo (521)

least developed countries countries that have been identified by the United Nations as showing the fewest signs of development in terms of income, human resources, and economic diversification (244)

países menos desarrollados países que la Organización de las Naciones Unidas ha identificado como los que muestran las menores señales de desarrollo en términos de ingresos, recursos humanos y diversificación económica (244)

life expectancy the average length of time that an individual is expected to live (238)

esperanza de vida la longitud promedio de tiempo que se espera que un individuo viva (238)

limiting resource a particular natural resource that, when limited, determines the carrying capacity of an ecosystem for a particular species (215)

recursos limitantes un recurso natural particular que, si está limitado, determina la capacidad de carga de un ecosistema para una especie en particular (215)

lithosphere the solid, outer layer of the Earth that consists of the crust and the rigid upper part of the mantle (65)

litosfera la capa externa y sólida de la Tierra que está formada por la corteza y la parte superior y rígida del manto (65)

littoral zone a shallow zone in a freshwater habitat where light reaches the bottom and nurtures plants (186)

zona litoral una zona poco profunda del hábitat de agua dulce donde la luz llega al fondo y nutre a las plantas (186)

livestock domesticated animals that are raised to be used on a farm or ranch or to be sold for profit (426)

animales de cría animales domesticados que se crían para usarse en una granja o rancho o para ser vendidos con el fin de obtener una ganancia (426)

lobbying an attempt to influence the decisions of lawmakers (583)

cabildeo un intento de ejercer una influencia en las decisiones de los legisladores (583)

M

malnutrition a disorder of nutrition that results when a person does not consume enough of each of the nutrients that are needed by the human body (407)

desnutrición un trastorno de nutrición que resulta cuando una persona no consume una cantidad suficiente de cada nutriente que el cuerpo humano necesita (407)

mangrove swamp a tropical or subtropical marine swamp that is characterized by the abundance of low to tall trees, especially mangrove trees (194)

manglar un pantano marino tropical o subtropical que se caracteriza por la abundancia de árboles bajos a altos, especialmente árboles de mangle (194)

mantle in Earth science, the layer of rock between the Earth's crust and core (65)

manto en las ciencias de la Tierra, la capa de roca que se encuentra entre la corteza terrestre y el núcleo (65)

mathematical model one or more equations that represent the way a system or process works (46)

modelo matemático una o más ecuaciones que representan la forma en que funciona un sistema o proceso (46)

mean the number obtained by adding up the data for a given characteristic and dividing this sum by the number of individuals (41)

media el número que se obtiene al sumar los datos de una característica determinada y dividir esta suma entre el número de individuos (41)

migration in general, any movement of individuals or populations from one location to another; specifically, a periodic group movement that is characteristic of a given population or species (237)

migración en general, cualquier movimiento de individuos o poblaciones de un lugar a otro; específicamente, un movimiento periódico en grupo que es característico de una población o especie determinada (237)

English and Spanish Glossary

mineral a natural, usually inorganic solid that has a characteristic chemical composition, an orderly internal structure, and a characteristic set of physical properties (441)

mineral un sólido natural, normalmente inorgánico, que tiene una composición química característica, una estructura interna ordenada y propiedades físicas y químicas características (441)

model a pattern, plan, representation, or description designed to show the structure or workings of an object, system, or concept (44)

modelo un diseño, plan, representación o descripción cuyo objetivo es mostrar la estructura o funcionamiento de un objeto, sistema o concepto (44)

municipal solid waste waste produced by households and businesses (520)

desechos sólidos municipales desechos producidos por las casas y negocios (520)

mutualism a relationship between two species in which both species benefit (222)

mutualismo una relación entre dos especies en la que ambas se benefician (222)

natural resource any natural material that is used by humans, such as water, petroleum, minerals, forests, and animals (14)

recurso natural cualquier material natural que es utilizado por los seres humanos, como agua, petróleo, minerales, bosques y animales (14)

natural selection the process by which individuals that are better adapted to their environment survive and reproduce more successfully than less well adapted individuals do; a theory to explain the mechanism of evolution (103)

selección natural el proceso por medio del cual los individuos que están mejor adaptados a su ambiente sobreviven y se reproducen con más éxito que los individuos menos adaptados; una teoría que explica el mecanismo de la evolución (103)

nekton all organisms that swim actively in open water, independent of currents (185)

necton todos los organismos que nadan activamente en las aguas abiertas, de manera independiente de las corrientes (185)

niche (NICH) the unique position occupied by a species, both in terms of its physical use of its habitat and its function within an ecological community (217)

nicho la posición única que ocupa una especie, tanto en lo que se refiere al uso de su hábitat como en cuanto a su función dentro de una comunidad ecológica (217)

nitrogen cycle the process in which nitrogen circulates among the air, soil, water, plants, and animals in an ecosystem (134)

ciclo del nitrógeno el proceso por medio del cual el nitrógeno circula en el aire, suelo, agua, plantas y animales de un ecosistema (134)

nitrogen-fixing bacteria bacteria that convert atmospheric nitrogen into ammonia (134)

bacterias fijadoras de nitrógeno bacterias que transforman el nitrógeno atmosférico en amoniaco (134)

nonpoint-source pollution pollution that comes from many sources rather than from a single specific site; an example is pollution that reaches a body of water from streets and storm sewers (305)

contaminación no puntual contaminación que proviene de muchas fuentes, en lugar de provenir de un solo sitio específico; un ejemplo es la contaminación que llega a una masa de agua a partir de las calles y los drenajes (305)

nuclear energy the energy released by a fission or fusion reaction; the binding energy of the atomic nucleus (476)

energía nuclear la energía liberada por una reacción de fisión o fusión; la energía de enlace del núcleo atómico (476)

nuclear fission the process by which the nucleus of a heavy atom splits into two or more fragments; the process releases neutrons and energy (476)

fisión nuclear el proceso por medio del cual el núcleo de un átomo pesado se divide en dos o más fragmentos; el proceso libera neutrones y energía (476)

nuclear fusion the process by which nuclei of small atoms combine to form a new, more massive nucleus; the process releases energy (479)

fusión nuclear el proceso por medio del cual los núcleos de átomos pequeños se combinan y forman un núcleo nuevo con mayor masa; el proceso libera energía (479)

observation the process of obtaining information by using the senses; the information obtained by using the senses (33)

observación el proceso de obtener información por medio de los sentidos; la información que se obtiene al usar los sentidos (33)

ocean thermal energy conversion the use of temperature differences in ocean water to produce electricity (abbreviation, OTEC) (501)

conversión de la energía térmica del océano el uso de diferencias en la temperatura del agua del océano para producir electricidad (abreviatura: OTEC, por sus siglas en inglés) (501)

oil reserves oil deposits that are discovered and are in commercial production (474)

reservas de petróleo depósitos de petróleo que son descubiertos y se encuentran en producción comercial (474)

ore mineral a mineral that contains one or more elements of economic value (442)

mineral metalífero un mineral que contiene uno o más elementos de valor económico (442)

organism a living thing; anything that can carry out life processes independently (101)

organismo un ser vivo; cualquier cosa que pueda llevar a cabo procesos vitales independientemente (101)

overgrazing the depletion of vegetation due to the continuous feeding of too many animals (390)

sobrepastoreo el agotamiento de la vegetación debido a la alimentación continua de demasiados animales (390)

overharvesting catching or removing from a population more organisms than the population can replace (423)

sobrecosechar capturar o sustraer de una población más organismos de los que la población puede reemplazar (423)

ozone a gas molecule that is made up of three oxygen atoms (73)

ozono una molécula de gas que está formada por tres átomos de oxígeno (73)

ozone hole a thinning of stratospheric ozone that occurs over the poles during the spring (360)

agujero en la capa de ozono un adelgazamiento del ozono estratosférico, el cual occure encima de los Polos durante la primavera (360)

ozone layer the layer of the atmosphere at an altitude of 15 to 40 km in which ozone absorbs ultraviolet solar radiation (359)

capa de ozono la capa de la atmó-sfera ubicada a una altitud de 15 a 40 km, en la cual el ozono absorbe la radiación solar (359)

parasitism a relationship between two species in which one species, the parasite, benefits from the other species, the host, which is harmed (222)

parasitismo una relación entre dos especies en la que una, el parásito, se beneficia de la otra, el huésped, que resulta perjudicada (222)

particulates (pahr TIK yoo lits) fine particles that are suspended in the atmosphere and that are associated with air pollution (552)

materia particulada partículas finas que se encuentran suspendidas en la atmósfera y que están relacionadas con la contaminación del aire (552)

passive solar heating the use of sunlight to heat buildings directly (492)

calentamiento solar pasivo el uso de la luz solar para calentar edificios directamente (492)

pathogen a microorganism, another organism, a virus, or a protein that causes disease; an infectious agent (297, 557)

patógeno un microorganismo, otro organismo, un virus o una proteína que causa enfermedades; un agente infeccioso (297, 557)

permafrost in arctic regions, the permanently frozen layer of soil or subsoil (172)

permafrost en las regiones árticas, la capa de suelo o subsuelo que se encuentra congelada permanentemente (172)

permeability the ability of a rock or sediment to let fluids pass through its open spaces or pores (293)

permeabilidad la capacidad de una roca o sedimento de permitir que los fluidos pasen a través de sus espacios abiertos o poros (293)

English and Spanish Glossary

pesticide a poison used to destroy pests, such as insects, rodents, or weeds; examples include insecticides, rodenticides, and herbicides (417)

pesticida un veneno que se usa para destruir plagas, tales como insectos, roedores o maleza; entre los ejemplos se encuentran los insecticidas, rodenticidas y herbicidas (417)

petroleum a liquid mixture of complex hydrocarbon compounds; used widely as a fuel source (472)

petróleo una mezcla líquida de compuestos hidrocarburos complejos; se usa ampliamente como una fuente de combustible (472)

pH a value that is used to express the acidity or alkalinity (basicity) of a system; each whole number on the scale indicates a tenfold change in acidity; a pH of 7 is neutral, a pH of less than 7 is acidic, and a pH of greater than 7 is basic (336)

pH un valor que expresa la acidez o la alcalinidad (basicidad) de un sistema; cada número entero de la escala indica un cambio de 10 veces en la acidez; un pH de 7 es neutro, un pH de menos de 7 es ácido y un pH de más de 7 es básico (336)

phosphorus cycle the cyclic movement of phosphorus in different chemical forms from the environment to organisms and then back to the environment (135)

ciclo del fósforo el movimiento cíclico del fósforo en diferentes formas químicas del ambiente a los organismos y de regreso al ambiente (135)

photosynthesis the process by which plants, algae, and some bacteria use sunlight, carbon dioxide, and water to produce carbohydrates and oxygen (125)

fotosíntesis el proceso por medio del cual las plantas, algas y algunas bacterias utilizan la luz solar, dióxido de carbono y agua para producir carbohidratos y oxígeno (125)

pioneer species a species that colonizes an uninhabited area and that starts an ecological cycle in which many other species become established (138)

especie pionera una especie que coloniza un área deshabitada y empieza un ciclo ecológico en el cual se establecen muchas otras especies (138)

placer deposit a deposit that contains a valuable mineral that has been concentrated by mechanical action (449)

yacimiento de aluvión un yacimiento que contiene un mineral valioso que se ha concentrado debido a la acción mecánica (449)

plankton the mass of mostly microscopic organisms that float or drift freely in the waters of aquatic (freshwater and marine) environments (185)

plancton la masa de organismos casi microscópicos que flotan o se encuentran a la deriva en aguas (dulces y marinas) de ambientes acuáticos (185)

poaching the illegal harvesting of fish, game, or other species (265)

caza furtiva la cosecha ilegal de peces, presas u otras especies (265)

point-source pollution pollution that comes from a specific site (305)

contaminación puntual contaminación que proviene de un lugar específico (305)

polar stratospheric cloud a cloud that forms at altitudes of about 21,000 m during the Arctic and Antarctic winter or early spring, when air temperatures drop below –80°C (360)

nube polar estrato-sférica una nube que se forma en altitudes de aproximadamente 21,000 m durante el invierno ártico y antártico o al principio de la primavera, cuando la temperatura del aire disminuye a menos de –80 °C (360)

pollution an undesirable change in the natural environment that is caused by the introduction of substances that are harmful to living organisms or by excessive wastes, heat, noise, or radiation (14)

contaminación un cambio indeseable en el ambiente natural, producido por la introducción de substancias que son dañinas para los organismos vivos o por desechos, calor, ruido o radiación excesivos (14)

population a group of organisms of the same species that live in a specific geographical area and interbreed (101, 211)

población un grupo de organismos de la misma especie que viven en un área geográfica específica y se reproducen entre sí (101, 211)

porosity the percentage of the total volume of a rock or sediment that consists of open spaces (293)

porosidad el porcentaje del volumen total de una roca o sedimento que está formado por espacios abiertos (293)

potable suitable for drinking (297)

potable que puede beberse (297)

precipitation any form of water that falls to the Earth's surface from the clouds; includes rain, snow, sleet, and hail (77)

precipitación cualquier forma de agua que cae de las nubes a la superficie de la Tierra; incluye a la lluvia, nieve, aguanieve y granizo (77)

predation an interaction between two organisms in which one organism, the predator, kills and feeds on the other organism, the prey (220)

depredación la interacción entre dos organismos en la que un organismo, el depredador, mata a otro organismo, la presa, y se alimenta de él (220)

prediction a statement made in advance that expresses the results that will be obtained from testing a hypothesis if the hypothesis is supported; the expected outcome if a hypothesis is accurate (34)

predicción una afirmación que se hace por anticipado, la cual expresa los resultados que se obtendrán al poner a prueba una hipótesis si ésta es corroborada; el resultado esperado si la hipótesis es correcta (34)

primary pollutant a pollutant that is put directly into the atmosphere by human or natural activity (325)

contaminante primario un contaminante que es colocado directamente en la atmósfera por las actividades humanas o naturales (325)

primary succession succession that begins in an area that previously did not support life (137)

sucesión primaria sucesión que comienza en un área donde previamente no podía existir la vida (137)

probability the likelihood that a possible future event will occur in any given instance of the event; the mathematical ratio of the number of times one outcome of any event is likely to occur to the number of possible outcomes of the event (42)

probabilidad termino que describe qué tan probable es que ocurra un posible evento futuro en un caso dado del evento; la proporción matemática del número de veces que es posible que ocurra un resultado de cualquier evento respecto al número de resultados posibles del evento (42)

producer an organism that can make organic molecules from inorganic molecules; a photosynthetic or chemosynthetic autotroph that serves as the basic food source in an ecosystem (126)

productor un organismo que elabora moléculas orgánicas a partir de moléculas inorgánicas; un autótrofo fotosintético o quimiosintético que funciona como la fuente fundamental de alimento en un ecosistema (126)

protist an organism that belongs to the kingdom Protista (110)

protista un organismo que pertenece al reino Protista (110)

R

radiation the energy that is transferred as electromagnetic waves, such as visible light and infrared waves (74)

radiación la energía que se transfiere en forma de ondas electromagnéticas, tales como las ondas de luz y las infrarrojas (74)

recharge zone an area in which water travels downward to become part of an aquifer (294)

zona de recarga un área en la que el agua se desplaza hacia abajo para convertirse en parte de un acuífero (294)

reclamation the process of returning land to its original condition after mining is completed (454)

restauración el proceso de hacer que la tierra vuelva a su condición original después de que se terminan las actividades de explotación minera (454)

recycling the process of recovering valuable or useful materials from waste or scrap; the process of reusing some items (525)

reciclar el proceso de recuperar materiales valiosos o útiles de los desechos o de la basura; el proceso de reutilizar algunas cosas (525)

reforestation the reestablishment and development of trees in a forest land (393)

reforestación el restablecimiento y desarrollo de los árboles en un bosque (393)

English and Spanish Glossary

renewable energy energy from sources that are constantly being formed (491)

energía renovable energía que proviene de fuentes que se están formando constantemente (491)

reproductive potential the maximum number of offspring that a given organism can produce (213)

potencial reproductivo el número máximo de crías que puede producir un determinado organismo (213)

reservoir an artificial body of water that usually forms behind a dam (300)

represa una masa artificial de agua que normalmente se forma detrás de una presa (300)

resistance in biology, the ability of an organism to tolerate a chemical or disease-causing agent (107)

resistencia en biología, la capacidad de un organismo de tolerar a un agente químico o causante de enfermedades (107)

risk the probability of an unwanted outcome (43)

riesgo la probabilidad de que se produzca un resultado no deseado (43)

risk assessment the scientific assessment, study, and management of risk; a scientific estimation of the likelihood of negative effects that may result from exposure to a specific hazard (551)

evaluación de riesgos la evaluación, estudio y administración del riesgo por medios científicos; un cálculo científico de la probabilidad de que ocurran efectos negativos debido a la exposición a un peligro específico (551)

river system a flowing network of rivers and streams draining a river basin (291)

sistema fluvial una red de ríos y arroyos en flujo que drenan una cuenca fluvial (291)

ruminant (ROO muh nuhnt) a cud-chewing mammal that has a three- or four-chambered stomach; examples include sheep, goats, and cattle (426)

rumiante un mamífero que mastica los alimentos dos veces, el cual tiene un estómago con tres o cuatro cámaras; entre los ejemplos se encuentran los borregos, cabras y ganado (426)

rural describes an area of open land that is often used for farming (381)

rural término que describe un área de tierra abierta que a menudo se usa para la labranza (381)

S

salinity a measure of the amount of dissolved salts in a given amount of liquid (80, 185)

salinidad una medida de la cantidad de sales disueltas en una cantidad determinada de líquido (80, 185)

salinization (SAL uh nie ZAY shuhn) the accumulation of salts in soil (416)

salinización la acumulación de sales en el suelo (416)

salt marsh a maritime habitat characterized by grasses, sedges, and other plants that have adapted to continual, periodic flooding; salt marshes are found primarily throughout the temperate and subarctic regions (194)

marisma un hábitat marino que se caracteriza por tener pasto, juncias y otras plantas que se han adaptado a la inundación continua y periódica; las marismas se encuentran principalmente en las regiones templadas y subárticas (194)

sample the group of individuals or events selected to represent a statistical population (42)

muestra el grupo de individuos o sucesos que se seleccionan para representar a una población estadística (42)

savanna a plain full of grasses and scattered trees and shrubs; found in tropical and subtropical habitats and mainly in regions with a dry climate, such as East Africa (165)

sabana una planicie llena de pastizales y árboles y arbustos dispersos; se encuentra en los hábitats tropicales y subtropicales y, sobre todo, en regiones con un clima seco, como en el este de África (165)

secondary pollutant a pollutant that forms in the atmosphere by chemical reaction with primary air pollutants, natural components in the air, or both (325)

contaminante secundario un contaminante que se forma en la atmósfera por medio de una reacción química con contaminantes primarios del aire, componentes naturales del aire o ambos (325)

secondary succession the process by which one community replaces another community that has been partially or totally destroyed (137)

sucesión secundaria el proceso por medio del cual una comunidad reemplaza a otra, la cual ha sido parcial o totalmente destruida (137)

sick-building syndrome a set of symptoms, such as headache, fatigue, eye irritation, and dizziness, that may affect workers in modern, airtight office buildings; believed to be caused by indoor pollutants (332)

síndrome del edificio enfermo un conjunto de síntomas, como dolor de cabeza, fatiga, irritación de los ojos y mareo, que puede afectar a las personas que trabajan en edificios modernos que cuentan con ventanas selladas; se cree que es producido por los contaminantes del interior del edificio (332)

smelting the melting or fusing of ore in order to separate impurities from pure metal (450)

fundir derretir una mena con el fin de separar las impurezas del metal puro (450)

smog urban air pollution composed of a mixture of smoke and fog produced from industrial pollutants and burning fuels (330)

esmog contaminación urbana del aire, compuesta por una mezcla de humo y niebla producida por contaminantes industriales y combustibles (330)

solid waste a discarded solid material, such as garbage, refuse, or sludges (517)

desechos sólidos un material sólido desechado, como por ejemplo, basura, residuos o sedimentos (517)

source reduction any change in the design, manufacture, purchase, or use of materials or products to reduce their amount or toxicity before they become municipal solid waste; also the reuse of products or materials (524)

reducción de la fuente cualquier cambio en el diseño, manufactura, compra o uso de materiales o productos para reducir su cantidad o toxicidad antes de que se conviertan en desechos sólidos municipales; *también,* la reutilización de productos o materiales (524)

species a group of organisms that are closely related and can mate to produce fertile offspring; also the level of classification below genus and above subspecies (101)

especie un grupo de organismos que tienen un parentesco cercano y que pueden aparearse para producir descendencia fértil; *también,* el nivel de clasificación debajo de género y arriba de subespecie (101)

statistics the collection and classification of data that are in the form of numbers (40)

estadística la recolección y clasificación de datos que encuentran en forma de números (40)

stratosphere the layer of the atmosphere that lies between the troposphere and the mesosphere and in which temperature increases as altitude increases; contains the ozone layer (73)

estratosfera la capa de la atmósfera que se encuentra entre la troposfera y la mesosfera y en la cual la temperatura aumenta al aumentar la altitud; contiene la capa de ozono (73)

subsidence the sinking of regions of the ground surface with little or no horizontal movement (453)

hundimiento del terreno el hundimiento de regiones de la superficie del suelo con muy poco o sin ningún movimiento horizontal (453)

subsurface mining a mining method in which ore is extracted from beneath the ground surface (446)

minería subsuperficial un método de explotación de minas en el que la mena se extrae de la parte inferior de la superficie del suelo (446)

English and Spanish Glossary

surface impoundment a natural depression or a human-made excavation that serves as a disposal facility that holds an accumulation of wastes (532)

separación superficial una depresión natural o una excavación hecha por el hombre que sirve como vertedero de basura para acumular desechos (532)

surface mining a mining method in which soil and rocks are removed to reach underlying coal or minerals (447)

minería superficial un método de explotación de minas en el que se remueven el suelo y las rocas para llegar al carbón o minerales subyacentes (447)

surface water all the bodies of fresh water, salt water, ice, and snow that are found above the ground (290)

agua superficial todas las masas de agua dulce, agua salada, hielo y nieve que se encuentran arriba del suelo (290)

survivorship the percentage of newborn individuals in a population that can be expected to survive to a given age (236)

supervivencia el porcentaje de individuos recién nacidos de una población que se espera que sobrevivan hasta una edad determinada (236)

sustainability the condition in which human needs are met in such a way that a human population can survive indefinitely (21, 573)

sustentabilidad la condición en la que se cumple con las necesidades humanas de una forma tal que una población humana pueda sobrevivir indefinidamente (21, 573)

symbiosis a relationship in which two different organisms live in close association with each other (223)

simbiosis una relación en la que dos organismos diferentes viven estrechamente asociados uno con el otro (223)

T

---

taiga a region of evergreen, coniferous forest below the arctic and subarctic tundra regions (163)

taiga una región de bosques siempreverdes de coníferas, ubicado debajo de las regiones árticas y subárticas de tundra (163)

tectonic plate a block of lithosphere that consists of the crust and the rigid, outermost part of the mantle; also called lithospheric plate (66)

placa tectónica un bloque de litosfera formado por la corteza y la parte rígida y más externa del manto; también se llama placa litosférica (66)

temperate deciduous forest a forest (or biome) that is characterized by trees that shed their leaves in the fall (162)

bosque caducifolio templado un bosque (o bioma) que se caracteriza por árboles a los que se les caen las hojas en el otoño (162)

temperate grassland a community (or biome) that is dominated by grasses, has few trees, and is characterized by cold winters and rainfall that is intermediate between that of a forest and a desert (166)

pradera templada una comunidad (o bioma) que está dominada por pastos, tiene pocos árboles y se caracteriza por inviernos fríos y precipitación pluvial que es intermedia entre la de un bosque y la de un desierto (166)

temperate rain forest a forest community (or biome), characterized by cool, humid weather and abundant rainfall, where tree branches are draped with mosses, tree trunks are covered with lichens, and the forest floor is covered with ferns (161)

selva tropical templada una comunidad de bosque (o bioma) caracterizada por tiempo frío y húmedo y lluvia en abundancia, en la cual las ramas de los árboles están cubiertas por moho, los troncos de los árboles están cubiertos por líquenes y el suelo del bosque está cubierto por helechos (161)

temperature inversion the atmospheric condition in which warm air traps cooler air near Earth's surface (330)

inversión de la temperatura la condición atmosférica en la que el aire caliente retiene al aire frío cerca de la superficie terrestre (330)

thermal pollution a temperature increase in a body of water that is caused by human activity and that has a harmful effect on water quality and on the ability of that body of water to support life (309)

contaminación térmica un aumento en la temperatura de una masa de agua, producido por las actividades humanas y que tiene un efecto dañino en la calidad del agua y en la capacidad de esa masa de agua para permitir que se desarrolle la vida (309)

threatened species a species that has been identified to be likely to become endangered in the foreseeable future (263)

especie amenazada una especie que se ha identificado como candidata para estar en peligro de extinción en el futuro inmediato (263)

topsoil the surface layer of the soil, which is usually richer in organic matter than the subsoil is (413)

capa superior del suelo la capa superficial del suelo, la cual normalmente es más rica en materia orgánica que el subsuelo (413)

toxicology the study of toxic substances, including their nature, effects, detection, methods of treatment, and exposure control (550)

toxicología el estudio de las substancias tóxicas, incluyendo su naturaleza, efectos, detección, métodos de tratamiento y control de exposición (550)

trophic level one of the steps in a food chain or food pyramid; examples include producers and primary, secondary, and tertiary consumers (130)

nivel trófico uno de los pasos de la cadena alimenticia o de la pirámide alimenticia; entre los ejemplos se encuentran los productores y los consumidores primarios, secundarios y terciarios (130)

tropical rain forest a forest or jungle near the equator that is characterized by large amounts of rain and little variation in temperature and that contains the greatest known diversity of organisms on Earth (156)

selva tropical un bosque o jungla que se encuentra cerca del ecuador y se caracteriza por una gran cantidad de lluvia y poca variación en la temperatura, y que contiene la mayor diversidad de organismos que se conoce en la Tierra (156)

troposphere the lowest layer of the atmosphere, in which temperature drops at a constant rate as altitude increases; the part of the atmosphere where weather conditions exist (72)

troposfera la capa inferior de la atmósfera, en la que la temperatura disminuye a una tasa constante a medida que la altitud aumenta; la parte de la atmósfera donde se dan las condiciones del tiempo (72)

tundra a treeless plain that is located in the Arctic or Antarctic and that is characterized by very low winter temperatures; short, cool summers; and vegetation that consists of grasses, lichens, and perennial herbs (172)

tundra un llano sin árboles que se ubica en la región ártica o antártica y se caracteriza por temperaturas muy bajas en el invierno, veranos cortos y frescos y vegetación que consiste en pasto, líquenes y hierbas perennes (172)

U

understory a foliage layer that is beneath and shaded by the main canopy of a forest (158)

capa sumergida una capa de follaje que se encuentra debajo de la bóveda principal de un bosque y está cubierta por ella (158)

urban describes an area that contains a city (381)

urbana término que describe a un área que contiene una ciudad (381)

urbanization an increase in the ratio or density of people living in urban areas rather than in rural areas (243, 384)

urbanización un aumento en la razón o densidad de las personas que viven en áreas urbanas en lugar de en áreas rurales (243, 384)

urban sprawl the rapid spread of a city into adjoining suburbs and rural areas (385)

derrame urbano la rápida propagación de una ciudad hacia los suburbios adjuntos y áreas rurales (385)

English and Spanish Glossary

V

value a principle or standard that an individual considers to be important (47)

valor un principio o norma que un individuo considera importante (47)

variable (VER ee uh buhl) a factor that changes in an experiment in order to test a hypothesis (35)

variable un factor que se modifica en un experimento con el fin de probar una hipótesis (35)

vector in biology, any agent, such as a plasmid or a virus, that can incorporate foreign DNA and transfer that DNA from one organism to another; an intermediate host that transfers a pathogen or a parasite to another organism (558)

vector en biología, cualquier agente, como por ejemplo un plásmido o un virus, que tiene la capacidad de incorporar ADN extraño y de transferir ese ADN de un organismo a otro; un huésped intermediario que transfiere un organismo patógeno o un parásito a otro organismo (558)

vertebrate an animal that has a backbone; includes mammals, birds, reptiles, amphibians, and fish (113)

vertebrado un animal que tiene columna vertebral; incluye a los mamíferos, aves, reptiles, anfibios y peces (113)

W

wastewater water that contains wastes from homes or industry (306)

agua de desecho agua que contiene desechos de los hogares o la industria (306)

water cycle the continuous movement of water between the atmosphere, the land, and the oceans (77)

ciclo del agua el movimiento continuo del agua entre la atmósfera, la tierra y los océanos (77)

water pollution contamination of water by waste matter or other material that is harmful to organisms that are exposed to the water (304)

contaminación del agua contaminación del agua con materiales de desecho u otros materiales que dañan a los organismos que están expuestos al agua (304)

watershed the area of land that is drained by a water system (291)

cuenca hidrográfica el área del terreno que es drenada por un sistema de agua (291)

weather the short-term state of the atmosphere, including temperature, humidity, precipitation, wind, and visibility (351)

tiempo el estado de la atmósfera a corto plazo que incluye la temperatura, la humedad, la precipitación, el viento y la visibilidad (351)

wetland an area of land that is periodically underwater or whose soil contains a great deal of moisture (185)

pantano un área de tierra que está periódicamente bajo el agua o cuyo suelo contiene una gran cantidad de humedad (185)

wilderness a region that is not cultivated and that is not inhabited by humans (394)

área silvestre una región que no ha sido cultivada ni está habitada por seres humanos (394)

Y

yield the amount of crops produced per unit area (409)

rendimiento la cantidad de cosechas producidas por unidad de área (409)

Index

bats, 61, 454, 654–657
bauxite, 443
Bayliss, Taylor, 515
bears, diet, 127, 127f
bedrock, 413, 413f
bell-shaped distribution curve, 41, 41f
benthic zone, 186, 186f, 188f
benthos, 185
bias, identifying, 20
biochemistry, 7t
biodegradable material, 15, 306–307, 519, 528, 528f
biodiversity, 259–275
  conservation strategies, 272
  critical areas of, 266–267
  ecotourism, 262
  endangered species, 15, 15f, 263, 268–269, 268f
  endemic species, 266
  extinction, 263–266, 263f
  hotspots, 268, 272
  keystone species, 260, 260f
  known versus unknown species, 259, 259f
  protective laws and treaties, 270–275, 270f, 271f, 272f, 575f
  population survival and, 261, 261f
  in the United States, 269
biodiversity hotspots, 268, 272
Biodiversity Treaty, 275
biological hazard, 557
biological magnification, 128
biological pest control, 419–420, 419f
biology, 7f, 7t, 634–635
  marine, 6f
  microbiology, 7t
biomagnification, 312, 312f
biomass fuel, 496
biomes, 153–173. *See also specific biomes.*
  altitude, 155
  chaparral, 168–169
  climate and, 153f, 154
  desert, 170–171, 171f
  latitude, 155

taiga, 153f, 154f, 163–164, 163f, 164f
temperate deciduous forest, 161–164, 161f, 162f, 163f
temperate grassland, 154f, 166–168
temperate rain forest, 161–164, 161f, 162f, 163f
tropical rain forest, 156–160
tropical savannah, 154f, 165–166, 165f, 166f
tundra, 172–173, 173f
vegetation and, 153, 153f
biomining, 534
biosphere, 84–85, 84f
biosphere reserve, 394, 394f
biotechnology, 266
biotic factor, 100, 102
birds, 113, 148, 264f
  habitats of, 163f, 188, 194
  sensitivity to pollution, 128–129, 265, 329
birth rate, 213, 213f, 239, 239f
botany, 7t, 266–267, 266f, 267f
bottleneck, population, 261, 261f
box turtle studies, 8, 8f
brackish marsh, 188
bridges, 61, 61f
Bromfield, Louis, 404
butterfly studies, 122–123
buttresses, 157

C

Cajun prairie, 182–183
California
  emissions controls in, 328, 583
  gold mining in, 448–449, 448f
  habitat conservation in, 273f, 392, 392f
  soil salinization in, 416
  threatened species in, 269
Calories, 129, **407,** 407t, 409
camouflage, 164f, 220, 221f

canopy, 158, 158f
captive-breeding program, 270, 270f
Carara Biological Preserve, 30–31, 30f, 31f
carbohydrate, 125, 129, 407t
carbon cycle, 132–133, 132f
carbon dioxide, 365t
  atmospheric levels of, 133, 133f
  in carbon cycle, 132–133, 132f
  emissions, 369, 369f, 664
  global warming and, 365, 365f
  in photosynthesis, 125
  from respiration, 128
carbon monoxide (CO), 325f, 326, 326t, 328f, 333f
carbon sink, 133
careers, 629–642
carnivores, 127, 127f
carrying capacity 214, 214f
Carson, Rachel, 6, 584t, 585, 585f
catalytic converter, 328f, 472
cell, 108, 109, 110
cell wall, 108, 109, 110
cellular respiration 128–129, 128f
CERCLA (Superfund Act), 313t, 530
CFCs (chlorofluorocarbons), 359, 359f, 362, 362f, 365, 379
  hormone-disrupting, 554–555
  hormone-mimicking, 554–555
  inorganic, 306t
chaparral biome, 153f, **168–169,** 169f
chemical equations, 626
chemical formulas, 626
chemicals
  CFCs (chlorofluorocarbons), 359, 359f, 362, 362f, 365, 379
  hormone-disrupting, 554–555
  hormone-mimicking, 554–555
  inorganic, 306t

chemical waste treatment, 534, 534f
chemistry, 7t
Chernobyl, 478
Chesapeake Bay, 192–193, 424–425, 425f
China
  aquaculture and, 424
  coal mining in, 454f
  integrated farming and, 427
  methane-generated electricity and, 496
  population issues, 246
  threatened species in, 268f
  waste disposal in, 519f
chlorination, 297f, 307f
chlorofluorocarbons (CFCs), 359, 359f, 362, 362f, 365, 379
chlorophyll, 125f
cholera, 39, 39f, 558, 558f
Clean Air Act (1970), 327, 580
Clean Water Act (1972), 312, 313t, 454, 580
clear-cutting, 391
climate, 154–155, 351–369. *See also* **global warming**
  altitude and, 155f
  atmospheric air circulation, 353–354, 353f
  biomes and, 154–155, 154f
  change, 37, 351f, 354–355, 354f, 355f, 358, 358f
  effects of volcanic eruption on, 69
  extinction and, 265
  geographic features and, 357, 357f
  global warming and, 363–369
  latitude and, 155f, 352, 352f
  mass extinctions and, 263f
  oceans and, 81, 81f, 356, 356f
  ozone layer, 359–362
climate regions,
  U.S., Canada, and Mexico map, 674f
  world map, 664f
climate researcher, 638–639

Index

Index

Index

Index

growth of, 235, 235f,
241–243, 242f,
245–246, 245f, 247,
247f
impacts on land and habitat, 243, 243f, 382, 518
lost civilizations, 257, 257f
migration, 237, 237f
nutritional needs, 407,
408
projections for, 241–243,
247, 247f
survivorship, 236, 236f
population pyramid, 236,
236f
porous material, 293, 294f
potential energy, 497f
poultry, 426t, 427, 561,
561f
Power Notes, 604–605
power plants
air pollution from, 326
coal-fired, 468f
geothermal, 498, 498f,
499f
hydroelectric, 497–498,
497f
mechanics of, 468
nuclear, 477, 477f
thermal energy conversion,
501, 501f
thermal pollution, 309
tidal power, 500, 500f
precipitation, 77, 77f, 289f.
See also **acid precipitation;** *specific biomes*
atmospheric air circulation
and, 353
toxic mold and, 571
predation, 218, 218t,
220–221, 220f
prediction, 34
preserves, 394–395, 394f,
395f
prevailing winds, 353f,
355, 355f
Pribilof Islands, 214
primary air pollutant,
325–326, 326t
primary succession, 137,
137f, 140–141
**primary wastewater
treatment,** 307f
probability, 42, 42f, 43
producer, 126–127t
products, 128
protective covering, 221,
221f

protein, 129, 407, 407t
protist, 108t, 110, 110f,
557t
protozoan, 259f
public hearings, 20f, 582
public land, 390, 394, 394f,
581

Q

quarries, 447

R

radiation, solar, 74–75f,
357
radioactive waste, 43t, 556
radon gas, 333f, 334
rainfall. *See* **precipitation**
rain forest. *See* **temperate
rain forest biome;
tropical rain forest
biome**
rangeland, 381t, 389, 390f,
404–405
reactant, 128
reactor, nuclear, 477, 477f
recharge zone, 83, 83f,
294, 310
reclamation, of mines, 454,
455f
recreational values, 47t,
50t
recycling, 505t, 521t,
525–527, 587. *See also*
conservation
composting, 526, 526t
household products,
526–527, 527t
reducing solid waste,
524–525, 524f
reforestation, 393, 393f
regulations
air quality, 327, 339, 580
economic implications of,
577
federal agencies, 580t
hazardous waste, 313t,
454, 522, 530
inherited laws, 580
marine protection, 313t
oil pollution, 43,
312–313, 313t
water quality, 312, 313t,
383t, 454, 580
renewable energy sources,
14, 14t, 491–502

biomass fuel, 496
geothermal power,
498–499, 498f, 499f
hydroelectric power,
497–498
hydrogen fuel, 501–502,
501f
ocean thermal energy
conversion, 501, 501f
solar energy, 491–494
tidal power, 500, 500f
wind power, 495, 495f
renewable resource, 14,
14t
replacement level, 237,
237f
replication, 35, 36
reproductive potential,
213, 213f
reproductive rate, 213,
213f
reptiles, 113, 264t
research, scientific. *See*
experimental method
reservoir, 300, 300f
residential energy use,
469, 469f
residential water use,
296–297, 296f, 297f,
297t, 302, 302f, 302t
resistance
evolution of, 107, 107f
to pesticides, 418
resource depletion, 14,
14t, 16–19, 151
resource limits, 215
respiration, cellular,
128–129, 128f
Richter scale, 67
riffles, 449
Ring of Fire, 68, 68f
risk assessment, 17, 551.
See also **toxicity**
earthquake hazards, 68
of genetically engineered
foods, 436–437, 436f,
437f
probability and, 43
versus risk perception, 43f,
43t
risk perception, 43f
river systems, 83, 83f, 186,
290–291, 291f
biomagnification in, 312
human impacts on, 190
rock formations, 293, 294f,
413

room-and-pillar mining,
446, 446f
Roosevelt, Theodore, 579,
579f, 584t
ruminant, 426
runoff
into estuaries, 193
as pollution source, 305,
305f, 452
into rivers, 190
threats to coral reefs, 195

S

Safe Drinking Water Act
(1975), 313t, 454
salinity, 80, 185, 188
salinization, 367, 416
Salmonella, 559
salt marsh, 188, 194
salt mining, 446, 446f, 448
room and pillar, 446, 446f
solar evaporation, 446
solution, 448
salt water, 290, 290f
sampling, statistical, 42
satellite images, 46, 46f,
445
savanna. *See* **tropical
savanna biome**
science, 8f, 33, 36, 38–39,
47t
scientific notation, 621
scientists, 38–39
scrubbers, 329, 329f, 523f
seasonal change, 358, 358f
Seattle, 12, 12f, 13f, 335f
secondary air pollution,
325. *See also* **air
pollution**
secondary succession,
138–140, 138f, 139f,
140f
**secondary wastewater
treatment,** 307, 307f
sedimentation, 453
seismic wave, 64, 64f
seismology, 64
selective cutting, 391
sewage treatment
population growth and,
242, 242f
plants, 12–13
toxicity of, 307
water pollution and, 195,
197, 304f
sewage sludge, 307
shopping, 646–647

Index

Reviewers continued

Steven Richard Reese, Ph.D.
Director, Radiation Center Instructor
Department of Nuclear Engineering and Radiation Health Physics
Oregon State University
Corvallis, Oregon

Dork Sahagian, Ph.D.
Research Professor, Stratigraphy and Basin Analysis, Geodynamics
Global Analysis, Interpretation, and Modeling Program
University of New Hampshire
Durham, New Hampshire

Miles Silman, Ph.D.
Associate Professor of Biology
Department of Biology
Wake Forest University
Winston-Salem, North Carolina

Marc Slattery, Ph.D.
Division Director, NIUST Ocean Biotechnology Center and Repository
Department of Pharmacognosy
University of Mississippi
University, Mississippi

Spencer Steinberg, Ph.D.
Associate Professor, Environmental Organic Chemistry
Chemistry Department
University of Nevada
Las Vegas, Nevada

Richard Storey, Ph.D.
Dean of the Faculty and Professor of Biology
Colorado College
Colorado Springs, Colorado

Ramesh Teegavarapu, Ph.D., P.E.
Assistant Professor (Adjunct)
Department of Civil Engineering
Assistant Director
Kentucky Water Resources Research Institute
University of Kentucky
Lexington, Kentucky

Martin VanDyke, Ph.D.
Professor of Chemistry, Emeritus
Front Range Community College
Westminster, Colorado

Judith Weis, Ph.D.
Professor of Biology
Department of Biological Sciences
Rutgers University
Newark, New Jersey

Elizabeth Wenk, Ph.D.
Adjunct Faculty
Department of Science
Cerro Coso Community College
Bishop, California

Mary Wicksten, Ph.D.
Professor of Biology
Department of Biology
Texas A&M University
College Station, Texas

TEACHER REVIEWERS

Robert Akeson
Science Teacher
Boston Latin School
Boston, Massachusetts

Dan Aude
Magnet Programs Coordinator
Montgomery Public Schools
Montgomery, Alabama

Lowell Bailey
Science Teacher
Bedford North Lawrence High School
Bedford, Indiana

Robert Baronak
Biology Teacher
Donegal High School
Mount Joy, Pennsylvania

Michele Benn
Science Teacher
Beaver Falls High School
Beaver Falls, Pennsylvania

David Blinn
Secondary Sciences Teacher
Wrenshall High School
Wrenshall, Minnesota

Bart Bookman
Science Teacher
Stevenson High School
Bronx, New York

Daniel Bugenhagen
Science Teacher
Yutan Community School
Yutan, Nebraska

Robert Chandler
Science Teacher
Soddy-Daisy High School
Soddy-Daisy, Tennessee

Johanna Chase, C.H.E.S.
Health Educator
California State University
Dominquez Hills, California

Cindy Copolo, Ph.D.
Science Specialist
Summit Solutions
Bahama, North Carolina

Linda Culp
Science Teacher
Thorndale High School
Thorndale, Texas

Katherine Cummings
Science Teacher
Currituck County
Currituck, North Carolina

Alonda Droege
Science Teacher
Evergreen High School
Seattle, Washington

Richard Filson
Science Teacher
Edison High School
Stockton, California

Randa Flinn
Science Teacher
Northeast High School
Fort Lauderdale, Florida

Jane Frailey
Science Coordinator
Hononegah High School
Hononegah, Illinois

Acknowledgments

Reviewers continued

Art Goldsmith
Biology and Earth Sciences Teacher
Hallandale High School
Hallandale, Florida

Sharon Harris
Science Teacher
Mother of Mercy High School
Cincinnati, Ohio

Carolyn Hayes
Honors Biology and Environmental Science Teacher
Center Grove High School
Greenwood, Indiana

Stacey Jeffress
Environmental Science Teacher
El Dorado High School
El Dorado, Arkansas

Donald R. Kanner
Physics Instructor
Lane Technical High School
Chicago, Illinois

Edward Keller
Science Teacher
Morgantown High School
Morgantown, West Virginia

Kathy LaRoe
Science Teacher
St. Paul School District
St. Paul, Nebraska

Clifford Lerner
Biology Teacher
Keene High School
Keene, New Hampshire

Stewart Lipsky
Science Teacher
Seward Park High School
New York, New York

Mike Lubich
Science Teacher
Mapletown High School
Greensboro, Pennsylvania

Thomas Manerchia
Environmental Science Teacher, Retired
Archmere Academy
Claymont, Delaware

Tammie Niffenegger
Science Chair and Science Teacher
Port Washington High School
Waldo, Wisconsin

Gabriele DeBear Paye
Science and Environmental Technology Lead Teacher
West Roxbury High School
West Roxbury, Massachusetts

Denice Sandefur
Fire Ecology and Science Teacher
Nucla High School
Nucla, Colorado

Jennifer M. Fritz
Science Teacher
North Springs High School
Atlanta, Georgia

Dyanne Semerjibashian, Ph.D.
Science Teacher
Pflugerville High School
Pflugerville, Texas

Bert Sherwood
Science/Health Specialist
Socorro Independent School District
El Paso, Texas

Dan Trockman
Science Teacher
Hopkins High School
Minnetonka, Minnesota

Jim Watson
Science Teacher
Dalton High School
Dalton, Georgia

Staff Credits

Mark Grayson
Robert Tucek
Executive Editors

Kelly Rizk
Debbie Starr
Managing Editors

Clay Walton
Senior Editor

Editorial Development Team
Bill Burnside
Jen Driscoll
Frieda Gress
Angela Hemmeter
Bill Rader
Jim Ratcliffe

Copyeditors
Dawn Marie Spinozza
Copyediting Manager
Anne-Marie De Witt
Simon Key
Jane A. Kirschman
Kira J. Watkins

Editorial Support Staff
Mary Anderson
Soojinn Choi
Jeanne Graham
Shannon Oehler
Stephanie Sanchez
Tanu'e White

Editorial Interns
Kristina Bigelow
Erica Garza
Sarah Ray
Kenneth G. Raymond
Kyle Stock
Audra Teinert
Jennifer Tseng

Online Products
Bob Tucek
Wesley M. Bain
Catherine Gallagher
Douglas P. Rutley

Book Design
Kay Selke
Director of Book Design
Christine Stanford
Designer

Media Design
Richard Metzger
Design Director
Chris Smith
Developmental Designer

Cover Design
Kay Selke
Director of Book Design

Publishing Services
Carol Martin
Director

Jeff Robinson
Manager, Ancillary Design

Production
Adriana Bardin Prestwood
Senior Production Coordinator
Eddie Dawson
Senior Production Manager
Diana Rodriguez
Project Manager

Technology Services Managers
Laura Likon
Director
Juan Baquera
Manager
JoAnn Stringer
Manager

Senior Technology Services Analysts
Katrina Gnader
Lana Kaupp
Margaret Sanchez

Technology Services Analysts
Sara Buller
Patty Zepeda

eMedia
Melanie Baccus
eMedia Coordinator
Ed Blake
Design Director
Kimberly Cammerata
Design Manager
Lydia Doty
Senior Project Manager
Marsh Flournoy
Technology Project Manager
Dakota Smith
Quality Assurance Analyst
Cathy Kuhles
Technical Assistant
Tara F. Ross
Senior Project Manager
Ken Whiteside
Manager, Application Development

Acknowledgments

Image Credits

COVER AND TITLE PAGE: (butterfly),Photodisc; (leaves), Yasushi Takahashi/Photonica; (droplets), Ken Hiroshi/Photonica.

FRONTMATTER: v(t), E.R. Degginger/Bruce Coleman, Inc.; (tl), Claus Meyer/Minden Pictures; (tml), Fred Bavendam/Minden Pictures; (bml), Yann Layma/Getty Images/Stone; (bl), Luis Vega/The Image Bank/Getty Images ; (b), Anthony Bannister/Photo Researchers, Inc.; vi(tl), Mark Moffett/Minden Pictures; vi(bl), Norbert Wu/Norbert Wu Productions; vii(tl), Earth Imaging/Stone/Getty Images ; vii(ml), S. Hanquet/Peter Arnold, Inc.; vii(bl), Gary Meszaros/Dembinsky Photo Associates; viii(tl), Martin Harvey/Peter Arnold, Inc.; viii(ml), Brandon D. Cole/Corbis; ix(tl), Mark Carwardine/Still Pictures/Peter Arnold, Inc.; ix(ml), Topham/The ImageWorks; ix(bl), John Shaw/Bruce Coleman, Inc.; x(tl), Ralph A. Clevenger/Corbis; x(ml), Chad Ehlers/ImageState; x(bl), NASA/Goddard Space Flight Center/Science Source/Photo Researchers, Inc.; xi(ml), Jim Wark/Peter Arnold, Inc.; xi(bl), Grant Heilman/Grant Heilman Photography Inc.; xii(tl), Dan Budnik/Woodfin Camp and Associates; xii(ml), Werner H. Muller/Peter Arnold, Inc.; xiii(ml), Rafael Macia/Photo Researchers, Inc.; xiii(bl), Andrew Rakoczy/Bruce Coleman, Inc.; xiv(tl), Argus Fotoarchiv/Peter Arnold, Inc.; xiv(ml) , Albert Normandin/Masterfile; xx(ml), John Cancalosi/Peter Arnold, Inc.; (tl), Bob Wolf; (tr), Sam Dudgeon/HRW; (br), Karen Allen; xx(bl), NOAA/Department of Commerce/NOAA Central Library; xxi(r), Gerhard Gscheidle/Peter Arnold, Inc.; (l), The Zoological Society of San Diego.

UNIT 1 OPENER: 2, E.R. Degginger/Bruce Coleman, Inc.; 3(t), Mark Moffett/Minden Pictures; (m), Norbert Wu/Norbert Wu Productions; (b), Earth Imaging/Stone/Getty Images.

CHAPTER 1: 4, Mark Moffett/Minden Pictures; 5, Courtesy of Cliff Lerner/HRW; 6(bl), Roland Seitre/Peter Arnold, Inc.; (br), Douglas Faulkner/Photo Researchers, Inc.; 7(br), Matt Meadows/Peter Arnold, Inc.; (bl), K & M Krafft/Photo Researchers, Inc.; 8(br), Courtesy of Gardner Watkins/Study conducted by the students of Dublin Scioto High School and supported by The Columbus Zoo Dublin Scioto H.S. Environmental Club; (bl), AFP/Corbis; 9(b), David Gillison/Peter Arnold, Inc.; (t), NorthWind Picture Archives; 10(b), M. Edwards/Peter Arnold, Inc.;(t), A. Murray/University of Florida/URL:http://plants.ifas.ufl.edu; 11(r), Color Blind Images/Blend Images/Getty Images.; (tl), Lambert/Archive Photos/PictureQuest; 12, NASA; 13, Joel Rodgers/Corbis; 14, Gene Aherns/Bruce Coleman, Inc.; 15(tr), Conor Caffrey/Photo Researchers, Inc.; (br), BIOS/Peter Arnold, Inc.; 18(l), Ric Ergenbright/Corbis; (b), Macduff Everton/Corbis; 20, Terry Farmer/Tony Stone Images; 21, Frank Pedrck/The ImageWorks; 22(t), Courtesy of Gardner Watkins/Study conducted by the students of Dublin Scioto High School and supported by The Columbus Zoo Dublin Scioto H.S. Environmental Club; (b), Ric Ergenbright/Corbis; 26, Sam Dudgeon/HRW; 28, Karen Allen; 29, Karen Allen.

CHAPTER 2: 32, Norbert Wu/Norbert Wu Productions; 33, Jeff & Alexa Henry/Peter Arnold, Inc.; 35, Courtesy of Cliff Lerner/HRW; 36, Tek Image/SPL/Photo Researchers, Inc.; 37, Courtesy of U of AK Tree-Ring Lab URL:www.uark.edu/dendro/stahle_bwr.tif; 38, K & K Ammann/Bruce Coleman, Inc.; 39, SPL/PRI/Photo Researchers, Inc.; 40, Cliff Lerner/HRW; 42, Kent Wood/Photo Researchers, Inc.; 43, Jim Olive/Peter Arnold, Inc.; 44, Eye Ubiquitous/Corbis; 46, Earth Satellite Corp./SPL/Photo Researchers, Inc.; 48(t), G. Lasley/VIREO URL: www. acnatsci.org/vireo; (b), S. Michael Bisceglie/Animals Animals/Earth Scenes; 49, Matt Bradley/Bruce Coleman, Inc.; 51, Richard Hamilton Smith/Dembinsky Photo Associates; 52(t), Jeff & Alexa Henry/Peter Arnold, Inc.; (m), Earth Satellite Corp./SPL/Photo Researchers, Inc.; (b), Richard Hamilton Smith/Dembinsky Photo Associates; 58, HRW; 59, HRW; 61, Merlin D. Tuttle/Bat Conservation International, Inc.

CHAPTER 3: 62, Earth Imaging/Stone/Getty Images ; 67, Jock Montgomery/Bruce Coleman, Inc.; 69, Gary Braasch/Corbis; 70, Dennis Flaherty/Photo Researchers, Inc.; 71, NASA; 73(t), NOAA/Department of Commerce/NOAA Central Library URL: www.photolib.noaa.gov; (br), Chris Madeley/SPL/Photo Researchers, Inc.; 77, Courtesy of Robert Cantor/Christian Grantham URL: www.christianandvince.com gallery/hawaii/diamondhead.jpg; 78, Peter Ryan/Scripps/SPL/Photo Researchers, Inc.; 79, K. Crane/WHOI/Visuals Unlimited; 81, Rosentiel School of Marine & Atmospheric Science, U. Of Miami; 83, Bernhard Edmaier/SPL/Photo Researchers, Inc.; 84(b), Provided by the SeaWiFS Project, NASA/Goddard Space Flight Center and ORBIMAGE/NASA/Seawifs;

(bl), Provided by the SeaWiFS Project, NASA/Goddard Space Flight Center and ORBIMAGE/NASA/Seawifs; 85, Geoff Kidd/SPL/Photo Researchers, Inc.; 86(t), Gary Braasch/Corbis; (m), NOAA/Department of Commerce/NOAA Central Library/URL: www.photolib.noaa.gov; 92, HRW; 93, Sam Dudgeon/Holt, Rinehart and Winston; 95, PhotoDisc.

UNIT 2 OPENER: 96, Claus Meyer/Minden Pictures; 97(t), S. Hanquet/Peter Arnold, Inc.; (tc), Gary Meszaros/Dembinsky Photo Associates; (bc), Martin Harvey/Peter Arnold, Inc.; (b), Brandon D. Cole/Corbis.

CHAPTER 4: 98, S. Hanquet/Peter Arnold, Inc.; 99, John Meilcarek/Dembinsky Photo Associates; 100(t, b), J.J. Alcalay/Peter Arnold, Inc.; 101(bl), Scott Smith/Dembinsky Photo Associates; (br), Fred Bruemmer/Peter Arnold, Inc.; 102, Joe McDonald/Bruce Coleman, Inc.; 103, Stephen Dalton/Photo Researchers, Inc.; 104, Tui De Roy/Bruce Coleman, Inc.; 105, Auscape/Parer-Cook/Peter Arnold, Inc.; 106(t), P. La Tourrette/VIREO URL: www.acnatsci.org/vireo; (bc), Tom Brakefield/Bruce Coleman, Inc.; (br), Klein/Hubert/Peter Arnold, Inc.; 109(t), Juergen Berger/SPL/Photo Researchers, Inc.; (bl), Rod Planck/Dembinsky Photo Associates; (br), Steven Mark Needham/Envision; 110(tl), Lawrence Naylor/Photo Researchers, Inc.; (b), F. Stuart Westmorland/Photo Researchers, Inc.; (tc), Jan Hinsch/SPL/Dembinsky Photo Associates; 111(t), Daniel Zupanc/Bruce Coleman, Inc.; (b), Kent Foster/Bruce Coleman, Inc.; 112(br), Mark J. Thomas/Dembinsky Photo Associates; (bl), Jim Steinberg/Photo Researchers, Inc.; (bc), Raymond A. Mendez/Animals Animals/Earth Scenes; 113(tl), Ed Reschke/Peter Arnold, Inc.; (tr),Gerard Lacz/Peter Arnold, Inc.; (tc), Klaus Jost/Peter Arnold, Inc.; 114(t), J.J. Alcalay/Peter Arnold, Inc.; (m), P. La Tourrette/VIREO URL: www. acnatsci.org/vireo; (b), Juergen Berger/SPL/Photo Researchers, Inc.; 120, Victoria Smith/Holt, Rinehart and Winston; 121, Manfred Kage/Peter Arnold, Inc.; 122(bl, br), 123, Lincoln Brower.

CHAPTER 5: 124, Gary Meszaros/Dembinsky Photo Associates; 125(bl), Phillipe Giraud/Sygma; (l), John Durham/SPL/Photo Researchers, Inc.; 126(tl), IFA/Peter Arnold, Inc.; (tc), Van deRostyne/BIOS/Peter Arnold, Inc.; (tc), Sharon Cummings/Dembinsky Photo Associates; (tr), Jeff LePore/Dembinsky Photo Associates; (bl), Ron & Valerie Taylor/Bruce Coleman, Inc.; (bc), Alfred Pasieka/SPL/Photo Researchers, Inc.; 127, Marilyn Kazmers/Dembinsky Photo Associates; 128, Harry Engels/Photo Researchers, Inc.; 129, Fritz Polking/Bruce Coleman, Inc.; 133, Ted Spiegel/Corbis; 134(bl), G. R. "Dick" Roberts/G.R. "Dick" Roberts Photo Library; (m), C.P. Vance/Visuals Unlimited; 136(t), E.R. Degginger/Color-Pic, Inc.; (l), G.R. "Dick" Roberts/G.R. "Dick" Roberts Photo Library; 137, Hans Reinhard/Bruce Coleman, Inc.; 138(b), Stan Osolinski/Dembinsky Photo Associates; (tl), Larry Nielsen/Peter Arnold, Inc.; 139(l), Scott Smith/Dembinsky Photo Associates; (r), Roger W. Archibald/Animals Animals/Earth Scenes; (tr), Patti Murray/Animals Animals/Earth Scenes; 141(l), Scott Smith/Dembinsky Photo Associates; (r), Norman Owen Tomalin/Bruce Coleman, Inc.; 142(t), Fritz Polking/Bruce Coleman, Inc.; (b), Hans Reinhard/Bruce Coleman, Inc.; (m), G.R. "Dick" Roberts/G.R. "Dick" Roberts Photo Library; 151(b), Stephen Rose/Rainbow; (t), FPG International/Getty Images.

CHAPTER 6: 152, Martin Harvey/Peter Arnold, Inc.; 154, Eastcott/Momatiuk/Animals Animals/Earth Scenes; 156(br), Dr. Morley Read/SPL/Photo Researchers, Inc.; (bl), Patti Murray/Animals Animals/Earth Scenes; (bc), Michael Fogden/Bruce Coleman, Inc.; 157(bl), Frans Lanting/Minden Pictures; (br), M. Gunther/Peter Arnold, Inc.; 159(r), Mickey Gibson/Animals Animals/Earth Scenes; (bl), E. Woods/Animals Animals/Earth Scenes; 159(br), Walter H. Hodge/Peter Arnold, Inc.; (l), Alan G. Nelson/Dembinsky Photo Associates; 160, Greg Baker/AP/Wide World; 161(l), Wayne Lawler/Photo Researchers, Inc.; (tr), Jim Steinberg/Photo Researchers, Inc.; 162(bl, bc, br), Scott W. Smith/Animals Animals/Earth Scenes; 163(r), George E. Stewart/Dembinsky Photo Associates; (tr), Anthony Mercieca/Dembinsky Photo Associates; (inset), Michael F. Sacca/Animals Animals/Earth Scenes; 164(tl), Walter H. Hodge/Peter Arnold, Inc.; (bc, br), S.J. Krasemann/Peter Arnold, Inc.; (inset), David Cavagnaro/DRK Photo; 166, Tim Davis/Photo Researchers, Inc.; 167(tl), Joel Bennett/Peter Arnold, Inc.; (tr), blickwinkel/Alamy; 168(t), Jim Brandenberg/Minden Pictures; (b), Coco McCoy/Rainbow; 169(t), Bobbi Lane/Stone; (inset), Ernest H. Rogers/Sea Images; 170(b), Jon Mark Stewart/Biological Photo Service; (inset), Frans Lanting/Minden Pictures; 171(bc), Anthony Bannister/Natural History Photographic Agency; (br), C. K. Lorenz/Photo Researchers, Inc.; 172, Jo Overholt/AlaskaStock Images; 173(r), Johnny Johnson/Animals Animals/Earth

Scenes; (tl), Gerald & Buff Corsi/Visuals Unlimited; 174(m), Dr. Morley Read/SPL/Photo Researchers, Inc.; (b), Tim Davis/Photo Researchers, Inc.; (t), Eastcott/Momatiuk/Animals Animals/Earth Scenes; 181(t), Adam Jones/Dembinsky Photo Associates; (b), D. Boone/Corbis; 182(t), Hugh S. Rose/Visuals Unlimited; (b), John W. Warden/West Stock; 183(t), Ken Graham/Tony Stone/Allstock; 182-183, Dr. Charles Allen.

CHAPTER 7: 184, Brandon D. Cole/Corbis; 185, Jan-Peter Lahall/Peter Arnold, Inc.; 186(t), Breck P. Kent/Animals Animals/Earth Scenes; (br), Roland Birke/Peter Arnold, Inc.; (bc), A.M. Siegelman/Visuals Unlimited; 187(t), David Overcash/Bruce Coleman, Inc.; (b), Stan Osolinski/ Dembinsky Photo Associates; 188, Dominique Braud/Dembinsky Photo Associates; 189(t), Brian Miller/Animals Animals/Earth Scenes; (bl), C.C. Lockwood/Animals Animals/Earth Scenes; (br), Bates Littlehales/Animals Animals/Earth Scenes; 190(t), R. Toms, OSF/Animals Animals/Earth Scenes; (m), Adam Jones/Photo Researchers, Inc.; 193(tr), Fred Bavendam; (m), Lynda Richardson/Corbis; 194(t), Peter Oxford/Nature Picture Library; (b), Ted Levin/Animals Animals/Earth Scenes; 195(br), Masa Ushioda-Visual & Written/Bruce Coleman, Inc.; (inset), Brandon Cole/CORBIS; 197(t), Norbert Wu/Peter Arnold, Inc.; (m), Image Life/Corbis/Corbis; 198(t), Breck P. Kent/Animals Animals/Earth Scenes; (b), Image Life/Corbis; 207(t), NOAA; (b), Vincent Laforet, POOL/ AP/Wide World Photos.

UNIT 3 OPENER: 208, Fred Bavendam/Minden Pictures; 209(t), Mark Carwardine/Still Pictures/Peter Arnold, Inc.; (m), Topham/The ImageWorks; (b), John Shaw/Bruce Coleman, Inc.

CHAPTER 8: 210, Mark Carwardine/Still Pictures/Peter Arnold, Inc.; 211(br), Fred Bavendam/Peter Arnold, Inc.; 211(bl), Stuart Westmoreland/Corbis; 212(tr), Norman Owen Tomalin/Bruce Coleman. Inc.; 212(tl), Michael Fogden/Animals Animals/Earth Scenes; 212(t), David Hughes/Bruce Coleman. Inc.; 214(bl), Bettman/Corbis; 215(tr), Richard Thom/Visuals Unlimited; 215(tl), Skip Moody/Dembinsky Photo Associates; 216(t), C.C. Lockwood/Animals Animals/Earth Scenes; 216(l), W. Metzen/Bruce Coleman. Inc.; 217(bl), Beverly Joubert/National Geographic Society; 217(bc), Tom Brakefield/Tom Brakefield Photography; 217(br), Y. Arthus-Bertand/Peter Arnold, Inc.; 217(br), Anne Wertheim/Animals Animals/Earth Scenes; 220(tl), Wyman Meizer/Photo Researchers, Inc; 220(r), J.T. Collins/Photo Researchers, Inc; 221(l), Bill Beatty/Visuals Unlimited; 221(r), Joe McDonald/Visuals Unlimited; 222(tr), CNRI/SPL/Photo Researchers, Inc; 222(tl), John Shaw/Bruce Coleman. Inc.; 222(bl), Patti Murray/Animals Animals/Earth Scenes; 223(t), R.F. Ashley/Visuals Unlimited; 224(t), Norman Owen Tomalin/Bruce Coleman. Inc.; 224(b), Wyman Meizer/Photo Researchers, Inc; 228(b), Dennis Kunkel/Phototake; 229(t), Dr. David P. Frankhauser URL: http://biology.clc.uc.edu/Fankhauser; 230(t), William bernarrd/Corbis; 231(t), Dan Grandmaison/Permission of International Wolf Center/URL: www.wolf.org.

CHAPTER 9: 234, Topham/The ImageWorks; 238(inset), Muriel Lasure/ShutterStock; (tl), Marcel & Eva Malherbe/The ImageWorks; (tr), Jeff Greenberg/Rainbow; 240, Sean Sprague/The ImageWorks; 241, Inga Spence/Visuals Unlimited; 242(b), Annie Griffiths Belt/Corbis; (t), Jean-Leo Dugast/Panos Pictures; 243(bl), Mark E. Gibson/Visuals Unlimited; (br), NASA/Johnson Space Center/NASA; 245, Jodi Cobb/ National Geographic/Getty Images; 246, Louise Gubb/The ImageWorks; 248(t), Jeff Greenberg/Rainbow; (b), Louise Gubb/The ImageWorks; 257(b), Phil Degginger/Color-Pic, Inc.; (t), Fritz Prenzel/Animals Animals/Earth Scenes.

CHAPTER 10: 258, John Shaw/Bruce Coleman, Inc.; 260(tl), Chip Clark/Smithsonian, NMNH; (bl), Nora Darbyshire/Selmer Ausland/ Memories of Deep River URL www.jkcc.com/evje/trapping.html; (bc), Norbert Wu/Peter Arnold, Inc.; (bc), Jeff Foott/Bruce Coleman, Inc.; (br), Jeffrey Rotman/Peter Arnold, Inc.; 262(t), Lineair/Peter Arnold, Inc.; 264, Art Wolfe/Stone/AllStock; 265, M. Timothy O'Keefe/Bruce Coleman, Inc.; 266, Alison Wright/Photo Researchers, Inc.; 267, M. Edwards/Still Pictures/Peter Arnold, Inc.; 268(tl, tr), Tom McHugh/Photo Researchers, Inc.; (br), S. Cordier/Jacana /Photo Researchers, Inc.; (bl), Merlin D. Tuttle/Bat Conservation International, Inc.; (tc), Sally A. Morgan/Corbis; 269(tc, tl), David Dennis/Animals Animals/Earth Scenes; (bl), Bill Lea/Dembinsky Photo Associates; (br), Jeff Foott/Bruce Coleman, Inc.; (tr), Tim Davis/Davis/Lynn Images; 270, David Clendenen/U.S. Fish and Wildlife Service; 271(b), Cameramann International; (t), ARS/RDF/Visuals

Unlimited; 272, Photo by Rodney North/courtesy of Equal Exchange/ URL www. equalexchange.com; 273, Phillip Roullard/Phillip Roullard Photography; 274(tl), Robert Caputo/Aurora; (tr), Louise Gubb/J.B. Pictures; 275, Baker/Greenpeace; 276(t), Chip Clark/Smithsonian, NMNH; (m), David Dennis/Animals Animals/Earth Scenes; (b), Phillip Roullard/Phillip Roullard Photography; 280, Sam Dudgeon/Holt, Rinehart and Winston; 283, Sam Dudgeon/HRW; 284, AP/Wide World; 285, Marc Halevi/Harvard Photographic Services.

UNIT 4 OPENER: 286, Yann Layma/Getty Images/Stone; 297(t), Ralph A. Clevenger/Corbis; (tc), Chad Ehlers/International Stock/ImageState; (m), NASA/Goddard Space Flight Center/Science Source/Photo Researchers, Inc.; (bc), Jim Wark/Peter Arnold, Inc.; (b), Grant Heilman/ Grant Heilman Photography Inc.

CHAPTER 11: 288, Ralph A. Clevenger/Corbis; 290, E.R.I.M./Stone; 293, John Warden/Index Stock Imagery; 298, Jim Zuckerman/Corbis; 299(tr, tl), Grant Heilman/Grant Heilman Photography Inc.; (b), Vanni Archive/Corbis; 300(br), Michelle Buselle/Getty Images/Stone; (l), Lloyd Cluff/Corbis; 301, Christi Carter/Grant Heilman Photography Inc.; 302, Dave G. Houser/Corbis; 303, Steve Raymer/National Geographic Society; 304, Thomas Del Brase/Getty Images/Stone; 305(bl), Gary Braasch/Corbis; (b), Grant Heilman/Grant Heilman Photography, Inc.; (br), Ben Blankenburg/eStock Photo/PictureQuest; 308(b), Nick Hawkes/ Ecoscene/Corbis; (bl), Siede Preis/PhotoDisc/PictureQuest; 309, AFP/ Anonio Scorza/Corbis; 312, Bettmann/Corbis;314(t), E.R.I.M./Stone; (m), Jim Zuckerman/Corbis; (b), AFP/Anonio Scorza/Corbis; 321, Victoria Smith/HRW; 320(t), IFA/Bruce Coleman, Inc.; 323(tr), Wolfgang Kaehler/Corbis; (bl), Liu Liqun/Corbis; (bc), Keren Su/Corbis.

CHAPTER 12: 324, Chad Ehlers/International Stock/ImageState; 327, Pictor International/PictureQuest; 328, Sam Dudgeon/Holt, Rinehart and Winston; 329, Michael Newman/PhotoEdit; 331, E. Tobisch/UNEP/Peter Arnold, Inc.; 332, Neal Preston/Corbis; 333, Geoff Tompkins/SPL/Photo Researchers, Inc.; 334(tc), Thomas Ives/Corbis Stock Market; (tl), Dick Blume/The ImageWorks; 335, Gary Braasch/Woodfin Camp and Associates; 337, Simon Fraser/SPL/Photo Researchers, Inc.; 338, David R. Frazier/David R. Frazier Photolibrary; 340(b), Simon Fraser/SPL/Photo Researchers, Inc.; (m), Geoff Tompkins/SPL/Photo Researchers, Inc.; (t), Pictor International/PictureQuest; 346, Victoria Smith/HRW; 348, C. Mayhew & R. Simmon/NASA/GSFC; 349, Pittsburgh Post-Gazette.

CHAPTER 13: 350, NASA/Goddard Space Flight Center/SPL/Photo Researchers, Inc.; 351(bl), Joe Sroka/Dembinsky Photo Associates; (br), Mark J. Thomas/Dembinsky Photo Associates; 354, From Degrees of variation: climate change in Nunavut, Geological Survey of Canada. Misc. Rept. 71, 2001, Natural Resources Canada/Reproduced with the permission of the Minister of Public Works & Govt. Services, 2002; 355(tr), GSFC/NASA; (r), CSIRO/Simon Fraser/SPL/Photo Researchers, Inc.; (l), Michael Sewell/Peter Arnold, Inc.; 356(t), JPL/NASA; 356(b), NASA; 357(br), GSFC/NASA; 360(tr, tc, tl), NASA; 366, Dr. Jeffrey Kiehl/National Center for Atmospheric Research; 367, NASA; 368(b), D. Allan/Animals Animals/Earth Scenes; (t), Terry Brandt/Grant Heilman Photography Inc.; 369, Bruce Brander/Photo Researchers, Inc.; 370(t), Mark J. Thomas/Dembinsky Photo Associates; (m), NASA; (b), Dr. Jeffrey Kiehl/National Center for Atmospheric Research; 376, Victoria Smith/HRW; 378, Louis Psihoyos/Matrix International; 379, R. Sanders/Courtesy of Susan Solomon; (tl), NASA/Visuals Unlimited.

CHAPTER 14: 380, Jim Wark/Peter Arnold, Inc.; 382(l), J. Messerschmidt/ Bruce Coleman, Inc.; (b), Hanson Carroll/Peter Arnold, Inc.; 384(bl, bc, br), University of Maryland, Baltimore County/Courtesy U.S. Geological Survey; 385(t), Brian Brake/Photo Researchers, Inc.; (b), Nicholas DeVore/Bruce Coleman, Inc.; 386(t), Mark Gibson/Index Stock Imagery; (b), Data:LandSat5 thematic Mapper, Data courtesy of C.P. Lo (U. of GA)/NASA/GSFC; 387(br, bc, bl), Reprinted with permission from the City of Seattle, Seattle Public Utilities' IT-Storefront; 388, Morton Beebe/ Corbis; 389, Douglas Peebles/Corbis; 390, E.R. Degginger/Animals Animals/Earth Scenes; 393(m), Tom McHugh/Photo Researchers, Inc.; (t), Peter Arnold/Peter Arnold, Inc.; 395, Scott Smith/Dembinsky Photo Associates; 396(t), Hanson Carroll/Peter Arnold, Inc.; (m), Nicholas DeVore/Bruce Coleman, Inc.; (b), Tom McHugh/Photo Researchers, Inc.; 404/405, Michael Murphy/By Permission of Selah, Bamberger Ranch/ URL: www.bambergerranch.org.

Acknowledgments

Image Credits continued

CHAPTER 15: 406, Grant Heilman/Grant Heilman Photography Inc.; 409(br), Chris Hellier/Corbis; (bl), Alan Bonicatti/Liaison Agency Inc; 410, David Austen/PictureQuest; 411, Grant Heilman/Grant Heilman Photography Inc.; 412, Arthur C. Smith III/Grant Heilman Photography Inc.; 415(b), Larry Lefever/Grant Heilman Photography Inc.; (tr), Alex S. MacLean/Peter Arnold, Inc.; (tl), Melinda Berge/Bruce Coleman, Inc.; 417(tl), Nigel Cattlin/Alamy; (tc), Nuridsany/Perennou/Photo Researchers, Inc.; (tr), Inga Spence/Visuals Unlimited; 418, John Zoiner; 419(tl), Nigel Cattlin/Holt Studios international/Photo Researchers, Inc.; (tr), Holt Studios International, Ltd.; 422, Patty Melander, permission of the Land Inst. URL www.landinstitute.org; 423, Roland Seitre/Peter Arnold, Inc.; 424, Doug Plummer/Photo Researchers, Inc.; 425, James L. Amos/Peter Arnold, Inc.; 426, Larry Lefever/Grant Heilman Photography Inc.; 427, Inga Spence/Visuals Unlimited; 428(t), Chris Hellier/Corbis; (m), Alex S. MacLean/Peter Arnold, Inc.; (b), Inga Spence/Visuals Unlimited; 435, Victoria Smith/HRW; 436(t), Science VU/ARS/Visuals Unlimited; (b), Scott Smith/Animals Animals/Earth Scenes; 437(b), Reuters NewMedia, Inc./Corbis; (t), Lynsey Addario/SABA/Corbis.

UNIT 5 OPENER: 438, Luis Vega/The Image Bank/Getty Images; 439(t), Dan Budnik/Woodfin Camp and Associates; (tc), Werner H. Muller/Peter Arnold, Inc.; (bc), Rafael Macia/Photo Researchers, Inc.; (b), Andrew Rakoczy/Bruce Coleman, Inc.

CHAPTER 16: 440, Dan Budnik/Woodfin Camp and Associates; 442(t), E.R. Degginger/Photo Researchers, Inc.; (b), Ken Lucas/Visuals Unlimited; 444(r), Mark A. Schneider/Visuals Unlimited; (b), Randy Jolly/The ImageWorks; 445, Paul A. Souders/Corbis; 446(b), David Barnes/Courtesy of New South Wales, Australia Department of Mineral Resources. New South Wales Mines Department; (t), By kind permission of K+S Aktiengesellschaft; 447(t), Michael Wickes/Bruce Coleman, Inc.; (b), Larsh Bristol/Visuals Unlimited; 448(t), Still Pictures/Peter Arnold, Inc.; (b), Carleton E. Watkins/California Historical Society; 449(tr), James L. Amos/Corbis; (m), Betty Sederquist/Visuals Unlimited; 450, Mireille Vautier/Woodfin Camp and Associates; 451, Phillip Richardson/Corbis; 452, Simon Fraser/SPL/Photo Researchers, Inc.; 453, Dean Purcell/AP/Wide World; 454, Courtesy of Dr. Prakash; U of AK, Geophysical Inst. Dr. Anupma Prakash; 455, Leo Touchet/Woodfin Camp and Associates; 456(tl), Ken Lucas/Visuals Unlimited; (m), Still Pictures/Peter Arnold, Inc.; (b), Simon Fraser/SPL/Photo Researchers, Inc.; 461, E.R. Degginger/Color-Pic, Inc.; 463, Victoria Smith/HRW; 465(b), Arnaud Zajtman/AP/Wide World; (t), Ryan McVay/PhotoDisc, Inc.

CHAPTER 17: 466, Werner H. Muller/Peter Arnold, Inc.; 467(bl), A.J. Copley/Visuals Unlimited; (br), Richard Hutchings/Photo Researchers, Inc.; 468, Bob Burch/Bruce Coleman, Inc.; 471, Leo Touchet/Woodfin Camp and Associates; 473(l), Gary Klinkhammer/College of Oceanic and Atmospheric Sciences; (r), Dr. Ian R. MacDonald/Texas A&M Univ./AquaPix, LLC; (t), GettyOne.com/Getty Images ; 474, Leonard Lessin/Peter Arnold, Inc.; 475, Keith Wood/Corbis; 477, George D. Lepp/Corbis; 478(inset), Courtesy Westinghouse Nuclear Fuel Division/Westinghouse Nuclear Fuel Division; 478(t), Inga Spence/Visuals Unlimited; 480(t), Keith Wood/Corbis; (b), George D. Lepp/Corbis; 486(br),HRW; (bl), Phil Degginger/Color-Pic, Inc.

CHAPTER 18: 490, Rafael Macia/Photo Researchers, Inc.; 491(br), Gunter Ziesler/Peter Arnold, Inc.; (bl), NASA; 492, Arnout Hyde, Jr./Dembinsky Photo Associates; 493, Permission of Rocky Mountain Institute URL: www.rmi.org; 495, Schafer & Hill/Peter Arnold, Inc.; 497, Carlos Sanuvo/Bruce Coleman, Inc.; 501, Warren Gretz/NREL/PIX; 504, Francis Dean/The ImageWorks; 506(t), Schafer & Hill/Peter Arnold, Inc.; (b), Francis Dean/The ImageWorks; 515(b), George Retseck; (m), Applied Innovative Technologies, Inc.

CHAPTER 19: 516, Andrew Rakoczy/Bruce Coleman, Inc.; 517, Michelle Bridwell/Frontera Fotos; 518, Mark Sands/SIPA Press, Headquarters; 519, Reuters NewMedia, Inc./TimePix.com; 520, Ray Pfortner/Peter Arnold, Inc.; 522, Prof. Rathje/The Garbage Project; 524, HRW; 525(bc), Randy Faris/Corbis; (inset), Phil Degginger/Bruce Coleman, Inc.; (br), Kay Park - Rec. Corp; (bl), Andy Christiansen/HRW; 526, Sam Dudgeon/HRW; 527, Sam Dudgeon/HRW; 528, Roger Ressmeyer/Corbis; 529, Roger Ressmeyer/Corbis; 531, Nancy J. Pierce/Photo Researchers, Inc.; 532, Krista Kennell/ZUMA/CORBIS; 533, Custom Medical Stock Photo; 534, Lawson Wood/Corbis; 535, Bernd Wittich/Visuals Unlimited; 536(t), Prof. Rathje/The Garbage Project; (b), Roger Ressmeyer/Corbis; (m), Phil Degginger/Bruce Coleman, Inc.; 543, Victoria Smith/HRW; 544, Sander/Gamma Liaison.

UNIT 6 OPENER: 546, Anthony Bannister/Photo Researchers, Inc.; 547(t), Argus Fotoarchiv/Peter Arnold, Inc.; (b), Albert Normandin/Masterfile.

CHAPTER 20: 548, Argus Fotoarchiv/Peter Arnold, Inc.; 552(b), Bourseiller/Hoaqui/Photo Researchers, Inc.; (t), John Elk III/Bruce Coleman, Inc.; 553(b), Mark Edwards/Still Pictures/Peter Arnold, Inc.; (r), Peter Turnley/Corbis; 555(m), J. Serrao/Photo Researchers, Inc.; (t), G. DeGrazia/Custom Medical Stock Photo; 556, UNEP/Peter Arnold, Inc.; 558, Jean-Marc Bouju/AP/Wide World; 559(t), George Turner/Animals Animals/Earth Scenes; (inset), David Scharf/Peter Arnold, Inc.; 561, Brad Rickerby/Bruce Coleman, Inc.; 562(t), Mark Edwards/Still Pictures/Peter Arnold, Inc.; (b), Jean-Marc Bouju/AP/Wide World; 568, Elvfis Barukcic/Corbis; 569, Dan McCoy/Rainbow; 571(inset), Brian Witte/AP/Wide World; (b), LisaLoucksChristenson/e-Compass Communications.

CHAPTER 21: 572, Alex Webb/Magnum Photos; 573, Rommel Pecson/The ImageWorks; 577(r), D. Seifert/UNEP/Peter Arnold, Inc.; (l), R. Sorensen/J. Olsen/NHPA; 578, Gunter Ziesler/Peter Arnold, Inc.; 579, Bettmann/Corbis; 581, C.C. Lockwood/Animals Animals/Earth Scenes; 582(bl), Spencer Grant/PhotoEdit; (br), Larry Kolvoord/The ImageWorks; 583, Louie Balukoff/AP/Wide World; 585(inset), Bob Schutz/AP/Wide World; 586(bl), Seth Resnick; (br), Pierre Gleizes/AP/Wide World Photos; 586, Fred Prouser/Reuters/Corbis; 587, Rhoda Sidney/The ImageWorks; 588(t), Gunter Ziesler/Peter Arnold, Inc.; (m), Bettmann/Corbis; (b), Rhoda Sidney/The ImageWorks; 594,HRW; 595, HRW. 596, Andrew Dunn; 597, Trevor Frey.

APPENDIX: 601, Sam Dudgeon/HRW; 629(tl), Ted M. Conde/Courtesy Niki Espy; (bl), Selvakumar Ramakrishman; 630, HRW; 631, HRW; 631(br), Louis Psihoyos/Contact Press Images; (bl), Solar Survivor Architecture, Taos; 633(t), Pamela Freund/Solar Survival Architecture, Taos; (b), Pamela Freund/Solar Survival Architecture, Taos, 634, Flavia Castro; 635, Ken Dudzik; 636(tl), Jonathan A. Meyers; (l), Jonathan A. Meyers; 637(t), courtesy Jana L. Walker; (b), Jonathan A. Meyers; 638(tl), Michael Newman/PhotoEdit; (b), Michael Newman/PhotoEdit; 639, Dian Russell/HRW; 640, Ken Dudzik; 641(t), Alex S. Maclean/Landslides; (b), Ken Dudzik; 642, courtesy Hanna Anderson; 643, Sam Dudgeon/HRW; 645, Bob Wolf; 648, Sam Dudgeon/HRW; 650(b), Hans Reinhard/Bruce Coleman, Ltd.; (t), Paul S. Conklin; 651(inset), George H. Harrison/Grant Heilman Photography; (b), Mae Scanlan; 652(t), Ken Cole/Animals Animals/Earth Scenes; (b), John Langford/HRW.

All other photos by HRW.